S0-BQJ-057

Democracy Denied, 1905–1915

Democracy Denied, 1905–1915

Intellectuals and the Fate of Democracy

Charles Kurzman

Harvard University Press

Cambridge, Massachusetts, and London, England | 2008

Library of Congress Cataloging-in-Publication Data

Kurzman, Charles.
 Democracy denied, 1905–1915 : intellectuals and the fate of
democracy / Charles Kurzman.
     p. cm.

 Includes bibliographical references and index.
 ISBN-13: 978-0-674-03092-3 (alk. paper)
 1. Democracy–History–20th century.   2. Intellectuals–Political
activity–History–20th century.   I. Title.
 JC421.K83 2008
 321.809'041–dc22   2008003837

Contents

Democracy Denied, 1905–1915

I

Intellectuals and Democratization

1

Introduction

On Monday, October 30, 1905, late in the afternoon, Tsar Nicholas II of Russia signed a one-page document promising to respect civil rights, share power with a parliament, and hold free elections. "There was no other way out than to cross oneself and give what everyone was asking for," Nicholas wrote to his mother two days later. General strikes gripped the major cities of his realm; his government's finances were a shambles; his sole candidate to lead a hard-line crackdown had refused the job that very morning, threatening to kill himself in the tsar's presence if reforms were not granted.[1]

Prodemocracy activists learned of the announcement several hours later. A journalist from the prodemocracy newspaper *The Russian News* raced across St. Petersburg and presented a still-wet proof sheet to a meeting where the country's first open political party was being founded. The activists were ecstatic. "We can congratulate each other on the realization of our cherished aspirations!" *The Russian News* editorialized. "Let us embrace as free people, as citizens of a free constitutional Russia!" Not everyone shared this optimism. Pavel N. Miliukov, a leader of the prodemocracy movement, spoke instead on the limitations of the pronouncement and the precariousness of the tsar's concessions. "Nothing has changed," he reportedly concluded. "The war continues."[2]

This was the first revolution covered "live" by international telegraph services, and by midnight, the news was all over Europe. Prodemocracy strikes had shut the St. Petersburg–Berlin telegraph lines, but telegrams were rerouted via Scandinavia and some European papers were able to include notice of the tsar's manifesto on Tuesday morning, October 31. "Only a few thousand people throughout Russia as yet know the glad news," wrote the correspondent of *The Times* of London. *The Dawn* of Paris, longtime supporter of the Russian prodemocracy movement, put the manifesto on its front page.[3]

3

Radiating from London, international telegraph services carried the tsar's manifesto around the world. In Portugal, the prodemocracy newspaper *The World* published its first comment on Wednesday, cautiously worrying about the tsar's real intent: "Hopefully a bloody deception will not follow [the Russian people's] generous hopes!" On Friday, *The North-China Herald* in Shanghai called the event "remarkable." The chief Iranian prodemocracy newspaper, *The Strong Bond*, published in Calcutta, India, mentioned the manifesto the following Monday. In mid-November, a prodemocracy socialist in Hong Kong commented, "the great ferment of the Russian Revolution has affected the entire globe like a clap of thunder." The editors of an Ottoman prodemocracy paper, which resumed publication in December in Cairo after a long absence, fulfilled their "duty, as staunch liberals, to send a fraternal salute to the champions of liberalism who are even now struggling in the vast Russian empire in the name of the Rights of Man and Citizen."[4]

Thus began a global wave of democratic revolutions. Though later upstaged by the Russian Revolutions of 1917, the Russian Revolution of 1905 gave an enormous boost to democracy movements around the world. *The Strong Bond* urged Muslims to "adopt the peoples of Russia as a model," and Iranians seem to have done just that. According to a British diplomat in Tehran, "the Russian Revolution [of 1905] has had a most astounding effect here. Events in Russia have been watched with great attention, and a new spirit would seem to have come over the people. They are tired of their rulers, and, taking example of Russia, have come to think that it is possible to have another and better form of government." Ottomans followed the Russian Revolution with "extra-ordinary interest," an opposition newspaper noted, concluding that "If we strive like Russians, . . . it won't be long before we see even the Sultan's aides-de-camp among our supporters." "Surely," the president of India's Congress Party commented in 1906, we British subjects "are far more entitled to self-government, a constitutional representative system, than the peasants of Russia." "The sparks of [the Russian Revolution] are still flying about," an Arab democrat wrote several years later. The Russian events "have echoed throughout the world like a powerful recurrent cry," according to a Portuguese democrat.[5]

These influences rebounded across the continents. Certain prodemocracy activists in Portugal called themselves "Young Turks," drawing on the image of Ottoman reformers, who themselves drew on the Young Italians of the nineteenth century. The Russian tsar and Ottoman sultan schemed to support the Iranian shah's antidemocratic campaigns. Mexican revolutionaries crossed paths with veterans of the Russian movement in exile in San Francisco. Chinese prodemocracy newspapers published numerous stories on lessons to be learned from recent movements in other countries.[6] And a wave of democratic revolutions emerged, consuming more than a quarter of the world's population by World War I:

- Russia, 1905
- Iran, 1906 and 1909
- Ottoman Empire, 1908
- Portugal, 1910
- Mexico, 1911
- China, 1912

This global reach places the wave alongside other clusters of democratic revolutions, such as the wave triggered by the French Revolution of 1789, the uprisings of 1848, the anticolonial movements after World War I and World War II, and the democratic movements of the late twentieth century.[7]

In addition to the influences and linkages that flowed among the democratic revolutions of the early twentieth century, these events followed parallel trajectories. In all of them, prodemocracy movements unseated long-standing autocracies with startling speed. The nascent democratic regimes held elections, convened parliaments, and allowed freedom of the press and freedom of association. Considerable disorder accompanied democratization, and the new regimes failed in numerous instances to uphold the rights and freedoms that they proclaimed. Coups d'état soon undermined the democratic experiments in every case but one, Portugal, where democracy survived an attempted coup d'état in 1915 and lingered until 1926. See Table 1 for a rough tabular chronology.

Naturally, each case has its own unique history. Yet the shared aspects of their trajectories distinguish the democratic revolutions of 1905–1912 from other movements of the same period: reformist democratizations, such as Austria in 1907, Sweden in 1909, Colombia in 1909–1910, Greece in 1909–1912, and Argentina and Italy in 1912; failed democracy movements, such as the Young Afghans, Young Bukharans, Young Khivans, and the Radical Civic Union's uprising in Argentina in 1905; anticolonial movements such as the Herero and Maji-Maji rebellions in southern Africa, Swadeshi in India, Sarekat Islam in Indonesia, Irish Nationalism, Korean resistance to Japanese rule, the Watchtower movement in Malawi, and Shaykh Ma al-'Aynayn's defense of the Sahara; and peasant uprisings in Moldavia and Burma.

Table 1. Democratic Revolutions of the Early Twentieth Century

	Russia	Iran	Ottoman Empire	Portugal	Mexico	China
Movement take-off	1905	1905	1908	1910	1910	1911
Democratic breakthrough	1905	1906	1908	1910	1911	1912
Parliamentary elections	1906	1907	1908	1911	1911	1913
Parliament convenes	1906	1907	1908	1911	1912	1913
Parliament subjugated	1907	1911	1909	1926	1913	1913

International observers at the time noted the flurry of democratizations. V. I. Lenin, the Russian communist, lumped several of these events together as "bourgeois-democratic revolutions." James Bryce, the British liberal, called them misguided attempts to "set a child to drive a motor car." British positivists noted that positivism played "so great a part" in them.[8] *The Journal of Despotism,* a satirical journal in Iran, ran an article written by fourteen-month-old "Democracy" to its half-brother "Parliament" in Russia likening various democracy movements around the world to siblings:

> My father [is] Justice-of-the-State, and my mother Iran-of-All-Lands. My father married a woman in every country that he visited; his first wife he married in England. . . . Now—praise be to God—I have 47 brothers[,] the majority of whose names I don't know, but I know [this much] that we all look alike except maybe with just a little difference in appearance. . . . Another thing that I've heard is that from India Justice-of-the-State intends to go to China, [and] I don't know where he will go first, the Ottoman country or China, undoubtedly he will not stay [put] in India; I know my father, where ever he goes he takes a wife and as soon as his wife becomes pregnant he leaves that country. [So] if you [happen to] know where he is going after India [please] write to me.[9]

As it happened, Justice-of-the-State appears to have visited the Ottoman Empire first, and then China several years later. In the decades since the wave crashed, however, these democratic experiments have receded into the province of area specialists. Plenty has been written about the individual cases—the present study relies heavily on this historiography—but the 1905 wave is rarely treated as an international event.[10] I propose that the wave is worth studying for contemporary and analytical purposes, in addition to its intrinsic historical interest.

In the late 1980s, a tentative liberalization in Russia once again generated a global wave of democratization. Dozens of countries toppled autocrats and experimented with democratic procedures.[11] Understanding the emergence of democracy has always been an important and prominent academic enterprise, but it has taken on added urgency as new democracies around the world struggle to survive. Studying the wave of democratic experiments set in motion by the Russian Revolution in 1905 offers a precedent for the study of new democracies at the end of the twentieth century. The sad fact that the democratic experiments of the earlier period all failed allows researchers to study both the upward and downward trajectories of democratization, and the linkages between them. Similar ideological contexts appear to have been involved in the democratizations of the early and late twentieth century: both periods witnessed a temporary downturn in tension between the competing ideals of democracy and national development. Indeed, in both periods democracy was often held to be a necessary, even, at optimistic moments, a sufficient, cause for national development. Both waves involve independent nations (with the exception of the Baltic and Adriatic coasts in 1989–1992), thereby avoiding the crosscutting issues of decolonization that affected the intervening waves of democratization. Similar international contexts also appear to have been involved in the democratizations of the early and late twentieth century: both periods witnessed the hegemony of capitalist democracies and economic (as opposed to ideological) competition among the Great Powers. In the pre-Soviet era this competition set Britain and its allies against Germany and its allies; the post-Soviet era pitted the United States against the European Union against Japan (though China's growing global presence may increase ideological diversity in this competition). As I will argue in the conclusion (Chapter 10), the new democracies of 1905–1912 were dress rehearsals for the new democracies of 1989–1996.

Hours before the announcement of the October Manifesto, Anna Sergeevna Miliukova stood at the founding conference of the Constitutional Democratic Party of Russia and demanded women's suffrage.

Women had participated actively in the prodemocracy movement, and feminist leaders such as Miliukova claimed the same political rights as male citizens of Russia. The matter was put to a vote, and the party agreed by a narrow majority to include women's suffrage in its platform. Pavel Miliukov, Miliukova's husband and a leader of the party, was furious. He berated two friends who had stepped outside and missed the vote, and managed to insert a clause indicating that the suffrage vote was not binding on party members.[12] With little pressure on this count from the main prodemocracy organization, the Russian government excluded women from elections in 1906 and 1907.

As the Chinese democracy movement came to power in early 1912, it too debated female suffrage, moving away from its earlier pledges to support women's rights. A group of women led by Tang Qunying—one of the democracy movement's earliest members and chief bomb-makers—burst into the provisional parliament at Nanjing and heckled the speakers so persistently that the session was adjourned. Over the next two days, the women scuffled with parliamentary representatives and guards, demanding equal rights for women. They too were denied the vote.[13]

Women were denied suffrage in all of the democratic revolutions of the early twentieth century, except Portugal, where one woman voted as a test case in 1911. The new democracy in Portugal then removed women's suffrage in 1913.[14] These regimes instituted other limits on suffrage as well: illiterate men were disenfranchised in Portugal, as were poor men in several countries. In addition, the newly implemented government institutions were disorderly and did not always follow their own rules. Some elections were rigged, some rights were repressed, some officials were venal and corrupt.

By the standards of the early twenty-first century, the new democracies of the early twentieth century were hardly full democracies. Even by the standards of the early twentieth century, the new democracies were not in the vanguard of democratizing reforms worldwide. Yet few countries at that time approached today's standards of democracy—in 1904, only four countries enfranchised more than half of their adult population. As a result, the democratic revolutions of the early twentieth century placed their countries in the middle of the pack along with various European countries that international observers classified as democratic at the time, including Britain, France, and the United States, all of which refused the vote to women. Prodemocracy activists studied these models intensely and considered their own movements as following in the path of existing democracies, paying special attention to the legacy of the French Revolution, which democracy movements around the world treated as an iconic ideal, despite the French Revolution's very imperfect record as a democracy. Democratic ambitions of the period were so limited that many activists venerated Japanese constitutionalism, an extremely restricted semidemocratic system that was widely credited with defeating Russian autocracy in the war of 1904–1905. Indeed, the terms used for democratic revolution at this time were sometimes ambiguous: *mashrutiyat* in Iran and *meşrutiyet* in the Ottoman Empire could refer either to constitutionalism or democracy, depending on the context, and the words for revolution in each country *(revoliutsiia, shurish, inkılâb, revolução, revolución, geming)* were not necessarily accompanied by modifiers specifying the goals as democratic. Nonetheless, these revolutions marked a major transformation in the direction of democracy: limiting the powers of the dictator, instituting competitive elections, and unleashing political debate through electoral campaigns, parliamentary sessions, and a vibrant press. If R. R. Palmer could call the late eighteenth and early nineteenth centuries an "age of the democratic revolution," based on the limited rights gained by the French Revolution and its global successors, then the early twentieth century deserves this label as well.[15]

Large numbers of citizens associated these revolutions with democratization and greeted them enthusiastically, almost apocalyptically, treating these events as significant political transitions. "In every corner of the Ottoman lands," an Istanbul newspaper effused soon after the reinstatement of the constitution in 1908, "hundreds of thousands of people—Muslims, Christians, and Jews, whole families, men, women, and children—have held unimaginable and indescribable celebrations, holidays, and feasts for the past 10 days. This joy will not disappear from the nation's heart til the end of days." In Mexico City, more than a hundred thousand people lined up to greet the leader of the democracy movement as his carriage arrived in the capital. In parts of China, celebrations were so widespread that the governor considered banning them: "Beijing opera, Sichuan opera, shadow plays and storytellers were making a clamorous noise everywhere, and actors and cooks did not get a day's rest." The arrival of a constitution was viewed by its most enthusiastic supporters as a panacea.[16]

In the early twentieth century, unsympathetic observers suggested that the masses did not comprehend the meaning of the new political system. Russian business officials suggested that "the magic word 'freedom,' understood by [workers] to mean that one can do what one wants, attracts the youth and creates scandalous behavior in the supposition that such behavior is necessary and demanded by the goal of achieving freedom." An upper-class Iranian man circulated a story about a lower-class protestor who thought that *mashrutiyat,* the Persian word for democracy and constitutionalism, was some sort of food. "I've been waiting for two days," the protestor said, "and I haven't gotten even a single piece of *mashrutiyat.*" Two Mexican peasants, welcoming the leader of the democracy movement as he made his way to the capital, are supposed to have said, "And what, *amigo,* is this *democracia* for which all are shouting?" "Why, it must be the lady who accompanies him."[17]

Contrary to these derogatory comments, millions of people participated knowledgeably in the political affairs of the new democracies. They voted in elections that were the freest in their countries' history, despite limited suffrage and considerable irregularities. They followed politics in the profusion of newspapers that sprouted after democratization. As a satirical journal in the Ottoman Empire joked, "Everybody is talking about the government and governmental affairs. What is this all about? Even a poor man standing next to his brazier at night talks with his mother-in-law about politics and discusses the issues. As soon as he gets up in the morning, he says, 'What is going on? What has been happening?' and dives into the newspapers."[18] Many people took advantage of their new liberties to organize in groups such as unions, as we will see in Chapter 6.

This is not to deny continuities between the old regimes and the new. Monarchs retained significant power in Russia and, for a time, in Iran and the Ottoman Empire. There and elsewhere, the new democracies maintained or rebuilt many of the old, repressive state apparatuses, and local elites frequently retained power. In addition, many of the old regimes had been committed to the modernization of economic and cultural life, and the new democracies built on some of the older reforms. The new legal codes that the Chinese democracy adopted in 1912, for example, had been drafted several years earlier under the monarchy.[19] Similarly, some of the new democracies' initiatives were maintained after democracy itself was suppressed, such as the top-down educational expansion called the "Tuba tree" policy in the Ottoman Empire, as we shall see in Chapter 4.

These continuities are clearer in hindsight than they were at the time, when historical disjuncture was the dominant experience. Holdovers from the old regime seem to have been viewed as temporary, to be swept away when the new democracy found its footing. The future was unpredictable, as attested by Ukrainian author Lesia Ukrainka, writing to relatives in the weeks after the October Manifesto: "We live as if we were persons in a romantic novel surrounded by contrasts, antitheses, impossibilities, tragedies, comedies, tragicomedies, chaos and among these some heroic scenes and figures, as if from a [classic] ancient drama. No one knows what will happen tomorrow; few remember what happened yesterday." These uncertainties tend to get short shrift in the study of the social bases of democratization, but I wish to put them front and center, in keeping with the approach in my earlier work on the Iranian Revolution of 1979.[20]

Observers of established democracies may be cynical about representative institutions. They may focus on how democracy can be co-opted by elites and dream about more radical measures of social change. But in countries that lack these institutions, democracy threatens "to change the relations between the people and those who have the power," in the words of a prodemocracy leader in early twentieth century China.[21] It often takes a wrenching social movement to force an entrenched autocrat to grant elections, to share power with a representative parliament, and to recognize the sovereignty of the people. Who is capable of carrying out such a movement? And who is capable of protecting democratic institutions against the challenges that seem to arise inevitably in their early years?

The usual suspects, according to social-scientific studies of democratization, are the bourgeoisie, the working class, and the middle class. The roles for antagonists are generally allotted to the landowners and the military. Foreign governments are sometimes accorded parts on either or both sides of the drama. But in the early twentieth century, as I contend chapter by chapter in the second part of this book, these characters played their roles inconsistently.[22] Groups of landowners sometimes supported democratization, for example; the bourgeoisie and the working class scarcely existed, in some cases. Many of these groups switched political affiliations rapidly, jumping in and out of the democratic movement in just months. Viewed in terms of the classic social-scientific scripts, the democratic revolutions of this period were a jumble.

One response to this jumble might be to focus on the process of democratic transition rather than the identities of the people who engage in this process. This approach, known half-jokingly among social scientists as *transitology*, proposes that the presence or absence of particular social groups is not required for democracy, and therefore group identities are not key to the analysis of democratization.[23] What are we to do, then, with evidence that a particular group identity mattered a great deal to the prodemocracy activists of the early twentieth century? Participants and observers consistently identified the democratic revolutions of the early twentieth century with a single social group: the emerging global class of modern intellectuals.

The term *intellectuals*, as a collective self-identification, had recently gained international popularity through the Dreyfus Affair in France in 1898, in which a movement of French writers and academics contested and eventually overturned the conviction of a Jewish military officer imprisoned for treason. Intellectuals around the world followed news of the campaign intently, as the reader will see in Chapter 2, and many sought to reenact the Dreyfusard mobilization in their own countries. The U.S. philosopher William James, for example, told the Association of American Alumni in 1907:

> We alumni and alumnae of the colleges are the only permanent presence that corresponds to the aristocracy in older countries. We have continuous traditions, as they have; our motto, too, is *noblesse oblige;* and unlike them, we stand for ideal interests solely, for we have no corporate selfishness and wield no power of corruption. We sought to have our own class consciousness. *"Les intellectuels!"* What prouder club-namecould there be than this one.[24]

James's definition of intellectuals as college graduates was one of many definitions that circulated in that era. For other self-proclaimed intellectuals, the defining feature was merely a high school education or any modern-oriented education or even a state of mind, regardless of formal education. This study does not impose any single definition, but rather attempts to track the political activities of people who identified themselves as intellectuals. In the more democratic nations of the world, the class consciousness of self-defined intellectuals manifested itself in statist social engineering. Intellectuals sought to reshape society along "rational" and "scientific" lines in the Progressive movement in the United States, Fabianism and New Liberalism in Britain, "Solidarism" and "Interventionism" in the Leftist Bloc in France. This trend drew leading segments of socialism and old-style liberalism into near unanimity.[25] In less democratic nations of the world, by contrast, the class consciousness of self-defined intellectuals manifested itself in prodemocracy movements.

Auguste Comte, the prophet of the modern intellectual class, scorned democracy as the rule of mediocrity. By the end of the nineteenth century, however, when the identity of "intellectuals" had gone global, their dominant ideology had shifted to a positivist liberalism, as I contend in Chapter 2. Among the pioneers of this shift were British academics who proposed democratic reforms that would allow an alliance of "brains and numbers on the one side" to carry the day against "wealth, rank, vested interest, possession in short, on the other." In the decade before World War I, intellectual organizations—student groups, alumni groups, professional associations, study groups, literary circles, and so on formed the backbone of prodemocracy movements around the globe, as Chapter 3 will demonstrate. This was true even in Mexico, where an earlier generation of intellectuals known as Científicos—also positivists—was closely associated with the authoritarian regime. The Mexican democracy movement rejected the Científicos' identification as intellectuals, claiming that title for "the poor intellectuals who have not suffered the corrupting influence of wealth. Among those one finds the thinkers, the philosophers, the writers, the lovers of the Fatherland and of Freedom." Moreover, as detailed in Chapter 2, intellectuals felt that democracy would bring them to power. The brains behind the alliance of "brains and numbers" anticipated that the "numbers" would recognize the intellectuals' right to rule and vote them into office. In this way, democracy was a self-interested ideology for intellectuals of the early twentieth century.[26]

In the years and months before the intellectuals came to power, as they confidently planned to inherit the reins of government, these dreams of grandeur seemed delusional. The intellectuals' numbers were miniscule and some of them were in exile, whereas their autocratic opponents were experienced and powerful. Perhaps the most startling aspect of the democratic revolutions of the early twentieth century is the hegemonic leadership that the intellectuals usurped, virtually overnight, from other social groups. That is, these other groups came to view the intellectuals and their democratic ideology as serving societal, and not merely self-interested, goals. Two of the intellectuals' key supporters were classes often identified by social scientists as the protagonists of democratization: the bourgeoisie and the working class. Activists in these groups viewed themselves not as leaders but as followers of the intellectuals, and to the extent that they favored democratization, they did so under the banner of the intellectuals' movement.

Workers joined the democracy movement despite the intellectuals' elitist treatment of working-class issues and personalities, as the reader will see in Chapter 6. For example, Francisco I. Madero, the leader of the Mexican prodemocracy movement, appealed for working-class support with the ambiguous slogan, "You do not want bread, you want only freedom, because freedom will enable you to win your bread." Yet crowds of workers came out to cheer Madero as he toured the country. João Chagas, a leading prodemocracy activist in Portugal, refused to promise workers "penny codfish" (that is, cheap food). Yet Portuguese workers participated actively in the democracy movement, suffering the bulk of casualties in the democratic revolution, and even standing guard, "defending the banks and the money of the rich, with the police and the Guard completely disarmed," as a prodemocracy intellectual recalled in amazement.[27] Moreover, democratic revolutions occurred in countries such as Iran and China that had almost no industrial working class.

The bourgeoisie's sporadic embrace of the intellectuals' hegemony has sometimes led the two groups to be lumped together as the "middle class," as I discuss in Chapter 5. In the early twentieth century, however, there were no self-proclaimed "middle-class" organizations, and middle-class political participants, such as shop owners or professionals, were as likely to oppose one another as to oppose other political groups. Yet an uneasy alliance did emerge between the bourgeoisie and the intellectuals in many countries in the decade before World War I, and the bourgeoisie's acceptance of the intellectuals' leadership was a crucial factor in the emergence of new democracies during that period. In Russia, for example, even conservative bourgeois organizations began to adopt the intellectuals' call for democratic reforms in 1905. Industrialist V. Belov explained his support for the democracy movement on the basis of self-identification with intellectuals, identification being the highest form of hegemony: "All of us intelligentsia, industrialists and non-industrialists, feel every minute that we are under surveillance." In Iran, merchants leading sit-ins against the state's arbitrary economic policies called in students and faculty from Tehran's new modern schools who lectured them on the need for democracy and inserted the call for a constitution and an elected parliament into the strikers' list of demands.[28]

The hegemony of the intellectuals was so strong in the first years of the twentieth century that even the past and future enemies of democracy, the landed elite and the military, exhibited signs of support, albeit briefly. Certain cosmopolitan aristocrats, for example, identified with the intellectuals and joined the democracy movement, and collective organizations of landowners, where they existed, dropped their resistance for a time, as detailed in Chapter 7. Modern-educated military officers were crucial allies in the democratic revolutions, as I will show in Chapter 8, though they later worked to undermine the fledgling democratic regimes they helped create.

The intellectuals' final pillar of support, as I will demonstrate in Chapter 9, was the Great Powers: Britain, France, Germany, and the United States. The Powers' support was supplemented by regional powers such as Austria-Hungary and Japan. (Russia, a regional power whose autocracy managed to undermine the democratic experiment within its own borders, played an unremittingly antidemocratic role in its relations with neighboring new democracies.) At crucial moments during the democratic revolutions, one or more of the Great Powers stepped in to assist them. The U.S. government allowed Francisco Madero to organize his invasion on Texan soil; Great Britain allowed Iranian prodemocracy sit-ins at its embassy grounds near Tehran; German military officials stationed in Ottoman Rumelia sent positive reports on the Ottoman democracy movement to the kaiser. France postponed loan negotiations with the Russian tsar until democratic political reforms were announced; Britain and Japan refused an emergency loan to the Chinese emperor while he was fighting against the prodemocracy revolution; British diplomats refused to summon British warships to protect the king of Portugal, despite the "fixed idea at the [Portuguese] Court that if a revolutionary movement were attempted we [British] should intervene."[29]

Many of the Great Powers' representatives expressed surprise and satisfaction at the attempt to mimic Great Power political formulas. The U.S. ambassador in Tehran commented on the Iranian prodemocracy movement, "The further development of this struggle will naturally attract the interest and sympathy of the friends of liberty throughout the world." Yet the Great Powers' sympathies were laced with racist misgivings about the possibilities of democratic self-governance in "backward" lands. The same U.S. ambassador in Tehran argued at length in the same memorandum that it was doomed to fail: "The great body of the Shah's subjects have no idea of the meaning of 'Constitutional Government'; the Persian language contains no equivalent of 'Constitution' as we understand the term. . . . History does not accord a single instance of successful constitutional government in a country where the Mussulman [Muslim] religion is the state religion; Islam seems to imply autocracy." A British ambassador characterized the Portuguese as "not everyday Europeans" and justified his interference in domestic affairs by writing to the Foreign Office, "I believe that if you found yourself face to face with this inert and corrupt mass you would be the first, now and then, to use the goad." Further examples of similar attitudes are presented in Chapter 9.[30]

Beyond ideological sympathies, the Great Powers cheered democratization because it sometimes served their economic and geopolitical interests. French government and business circles were jubilant over news of the October Manifesto, according to the Russian ambassador in Paris, because they felt that political concessions would help to restore order in Russia, preserving the country's value as an ally and a field of investment. The British foreign office was pleased that the restoration of the Ottoman constitution might balance the pro-German affinities of the court with the pro-British affinities of the prodemocracy coalition: "If only this Young Turk party can consolidate itself and introduce a really good administration, they will have been playing our game entirely, but perhaps not the game of other more interested Powers." Yet the Powers soon soured on the democracies. As it turned out, the game that the new democracies played was not that of the Great Powers, but rather that of the ruling intellectuals.[31]

The intellectuals calculated correctly. Their hegemony in the prodemocracy movement, based on the confident alliance of "brains and numbers," launched large numbers of intellectuals into power in the new democracies (see Chapter 4). In Russia, a hostile tsarist official called parliament "the dregs of the Russian 'intelligentsia'"; 42 percent of parliament had a higher education. In Portugal, the leading prodemocracy newspaper called for "the heroes of the field of battle"—those who had participated in the days of the revolt—to give way to "the heroes of thought," who would rule the new democracy. Old-style intellectuals opined, "The diploma in this country is everything—wisdom, nothing," and less-educated republicans complained that all the best government jobs were going to youths whose sole qualification was "having spent years of their youth eating sardines and strumming guitars alongside the learned teat of the University." In Mexico, young intellectuals "picked up the plums of office, while the real captains of the revolution"—the nonintellectuals who had actually fought against the dictator's army—"were fobbed off with, at best, lowly commissions in the *rurales* [gendarmes]." In the Guangdong province of China, where the democracy movement was most entrenched, foreign-educated men occupied "practically all the important government posts for the province."[32]

The intellectuals miscalculated, however, the stability of hegemony. The pillars of support that had carried them into office crumbled, sometimes within months, as the new ruling class ruled in its own interests. The working class was the first to defect from the prodemocracy coalition. Or rather, the working-class mobilization that had served the prodemocracy movements simply continued once democracy had been announced. With strikes now legal, and the new governments hesitant at first to use force against their own citizens, working-class activists escalated their demands for higher wages, shorter hours, and better working conditions. A flurry of strikes struck the new democracies, and the ruling intellectuals soon struck back at this challenge to their authority. In Russia, one prodemocracy leader called continued strikes "a crime against the revolution"— though he later used the threat of strikes to try to wrest further concessions from the tsar. In Portugal, the state invented a monarchist plot to subvert the republic through worker unrest and used this as a pretext to clamp down on worker activism. Even British ambassador Arthur Hardinge, who was generally hostile to the new democracy in Portugal, commended it for the "vigorous measures" taken to suppress railway strikes in mid-1912. In Mexico, the government's new Department of Labor worked with textile-mill owners to calm the strikers. In China, public health officials tried to regulate the "night-soil coolie" industry, which involved the carrying of city-dwellers' feces in buckets to dumping sites outside of town; when the workers resisted, they were arrested. In the Ottoman Empire, the government struggled to commandeer the port strikes that broke out when Austria annexed Ottoman Bosnia-Herzegovina. As a result of these tensions, the working class sat idly by when the new democracies lurched into crisis.[33]

The next group to defect was the bourgeoisie, which resented the disorder of the new democracies, the intellectuals' monopoly on power, and the taxes being foisted upon the wealthy to pay for positivist-inspired government programs. In Portugal's new democracy, a sympathetic British diplomat noted, "Taxation is high, but now all pay their share, and before the republic, the influential and rich escaped almost scot free. Commerce has fallen off, nevertheless the amount of customs duties collected has increased, as evasion has now become difficult, if not impossible. Formerly anyone with money could make an 'arrangement' with the officials." In Iran, a German diplomat reported, the wealthy tired of democracy as parliament "begins to question even their traditional prerogatives and their most sacred possession: their freedom to steal and their freedom from taxes." In Mexico, the government debated major tax increases to solve the three most pressing problems facing educational reform in the country, as identified by an intellectual in Yucatán: "money, money, and money." In the first weeks of the new democracy in China, the French consul in Shanghai noted, "The bankers and the wealthy wholesalers and compradores have all had to contribute and there is no doubt that many of them are beginning to find the new regime very burdensome."[34]

In Portugal, five major business groups were so "disgusted" with "the agitated life of party politics" that they wrote the president requesting "a rapid solution of the political crisis, so as to assure peace and domestic tranquility"—catchwords for authoritarianism. One business group complained in 1915 that popular suffrage resulted in the election of stupid men, rather than representatives of the "conservative classes." In Mexico, business groups became openly critical of the democratic regime by early 1913, and several leading businessmen supported the military coup d'état of February 1913. In the Ottoman Empire, much of the bourgeoisie consisted of ethnic minorities, in particular Greeks, Armenians, and Jews, who eventually turned from Ottoman democracy to nationalist separatism, supporting Greek annexation of Ottoman Cyprus, Armenian revolutionary movements, and Zionist settlement—though this turn occurred after democracy had been undermined.[35]

Landed elites, whom scholars expect to be the social group most hostile to democracy, resumed their assigned role in several countries, including Portugal, where some aristocratic landowners supported monarchist invasions. Only in Russia, however, did the landowners' monarchist plots succeed, when the tsar's government reasserted control and rewrote the election rules to favor landed elites. More often, democracy was undone by military officers and their coups d'état: Mahmud Şevket Pasha in the Ottoman Empire, Samsam al-Saltanah in Iran, Félix Díaz and Victoriano Huerta in Mexico, Yuan Shikai in China, plus Joaquim Pimenta de Castro's near-coup in Portugal. None of these would-be dictators lasted much longer than the democratic experiments that they toppled, and years of chaos and war ensued.

The plotters who undermined these new democracies in the early twentieth century were keenly aware of the international context of their actions.

They eagerly courted Great Power support, as did the prodemocracy forces, and searched for cues of Great Power sympathies. The governments of Britain, France, and the United States—as well as less-democratic governments in Austria-Hungary, Germany, Japan, and Russia—obliged the antidemocracy forces by withdrawing support from the new democracies in various ways. The Great Powers offered unconstitutional loans to the leaders planning coups in China and Russia. In Mexico the U.S. ambassador actually helped to arrange a coup d'état. The British gave permission that the Iranian coup-makers requested, and the British and Germans cooperated to cover the Ottoman coup-makers' Balkan flank through diplomatic pressure on Ottoman neighbors. In Portugal, too, the British expressed satisfaction with the military government of 1915: "I trust Portugal has at last been endowed with a moderate and sensible government."[36]

Yet the Portuguese coup did not succeed, presenting us with an instructive comparison: Why did this attempted coup fail to undermine the new democracy, while coups succeeded in all the other cases? Chapter 9 takes up this question and concludes that the Portuguese democracy survived because of a failed alignment of resources among the antidemocratic forces. The military coup planners in Portugal were so pro-German that they refused to seek British assistance, and the British, despite their preference for a military dictatorship in Portugal, recognized that prodemocracy intellectuals were more staunchly pro-British. In the other cases under study, no such accidental discrepancy barred the alignment of resources among the military, the bourgeoisie, the landowners, and the Great Powers.

The story of new democracy that emerges in these case studies, then, is one of alliances gained and lost. On the prodemocracy side, the intellectuals gained hegemony over and support from workers, capitalists, portions of the military, and the Great Powers. When this hegemony disintegrated, the military and landowners attempted to woo the capitalists and the Powers to an alternative, antidemocratic alliance. In Portugal, the two alliances clinched in virtual stalemate for a decade, until the fascist coup of 1926. In the Ottoman Empire and China, the antidemocratic alliance won the capital but lost the provinces to centrifugal disintegration. In Mexico, the antidemocratic alliance's victory lasted only a year, but the prodemocracy forces emerged from a decade of civil war looking like the antidemocratic regime they had ousted. In Iran, the antidemocratic alliance lost power to foreign occupation during World War I. Only in Russia did the antidemocratic alliance return to power for any length of time, about a decade, succumbing to a second democratic revolution in 1917 that lasted no longer than the first.

The failure of the new democracies devastated the intellectuals. Their newspapers were closed, their parties were driven from parliament, their state sinecures were purged, and many were driven into exile. The new authoritarians adopted parts of the intellectuals' ideology—mass education and public health reform, for example—but incorporated intellectuals selectively and only in subordinate roles. Many intellectuals plunged into despair, and themes of hopeless bleakness emerged in the literatures of all of the former democracies. In Russia, a leading poet worried: "Already, as in a nightmare or a frightening dream, we can imagine that the darkness overhanging us is the shaggy chest of the shaft-horse, and that in another moment the heavy hoofs will descend." A prodemocracy poet in Iran brought his audience to tears with the lament, "These ruins of a cemetery are not our Iran. These ruins are not Iran, where is Iran?" An Ottoman author opined: "My friend, sometimes the environment is like a bad omen, like a graveyard. What intelligence, what wisdom, what talent can survive there?" A well-known Mexican novelist came to the "basic conviction that the fight is a hopeless one and a thorough waste." In Portugal, after the coup of 1926, the journal *School Federation* warned, "Black days await us. Days of hunger threaten us. Days of slavery await us."[37] A Chinese writer offered this extreme metaphor: "Imagine an iron house having not a single window, and virtually indestructible, with all its inmates sound asleep and about to die of suffocation. Dying in their sleep, they won't feel the pain of death. Now if you raise a shout to awake a few of the light sleepers, making these unfortunate few suffer the agony of irrevocable death, do you really think you are doing them a good turn?"[38]

With their class mobilization in ruins, intellectuals began to criticize the collective identity of "intellectual." In Russia, a widely noted book of essays berated the intellectuals' class mobilization, one figure bemoaning the great breech between "the people and the intelligentsia; a hundred and fifty million on the one hand, and a few hundred thousand on the other, unable to understand each other in the most fundamental things." In the Ottoman Empire, a popular pamphlet denounced prodemocracy intellectuals for aping the West, and in Iran, prodemocracy intellectuals were mocked as "national goody-goodies." In China, leftist intellectuals adopted the slogan "Down with the intellectual class." In place of prodemocracy activism, intellectuals turned to nonpolitical pursuits or shifted to serve other masters.

Instead of ruling in their own name, the intellectuals adopted ideologies that allowed them to rule in the name of the working class, the bourgeoisie, or the "nation." The sociology of intellectuals emerged at this time with the founding insight that intellectuals are to be found on all sides of every political debate.[39]

Today, a century after the October Manifesto, the identity of "intellectual" no longer carries the global cachet that it did for educated people in the early 1900s. To many ears, my own included, it sounds old-fashioned and elitist. Yet in various parts of the world, the term once again came to inspire and impress in the late twentieth century, and the identity of the intellectual was linked once again with democracy movements. As I will argue in Chapter 10, the linkage between intellectual identities and democratization reemerged at this time, with potentially important implications for new democracies in the early twenty-first century.

This on-again, off-again linkage between intellectuals and democratic ideologies underlines the fluidity of class politics. In the decade before World War I, large numbers of educated people came to identify themselves as intellectuals and commit themselves to democratic activism; in the decade after World War I, many of the same people—and their successors—lost confidence in the class identity of intellectuals and devoted themselves to nondemocratic causes. Similarly, segments of the bourgeoisie followed the intellectuals' lead and supported democratic revolutions, then turned against democracy within a year or two. Working-class activists opposed dictatorship, then opposed democratic government. Portions of the landowning class did the same. The politics of a class, including the self-definition of a class, can change, and change quickly.

This study tracks these changes as closely as possible. It pays less attention to the long-term causes of change, which are well covered in other academic work, as summarized in Chapter 10. Rather, this study examines the self-understandings of democratic activists and their opponents during the emergence, the brief life, and the demise of democratic revolutions in the early twentieth century. It presents evidence of their collective identity, their organizational affiliation, their political ideology, and their joint activities. The rapid shifts in these self-understandings suggest that long-term causes may not be so important as short-term expectations: the more closely we examine the junctures of dramatic change, the more evidence we see of ideological and political fluctuation.

The evidence examined in this study is of four types: academic histories of each democratic revolution, memoirs by activists and observers, contemporaneous reports by journalists, and contemporaneous reports by government officials. As is typical in comparative studies of this scope, language barriers prevented entirely parallel evidence for all six cases.[40] I did not learn Chinese or Russian for this project. However, I was able to study national-language material for the other four cases. The case studies took their initial framework from a handful of books that I took to be the best overall histories of each case: Abraham Ascher's *The Revolution of 1905* and Shmuel Galai's *The Liberation Movement in Russia;* Janet Afary's *The Iranian Constitutional Revolution;* M. Şükrü Hanioğlu's *Preparation for a Revolution* on the Ottoman Empire; Vasco Pulido Valente's *O Poder e o Povo* and A. H. de Oliveira Marques' *Nova História de Portugal,* volume 11; François-Xavier Guerra's *Le Mexique de l'Ancien Régime à la Révolution* and Alan Knight's *The Mexican Revolution;* and Edward Friedman's "The Center Cannot Hold" on China. These were supplemented with an attempt to review historiographical and memoir accounts in English, French, Persian, Portuguese, Spanish, and Turkish as comprehensively as possible. In addition, I explored contemporaneous accounts by journalists and government officials. I sampled as strategically as I could from the huge number of newspapers that proliferated during the democratic revolutions, seeking representation from diverse ideological positions and focusing my limited time on key episodes such as the emergence and demise of democracy. For government reports, I examined published documentary collections, which are exceptionally rich owing to competition among governments in the 1920s and 1930s to air documents related to the outbreak of World War I. In addition, I consulted the national archives in Istanbul, London, Lisbon, Mexico City, and Washington, thanks to the financial support of the Sociology Program of the National Science Foundation and my home institutions, first Georgia State University and then the University of North Carolina at Chapel Hill. I was also fortunate to be able to consult private archives at the Condumex Center for the Study of the History of Mexico, the National Chamber of Commerce of Mexico City, and the Chamber of Commerce in Lisbon. With the help of research assistants, I focused on archival documents pertaining to the mobilization of intellectuals, such as educational policy reports, finance ministry documents on budget priorities, interior ministry monitoring of oppositional activities, and the flurry of political bargaining that surrounded democratic collapse.

The details of these revolutionary transitions generally bear out the observation I made in my last book, *The Unthinkable Revolution in Iran*

(2004), that in moments of revolutionary confusion, people replace their old routines with new paths based largely on estimates of what they think others will do. They join the revolution when they think others are going to join, and if enough people make the same calculation at the same time, revolution occurs. If not enough people do so, then the revolutionary movement fizzles. There is no way to tell in advance how such a situation will play out, or even to explain the outcome afterwards in terms of preexisting conditions. In other words, my only prediction is that prediction—even retroactive prediction—is impossible. In place of explanation, we are left with the attempt to understand the experience of people living in such unsettled conditions.[41] The experience of the democratic revolutions of the early twentieth century, I argue, included attempts by self-described intellectuals to form a class and take power through the hybrid ideology of democratic positivism. The outcome of these movements cannot be predicted retroactively. Instead, I will make one more prediction: No documents will surface to contradict the narrative I have constructed about the democratic revolutions of the early twentieth century.

2

Intellectuals and the Discourse of Democracy

Intellectuals have long aspired to power. They have justified this aspiration on the grounds that intelligence is a superior basis for the selection of leaders than is heredity, warfare, or divine nomination. It is worth noting that this justification is not based on evidence: intellectuals rarely demonstrate that they make better leaders than others, whatever the criteria of comparison may be. Indeed, the evidence in some limited historical realms, such as the mid-twentieth century, is less than favorable.[1]

Plato's ideal philosopher-king is sometimes cited as the font of a tradition that runs through the "enlightened despotism" and Jacobin revolutionaries of eighteenth-century France to the revolutionary intellectuals of the twentieth century. This tradition involves individual aspiration to power, a single intellect deemed worthy to lead. In the nineteenth century, however, intellectuals began to aspire to lead collectively, as a class, adopting an ideology closer to the Confucian examination system than to Plato. A global intellectual identity emerged at this time, a "universal market of world trade" in "spiritual commerce," as J. W. von Goethe put it.[2]

The prophet of this modern intellectual class was Auguste Comte. Much as Karl Marx championed the proletariat as the class destined to lead society, Comte predicted the inevitable rule of the "savants." Also like Marx, Comte's belief in the certainty of this eventuality did not prevent him from adopting an attitude of fervent proselytization. In Comte's view, history was divided into two stages, the premodern and the modern, with a difficult transitional period in between that Europe was then experiencing. Premodern society was based on military conquest, with ideological support from religious leaders. Modern society is based on production, but has progressed thus far, he emphasized, without appropriate ideological support, having failed to break with the religious ideology of the old system. The problems of Europe, therefore, are "the consequence of having directed attention exclusively to the practical side of the reorganization [of society] without having first decided on the theoretical part or even thought of constituting it." The only group capable of developing the new ideology, Comte argued, was the intellectual class:

> The nature of the works to be executed, of itself sufficiently indicates the class on which their execution must devolve. Since these works are theoretical, it is clear that those whose professed aim is to form theoretical combinations, in other words savants, occupied with the study of the sciences of observation, are the only men whose capacity and intellectual culture fulfill the necessary conditions.

Distinguishing himself from the philosopher-king intellectual tradition, Comte noted that one may find more intelligent individuals outside of the savants, but "we must consider classes and not individuals." Education, not intelligence, was the defining characteristic of intellectuals. In addition, Comte considered the savants to be the only group with the popular authority to gain the people's consent for the new ideology. "Thus the savants in our day possess, to the exclusion of all other classes, the two fundamental elements of spiritual government, Capacity and Authority in matters of theory." Moreover, he argued, the social transition affecting Western Europe was supranational; therefore the solution must be supranational, and only scientific men had "mutual understanding" and a social network on this international scale.[3]

These statements by Comte contain many of the themes that would mark the intellectual class mobilization of the late nineteenth and early twentieth centuries. These themes included the following:

- the definition of intellectuals as a discrete social group (Comte distinguished intellectuals from the clergy and the uneducated, as well as from engineers [not theoretical enough] and lawyers. Although boundaries of this definition would be continually contested and modified, the concept of a discrete group would not.)
- the transnational nature of this group
- the sense of the historical destiny of this group
- the abiding belief in the power of science to solve social problems, given science's successes in the natural world
- the faith in popular support for this group

This final element became all the more central at the end of the nineteenth century when intellectuals attempted to reconcile democracy, the rule of *demos* (the people), with a modern aristocracy, the rule of *aristos* (the best).

The term *intellectuals*, as a collective self-identification, was popularized in 1898 during the Dreyfus Affair in France, a scandal over the wrongful conviction of a Jewish military officer. In January, author Émile Zola published his famous essay, "I Accuse!" protesting the miscarriage of justice. In the following weeks, hundreds of college graduates from around France signed petitions supporting Zola, with their educational credentials listed in the newspaper after their names. "Is it not a sign," wrote Georges Clemenceau, the newspaper editor who published Zola's essay and the subsequent petitions, "all these *intellectuals* come from the corners of the horizon, who gather over an idea?"—Clemenceau's use of italics indicating the novelty of the term. The following week, the term gained greater circulation when an anti-Zola nationalist published an article, "The Protest of the Intellectuals," attacking the petition-signers as Jews, Protestants, simpletons, foreigners, and only "a few good Frenchmen." This insult suited the intellectuals fine; one wrote in response to praise the intellectuals as "the uprooted, or, if you will, the disinterested, the majority of men who know how to put the law and an ideal of justice ahead of themselves, their natural instincts, and their group egoisms." Indeed, French intellectuals conceived of themselves, as Comte had, as a supranational group, and were roundly criticized for this by French nationalists, who refused to identify themselves as intellectuals because of the term's antinationalist connotations.[4]

News of the Dreyfus Affair was followed intently by educated people around the world. Thousands wrote letters of support to Dreyfus and his family. A decade later, an Iranian newspaper could still comment, "Of course, the Dreyfus Affair is implanted in [our] memories." In the Ottoman Empire, the sultan was reportedly concerned that the scandal might encourage the Ottoman opposition. Indeed, many educated people, drawing inspiration from the mobilization of their French comrades, adopted the activist identity of "intellectuals." In Spain, where virtually "all the literate men" of Barcelona signed a manifesto in support of Zola, the term *intelectuales* gained currency almost immediately. Leading self-identified intellectuals called on their peers to dedicate themselves to self-abnegating political mobilization; the problem with Spain, one wrote in 1908, was that "the number of intellectuals is so limited that it cannot form enough of a mass to call itself a people." In Egypt, a leading Islamic modernist reported on the difficulties of the French *'uqala,* an Arabic term for rational intellectuals, as contrasted with religious scholars. In Iran, the terms *danishmandan* (knowledgeable ones) and later *munavvaran al-fikr* (enlighteners of thought), borrowed from Ottoman Turkish, became popular terms of self-identification among those with modern education, as did the term *ziyalilar* (enlightened ones) in Central Asia. In Russia, the older term *intelligentsia,* previously used to refer to alienated, radical youths, changed in meaning to encompass the broader meaning of *intellectuals.* China, by contrast, lacked a specific term for intellectuals at this time, as evidenced by the use of the descriptive phrase "people of education and knowledge" to translate the Russian word *intelligentsia* in 1906. Only in the late 1910s was the term *zhishi jieji* (knowledge class) adapted from Japanese.[5]

Who were the intellectuals? In crude terms, they were the holders of advanced degrees in higher education, which in some countries meant the equivalent of a high school degree. A more accurate definition, though, is that intellectuals consisted of people who called themselves intellectuals. In other words, the category was a contested badge of honor or insult. On one hand, intellectuals were constantly inventing and defending definitions of their group that would include themselves and exclude others. On the other hand, anti-intellectuals—including writers and other educated individuals who "objectively" belonged to the intellectual class—derided the group as effete (as opposed to men of action), deracinated (as opposed to good nationalists), and freethinking (as opposed to those who respected authority).[6]

Two boundaries consistently delineated the intellectuals' self-definition in the nineteenth century. The first was their exclusion of and hostility toward their competitors in the field of cosmic transcendence, namely, the clergy. "Modern" intellectuals—the term would have been considered redundant at the turn of the century because clerics were generally not deemed intellectuals—demonized religious figures as backwards and irrational. As one British intellectual stated in the 1820s, "A Representative System of Government would soon see the propriety of turning our Churches and Chapels into Temples of Science and . . . cherishing the Philosopher instead of the Priest." In Portugal, almost a century later, the prodemocracy intellectuals felt they were on the verge of accomplishing such a transformation. "The school, once modernized, clean, disinfected of customary methods, will be the beloved temple of the people." In China and Portugal, as described in Chapter 4, the intellectuals threatened to expropriate religious

buildings when they came to power in the 1910s. In some countries, however, intellectuals considered the religious scholars too powerful to be
threatened openly. In Iran and the Ottoman Empire, lay intellectuals attempted to forge an alliance with progressive religious scholars. One group
of Iranian prodemocracy activists, for example, pledged to win over Islamic
authorities "without letting them know of our real goals." A Turkish intellectual later blamed respectfulness toward religious scholars as "the mistaken starting point" of the Ottoman democracy movement, "which bound
its feet like fetters." In Mexico, one intellectual noted that the clergy ran a
good number of schools, and that the country needed education; perhaps
secular intellectuals should ally with them in the push for national education, even if this is like "making the cat the butler of the grease," a Spanish
phrase roughly equivalent to the English phrase "putting the fox in charge
of the hen house."[7]

The second boundary was set by the intellectuals' definition of themselves as outside the realm of capitalist production. By this definition, intellectuals were not so much a class, in the economic sense of having a relationship to the means of production, as an anticlass. If workers in the
late nineteenth and early twentieth centuries organized around their
common economic position, so did intellectuals—only their position was
one of detachment from the means of production. They saw themselves as
being above material interests and as "natural adversaries of [the bourgeoisie's] narrow and mundane spirit," as one of the Dreyfusard newspapers put it. They were not to be sullied by such base motives, but imagined their lives to be governed by rationality. "Our arms will be simply
inductive and deductive analysis," wrote one Dreyfusard intellectual. "We
will support ourselves solely on known and uncontested facts."[8] Julien
Benda was one of many Dreyfusards to emphasize intellectuals' ability to
transcend personal self-interest:

> [H]ere is an entire phalanx of people who not only conceive of gen-
> eral ideas, but for whom ideas determine the corresponding emo-
> tions, which in turn determine their acts, which are, much of the
> time, directly opposed to the immediate interest of the individual.
> Here is a lieutenant-colonel [Georges Picquart] who, through devo-
> tion to an abstraction, ruins his career, accepts three months of de-
> tention; a novelist [Émile Zola] who confronts the savagery of the
> crowds; thousands of young men who sign manifestos that may com-
> promise their future, perhaps even their security.[9]

The intellectuals' professed lack of self-interest was disingenuous. They had interests just like any other class. They may not have been workers or owners, but they had to make a living too, as writers, teachers, lawyers, and so on. Two narratives emerged in the nineteenth century about the material interests of the intellectuals. The first, generally marshaled by rightists, involved the overproduction of intellectuals. In this view, expanding educational opportunities were churning out graduates faster than jobs emerged to employ them, creating a mass of anomic, overeducated rabble-rousers. No international survey of intellectual underemployment occurred until the 1930s, but similar arguments were being publicized in the early 1800s.[10]

A second narrative, more congenial to intellectuals themselves, concerned the working conditions of the intellectuals. The bureaucratization of science and academia led intellectuals to fear a loss of guild autonomy through "proletarianization." One French author wrote in 1898, in an article on "Intellectual Proletarians in France," that young intellectuals, "who have acquired a considerable knowledge by force of labor and sacrifice, men who demand entrance into the administrative ranks by virtue of their university grades . . . have remained proletarians like their fathers, the peasants, workers, or employees—with this simple difference that having believed they were to become free men, they feel themselves all the more slaves." In the United States, professors complained about being "mere employees to be hired as cheaply, [and] worked as hard, as possible" and having the "stigma of servility" attached to "the noblest of callings." In Germany, Max Weber argued that academic institutions increasingly involved "the 'separation of the worker from his means of production,'" making young academics' position "as precarious as is that of any 'quasi-proletarian' existence."[11]

Moreover, the intellectuals' professions were particularly vulnerable to state control, either through sponsorship or regulation. The expansion of public education promised to create thousands of jobs for school and college graduates, as well as reproduce and increase the intellectual class. Laws widening freedom of the press allowed journalists to earn their living more easily; legal systems provided career opportunities for attorneys; and so on. The intellectuals' aspiration to state power promised to promote these class interests.

Yet the intellectuals' aspiration to state power was consistently phrased in terms of the public interest, not class interest. Indeed, the intellectuals argued that their detachment from self-interest entitled them to govern, much as monarchs claimed the divine right to rule in an earlier age. Intellectuals, like medieval monarchs, were closer to the higher cosmic spheres than economically motivated individuals. William James's comment that intellectuals were the successors to the aristocrats (quoted in the Introduction) makes the analogy explicit, as does the argument of Portuguese writer Latino Coelho, a half-century earlier, who said that those "whom God has privileged with talent" form a modern nobility, distinguishable from the premodern nobility by its altruism. "[T]he estate that this nobility founds is not for itself. All of humanity partakes of it."[12] Abdullah Cevdet, a leading prodemocracy figure in the Ottoman Empire, emphasized the catalytic role of the intellectuals: "We learn that in chemistry . . . two particular elements mix and transform into a novel, valuable compound. Let us [intellectuals] all unite to form such an immense power. Then let us attack and destroy, with our own hands, this bastion of the castle of despotism established against us."[13] Henry Bérenger, who may have coined the noun *intellectuels*, adopted an almost messianic position in *The Intellectual Aristocracy*, published in 1894: "If a free solidarity is possible among all the members of the social organism, it is the intellectual aristocracy which alone can prepare and maintain it. It does not partake of the vices that have ruined its precursors. It is above violence; it is not recruited by heredity; it is not founded upon interest. It has no reason or even possibility for existence except in justice, except in liberty, and in the conquest of the Ideal."[14]

The Dreyfus Affair built on such expectations and savior complexes. Benda, for example, by contrast with the more well-known pessimism of his *Betrayal of the Clerks*, written in the 1920s, believed at the turn of the century in "the religion of the intellect":[15]

> After its prophets, it must have, on pain of failure, its martyrs and its fanatics; like all the preceding [religions], the intellectual religion will only become a real fact through the spilling of blood. . . . [W]e will have triumphed, because our movement is directed in the main sense as that of the general and current evolution of the human spirit, while the movement of our adversaries is directed in the opposite sense; we will have triumphed because humanity of the 19th century, whatever one may say of it, tends toward civilization. . . . [T]he [Dreyfus] Affair will have marked a particularly sensitive stage in the slow formation of superior beings; it will have been a violent distention in the meaning of human progress.[16]

Comte himself was thoroughly skeptical of majority rule, as well as the civil liberties that the Dreyfusards considered central: "The 'sovereignty of the people' tends to dismember the body politic by placing power in the least capable hands; while the 'right of private judgment' tends to the complete isolation of thinkers by investing the least enlightened men with an absolute right of control over the system of ideas conceived by superior intellects for the guidance of society."[17] But by the end of the nineteenth century, such antidemocratic sentiments were considerably less popular among intellectuals, though iconoclasts like Friedrich Nietzsche of Germany and José Enrique Rodó of Uruguay—both widely read regionally—might scandalize themselves by embracing elitism and rejecting democratic sovereignty.

As Comte's positivist philosophy spread throughout Europe and the Americas in the nineteenth century, it underwent a political transformation. Instead of disparaging democracy, followers of Comte began to develop a positivist liberalism. In Britain, a positivist movement centered at the University of Oxford in the 1860s, argued, as did Comte, that intellectuals should rightfully succeed the landed aristocracy as rulers of the country. However, unlike Comte, they would rule *democratically*—they favored electoral reform and were confident that the bulk of the British people would support them if parliament were elected on a fair basis. One intellectual characterized the transition as "brains against acres." Another argued that "the contest will lie between brains and numbers on the one side, and wealth, rank, vested interest, possession in short, on the other." In the United States, too, Comtean ideas combined democratic elections with "the guidance of the elite and the genius." In Canada, a new generation of intellectuals considered it their duty to serve their country, because, as one put it, "Democracy has never succeeded, or monarchy either, where the 'best men' followed their own pleasures and allowed the worst men to seize the reins of government." In Portugal, where an opponent bemoaned "the positivist epidemic," a leading prodemocracy Comtean held that "politics transformed into the object of a science can only be conducted by the most competent."[18]

Similarly, the French mobilization on behalf of Dreyfus came to adopt a prodemocracy stance. Initially, Dreyfusards made use of and emphasized the importance of civil liberties protected by democracy: the freedom of speech, guaranteed by articles of law cited in Zola's famous open letter "I Accuse"; the freedom of assembly, including the right to form civil associations such as the League for the Defense of Human and Civil Rights.[19]

However, the defense of these rights did not at first lead to a defense of democracy. Zola, for example, praised "a hundred years of democratic conquests," then three paragraphs later expressed reservations about turning over the state to an anti-Semitic and xenophobic electorate:

> Although universal suffrage seems so fair and logical, it has a frightful drawback: the instant a man is elected by the people he becomes nothing more than tomorrow's candidate and hence the people's slave, so overriding is his need to be re-elected. Thus, when the people suffer an attack of madness such as we are witnessing now, the elected man is at the mercy of that collective madness. He goes along with it if he is not stouthearted enough to think and act as a free man.[20]

The "amalgam of Dreyfusism and what one may call the democratic counter-offensive" took place over several years, according to one of the Dreyfusard activists. After 1902, "all the Dreyfusards were integrated into the republican bloc, radical and socialist, and conversely, with negligible exceptions, all the elements of the bloc have, more or less, become Dreyfusards."[21]

Positivist liberalism faced a theoretical problem that Comte's elitism had avoided: how to reconcile the openly desired rule of the intellectuals with the oft-proclaimed sovereignty of the people. The solution lay in the belief that an enlightened population would freely choose enlightened leaders. With proper education, the voters would be able to identify and would surely prefer the expounders of truth and progress, namely the intellectuals. Hence the importance of mass education in the intellectuals' political plans: they recognized that, as it stood, the "backward" majority would refuse to support them. The next generation—even, if possible through adult education, the current generation—had to be taught how to vote. By the mid-1910s, this argument was so pat that a leading U.S. intellectual tried to go beyond the "superficial explanation . . . that a government resting upon popular suffrage cannot be successful unless those who elect and who obey their governors are educated."[22]

Mass education, therefore, formed the crux of the hegemony of the intellectuals. *Hegemony*, a term associated with the Italian communist Antonio Gramsci, is the acceptance of the interests of the ruling group as though they were the interests of the whole society. Gramsci and most Marxists apply this concept to the bourgeoisie, as in the famous statement, "What's good for General Motors is good for the United States." The hegemony of the intellectuals, by analogy, suggested that what was good for intellectuals was good for the country. Let's not avoid the obvious: mass education and other elements of the Comtean class project were very good for intellectuals.

The rest of this chapter examines the combination of positivist elitism and democratic populism in the discourse of prodemocracy movements in the six countries that underwent democratic revolutions in the early twentieth century. Positivist liberalism might seem to be a contradiction in terms—as previous and later generations of intellectuals would argue—but intellectuals in the first decade of the twentieth century considered the two ideological elements to be necessary complements.

Russia

Pavel N. Miliukov, the leader of the democracy movement in 1905, identified his intellectual lineage as positivist: "I experienced as early as my student years the impact of the two founders of contemporary sociology—the creator of positivist philosophy, Auguste Comte, and the author of synthetic philosophy, Herbert Spencer." Miliukov adopted a Comtean framework for his masterwork, a history of Russian culture that identified the emerging intellectual class of the eighteenth century as the future savior of the nation. His political activities conformed to his academic analysis. In keeping with "the laws of political biology," Miliukov emphasized the importance of unity among intellectuals in the democracy movement. Comte's work, introduced to Russia in the mid-1860s, quickly became "the bible of the Russian intelligentsia," according to a contemporary, though it did not merge with prodemocracy political activity until the end of the century.[23]

Not all members of the prodemocracy movement shared Miliukov's positivism. Petr B. Struve, founder and editor of the leading prodemocracy newspaper in 1902–1905, repudiated positivism in 1900 and had long dismissed the idea that the intellectual class was a prime mover of history. Sergei Bulgakov, another former Marxist and critic of positivism, criticized the emerging prodemocracy parties in September 1905 as espousing "different varieties of positivism and materialism." For all the attention paid to these opponents of positivism, their numbers were quite small among intellectuals at this time. Publication runs for positivist works numbered in the tens of thousands, while their opponents' works numbered in the hundreds. Even the antipositivists recognized their minority status under "the reign of positivism." Moreover, antipositivists were less likely to participate in the democracy movement than their positivist colleagues.[24]

The most telling example of antipositivism in the democracy movement was the Slavophile faction of the gentry-intellectuals, led by Dimitri N. Shipov. Shipov, a longtime activist in the Moscow provincial assembly, shared many of the ideals of the democracy movement, including the need for constitutional limits on the tsar's power and the state's duty to provide educational and social-welfare services to its citizens. At the same time, however, he favored Russian solutions, not universal positivist approaches, to Russia's problems. He envisioned a constitutional order based on traditional Russian social groups, whose representatives would complement the authority of the tsar without undermining it. When the democracy movement began to gain steam at the end of 1904, under the auspices of the gentry-dominated assemblies, Shipov participated actively and tried to steer the movement in a Slavophile direction. Six months later, however, Shipov decided that he was unable to sway the democracy movement and disassociated himself from it.[25] Shipov retained his prodemocratic ideals—for example, protesting the dissolution of parliament in 1906 and working to stem the right-wing backlash among the gentry—but he remained aloof from mainstream prodemocracy organizations.

In contrast to Shipov's emphasis on Russian traditions, the prodemocracy movement emphasized positivist themes such as the universality of progress. For example, the founding statement of the main prodemocracy organ, *Liberation,* announced in 1902:

> Free forms of political life are as little national as are the use of the alphabet or of the printing press, steam or electricity. These are merely forms of higher culture—broad and flexible enough to contain the most varied national content. The adoption of these forms becomes necessary when public life becomes so complicated that it can no longer be contained within the framework of a more primitive public structure. When such a time arrives, when a new era of history knocks at the door, it is useless to place restraints and delays in its path. It will come just the same.[26]

The democracy movement also emphasized the universality of democracy (or rights or liberty) and rationality (or science or intellectuals), and especially the linkage between these two concepts. For example, engineers in southwest Russia supported the democracy movement on the grounds that the country needed "a rational solution of many questions which are supremely important for the successful development of engineering activities in [various] areas of government life," meaning increased scientific oversight of public affairs. A national physicians' conference endorsed the goals of the democracy movement on analogous grounds: "Only if these preliminary conditions [political and social reforms] are realized will it be possible to organize a fruitful and planned struggle against the poverty of the people and against epidemics." The chair of a national teachers' conference, though personally conservative, was forced to admit that the Russian "teacher refuses to be a narrow professional, but wants his efforts to be closely aligned with the needs of the popular masses, and to satisfy these needs teachers must participate in public activity."[27] The professoriate joined the democracy movement with the *Declaration of 342*, signed by more than 1,650 academics: "Our school administration is a social and governmental disgrace. It undermines the authority of science, hinders the growth of scientific thought and prevents our people from fully realizing their intellectual potentialities. . . . Only a full guarantee of personal and social liberties will assure academic freedom—the essential conditions for true education."[28]

Despite the clear identification of democracy and professional self-interest, intellectuals viewed themselves and their prodemocracy movement as entirely un-self-interested. They used the terms *above-class (nadklassnye)* and *estate-less (bessoslovnye)* to describe themselves, in contrast to workers, capitalists, landowners, peasants, and other groups in society that were unable to rise above self-interest. Students, for example, embraced self-sacrifice as an ideal and reviled "place-hunters" for being more interested in a career than in ideals. Indeed, sacrificing for ideals has been called one of the original defining characteristics of the Russian intelligentsia. One of the founders of the idea of a Russian intellectual class project, Nicholas Shelgunov, wrote in 1864: "The intelligentsia of the eighteenth century was purely bourgeois. . . . Only the intelligentsia of the nineteenth century, schooled in generalization, has posed as the aim of all its effort the happiness of all . . . equality." In 1905, Miliukov argued that the closed political system of monarchist Russia precluded the development of interest-groups politics: "There being no 'spoils,' political opinion, having had no chance to back the private interests of any particular group or person, is disinterested, abstractly humanitarian, largely democratic, and thus naturally radical."[29] According to historian James McClelland,

the advocates of this view [of the intellectuals' duty to apply themselves to social problems] never saw their actions as benefitting narrow political or class interests. They thought that *nauka* [science], while standing above partisan struggles and debates, nonetheless carried within itself the seeds of a broadly liberal and democratic system, so that in working for one they were automatically benefiting the other. Their attitude was similar to that of the Kadet Party (which many of them joined), which proclaimed its *nadpartiinost'* [above-party-ness], its determination to stand above all parties and special interests and to represent instead the interests of all the people.[30]

The universal interests of the intellectuals made them uniquely suited to lead the nation. In 1876 a progressive Russian newspaper posed the question: "What should be the duty of that numerous, educated, and industrious class in Russia which with complete justice calls itself the intelligentsia, which represents the flower of the Russian land, and which with us more than elsewhere ought to be the medium for the understanding and manifestation of true national thought. . . . ?" By the end of the century, such questions no longer needed to be asked; the duty of the intellectuals to lead the nation's battle against the monarchy was a given. The "vast majority" of professors in Russia believed that scientists, or science itself, would generate democratic reforms. During the final year of the democracy movement, demands for "public enlightenment" were second only to demands for parliamentary rule. A union of secondary school teachers, for example, referred to the "important role that the school is conceded to play in society's advance" and its "high national purpose of awakening and renewing the country." According to a recent analysis, "The intelligentsia culture included a strong sense of social responsibility, far more demanding than simple noblesse oblige. Members of the intelligentsia felt not merely a responsibility but a compelling duty—to their peers, to their country, and to the *narod* [people]—to fulfill the mission of education, uplifting, and modernizing the Russian masses."[31]

The two ideological strands in the prodemocracy movement stood in potential conflict: the liberal ideology granting popular sovereignty and the positivist ideology emphasizing the leadership of the intellectuals. As Petr Struve noted in 1901, "How can one reconcile the striving for absolute truth and beauty with the absolute postulate of equality, of the equal value of all people?" Similarly, Maxime Kovalewsky complained in early 1906 about plans for universal suffrage (in a sentence equating "intellectuals" and "liberals"): "In a country where the intellectuals are far from forming a majority, one would think that the liberals would express the desire to make the deputies . . . the interpreters of the needs of the entire country." On occasion, the intellectuals' eagerness to reshape Russian society exposed this tension: some have criticized the movement's 1906–1907 agrarian reform plans in just these terms, as expressions of an antiliberal attempt at social engineering.[32]

Prior to October 1905, however, the tension between the positivist and democratic ideologies remained almost invisible. What prevented the tension from emerging was the intellectuals' popularity among members of other classes. The "mystique of *nauka* [science]," the intellectuals' claim to leadership of Russia, and their prodemocracy ideology, became hegemonic throughout all classes of Russian society. As will be discussed in upcoming chapters, worker activists adopted the intellectuals' prodemocracy discourse, and leftist intellectuals grudgingly followed suit. Sympathetic capitalists, who briefly captured the leadership of the bourgeoisie, adopted both the discourse of democracy and the intellectuals' rationale that intellectual activities such as science and education were crucial for the progress of the nation. In a statement of early 1905, for example, these capitalists wrote: "it is undoubted that industry is closely tied with stable legal organization of a country, with the guarantee of freedom to science and scientific truth, with the enlightenment of the people from which it recruits its working hands, which are less productive, the more ignorant they are." Even landowners granted leadership of their class to gentry-intellectuals who were enthusiasts of mass education, public health measures, and other intellectual class projects. In Saratov province, to give one example, a conservative gentry landowner made an impassioned plea on behalf of the peasants: "And what is so surprising if our teachers, having heard such lectures [on psychology], disperse to their villages and begin to preach that we do not have souls, but only an [empty] cavity, that immortality and life beyond the grave is all nonsense. They will deprive the peasant of his last faith, take from him the last comfort. . . . [T]his is unforgivable and cannot be tolerated." His colleagues were not swayed by this argument and approved a project of mass education.[33] After 1905, the hegemony of the intellectuals fell into tatters. What remained, as we will see in Chapter 10, was an authoritarian program of mass education that subjugated the intellectuals to other class projects.

Iran

Positivism was popularized in Iran primarily through the efforts of Mirza Malkum Khan, a diplomat, embezzler, and essayist who was also one of the founders of the prodemocracy movement. Malkum, educated in France, returned to Iran in 1858 and founded a secret society, the Faramushkhanah (House of Forgetting), that drew heavily on Comtean imagery and ideals. Like Comte, Malkum described this organization as a new religion, one based on the fusion of spirituality and reason, grounded in the findings of modern science, and tended by the contemporary equivalents of religious adepts, namely the modern intellectuals. Like Comte's positivism, Malkum's new religion also aspired to state power and sought to reshape society along more rational lines, including the promotion of two kinds of factories: one for producing goods, and the other for producing "men," taking in "ignorant children and turn[ing] out engineers and accomplished thinkers."[34]

Malkum also pioneered prodemocratic, or perhaps more accurately protodemocratic ideas through his espousal of a routinized, written legal system. Malkum introduced the term *qanun* (law) into Persian in his mid-nineteenth century writings, borrowing from Ottoman Turkish, and helped to popularize the term in the 1890s with his newspaper of the same name. "Who is the greatest of Iran's kings?" Malkum wrote. "He who rescues God's worshipers from the courtiers' oppression by spreading knowledge and by establishing the law." In general, however, Malkum used "the law" to refer to an enlightened despotism, with himself serving a prominent advisory role, much as Comte envisioned for himself; only once, in the 1890s, did Malkum espouse democracy itself, with a popularly elected lower legislative body and an upper body consisting of intellectuals and other "accomplished" individuals.[35]

Malkum's writings, especially his newspaper *Law*, were very popular among the emerging class of modern intellectuals, and his combination of appeals to rationality and law continued to characterize the prodemocracy movement. A number of prodemocracy intellectuals adopted surnames symbolizing their positivist values, among them 'Abbas Quli Khan Qazvini "Adamiyat" (Humanity, a tribute to Comte's positivist Religion of Humanity), Husayn " 'Adalat" (Justice), Taqi "Danish" (Knowledge), Sayyid Muhammad Riza "Musavat" (Equality), Mirza Hasan "Rushdiyah" (Elementary School), and Muhammad 'Ali "Tarbiyat" (Education). Adamiyat founded a "Society of Humanity" at the turn of the century to unite the small, secret groups of intellectuals committed to the twin ideals of democracy and truth. One of the society's founding documents linked these two ideals explicitly: "Avoidance of the bad, steps toward the good [a Qur'anic expression], removal of oppression, unity, search for knowledge, promotion of humanity, and protection of order. That which is contrary to truth is oppression."[36]

The prodemocracy movement debated which would have to come first, cognitive enlightenment or political reform. For some, democracy would have to wait until the intellectuals had enough power and time to prepare the populace. "As long as the people do not have education, they will remain ignorant of their rights, and as long as they do not know their rights, one should not hope for anything from [political and social] reforms," according to one activist. Given the country's "almost total illiteracy," another argued, the people would "remain the slaves" of their social superiors even in a democracy. The dominant opinion, however, was that intellectuals would never get the chance to enlighten the masses unless the autocracy was overthrown. Under autocracy, even when reformers were named to high positions, fickle royal favor and the opposition of entrenched reactionaries limited their ability to make significant reforms—a theme repeated in much of the critical literature of the nineteenth century. As Malkum Khan put it: "in Iran one can be appointed minister even if one has no education. . . . But I, even if I knew seven languages, would still have to be the servant of a vacant-minded illiterate."[37]

Here the self-interestedness of the intellectuals' prodemocracy ideology surfaces. The intellectuals felt they deserved to hold power, and the democracy movement was intended to bring them to office. Malkum Khan: "some uninformed *mullas* [religious leaders] say that if these ministers are removed then there will be no one left to talk to foreign governments and that then all will be lost. God save us from ignorance! . . . We have two hundred students of the *Dar al-Funun* [House of Sciences] who can give a decade of lessons to our great ministers." "Aren't you aware," a prodemocracy organization wrote in an open letter, "that the wisest of the country, the nation's intellectuals and graduates, unemployed and inactive, have crawled into a corner of poverty and have experienced degradation, while ignorant and vulgar men are in charge of all the important things and make fun of science?" Prodemocracy activists argued that the "the intellectuals of the country" should be in charge of the country in a democratic system. "I am not saying that all the affairs of the country should really be given over to four foreign-educated or European-trained youths," wrote a prodemocracy poet, "but I am saying that, by all means, the number of this sort of people in the parliament should be increased." Even a traditional intellectual, one of the leading religious scholars of the Shi'i world, agreed that "democracy means that intellectuals [literally, owners of rationality] would be selected to protect and secure the rights of the state and the subjects."[38]

Yet the prodemocracy intellectuals, naturally, preferred more often to emphasize the coincidence of their own interests and the interests of the nation as a whole. One prodemocracy activist exhorted the students of a new secular school along these lines: "Your destiny, and that of your nation and of your children, lies under the banner of science and nothing else. . . . Only through knowledge can you raise your nation to the level of the live nations of this world." "In short, every place that raises the banner of science removes the cloak of misery and misfortune," the leading prodemocracy newspaper wrote.[39] This ideology came to be accepted by the intellectuals' partners in the democracy movement.

Ottoman Empire

The primary goal of Ottoman prodemocracy activists was salvation of the empire, which was breaking apart under the influence of nationalist separatism and European imperialism. "They believed that in order to rescue the Ottoman Empire it would be sufficient merely to proclaim the constitution," one activist recalled, and "that if the parliament were convened and allowed to act, then all the complaints and evils would be abolished."[40]

In the late 1860s, a series of state officials, devout Muslims, urged the adoption of European-style government, both on pragmatic and revelatory grounds. These pioneers transformed the word *meşrutiyet,* previously a technical term in Ottoman estate law, into a new meaning of constitutionalism. Whether by coincidence or design, this new usage combined the Arabic root *shart* (conditionality, as in setting conditions on state power) and the French prodemocracy term *la charte* (constitution, from the same Latin root as the English precursor, the Magna Carta). Ottoman constitutionalists of this period were not unanimous about how democratic *meşrutiyet* ought to be; some had reservations about democratic elections.[41] By the end of the nineteenth century, however, Ottoman constitutionalists had redefined *meşrutiyet* as the equivalent of Western European democracy.

This transformation coincided with a shift toward positivism. While only a few of the early Ottoman constitutionalists had positivist ties, the movement became thoroughly imbued with Comtean ideology. The main Ottoman prodemocracy newspaper, *Mechveret* (Consultation), adopted the positivist slogan Order and Progress in its initial issues in 1895 and used Comte's dating system alongside Islamic and Gregorian dates. The editor of *Meçveret* and leader of the movement at the time, Ahmet Rıza, was a disciple of positivist leader Pierre Laffitte and a friend of Dreyfusard intellectual Georges Clemenceau. "I was totally taken with positivist doctrines," he wrote. In 1906, Ahmet Rıza participated in the founding of the International Positivist Society.[42]

Ottoman intellectuals linked the positivist vision of an orderly society ruled by experts with the democratic vision of public opinion, as in this statement by Ahmet Rıza: "Society is a unified being that is tied to natural law. This society periodically suffers illnesses. In order to diagnose the illness, the patient must be made to speak up, so that the people's condition and health, their pain and needs, will be made known to the doctors of the nation. If it is not made clear, no antidote can be found." The implicit challenge to royal authority was not lost on Sultan Abdülhamid II, who castigated a former minister of education for similar comments: "Those doctors you mentioned forced our forebears to swallow medicine whose ill effects are still with us. . . . In the end, when you say that refusal to accept the doctors' prescriptions is dictatorship, you are attacking the position of the sultanate."[43]

The intellectuals' elitism meshed uneasily with their support for democracy. "The mass feels more than it thinks," wrote Ahmed Rıza, and it was therefore incumbent upon "enlightened" activists to think for ordinary Ottomans and "to work to enlighten the people about their rights and responsibilities." If attempts were made to democratize prior to mass education, he concluded, the results would be disastrous.[44]

This tension between elitism and support for democracy led intellectuals to emphasize two ideological tendencies. The first was a fixation on mass education, by which the intellectuals meant mass acceptance of expert knowledge. "Education is the basis of civilized progress," wrote Ahmet Rıza. "If education is not advanced and the people are not involved, there will be no educated people in the country, and if there are no educated people the future of the state cannot be saved from danger." Even opponents of democracy linked it with education, as in Sultan Abdülhamid II's grudging speech welcoming the new parliament in December 1908: democratic reforms had been "postponed until, by the progress of instruction in my empire, the capacity of my people should be brought up to the desired level." Now that "the level of ability of the various classes of my people [has] been raised, thanks to the spread of instruction, I . . . proclaimed the constitution anew without hesitation."[45]

The second approach was the adoption of modernist Islamic discourse to appeal to ordinary Muslims, in keeping with the saying, popular among Ottoman intellectuals, that "Science is the religion of the elite, whereas religion is the science of the masses." Even atheist or deist intellectuals went to considerable trouble to present Islamic arguments for their cause. The positivist prodemocracy newspaper, *Mechveret,* included a Qur'anic quotation on the masthead of its Turkish-language edition (along with the positivist calendar on the French-language edition): "And consult them in the matter." The quotation was a prodemocracy interpretation introduced into modernist Islamic discourse by publicist Namık Kemal a generation earlier. The title of the newspaper, meaning "consultation," drew on this Qur'anic reference, and the editor stressed that "Consultation is the most important aspect of Islamic law." As the prodemocracy movement mobilized inside the Ottoman Empire, it continued to play on these themes. For example, activists posted a folk poem in public places in 1907 that invoked Islamic precedent: "The heirs of the Prophet were only four: Abu Bakr, 'Umar, 'Uthman, and 'Ali [the first four caliphs, or successors to Muhammad]. All who came after are shahs or sultans. Sultan means a cruel enemy." On the eve of the revolution, prodemocracy activists sent an open letter to provincial officials in Rumelia that condemned the regime both in terms of "natural law" and "Islamic law."[46]

Some argued later that the concern for Islam was their undoing. Hüseyin Cahid Yalçın, a prodemocracy activist already quoted briefly in the Introduction, proposed decades afterward that "the mistaken starting point of the constitutional revolution, which bound its feet like fetters, was the concern that every movement and plan be consistent with the *shari'a,* the fear that they would be seen in the country as opposed to religion, and the politics of respecting and protecting public opinion, or more precisely, the guild of religious scholars." At the time, however, the intellectuals appear to have considered the support of the devout to be necessary. As a result, Ottoman intellectuals did not emphasize the secular aspect of their intellectual identity in the same way that their fellow intellectuals in Russia and Western Europe did. Rather, they used terms such as *münevverler* (enlighteners) and *mütefekkirler* (thinkers) to describe themselves—terms that were Arabic in origin, and could encompass progressive religious scholars as well as secular-trained intellectuals. The same was true in Iran, where intellectuals identified themselves during the democratic revolution of 1906 as *danishmandan* (knowledgeable ones), later adopting the term *munavvaran* from Turkish. An Iranian prodemocracy newspaper visualized the alliance between modern and traditional intellectuals on its masthead, which pictured a group of men with hats (the moderns) and a group of men with turbans (the seminary scholars) both greeting an angel's message of "freedom," "equality," and "fraternity." Between them lay an inert mass of people sleeping unaware.[47]

Unlike in Iran, the Ottoman democracy movement received little support from progressive clerics until after the constitution was reinstated, when influential Muslim religious scholars, even the sultan's chief religious official, sided with the intellectuals. The day of the constitution's reinstatement, the religious scholar Musa Kazım, later appointed the chief religious official of the empire, issued a pamphlet enjoining democracy—citing Sura 3, Verse 159, of the Qur'an, as had Namık Kemal and others—and associating it with "entrusting the affairs of the country and the interests of the *umma,* which are a divine charge, to qualified persons," where "qualified persons" may indicate the placement of modern-educated intellectuals in high government positions.[48] Certainly this was the goal of the modern-educated intellectuals themselves.

Portugal

The new democracy in Portugal took as its motto the very Comtean-sounding Order and Work, and not by accident. The ideals of democracy and positivism had been linked for decades in the person of Teófilo Braga (1843–1924), the first president of the republic after the democratic revolution of 1910, professor of literature, longtime prodemocracy leader—"the highest representative of the Portuguese mentality," another prodemocracy leader called him in 1907—and ardent follower of Comte. Braga's writings included *Positivist Solutions to Portuguese Politics* (1879), *The History of Republican Ideas in Portugal* (1880), and *System of Sociology* (1884), in which he alternated and combined prodemocracy and positivist ideals.[49]

The central theme of these ideals was a stage theory of history drawn explicitly from Comte. The stage theory proposed the monarchy and old forms of knowledge belonged to a stage of time that was ending; democracy and positivism belonged to a stage of time that was arriving. One of the crucial indicators of the progression of stages, according to Braga and other Comteans, was traditional religion. Braga took Catholic Christianity in Portugal as a symptom and a bastion of the old order, and his hostility to the established church carried over into the early years of the new democracy, when the new government pursued aggressive, even foolhardy, measures against the church, expelling the Jesuits, expropriating church property, and jailing clerics who objected. Theocracy must give way to sociocracy, Braga argued, echoing Comte.[50] In our terms, the modern intellectual class sought to displace the premodern intellectual class.

The twin goals of democracy and positivism were inseparable for Braga. Positivism justified democracy—"Science tells us that monarchies have no *raison d'être*"—and was dependent on it: "All the evils which our national organism suffers are derived from the monarchical institution; let us extirpate this cancer which will impoverish us, with the same impassiveness and experimental knowledge that the surgeon attacks a morbid degeneration." According to Braga, the "reorganization of temporal power" (democracy) was a necessary condition for "the reorganization of spiritual power" (positivist intellectual reform); elsewhere he argued the reverse, that "we must begin by exercising philosophical liberties . . . because it is the instrument by which all the other activities [political reforms] are amplified."[51]

Braga's positivist vision of democracy centered on "the necessity of reorganizing politics as a science applied to the relations of social collectivity." From this he deduced that "politics transformed into the object of a science can only be conducted by the most competent." Similarly, the leading republican journal in 1910 placed great faith in "the science of governing, which is today almost a laboratory science, based above all on experimentation." As prodemocracy leader Bernardino Machado put it in a famous speech, to be discussed further in a moment: "If the thinkers do not govern, the interests and passions will govern without the bridle of reason." The idea of a rational politics was predicated on the existence of a rational class, the intellectuals, whose reason allowed them to put aside base interests and passions.[52]

Prodemocracy intellectuals commonly contrasted their own ideals with the "interests" of ordinary economic actors, both modern and premodern. Oliveira Martins, a prominent historian and prodemocracy activist, inveighed against utilitarianism on these grounds: it "is the enemy of ideologies," he wrote, using the term *ideology* in a positive sense different from later definitions, "because ideology is the equivalent of abnegation, of sacrifice, of enthusiasm, of disinterestedness, which are not compatible with egoism."[53]

The democracy movement did not appear to notice the potential conflict between a politics based on popular election and one based on "science." Braga, for example, slipped unself-consciously from a discussion of "democratic ideas" to "the necessity of avoiding all partisan agitation."[54] I have been unable to find any statements by Braga or other republicans dealing with Comte's well-known opposition to democracy.

Switching from theoretical prophecy to political demands, we find a similarly close identification of democracy with the interests of modern intellectuals. In 1878, a list of republican demands began with freedom of conscience, freedom of education, and freedom of the press, freedoms that serve the professional interests of thinkers, teachers, and writers—securing elections and protecting private property came farther down in the list. Similarly, in 1910, the founding issue of *Soul of the Nation,* the prodemocracy newspaper, led with a quotation from Georges Danton, a leader of the French Revolution: "After peace, education is the first necessity of the people."[55]

These vague demands were operationalized in terms of specific professional interests. For example, prodemocracy Professor Bernardino Machado, later president of the republic, made a famous speech on "The University and the Nation" in 1904, linking republican ideals with reform of the ancient university of Coimbra, which was dominated by old-style intellectuals but was home to a growing group of modern-oriented intellectuals. "Despotic education: despotic government," he said. "Only let there be a savior education, . . . in order to transform ourselves, this debased Portugal of today, into the grand Portugal of tomorrow." He concluded: "In sum, I identify, in my thought and in my heart, the image of the school with the image of the fatherland, both in my sadness over its reverses and decadence, and in my inextinguishable confidence in its resurgence." António José de Almeida, later minister of the interior, argued in 1907 that education was "a fundamental condition of the democratic state," that the educator was "the irreplaceable champion of the progress of peoples," that Portugal had fewer schools per capita than other countries in Europe, and that educators' salaries barely covered necessities such as a household servant and a new suit of clothes each year. Another example: Both Portuguese journalists' associations, largely composed of prodemocracy activists, marched on parliament in 1906 to protest press censorship and identify their professional interests with the salvation of the nation: "the financial, economic, moral, and intellectual reconstitution of the Nation is impossible with an unfree press."[56]

Mexico

Mexico presents an anomaly. There positivist ideals of "scientific politics" had gained power in the 1870s, and were part of the ruling dictatorship in the early 1900s. The prodemocracy movement emerged among a younger generation that was disillusioned with what they saw as the betrayal of positivist principles by their elders, the generation of Científicos (Scientists). "These Bank counselors, these Corporate lawyers, . . . these creatures of great national businesses" "measured all value in gold." "There are no poor Científicos."[57]

The young intellectuals defined themselves, by contrast, as standing for the denial of economic self-interest. Some of the younger intellectuals saw themselves as suffering economically, with "hunger at the gates." Others were apparently doing fine economically. But the central ideological thrust of the new Mexican intellectuals seems to have been a rejection of economic motivation. Indeed, Francisco I. Madero, the leader of the democracy movement, began his campaign precisely on this theme: I ought to "affiliate solidly under the flag of Porfirianism [a reference to the dictator, Porfirio Díaz] if I were only seeking the satisfaction of narrow ambitions, if I were only content to live for myself, if I were worried only about my own tranquility, the prosperity of my business affairs." Indeed, as quoted in the previous chapter, Madero suggested that the democracy movement would appeal precisely to intellectuals untainted by economic interests, "who have not suffered the corrupting influence of wealth." The young intellectuals who joined the movement similarly renounced all self-interest and embraced the rhetoric of sacrifice and national duty: "Our times demanded heroism . . . forcefulness and decisiveness in the face of responsibility . . . perennial sacrifice and the struggle of the revolutionary."[58]

Such self-abnegation, they felt, entitled them to govern. One review of the thought of three oppositional intellectuals, widely varying in their political ideologies, found similarities entirely parallel to the positivist intellectuals who were waging prodemocracy movements elsewhere: "Democracy and progress were unquestioned goals, but elitism—that is to say, the perception of special responsibilities and positions for a select group that would act on behalf of the majority—was one of the premises of their thought." This was the case even for Madero, who presents a somewhat anomalous figure in that his philosophical leanings were transcendentalist, not positivist. His fragmentary memoirs claimed that spirit mediums had communicated with him and spurred his entry into politics—yet the politics he plunged into adopted the same positivist themes as his less spiritually sensitive colleagues.[59]

For example, Madero emphasized repeatedly that the intellectuals needed to assume special responsibilities in public affairs, that the "intellectual element . . . would lead the country." "Civilization does not arrive on the point of bayonets, but in the books of teaching; it is not the soldier who must be its herald, but the schoolteacher." "Intellectual progress [is] the only true [method] for the country to grow." "The only way to make a people strong is to instruct it. . . . This only follows by means of the union and assistance of the press, since the reading of the daily press puts the humble masses in contact with the thinkers, the intellectuals, and those of firm and powerful will, the only ones who can lead the people successfully." And other ideologues of the Mexican Revolution, as Arnaldo Córdova has pointed out, were even closer to positivism, in particular Andrés Molina Enríquez (though some have raised questions about how widely his work was read within the prodemocracy movement).[60]

The intellectuals of the Mexican Revolution may have been hostile to prominent positivists, called the Científicos but they were not necessarily hostile to positivism. Only one small faction opposed positivism itself: the Ateneo de la Juventud (Atheneum of Youth), a group of young intellectuals in Mexico City who met regularly after 1908 to discuss philosophy and culture. Ateneo members felt that positivism undervalued the humanities and philosophical speculation, and in a series of lectures in 1909, they set out to demolish the premises of positivism, though even this group considered Comte a genius whose principles were debased by his followers.[61]

However, the Ateneo was one of the few organizations of young Mexican intellectuals that did not participate in the democracy movement, though some of its members took up politics after the movement came to power. As the democracy movement mobilized electorally in 1910, the leading intellectual figure of the Ateneo, Antonio Caso, spoke at a political rally supporting the dictator. One of the group's members, José Vasconcelos, was critical of his colleagues in the Ateneo who "read, quoted, and debated for the sole love of knowledge. . . . For my part, I never thought highly of knowledge for its own sake." His colleagues could not understand his desire to go off and fight for democracy. In a speech to the Ateneo in 1911, Vasconcelos urged them not to fear the "frenzy of the liberating enthusiasm," but rather trust that "the intellectual class will emerge among us, and the public power will become accustomed to respecting it." By contrast, other organizations of young intellectuals were formed in large part to wage the democracy movement, including a small political club called Order and Progress, the Comtean slogan. Prodemocracy intellectuals sought an activist reign of reason, and felt they were just the people to lead it.[62]

China

Western ideologies flooded into China in the nineteenth century, and especially after 1895, when China was defeated in war by much-smaller Japan. The defeat illustrated for many Chinese the need to follow Japan's lead in adopting Western ways. Western works and words were translated into Chinese, or more often retranslated from Japanese; Western teachings were promulgated in newly founded modern-style schools; recently founded periodicals relayed news of political and social developments in the West. The result was an ideological hodgepodge of socialism, anarchism, liberalism, and other positions, adopted wholeheartedly and with relatively little notice taken of the potential contradictions among them. Nevertheless, two elements recur throughout the Chinese intellectual scene during this period: "Mr. Democracy" and "Mr. Science," as a Chinese scholar labeled them in the late 1910s. These names were briefly adopted into Chinese directly from the English, before more suitable words were created from Japanese.[63] Although the concepts themselves were not adopted directly from the works of positivists—there were no prominent disciples of Comte in the Chinese democracy movement, as in the Russian, Ottoman, and Portuguese—they corresponded to the basic tenets of positivism.

Mr. Democracy represented such an uncontested ideal that "even the imperial government has been shrewd enough to send lackeys abroad to inquire into the political situation there so that they can concoct some imperial edicts having to do with constitutionalism," as revolutionary leader Sun Yatsen commented bitterly in 1906. The imperial state's promise of a future constitutional monarchy split the prodemocracy movement, with one faction favoring a gradual transition to constitutional rule within the framework of the imperial regime, and the other, larger faction favoring immediate deposition of the monarchy. The moderates, discussed further below, felt that China needed an extended period of tutelage before it would be ready for full democracy. Sun, the leader of the revolutionary faction, was somewhat more optimistic, noting the tradition of primitive forms of self-government in China's rural areas and commenting that the recently cannibalistic Hawaiians and the recently enslaved African-Americans were citizens of a republic; surely Chinese racial development was "somewhat higher" than that of these groups. Several years later, after the failure of the new democracy, Sun and others would revert to a tutelary perspective analogous to that of the constitutional monarchists (see

Chapter 10). Yet even before the revolution, Sun spoke of a transitional period of military dictatorship before the granting of full democratic rights, and his vision of full democracy included a leading role for intellectual guidance.[64]

This guidance was to take the form of an additional branch of government, on top of the executive, legislative, and judicial branches he wished to adopt from Anglo-American practice. This branch he called "examination power," analogous to the ancient Confucian examination system but thoroughly modern and updated, which would determine whether state officials were qualified to hold office. The need for this branch reflected a mistrust of the popular will: "foolish and ignorant people" may win elections, he argued, and fill the civil service with followers unqualified for their positions. "Therefore, the future constitution of the Republic of China must provide for an independent branch expressly responsible for civil service examinations." Sun even suggested that *all* state officials, "elected or appointed, . . . must pass those examinations before assuming office." Here then was an open declaration for the class rule of the intellectuals.[65]

Mr. Science held a similar "position of respect" during this period, as one intellectual later recalled. An ancient word for knowledge reentered Chinese usage through a reverse borrowing from Japanese. "[N]o one, whether informed or ignorant, conservative or progressive, dares openly to slight or jeer at it." Some authors limited the scope of science to the study of nature: "The only education that deserves the name is in the physical, chemical, and mechanical sciences and industries," one wrote in 1908. Many others, however, included the human sciences as well. In particular, theories of social evolution, which first appeared in Chinese translation in the last years of the nineteenth century, attracted a tremendous following. Young intellectuals adopted evolution-linked names as pseudonyms, such as Hu Natural Fitness, Yang Natural Selection, and Chen Struggle for Existence.[66] (The family name precedes the personal name in China.)

The positivist theme of social evolution was held to mean not just that society could be understood scientifically, but also that it could be steered and directed scientifically. The first issue of the revolutionary weekly *New Century* expressed the shift between the two positions in 1907:

The discovery of scientific laws and the expansion of waves of revolution are truly the characteristics of mankind during the nineteenth century. These two mutually complement and affect each other, so that society may merge into the laws of nature. . . . [T]he revolution of the New Century considers that all that does not conform to the laws of nature is undesirable and must be changed. Not only that, but this revolution will persist, forever nearing the right and the truth. Therefore, this is a relentless and progressive revolution, a revolution that has as its object the happiness of mankind.[67]

The quotation is confusing but indicative of the positivist ideology of the period: confidence in intellectuals' ability to discover the laws of nature, including natural laws governing the functioning of society, mixes unselfconsciously with confidence in intellectuals' ability to give these natural laws a helping hand through revolutionary activism.

Similarly, Sun Yatsen combined a belief in the inevitability of social evolution with a sense of mission about aiding the process. Sun's stage-theory of social evolution sketched three principles governing the "natural and inevitable . . . advance of civilization." The first was nationalism, whereby nations throw off foreign rule; the second was democracy, whereby nations replace monarchies with republics; and the third was "people's livelihood," whereby nations solve the social problems generated by capitalism. The West had accomplished the first two principles but was baffled by the third: "every informed person knows that a social revolution is inevitable in Europe and America." (On Sun's socialism, see Chapter 6.) Yet China could accomplish all three principles at a single stroke, ousting the foreign Manchu rulers, establishing a republic, and implementing unspecified social reforms, thereby leaping from a position of backwardness to the vanguard of global progress. "Then we can look back and find Europe and America looking ahead to us." Sun's optimism was based on his judgment that China had developed the intellectual capacity to solve social problems before it had developed the social problems themselves, while in Western countries the reverse was the case. "Social problems" for Sun meant specifically capitalist inequalities; he made little mention of precapitalist social problems, and indeed at one point denied that such problems existed: "land is entirely or almost entirely common property in China. That is to say, there are few or no great landowners . . . [and] the lives of Chinese workers today are far from being pitiable. There are few poor people but there are even fewer who are really rich." By this definition, China's social problems had not yet reached an "incurable" stage, Sun suggested, using a metaphor of disease that must have been natural for a physician. "Let us devise preventive measures now," he said. Sun's proposed prophylactic was a tax on land valuation that he borrowed from the U.S. economist Henry George (discussed in Chapter 7); behind the specifics of this proposed policy was a general belief in the role of intellectuals as national leaders: "Within any group, there are always a few who, possessing an enlightened outlook, spur on the rest, applying the most appropriate principles of government to our people and then apply those principles that have advanced our people to the rest of the world. This is the heavenly duty of those who are prescient."[68]

These prodemocracy movements of the early twentieth century were imbued with positivist ideology. Half of the movements were led by outright followers of Comte: Pavel Miliukov in Russia, Ahmed Rıza in the Ottoman Empire, and Teófilo Braga in Portugal. The others picked up the ideology indirectly, tapping into currents of positivist liberalism that were in the air at the time. This was the case even in Mexico, where the prodemocracy leader was a spiritualist who eschewed natural laws of society. Notwithstanding his communication with the spirit world, Francisco Madero espoused a political vision that was fully in line with the positivist democrats in Mexico and other countries of the time.

The basic elements of this ideology were faith in science and faith in democracy. Science would solve not only the challenges presented by the natural world, in this view, but also the challenges presented by the social world. Rational, scientific administration would eliminate the social vices that arbitrary government had encouraged or permitted. Democratic procedures, on the other hand, were a moral good in themselves, even above the benefits they bestowed by restraining arbitrary government.

All of these movements argued forcefully for popular sovereignty—elections, parliaments, and institutional expressions of public opinion—and just as forcefully for stewardship by a modern elite, the intellectual class. They justified this stewardship through association with the truthtelling of science, sometimes using a medical analogy: to thrive, society needed the diagnosis and care of a class of social physicians, namely intellectuals. To merge their elitism and their populism, prodemocracy movements emphasized the need for mass education—that is, for a system that would train people to recognize the intellectuals' superior qualifications for rule. Left untutored, the people might vote for reactionaries, demagogues, or other unsuitable candidates.

Yet the intellectuals were impatient to rule, and soon. They could not wait for the people to become educated and did not trust the autocracy to educate people properly in large enough numbers. Thus, the intellectuals adopted an ideology of democracy-first, education-second. This position required considerable confidence that democratic elections would send them into office. As it turned out, the intellectuals were right, at least in the short term. The next two chapters show how intellectuals won power through democratic revolutions, and how they ruled in their own hegemonic interests.

3

Intellectuals and Democratization

On average, the six countries that underwent democratic revolutions in the early twentieth century had more educated people than did other nondemocracies of the period. Leading the way, statistically speaking, was Russia, which had dozens of institutions of higher education and tens of thousands of university students in 1904, at the start of the wave of democratization.[1] University graduates played a central role in many of Russia's national institutions. Although they comprised a tiny percentage of the Russian population, they constituted a sizable cadre that mobilized in the prodemocracy movement. This chapter describes how such mobilizations occurred in the democratic revolutions of the early twentieth century.

Afghanistan, by contrast, had very few modern-educated people in the early twentieth century, only perhaps one hundred university graduates in 1905, many of them associated with the newly formed Habibiyah School, the first modern-style high school in the country. Like other intellectuals around the world at that time, they organized themselves into a prodemocracy movement, the National Secret Party, and began in 1906 to publish a newspaper, *Lamp of the News of Afghanistan*. A poem in the first issue linked education with prodemocracy activism: "Literacy . . . added the brightness of knowledge to the rays of religion, [and] wiped oppression off the mirror of time." But Afghan intellectuals were unable to garner support from other social classes, as intellectuals in neighboring Iran—only slightly more numerous—were doing at the same moment. They could not protect themselves when royalists denounced the party to King Habibullah. The monarch, a self-described "advocate of Western learning" (he had founded the Habibiyah School and named it after himself), considered democratic demands a threat to his prerogatives, and in any case premature, as Afghans "needed thirty years of education to be fitted for the post" of democratic citizenship. In 1909, many of the prodemocracy activists were arrested, including officials of the Habibiyah School, and some were executed. Thereafter, intellectuals downplayed democracy and addressed reform projects to royal patronage.[2]

The correlation of high education figures with democratic revolutions is robust, but not perfect. Colombia, for example, is a "deviant" case: by the early twentieth century, it had generated the largest cadre of university students in Latin America and far more than, say, China or Iran. Like China and Iran, Colombia had an intellectual-led prodemocracy movement. Colombia's movement was headed by Rafael Uribe Uribe, a lawyer, military officer, publisher, and coffee magnate, who—like intellectuals around the world at the time—combined faith in democracy with belief in the vital role of the "an intellectual aristocracy." "I repeat," Uribe Uribe said, "dictatorship is a vulgarity; to disdain it, one need only be somewhat learned, somewhat intelligent, and have a somewhat good education." However, Colombia did not undergo a democratic revolution in the decade before World War I. Colombia's relatively large number of educated individuals was, by itself, insufficient, because Colombian intellectuals lacked a sense of class unity. They were deeply split into two camps, the Red (liberal), who were educated in lay schools, and the Blue (conservative), who were educated in Catholic Christian schools. The two camps disagreed vehemently over what it meant to be educated. "The unfortunate system of education that predominates in Colombia is the prime cause of all our mistakes and disgraces," wrote Uribe Uribe. "Whenever I think of the children in Colombia's schools, I am overcome with a feeling of profound compassion. Poor things! Poor things!" For its part, Colombia's Catholic leadership tried in 1898 to force all intellectuals in the country to sign an oath of faith that read in part: "I . . . condemn with the Holy Father without any qualms all types of Liberalism—religious or political. I condemn with all my heart all those false freedoms which threaten and damage our Catholic faith." Intellectual debate became violent on several occasions, most recently in 1899, when liberals launched a revolutionary movement that came to be known as the War of a Thousand Days. The liberals achieved surprising early victories, but, unlike the victorious democratizations elsewhere, their movement sputtered and failed amidst terrible battlefield carnage.[3]

The Colombian case suggests that objective factors such as the absolute numbers of educated people may not have been as central to democratization as subjective factors such as class solidarity among self-identified intellectuals. The argument that I propose is circular: In the early twentieth

century, intellectuals mobilized for democracy when they had gained sufficient solidarity around the liberal positivist collective identity of themselves
as "intellectuals." Their prodemocracy mobilizations succeeded, as I argue
in the following chapters, when other groups in society acknowledged their
leadership as intellectuals. How do we know whether these conditions were
sufficient to effect their desired change? We know, and they knew, because
democratic revolutions ensued. As with other critical-mass behaviors, cause
and effect are one and the same.[4] Democracy movements of the early twentieth century grew hand-in-hand with the intellectual class consciousness
and organizations that provided their identity and infrastructure. The following sections examine the intertwined histories of intellectual class formation and prodemocracy activism in each of the six democratic revolutions of
the period.

Russia

The Russian prodemocracy movement self-consciously considered itself a
movement of the intellectual class. Months before historian Pavel N. Miliukov returned to Russia and assumed leadership of the democracy movement in 1905, he stated this perception clearly:

> [T]here exist two Russias, one quite different from the other, and
> what pleases one is quite sure to displease the other. . . . Were I to
> label these two Russias, I should designate the one as the Russia of
> Leo Tolstoy, the great writer; and the other as that of [Konstantin]
> Plehve, the late minister of the interior. The former is the Russia of
> our "intellectuals" and of the people; the latter is official Russia. One
> is the Russia of the future, as dreamed of by members of the liberal
> professions; the other is an anachronism, deeply rooted in the past,
> and defended in the present day by an omnipresent bureaucracy. The
> one spells liberty; the other, despotism.[5]

"Russian liberalism was not *bourgeois*, but *intellectual*—to use the
French terms," Miliukov wrote. *Intellectual* was still a newfangled term,
and Miliukov put it in quotation marks throughout his book. However,
Russians had an older term, *intelligentsia*, which emerged in the 1860s to
denote the "aristocracy of intellect, knowledge, and talent," as one enthu-
siast put it in 1868. The intelligentsia was never clearly defined—in 1895,
one Russian writer called it "a highly significant concept . . . which not a
single person understands"—and it had often been associated with the

subgroup of alienated, radical intellectuals rather than with the intellectual class more broadly. By the end of the century, however, the term was widely used in the latter sense. Anton Chekhov used the word in 1898 to describe the Dreyfusard intellectuals: "I first of all take the obvious into consideration: on the side of Zola is all the European intelligentsia." Similarly, an organizer of the prodemocracy movement's "banquet campaign" of 1904 sought to unite "the bulk of the country's intelligentsia around the constitutional banner." Russian Orthodox clerics understood that the term did not refer to them, noting that "church and intelligentsia are deeply divided."[6]

Prodemocracy agitation among Russian intellectuals may be dated to the late 1700s, but concerted activity did not begin for another century. In 1880, two dozen intellectuals stated in an open letter to the tsar:

> Educated society as a whole, irrespective of rank, position, or opinions, is intensely dissatisfied, and out of that dissatisfaction arises the existing agitation. . . . The only way to extricate the country from its present position is to summon an independent parliament consisting of representatives of the *zemstvos* [provincial assemblies]; to give that parliament a share in the control of the national life; and to securely guarantee personal rights, freedom of thought, and freedom of speech.[7]

"[T]he majority of the 'intelligentsia' . . . call themselves liberal," an opponent of democracy concurred in 1880.[8] The Marxist Elena D. Kuskova, breaking with the Social Democrats in 1898, referred explicitly to the linkage between intellectual self-definition and prodemocracy activism:

> As long as an *intelligent* [member of the intelligentsia] identifies himself with the workers he has no right to impose upon them ideas which do not invoke a practical response from their side [since, Kuskova argues, workers are interested only in economic benefits]. But if he considers himself a democrat he has to identify himself with all the democratic circles, including the bourgeoisie. . . . I have nothing against the political aspirations of such an *intelligent*. On the contrary. It would, however, be much better if he would actively try to fulfil his aspirations and if, without duplicity, without trying to identify his own aims with the aims of the working class, he would work in the circles of the liberal and especially radical bourgeoisie for the achievement of political freedom.[9]

Historian Shmuel Galai dates the organizational mobilization of the prodemocracy movement to the short-lived People's Rights Party of 1893–1894, which emerged from the interaction of Populists, Marxists, and prodemocracy intellectuals. Its program declared: "There are moments in the life of states when one question occupies the foremost place, thrusting into the background all other interests, however essential they might be in themselves. . . . Such a moment Russia is now living through and the question, determining her future destiny, is the question of political freedom."[10] In the early years of the twentieth century, three distinct groups of intellectuals joined the democracy movement:

- Gentry-intellectuals, whose prodemocracy agitation took advantage of their privileged legal status in provincial assemblies (*zemstvo*'s). These groups pioneered prodemocracy activism in Russia ("I can't understand why Russian noblemen would rebel in order to lose privileges," one opponent commented), but were no longer the dominant group in the movement by the end of the nineteenth century. Prodemocracy gentry were more likely than other gentry to have a higher education and to earn a living as a professional rather than as a landowner. As a result, they sympathized more with nongentry-intellectuals than with nonintellectual gentry. Prince Sergius N. Trubetskoi, to take one outstanding example, "though allied by birth and position to many other interests, was specially a champion of the Russian Intelligence."[11]

- University students, whose move from individual terrorist activity to collective political organization in the 1890s coincided with a shift from social revolutionary to democratic goals. "These Young Turks have indeed organized their own university," a faculty member complained in 1897. In the words of one student activist, the weakness of the Russian bourgeoisie leaves intellectuals as "the political and moral vanguard of the nation." "We, the students of St. Petersburg University, demand . . . the introduction of a constitution into Russia," student protestors proclaimed in 1901. A popular play in 1905 joked that in other countries, cattle are butchered rather than students, but "here we have the opposite."[12]

- Professionals, sometimes castigated by activists for abandoning the ideals of their student days, who began to organize themselves professionally—and politically—at the turn of the century.[13] The traditional division between *zemstvo* employees and the private sector tumbled as professionals assembled a series of congresses and organizations culminating in the professional unions of 1905, to be discussed later.

The Union of Liberation, the central organization of the prodemocracy movement, emerged in 1901–1903 from precisely these social groups. Its conception followed a mass demonstration in St. Petersburg, the first to bring students and professionals together in large numbers. Its first organizers, gentry-intellectual Prince D. I. Shakhovskoi from the Iaroslavl provincial assembly and historian V. Y. Bogucharskii of the Writers' Union, traveled in gentry and professional circles, respectively, urging these groups to ally themselves in a broad prodemocracy movement. Three-quarters of the Union of Liberation's members were between 30 and 45 years old; all had secondary degrees (in a country more than half illiterate), and 82 percent had a higher education; 21 percent worked in journalism, 20 percent in science and academia, and 16 percent in law.[14]

The prodemocracy movement succeeded insofar as these groups identified themselves as members of a single intellectual class. The dynamics of this identification differed in each of these groups. Among the gentry, as I will contend in Chapter 7, the prodemocracy gentry-intellectuals had to co-opt or overcome their colleagues' premodern ideals (the Slavophile model of old-time Russian consultative bodies) and their class mobilization as landowners (the Union of Landowners) and gentry (the United Nobility). For a time in 1904–1905, this project was a success. Among the university students, the competing identity was solidarity with workers (Social-Democratic Labor Party factions) or peasants (Socialist Revolutionary Party). The Union of Liberation was slow to mobilize student support, broaching the issue only in September 1904, apparently because it was assumed that students were wholeheartedly leftist. After Bloody Sunday, in January 1905, however, the students joined the democracy movement en masse: virtually every student body in the country voted to strike until September and called for a constituent assembly to establish a new democratic order.[15]

Among the professionals, intellectual class mobilization had less competition. Trained specialists aspired to intellectual status, identified with their colleagues abroad, and had already begun to organize collectively along professional lines when prodemocracy activists decided to mobilize them in late 1904. In November 1904, the Union of Liberation called for "a propaganda campaign for the formation of unions of advocates [lawyers], professors, writers and other members of the liberal professions, for the organization by

them of congresses which would elect permanent bureaux and for the amal-
gamation of these bureaux . . . into a single Union of Unions." Within
months, the Union of Unions had signed up fourteen professional associations, representing fifty thousand intellectuals and their allies. "Under the
present conditions," the Union of Unions announced in May 1905, "we
members of the intelligentsia have for too long protested merely by word.
The government is accustomed to this and it hardly responds. If we are to
have any influence on the course of events we must add to these words [with
action]."[16]

The mobilization of the intellectual class attracted members of other
classes: military officers and capitalists with engineering degrees, for example, joined the All-Russian Union of Engineers and Technicians, which
demanded the convocation of a constituent assembly. The industrialist V.
Belov, quoted in Chapter 1, explained his support for the democracy
movement on the basis of this self-identification: "All of us intelligentsia,
industrialists and non-industrialists, feel every minute that we are under
surveillance."[17]

In the summer of 1905, the prodemocracy movement nearly split in
two, with gentry-intellectuals, academics, and some elements of the professional intellectuals favoring participation in a consultative—not legislative, and far from democratic—assembly. Such an assembly was promised
by the tsar in February, and its general outlines were made public in late
spring. The rest of the Union of Liberation opposed this participation and
held out for a fully democratic system. The friction at one congress of the
Union of Unions was so embarrassing that Pavel Miliukov, the leader of
the moderate faction, denied in his memoirs that he attended. Underlying
this division were differing perceptions of the intellectual class. As more
groups sought to identify themselves with the intellectual class, elite
groups such as university professors wished to distance themselves from
such a categorization—and from the prodemocracy movement linked to
it.[18] In addition, moderates were unsure of the extent to which other social groups supported the intellectuals' democratic goals, and were hesitant to force the issue. Hard-line prodemocracy intellectuals, by contrast,
were confident that they enjoyed widespread support. They proceeded to
prove it in the general strike of October 1905, which brought moderates
back on board and allowed the intellectuals to close ranks.

The general strike of October 1905 convinced the tsar to grant democratic reforms and marked the high point of the Russian democratic revolution. The strike was initially planned by the Union of Unions, and in

particular its member-association, the Union of Railway Workers and Employees. This group, unlike others in the Union of Unions, had a large working-class membership as well as professional members and was the only working-class union at the time with a prodemocracy leadership (the others being leftist groups with an ambiguous attitude toward democracy, as I will detail in Chapter 6). The railway union also played a key role as the capital's only link to eastern Russia, where a large portion of the military was still located in the wake of war with Japan. To transport the military west to suppress the democracy movement, or even to communicate with its forces in the east, the state relied on the rails. The railway union began to organize a strike in the spring of 1905, and grabbed the opportunity to put their plans into action at the end of September, following a congress of railway worker representatives.[19]

Within weeks, huge sectors of the country had joined in a general strike, embracing prodemocracy demands. Even Marxists noted that the general strike "was to a considerable extent caused by the participation of that part of the intelligentsia which performs organizing functions in a capitalist economy and in state activities and, owing to its social position, can act as a link between the movement of the masses and that of the propertied upper classes." Supporters of the autocracy also identified intellectuals as the prime agents of the prodemocracy movement. In 1902, the minister of the interior identified the prodemocracy movement with "the so-called educated classes" and "all their theories and utopias," and banned statistical research, blaming statisticians for inciting peasant unrest. In 1905, Russian statesman Sergei I. Witte—pressing the tsar to issue the October Manifesto that Witte had drafted—emphasized the "ideological revolution" within educated society. Throughout 1905 and 1906, the police and monarchist mobs targeted students—identifiable in their student uniforms—and "other intelligentsia" for attack.[20]

Most of Russia supported the intellectuals' prodemocracy movement, or so it appeared. Yet even before the tsar relented, granting a legislative parliament in his October Manifesto, the intellectuals had lost control of the general strike. Within two years they had lost control of parliament as well.

Iran

The prodemocracy movement in Iran emerged and triumphed in the summer of 1906, during a monthlong sit-in held on the British legation grounds in Tehran. The event did not begin as a prodemocracy movement, but rather as a protest led by merchants and inspired by senior religious leaders (see Chapter 5) against recent arbitrary oppressive actions by the monarchy. It acquired its prodemocracy character when a delegation of teachers, graduates, and students from modern schools joined the sit-in and commandeered it. Setting up their own tent alongside those of the various guilds, these modern intellectuals lectured on democracy, teaching that "when the nation no longer wants a shah [king] he is not recognized" and turning the sit-in into "one vast open-air school of political science." "Since those who took refuge in the Embassy had absolutely no concept as to what a constitution was or what it required, a special group kept them informed and instilled in them its own ideas," according to a socialist prodemocracy activist. Intellectuals dominated the sit-in's negotiating committee and added a state constitution and an elected parliament to the protesters' list of demands. They convinced various groups not to leave the sit-in as negotiations continued over these demands.[21]

The Iranian intellectual class that seized this prominent position was tiny in comparison with the Russian intellectual class, whose democracy movement of 1905 inspired the Iranians. Whereas Russia had nine universities and hundreds of thousands of secondary-school students in 1905, Iran had no full-fledged universities, only several thousand secondary-school students, and possibly several hundred graduates of European schools. Yet this small group enjoyed a solidarity that was perhaps greater than their Russian counterparts. In Iran, the identity of "modern-educated intellectual" was conceived from the outset as a "class," just as merchants, guilds, aristocratic ranks, and other social groups were considered to form "classes." One early indication of this position was the state's allotment of convicts to various "class[es] of the people" in 1852 for them to execute. The newly founded modern school, Dar al-Funun (the House of Sciences), received its allotment of convicts along with other "classes."[22]

The intellectual class soon fell under royal suspicion itself. It came to be associated with antimonarchist agitation through the founding in 1858 of a Masonic-type organization, the founder and many of the members of which were associated with the Dar al-Funun. The secret organization was banned in 1861, and the monarch, Nasir al-Din Shah, came to "hear the name of the school with hatred" as a result of the episode. He is said to have preferred obedient ignoramuses to "progressive" and disobedient intellectuals. "The educated youth are very, very, very wrong," Nasir al-Din Shah stressed upon hearing of the formation of an apolitical organization of intellectuals in 1890. This royal antipathy, though it relaxed periodically, slowed the growth of the modern intellectual class. It was only at the end of the nineteenth century, after the death of Nasir al-Din Shah, that modern schools began "flourishing all over," as one student recalled.[23]

By then, the intellectuals' class consciousness was already well established. Throughout the second half of the nineteenth century, modern-educated Iranians appear to have flaunted their identity as people of enlightened thought. Malkum Khan, arguably the prototype and certainly a hero of the modern intellectuals in Iran, defended his reformist proposals in the 1850s on the basis of this identity: "If they ask me what my proof is for all of this, I will say: my proof is that I went to Europe, that I spent there ten years of my life, and that I learned the science of economics, which is the broadest in scope of all the sciences." A later prodemocracy activist asserted in a private letter, "Two days in a modern school or limited training in a foreign language is a thousand times closer to the judgment of these needs [of the country in the present era] than embarking on a hundred marginal commentaries and two hundred exercises on the *Treatments* of Abu 'Ali [Ibn Sina, the famous eleventh century scholar]." Similar attitudes were apparently widespread enough that even some observers who favored social and political reform objected to the pretensions of the modern intellectuals. One commentator said the intellectuals were "neither Western nor Eastern, but something floating between the two." Another, called them "chameleons who have returned home from St. Petersburg and other cities and for whose sake the state had to suffer great losses. Of all the sciences at their disposal [the intellectuals] have learned two things: contempt for the people [of their own country] and dishonor to their nation." Others testified to the class consciousness of the intellectuals in more positive terms, linking it with the prodemocracy movement: "If those of us who consider ourselves among the outstanding group of the country would not engage in such services [to the country], who else would?"[24]

A hundred to 150 thousand tumans of Iranian money go into the pockets of French and German teachers annually, and the intellectuals [*danishmandan*] of Iran are forced to go hungry. . . . It should also be mentioned that Belgians were hired in the [Iranian] customs service and the post office and given 800 thousand tumans while the educated, experienced Iranian youths were left unemployed. In any case, although the existence of these students was of no use to the state, it was of great use to the nation. Among other things, they who had seen the condition of the French and English state [in their studies abroad] gradually became offended by the deplorable conditions of oppression and dictatorship in Iran, and laid the foundation for complaints about this and stories about that, and awakened the people.[25]

For all their solidarity, the modern intellectuals were also keenly aware of their tiny numbers. For this reason, Iran's modern intellectuals proceeded far more carefully with their political mobilization than did other countries'. Throughout the nineteenth century, they limited themselves almost exclusively to writings, frequently anonymous (summarized in Chapter 2). Only at the turn of the century did small secret societies of intellectuals begin to organize in anticipation of playing a political role. These organizations owed their origin to the example of Malkum Khan's pseudo-Masonic organization, the Faramushkhana (House of Forgetting), founded and then banned in the mid-nineteenth century; and to Malkum's second organization, the League of Humanity, founded and disbanded in the 1890s. Most of these intellectual organizations engaged in educational activities: establishing schools, libraries, and bookstores to serve and build the intellectual class, or in their own terms to enlighten the Iranian people in preparation for future prodemocracy activities: "As long as the people do not have education, they will remain ignorant of their rights."[26]

The first intellectual organization devoted to prodemocracy mobilization—the first organization of any kind devoted to such a task—was the Revolutionary Committee, formed in May 1904. Its fifty-plus founders "reflected both the ideological homogeneity and the sociological diversity of the early intelligentsia." Some were aristocrats, some tribal leaders, some from clerical or business backgrounds, some belonged to the professions—but almost all had a modern education in one form or another, either at the Dar al-Funun or through informal study of European languages or ideas.[27] A leader of the organization announced the class basis of the movement at the first meeting:

> However benevolent, intellectual men may mobilize a force of intellect and faith, they will not succeed in anything without gaining power and strength. . . . Power in this country is in the hands of two classes—the state officials and the religious scholars—and these two classes rule the county by joint agreement. After great thought and reasoning and research, we have concluded that because our goal is

just and true, comprising the welfare of this world and the next, the salvation of the homeland and the well-being of the nation, we must resort to all possible means to achieve this goal. We must assemble a class whose thoughts and interests are closer to ours and add them to our own force. We must strive and endeavor to establish a movement through the propagation of thoughts and the publication of doctrines, showing the evils of despotism and revealing the acts of the oppressors.[28]

A second prodemocracy organization, the Secret Society, was founded in early 1905 with a similar self-understanding. One of the founders opened the first meeting with these words:

Oh gentlemen, oh intellectuals, oh patriots, oh supporters and reformers of Islam, oh zealous ones, are you sleeping or are you awake? Is there zeal for your homeland among you, and any kind of honor, and national and religious feeling? Do you love the state and worship the nation and desire education? Do you count yourself as human or not? If you have any sentiment of humanity, why do you give no thought to the wretched condition of yourselves and your compatriots and coreligionists? Why don't you notice the conditions of the learned ones?[29]

Neither prodemocracy organization appears to have engaged in any open political acts prior to the 1906 sit-in that resulted in the promulgation of the constitution. Behind the scenes, however, they were active in prodding businessmen and religious scholars to oppose the monarchy. In December 1905, an intellectual from the Revolutionary Committee helped create a crisis that involved the public beating of two leading merchants by the governor of Tehran: "since our goal is to start the revolution," he reported, "instead of opposing [the authorities'] action, I instigated it." During the protest that followed, the merchants' demands were delivered to the government by a member of the Secret Society, who "added the establishment of a 'House of Justice' to what these gentlemen had written."[30]

A second form of behind-the-scenes activity was outreach to reform-minded religious scholars whose popular following was far greater than that of the modern intellectuals. Indeed, unlike other regions of the world, the Iranian intellectuals' term for themselves—*danishmandan*, knowledgeable ones—deliberately included both modern-educated and traditional seminary-trained scholars. Only later, as the new democracy was crumbling and religious scholars were turning against it, did modern-educated intellectuals begin to refer to themselves with an Ottoman term—*munavvaran al-fikr,* enlighteners of thought—that had exclusively modern, Enlightenment connotations.[31]

Prior to the emergence of democracy, however, certain traditionally educated intellectuals were among the most outspoken proponents of democracy and modern education. This was possible because Islamic education at the beginning of the twentieth century—unlike, for example, Russian Orthodox education—was undergoing a period of modernist reform. Istanbul University in the Ottoman Empire, al-Azhar in Cairo, the Muhammadan Anglo-Oriental College in Aligarh, India, the *jadid* (modern) schools in the Islamic regions of Russia, the Muhammadiyah schools in Southeast Asia all sought to produce Muslim scholars who valued modern approaches to social problems. Islamic education arguably underwent less reform in Iran and in Najaf, the Shi'i seminary city in the Ottoman Empire where many Iranian religious scholars studied. However, a number of young religious scholars in Iran were strongly affected by the international reformist currents, and they found a patron in Ayatullah Sayyid Muhammad Tabataba'i, and to a lesser extent in the more conservative Ayatullah Sayyid 'Abdullah Bihbihani. When the lay intellectuals sought to ally themselves with the clerical establishment, this pool of modern-oriented religious scholars formed a natural bridge. Fourteen such clerics were among the fifty-seven founders of the Revolutionary Committee.[32]

These prodemocracy clerics—some of them apparently closet members of heretical offshoots of Islam—sought to push the more conservative religious scholars toward the democracy movement. They established an organization of seminary students to "pressure the religious scholars"; they distributed anonymous "night-letters" praising the religious scholars' supposed support for democracy and denigrating backsliders; at times they spread misinformation in order to block the convergence of religious and state conservatives; at other moments they tried to bring religious and state leaders together around a prodemocracy compromise.[33]

These efforts succeeded, as many of the major religious scholars of Iran sided with the intellectuals' prodemocracy movement in spring 1906, coordinating their efforts with lay intellectual organizations and mobilizing their followers in support. Despite the backstage role of the modern intellectuals, the public face of the democracy movement at this time was almost entirely clerical. The precipitating event in Iran's democratic revolution also involved conservative religious scholars. The arrest of a prodemocracy religious scholar spurred Bihbihani to arrange for a group of seminary students to free him by force; when one of the students—a descendant of the Prophet Muhammad—was killed by troops, Bihbihani called on other senior clerical leaders to join him at a sit-in at Tehran mosque. As the sit-in moved to the nearby seminary city of Qum on July 15, 1906, Bihbihani advised the merchants of the Tehran bazaar to seek refuge on British diplomatic grounds, which they proceeded to do four days later. During the British legation sit-in, the modern intellectuals finally entered the fray in their own name, as noted previously. The irony of these clerical protests is that neither Bihbihani nor many of the other senior religious scholars who joined him in this protest favored democracy per se.[34] They were seeking only to have a hated minister replaced and felt they were using the democracy movement for their own ends. At the mosque sit-in, a prodemocracy activist despaired when he overheard their plan:

> I saw a group of sons of senior religious scholars laughing heartily as they looked at the wretched people [their fellow protestors] and said: "Oh, tool for the execution of [our] intentions, our battle is not with the state, or we would have prepared weapons. Our quarrel is personal politics. Shout 'Oh, God!' louder, so that the 'Turks' of the city will be roused to take the news to the shah and [chief minister] 'Ayn al-Daulah will be removed from office."

A prodemocracy colleague reminded the activist who was using whom: "Our goal must be accomplished through such things, such people, and such motives. Any sacred goal generates profane [literally, discarded] goals and motives."[35] When the monarch agreed a month later to a constitution, a parliament, and elections, the modern intellectuals' plan had succeeded: not only had the hated minister been dismissed but the intellectuals' demand for an elected parliament had also overcome the objections of conservative religious scholars. These opponents were explicit in naming the evildoers who had forced democracy upon Iran: They were "clearly nineteenth-century Babis [a sect considered heretical by the conservatives], that is, the intellectuals of the nation, that is, renovators, atheists, and superstitious people, since true Muslims would never enter parliament. They would consider doing so to be harmful to the [religious scholars'] leadership [of the community]."[36]

Ottoman Empire

The Ottoman prodemocracy movement first emerged in the 1860s, when a small group of educated young men gathered for a picnic meeting in a forest near Istanbul. This group was familiar with Western political thought—most of them worked at the government's Translation Bureau—and wished to turn "absolute into constitutional rule" in the Ottoman Empire. Several of these men were vaulted into positions of power a decade later when a coup brought the empire's first protodemocratic interlude, a period of months in 1876–1877 that saw the proclamation of a constitution and the convening of parliament, but no direct elections or institutional checks on royal authority. Sultan Abdülhamid II soon dismissed parliament, exiled the activists, and suspended the constitution.[37]

A decade later, prodemocracy activism reemerged, once again concentrated among young educated men. The first organized group was the Ottoman Union, founded in 1889 by four students at the Military Medical School in Istanbul. The group grew to encompass the entire student body. According to the memoir of Rıza Nur, a graduate of the school, upper-class students told newcomers, "This school is the hearth of science and liberty. Here it was a duty [to study] science [and] to save the nation from dictatorship." "There was such a discipline among the students," Rıza Nur recalled, that "even though we openly practiced politics and read newspapers that were banned [by the government] as harmful and seditious, no one dared to report us to the administration. During the six years [I was in school], only three spies emerged among us."[38]

This and later prodemocracy organizations "recruit[ed] their ranks, for the most part, among the intellectual youth," according to one participant, and many of them worked in the field of education. On the eve of the 1908 democratic revolution, the seventy-eight members of the Society for Union and Progress in Istanbul consisted largely of professors, poets, and littérateurs, as well as a chemist and an astronomer. An activist in Rumelia characterized his cell as composed of "general staff, young officers, schoolteachers, junior officials, engineers, lawyers and some energetic preachers, young-thinking professors, all concerned students, and experienced elders." Among these were military officers who had been trained in modern-style schools and considered themselves intellectuals too, as in the reference by one longtime prodemocracy activist, himself a professor at a military academy, to "intellectuals (*münevverler*), especially educated military officers."[39] (On the military, see Chapter 8.)

The almost all-intellectual makeup of the prodemocracy movement co-incided with an ideology that linked reform with the intellectual class identity. A leading prodemocracy Ottoman newspaper, published in Paris, characterized its struggle as one between "crowned tyrants" and "Sorbonnes, Tolstois, and Hugos."[40] The newspaper later editorialized along these lines:

> Thus whether the people get upset about something—for example, whether or not they will oppose despotism—depends on the intellectuals of the nation. . . . In sum, it may be said that if a small rudder can by itself steer a ship ten or twenty thousand times its size, the intellectual notables can similarly manage the ordinary masses, steering them forward or backward. . . . The people of Istanbul endures its most sacred rights being trodden upon, and the shame that derives from this belongs not to the masses but to the intellectuals of the Muslim society.[41]

The exiles actually hoped at one point, according to the memoir of an intellectual activist studying in Switzerland, that when the situation was ripe, "all the intellectuals in Istanbul would soon join us."[42] In a prison in Anatolia, too, prodemocracy intellectuals discussed the need to target intellectuals:

> If there is no freedom and liberty of the press, how will everybody in the nation be taught these [goals]? But in order to write about these goals, first our thinkers must understand them. Today, however, our intellectuals have not made up their minds decisively. The thing I fear the most is that when the constitution is promulgated, the intellectuals will not have been prepared in advanced. If such a thing comes to pass, then freedom of the press at that time will be of no use to our nation.[43]

Ottoman intellectuals distinguished themselves from seminary-trained Islamic scholars but asserted their own right to interpret sacred sources, as did lay intellectuals in Iran and other Muslim societies of the period.[44] As Chapter 2 noted, the Ottoman prodemocracy movement draped itself with Islamic justifications, and some modernist clerics sympathized privately with the movement, as they noted after democratization in August 1908. But, unlike in Iran, few if any Ottoman clerics actually engaged in prodemocracy activism prior to that moment.

Indeed, just days before they came to power, some intellectuals were not at all convinced that their forces were yet sufficient to make the revolution they were planning. Others were more confident. Yet they seem to have been unanimous on one point: they all considered the mobilization of intellectuals as the natural and necessary path to democratic change. Opponents of the movement noted this as well, deriding prodemocracy leaders as "Turkish Dreyfuses."[45]

Portugal

The democracy movement in Portugal and the student movement at the University of Coimbra are nearly identical in their careers. Both began in the 1860s, suffered setbacks at the end of the century, and gained force in the first decade of the 1900s. The coincidence is not accidental. Coimbra, the sole university in Portugal, was dominated by conservative professors and theologians and tightly linked to the monarchy through ritual and the power of appointment. Yet the student body it attracted in the late nineteenth and early twentieth centuries found both the old-style education and the old-style politics it stood for to be profoundly unsatisfactory. They were interested in modernist art, experimental science, and positivist politics. The contrast between students and professors at Coimbra represented, in microcosm, the conflict between the modern and premodern intellectuals. The students felt this keenly. "At Coimbra," one prodemocracy intellectual recalled, "the only superior and heroic creatures were ourselves, the students. The professors—we considered them inferior creatures, and, it goes without saying, irrational."[46]

Student activists at the University of Coimbra understood this as a historic conflict with tremendous consequences for the nation. What was at stake was not just reform of the university, they felt, but the destiny of Portugal. In late 1862, 316 students signed a manifesto protesting the illiberal administration of the university, linking the future of the nation with the treatment of "the best of its sons." In 1890, 120 students protested the monarchy's capitulation to British economic demands: "The King is the origin of all our ills," they wrote. "Without pride we say it: any one of us is infinitely superior to that degenerate product of a dynasty of failures." In 1907, the student body went on strike, calling academic reform "an immediate necessity for the intellectual and moral renewal of the Nation, in the sense of integrating it into modern civilization."[47]

Student activism at Coimbra was a crucial component of the class formation of modern intellectuals. They came to see themselves, as Rui Ramos has noted, as a cohesive social group endowed with "the sacred mission" of transforming the nation. As prodemocracy leader Bernardino Machado proclaimed in 1883, "The university must go in the vanguard of the legion that will propel us into the future."[48]

When they graduated, student activists focused their efforts on the larger arena and formed the core of the democracy movement (unlike Russia, where graduates were roundly accused of abandoning the activism of their student years). Vasco Pulido Valente's tabulation of republican candidates during the period 1903–1910 finds that 78 of 188 were educated professionals of one sort or another, including 36 doctors, 19 lawyers, 13 teachers and professors, and 4 journalists. Others listed under commercial professions may also have had a higher education. Valente goes on to make a distinction between these leaders and the petty bourgeoisie and workers who comprised the bulk of the democracy movement's activists. Still, the democracy movement's self-conception appears to have centered on the "enlightened" elements that compose "the great base of the Republican Party."[49]

Mexico

Liberalism emerged earlier in Mexico than in the other countries in this study. By the mid-nineteenth century, democratic thought dominated political discourse. Over the last quarter of the nineteenth century, however, many prominent Mexican politicians and intellectuals turned against democracy, arguing on positivist grounds that Mexican society needed order more than it needed democratic rights. Drawing on the work of Auguste Comte, these thinkers called for "scientific politics" in place of politics based on local traditions, liberal idealism, or mass fads. The Científicos (Scientists), as they came to be known, supported the rise of "strong" government under President Porfirio Díaz, though they disagreed at times with his dictatorial ways. These scholar-administrator-politicians opposed the democracy movement that began to gain momentum in 1908. Indeed, members and sympathizers of the Científicos later commented that few if any intellectuals—using a definition that restricted the term to themselves—supported the Mexican Revolution.[50]

This was true only if one ignored the emerging generation gap among Mexican intellectuals. In the early twentieth century, owing to the spread of modern educational institutions that the Científicos and the Díaz regime had established, a younger generation of intellectuals came of age with a keen sense of group identity and a hostile attitude toward their

Científico predecessors, whom they regarded, with a couple of exceptions, as sellouts.

> The Científico group, with strictly personal intentions, has put itself under the patronage of the neo-conservatives. . . . It has taken the pompous name "Científico" presuming to base its conduct on science; and though this name has dazzled many, it must be noted that it has taken from science only those postulates that are in accord with its interests.[51]

Indeed, *científico* remained a term of insult for years after the revolution.

By contrast, younger, nonelite intellectuals were to form the crucial basis for prodemocracy mobilization, according to movement leader Francisco Madero:

> [T]he only ones who are not satisfied [with dictatorship] are the poor intellectuals who have not suffered the corrupting influence of wealth. Among those one finds the thinkers, the philosophers, the writers, the lovers of the Fatherland and of Freedom; the Middle Class that does not have many distractions and that dedicates itself to study, that does not receive any benefit from the present regime of government and that class, in the shop, while it has at stake its physical strength for the discharge of its daily task, lets its restless imagination wander through the spacious field of thought, conceiving brilliant dreams of redemption, of progress, of equality. And finally, among the working classes the select element which aspires to improve and which has managed to form powerful leagues to obtain by means of the union the force necessary for the recovery of its rights for the realization of its ideals.[52]

Notice that Madero included the middle class and even enlightened elements of the working class within his definition of intellectuals, though educated persons led the list. According to François-Xavier Guerra's study of the prodemocracy movement, Madero's predictions came to pass. Educated professionals and students formed the backbone of the movement, a third of Guerra's sample of "anti-reelectionists." Two-thirds of the sample had an advanced education, and a majority were under 30 years old.[53]

The democracy movement coincided with a dramatic rise in student organizing. A variety of student groups sprang up toward the end of the first decade of the twentieth century, gathering their forces in a Student Congress in 1910. This event was ostensibly intended to celebrate the centenary of Mexico's independence from Spain. In fact, one of the attendees recalls, "it was at heart a revolutionary assembly, with attacks on the dictatorship of Porfirio Díaz." The students held a demonstration march that was dispersed by the police, further radicalizing their peers around the country.[54]

Young intellectuals self-consciously formed "the nucleus of the democratic resurgence of 1909," as one participant later commented: schoolteachers who helped to mobilize rural areas; graduates, engineers, and journalists who corresponded profusely with Francisco Madero; youths who were "possessed of the absurd belief that the world ought to be governed by college students or professional men still in the infantile stages of their intellectual development."[55]

Young intellectuals were not the only participants in the Mexican Revolution, by any means. If they had been, it could not have succeeded. But they held most of the leading positions in the movement—the Anti-Reelection Center, which coordinated the democracy movement, was run by a schoolteacher-engineer, two lawyers, two journalists, and two well-educated landowners[56]—and largely determined the movement's goals and tactics.

China

When the Chinese state began to found modern-style schools in the second half of the nineteenth century, it was concerned about creating a class of culturally distinct and politically active intellectuals. An imperial official who founded several modern schools in the Huguang provinces contrasted the experience of Japan and Russia:

> We definitely must translate and use foreign books. Japanese education fully imitates Western method [with the exception of religious education] . . . Recently it has seemed that [the Japanese] are continually selecting, inspecting, and using [foreign books], and a wealth of human talent is steadily produced. This is using the books of other countries and obtaining great profits. Russian schools use textbooks of the French Republic, and their students repeatedly stir up troubles. This is using the books of another country and reaping great disadvantages.[57]

The development of a modern intellectual class in China was unintended, but not unexpected. And the state gave a massive impetus to the formation of this new class after 1903 by phasing out the traditional examinations that had for centuries vetted candidates for state employment. These civil-service examinations rewarded ancient forms of scholarship and shaped the aspirations of the premodern intelligentsia. When they were abolished, promising students turned to Western models of academic achievement. The number of modern schools grew from around 4,000 in 1904 to around 50,000 in 1909, according to one tabulation. Enrollment in these schools leaped from approximately 100,000 in 1905 to 1,600,000 in 1909, according to another set of statistics. Enrollment in normal and teacher-training schools increased from 80 in 1903 to 38,019 in 1909, prompting the imperial government to restrict attendance in these programs in 1910.[58]

By this time, however, modern education had largely escaped state control. Local schools far outnumbered official state schools, and a growing number of advanced students who could afford to went abroad for their higher degrees. Japan, nearby and linguistically similar, was the primary destination for these students. The Chinese student population in Japan multiplied from several hundreds at the turn of the century to several thousands by mid-decade, peaking at 13,000 in 1906 just after the abolition of the traditional civil-service examinations. Most of these students were enrolled in short-term training courses that the more serious students disdained as a "speculative rush" for "the name of being returned students, and for the prospect that was held out to them of becoming officials"; "all the opportunists rushed to Japan to study, as a shortcut to high office, and those veritable cats and dogs coiled up to buy their quickie diplomas."[59]

Despite these recriminations, Chinese students in Japan developed a sense of collective identity and a messiah complex. One returned student in Shanghai called them "the primary motive force of the entire country and the mothers [*sic*] of the progress of civilization." A Chinese student in Japan wrote in 1903: "Only students, placed between the upper class and the masses, may be able to save China from total collapse." Indeed, a returned student wrote in 1917, "the student class has been encouraged officially as well as unofficially to regard themselves as the leaders, if not the saviours, of the nation." Later leaders of the democracy movement got their first taste of oppositional politics in protests against Japanese regulations and the Chinese government's attempts to control the student body abroad. Prodemocracy organizations recruited successfully among these students.[60]

Back in China, these "returned students" formed the core of the class mobilization of the modern intellectuals. One Westerner reported, "It is estimated that at least ninety-five percent of those who received part of their education in other lands became, on their return, leaders of revolutionary thought."[61] A less sympathetic Western portrait noted the emerging class identity as early as 1905:

> [T]he young men, who already form a class apart in China, called "the returned students," are pro-Japanese scholars, who have assimilated a superficial knowledge at the Tokyo schools, and being in a transition stage, with one foot on the rock of Chinese classics, and the other on the bobbing raft of the dangerous New Learning, they must necessarily halt at the treaty ports, and attempt to make for themselves positions which are as yet denied them in the interior. Such men drift into journalism.[62]

Even more than journalism, teaching constituted the primary profession of the modern intellectuals. By 1910, modern-school graduates held more than half of all teaching jobs in China, clashing culturally and professionally with the traditional intellectuals whose jobs they were taking. "One old scholar in Sichuan altered the self-congratulatory couplet left by visiting schoolteachers at a famous beauty spot to refer to stinking ignoramuses; the resulting feud was taken to court." Yet for many modern intellectuals, teaching was devalued as merely "a stepping stone to more lucrative employment," as a contemporaneous study found. A well-known author, for example, admitted in his memoirs that he gave up teaching because it earned only one yuan per hour, while novels paid three yuan per thousand words.[63]

Lucrative employment, however, was in short supply as the new educational facilities churned out more and more graduates. Civil-service examinations had to be reconfigured in 1910 because too many modern-school students were passing; engineers, agronomists, and business school graduates found no outlet for their training except in teaching, leading later observers to label the process "circular education," whereby teachers teach pupils to become teachers.[64]

The democracy movement in China grew out of the professional grievances of the modern intellectuals. Its leaders were exiled intellectuals whom Jerome Grieder has labeled "political entrepreneurs." Its ideology reflected the intellectuals' defensive response to Western education, as described in Chapter 2. Its mobilization occurred largely through intellectual milieux. In Shanghai and Zhejiang, the maltreatment of students in Chinese schools was prime fodder for revolutionary organizing. In

Jiangsu and elsewhere, the democracy movement opposed cuts in the education budget. Scholarly societies, beginning in 1895, and education associations, beginning in 1905, proposed administrative reforms and improved training for state officials; by mid-1911 delegates from these societies were meeting in Shanghai to coordinate their efforts. By the fall of 1911, the revolutionary democracy movement met "with almost universal sympathy" among modern-educated Chinese, according to a British observer. As a result, the geography of the democracy movement paralleled the distribution of modern education in China. Y. C. Wang has noted that the provinces most committed to modern education, such as Hubei, were also the provinces most active in the democracy movement; even within a single province, such as Xinjiang, the regions exposed to modern education were more supportive of the movement than the regions that were less exposed.[65]

Young intellectuals were not the only participants in the democracy movement. Also playing crucial roles were poor people who formed the bulk of the membership of the secret societies; merchants who funded the movement; and progressive gentry whose opposition to state centralization made them allies of the democracy movement, as the reader will see in the chapters to come. Yet the modern intellectuals were so closely identified with the democracy movement that in late 1911, when the democratic revolution had broken out, imperial forces executed young men in at least one city "for no more reason than having their queues cut or wearing modern school uniforms."[66]

In all six countries where democratic revolutions succeeded in the early twentieth century, prodemocracy mobilization was linked with the emergence of a self-conscious intellectual class. The size of this class varied widely, from tens of thousands of university graduates in Russia to several hundred in Iran. In addition, the class's historical trajectory differed in each case, from the early-nineteenth-century dominance of intellectual liberalism in Mexico to the early-twentieth-century emergence of intellectual liberalism in China. The organizational form taken by these movements differed as well, from professional associations in Russia to secret societies inspired by Freemasonry, either directly through the Masons' international networks or indirectly as a model for underground organization, including oaths, codes, handshakes, and other secret practices.[67]

More important than the objective characteristics of the intellectual class were its self-understandings. In each case, the intellectuals viewed themselves as a class and mobilized around this class identity. The boundaries of the intellectual class were not uniform. In Iran, for example, perhaps because of the intellectuals' small numbers and precarious position, intellectuals were open to alliances with traditional Shi'i Islamic scholars. Ottoman Muslim intellectuals, by contrast, appear to have made less of an effort to forge alliances with Sunni Islamic scholars, and intellectuals in the other prodemocracy movements were generally hostile to Orthodox, Catholic, and Confucian scholars. Older lay scholars were often defined out of the intellectual class as well, most strikingly in Mexico, where young activists derided the positivists of the preceding generation who had supported authoritarianism. Mexican prodemocracy activists considered these forebears to have betrayed the intellectual class for personal benefit.

Despite this variation, a central commonality remains. The institutions with which intellectuals organized themselves into a class were also the key institutions of the prodemocracy movement: the Union of Unions in Russia, various secret societies in Iran and China, the Society for Union and Progress in the Ottoman Empire, and student associations in Portugal, Mexico, and China. In this way, the intellectual identity was bound up with commitment to democracy: the very terms *intelligentsia* in Russia, *danishmandan* in Iran, *münevverler* in the Ottoman Empire, *intelectuales* in Portugal and Mexico, and "returned students" in China were reserved for educated people who shared this ideological stance. It was these intellectuals who took power in the democratic revolutions, as we shall see in the next chapter.

4

The New Democracy:
Intellectuals in Power

The democratic revolutions of the early twentieth century surprised virtually everybody, including the intellectuals who considered them necessary and inevitable. One year prior to each of these revolutions—even one week prior to the Portuguese revolution of 1910—autocratic regimes appeared fully in control. In China, the Ottoman Empire, and Portugal, democracy movements were spurred to mobilize for revolution by fears that they were about to be suppressed entirely. Portuguese pro-democracy leaders called for revolution within hours of learning that a leading intellectual activist had been murdered; two days later, the king sailed into exile and the country was theirs. In the Ottoman Empire, pro-democracy military officers mutinied and fled to the countryside when they learned that they were about to be court-martialed; two weeks later, the sultan reinstated the constitution. In Iran, the democracy movement piggybacked on a sit-in by merchants, and the constitution was granted within a month. The Mexican democracy movement took power eight months after revolting. In China, prodemocracy revolutionaries were raided by the police on October 9, declared an uprising on October 10, controlled the province on October 11, and had toppled the monarchy by the end of the year. In Russia, the revolution took longest to develop, more than a year from the first major mobilization to the October Manifesto granting democratic rights, though it seemed longer at the time. As one minister recalled: "We had lived not a year between December 12, 1904 [when the tsar first offered concessions], and October 17 of the following year [when the October Manifesto was issued], but perhaps half a century."[1]

The leaders of these democracy movements were not prepared to take power so rapidly, but they made the best of the situation. In particular, they placed themselves in office whenever possible. Not all offices were available. In Russia, Iran, and the Ottoman Empire, monarchs managed to retain significant powers, at least for a time. In all of the democratic revolutions, parts of the old state bureaucracy remained largely in place, even as purges opened positions for young intellectuals. Prodemocracy intellectuals had their best showing, as they had predicted, in elected bodies, where they gained a disproportionate percentage of seats. In the months after democratization, voters endorsed the intellectuals' self-image as the rightful leaders of their nations. What did the intellectuals do with their mandates? This chapter examines how they gained office and the state projects and policies that occupied them once in power. In general, the intellectuals stayed true to their hegemonic mission (described in Chapter 2) and pursued policies that benefited all of society, but especially the intellectual class.

Russia

The October Manifesto's promise of limited democratic reforms led intellectuals to think their time would soon come. According to one professional in Poltava:

> [T]he rural intelligentsia breathed more freely and believed, as did all moderate elements of Russian society, that a Rubicon had been crossed and there was no returning to the past. At that time the intelligentsia lived through a period of political romanticism, instinctively believing that all the principles of the October Manifesto would be realized in the very near future . . . naive, but this was a wonderful time![2]

Yet, in contrast to the other new democracies of the period, the Russian democracy movement did not fully take power, and therefore did not develop as extensive a track record as the other cases in this study. As policymaking remained in the hands of the tsar and his appointees, leaders of the democracy movement sought to use parliament to push toward a truly democratic system, devoting much of its time to constitutional issues involving parliamentary power and devoting relatively little time to concrete legislation. The monarchy contributed to parliament's ineffectiveness by refusing to initiate substantial legislation—the first bill submitted was to establish a laundry and greenhouse at a provincial university. Still, monarchists said parliament's behavior proved its uselessness and revolutionary tendencies, and the lack of legislative output was one factor cited by the tsar in his order dissolving the first parliament (April–August 1906).

When popular support for parliament failed to develop in the weeks after its dismissal, prodemocracy activists recognized that their intransigence had backfired. During the second parliament (March–June 1907), they tried instead to develop a track record of productive legislative activity. This effort was stymied, however, by the continued intransigence of the monarchist government and radicals within parliament, and by a lack of time. When it became clear that the government planned to dismiss parliament again, a delegation of parliamentary moderates made a last-ditch personal appeal to prime minister P. A. Stolypin, emphasizing parliament's productivity in the past several weeks. Stolypin was unmoved; apparently, it was not parliament's productivity or lack thereof that the government objected to, but its very existence.[3]

All of the foregoing explains why it is difficult to tell, in the Russian case, how the new democracy's policies related to the class basis of the prodemocracy movement. Several aspects of this relation, however, are clear.

First, representatives of the intellectual class, who formed the bulwark of the prodemocracy movement, disproportionately led the new democracy. The Constitutional-Democratic (Kadet) Party, founded the week of the October Manifesto by the prodemocracy movement's main organizations, was a "professors' party," according to its leader, Pavel N. Miliukov. Another party activist called it a "faculty of politicians." Analysis of party membership has confirmed these impressions; for example, professionals comprised 60 percent of the party's candidates for office in early 1906, and another 25 percent were educated, salaried employees. This party of intellectuals fared well in the 1906 parliamentary elections (in part because leftist groups largely boycotted the elections) and won 153–182 seats (the number fluctuated), or 34–40 percent. A hostile tsarist official called parliament "the dregs of the Russian 'intelligentsia'"; 42 percent had a higher education, though members of intellectual professions constituted barely a quarter of the parliament's membership. Intellectuals held a lower profile in the second parliament, with only 23 percent of members having a higher education.[4] Still, no other party came close to the Kadets' plurality, and Kadet intellectuals were able to dominate parliamentary leadership and proceedings.

Second, the Kadets' party platform emphasized policies that served the class interests of the intellectuals. Freedom of expression was listed third in the program's first section, after equality before the law and freedom of conscience and religion: "Every person is to be free to express his thoughts orally and in writing, as well as to publish and disseminate them through the press or by other means." Judicial autonomy had its own section (the fourth), as did education (the eighth), which called for "complete autonomy and freedom of instruction in universities and other higher schools. Increase in their number. Decrease in tuition. Organization, by the higher schools, or educational work for the entire populace. Freedom of student organization. . . . Establishment of universal, free, and compulsory primary education." Unlike the other new democracies of the period, which aspired to large-scale educational expansion under the aegis of their central governments, Russian intellectuals were wary of centralized control, given their government's continued domination by monarchists. They called instead for decentralization. These expressions of intellectual class interests did not prevent the Kadets from supporting issues of interest to other classes as well: the party platform included sections on land reform (sixth) and labor legislation (seventh), which appealed to peasants and workers. This sensitivity to popular, nonintellectual issues set the Russian prodemocracy party apart from the other cases in this study. However, their legislative track record was too limited to maintain popular support for democracy, as I will contend in Chapter 6.[5]

Third, the autocratic regime recognized the intellectuals as the primary force behind the democracy movement (see Chapter 3) and made its greatest concessions to them. Censorship was lifted partially, for example, allowing journalists and playwrights to reach larger audiences. Among the most important concessions was the naming of a liberal intellectual, Count Ivan Tolstoi, as minister of public instruction in October 1905. Tolstoi quickly set about implementing the intellectuals' program of educational reform. In January 1906, he convened a meeting of university rectors, recently elected by professors, to advise him on higher-education policy; the group recommended that universities be completely autonomous from the state, governed by faculty, and open to all regardless of religion (removing the quota on Jews) or gender (allowing women to enroll as adjunct students for the first time). Tolstoi accepted the recommendations. In the field of primary education, too, Tolstoi adopted the intellectual position, proposing universal access.[6]

Iran

Soon after democratization, the Iranian ministerial cabinet came to be composed almost entirely of "the civilized class that was trained in Europe."

Some Iranians commented that "the meaning of democracy [was] to elect intellectuals [literally, the owners of intellect]." Indeed, intellectuals were greatly overrepresented in the new parliament, as in Russia and the other new democracies of the period. Fifty-four percent of the members of the first parliament (1906–1908) and 50 percent of the second (1909–1911), had a modern education—in a country with only a few dozen modern schools. Intellectual leaders thus had a disproportionate influence on the parliamentary proceedings, employing European terms and sitting European-style on chairs instead of rugs.[7] At the outset of the democratic period, even reactionary leaders with no modern education, including the shah, symbolically aligned themselves with the intellectuals by enrolling in the Society of Humanity (described in Chapter 2). Nonintellectual prodemocracy activists, by contrast, were frozen out of office, most notably Sattar Khan and Baqir Khan, the horse dealer and the stonemason who led the prodemocratic movement's defense of Tabriz in 1908–1909.

The intellectuals in parliament did not always agree with one another. Factions emerged between "moderates" (typically wealthier men, with links to landowners or businessmen) and "democrats" (typically younger men, with links to social-democratic movements in the Caucasus). But they did agree on a large set of positivist social reforms. Unlike the Russian parliament, the Iranian *majlis* was able to establish a track record of reform legislation during its three-and-a-half years of operation— tentatively at first, then more aggressively after the reactionary interlude of 1908–1909. As in Russia, the Iranian democracy movement never fully displaced the authority of the monarchy. While attempting to fend off challenges from absolutists, the Iranian parliament passed important reforms serving the hegemonic interests of the intellectual class. In the name of efficient governance, parliament instructed provincial and local authorities to hire graduates of modern schools. Modern-educated lawyers and judges were granted a significant, and then a dominant, role in the legal system. The Supplementary Constitution of 1907 established a secular court system separate from the long-standing religious court system (a first draft had abolished the religious courts entirely). In 1908, parliament created a new court to adjudicate disputes between the two systems. In 1910, an attorney general's office was founded. And in 1911, the entire legal system was reorganized, subordinating religious courts to state courts. Though the reorganization was never fully implemented, a leading religious scholar—one of whose traditional duties was judicial— "expressed some doubt, perhaps not without a touch of grim humour, as to whether there would be anything left for the Mollahs to do after the institution of these Courts." Modern-educated physicians were protected from traditionally trained competition through reform of the medical industry in 1911, though, for lack of credentialed physicians, experienced traditional healers in the provinces were allowed to continue practicing for the time being. Modern-educated doctors requested and were granted new powers in the field of public health, with specific tax revenues dedicated to their efforts. Censorship systems were dismantled and intellectuals dove into the profession of journalism: 190 newspapers were founded in the two-and-a-half years after the constitution was announced. According to one of these newspapers, "the strongest sign of the progress and supremacy of a nation is considered to lie in its large number of newspapers. A thriving press is seen as evidence of the presence of an awakened people." Parliament demanded a modern state budget, which meant hiring modern-educated accountants. So few such accountants existed and the state's finances were such a mess that the finance minister reported sadly to parliament that "it should not count too much on the revenue figures I've presented."[8] Indeed, for lack of a budget, no overall figures can be given for the growth of the intellectuals' state expenditures on social reform.

The greatest campaign of the intellectuals was in the field of education. Prodemocracy activists frequently defined education as their first goal, as in one newspaper editorial: "in this regard, there is never any room for protest, because the matter cannot be objected to. Every place, every country, desires the establishment of a system and good principles for schools." Articles 18 and 19 of the Supplementary Constitution of 1907 guaranteed the freedom to pursue education, required the government to establish and fund schools, and made school attendance compulsory. This school system would have to be built from scratch, beginning with a modest system of nine primary schools, with 180 students per school. In 1910, parliament reorganized the Ministry of Science and Arts, reaffirming a commitment to compulsory elementary education and placing the school system more firmly under the control of the ministry, which was to report to parliament.[9] In 1911, parliament outlined its ambitious educational goals:

All school curricula will be planned by the Ministry of Education so as to provide for the growth and development of scientific, industrial, and physical education. . . . Elementary education is compulsory for all

Iranians. . . . Although the pursuit of learning is free, everyone must complete the amount of elementary education prescribed by the government. . . . Regardless of the extent of his education, no individual will be accepted as a teacher in official schools until he has passed an examination. . . . The Ministry of Education may ban the study of any books which are detrimental to the ethics and religion of the students; books which are rejected on this basis may not be brought into any school. . . . Civil Service eligibility will be contingent upon possession of a diploma . . . Higher institutions will be built in Tehran and other principal centers. . . . The government will finance elementary schools in the villages and cities. Funds for meeting these expenses will come from a tax, collected according to law.[10]

This statement of principles, called the "Fundamental Law of the Ministry of Education," also continued the Iranian intellectuals' practice of making concessions to religious leaders: non-Muslims were not granted the right to study their own religions in state-run schools, and Islamic schools were given a partial exemption from state regulations.[11] However, the overall intent of the bill was to replace traditional intellectuals with modern intellectuals in the field of education. Religious education now faced potentially widespread competition from state-run schools, which were required to offer Islamic training. Traditional schools were supervised by state educational officials, even to the extent of selecting texts for study.

Moreover, government positions were reserved for modern intellectuals, defined as those in possession of a diploma. The constitutional article on civil-service eligibility was not limited to the Ministry of Education, but referred to virtually all state employment. Yet there were not enough intellectuals to fill these positions in 1911, much less the additional positions needed to carry out the intellectuals' social reform plans. The prodemocracy intellectuals hurried to expand their class. Despite the stated commitment to universal elementary education, the requirement that schoolteachers (and other civil servants) have at least a secondary-school diploma meant that efforts had to be geared more to higher education than to elementary education, at least in the short term. In 1911, the Ministry of Education budgeted almost twice as much money for high schools and colleges as for primary schools, to which parliament added 3,500 tumans for new primary schools and 3,600 tumans to send thirty-four students abroad for advanced education. Indeed, some intellectuals later complained that these educational efforts were "not on a large scale, not systematically on firm foundations." "Unfortunately, it did not take long for the problem of education, like its other friend—constitutionalism—to put on the attire of forgetfulness and oblivion," a newspaper commented in 1913.[12] A poet suggested that the twin ideals of democracy and science seemed somewhat loftier in principle than did the reproduction of the intellectual class in practice:

> Constitution's star shone to no avail;
> The sun of science rose, but what did we gain?
> In cities and towns you now want to base
> Training centers, there teachers to raise.[13]

Ottoman Empire

As with the intellectuals in other new democracies of this period, Ottoman intellectuals immediately attempted to colonize the state administration. A memorandum from the Society for Union and Progress, the main organization of the prodemocracy movement, insisted that all ministers, educational personnel, judicial personnel, and public works officials "be chosen from our loyal and self-sacrificing members." Employment possibilities in the new democracy appeared fairly clear at the founding meeting of the Club of Educated Ottoman Youth, one week after democratization: interpreting Article 15 of the 1876 constitution, which promised public education, a speaker concluded that "the people will complete their instruction under the direction of eminent teachers and honest patriots heretofore condemned to silence." Article 12, promising freedom of the press, meant that "the people will be able to read and listen to the opinion of these same teachers on everything of public concern."[14]

On a more theoretical plane, this power grab was wrapped in positivist principles: "All thinkers agree that if statesmen's efforts at renewal and reform do not consult the latest trends in social science, these efforts will not be fully assured of determining a secure path, and the development and reform of the country will be impossible." The politicians of the old regime "do not look to the events of history and causal patterns; they are not equal to the knowledge of the era." Education should trump experience. Cynics mocked such aspirations. One cartoon showed a child crying in a government ministry because he received a high-paying appointment, "but I was not made the boss."[15]

Beginning with the department of tax collection, old-style officials were fired en masse under the rubric of "reorganization," which one cynical newspaper likened to "swinging a stick at a crowd in the dark." In Sivas, in eastern Anatolia, an American missionary commented that the old civil servants were all laid off, and "only one out of ten of the vacancies was filled during three months following July 24 [the announcement of the constitution]. The supply to the vacant places was filled by substitutes, usually from the assistant in the offices." One such assistant in the Interior Ministry recalled that "most officials left or were forced to leave, one by one, so that not a single cabinet secretary remained." Elsewhere, the Interior Ministry told provincial governors to demote officials to menial jobs. In some areas, experienced officials had to be rehired in order to get the state's business done.[16]

At the head of the government, Sultan Abdülhamid II remained in office, as did the Russian tsar and the Iranian shah. The sultan's legal authority was now limited by the constitution, but he retained considerable powers, including—for half a year—the right to name key cabinet ministers. Initially, he kept several old-style politicians in high office, including two successive prime ministers ("the old regime did not prepare any of us as men of administration," one young intellectual explained). The lower, elected house of parliament was led by Ahmed Rıza, the positivist activist who returned from exile in Europe after democratization, and was comprised of large numbers of young, educated men (and no women): half of the representatives were younger than 44 years old, and approximately three-quarters had some modern education. Behind the government and parliament, however, stood the Society for Union and Progress, whose leaders were modern-educated men with an average age of 32, according to a British observer who met with many of them. "The order that we established in this country may be called an intellectual dictatorship, but in truth, we don't have enough intellectuals for that," prodemocracy activist Talat Bey—later a repressive government official—told a colleague.[17]

These intellectuals embarked on an ambitious reform program along hegemonic lines. As a satirical newspaper in Istanbul joked, "The constitution and the regime that resulted have had the benefit of exciting investigators and inventors of all sorts. No day passes where the government is not called to examine some project of improvement or transformation of this or that lever of the state machine. The producers and importers of formulas have become legion in Istanbul." State expenditures in 1909–1910 were one-third greater than in 1905–1906.[18]

Primary among the new projects was educational reform. Educational reform had been a catchphrase of the Ottoman state since the 1860s, and the old regime had greatly expanded the school system over the past generation, to the point where an estimated two-thirds of the population above the age of 10 was literate. The intellectuals pledged to do better. "Above all," said one official of the Society for Union and Progress soon after it came to power, "it is the lack of education to which we intend to address ourselves." Newspapers dwelt frequently on educational issues, calling schools "the spirit of the nation" and counting on them for national salvation.[19]

Within a month, the new administration replaced the entire Grand Education Council, the policy-making body in the Ministry of Education. Several months later, every state school principal was replaced. Numerous teachers and school administrators were offered raises of more than 40 percent.[20] Still, the minister of education complained to parliament that schools were starved for money:

> You realize that our Education [Ministry's] budget is in no state to speak of. For such a country, from Baghdad [now in Iraq] to Shkodra [now in Albania], our budget is 390,000 liras. We have annual public expenditures of 448,000 liras. We have a deficit of more than 50,000 liras. Do you understand, sir? Salaries cannot be paid. Anything could happen. Work is not going well, because of this, only this. Our funds are extremely scarce, nothing can be done with this amount of money.[21]

The empire's first public budget proposal, presented to parliament in February 1909, contained a 60 percent increase in education spending, with the following explanation:

> Our country's greatest need is the spread and progress of education. If this is taken seriously, it goes without saying that the budget currently accords a tiny and insufficient amount for this matter. The aspect whose achievement and progress needs the greatest care is the establishment and extension of primary education. Turning to secondary and higher education before this goal has been ensured will not bring about the desired results. First and foremost, to guarantee the establishment of primary education throughout the Ottoman lands, primary schools must be opened everywhere, and to train teachers for these [primary schools], Primary Teacher Training Schools must be immediately reformed and expanded.[22]

Nonetheless, parliament rejected a proposal to offer free and compulsory primary education. To generate teachers for primary schools, the budget allocated more money to secondary and higher education combined, than to primary education. Nail Bey, education minister for much of 1909, helped found Teacher Training Schools in every province. Still, he wrote, "We need more than 200 high school teachers; we are looking for teachers, but there are none. Their salary is at least 800 kuruş. However, nobody wants these teaching positions. . . . In the face of these conditions, what can the Ministry of Education do? We cannot train teachers in an instant. The only thing we can do is prepare teachers for the future."[23]

The figure most associated with this top-down approach was Emrullah Efendi, a prodemocracy activist and educational administrator who was appointed director of the scientific department of the Grand Education Council in the days after democratization. Emrullah, who later served as minister of education, likened school expansion to the sacred Tuba tree mentioned in the Qur'an, which has roots in heaven but bears fruit on earth: "The increased number of people educated in these [advanced] schools will enlighten the people. . . . To diffuse and reform primary education will take a long time, at least three generations. . . . We cannot wait this long. To progress, the efforts of individuals with higher education is quite necessary."[24]

In keeping with the self-definition of the intellectuals during the prodemocracy movement, the new government emphasized the empire's Islamic identity, notwithstanding the significant non-Muslim presence in the prodemocracy movement and in the population at large.[25] Curricula submitted to central authorities by a high school in Serfice (now the city of Serbia in northern Greece) show the changes mandated by the new authorities: in fall 1908, after democratization, classes on morals were renamed Morals and Civilized Manners. Islamic studies, neutrally labeled Religious Studies, shifted from a focus on ritual to a focus on the Qur'an. The new authorities, despite their positivist ideology, retained a significant Islamic element in state schools—they did not want to break too fast with tradition. Nonetheless, the incorporation of positivist grounds, not just religious morality, to define "civilized" behavior challenged Islamic scholars' monopoly on this subject. In addition, the shift of focus from ritual to the study of the Qur'an challenged the traditional religious authorities' control of interpretation, by teaching nonclerics to read the sacred text for themselves, and not simply follow the interpretations of seminary-trained scholars—a move characteristic of the modernist Islamic movement globally. In keeping with these new priorities, a government proclamation in September 1908 reduced religious officials' numbers and salaries.[26]

These shifts aroused opposition from religious conservatives. Derviş Vahdeti, a clerical activist who led an uprising against the new democracy in April 1909, railed against the intellectuals' meddling in religious affairs: "among these irreligious people, as education advances, religion declines in the same proportion. . . . To expect religion from those who don't know their religion and have no Islamic training is like extracting oil from a cucumber. The offspring of these cucumber people will have the same training. Wait and see what good comes from these children." Nonetheless, these opponents were in the minority. After democratization, the intellectuals built an alliance with Islamic scholars who shared their modernist vision, as well as with pragmatists such as the chief Ottoman religious authority, Cemaleddin Efendi, an appointee of the sultan who gave his blessings to the intellectuals' reform projects.[27]

Other hegemonic reforms included freedom of the press. Just after the promulgation of the constitution, four newspapers refused to send their articles to the censor. The government was forced to accept this change, and censorship was abolished entirely. As a result, more than two hundred new papers emerged in the following months, about as many as had appeared in the past three decades. "After July [1908], we saw family newspapers appearing with father as director, son as editor, uncle as bookkeeper, and sister as translator," and, for the first time, one's "ears are assailed by the hoarse cries of many-tongued newsboys furiously selling the latest editions." "Everyone has turned into a writer, a poet, or a satirist," a provincial newspaper commented in February 1909. Plays proliferated, many of them dramatizing the evils of dictatorship and the blessings of freedom. Publishers organized their first trade association. A commission had just proposed further press protections when the coup of April 1909 undermined the new democracy.[28]

Even before the coup, however, press freedoms were under assault. A cartoon in February 1909 showed a skeleton labeled "Censorship" trying to get out of a coffin, with journalists jumping on the coffin to keep it closed. The caption read, "The vampire is escaping." Hüseyin Hilmi Pasha, a member of the Society for Union and Progress, was named prime minister soon thereafter, following a show of force in parliament by pro-Society military officers. Hüseyin Hilmi reintroduced a restrictive publications bill to parliament, which refused to vote on it. To protest against encroachments on freedom of the press, the opposition newspaper *Serbesti* (Freedom) announced a public meeting for early April 1909. Two days before the meeting, the editor of the newspaper was assassinated. The fact that he was shot on an Istanbul bridge with police posts at either end, yet the assailant escaped, led to suspicions that the government was complicit in his murder.[29]

This event and others reflected the intellectuals' split into two camps: one side allied with the military (see Chapter 8), favoring order over freedom; the other, allied with liberal opposition parties and favoring freedom over order. These camps clashed over national policies, including regulations in February 1909 requiring police permission for public gatherings, as well as over local issues, as when two pro-Society professors at the Administrative College in Istanbul threatened to resign unless a pro-opposition colleague was fired. An opposition intellectual asked the Society for Union and Progress to stop calling its opponents "traitors" and "reactionaries." Several student groups mobilized on the liberal opposition side, enough for the Society's newspaper to condemn them: "The students' most important patriotic duty, in order to secure the homeland's future, is serious scientific effort. For students to occupy themselves with daily politics is a dangerous flame and a grievous loss." When a mutiny in Istanbul threatened the new democracy in April 1909, student groups offered to help suppress the revolt, but the Society declined their offer.[30] Instead, the Society brought in the army and used the mutiny as an excuse to suppress the new democracy itself.

Portugal

Intellectuals in Portugal's democracy movement immediately took the top positions in the postrevolutionary regime. Of eight cabinet positions in the provisional government, three were filled by teachers, one by a doctor, and one by a lawyer. The next cabinet included two teachers, two doctors, two journalists, and one lawyer. Subsequent cabinets were similar. More than three-quarters of the 272 members of parliament in 1911–1915 had some higher education, including 70 lawyers, 65 doctors, 27 journalists, 26 professors, 9 engineers, 5 schoolteachers, 5 pharmacists, and 3 librarians.[31] At least one intellectual, a young lawyer who had studied at the University of Coimbra, admitted in his memoirs that democracy was good for his career:

> The republican regime was installed in the country. This historic event, with its transcendental effects and transformations, offered me

hopeful prospects for a prosperous career. . . . My situation as a republican was notorious in Coimbra, allowing me to approach the political chiefs and other important persons of the new regime installed
in 1910, and to cultivate sympathies and friendships. By a decree of
February 10, 1912, I was named administrator of the 4th district of
Lisbon.[32]

The intellectuals did not set aside their identities as intellectuals when
they stepped into public office. For example, provisional president Teófilo
Braga proudly commented: "Everyone who saw me, during my term of
office, passing on foot through the streets, could say: 'There goes the
same man who still is the master of Literature in the Advanced College of
Letters [Braga's university department].'" The editors of the prodemocracy newspaper *The World* urged "the heroes of the field of battle"—those
who had participated in the days of the revolt—to give way to "the heroes
of thought," who would rule the new democracy. This self-image was
matched by outsiders' testimony as well. Old-style intellectuals complained, "The diploma in this country is everything—wisdom, nothing."
Less-educated republicans complained that all the best government jobs
went to youths whose sole qualification was "having spent years of their
youth eating sardines and strumming guitars alongside the learned teat of
the University." Historian Vasco Pulido Valente gives the example of
Fernão Botto Machado, a solicitor and prodemocracy activist named to a
government position and then forced to resign for lack of academic qualifications.[33]

A great debate sprang up over whether to vet public appointees on the
basis of "competency" or on their loyalty to the prodemocracy cause.
After the fall of the monarchy, many professionals who had previously
been apolitical now expressed a newfound zeal for democratic ideals.
Moderates in the democracy movement felt these *adesivos*—literally "ad-
herents," with a connotation of "bandwagoners"—ought to be embraced
as fellow intellectuals, not just "those who had fought for the Republic,"
but also "those who did not fight," and even "those who fought against
it," in the words of António José de Almeida.[34] This apolitical vision of
the intellectual class contrasted with the dominant radical perspective,
which held that prodemocracy activism was part of the intellectual
identity. In Mexico, where a similar debate occurred, the apolitical perspective won out. Not in Portugal. There the politicized faction maintained vigilance through a constant series of newspaper exposés on the

monarchist past of various state appointees. This faction managed to oust the moderates from the cabinet in 1913.

Both moderates and radicals immediately ruled in the class interests of the intellectuals, however one defined the group. As with the other cases in this study, the primary reforms in Portugal were in the field of education. Once the provisional cabinet replaced the monarchist governing bodies, among its first decrees were the expulsion of the Jesuits—paragons of premodern intellectuals—and the replacement of agency heads for primary, secondary, and higher education. That was in the first week of the new democracy. In the second week, primary school inspectors were replaced; new guidelines for high school teachers emphasizing modern degrees were declared, and high school rectors were fired, their administrative tasks to be assumed by councils of scholars. In the third week, Christian teaching in primary schools was replaced with civic education; tuition was made free at the University of Coimbra and the Polytechnical School of Lisbon; the Academy of Sciences was reorganized; and the cabinet began micromanaging the University of Coimbra, abolishing caps and gowns, oaths, and a first-year theology requirement. In the fourth week, the minister of the interior announced, "Of all the tasks that the Republic must undertake, national education is the one to which it should dedicate its greatest forces."[35]

This prioritization continued throughout the years of the democratic regime. In 1911, the new constitution mandated free and compulsory primary education, and two new universities were organized to compete with the tradition-bound University of Coimbra. In 1913, a Ministry of Education was founded. Enrollment in universities and high schools rose 50 percent during the democratic era. The intellectuals in power justified these educational reforms in terms of their benefit to the nation, their ability "to form new men for a new world." Yet the intellectuals clearly enjoyed disproportionate benefits. Hundreds of new teachers were hired, and teachers' salaries increased. Government budgets for secondary and higher education rose 10 percent from the 1910–1911 prerevolutionary budget to the 1911–1912 postrevolutionary budget, while funding for primary education fell 15 percent. By the 1914–1915 budget, funding for secondary and higher education had climbed another 36 percent, but had dropped another 15 percent for primary education. The promised (and obligatory) primary education was not made available to all Portuguese youths: the number of primary schools rose only 10 percent during the democratic period. The emphasis on advanced education assured the social reproduction of the intellectual class, but flouted both the intellectuals' hegemonic claims to reshape Portuguese society and the need for basic education in a country with an illiteracy rate of 70 percent. After fifteen years of rule by intellectuals, the illiteracy rate remained above 60 percent. Later observers have marveled at how this could be, given the great efforts devoted to education[36]—the answer lies in the focus of these efforts.

Teachers were not the only intellectuals favored by the new regime. Judges were granted the right to judicial review of the constitutionality of laws, Portugal being the first country in Europe to adopt this principle from the United States—though in practice the executive maintained extensive political control over the judiciary. Journalists were granted freedom of the press, and 337 newspapers were published in 1919 for fewer than two million literates—though this freedom was sometimes contravened by progovernment mobs that attacked the opposition press. "Holy name of God!" one journalist exclaimed after being attacked (and then arrested for disturbing the peace). "I never imagined that liberty of thought would involve such a beating to the loins of a journalist!"[37]

Two anecdotes further illustrate the extent to which the regime would protect intellectuals' interests. The first involves two Chinese oculists who ran a successful practice in Lisbon, competing with modern-educated doctors in the treatment of conjunctivitis: "[T]he authorities, at the instigation of the medical faculty, issued an order expelling these women, on the ground that their practising medicine without a diploma was illegal." Outraged patients marched on government offices and surrounded the oculists' house, but authorities expelled the two to Spain. The next day, "after some inflammatory speeches, reviling the Portuguese doctors and the Government, a crowd marched down the Avenida da Liberdade," smashed two Republican newspapers, stoned the Ministry of the Interior, attacked Machado Santos—a prodemocracy hero who had tried to calm the crowd—and fought with security forces into the night. Several dozen were reported wounded, with several fatalities. The second anecdote involves the opera, which was traditionally held in a small, elegant building that catered to the aristocratic elite. In a democratic era, opera was to be made available to all—meaning, to all intellectuals, because workers had neither the interest nor the means to attend. Accordingly, the opera was moved to a five-thousand-seat coliseum, and the old building was closed. When the traditional elite attended a show at another, smaller opera house—a benefit for impoverished monarchists—the government raised a crowd to harass the event. As the show ended and the patrons left the building, shots were fired, confusion reigned, and the police arrived to further harass the elite.[38]

Mexico

When the revolution succeeded, young intellectuals virtually monopolized available government positions, "pick[ing] up the plums of office, while the real captains of the revolution"—the nonintellectuals who had fought against the dictator's army—"were fobbed off with, at best, lowly commissions in the *rurales* [gendarmes]." One telling example is the case of Gabriel Gavira, an artisan with some education who considered himself an intellectual. A longtime prodemocracy activist, Gavira expected, but did not receive, Madero's support in the postrevolutionary elections in Veracruz: "Madero, democratic as far as possible for a man of his class, preferred *a priori* the lawyer to the carpenter." As in Portugal, an elderly, respected Francophile intellectual was installed as a figurehead transitional leader. The real leader, elected president at the end of 1911 almost unopposed, was Francisco I. Madero, a 37-year-old graduate of business programs in the United States and France. His nine-member cabinet had only one minister over 49 years old and only one without a higher education (but included five lawyers and two engineers).[39]

The young intellectuals-turned-politicians embarked on a policy of national development through education. In Mexico as elsewhere, the modern intellectuals believed that ignorance was the primary barrier to progress and the primary indicator of the lack thereof. Some worried, as one put it, about the "manifest incapacity of the people to perform its electoral function appropriately"; with an 84 percent illiteracy rate, as Madero himself noted, "it would not be the illiterate masses which would lead the country, but the intellectual element. . . . We have tried to show that ignorance is not an obstacle that should deprive us of democratic practices."[40]

Once in power, the intellectuals acted on the hegemonic principle that identified their interests with those of the nation. Intellectual "experts" began to exert their class influence through government regulations on industry (see Chapter 6), but their primary hegemonic thrust was in education. One of the first policies of the new era, adopted on June 1, 1911, was an educational reform bill that budgeted 900,000 pesos for elementary education, especially for indigenous populations, which previously had been largely left out of the educational process. By fiscal year 1912–1913, the federal education budget had climbed 17 percent over the last prerevolutionary budget (1910–1911), while the rest of the budget rose only 7.3 percent. At the regional level as well, Madero allies and appointees proved to be ardent boosters of education: in Nuevo León, the new governor's three planks included the "imperative necessity" of mass education to create a new society; in Coahuila, the governor "sacrificed other reform programs to finance the costs of revamping the state's education system," which included raises for teachers. In Sonora, "education represented the largest single allotment in the state budget." In Puebla, the governor raised teachers' salaries and made competitive examinations, rather than connections, a prerequisite for employment. In Yucatán, the legislature required four years of elementary education for boys and girls.[41]

As one intellectual in Yucatán noted, however, these reforms faced three problems: "money, money, and money." A report by the undersecretary of public education, released a year after the 1911 federal education bill, stated the magnitude of the problem: to educate all Mexican children would require not 900,000 pesos annually but 40,500,000 pesos. A vigorous debate broke out over this report. Some intellectuals, even visionaries who had previously advocated an education tax on industrialists and landowners, now cited changed "economic circumstances" that made it less "opportune even to speak of a new tax," as one intellectual put it. Other intellectuals saw nothing wrong in "requesting further the cooperation of the landowners, the industrialists, the great property owners, prescribing to them the duty of supporting appropriate schools for all the children of the wage-earners and workers they employ." The executive branch of the government scaled back its ambitions, postponing for the moment the massive attack on illiteracy to focus on higher-level education, especially normal schools to prepare new teachers. Federal spending on secondary and higher education rose by more than 40 percent between 1910 and 1912, while spending on primary education increased only 3 percent. Meanwhile, intellectuals in the legislative branch held out for the full plan. In November 1912, they proposed a law to force landowners to open schools for agricultural employees.[42] Neither side was able to accomplish much before the coup d'état of February 1913.

Already, the intellectuals' prodemocracy coalition was splitting apart. Peasant groups that had contributed to the victory of the democracy movement now continued their struggle against the democratic regime; the largest of these, led by Emiliano Zapata, threatened the capital city itself. Workers, too, continued their militancy (see Chapter 6), and large sections of the bourgeoisie continued to be disaffected (see Chapter 5). Speculation continued about the loyalty of the military (see Chapter 8). The government's attempts to mollify its class allies led only to further disillusionment from within. Leftist intellectuals criticized the government for not pursuing land reform, while rightist intellectuals criticized the government for not cracking down on strikes. One group of students objected to the government's harsh treatment of an anti-U.S. speaker; another group of students petitioned the government to show leniency toward a pro-U.S. coup plotter. The result, as an opponent gleefully noted, was a "marked autophagism": "The elements that have taken on the task of destroying, disturbing, unmasking, discrediting, and revealing Maderismo have emerged . . . from Maderismo itself!"[43]

Intellectuals in the government tried to define the opposition out of the intellectual class, just as the Científicos had done with them. On the occasion of one student protest, José Vasconcelos apparently wrote:

> One of the most degraded social classes, which the dictatorship left in a state of agitation, is the student class, where there is nothing but debility and stultification. I am sure that people who cannot read or write have a cleaner moral sense and clearer standards than the semi-intellectuals who, for having attended school, think themselves to be the representatives of culture.[44]

All this infighting led to severe disillusionment among the government's supporters. "Two things were evident at the beginning of January, 1913: the total discredit of Madero among the conservative classes . . . and the profound discontent, dismay, and despair with which all his supporters, even the most fervent, watched him persist in the politics of tolerance and conciliation." In parliament, a group calling itself the "Renovators" issued a sharp rebuke to Madero for having compromised the ideals of the revolution. Through "unfortunate conciliation, the deformed hybridism that appears to have been adopted as a system of government[,] . . . [t]his government is killing itself little by little." Despite this disillusionment, at least some intellectuals tried to come to the democracy's defense during the coup of February 1913. A student organization tried to gather at its central office in the capital, according to its president, but was unable to do so because of bombardment and military maneuvers, which I describe in Chapter 8.[45]

China

In the provisional republican government, based in Nanjing, ten of twelve cabinet members were educated abroad. Yet these intellectuals controlled only half of China; the monarchist government in Beijing, headed by General Yuan Shikai, retained command of the rest. As the two sides entered negotiations, the provisional government limited itself largely to public exhortations: to populate the sparsely populated regions of the country, pave the way for women's rights, relieve poverty through private charity, assist peasant agriculture through loans of farm tools by landowners, publicize the evils of opium, and allow freedom of the press. These exhortations did little to implement the class rule of the intellectuals, though more concrete action was taken on at least one item: telegraph rates for news reports were discounted as a boon to journalism.[46]

The Nanjing government resigned after just three months, bowing to the Beijing government, which had renounced the monarchy. Many of the intellectuals serving in Nanjing then scurried to Beijing "in search of official position and wealth," as one of their colleagues put it derisively. One intellectual in the Nanjing government, realizing that his job was about to end, appointed himself as an official in his home county. "Before the revolution I imagined you were all public-spirited," one man wrote to the leading prodemocracy newspaper in mid-1912. "I have been deceived. All you who are revolutionists have your thoughts turned to honours and wealth." The desire for official position may have been a function of Western-educated students' heightened expectations: "Generally, he [the modern intellectual] is freshly graduated, puffed with book learning, self-conscious of his dignity and importance, and valuing himself 50 percent above par—in short, he is like an ex-President of the United States just left the White House, embarrassed at what he is next to do." A more charitable explanation suggests that intellectuals sought state power to effect social reforms.[47]

Within Yuan's federal government, intellectuals occupied several ministries. They wrote new regulations privileging modern-educated lawyers over old-style attorneys and modern actors over old-style boy actors. Most significantly, they mobilized to establish the new Ministry of Education. Cai Yuanpei, provisional minister since the beginning of 1912, had been active since the turn of the century in the interlinked movements for democracy and intellectual class formation. A prominent member of the Chinese Educational Association in Shanghai, he was principal of the organization's Patriotic School, a controversial and short-lived attempt to combine Western learning and revolutionary military training. Later he studied Western educational philosophies in Germany.[48]

On his return to China as minister of education, Cai published a paper spelling out the intellectual class's hegemonic project: to apply the powers of the state in the name of popular will to the transformation of the popular will. On one hand, Cai wrote, education in a democracy "conforms to the will of the people." On the other, he continued, the goal of education in a democracy is not "securing present-day happiness," but "developing a true conception of realities"[49]—which only modern intellectuals correctly understand. The great majority of the Chinese people must be brought to this understanding, even if they resist. The positivist contradiction between democracy and intellectual hegemony lurks in this formulation, as it does in Cai's subsequent government career.

In the first weeks of the provisional government, Cai's Ministry of Education immediately began to reorganize Chinese education along Western lines. A dispatch in mid-January 1912 called for the replacement of texts, reform of the curriculum, and coeducation at the primary level. In the following months, a conference was held to discuss the development of a phonetic alphabet. Funds were made available to young intellectuals who had served in the revolution, allowing them to study overseas. Education budgets were increased and new schools founded, enrolling 85 percent more students in 1912 than in 1909. The government announced plans to re-organize Beijing University along modern lines and to open new universities in the prodemocracy strongholds of Nanjing, Wuchang, and Guangdong. As in Mexico, the Ottoman Empire, Portugal, and elsewhere, the focus of the expansion was on advanced, not primary, education, though some intellectuals criticized Cai on this account. China had many potential students but few teachers, wrote Song Jiaoren, a leading prodemocracy figure, in March 1912. "The first step to popularize education must be middle-school and primary-school normal education, which supplies teachers." In keeping with demand, schools rushed to add "normal" to their name. Educational reforms were moving too fast, according to some intellectuals. "The reform process is a good deal like trying to cook an immense lump of dough," wrote one educator. "If the fire is too hot, the outside is burned black and the inside is still raw."[50]

Hoping to rally the intellectuals of China for a unified educational policy, Cai convened a conference in Beijing in the summer of 1912. Although many of the provisional government's major reforms were ratified at this conference, there was less consensus about the content of instruction. In a classic debate between liberal and positivist educational philosophies, disagreed whether to focus more on students' personal development or on mobilizing students for social goals. The positivist position won out.[51] But even before the conference ended, Cai and three other prodemocracy intellectuals had resigned from the cabinet to protest the authoritarian leanings of the provisional president, Yuan Shikai.

These resignations removed the intellectuals from one of their main power bases in the federal government. They retained control, though, of more than ten provincial governments, which embarked on intellectual class projects of their own. Several of these provinces committed themselves to closing traditional *sishu* schools that did not adapt to modern educational standards. Hunan tripled its education budget from 1911 to 1912, and raised the budget for legal affairs by a factor of nine. The 25-year-old Japanese-educated police chief in Chengdu opened a police academy and various social welfare institutions. Shandong required the land-tax to be devoted entirely to education. Guangdong, where the democracy movement was most entrenched and foreign-educated men occupied "practically all the important government posts for the province," moved toward universal, compulsory primary education. Two hundred lecturers were hired to canvass the province and encourage people to support the republic and send their children to school. The Guangdong commissioner of education announced controversial plans for coeducation up to age 11, a census of the educable population, and the conversion of Confucian temples into schoolhouses. These plans were in addition to other modern-oriented reforms in the area of public health, public works, the emancipation of household slaves, and the abolition of opium smoking, gambling, and prostitution. Officials even stood at the capital entrance and forcibly cut off men's queues—the ponytail symbolic of obedience to the Qing dynasty—on the feeble public health ground that they might be infested with lice.[52]

The British governor of Hong Kong urged the Guangdong governor to abandon these "foolishly embarked on" reforms and focus on maintaining law and order, but financial pressures proved more convincing than advice. By the end of 1912, the province's financial crisis was so severe that newly founded schools had to be closed, plans for others were shelved, subsidies for local schools were ended, and the Commission on Education's budget was cut, among other retrenchments. The provincial government reintroduced several imperial taxes and tried to raise land taxes, but these did not meet the need. It tried to borrow money abroad, but was blocked by Yuan's central government. It tried to sell government bonds, with little success. Ultimately, the Guangdong reformers had to accept a bailout by Yuan Shikai's hostile central government. "Foreign ways of government cannot be adopted in a day," Yuan's representative lectured them. The governor should replace young intellectual officials with "men of ability and experience."[53]

In 1912 and early 1913, intellectuals were purged from the top ranks of the federal government and financially crippled in the provinces. Still, intellectuals managed to gain one final stronghold: parliament. Elections in early 1913, won by the prodemocracy movement's new party, populated the bicameral legislature with young intellectuals. Their average age was 36; 81 percent had modern educations; 53 percent attended schools abroad, and 21 percent had worked in the field of education. As we might expect, the revolutionary prodemocracy party's representatives were slightly younger (by about two years) and slightly more likely to have a modern education (84 percent versus 78) than were the representatives of other parties. (An alternative listing of representatives shows a considerably higher percentage of educators in parliament and a more dramatic difference between revolutionary and nonrevolutionary representatives' educational backgrounds.)[54]

Parliament, however, was undermined before it could get started. In its first days of deliberation, President Yuan Shikai signed an unconstitutional loan with the Great Powers and was able to ignore parliamentary objections. As Chapter 9 will detail, these funds allowed Yuan to send troops to subdue the prodemocracy provinces in the summer of 1913; to reorganize the police force, which he used to arrest the prodemocracy members of parliament in the fall of 1913; and to dismiss the parliament entirely in early 1914. A new assembly was elected in 1914, but only the extremely wealthy were allowed to vote. Yuan's supporters shifted education funds to military expenditures.[55]

Democratic revolutions brought modern-educated intellectuals to power in the early twentieth century. To a greater or lesser extent in each country, intellectuals occupied the state administration, most dramatically in the Ottoman Empire, where they took the offices of bureaucrats who were fired en masse. Everywhere but Russia, where monarchists retained control of the bureaucracy, patronage positions went to intellectuals who passed their youth "eating sardines and strumming guitars alongside the learned teat of the University," according to a critic in Portugal. In all six cases, intellectuals dominated parliament—they had calculated correctly that "numbers" (the masses) would vote for "brains" (the intellectuals) against "acres" (traditional elites), in the words of one nineteenth-century British intellectual (see Chapter 2).

The priorities of the newly empowered intellectuals were remarkably similar among the six new democracies. First, the intellectuals sought to solidify their power—demanding greater rights for parliament, as in Russia, Iran, and the Ottoman Empire, or rebuilding the state administration in their own image, as in the Ottoman Empire, Portugal, Mexico, and some provinces of China. Second, the intellectuals sought to reproduce themselves, proposing educational initiatives that focused on expanding high schools and universities. Third, they favored policies to promote intellectual professions, such as freedom of the press for journalists, judicial reforms for modern-educated lawyers, and public health projects for medical doctors. Fourth, the intellectuals sought to raise taxes to remake society along positivist lines (see Chapter 5). In sum, intellectuals sought to rule in their own class interest.

The intellectuals did not always succeed in these ambitions. In particular, the intellectuals' positivist search for order generated considerable disorderliness. Not only did popular mobilizations continue, as we will see in Chapter 6, but a weakened governmental authority also gave rise to criminality and uncertain systems of justice and state administration. In addition, in several countries the democracy movements maintained private militias that used thuggish lawlessness to suppress what they perceived as threats to the rule of law: the *anjuman* associations and Bakhtiyari tribal forces in Iran, the White Ants in Portugal, and the Porra (meaning truncheon or gang) in Mexico. "The Porra has extended itself throughout the country and constitutes the current form of tyranny, a demagogic tyranny much more brutal than Porfirism [the old regime], much more insolent and disturbing of public order than the previous [form of tyranny]," wrote an opposition newspaper in Mexico City. "What irony! The sword of Don Porfirio [the deposed dictator] in the hands of the Porra!"[56]

It should also be noted that the governmental achievements of the democratic revolutions were somewhat limited. In Russia in particular, the monarchy allowed very few legislative accomplishments before quashing parliament. Even in Iran, where parliament enacted relatively far-reaching reforms, few plans were implemented before coups and civil war undermined its efforts. None of the new democracies lasted long. Yet some of the intellectuals' achievements were remarkable. The removal of censorship, for example, led to a huge flourishing of the periodical press, with hundreds of newspapers emerging in the new democracies. Political papers engaged in sharp debates, and satirical papers poked fun at government leaders and their policies with a directness that was unimaginable before the democratic revolutions.

Debates grew so serious at times that they appeared to threaten the continued class rule of the intellectuals. In Mexico, students clashed with a government that had counted on students as one of its main pillars of support. In Portugal, factional maneuvering kept the new democracy unstable throughout its existence. In the Ottoman Empire, educated military officers in the Society for Union and Progress tried to limit press criticism, and ultimately abandoned democracy entirely (see Chapter 8). In Iran and elsewhere, threats from antidemocracy movements divided the prodemocracy side into hard-liners and appeasers (see Chapter 9). These divisions were not initially fatal to the new democracies, but became so when combined with the loss of support from other groups. Part 2 of this book considers these other groups and their on-again, off-again allegiance to the intellectuals and democracy.

II

Erstwhile Allies

5

Democracy and the Bourgeoisie

Bourgeois democracy was supposed to be the work of the bourgeoisie. According to Karl Marx, rising capitalist elites use democracy to displace the declining feudal elites who control monarchist autocracies. The "Manifesto of the Communist Party" identified a series of stages in this conquest:

> Each step in the development of the bourgeoisie was accompanied by a corresponding political advance of that class. An oppressed class under the sway of the feudal nobility, an armed and self-governing association in the mediaeval commune, . . . the bourgeoisie has at last, since the establishment of Modern Industry and of the world-market, conquered for itself, in the modern representative State, exclusive political sway. The executive of the modern State is but a committee for managing the common affairs of the whole bourgeoisie.[1]

In Barrington Moore's memorable phrase: "No bourgeois, no democracy." In the late twentieth century, the bourgeoisie played a prominent role in democratization in South America, South Africa, South Korea, and other countries.[2]

A mystery about this passage from the "Manifesto" has occupied social scientists for more than a century: How does the bourgeoisie, an elite minority, manage to retain "exclusive political sway" in a "representative State" that privileges majority rule? Numerous studies have examined this question. But a second mystery has attracted less attention: Why would the bourgeoisie drape its political conquest in the flag of majority rule, mass suffrage, and a "representative State"? Would it not be simpler for the new ruling class to adopt authoritarian political structures and impose its interests in the name of "economic progress" or "law and order" and thereby avoid the nuisance of elections, judicial challenges, and a snooping free press? In other words, what is the connection between the political interests of the bourgeoisie and the emergence of democracy?

This connection appears all the weaker in light of well-documented instances of the bourgeoisie's abandonment of democracy. Marx's famous case study of the French "Second Republic," the democratic revolution of 1848–1851, argues that the French bourgeoisie turned against democratic ideals when its control over the state was challenged: "all the so-called bourgeois liberties and organs of progress were attacking and threatening [the bourgeoisie's] *class rule* both at the social foundation and the political summit, and had therefore become '*socialist*'." Parliamentary debates, appeals to public opinion, majority rule, and the like opened the door for working-class challenges to bourgeois political control. "Thus, by now branding as 'socialist' what it had previously celebrated as 'liberal,' the bourgeoisie confesses that its own interest requires its deliverance from the peril of its own self-government; that to establish peace and quiet in the country its bourgeois parliament must first of all be laid to rest."[3] Writing about Russia in 1906, Max Weber also questioned the relationship between the bourgeoisie and "bourgeois democracy":

> It is absolutely ridiculous to attribute to the high capitalism which is today being imported into Russia and already exists in America—this 'inevitable' economic development—any elective affinity with 'democracy' let alone with 'liberty' (in *any* sense of the word). The question should be: how can these things exist at all for any length of time under the domination of capitalism? In fact they are only possible where they are backed up by the determined *will* of a nation not to be ruled like a flock of sheep.[4]

Later in the twentieth century, analyses of Latin America noted a similar phenomenon, capitalists rejecting democracy when forced to choose between profits and principles. In recent years, scholars have frequently noted that the bourgeoisie supports new democracies only when democracy appears to serve its interests.[5]

In the democratic revolutions of the early twentieth century, the bourgeoisie was generally a latecomer to prodemocracy mobilization. In some cases, it did not support democratization at all until after the fact. Indeed, in some cases there was scarcely any "bourgeoisie" to speak of, in the sense of a modern, investment-oriented capitalist class. Even in those countries where a bourgeoisie existed in an objective sense—that is, according to the judgment of social-scientific observers—it was not always organized as a class. Portuguese industrialists, for example, opened a new publication in 1915 with an appeal for bourgeois class consciousness: "We have the honor of presenting [this publication] today to the country's industrial class, in the hope that it will support it with dedication and affection, in way that will convert it into a weapon of defense . . . and consider it at the same time a battle flag to rally those whose daily life is dedicated to the noble duty of enriching the entire Portuguese economy."[6]

The case studies discussed in this chapter explore how certain business people came to hail democracy, and how they soon regretted it. In particular, the cases illustrate the mutual fascination and recurrent tensions between the bourgeoisie and the intellectuals. The bourgeoisie and the intellectuals are sometimes combined in the category of "middle class," which is often associated with democratization. Seymour Martin Lipset, the most influential exponent of this approach, traces this analytical lineage back to Aristotle:

> Thus it is manifest that the best political community is formed by citizens of the middle class, and that those states are likely to be well administered, in which the middle class is large. . . . And democracies are safer and more permanent than oligarchies, because they have a middle class which is more numerous and has a greater share in government.[7]

As elaborated in Lipset's more recent work, "People with more income, in complex and widely interdependent work situations, with more education, and more access to health and other services are more likely to ask for increased political freedom." This combination of economic and educational criteria to define the middle class is characteristic of studies of the phenomenon, and of certain theories of "civil society." However, this combination rarely exists in the subjective understandings of democracy movements. In the cases in this study, the main references to the "middle class" came from Portuguese business groups who were critical of democracy.[8] The reification of the "middle class" masks the intriguing history of negotiation, conflict, and occasional alliance between capitalists and intellectuals, the category's two constituent parts.

Russia

The Russian bourgeoisie was far stronger than any of the other emerging capitalist classes covered in this study. Russian industry boasted some of the largest factories in Europe. The Russian Empire had the second greatest railway mileage in the world. Its exports were the fifth highest in the world, greater than Austria-Hungary and Japan (though not in per capita terms). Recession since 1899 had not erased two decades of phenomenal economic growth, during which the tsarist government had made a concerted effort to promote industrialization.[9]

Despite the proven economic benefits of tsarist protection, the Russian bourgeoisie harbored significant grievances that mounted in the years before 1905. They objected, as the bourgeoisie always does, to the periodic recessions caused by capitalist business cycles; in addition, they objected to the artificial recession in 1904 caused by the tsar's war against Japan. They despised government factory inspectors who personified the state's reach into the economic domain. "Factory Inspectors always want to show their power, and take the side of the [working] men," a Russian industrialist told a British scholar. "This stirs up trouble."[10] Most of all, they opposed the state's policy after 1902 of encouraging "police unions," government-sponsored organizations created to press workers' economic demands and steer workers away from political demands. (It was a police union, Gapon's Assembly of Mill and Factory Workers of St. Petersburg, that—contrary to the government's plan—turned from economic to political demands and escalated the democracy movement through the demonstration that became known as Bloody Sunday.)

As a result, significant elements of the Russian bourgeoisie were willing to join the prodemocracy movement in 1905. A handful of capitalists were already devoted to the democracy movement on ideological grounds, some, such as the Moscow textile industrialist Sergei I. Chetverikov, through their interaction with gentry intellectuals in the *zemstvo*s (provincial councils). In fall 1904, Savva T. Morozov, another Moscow capitalist, helped fund the Union of Liberation's new newspapers. In November 1904, four liberal Moscow manufacturers joined *zemstvo* liberals in signing an eleven-point prodemocracy declaration.[11]

As prodemocracy unrest continued, this faction began to move into the leadership of the Russian bourgeoisie. In late November 1904, the bourgeois-dominated Moscow City Council approved a statement supporting the *zemstvo* declaration; conservative capitalists walked out in protest. In the capital in January 1905, after a week of daily meetings, the St. Petersburg Society to Assist in the Improvement of Factory and Mill Industries—an influential group of industrialists—issued a modestly liberal statement denouncing workers for "unrealizable" and "nonsensical" aspirations but expressing mild sympathy with their plight and calling for government policies to resolve the current unrest. In Odessa, *Commercial Russia*, which represented the local bourgeoisie, opened its pages in February to a variety of political and economic complaints.[12]

What appears to have pushed the prodemocracy faction into the lead, in all but the last-mentioned case, was the state's response to the ongoing protests. The monarchy sought to alleviate the unrest through economic concessions paid out of the bourgeoisie's pocket; the bourgeoisie objected and sought to alleviate the unrest through political concessions reducing the authority of the tsarist government. Prodemocracy capitalists thus became the defenders of the bourgeoisie's material interests; capitalists predisposed ideologically to be loyal to the tsar were unwilling to subsidize the tsar's retention of power. This dynamic became evident soon after Bloody Sunday in January 1905, when Finance Minister V. N. Kokovtsov reversed his earlier no-concessions position. He called in a group of industrialists, reported that the preparation of labor reforms would take months, and urged them to make concessions to striking workers in the meantime.[13] In an outpouring of petitions and memoranda to the government from around the Russian Empire, the bourgeoisie refused. The St. Petersburg Society, for example, abandoned the caution that characterized its statement of January 20, one week earlier:

> [T]he workers' movement did not arise out of a general recognition by the workers of economic adversities but is provoked and sustained by the surrounding atmosphere. It is impossible to isolate the workers, and it is also impossible to pacify them with concessions while the surrounding milieu is in ferment. The government is aware of widespread dissatisfaction in all levels of Russian society—the press, public organizations, *zemstvo* and municipal bodies, institutions of higher learning, and not only among students but among professors as well— all levels of society are showing signs of general suffering. . . . [N]either concession of any kind to the workers on particular questions nor a review of factory legislation can produce real pacification of the troubled state of the workers. It is beyond doubt, in the opinion of the meeting, that the only genuine means of appeasing the workers' movement . . . are more fundamental reforms of a general political nature.[14]

In Moscow, more than two hundred factory and mill owners enthusiastically endorsed a statement drafted by Morozov and other prodemocracy capitalists that demanded individual rights, an elected legislature (divided by class), and the removal of state interference in industrial relations. Significantly, the conservative leadership of the Moscow Stock Exchange did not approve; it presented its own petition to the tsar, pledging "limitless devotion." But the majority of the Moscow bourgeoisie had shifted to a limited devotion.[15]

Even the Moscow Stock Exchange jumped ship in May 1905, when news arrived of Russia's disastrous naval defeat by Japan at Tsushima. G. A. Krestovnikov, a merchant-capitalist and president of the Moscow Stock Exchange, withdrew the bourgeois participants from a labor-legislation commission—they were unenthusiastic in any case about the state's plans to solve its crisis through limited labor reforms. The following day, he signed a telegram to the Finance Minister along with the prodemocracy capitalists, expressing "our profound and sincere conviction that only the convocation without delay of the elected representatives of the people, promised in the Supreme Rescript of February 18, can bring the country out of its present difficult position, return the whole population to peaceful work and provide a correct solution for the state questions that have come to a head."[16]

The bourgeoisie's refusal to come to the aid of the monarchy in its moment of crisis was not the primary factor in the democracy movement. It is unlikely that limited economic concessions such as the government envisioned would have calmed the populace and undermined the democracy movement, as the government hoped. (As we will see, lockouts and firings were far more effective in this regard.) In addition, the bourgeoisie's refusal to aid the monarchy did not translate into a willingness to aid the democracy movement. Few capitalists were willing to go beyond public statements favoring modest political reform. Chetverikov, one of these few, proposed in July 1905 that capitalists boycott the consultative assembly that the tsar promised to convene, refuse to buy new government bonds or pay industrial taxes, and close their factories to aggravate worker unrest. Prodemocracy capitalists rejected these measures for the time being, however.[17]

The democracy movement spurned bourgeois support. A telling vignette occurred during the *zemstvo* congress of July 1905, where the gentry-intellectuals and nongentry intellectuals merged their reform movements. The prodemocracy capitalists, who were also meeting in Moscow to forge a nationwide bourgeois organization, sent a delegation to greet the *zemstvo* congress. The delegation was turned away at the door. The capitalists were furious and asked the *zemstvo* organization to consider that "this visit had not taken place."[18] Presumably the democracy movement, which had organized itself into unions along working-class lines and followed a policy of "No enemies on the left" (see Chapter 6), did not wish to be seen as an ally of the bourgeoisie. Underlying this decision was the democracy movement's reliance on worker unrest to force reforms upon the tsar; the capitalists, even most prodemocracy capitalists, were ultimately opposed to ongoing worker activism.

This split became clear after the tsar's October Manifesto promised a legislative parliament—not just a consultative assembly, which had been promised earlier in 1905. The bourgeoisie, even the prodemocracy faction, deemed that political reform had been won, and that normal working conditions could now be reestablished. The democracy movement, keenly aware of the limitations the Manifesto placed on democratic institutions, wished to continue the battle. In the days before the Manifesto, Chetverikov and other prodemocracy capitalists urged the government not to call in the Cossacks to suppress the general strike that paralyzed Russia. In the days after the Manifesto, bourgeois sympathies shifted. In the political arena, prodemocracy capitalists remained aloof from the Kadet party formed by the prodemocracy movement. Instead they formed their own party, the Moderate Progressive Party, whose platform mimicked Kadet positions on almost every issue, though the capitalists wished to abolish state inspections of factory conditions, while the Kadet platform favored positivist state oversight of the economy. The Moderate Progressives aligned themselves with other bourgeois parties that formed to defend the October Manifesto, most notably the Union of 17 October (named after the old-style date of the Manifesto) under Alexander Guchkov, himself the heir of Moscow textile manufacturers. These bourgeois parties failed at electoral politics, even in a semi-democratic system that favored wealthy voters. They would not deign to mobilize electoral campaigns and simply did not believe that intellectuals could be popular. As the Progressive Economic Party of the St. Petersburg Society of Factory and Mill Owners put it, voters would "sooner vote for men of experience and reason than for *belletristy*"—writers of belles lettres, that is, intellectuals. Bourgeois districts appear to have voted less heavily than others for the Kadet party, but the bourgeois parties were limited to 28 representatives in a parliament of 448, or 6 percent.[19]

The bourgeoisie was far more successful in restoring its authority in the workplace than in exerting its authority in the political realm. But restoring its workplace authority had significant political effects that helped to undermine the new democracy. After the October Manifesto, employer associations began to take the initiative in combating worker activism. "Abandon your foolish demands," one industrialist group announced. "Everything necessary has already been given to the people; it is called to the State Duma, and on its own it will forge its destiny." Weeks after the Manifesto, the St. Petersburg Society formed a strike committee, and the Moscow Stock Exchange Committee's Labor Commission (formed earlier in the year) turned from debating reformist labor legislation to coordinating strikebreaking. Chetverikov, the prodemocracy manufacturer and head of the Labor Commission, became one of the most energetic proponents of the effort to "fight against the workers' movement. . . . I used the word 'fight' and I think that there is no need to be afraid of the word. The old foundations are crumbling; many prerogatives of capital are turning out to be unstable; a fight, in the sense of a test of respective strength, is completely inevitable."[20]

The industrialists developed two primary strategies in this fight: lockouts and firings. In the month after the October Manifesto, more than nineteen thousand factory workers were locked out in St. Petersburg and almost sixty thousand were locked out in Moscow. Firings were more selective but just as significant, removing leading activists from the workplace, or as the instructions in one plant called them, "those worthless and undesirable elements who interfere with the peaceful and normal conduct of work." Indeed, firings were critical enough to the workers that they could on occasion lead to strike activity where ideological appeals failed. At the Golutvinskaia cotton mill in Moscow and the Putilov metalworking plant in St. Petersburg, for example, workers unwilling to strike for an eight-hour workday struck on behalf of dismissed colleagues. The owners followed up these firings with the development of blacklists in 1906. Such strategies proved highly effective. They exacerbated the growing unemployment in Russia's largest cities—according to a survey of 330 unemployed people in St. Petersburg in 1906, half said they were fired for their political activities—and contributed to the demoralization of workers. Unemployed workers began an "epidemic flight to the countryside," according to a Moscow labor organizer. Although worker activism picked up in the spring of 1906, workers' feeble reaction to the dissolution of the first two parliaments is in part a testament to the bourgeois counterattack.[21]

The bourgeoisie also cooperated with state repression of worker activism, an indication of how quickly the prodemocracy capitalists had lost their fragile leadership of the bourgeoisie. In the southern Donbass region, a leading mine manager reviewed his 1905 diary in 1906 and was "abashed and even frightened" by the politicized tone of management's statements, which "followed the stereotypical pattern of days which were already long gone." In July 1905, conservatives ousted the liberals from the Moscow Stock Exchange Committee. In November they regained control of the Moscow City Council, which promptly fired activist city workers and supported the execution of prodemocracy mutineers. In December they donated funds to support the military and police forces that were busy executing labor leaders. A similar trend in the capital led to a statement by the St. Petersburg Society in December supporting the use of force against strikers: "the use of military protection against violence can in no way be considered blameworthy, but it is only a sad necessity." Only in the southern city of Ekaterinoslav do we find continued bourgeois support of the general strike after the October Manifesto, until the military suppressed the opposition in December.[22]

The bourgeoisie's withdrawal of its limited support for democratization had an important, though indirect, effect on the failure of the new democratic institutions: As I will argue in Chapter 6, prodemocracy intellectuals had counted on a massive worker uprising to protect the parliament should the government try to shut it down. When this support failed to materialize following the suppression of the first parliament in the summer of 1906, the intellectuals continued to threaten a worker uprising, but with far less confidence. Indeed, the government's decision to dismiss the second parliament in the summer of 1907 was made only after a careful police study of the probable public reaction.[23] The bourgeoisie had done its part to create an atmosphere of timidity.

When the democratic experiment was destroyed, the bourgeoisie was pleased with the results. In Russian Central Asia, for example, local businessmen picked this moment to start a newspaper that promoted itself as a "friend and supporter of the Russian state." In St. Petersburg, printing-industry owners took advantage of their renewed power in labor relations to rescind concessions made when parliament was in session and the workers were unionized. "Now that your union no longer exists, you will work under the earlier conditions," one owner said. A similar turnabout transpired in the St. Petersburg baking industry, home to some of the strongest and best-organized unions in the country. Within a year the government shut down half of the unions in St. Petersburg and more than half in Moscow. Only in the southern Donbass region did workers gain pay increases, improved medical care, and other benefits in the years after 1905.[24]

The bourgeoisie's short-lived sympathies for the democracy movement did not translate into effective support, and its strikebreaking activities undermined one of the main threats that prodemocracy forces in parliament had come to rely on. In short, the bourgeois revolution of 1905 was hardly a revolution of the bourgeoisie. The prodemocracy faction of the bourgeoisie admitted as much in 1912, when it tried once again to organize its class on behalf of political reform:

> Hitherto, the task of liberalism has lain wholly on the Kadet party. No one will think of reproaching them with betraying their ideals. But by its very nature the party has a weakness. It is a party of the intelligentsia, shorn therefore of any economic strength, and consequently does not have any real weight in the eyes of the government. . . . Once the intelligentsia has played the part, which always falls to its lot and to which it is suited, of the political avant-garde, its work in parliament is more fruitful if alongside it there stands another party—also one of justice, but in addition possessing strength.[25]

Iran

Compared with the other cases considered in this study, the Iranian bourgeoisie was considerably less developed in its economic activities, its transition to modern means of production, and its organization as a class. Imports and exports were far lower than any of the other cases, though large enough to disrupt the previously self-sufficient economy and drag it into the periphery of the world system. The country had little infrastructure for modern commerce and no modern banks aside from the British and Russian concession-holders, which did not often loan to Iranians and crushed local competition that would have. The British bank's monopoly on issuing banknotes, its manager noted with surprising frankness several years later, "has made competition impossible, and has established an economic supremacy which allows the Bank to dictate its own terms to government and people."[26]

The traditional merchant class of Iran had made tentative forays into modern industrial production, but "as regards factory industry, even by Middle Eastern standards Iran remained backward." Attempts by the merchant class to organize itself into a modern Chamber of Commerce failed in the 1880s, when newly founded merchant councils criticized the government's economic policies and were banned. The emerging bourgeoisie remained organizationally locked into traditional guild associations. Unlike similar associations in China, however, the guilds were unable to form lasting coalitions representing the collective interests of the business community. "You have not as yet established a chamber of commerce in Tehran and are not aware of its benefits," *The Strong Bond*, a prodemocracy newspaper published by Iranian merchants in India, chided the bourgeoisie of Iran.[27] In Iran, would-be industrialists and financiers operated individually, or in ad hoc delegations.

One such delegation emerged to lead the sit-in at the British legation grounds in the summer of 1906 (see Chapter 3) and arranged for funds to feed several thousand participants for weeks. Another delegation mediated between the government and the sit-in, passing along the escalating demands for democracy that the intellectuals insisted upon. "The merchant class played the leading role in the democratic revolution," *The Strong Bond* suggested in the fall of 1906. "Without the merchants there would been no revolution." Industrialist Sani' al-Daulah, later minister of finance, agreed: "It was the middle class of businessmen, merchants, and the educated youth that undertook the fundamental reform of the country."[28] (Notice that this formulation of the "middle class" corresponds to later academic definitions by combining economic and educational criteria.)

This was not the first time the emerging Iranian bourgeoisie had mobilized against the monarchy. In addition to the short-lived merchants' councils of the 1880s, merchants actively participated in the national protests of 1891–1892 against the Reuter concessions, which would have turned much of Iran's natural resources over to a British company. In 1905, importers and exporters protested a large increase in customs fees. At the end of that year, Iranian merchants protested the punishment of some of their colleagues for alleged overpricing.[29] The year 1906, however, marked the first time that the bourgeoisie rallied around democratic ideology.

The prodemocracy movement had long included bourgeois economic interests in its appeals to the Iranian nation. Malkum Khan (discussed in Chapters 2 and 3) addressed these interests directly, accusing the Iranian monarchy of selling the country to foreigners, to the detriment of Iranian commerce. "Dear Merchant," he wrote, "the government has mistaken our inaction for our death." A leading prodemocracy figure in Isfahan wrote a treatise extolling the virtues of Iranian industry, and others proposed a buy-Iranian campaign similar to—though not aware of—the Swadeshi movement in India. Some social democratic intellectuals in Iran argued, as did Sun Yatsen in China, that the underdevelopment of the "small capitalist class" was an advantage for Iran, because the bourgeoisie would grow within limits set by democratic institutions, rather than dominate these institutions, as it did in Europe.[30]

The leaders of the bourgeoisie had for some years subsidized the formation of a modern intellectual class, supporting the founding of modern schools and sending their own sons abroad for education. The rise of these foreign-educated businessmen coincided with the shift of the emerging Iranian bourgeoisie to a prodemocratic ideology. One of the strongest supporters of the democracy movement, for example, was Hajj Muhammad Husayn Amin al-Zarb, perhaps the leading Iranian businessman of the period and founder of Tehran's only electricity plant. Amin al-Zarb studied in France, spent time in London, and financed modern schools in Iran. A more indirect example was 'Ali-Quli Khan Sardar As'ad, a tribal leader turned businessman who leased land to a British oil company operating in Bakhtiyari territory and subcontracted tribesmen as security teams. Sardar As'ad spent several years in Europe, joined the Freemasons, learned French, and acquired an appreciation for modern education, including the founding of a school in tribal territory. On his return to Iran, he participated in the establishment of the prodemocracy Revolutionary Committee and later convinced his fellow Bakhtiyaris to march on Tehran to restore the democratic regime after the coup d'état of 1908 (see below). For a time, it appears, many business leaders may have shared the intellectuals' hegemonic linking of science and democracy, as expressed by one merchant of Tehran in a letter to a prodemocracy newspaper: "The shining lamp of science has been diminished in the citizens of our dear eternal native land by the negligence of the respected trustees of the state."[31]

Among the issues that brought Iranian business leaders to the cause of democracy was the creation of a national bank. Iranian business leaders had called for the creation of such an institution since the 1870s, and business representatives brought the issue to parliament when it met in late 1906, even before all of its members had arrived from the provinces. But prodemocracy intellectuals accused the plan of containing concessionary terms as onerous as those demanded by foreigners: exclusive rights to mining, pearl fishing in the Gulf, and railroad and road construction, combined with 9 percent interest guaranteed by custom, post, and telegraph receipts. The emerging Iranian bourgeoisie felt unappreciated: "When we wish to be of service to the nation, foregoing profit, and this is the result, that we are written off as untrustworthy, we will never take up this task," one of the five businessmen proposing to underwrite the bank complained in parliament. "Yes, you wish to defraud the nation and the state," a fellow representative countered. In the ensuing debate, one merchant was asked to leave the floor, and the whole business delegation walked out in protest. They returned a few minutes later, but business support for the new democracy was not the same afterward. The bank did not become a reality until decades later.[32]

Another attraction of democracy that became a grievance against it was the expectation of greater law and order. Lawlessness, especially on the roads, was a long-standing problem. When disorder continued in the new democracy, business people held the government responsible. Already in the first months after parliament convened, business leaders in southern Iran were writing to complain. In following years, banditry continued in the region. By late 1911, a British observer in Isfahan wrote, conditions were so "miserable" that Iranians were "ready to accept any form of government which will give them security."[33] The new democracy sought to create a national police force and a gendarmerie to establish order, but these plans barely got off the ground (see Chapter 8).

To develop the police and gendarmerie, as well as fund social reforms, the intellectuals tried to raise taxes. "In no country are modern reforms feasible without an investment of cash," one newspaper editorialized in the first year of the new democracy. Under the old regime, merchants were taxed through elaborate but inefficient customs duties, much of which was "heavily pledged" as collateral for foreign loans. Merchants recognized that this system was going to change. One prodemocracy figure noted that "money is needed for all the reforms, and money is not being collected without reform of the tax budget." The prodemocracy industrialist Sani' al-Daulah agreed: "Many people pay nothing [in taxes], or pay less than they should, and others pay way more than they are able." But many business people were not pleased by the new democracy's attempts to increase tax income. German diplomats noted in late 1911 that this was one of the factors causing "the wealthier businessmen," as well as landowners and clergy, to become disillusioned with democracy. They "are all sick and tired of the ruling parliamentary demagoguery, primarily because this now begins to question even their traditional prerogatives and their most sacred possession: their freedom to steal and their freedom from taxes."[34]

At the same time, business flourished. Customs revenues leapt by 48 percent in the first year of the new democracy, and the value of imports was on average a third higher during the period of democracy than during the previous five years. Industrialization "accelerated" during the life of the new democracy, with sixty factories and shops founded during the years 1905–1911. But almost all of these were foreign-owned businesses. Only 4 percent of the modern industrial labor force, as tiny as it was (see Chapter 6), was employed by Iranians. Not all merchants enjoyed the same success. One man recalled the disastrous situation of his father's business during this period, and a prodemocracy activist attributed several prominent merchants' disenchantment with democracy to the ruinous condition of their businesses.[35]

The business community's support for democracy, so strong in the summer of 1906, soon wavered. By the spring of 1908, this support had dwindled to the point that Amin al-Zarb, who remained steadfastly prodemocracy, considered himself almost entirely isolated among his merchant friends. Although Amin al-Zarb was a leader of the business community, his ability to finance the defense of parliament may have been limited at this time, because the British-owned Imperial Bank of Persia was calling in a large debt of his. Other merchants hid weapons from prodemocracy activists; one merchant loaned money to the shah in early 1908 as he threatened to shut down parliament. Perhaps the most prominent single business defection from the cause of democracy was that of Mirza Javad Khan (Sa'd al-Daulah), an industrialist from Tabriz with a French missionary education who had helped to write the Iranian constitution in 1906. By 1907, he had gone over to the antidemocracy side. "Merchants, traders, and others like dictatorship better than democracy; this is why parliament was destroyed," one prodemocracy activist commented bitterly. "At the start of the affair we were out in front of everybody," a prodemocracy member of the Merchants Association wrote. "Now, unfortunately, we are behind everybody, we have no program, and our policy is unclear."[36]

When the shah bombarded parliament in June 1908, the merchants in Tehran did little to protest. "We must stand aside and not get involved in this matter," one guild association announced, "otherwise we'll be arrested." "All of the merchants and shopkeepers agree: for years we have been monarchists, we are nothing but monarchists," Sani' al-Mamalik, the leader of one business group, told the shah. "We don't want democracy or parliament. We have no need for such games." Other merchants disagreed: "Sir! Sani' al-Mamalik speaks only for himself. We want both a parliament and democracy." But organized support for democracy emerged only in two locales, Tabriz and Isfahan. In Tabriz, the assistance was not entirely voluntary. The democracy movement, in need of money to fight the shah's troops, levied "forced contributions on the richer native members of the community, whose reluctance to pay up is overcome by threats of assassination, and, in some instances, by the infliction of corporal punishment." But the antidemocratic forces were even more rapacious, and business support for democracy could be reinvigorated on occasion with rousing calls to sacrifice for the homeland. In Isfahan, the merchants went on strike immediately, refusing to obey the new governor. They were joined by Sardar As'ad, the Bakhtiyari tribal leader turned Francophile businessman, who snuck into Isfahan and made contact with the leaders of the democracy movement. Together, Sardar As'ad and the activists in Isfahan were able to convince the Bakhtiyari tribal factions to make peace with one another and march on Tehran to reinstate democracy.[37]

But the form of democracy that merchants wanted was an orderly democracy, free of debate and criticism. Sardar As'ad urged "unity" on parliament and said party debates were "ruining our house. . . . Until we throw this talk out of parliament, we will never achieve our goals." Merchants supported the conservative prime minister in 1910, according to British diplomats. In 1911, as Russia occupied parts of northern Iran and pressured the Iranian government to accept onerous conditions for withdrawal, the Iranian business community was as outraged as the intellectuals and other Iranians. One group of merchants telegraphed the British Chamber of Commerce—presuming homologous social positions, perhaps—and asked for British pressure on Russia, appealing to the "feelings of justice and humanity of British commercial circles." This sense of outrage translated briefly into renewed activism for democracy, as merchants and other Iranians boycotted foreign goods and encouraged parliament to stand firm. But in late 1911, Sardar As'ad and others shut down parliament (see Chapter 8). Some merchants in Tehran objected briefly, then went back to business.[38]

Ottoman Empire

Ottoman prodemocracy activists had sounded the theme of economic development for more than a generation. Midhat Pasha, one of the heroes of the first Ottoman constitutionalist interlude in the 1870s, stressed at his trial the regrettable condition of Ottoman industry, which he attributed to the lack of freedom and laws:

> The companies which are formed in our country are . . . totally unprotected [from state expropriation] and therefore lose their capital and profits. . . . [In addition,] money is not available in our country except at exorbitant rates of interest. We have no banks which facilitate the undertaking of useful business and enable businessmen to make profits and benefit others.[39]

In 1907, on the eve of the Ottoman Revolution, the platform of the prodemocracy movement continued to emphasize grievances that were presumably shared by the bourgeoisie, such as corruption, excessive taxation, ineffective state spending, and the difficulties in obtaining passports.[40]

In terms of capital accumulation and industrialization, the Ottoman bourgeoisie was not nearly so developed as its Russian counterpart, but was considerably stronger than its counterpart in Iran. In the late nineteenth and early twentieth centuries, the Ottoman Empire had developed increasing international trade, though foreign investors, whose businesses were capitalized at a far greater rate than Ottoman-owned businesses, controlled much of this. In terms of collective representation, too, the Ottoman business community lay partway between the Russian and Iranian bourgeoisies. It had been organized into local chambers of commerce for several decades and had experience lobbying the government for policy change.[41]

Prodemocracy activists solicited funds from certain businessmen, but in general made few alliances with the Ottoman bourgeoisie prior to coming to power. One young intellectual, Ziya Gökalp—who later became one of the empire's most influential thinkers—briefly served as secretary to the Diyarbakır Chamber of Commerce in 1902, and a prodemocracy leader in Trabzon was related to a major business figure, but these appear to have been anomalous intersections between the two worlds.[42]

One reason for this relative lack of alliance may have been the diverse ethnic makeup of the Ottoman bourgeoisie. In 1908, the executive committee of the Istanbul Chamber of Commerce, the leading business organization in the empire, consisted of five Muslims, five Armenians, four Greeks, two Jews, two Western Europeans, and one Bulgarian. The democracy movement demonstrated that it could ally itself with varied ethnic groups when need be, and some of the leading prodemocracy intellectuals were themselves non-Turks. Nonetheless, many in the Ottoman democracy movement considered the lack of a Turkish bourgeoisie to be a significant problem. Several months after coming to power, an intellectual close to the ruling circles noted that "governments in Europe rely either on the working or the bourgeois classes. They enjoy a social support which they can draw on in difficult moments. Which class shall we rely on?" The most relevant ally, he concluded, would be an ethnically Turkish bourgeoisie. "Is there such a powerful class in Turkey?" he asked rhetorically, then answered in the negative. "Since there is none, why shouldn't we create one?"[43]

When the democracy movement suddenly came to power in July 1908, the business community's "nervousness" quickly gave way to a "marked return of confidence," according to a British journalist. The Istanbul Chamber of Commerce soon worked up a "petition of gratitude" welcoming "the effect of the declaration of the constitution on our economic progress." Business associations and prodemocracy activists alike blamed the empire's lack of economic progress on the old regime's rapaciousness.[44]

It was not until World War I that the Society for Union and Progress embarked on major efforts to build a Turkish bourgeoisie. Already in the first months of the new democracy, however, officials expressed a commitment to "taking immediate measures for the promotion of industry and commerce," the British director of the Ottoman debt administration reported in October 1908. Ottoman officials planned a big extension of railway projects aimed at improving transportation throughout the empire, a plan that the Istanbul Chamber of Commerce applauded (so long as the railways would guarantee "exceptionally reduced" cargo fees). Parliament discussed expropriating the foreign tobacco concession. Government officials sought to break down the monopolies held by guilds such as the longshoremen of Istanbul, and opposed labor mobilization (see Chapter 6).[45]

At the same time, the bourgeoisie requested increased state expenditures for itself: not just major financing for railways but also annual subsidies for the empire's hundreds of chambers of commerce and for industry and agriculture. These expenditures were slow to materialize, and some of the new democracy's economic policies pleased the bourgeoisie less well. The Istanbul Chamber of Commerce repeatedly objected to the state's positivist attempts to manage markets. "The state is bad at commerce," the chamber's newspaper repeated. One of the most threatening aspects of the new democracy pertained to taxes. Desperate for revenue and eager to organize the social world, the minister of commerce and public works required the empire's governors to register all factories and tax them at the proper rate.[46]

Conversely, the government also considered removing import tariffs, in accordance with the free trade teachings of economist Mehmed Cavid Bey, a prodemocracy activist and member of parliament who became minister of finance in mid-1909, after the Committee on Union and Progress's coup. Cavid railed against protectionism: "I am not a protector of industry," he wrote in late 1908. "There will never be progress in this country for industries that need artificial means of protection." Protectionist tariffs would not help the Ottoman economy to develop, he argued elsewhere. They would only prevent competition, feeding "an empty and prideful greed."[47] The Ottoman bourgeoisie begged to differ. A business newspaper promoting agricultural interests published an extended critique, arguing that unfettered exposure to foreign competition would destroy some Ottoman industries:

> Although our respected teacher Cavid Bey Efendi argues in the *Journal of Economic and Social Sciences* for unconditional free trade, we disagree. We support complete free trade for some goods, and protectionist principles for others. The resuscitation of some of our ailing domestic industries requires that the government adopt protectionist principles. . . . From now on, our democratic government is expected to pay great attention to advancing Ottoman interests, and to inquire into the views of our merchants and economists when making commercial treaties, now and in the future.[48]

The newspaper of the Istanbul Chamber of Commerce, more attuned to international trade, focused its concern on lawlessness in the customs offices and on export taxes, rather than import tariffs. The newspaper lobbied the government to remove the 1 percent export tax, which it said benefited nobody "except some *budgetivores,* some parasites, [who are] associated with our Customs Service and doing . . . immense damage to the economic progress of the Ottoman Empire." Parliamentary representatives railed against a variety of other taxes—the livestock tax, the cereal and fruit tax, the inheritance tax—but none of these was abolished. The new democracy was determined to raise, not reduce, taxes to support educational and other ambitions (see Chapter 4). Intellectuals wanted taxation to be more efficient than under the old regime: everybody should pay, Cavid wrote in fall 1908, not just disadvantaged groups. Tax revenues were up in early 1909, and so were projected expenditures. The prospect of rising budget deficits prompted a satirical newspaper to run a cartoon showing the finance minister writing "$2+2=3$" on a blackboard, while a child laughed hysterically and said, "I know that it is easy to be appointed Minister of Finance, but you see, I must teach you to balance the budget."[49]

Despite their grievances, I have seen no evidence that the Ottoman bourgeoisie was involved in the mutiny and coup d'état of April 1909, either for or against. The main business newspapers make little mention of the episode, and the Istanbul Chamber of Commerce, the most important business organization, no longer has records from this period. The most that can be said, it appears, is that the suppression of Ottoman democracy may have played into the hands of autonomist movements among the non-Turkish segments of the business community.

In the summer of 1908, the restoration of the constitution had generated a brief honeymoon of Ottoman patriotism among the disparate communities of the empire. Armenians, Greeks, Jews, Macedonians, and other groups celebrated democratization alongside Turks, Arabs, and others. In Ottoman Jerusalem, for example, a crowd estimated at forty thousand—larger than the permanent population of the city—gathered for a public proclamation by the governor, who wrote to Istanbul:

> The voices of joy in the city of Jerusalem, which has no equal in the world to the contrast of religions, sects, and races in it, were raised to the heavens in a thousand languages and styles. Speeches were given. Hands were shaken. Pleasant tunes were played. In short, the proper things were expressed for the honor of liberty.

Some of this bloom wore off during the parliamentary elections of fall 1908, when several communities complained that the Society for Union and Progress had maneuvered to obtain strict proportions for ethnic representation. Still, the leaders of the major non-Muslim communities hewed to a line of participation in the new Ottoman politics: Greek leaders predicted optimistically that Greek capital and education would come to dominate the Ottoman Empire, restoring the Byzantine heritage. The conservative leadership of the Armenian community emphasized cooperation with the new government. Armenian, Bulgarian, and Greek militants abandoned revolutionary violence in the months after the constitution was reinstated. At the same time, the Jews of the Ottoman Empire elected a new chief rabbi who was friendly to the Society for Union and Progress and opposed Zionism.[50]

Within each of these communities, however, there were movements that rejected Ottoman politics and saw democracy as a trap that would ensnare non-Turks in a common Ottoman citizenship. This was, after all, among the main stated goals of the Turkish prodemocracy intellectuals: in their eyes, democracy was supposed to save the empire from splintering (see Chapter 2). Several independence movements gained strength when the new democracy stumbled. At least two Greek newspapers in the Ottoman Empire cheered the mutiny of April 1909, for example, rather than condemning its Islamic-law message. Armenians mourned the mutiny instead, as it coincided with a terrible massacre in Adana, which contributed to the radicalization of Armenian aspirations for independence. In a less bloody way, the suppression of democracy may have spurred Arab nationalism, too. Ottoman Jews, by contrast, rallied to the Society for Union and Progress: a unit of several hundred Jews joined the march on Istanbul that suppressed parliament, solidifying ties with the central government and rejecting Zionism.[51]

Over the next several years, these communities—their bourgeoisies included—would turn away from Ottoman democracy and toward the Greek annexation of Cyprus, Armenian independence, Arab nationalism, Zionist settlement, and multiple Balkan separatisms. When Ottoman democracy came under threat in the spring of 1909, most of these transitions had only just begun. Yet there is little indication that the non-Turkish segments of the Ottoman bourgeoisie were prepared to defend the new democracy, whose arrival they had cheered eight months before.

Portugal

The bourgeoisie in Portugal, as elsewhere, was closely linked to the old regime. In social terms, it was not yet free of aristocratic pretensions—industrialists and merchants purchased noble titles and barred social inferiors such as politicians from their salons because "the women become nauseous." In political terms, the bourgeoisie had been integrated into the monarchist regime, displacing aristocrats at the highest level of government. Economically, the bourgeoisie fared well, as industrial production doubled between 1885 and 1910. Organizationally, the bourgeoisie had not yet developed collective mechanisms that might have allowed it to pursue an autonomous path. In contrast to Mexico, Portuguese commercial and industrial associations were mutually exclusive; it was only after democratization that the first joint organization was formed, and no national organization was established until the 1920s.[52] The bourgeoisie was organizationally divided and therefore unable to act as a body.

Still, capitalists had grievances with the monarchy. In 1893, during a recession, the catalog for a Portuguese industrial exposition expressed these grievances vehemently: "The finances of the State are ruined, the tax rate has reached the limits of tolerance, the nation is wasting away, emigration is rising, metal currency is disappearing, the large banking houses are either failing or approaching insolvency, political questions are becoming bitter, ministerial crises are multiplying." The democracy movement played on these grievances in its appeals to the bourgeoisie. In 1880, a "Republican Catechism for the Use of the People" took care to define the right of property in terms of free acquisition and transfer without traditional impediments. Democracy "is going to accomplish the work that the monarchy was never able to put into practice, because it is the just expression of the dominant bourgeois class," wrote the leading republican newspaper in 1910, just before the overthrow of the monarchy. "The democratic bourgeoisie is going to have, in the republican institutions, indispensable political sanction for its economic expansion."[53]

The extent to which such statements attracted the support of the bourgeoisie to the democracy movement is unclear. The democracy movement had its bourgeois sponsors, such as Francisco de Almeida Grandela (1852–1934), founder of the Armazéns Grandela department store—but it also had committed bourgeois enemies, including the prominent financier Count Henrique Burnay and the millionaire Henrique Monteiro, who conspired with monarchists. We might well be skeptical of claims such as that of the republican paper *The Century,* which wrote in the days after the revolution: "The bourgeoisie is the safe of the nation, and it is nearly all on the side of the Republic." Somewhat more credible are the worried comments of prodemocracy intellectual Abílio Manuel Guerra Junqueiro in early 1911: "We are turning against us the same bourgeoisie that allowed us to make the republic. . . . Do you not recall that the ox that feeds can change into the ox that gores."[54]

The new government sought to keep the ox from goring them by cultivating bourgeois support. First, as in China, positivist officials sought to develop national industry. In the first months of the new democracy, the provisional government banned the export of raw cork, hoping to boost the domestic cork-processing industry, and proposed changes in tariff collection that industrialists favored, over the protests of agricultural and retail sectors. Second, the government used force to undermine labor activism (as Chapter 6 will describe), with the result that industrial production climbed more than 10 percent in 1911, despite hundreds of strikes. Third, the new government made bringing the state deficit under control a priority. "When we have balanced our accounts," one leader announced in 1911, "we will have guaranteed the welfare of the nation." The new democracy passed an arguably balanced budget in 1913.[55]

Yet in Portugal as elsewhere, the intellectuals in power were primarily concerned with the project of intellectual class formation, not with the interests of the bourgeoisie. At times, business associations complained bitterly that the new democracy was not cracking down harshly enough on strikers. During a strike by longshoremen in Lisbon, the leader of a federation of local business groups reported to the federation's consultative council that the minister of the interior "promised to guarantee freedom of work"—that is, the strikers would not be allowed to prevent others from working—"but that since a democratic government was in power, it could not take energetic measures." A member of the council declared himself "fed up with hearing friendly words from the ministers. The government pursues its own politics and nothing more. If it wanted to enforce the law, it has the power to do so. It is all rotten, and we are rotten too, since if we weren't, we wouldn't allow them to dominate politics. Everyone gets what they deserve." The head of the business federation "cited various facts tending to prove that the action of the [business] associations had achieved absolutely nothing," and the council resolved to appeal to the president of the republic along with a large number of associations.[56]

Another point of contention was taxation. The intellectuals sought to raise funding for education and other intellectual class projects, while also balancing the budget, a key element in the "rational politics" that the democracy movement had promised. The intellectuals' solution was to tax the rich. One year after the ouster of the monarchy, the prime minister was said to be counting on "a new 'Properties' or graduated tax on land and industries [that] would enable the Finance Minister to meet the deficit of nearly 500,000 pounds. (I hear elsewhere that this is deemed a low estimate.)" In May 1912, parliament voted to assess this property tax, but opposition by property owners prevented implementation. "Taxation is and always has been the sole honorable and logical method for a state to obtain the resources to meet its commitments," the finance minister told parliament in late 1912, detailing the budget deficit. "Sooner or later—sooner rather than later—we will have to come back to it." In response to the finance minister, the business federation in Lisbon drafted a strongly worded letter to parliament objecting to increased taxation: "It is beginning to appear to us that the state aspires to be nothing more than a wanton parasite of taxation." The group decided against sending the letter, viewing its role as "pacification and not imitation of political passions."[57] By 1913, the Democratic Party had consolidated enough power to collect the tax. The new British ambassador commented sympathetically:

> Taxation is high, but now all pay their share, and before the republic, the influential and rich escaped almost scot free. Commerce has fallen off, nevertheless the amount of customs duties collected has increased, as evasion has now become difficult, if not impossible. Formerly anyone with money could make an "arrangement" with the officials.[58]

Business organizations decided to do something about their lack of influence. "We have not made our organizations solid and important," a business leader in Lisbon told his colleagues. "For if we had, [business people] would not go to foreign embassies but to those associations to demand the defense of their interests." The Lisbon business federation pledged to involve itself more actively in electoral politics, supporting candidates in upcoming elections. This strategy seems to have paid off in early 1914, when the new prime minister appointed as finance minister one of the founding members of the Lisbon business federation. The prime minister himself soon attended a meeting of the federation, which elected him honorary president. "The Republic is with the [business] federation," the prime minister told them. To combat "the so-called autonomy of politics and the live forces"—a phrase that business leaders used for themselves—they should "fight politics with politics" and support him in future elections. The business group started to draw up an economic policy platform for "class candidates" around the country to adopt.[59] The bourgeoisie was beginning to engage in democratic politics when World War I broke out in August 1914 and threw Portuguese politics into turmoil.

In early 1915, when the military government of Pimenta de Castro threatened the new democracy (see Chapter 8), some of the bourgeoisie were pleased. A business newspaper in Porto suggested that democracy is appropriate only for "greatly cultured peoples," but not for the Portuguese, who have transformed it into a "libertinism" that is "capable of all excesses and all demands." The solution: "Permanent dictatorship, or . . . [ellipsis in original, implying that there is no other solution]." Another business newspaper published a nine-part series proposing the less radical but still antidemocratic solution of corporatist representation in parliament, with a view toward reducing the influence of "the so-called intellectuals." "It is not proven that the capacity to govern well and administer a country is inseparable from graduation honors," the newspaper noted snidely. In Lisbon, two thousand "proprietors" took the opposite tack and demonstrated in favor of wider suffrage, presuming that illiterate rural residents would vote monarchist.[60] Intellectuals shared this presumption, and this was one reason they had disenfranchised illiterates in 1913 (see Chapter 6).

The private minutes of Lisbon business groups show no antidemocratic mobilization. Leaders of the Commercial Association of Lisbon complained about "the lack of continuity in matters of public administration, resulting from successive changes of ministers," and proposed to meet with the president of the republic to impress upon him "that the worst evil for the country was this lack of continuity in its affairs." Despite this potential sympathy for authoritarian consistency in politics, neither this organization nor the Union of Agriculture, Commerce, and Industry appears to have taken any steps to support Pimenta de Castro. They remained on the sidelines when an uprising reinstated multiparty democracy in May 1915. One industrialist in Oporto even helped the uprising. Several months later, the Commercial Association of Lisbon seems to have regretted this lapse: "Crowning this very sad episode in our national life [is] a government whose weakness and incompetence has risen to an original and novel doctrine." Bourgeois support was not enough to dictate the survival or demise of democracy in Portugal. It was not until the mid-1920s that the bourgeoisie became sufficiently organized to mobilize decisively against the new democracy.[61]

Mexico

The Mexican bourgeoisie was divided over the prodemocracy movement of 1910. Certain regional capitalists, out of favor with the Díaz regime, supported the movement. The Madero family, which operated a significant agribusiness in the northern state of Coahuila, fell into this category, although they opposed black-sheep Francisco's oppositional political activities until he showed decent prospects of success. Other bourgeois supporters of the democratic revolution included plantation-owner José Rodríguez Cabo in San Luis Potosí; mining entrepreneur Pascual Orozco and other capitalists in Chihuahua; and Venustiano Carranza, a Coahuila rancher who wrote that he got involved in politics "without separating myself from [my] business dealings."[62]

Most capitalists, however, were opposed to the revolution. Those who had benefited from the considerable economic growth under Díaz's three-decade rule were understandably appalled by threats to that system. When the revolution was formally declared in November 1910, *The Mexican Economist* deemed the event worthy of a rare political editorial:

> There is no need for us to describe the already well-known events, nor to put in relief the deep and disagreeable impression that they have caused among the sensible part of society. . . .

> Enough has been said about the advantages obtained by peace, and there is no need to insist further on a topic which brooks no contradiction; to fall once again back into the ancient epoch of revolutions would be to lose irremediably the benefits obtained in the space of more than 30 years of constant effort. . . .

> The revolutionary form is repugnant to all constituted interests, whose links and roots offer conditions of such resistance as to suffice, to our understanding, to hold in check the small group of rebels, true laggards in the useful transformation of forces that has been accomplished in the Republic.[63]

This editorial touched on several themes central to the bourgeoisie: the preference for order over democracy; the capitalist transformation of the country; and the self-definition of the emerging capitalist class, which described itself as "the sensible part of society" and excluded the "laggards" left behind by capitalist transformation.

One of the key means of capitalist self-definition was self-organization, which took the form of a chamber of commerce in each major Mexican city. In 1908, the Díaz government passed a law naming these chambers the authorized representatives not only of merchants, whom they had represented since the 1870s, but also of industrialists and shipowners. In response, the Mexico City Chamber of Commerce, the nation's oldest and largest, rewrote its bylaws accordingly: "1) To promote and direct the actions of commerce or industry that may have as their object the development of these spheres. 2) To solicit from the Government the changes and modifications of laws or [executive] orders that may affect commerce and industry," and so on.[64]

In early 1911, as the revolution progressed, the Mexico City Chamber of Commerce began to become alarmed by the "grave political events." The executive board sent a commission to two government ministries "with the object of communicating to them the idea that commerce might arm itself in defense of its interests in case the population were to attack commercial establishments." The ministers downplayed the danger but said they would help arm the chamber of commerce as an act of prudence. In a special general assembly, the chamber decided not to organize its own paramilitary defense, but it was clear that the chamber's sympathies were not with the revolutionaries, whom it termed a "crowd of malefactors."[65]

The revolutionaries, however, did have sympathies for the bourgeoisie. Madero wrote that he was "very much in agreement that the propertied faction will influence greatly the development of agriculture and national wealth. That's not all I believe. I believe that the propertied faction will be one of the firmest bases of democracy."[66] Much of the ideology of the democracy movement coincided with the interests of capital, as demonstrated in this manifesto by governor Venustiano Carranza in 1911:

> In the short period of two months that I headed the state administration, I have endeavored principally to dedicate all my time and all my attention to reestablishing public tranquility and the constitutional order disturbed by the recent events of the Revolution; and at the same time, to improve as far as was possible the economic condition of Society and of Commerce in general, abolishing entirely, or reducing in other cases, the most onerous taxes, or the most unjust and anti-economic at first glance, already liberating employees, public as well as private, from an anomalous and positively personal tax, as well as others on the introduction, free transit, and mere consumption of goods—targeting property-owners, merchants, and consumers.[67]

As a result of these promises—law and order, free trade, lower taxes— the bourgeoisie did not find it overly difficult to accommodate itself to the new political order once the democracy movement gained power. According to one study, entrepreneurs comprised 30 percent of Madero's cabinet. In Monterrey, the businessmen who had pledged their "unconditional support" to President Díaz in May 1911 welcomed president-elect Madero with receptions and balls in October 1911. In Yucatán, the "planter-merchant bourgeoisie" adapted "skillfully to changing political circumstances [and] maintained a firm hold on the levers of political and economic power." In Jalisco, "Rich men with foresight suddenly appeared as supporters of the new cause and devotees of the winning leader." In Mexico City, the chamber of commerce requested a congratulatory meeting with the newly elected president.[68]

The intellectual-led government, however, may have supported free trade in the abstract; in practice, however, it was unwilling to leave matters to the market. Intellectuals, in keeping with the positivist tradition, saw their role as the maintenance of social order and the furtherance of progress. In the industrial sphere, intellectuals wrote detailed regulations on safety, minimum wages, maximum hours, and so on, intended to quiet labor militancy and improve industry. New mining regulations in 1912, for instance, required the hiring of engineers and first-aid attendants. New oil industry regulations required detailed reporting of assets and prodution.[69]

Interestingly, much of the bourgeoisie did not mind the government regulations that the intellectual-politicians imposed on virtually every industry. In the textile industry, for instance, factory owners seemed willing to accept minimum-wage and maximum-hour policies, so long as this would induce workers to stop their constant strikes. In a meeting at the Ministry of the Interior in January 1912, factory owners readily agreed to a ten-hour workday and a 10 percent wage increase. In May, the factory owners organized themselves into a Mexican National Manufacturing Confederation "whose program gives one to understand that the manufacturers are preparing for war," as *The Mexican Economist* put it. In July, the confederation convened a nationwide conference of industrialists. Still the industrialists continued to support labor regulations. In return for this support, they wanted a substantial reduction in taxes on the textile industry, which they received.[70]

The new democracy was no more than a few months old, though, when the bourgeoisie began to turn against it. In early March 1912, the Mexico City Chamber of Commerce was again considering a special general assembly, this time "with the object of considering means that will have to be adopted in the abnormal state of things that the country is currently experiencing, in order to ensure that the interests of all the merchants, bankers, farmers, industrialists, miners, and other workers in the Republic [the capitalists considered themselves workers, too] will not continue on the path of ruin that they are headed toward." The general assembly appealed for peace and blamed the new democracy for the unsettled conditions. Throughout 1912, the bourgeoisie continued to complain loudly about increased taxes and other matters. The Chihuahua Chamber of Commerce wrote to Madero, "Before burdening us with the onerous weight of a double payment of taxes, you ought to grant us the opportunities that will allow us to regain all the losses [we have] suffered." In Saltillo, a state capital, "commerce as well as property-owners and almost all of Society and the people are supremely upset with the authorities here owing to the tax increase they have imposed on commerce which amounts to a 40 percent increase."[71]

By early 1913, these complaints had reached a fever pitch. "What happened to the good work of the mercantile revolution of 1910?" a newspaper in Puebla asked. "The reserves have been exhausted, the public posts have been assaulted, . . . taxes have been increased every day, and grave international conflicts have been provoked."[72] In an executive board meeting of the Mexico City Chamber of Commerce, one board member

> stated that the recent initiatives of the national Executive on the increase in taxes, modifications of the customs tariffs, etc., etc., had alarmed commerce and industry, and that he believed that it is a duty of the Chamber to do what is necessary so that the Executive does not proceed to modify, alter, or increase taxes, in whatever form, that might affect commerce and industry, without prior consultations with the Chamber of Commerce, the genuine representative of these interests.[73]

The chamber's response was to hire a lawyer, but other capitalists expressed their opposition to the democratic government more aggressively. Their rallying point was the former general and governor Bernardo Reyes, who had agitated against Díaz himself in the years before the 1910 revolution. Indeed, his influence on the democracy movement was such that one newspaper joked, "What do Francisco I. Madero and the constitution[s] of Europe have in common? They were both imposed by 'Reyes' ['kings']." Reyes ran for president against Madero in 1911, drawing most of his support from "the stable elements" and "the propertied interests," according to U.S. consul reports, "the common opinion being that he will create a benevolent dictatorship following the Díaz line." After a hostile riot, with popular support possibly dwindling, Reyes dropped out of the race and moved to Texas, where he began to prepare a coup d'état. "The better classes" in Mexico are with Reyes, his leading supporter told the press; only the "peon classes" favor Madero. According to an unsigned Mexican intelligence report from early 1912, the Reyes plot was linked to a seemingly contradictory assortment of capitalists, landowners, peasant rebels, and U.S. speculators.[74] With the U.S. government threatening imminent legal action against him, Reyes launched his plot prematurely in December 1911. It failed miserably, and he was imprisoned.

In late 1912, however, Reyes became the focal point for another rightist plot. Go-betweens arranged an alliance between Reyes and another failed coup plotter, Félix Díaz, the nephew of the deposed dictator (see Chapter 8). Rodolfo Reyes, Bernardo's son and self-proclaimed " 'leader' of the intellectual youth of Mexico," noted in his memoirs that the conspirators relied heavily on fund-raising activities—"money is the nervous system of war." Another conspirator listed several businessmen who took charge of the movement's finances, including Cecilio Ocón, who had lost lucrative stevedore concessions in Sinaloa under the new democracy, and Tomás Braniff, an Oklahoma-born industrialist, banker, and coffee exporter. Yet another conspirator called on the support of José Sánchez Juárez, the taxi boss of Mexico City, who provided vehicles for the plot.[75]

I found no evidence linking these individuals with the chambers of commerce, evidence that would conclusively indicate the Mexican bourgeoisie as a whole supported the coup d'état of early February 1913. There is plenty of evidence, however, that the bourgeoisie was pleased with the event. In Guadalajara, a club of wealthy Mexicans cheered the February 1913 uprising, according to a club worker who wrote to Madero:

> [Y]esterday one of them brought the news that you had resigned, and that Félix Díaz had come to power. Everyone clapped their hands and started to talk about signing a public statement and taking it to a newspaper. . . . The past Monday, at one in the afternoon, a Félicista propaganda was organized with the employees of the Commercial Houses which are in the front portal of the university temple and they succeeded in getting twenty individuals to rise up with a Félix Díaz banner.[76]

In Monterrey, as in other towns, the chamber of commerce helped the new government maintain public order after the coup. In Jalisco, the new government reimbursed the chamber of commerce for 1,000 pesos expended "in the organization and maintenance of a corps of volunteers, which will be dedicated to the defense of the city itself." One prominent Mexican businessman traveled to the United States and convinced his associates in the U.S. Chamber of Commerce to support recognition of the new regime. In Mexico City, the chamber of commerce donated funds to a Reyes-Díaz Club—the political party founded by the coup planners—for unspecified "victims" of the coup d'état.[77]

Ideologically, the bourgeoisie was largely in accord with the new regime's preference for discipline over democracy. A capitalist in Aguascalientes wrote to one of the nation's leading business journals, "It is time for us to leave off politics and dedicate ourselves to work," and the journal's editors agreed that this observation "is applicable to the whole Republic, where politics has invaded everything. . . . The cancer of Latin America in general has been politics." The newspaper of the Mexico City Chamber of Commerce opined that "much has been lost in the last two years and some months of the revolution," but expressed satisfaction that "a wave of peace, a yearning for the tranquility that permits devotion to healthy and honorable work, appears to be bathing all of the Republic, something like the awakening of the public consciousness from a bad dream and a recovery of its old energy, its previously vigorous drive, which raised Mexico to such a conspicuous place among the civilized nations."[78] Nothing good, in this view, had come of democracy.

China

The emerging bourgeoisie in China was divided into two groups. The first group overlapped with rural landowners and members of the government bureaucracy. Its industrial and large-scale commercial operations took the form of state monopolies, as typified by the businesses of Sheng Xuanhuai, an imperial official who held monopolies in textiles, steamships, and banking. The second group leaned instead on foreign circuits of capital and power. Concentrated in and around "treaty ports"—colonized or semicolonized outposts of European states—this group has long been tarred with the insulting term *comprador*. Yet, as Marie-Claire Bergère and Wellington Chan have argued, these two groups were not so distinct as commonly imagined, because both relied on foreign capital and domestic political protection.[79]

Unlike, say, the Russian bourgeoisie during the same period, the Chinese bourgeoisie developed enough collective organization in the first decade of the twentieth century to begin to claim independence from its state sponsors. Chambers of commerce, established by government decree at the beginning of the twentieth century, numbered almost eight hundred by 1911, organizing militias to supplement the government security forces and pioneering democratic procedures for their internal affairs. In 1907, a national project of class mobilization was proposed, as delegates from around the country met in Shanghai to discuss a federation of chambers of commerce.[80]

Organizational autonomy allowed the bourgeoisie to critique the Chinese monarchy for handicapping capitalism through governmental monopolies, lack of infrastructure investment, and complex internal customs taxes that penalized domestic commerce. In 1907, chambers of commerce began to draft commercial codes, hoping to see them implemented in the future. By 1910, chambers of commerce were contributing to demands for the convocation of a parliament.[81]

The democracy movement sought bourgeois support by promising to encourage capitalist industry and trade. Quieting talk of socialism after 1907, the movement began to speak of "merchant power" and the use of "political power to protect and assist the development of commerce," as one prodemocracy activist said in a speech to merchants. Specifically, the democracy movement made tax relief a central tenet of its platform.[82] Sun Yatsen's manifesto of January 5, 1912, just after he took office as provisional president, attacked taxation without representation:

> They [imperial officials] created privileges and monopolies. . . . [T]hey subjected us to illegal taxes. . . . [T]hey limited the development of external trade to the treaty ports, they imposed *lijin* dues on the circulation of merchandise and paralyzed internal trade. . . . We will revise . . . our commercial and mining legislation and abolish the restrictions that are impeding trade.[83]

Sun Yatsen even offered shares in the revolutionary movement, promising a 200 percent return on investments.[84]

A significant portion of the bourgeoisie, including compradors, responded positively. In Tianjin, in the north, merchants reportedly felt that "the old regime had outlived its usefulness and they would welcome the abdication of the Manchus and the organization of a new form of government, if the change can be effected without great disorder." In the south, British observers noted the "great efforts . . . made by the merchant class in Canton [Guangdong] to effect a peaceful change of Government." In Hankou and other cities, chambers of commerce armed and funded revolutionary uprisings. The revolutionary cause solicited and received financial support from wealthy Chinese throughout Southeast Asia, though the support was not as generous as the revolutionaries desired.[85]

In Shanghai, in the east of China, "the bourgeoisie did not simply cooperate with the revolutionaries after the uprising, in fact they helped to prepare for it." More commonly, however, the emerging bourgeoisie responded to the democracy movement rather than help to initiate it, and joined only when success appeared sure. Such was the "nature of the merchants," according to Hu Hanmin, a prominent figure in the prodemocracy movement despite his personal reservations about democratic procedures. In some cities, militias organized by chambers of commerce assumed police functions during the revolutionary turmoil, approximating Adam Smith's utopia of a bourgeois "nightwatchman" state limited only to the protection of private property. Elsewhere, the bourgeoisie subsidized revolutionary troops to maintain order. In addition, the bourgeoisie loaned the revolutionaries money to set up government institutions, perhaps with the intention of controlling the new government's purse strings.[86]

The bourgeoisie's prodemocracy stance initially showed signs of paying off in terms of government policy. A number of leading capitalists were appointed to high office, including Zhang Qian, who was offered the minister of commerce seat in both the interim prodemocracy cabinet and the imperial cabinet (he chose the former). Internal customs taxes, hated by the bourgeoisie, were abolished in several provinces. In the central provinces of Hunan and Hubei, state funds were used as investment capital; elsewhere, provincial governments passed protectionist legislation intended to promote Chinese industry (on foreign fears of this economic nationalism, see Chapter 9). In Guangdong, the new governor promoted a Society for the Protection of Domestic Products and cut taxes on Chinese-made goods. In Shanghai, silk manufacturers received a tax break. Leaders of the democracy movement joined with leading capitalists to found a major bank, and the conducive economic climate generated a small boom in the founding of banks and factories.[87]

At the same time, positivist reforms did not always benefit the bourgeoisie. For example, the provincial government in Guangdong—the showcase of the democracy movement—pursued morality campaigns that inconvenienced the lucrative gambling, opium, and prostitution industries, notwithstanding the well-publicized collections taken up by four wealthy prostitutes on behalf of the prodemocracy movement. The Guangdong bourgeoisie protested the imposition of public health regulations on the coffin industry and the freeing of household slaves. Sun Yatsen argued that significant social reform was possible only because China had not yet developed a bourgeoisie large and powerful enough to block it. An anecdotal indication of the ill will that had begun to develop between the intellectuals and the bourgeoisie comes from Shanghai: a wealthy merchant, the leader of the merchants' private militia, sought a gun permit. French officials in the International Settlement quickly approved the request, but the intellectual-controlled Shanghai Municipal Council refused, warning of "accidents caused through carelessness or bad men." The merchant took this as "nothing else than an insult to a well-known Chinese gentleman, comparing him with 'bad men' or something like that."[88]

In addition, positivist reforms required higher state revenues, which the positivists sought to obtain from the bourgeoisie. Even in the first weeks of the new democracy, the French consul in Shanghai noted, "The bankers and the wealthy wholesalers and compradores have all had to contribute and there is no doubt that many of them are beginning to find the new regime very burdensome." One overly zealous revolutionary official resorted to kidnapping in order to extort money from the bourgeoisie. The budget crisis did not ease as revolutionary measures gave way to legalistic ones (Chapter 4 discusses the reforms that were scaled back for lack of funds). Several provinces that had promptly abolished the internal customs tax at the end of 1911 restored it, under different names, in 1912, and plans for increased property taxes instilled fear that the bourgeoisie was being called upon to pay more than its fair share.[89]

The bourgeoisie began to refuse. In Guangdong in early 1913, the bourgeoisie failed to purchase government bonds to finance public works. One merchant spokesman urged the government to stop reform plans (except for education) and focus on maintaining order. A guild newspaper reported that "rich merchants . . . cannot be expected to be as liberal as hitherto" in supporting the government through subscriptions. Hoping to shift the financial burden elsewhere, the Guangdong bourgeoisie urged the provincial government to approve a bailout by the central government.[90] But this step had serious political ramifications, for the bailout was predicated on an unconstitutional loan that Yuan Shikai was negotiating with a cartel of Great Powers.

As the Powers recognized approvingly (see Chapter 9), this loan would enable Yuan to undermine the new democracy, not least in its cash-strapped bastion, Guangdong. Bourgeois organizations in the province and around the country telegraphed their support to Yuan:[91]

> Since the Revolution which took place the year before last, the business community has suffered very severely, and the heavy discount of Government notes in Kwangtung [Guangdong] has resulted in an additional heavy loss. . . . The recent conclusion of a foreign loan was indispensable in saving the country; and the difficulties which Yuan encountered should arouse the sympathies of all. The merchants of the 72 Guilds are all willing to elect Mr. Yuan Shih-k'ai to be the formal President.[92]

When Yuan used the new loan to suppress the new democracy in mid-1913, the bourgeoisie again approved. Even where the bourgeoisie was less than enthusiastic about Yuan's intentions and his marauding troops, as in Shanghai, chambers of commerce chose to maintain neutrality rather than assist the prodemocracy forces.[93] A prominent merchant explained the bourgeoisie's abandonment of democracy:

> [I]f we trace [the prodemocracy] Party's action with regard to the merchants, we see that although they at first used the pretext of protecting the merchants, they proceeded to building-to-building plundering till the goods in the independent area were exhausted. They are so evil and wily as to be indistinguishable from pirates. The Merchants Corps of the various provinces saw the traitorous intentions and warned each other. . . . In 1911 when armies rightfully rebelled at Wuhan [leading to the overthrow of the monarchy] the Chamber of Commerce was the first to welcome it. When calamity struck this time [fighting between Yuan's forces and supporters of the new democracy in 1913] the Merchant Corps of the various places entirely opposed it. That [prodemocracy] Party expected aid as in the former case. But the merchants suddenly changed their direction and turned their backs on them.[94]

For example, Zhang Qian, the businessman who had been offered the ministry of commerce in both the prodemocracy cabinet and Yuan's cabinet in early 1912, prior to their merger, and had rebuffed Yuan, now embraced the general, and returned to the post in October 1913 just as parliament was being disbanded. In 1914, the first meeting of the all-China Chamber of Commerce supported Yuan. Having achieved supremacy, however, Yuan had no need for potentially autonomous organizations and moved to make chambers of commerce subordinate to the state.[95]

V. I. Lenin, the Russian communist, called the democratic revolutions of the early twentieth century "bourgeois-democratic revolutions": "Only a blind man could fail to see in this chain of events the awakening of a *whole series* of bourgeois-democratic national movements which strike to create nationally independent and nationally uniform states."[96] But if these were bourgeois revolutions, it is striking how small a role the bourgeoisie played. Iran, which had almost no modern bourgeoisie, underwent a revolution of the same sort as Russia and Mexico, which both had much larger capitalist classes and considerable enclaves of advanced industrial manufacturing. China, which had the beginnings of a national business association in 1907, underwent the same bourgeois revolution as Portugal, which did not develop national business associations until after democratization.

Moreover, the bourgeoisie—or the emerging bourgeoisie—did not lead these democracy movements, but rather followed. A handful of capitalists sponsored the movement before democratization, such as Chetverikov and Morozov in Russia, Amin al-Zarb and Saniʿ al-Daulah in Iran, Grandela in Portugal, Madero and Carranza in Mexico, and Zhang Qian and Shanghai business circles in China. Outside of China, however, the bourgeoisie as a whole was more likely to oppose democratization than to favor it, as exemplified in the earlier-quoted comment in a Mexican business journal that the democracy movement was composed of "laggards" in the country's economic transformation and was making a "deep and disagreeable impression" upon "the sensible part of society."

Significant segments of the bourgeoisie joined the democracy movement only when it appeared to be on the brink of success. Russian capitalists, meeting in Moscow to form a national organization in the summer of 1905, sent a delegation to the democracy movement, and were furious when they were turned away. Iranian merchants allowed the democracy movement to commandeer their sit-in at the British legation in 1906, and helped to negotiate the movement's escalating prodemocracy demands. Chinese business associations subsidized law enforcement and other government functions in the transitional months of the democratic revolution. Business organizations in the Ottoman Empire, Portugal, and Mexico offered congratulatory messages and celebration banquets when the democracy movement came to power.

This support did not last long. Soon after democratization, business groups began to express serious doubts about democracy. In Russia, prodemocracy capitalists formed their own political group, the Moderate Progressive Party, which supported the rights of the monarchy against further encroachment by parliament. The Mexico City Chamber of Commerce worried about the "path of ruin" that the new democracy seemed to be following and considered arming its members for self-defense. A Chinese businessman called the intellectuals in charge of the new democracy "so evil and wily as to be indistinguishable from pirates." The Industrial Association of Oporto concluded that elections resulted in government by fools, and proposed a corporatist system that would give greater influence to representatives of the "conservative classes."

I have seen little evidence that the bourgeoisie conspired to undermine the new democracies, despite its hostility. Business associations withheld funding from the new democracy in Iran and China, but even there they do not appear to have financed antidemocratic movements. In Russia, business groups supported right-wing suppression of strikes, destroying the new democracy's trump card in its negotiations with the monarchy, but the historiography does not suggest that they did so to weaken the new democracy. In general, the organized elements of the bourgeoisie limited themselves to agitating for policy change, not regime change.

Which policies did they object to? In Russia and to some extent in Portugal, the bourgeoisie objected to the new democracy's empowerment of workers. In Mexico, by contrast, the bourgeoisie seems to have accommodated itself to the government's positivist intervention in labor relations, accepting compromise settlements imposed on owners and workers as the surest way to reduce worker activism. Outside of Russia, where the new democracy never won the power of taxation, the bourgeoisie objected primarily to the increased taxation that intellectuals sought to finance positivist social reforms. The main Ottoman business association complained about *budgetivores* in the customs office. Similarly, the main business association in Mexico complained that "the recent initiatives of the national Executive on the increase in taxes, modifications of the customs tariffs, etc., etc., had alarmed commerce and industry." In Iran, a German diplomat noted, "the wealthier businessmen" are "sick and tired" of parliament questioning "their most sacred possession: their freedom to steal and their freedom from taxes." In Portugal, the British ambassador commented, "the influential and rich" could no longer make an "arrangement" to avoid taxation "scot free." In China, a French diplomat reported, the "bankers and the wealthy wholesalers and compradores have all had to contribute and there is no doubt that many of them are beginning to find the new regime very burdensome."

These grievances suggest that the bourgeoisie's gripe with democracy was not over control of the means of production. Indeed, the fundamentals of the bourgeoisie's economic position did not change during the short lifespan of the new democracies. If anything, economic production seems to have increased in many of these countries after democratization, and the new democracies went out of their way to suppress challenges to capitalist control of the workplace, as I will detail in the next chapter. Rather, the bourgeoisie's gripe appears to have centered on control of the state. Business organizations apparently expected to have a greater say in state policy than the newly elected representatives allowed them, and they were reminded of this subordinate status repeatedly. Far from comprising a consolidated "middle class," business organizations and intellectuals were rivals in the new democracies of the early twentieth century.

6

Democracy and the Working Class

If the bourgeoisie is a fair-weather ally for the democracy movement, the working class is generally considered more dependable. While the bourgeoisie favors only limited political openings that they can control, the working class stands to gain by broader democratization, not least because its numbers are larger than any elite's. Dietrich Rueschemeyer, Evelyne Huber Stephens, and John Stephens have presented the most extensive case material for this theory:

> It is especially the working class that has often played a decisively pro-democratic role. Labor's role was concealed to the superficial eye precisely because in many countries workers were long excluded from the political process and thus from visible participation in democratic politics. This role becomes clear, however, if one looks at the struggles that led to an extension of political participation beyond the social circles surrounding the dominant classes.

These authors propose the "crucial hypothesis that the relative size and the density of organization of the working class—of employed manual labor outside of agriculture—are of critical importance for the advance of democracy." Working-class organizations played key roles in democratization in numerous countries in the late twentieth century.[1]

In the early twentieth century, however, democratization was a subject of considerable debate within working-class organizations. A variety of global social movements, including anarchism, producerism, socialism, and trade unionism competed for the loyalty of the working class, and it was not obvious at the time which ones would prevail where. Each of these movements had complicated relationships with democracy. Trade unionism, for example, sometimes sought the protection of laws regulating workplace safety, maximum hours, and minimum wages, which led it to demand effective parliaments, competitive elections, and broad suffrage. At other times, trade unionism sought the protection of patrons, corporate or governmental, which led it to resist challenges to the patron's power.

Socialism sometimes demanded the overthrow of the state through mass industrial action, and sometimes—with the emergence of "evolutionary" or "democratic" socialism at the turn of the twentieth century—demanded the commandeering of the state through electoral participation. These contrasting views were the subject of sharp debate. At the Sixth International Socialist Congress in August 1904, for example, French socialist leader Jean Jaurès defended democratic participation with the claim that socialists had "helped to save the [French] republic" during the Dreyfus Affair. Facing jeers, he continued, "And if some of our comrades no longer remember those detestable days of six years ago when clerics, monks, and coup-plotting generals sought to revive the war of religions, the war of races . . . human conscience has not forgotten, and the conscience of the universal proletariat has not forgotten." Jaurès's rival Jules Guesde dismissed the claim. The republic was not in danger, he said, and socialists are "dupes" if they collaborate with the bourgeoisie by investing any hopes in democratic politics.[2]

For their part, democracy movements were inconsistent in their approach to the working class, as the case studies in this chapter will demonstrate. On one hand, they repeatedly sought to mobilize working-class support, sometimes adopting the recently invented discourse of democratic socialism. On the other hand, they generally refused to promise workers material benefits. Instead, they suggested that procedural democracy would allow workers to organize to gain such benefits, if they wished.

Overarching these debates was the question of nonindustrial and rural workers, who comprised the bulk of the labor force in the early twentieth century, even in most of Western Europe. Socialist organizations and democracy movements largely ignored the peasants in favor of urban populations. In the cities, would democracy movements seek alliances with artisans and popular organizations? Or would their elitism prevent them from associating with the rabble, "the ignorant people who misunderstood equality and liberty," as prodemocracy leader Sun Yatsen in China—a self-proclaimed socialist!—called working-class activists?[3]

Russia

The Russian working class emerged rather suddenly in the 1890s when the monarchy embarked on a policy of rapid industrialization. In this single decade, the number of industrial workers grew by 1 million persons, from 1.4 to 2.4 million. Still, even if we expand the count to include nonfactory workers, who comprised three-quarters or more of the working class, the proletariat comprised a small minority in the Russian population.[4] Yet this group played a disproportionately large role in the Russian democracy movement. Its activism in October 1905 ensured the victory of the movement, and its subsequent lack of activism in 1906 and 1907 contributed to the movement's demise.

Leaders of the democracy movement, recognizing its limited social base, sought to solicit the support of the working class. At first, their methods were indirect. They did not make speeches to groups of workers, as Francisco Madero did in Mexico; or ally themselves with traditional working-class organizations, as prodemocracy movements did in China and Iran; or support unionization, as Portuguese prodemocracy groups did on occasion. Rather, they in effect subcontracted the mobilization of working-class support to leftists. This policy was first formulated by a prodemocracy gentry-intellectual in 1902. Y. Y. Gurevich urged the democracy movement to make "no enemies on the left"—in other words, to court the socialist parties that claimed to represent Russian workers.[5] In 1904, the democracy movement adopted the policy wholeheartedly, incorporating social-reform language into the prodemocracy campaign and seeking allies among the socialist parties. P. B. Struve, editor of the prodemocracy journal *Liberation*, framed the idea of alliance as follows:

> This is how we visualize the matter: The local committees of the "Union of Liberation" enter into an agreement with the local Social-Democratic committees and, having enlisted in the cause some influential members of the [radical] intelligentsia and the more advanced workers, press for the authorization of economic labor organizations. . . . [W]e do not at all visualize [outreach to workers] as some sort of contest with the Social-Democrats. On the contrary, we should like the "Liberationists" to persuade the Social-Democrats that major social achievements are not brought about by verbal incantations and to begin systematic organizational work among the working class together with the Social-Democrats.[6]

It appeared that the entire liberal movement was becoming "Marxified," as a 1906 study of Russian intellectuals put it. Pavel N. Miliukov argued several months later that such a development was inevitable: "Russian liberalism was always tinged with democratism, and Russian democratism has been strongly impregnated with socialistic teachings and tendencies ever since socialism made its appearance." The culmination of this trend was the summit meeting of the Russian opposition (minus the Bolshevik fraction the Social Democratic party) that took place in September 1904 in Paris, where the leading prodemocracy group, the Union of Liberation—represented at the meeting by Miliukov and three others— adopted a statement of mutual support with seven revolutionary parties.[7]

In the following months, the opportunity arose for a direct alliance between the democracy movement and the working class. Prodemocracy activity among intellectuals attracted the attention of working-class activists, who discussed whether to join the "general protests of Russian intellectuals." A meeting of working-class leaders in St. Petersburg resolved in November 1904 to offer unspecified "support for the intelligentsia, demanding freedom"; and Father Georgii A. Gapon, the leader of the Assembly of Mill and Factory Workers of St. Petersburg, established contacts with the Union of Liberation. Earlier in the year, Gapon had prepared to break with his government benefactors by drafting a secret program calling for political and social reforms—freedoms of speech, press, assembly, and religion, and equality before the law (but not a parliament); universal education, the right to unionize, an eight-hour maximum workday, and minimum wage rates (but not socialist control of production). In the fall of 1904, Gapon shared these plans with "several intellectual Liberals" and "invited students and other educated people to deliver lectures at all our branches on political questions." Gapon refrained from announcing his liberalism publicly until early January 1905, when the assembly represented virtually the whole working class of the capital, with more than one hundred thousand workers on strike. When the demands were read at assembly meetings on January 7 and 8, they received enthusiastic approval with almost messianic overtones. The reading of the demands at one meeting "brought the listeners to a frenzy," according to one eyewitness.[8]

On January 9, 1905, Gapon and thousands of his followers carried these demands to the tsar's palace in a massive demonstration. The tsar was not there to receive them; instead, the military blocked the protestors' path and then fired on them, killing hundreds. The event known as

Bloody Sunday ignited the anti-tsar movement. "On this day I was born a second time, but now not as an all-forgiving and all-forgetting child, but as an embittered man, prepared to struggle and be victorious," one worker recalled. "The events of January 9 completely changed my world view and left an indelible imprint on me for the rest of my life," said another. Even V. I. Lenin, the communist leader who had scorned the democracy movement a year earlier, urged "the proletarian not to keep aloof from the bourgeois revolution" but "to take a most energetic part in it."[9] Strikes cascaded around the country for months, culminating in the general strike of October 1905, which convinced the tsar to grant a semi-democracy.

But the opportunity for direct cooperation between the democracy movement and working-class organizations passed. The prodemocracy activists who wished to reach out to workers—primarily the democratic socialists of the St. Petersburg "Big Group," who had met with Gapon in late 1904 and again in early 1905—were unable to follow up on this lead. Although they had some influence among printers and several white-collar employees' groups and made contacts with metalworkers and others, the democracy movement "recruited only a small following among unionized workers" in Russia's two largest cities.[10]

Instead, the democracy movement and the workers' movement traveled separate paths during 1905, reuniting only during the general strike in October. The organizations were largely separate and the rhythms of the movements were not in sync. In terms of ideology, the workers' movement focused primarily on economic issues. When a worker shouted, "Down with the autocracy!" at a meeting in Ivanovo-Voznesensk—the textile center known as the "Russian Manchester" and site of Russia's first *soviet* (workers' council)—his colleagues urged him to leave aside political questions. When politics did enter the workers' movement, it was generally socialist politics. The relationship of Russian socialists to the democracy movement is extremely unclear, and was heatedly contested at the time, so I will not attempt to describe it in any detail. Leftists wished to use the democracy movement to usher in a socialist era, just as the democracy movement wished to use the socialists to usher in a democratic era.[11]

These different agendas coincided in the general strike of October 1905, a strike triggered by the railway workers' union, one of the few working-class unions that had a significant white-collar membership and a largely prodemocracy ideology. Other working-class organizations and leftist parties followed suit, generally adopting prodemocracy demands along with socialist demands. In Moscow, where the general strike began, the strike committee was dominated by prodemocracy intellectuals who welcomed working-class agitation as a means to pressure the monarchy to reform. The Constitutional-Democratic (Kadet) Party, an outgrowth of the Union of Liberation, also meeting in Moscow at this time for its founding congress, stated that it "warmly welcomes the enormous step taken by the people in the same direction it [the Kadet Party] has chosen itself: [it welcomes] the organized mobilization of the Russian working class." Miliukov, the leader of the Kadets, said that "our Party stands closest to those groups among the Western intellectuals who are known under the name of 'social reformers'" and "our program is undoubtedly the most leftist of all those advanced by similar groups in Western Europe." For their part, many workers appear to have supported the prodemocracy ideology: "The extent of such sentiments is difficult to judge," according to one major study, "but there can be no doubt that demands for civil liberties and for a constitutional system of government had the support of a great many workers during the final months of 1905."[12]

The general strike was weakening in Moscow by October 17, when the tsar issued the October Manifesto granting limited democratic reforms. The *soviet* in Ekaterinoslav had actually conceded defeat on the 17th and voted to call off the strike; news of the Manifesto did not reach the southern city until the next morning. But the pressure was kept up in St. Petersburg, Odessa, and elsewhere, and apparently this was enough.[13]

The October Manifesto shattered the alliance between leftists and workers, on one hand, and the prodemocracy movement, on the other. The Kadet Party hoped to continue its policy of "no enemies on the left" while taking advantage of the democratic institutions promised by the tsar, limited though they might be. Miliukov argued that the forthcoming parliament "can serve for the [Kadet] Party only as one of the means towards realization of the above-mentioned aim [constitutional democracy and social reform], while a permanent and close contact should be maintained with the general course of the liberation movement outside the Duma [parliament]." However, the socialists scorned the forthcoming parliament and refused to participate. Even the "Big Group" of democratic socialists, though it supported participation in parliament, considered the revolution only half-won and distanced itself from the Kadet Party: "They [the Kadets] are not against the revolution in general," the

Big Group's journal editorialized in early 1906, "or at least they are not unequivocally against it. But they are not with the Russian revolution, or at least they are not in it. They are on its sidelines. They are its spectators, its critics." The Big Group's aloofness to the Kadets severed the democracy movement's only direct link with working-class organizations.[14]

Many workers were also dissatisfied with the semidemocratic promises of the October Manifesto. Some of this sentiment may have been linked to the workers' resentment of intellectuals, for whom political rights took precedence over the improvement of economic conditions. During the October general strike, for instance, workers clashed with liberal legal scholar S. A. Muromtsev, future president of parliament and at that time a member of the Moscow City Council. Muromtsev expressed sympathy with striking city council employees but urged them to postpone their economic demands until political reforms had been won. In Ufa, striking railway workers objected to the linkage of their economic goals with demands for democratization, then attacked student activists who had mocked their pious devotion to the tsar. As intellectuals prepared to participate in parliament after the October Manifesto, workers in the south argued that political freedom was useful only for socialists and "the well-educated." "For what do we need a constitution!" they shouted. Two weeks after the Manifesto, an assembly of railway workers in Ekaterinoslav called for the establishment of a "kingdom of socialism" to expropriate the intellectuals along with the landowners and capitalists: "all—land, factories, and establishments of art and science—will belong to the people." In Odessa, though the Kadets generally maintained better relations with workers here than elsewhere, one rally heckled a Kadet speaker and his "liberal prattle." Another group of workers in Moscow several weeks later refused to listen to a union leader until they were assured he was not an intellectual or a student. A prominent liberal intellectual worried that "the embittered masses" might revolt and "subject to destruction the entire intelligentsia."[15]

As general strikes continued to pressure the government in November and December, prodemocracy intellectuals grew increasingly hostile. Miliukov wrote in early December, "In October, the political strike was a heroic civilian feat. It was doubtless a political mistake in November. Now, a political strike could turn out to be a crime—a crime against the revolution!" With limited support, these strikes were crushed, an outcome that may well have increased the bitterness of workers toward the prodemocracy intellectuals, some of whom worried that "the workers' distrust of the intelligentsia . . . had created insurmountable barriers against [our] enlightenment (in the broadest sense of the word) work among the property-less and 'dark' strata of the population."[16]

A sign of workers' bitterness was their limited participation in the parliamentary election of early 1906. In one Moscow bakery, for example, management gathered the workers together and tried to force them to vote, but most workers would not. With socialists refusing to stand for office and the more radical workers refusing to vote, the Kadet Party scored an impressive victory. However, this outcome did not represent real support. Interestingly, such support began to emerge after the opening of parliament in the spring of 1906. The St. Petersburg Central Bureau of Trade Unions announced, "Of course the Duma [parliament] is powerless, but it can provide us with a great service if we succeed in turning it into a forum for disseminating loud and brave voices in defense of the working class, and together with it, the entire laboring population." At the same time, the legalization of trade unions in March 1906 led to a profusion of worker organizations, and strike activity increased again in the spring of 1906.[17]

Within parliament, the Kadets saw the renewal of worker activism as a sign of support for their labor-reform policies. In their reply to the tsar's opening address to parliament, the Kadets listed labor legislation among their principal goals for the parliamentary session. During the first session they introduced legislation to liberalize the March 1906 trade-union law. Maxim Gorky, the famous socialist writer, continued to agitate on behalf "the necessity of placing in unison and harmonizing, in any great public movement, the thought of the intellectuals and the action of the proletarians."[18]

As the threat of socialist uprising passed, the Kadets reverted to their earlier stance that worker agitation presented useful leverage against the monarchy, a position that they held to the end of the democratic experiment. No longer were political strikes "a crime against the revolution," as Miliukov had termed them in December 1905. Instead, the Kadets' reply to the tsar argued, "Pacification of the country is impossible so long as it is not clear to the people that from now on the authorities cannot govern by force." The extent of working-class support for parliament became a major factor in parliament's relations with the monarchy. In April 1906, one leading Kadet suggested that suppression of the new democracy would stir such popular outrage that it "will be the government's last act, after which it will cease to exist." In mid-June, the Kadet newspaper concluded that parliament could not be dissolved "without risking an enormous convulsion." In late June, a member of parliament urged the assembly to "take into its hands the executive power. . . . I know that the people and half the army are bewildered by the composure of the State Duma and only wait . . ." [ellipsis in the original]. In early July, Miliukov wrote that "dissolution of the Duma—there can be no doubt of that— would lead to civil war." In the first weeks of the new parliament, the monarchist government was already considering dissolving parliament and ending the democratic experiment; one of the arguments against doing so, voiced by the minister of war, was that people "had placed such great hopes in it [parliament] that an immediate dissolution would be a great disappointment to them." As late as early July, some within the government still felt that dissolution would lead to the "most fateful consequences—including the collapse of the monarchy." In view of these warnings, the government's decision to dissolve parliament on July 9, 1906, was accompanied by large-scale military mobilization to prevent popular protests.[19]

Barred from the parliamentary building, the Kadets and other representatives met in nearby Vyborg, Finland, where they called on workers and peasants to engage in civil disobedience in defense of parliament: "don't give a kopek to the treasury or a soldier to the army. Be firm in your refusal, stand up for your rights, all as one man."[20] Most workers did not heed the call. Scattered protests occurred, the most serious being three naval mutinies near St. Petersburg. Several *soviets* announced a general strike to support the mutinies, but it did not attract popular support and was quickly abandoned. Humbled by their isolation, the Kadets soon retreated from the adamancy of the Vyborg Manifesto and prepared for the new parliamentary elections, this time with the slogan, "Save the duma at all costs."

Workers were not willing to make sacrifices for democracy in the summer of 1906 as they had in October 1905. But this did not mean they were hostile to democracy, as the winter 1906–1907 elections demonstrated. Workers actively participated, as did members of the socialist parties who had boycotted the first parliamentary elections a year earlier. A Social Democrat in St. Petersburg noted in December 1906 that "there is not a single union which has a negative attitude toward the Duma elections." Leftist candidates fared well in these elections, winning 118 seats, with Kadets winning only 99 seats (down from 195 seats in the first parliament). But leftist participation in parliament was not intended, and did not serve, to prolong the democratic experiment. Rather, leftists sought to use parliament as an organizational center for a revolutionary uprising. While the Kadets tried to "protect the duma" through conciliation and moderation, the leftists were outspoken and provocative. They booed government ministers, proposed legislation to bring about an immediate dissolution of parliament, and made speeches calling for armed revolution. Ironically, given this record, the monarchists resorted to fabricated evidence to charge the socialist parliamentary bloc with subversion, which served as a pretext for dissolving the second parliament in early June 1907. As with the first dissolution, the government made careful preparations to prevent protests, including two detailed police reports that predicted the country would remain calm. The Kadets' last-ditch negotiations to save the second parliament appealed (as before) to the specter of unrest. Prime minister P. A. Stolypin replied that he anticipated "purely local [incidents]; but this is not important." This assessment proved accurate. As in the previous summer, workers failed to rise in defense of democracy. When democracy was suppressed, so were working-class organizations.[21]

Iran

In October 1908, a group of social democrats assembled in Tabriz, Iran. Twenty-eight members—Armenian intellectuals from Tabriz and the Caucasus—debated whether Iran had a working class or not. After extensive discussion, the group voted on two proposals. One argued that "Iran has already entered into the domain of capitalist production, and that industrial production (tobacco and [cigarette] tube factories, steam-powered mills, cotton-cleaning factories, et cetera) has been generated alongside large-scale manufacturing." As a result, "there exists a proletariat in Iran as well as small artisans." The second proposal argued, by contrast, "that Iran does not find itself in the [historical] phase of industrial production, that it is just entering the path of capitalism, and that a modern proletariat has not been created." The group voted 26 to 2 in favor of the first proposition and committed itself to prodemocracy work on behalf of the proletariat. In 1910, a separate group of social democrats in Tehran came to the opposite conclusion. Capitalism was so little developed in Iran, they said in the introduction to their party platform, that the tasks of introducing bourgeois democracy and agitating on behalf of poor people fell to intellectuals—"the possessors of education, who are, unfortunately, all too few"—and to reputable nationalists.[22]

The Iranian proletariat, if it existed, was numerically tiny, involving about seven thousand workers in 1910, less than one-fifth of 1 percent of the economically active male population, according to a recent estimate. Many of these jobs had emerged after democratization in 1906. Tehran's first electrical plant began operating only in 1904; Mashhad's first plant was burned down by a crowd claiming religious objections. Iran had two railways, totaling only eight miles, plus twenty-six cotton gins, five oil re-fineries, and eighteen other factories. This small working class was not ac-tive in the democratization movement, but after parliament convened in 1906, it began to test the new atmosphere of freedom. Fishermen in En-zeli, a Caspian port, were the first to go on strike, followed by a dozen other groups over the next several years. The central government played no systematic role in these events, though various officials intervened per-sonally on behalf of one side or another, sometimes confronting one an-other on both sides of the dispute. In Tabriz, where social democrats came to hold significant positions, the local council was somewhat more sympathetic to working-class issues, adjudicating individuals' grievances about mistreatment by powerful persons and price gouging.[23]

By contrast, the prodemocracy movement enjoyed widespread support among another working class, the premodern artisanal workers, who were traditionally organized in guilds. Wealthy owners (discussed in Chapter 5) dominated some guilds. Other guilds were primarily composed of workers with more modest occupations. Both sorts of guilds participated enthusi-astically in the prodemocracy movement of 1906. They went on strike, encamped at the sit-in at the British embassy, and supported the intellec-tuals' demand for parliamentary democracy. After this demand was achieved, emboldened artisans—as well as peasants—organized collec-tively in many regions of the country and demanded recognition of their rights. A committee of intellectuals in the capital tried to coordinate pop-ular movements, but it appears that mobilization around the country oc-curred outside of any central control.[24]

Intellectuals were uneven in reciprocating this support from workers. They wrote and passed a constitutional amendment granting Iranians the right of association, so long as they carried no arms, obeyed police regula-tions in public places, and did no harm to Islam, the state, or the public order. Some intellectuals were consistent in supporting the use of the right of association, such as the Tabriz activist Sayyid Javad Natiq, who ar-gued, "In every civilized nation, and according to our Muslim tradition, people are allowed to form organizations." Some also cheered working people's newfound assertiveness, as did a Western-educated Iranian who told a story about an ironworker who arrived to fix a cabinet minister's fireplace soon after the constitution was declared: "On entering, he saluted the Minister. The Minister's servant bade him do obeisance. He replied, 'Knave, do you not know that we now have a Constitution, and that under a Constitution obeisances no longer exist?'" A newspaper in Tehran commented, "Whatever one may think of it, the people are evidently not the same people as last year! Everywhere you go, talk is of parliament. Everybody you see is speaking of Iran." On the other hand, Iranian intellectuals frequently disparaged the political acuity of working people. Their self-image was based on a strong distinction between the "knowledgeable" and the "ignorant," and they placed the vast majority of the population in the latter category. One of the leading prodemocracy activists said that the majority of Iranians "are plunged in the sewer of ignorance and illiteracy."[25]

As soon as Muzaffar al-Din Shah acquiesced to convene parliament, debate emerged whether this "ignorant" majority should be allowed to dominate elections. A prodemocracy newspaper suggested that they should: "if the decision is made on the basis of scholarly worthiness, [then] the rights of the nation's many ignorant classes, which are widespread, will be wasted. . . . If we judge the basis of worthiness to be reading and writing, the common classes, which are larger than all others, will be deprived [of the right to vote] on account of illiteracy or weak reading and writing." By contrast, a prodemocracy intellectual commented somewhat later, "Of course, universal suffrage is the fundamentally correct system, but this system is advisable only when a people has progressed in political affairs and has gained sufficient insightfulness. In many countries of Europe, suffrage is still limited in elections." This view prevailed.[26]

The electoral law of September 1906 rewarded the guilds' activism with thirty-two reserved seats in the first parliament, more than a fifth of the total. However, it also disenfranchised the poor. Certain low-paid occupations were excluded, and members of guilds that were enfranchised had to "be in possession of a shop of which the rent corresponds with the average rents of the locality"; peasants were required to "possess property of the value of at least one thousand tumans," about 200 British pounds at the time. A group of intellectuals offered an alternative electoral law, with suffrage for all adult males, but the merchants rejected it. When talk in parliament turned to widening the electorate, it was turned aside on the

grounds of "ignorance": this might work in places where "at least 90 percent of the people are educated, but it is not this way here and now."[27]

Owners of modest shops could be and were elected to parliament,
though they generally kept quiet during debates. Less than a tenth of the
speakers in the first parliament (1906–1908) were guild representatives,
who comprised a fifth of the chamber. On at least one occasion, however,
a shopowner spoke out forcefully in favor of democracy. A grocer, representing Tehran's grocers, wholesalers, nut sellers, fruit sellers, corn sellers,
and rice sellers, defended democratic constitutionalism *(mashrutiyat)*
against religious law *(mashruʿiyat)* in a crucial debate: "We guild members and the dirty collared and the common people don't understand
these deep-sounding Arabic words; what we have acquired with so much
hardship and bloodshed is called *mashrutiyat,* and we shall not part with
our *mashrutiyat* with a play on words."[28]

Outside of parliament, the traditional working class's support for democracy was voluble. Guild artisans and poor people formed the backbone
of numerous popular associations that sprouted after democratization—a
hundred or more in Tehran alone. The prodemocracy movement came to
rely heavily on these groups. In 1907, when the shah refused to sign supplementary laws to establish parliamentary rights vis-à-vis the monarch,
widespread strikes broke out across the country—"the whole of the trades
and employment of the bazaar, down to the porters" in Kermanshah, according to a British diplomatic account—and the shah felt compelled to
sign. At the end of 1907, when the shah sent troops to menace parliament,
popular associations gathered in force and camped outside the parliament
building for a week. On another occasion, the threat of convening popular
associations was sufficient to convince the speaker of parliament, whom the
prodemocracy forces considered a liability despite his earlier support for
democracy, to resign. The speaker complained, "Do popular associations in
any democratic or republican country have such a right to remove the president of the National Consultative Assembly, duly elected by the nation, on
the whim of a single ignoble member of parliament? This is a disgrace!"[29]

As this last example implies, the defense of democracy sometimes involved violations of democratic procedures. The state had a limited ability
to control the activities of the popular associations, a few of which were
armed, and a British diplomat was not the only one to worry that Iran was
"fast drifting into a state of government by the semi-secret and wholly ir-
responsible political Societies of Tehran." Similarly, ʿAbdulrahim Talibuf,
a prodemocracy intellectual in Russian Azerbaijan who was elected in

absentia as a parliamentary representative in Iran—and declined to serve—wrote in a Tabriz newspaper, "Up until now Iran was captive to the double-horned bull of arbitrary government, but from now on—if it does not succeed in bringing order to itself—it will be struck by the thousand-horned ox of the rabble and the mob."[30]

Some of the popular associations, for their part, were exasperated with the ineffectiveness and pretentiousness of parliament. An open letter from a women's organization said that parliament had wasted its first year. "We are fed up, we can no longer remain patient." A flyer from another organization opined: "Good God, we elected a representative to parliament in order to reclaim our unrecognized rights from the hands of the oppressors. We never wanted him to give away our just rights to the oppressors. . . . If they used to arrest us before [democratization] without any legal basis, today they do it legally, on the vote of the representatives."[31]

But when the shah prepared to suspend the constitution in June 1908, many popular associations rallied to defend parliament by force of arms, gathering in large numbers in and around the parliament building in Tehran. Hasan Taqizadah and other prodemocracy intellectuals had lost their great hopes for armed confrontation and now considered resistance futile. "The foreigners say that the committees are excessive," Taqizadah told colleagues. On the contrary, he continued, the real problem is that "we don't have enough power to defend ourselves." For this reason, intellectuals in parliament dispersed most of their working-class defenders just before royalist troops bombarded parliament.[32]

Democracy survived this coup d'état only because of resistance in places where intellectuals had strong links with other classes. In the southern province of Isfahan, intellectuals made an alliance with tribal forces, headed by a Francophone businessman named 'Ali-Quli Khan (Sardar As'ad) (see Chapter 5). In the northern province of Gilan, they made an alliance with one of the largest landowners in Iran, Muhammad Vali Khan (Sipahdar) (see Chapter 7). In the northwestern province of Azerbaijan, the intellectuals maintained an alliance with the working class. Popular association leaders Sattar Khan and Baqir Khan, a horsedealer and a stonemason, were invited to join the city council, and they proved crucial in organizing the uprising that held off a royalist invasion. The alliance had its tensions. Sattar Khan was furious that the "educated and schooled" prodemocracy leaders did not appreciate the contributions of his uneducated followers, and the intellectuals worried that the lower classes would switch sides if the reactionaries made them a better offer.[33] Still, the alliance held.

These groups conquered Tehran in mid-1909 and reestablished democracy. Yet for their efforts, the traditional working class was removed from parliament. A committee of notables rewrote the election law, removing the thirty-two seats reserved for guild representatives. The poor were still barred from voting, with suffrage limited to men who owned 250 tumans (50 pounds) of property, or paid 10 tumans (2 pounds) in taxes, or earned 50 tumans (10 pounds) a year, "or have studied"—this last stipulation allowing intellectuals to vote. At least one prominent prodemocracy intellectual indicated that it was okay by him to "change the law in consideration of the needs of the time." The committee also accepted advice from the Russian foreign ministry, which blamed the original electoral law for a parliament that "was dependent upon the revolutionary anjumans [popular associations]" and that "gave unmistakable proof of its complete incapacity to guide the affairs of the country in a new direction." What was needed, the Russians suggested—drawing perhaps on the tsar's own experience in subduing the Russian parliament—was "a rational form of representative government . . . in accordance with the historical usages and customs of the Persian people." In short, suffrage should be limited. The British foreign minister "entirely" concurred with the need for "a scheme of elective Government in conformity with the civic ideas of the Persian people." The British ambassador in Tehran called the new electoral law "most democratic," urging the Iranian government to ignore criticism of the law from Tabriz, because "it was hopeless to expect to satisfy all sections of the community." There were no guild representatives in the second parliament, which convened in late 1909.[34]

Perhaps as a result of its reduced representativeness, the second parliament sought to initiate or increase a series of taxes on poor people, including a particularly unpopular salt tax. Radical intellectuals, in conjunction with the new treasurer, an American named Morgan Shuster, managed to reverse the salt tax. They also continued to mobilize popular support for parliament, but on a far smaller scale than before 1908. Instead of mass demonstrations, popular associations turned to assassination, which multiplied after the first and most prominent victim, prime minister Amin al-Sultan, was shot outside parliament in late summer 1907.[35] In 1910, the government disarmed and dispersed Sattar Khan's followers, the last major independent force. In 1911, the government sought and received parliamentary approval to ban popular associations that it deemed injurious to the public order.

In its final weeks, parliament passed a new electoral law, removing the property requirement. Even a defender of property restrictions admitted that "I believe nobody in the National Consultative Assembly of Iran thinks that poor people shouldn't have the right to vote and participate in political affairs."[36] But this bid for popular support was futile. The popular associations that had defended the constitution in 1907 and 1908 were no longer around in 1911.

Ottoman Empire

The modern working class in the Ottoman Empire numbered as many as a quarter-of-a-million persons, according to one oft-cited study, a size falling somewhere between that of the working classes in Iran and Russia. Major Ottoman ports joined the world economy in the eighteenth and nineteenth centuries, reaching into adjacent regions through agricultural markets and piecework manufacturing. In Salonica alone, there were twenty factories by 1908. But this large working class was divided by ethnicity—many of the industrial workers were non-Turks—and by region and economic sector, with the result that virtually no working-class organization existed until after democratization. Possible exceptions to this were underground socialist groups such as the Armenian Revolutionary Federation and leftist factions of the Internal Macedonian Revolutionary Organization, which sought regional autonomy as much as social revolution. The Ottoman democracy movement allied with these groups in 1907, but not out of an ideological commitment to the working class.[37]

Few Ottoman intellectuals trusted the uneducated majority of the general population. For years, Ahmed Rıza, leader of the prodemocracy movement, urged his followers not to precipitate a revolution, out of concern that political mobilization might lead to anarchy and bloodshed. Even when he shifted position and urged the movement to engage in armed revolution, he still opposed mass mobilization: "In a country the population of which is composed of elements that possess contradictory political ideas and are affiliated with different faiths, a [mass] revolution would only strengthen the tyranny and benefit the foreigners who are seeking a pretext with which to legitimize their intervention."[38]

Perhaps as a result, the prodemocracy movement organized almost no popular protests. There were scattered tax revolts in the first years of the twentieth century, as well as food riots, petitions, and other forms of popular protest, but these were rarely part of the democracy movement. Two of the few documented instances of cooperation between the movement and the working class prior to the 1908 revolution occurred when the Society for Union and Progress made contact with a workers' society in Istanbul and actively assisted a strike among carpet weavers in the town of Uşak.[39] Unlike in Iran, the prodemocracy movement in the Ottoman Empire made little effort to mobilize premodern popular organizations.

Nonetheless, the restoration of the constitution triggered a huge outpouring of popular support. In Beirut, for example, large crowds took part in "public rejoicings" and "vociferously cheered" speeches about liberty, democracy, and popular sovereignty. After a few days, the Society for Union and Progress, the main prodemocracy organization and the power behind the throne after democratization, told people to stop demonstrating, get back to work, and leave politics to the intellectuals: "All the people of the nation [should] attend to their work, toil, and duties. . . . From today on, the council of ministers must be able to work with complete authority; . . . it needs only for the people not to interfere in the administration of government affairs."[40]

The Ottoman people did not heed this advice. A satirical newspaper parodied the spread of political activism with a cartoon of stray dogs presenting a petition to the Istanbul government, objecting to the plan to eradicate them. As in other countries, intellectuals ridiculed the populace for their supposed ignorance:

> Yes, experience shows that some humans consider liberty to be completely limitless independence. In some villages, in my experience, liberty means the right and ability not to pay taxes to the government, or to smuggle freely. Some people suppose that [liberty means] doing anything they want wherever they want and saying anything they want wherever they want.

Ahmed Rıza's positivist elitism overrode his democratic convictions in a diary entry from this period: "Fools should not be allowed to enter politics; however, they have unfortunately even become deputies, and this is a defect of liberty that enables the masses to assume a role in the life and future of the state and nation."[41]

One of the main avenues for popular participation was labor activism. Just days after democratization, dockworkers in the port of Izmir went on strike, marching to government buildings to present their demands. Over the next five months, according to one count, this strike was followed by 110 more, compared with 50 strikes in the previous 36 years combined. Various studies estimate that at least one-quarter of the urban working class and three-quarters of its industrial labor force participated in strikes. Many of the strikers appear to have taken the demands of railway workers as a model: union recognition, delimited working hours, paid holidays, better working conditions, and set procedures for hiring and firing.[42]

The Society for Union and Progress quickly intervened in this wave of working-class protests. The Society hoped to combine social order with social justice, but it was clear that order came first. One day after the first strike in Izmir, the Society issued a declaration forbidding "mass demonstrations." As strikes multiplied around the country, the Society's members mediated, sometimes at the request of the workers or the owners, and sometimes through the threat of state coercion. Concessions invariably ensued. In October 1908, the Society's new platform included a paragraph promising laws "to regulate the mutual responsibilities between workers and employers"—a common positivist theme in other countries as well. Within a week, the government promulgated new regulations banning strikes in the public sector and preventing strikers from demanding the removal of company executives.[43]

Complicating these regulatory efforts were the international implications of the strikes. Many capitalists in the Ottoman Empire had European citizenship or protection, and work stoppages quickly turned into diplomatic incidents. During a strike of a British-owned railway, for example, British diplomats considered stationing a British naval vessel near Izmir "in view of the threatening state of affairs." Diplomatic incidents, conversely, could turn into labor issues, too. Three months after democratization, several Ottoman provinces were wrested from Istanbul's control: Austria-Hungary annexed Bosnia-Herzegovina, Crete seceded and joined Greece, and Bulgaria declared independence. In the case of Bosnia, the Society for Union and Progress sought to use labor unrest as part of its foreign policy. The Society helped to promote a massive strike and boycott against Austrian companies: port workers refused to unload Austrian goods from ships, then refused to unload any goods from ships that had sailed from Austrian ports, then refused to unload any goods that did not have a license from the boycott syndicate. When workers in the ports of

Izmir, Beirut, and Haifa relaxed these restrictions, the Society ordered them to continue the strike.[44]

The Society for Union and Progress was also concerned about the prospect of socialism. The Society had very little truck with socialism, or even social-democratic thought. One activist's memoirs recalled a bizarre plan to establish an Ottoman commune in New Zealand, but dismissed this as youthful daydreaming. Among Society members in power after democratization, only one midranking official is supposed to have been something of a socialist. The more influential position within the Society was expressed in a Society newspaper in late October 1908: "If we follow an extremist policy and take a step toward socialism, we will scare the capitalists, whom we need to give more security than ever." Even Ottoman leftists shared this concern, preferring the protection of democratic gains to the improbable odds of imminent socialist transformation. One of the few social-democratic members of parliament—an ethnic Bulgarian and opponent of the Society—questioned whether the working class, or any class, in the Ottoman Empire was well-developed enough to defend democracy. Similarly, a union official urged workers to stop striking, for fear that capitalists and reactionaries would join together and destroy democracy.[45]

As it turned out, the most dangerous threat to democracy came not from capitalists and reactionaries, but from military officers in the Society for Union and Progress (see Chapter 8). When they marched on Istanbul and undermined democracy in April 1909, the Ottoman working class stood idle. Two months later, worker-activists appear to have regretted this decision. The Society was now bent on imposing order in the economic realm, as in other realms, even at the expense of democratic rights. A new labor law, written in part by a railway executive, virtually outlawed striking by prohibiting the impairment of business or the organization of demonstrations. One cabinet member, speaking to parliament in favor of the law, threatened to go even farther and ban trade unions altogether—"only to protect the workers, not in order to protect the capitalists. For, be sure, workers will become slaves in the hands of trade unions."[46]

Several thousand workers in Salonica, perhaps the most socialist-influenced city in the Ottoman Empire, rallied to oppose the strike law, distributing leaflets in multiple languages (including Bulgarian, Greek, Ladino, and Turkish) to reach the city's ethnically diverse population. Perhaps because these ethnic divisions were becoming increasingly salient, the rally did not result in an organized campaign, and the law was passed.

The number of strikes dropped from more than one hundred in the fall of 1908 to five in 1909.[47]

Portugal

In a population of roughly six million, Portugal's industrial workers numbered perhaps 180,000 on the eve of the 1910 revolution. Half of these were artisanal workers in small shops. Only 27,000 were unionized. The largest single industry, cotton textiles, numbered only 20,000 workers and had shrunk in the previous two decades due to foreign competition. In sum, Portugal's modern working class was a small fraction of the social scene. Yet it attracted a disproportionate amount of attention through its increasing militancy, its presumably greater role in the future, and its active propagandists. These propagandists—trade-unionists, socialists, and anarchists—treated the democracy movement as competition. The Portuguese workers' movement and democracy movement had begun life in the early 1870s intertwined: one early prodemocracy intellectual, a poet, was the head of a radical workers' organization, for example. But the two movements quickly fell out, with the workers turning against "scientific authorities" and the positivist intellectuals entertaining serious doubts as to the mental abilities of the popular classes. After this point, leftist intellectuals and prodemocracy intellectuals tried to undermine each others' claims to represent the working class. A writer for the hatmakers' union, for example, identified the democracy movement with the humanitarian pretensions of the bourgeoisie: "O model-boss, great benefactor of humanity, apologist of the sympathetic trilogy of the French Revolution—Liberty, Equality, Fraternity—the result of which is a simple man of business, with a coin in place of a heart."[48]

One result of this split lay in the prodemocracy intellectuals' disparaging attitudes toward the workers. There were populist strains in the democracy movement—Bernardino Machado praised the workers' "popular knowledge," for example, and the democracy movement held that the "effectiveness of the fundamental political principle of Popular Sovereignty resides in universal suffrage" (a principle that the prodemocracy leaders soon reneged on). Still, the dominant outlook was decidedly elitist. As prodemocracy propagandist França Borges put it, "The people will go where they are ordered." In the 1860s, a prodemocracy leader argued that ordinary Portuguese were not yet "in a state of moral and intellectual culture to comprehend democracy" and that the movement had better continue "the holy propaganda of the ABC's," meaning education. On the eve of the revolution of 1910, prodemocracy intellectuals continued to worry about the backwardness of Portugal's "conservative majority."[49] Indeed, the ongoing vehemence of the clamor for education could itself be interpreted as disparagement.

The intellectuals also disliked the self-interestedness of the workers' demands. (The intellectuals' self-image placed themselves above such pettiness.) João Chagas, later a prime minister of the republic, angrily denied in 1908 that the Republican Party had ever promised workers "penny codfish" (cheap food). All we can tell the workers, he continued, is *Surge et ambula*, a Latin phrase that might be translated uncharitably as "Get up and walk."[50] Both the unsympathetic sentiment and the foreign language it was expressed in could hardly have been calculated to attract proletarian support.

Various prodemocracy figures appear to have recognized that their message was not a populist one. "Energetic propaganda around the grand principles of liberty cannot exploit misery," wrote Miguel Bombarda, the psychiatrist whose murder precipitated the democratic revolution of October 1910. "Radical or moderate, the republican programs do not resolve the social question," wrote another intellectual in 1902. *Soul of the Nation,* the premiere republican newspaper in the last year of the monarchy, chimed in: "Without a doubt, they [the people] aspire to republican government in its greatest democratic expression—socialism; but they do not believe in the bourgeois and conservative republic, that intermediate formula through which we must pass, we too, the peoples of the Latin race."[51]

As a result, some prodemocracy intellectuals took steps to woo the workers. António José de Almeida, for example, who as minister of the interior after the revolution showed little sympathy for workers' movements, wrote before the revolution: "With regard to the working class, what orientation shall we adopt? Must we make a conservative and bourgeois republic, or shall we make, as is just, a socialist republic, giving satisfaction to the legitimate aspirations of the immense multitude of workers?" Bernardino Machado, who later helped to repress workers' movements as president of the republic, wrote to workers that he considered anarchism—which enjoyed a strong following among Portuguese workers, as among Mexican workers—"a sublime ideal." Striking metalworkers sometimes received financial assistance from republicans, and the democracy movement launched peacemaking efforts toward certain unions.[52]

Whether because of these appeals or because of an inherent proletarian interest in democracy, workers supported the democracy movement in large numbers. The anarcho-syndicalist newspaper *Strike* lamented that a majority of industrial and office workers had "abandoned the struggle" and were following the republicans. In October 1910, when revolution erupted, working-class towns near Lisbon were the first to join the republican side. Workers comprised almost half of the membership of republican organizations in 1910 and provided the bulk of casualties during the prodemocracy revolution. Contemporary observers noted the irony of poor workers standing guard during the revolution, "defending the banks and the money of the rich, with the police and the Guard completely disarmed."[53]

As in other new democracies, workers acted quickly on proclamations of liberty. Strikes jumped from a dozen a year to 247 in the fourteen months after the democratic revolution. Even rural workers, whom urban socialists thought to be hopelessly backward, turned militant in several regions: "The spontaneity and solidarity that our rural brothers have recently exhibited are truly impressive," wrote *The Syndicalist* in mid-1911.[54]

The response of the new democratic government was typically positivist, aspiring to manage labor disputes as a neutral broker. The key piece of legislation legalized strikes in early December 1910, just two months after the overthrow of the monarchy. The decree itself was rigidly evenhanded, granting parallel rights to owners and workers: both may stop work, both may form organizations, and so on. Naturally, both sides said the law favored the other side: workers' organizations called it a "joke-decree"; the wealthy called it "an explicit incitement to disorder." Labor activism continued. For a short while, the state could call upon its revolutionary prestige to settle strikes: metalworkers in Lisbon agreed in early January to return to work "considering that, according to the explanation made by his honor the civil governor of Lisbon, strikes are damaging the normalcy of the country and, should they spread, will be stirred up by enemies of the Republic."[55]

By March, 1911, this goodwill was gone. Strikers refused to heed the government's call for calm, and the state responded with force, shooting striking workers in Setúbal. The attempt at high-minded evenhandedness having failed, the state turned to a more aggressive positivist management of labor disputes. Strikes—though legal in principle—were banned in practice. The state invented a monarchist plot, to subvert the republic through worker unrest, and used it as a pretext to clamp down on worker activism. Even British ambassador Arthur Hardinge, who was generally hostile to the new democracy, commended the regime for the "vigorous measures" taken to suppress railway strikes in mid-1912, and the foremost Portuguese historian of this period argues that repression of worker activism was even greater than under the monarchy.[56] The intellectuals in power also stripped illiterates of the right to vote in 1913.

At the same time that the government disenfranchised workers and used armed force to break their strikes, it granted many of the workers' demands. Bernardino Machado, a leading intellectual politician, made this approach explicit: workers are "good," he said. To lead them, one need only show some "interest in their cause . . . feel their needs . . . be their friend." They will let themselves be "led to sacrifice." Similarly, Afonso Costa, the premier leader of the Democrats in the first years of the republic, derided workers' organizations but praised social democracy. One demonstration of this attitude was the granting of wage demands: for example, workers in the cork industry, which produced half the world's cork, struck and received state-imposed concessions in 1911.[57] By the revolution's second anniversary, a British diplomat noted that "a general rise in wages has resulted."

> [T]he manufacturers of cheap goods and middlemen and retailers of them have, I am given to understand, been enjoying a time of considerable prosperity owing to the purchasing power of the working classes. With the lower and lower-middle classes in the large towns[,] the republic may therefore be said to be popular.[58]

In addition, the new government shortened the work week to six days, made owners liable for labor accidents, limited the working day, and in 1916 established a Ministry of Labor.[59]

Working-class mobilization shrank to fewer than two dozen strikes a year by 1913, but increased in intensity. Anarchists and socialists launched a general strike in 1912, two attempted revolutions in 1913, and a wave of activism in early 1914 that led the British ambassador to comment, "Many persons consider that a social revolution is imminent."[60]

The intellectual leaders of the new democracy calculated correctly, however, that the working class would support the regime against right-wing challenges. When General Joaquim Pimenta de Castro took power in early 1915 and appeared to be establishing a military dictatorship, even his supporters felt it was a mistake to shut workers out of administrative positions. Pimenta de Castro's labor rhetoric sought a balance similar to the prodemocracy positivists' position—"caring for the proletariat" and "tending to be useful to the poor without aggravating the rich."[61] But when the intellectuals sought to oust Pimenta de Castro and reestablish multiparty rule, the workers of Lisbon responded to the call, as they had in October 1910.

Mexico

In a triumphant speech soon after the ouster of the Díaz dictatorship, democracy-movement leader Francisco I. Madero concluded:

> I wish to direct myself to the working people who are present here in great numbers. The situation of the working people during the administration of General Díaz was very sad and very painful. The suffering people were the first to rally to me when I traversed the territory of the Republic, seeking out fellow citizens to invite them to the struggle. . . . One of the methods that workers value for obtaining better salaries or to better their situation in many cases is the strike. That right has been recognized by the civilized nations; but the workers, in declaring a strike, do not have the right to attack property, and the Government must give guarantees to all. . . . But in the current circumstances [of economic depression and labor oversupply] strikes are inconvenient, because it is not the appropriate economic moment for them.

Madero closed with a request that workers refrain from strikes for the time being "to demonstrate to the entire world that the Mexican people are capable of democracy."[62]

This half-hearted thank you typifies the democracy movement's attitude toward workers, both in its defense of their right to strike and in its limited enthusiasm for their cause. Prior to the revolution, Madero's appeals to workers typically refused to promise governmental action on their behalf outside of increased education, worker-safety legislation, and the protection of the right to collective organization. In a major speech to workers on May 22, 1910, just before the revolution, Madero stated clearly:

> Neither increases in wages nor decreases in working hours depend upon the government. . . . You want freedom. You want your rights to be respected so that you will be able to form powerful associations

in order that, united, you will be able to defend your own rights. . . .
[Y]ou do not want bread, you want only freedom, because freedom
will enable you to win your bread.[63]

Other prodemocracy activists apparently were less scrupulous than
Madero and simply promised higher wages if the democracy movement
came to power.[64]

Yet the right to unionize and strike may have been sufficient to attract
working-class support for the democracy movement, as suppression of
these rights was a major obstacle to working-class mobilization under the
dictatorship. Rodney Anderson has gathered considerable evidence of
working-class rhetoric and activity around the themes of citizenship rights
and the rule of law, and of working-class participation in the democratic
revolution. It seems significant that workers were not nearly so supportive
of the simultaneous revolutionary mobilization of the anarcho-syndicalist
party,[65] which later scholars have frequently deemed the "objective" representative of working-class interests.

The importance of this working-class support is hotly contested. Alan
Knight, noting that Mexican industrial workers numbered fewer than one
hundred thousand in 1910 and that revolutionary military victories were
quite separate from instances of worker activism, concluded that "the urban
working class made a negligible contribution to the success of the 1910–11
revolution." Yet working-class activism in the years prior to the revolution
has been widely credited with weakening the dictatorship.[66] This sort of debate is not easily amenable to empirical adjudication.

What is clear is that workers had great expectations of the new democratic era. The legalization of strikes had predictable effects. Strikes broke
out immediately throughout the nation. Two months after the ouster of
the dictatorship, for example, the U.S. consul in Durango commented
that "more strikes have taken place in the last two months than in the
whole history of this district." In January 1912 there were reportedly
more than forty thousand workers on strike.[67]

Along with strike activity, union organizing mushroomed: among the
new unions were the Society of Lightermen in Tampico, the Mexican
Miners Union of the North, the Confederation of Labor in Torreón, the
Confederation of Labor Unions of the Mexican Republic in the port of
Veracruz, the Stonecutters Union and the Printers Federation in the capital, and railworkers' unions around the country. A Society of Free Employees, organizing retail workers in Mexico City, signed contracts with

ninety-seven stores in less than a year.[68] Unionists, leftists, and anarchists founded a House of the Global Worker in Mexico City that served as the sentimental headquarters of the Mexican workers' movement, at least in the view of subsequent leftist scholars.

The breadth of labor activism apparently took prodemocracy leaders aback. Twice in late 1911 Madero attributed worker activism to right-wing plots seeking to destabilize the new democracy. The main prodemocracy newspaper, *The New Era,* opined about the irony of strikes mushrooming "now that the present government is no longer at the disposition of the capitalists."[69] Madero lectured workers not to expect their material conditions to improve "abruptly" and suggested that workers adopt the values that the intellectuals prided themselves on:

> You must know that you will only find happiness within yourselves, in the domination of your passions and the repression of your vices; and that you will only succeed in achieving wealth and prosperity by saving your money and developing your will-power, in order always to act according to the dictates of your conscience and of your patriotism, not those of your passions.[70]

Yet the democratic regime was hesitant to suppress worker activism. There were instances of repression, including one in which thirty strikers were shot dead, but in general the government took pains to avoid confrontations. One example of this approach, unfortunate in its results, occurred at a textile plant in Puebla, where clashes between strikers and management led to a riot in which four German managers were killed. The German ambassador demanded that the perpetrators be rounded up and executed, and Madero's government refused to undertake such Porfirian measures, contributing to the German's disaffection with Mexican democracy. These "half-savages," the ambassador concluded, "can live with no regime other than enlightened despotism." The ambassador helped impose such a regime in early 1913 (see Chapter 9).[71]

Instead of repression, the government's response to worker activism was to abandon free-market prescriptions and seek to broker or impose labor agreements. One of the new government's first plans was to create a Department of Labor charged with the explicit goal of calming unrest. The department helped build a corporatist workers' organization, called the Central Committee of Workers, and sent its representatives to sites of labor strife to urge the workers not to strike. The department took even stronger action with regard to the textile industry, which was Mexico's largest industry and one of its most oppressive. Strikes wracked the industry after mid-1911, with workers demanding salary increases, a ten-hour workday, protection against capricious firing, and the recognition of unions, among other reforms. The department, declaring its "neutrality," reduced these demands to two—a shorter workday and a minimum wage—and convened two meetings of textile mill owners to pressure them to agree. The workers, on the other hand, having been shut out of these negotiations, were not inclined to accept the proffered compromise. They continued to strike.[72]

Despite their disagreements with the new democracy's labor policies, many workers' organizations supported the democratic regime. The contrast with the repression of the dictatorship must have been obvious enough. Workers' sympathy for President Madero was so great that one union at Río Bravo, the site of some of the most violent repressiveness in Mexican labor history, wrote and asked Madero to join. (Madero declined, writing that "an agreement of this nature would bring with it the censure of the enemies of the Government.") In early 1913, a Mexico City union invited Madero to speak at a rally. When democracy was threatened by a coup d'état in February 1913, several groups of workers offered to help defend it. Miners demonstrated in favor of democracy in the north of Mexico, and "lower class" volunteers organized a prodemocracy brigade in the east. One group of labor representatives met with Madero in person, skirting military blockades to reach the presidential palace, but he turned down their assistance, confident that the military would remain loyal.[73] This confidence, as we will see in Chapter 8, turned out to be misplaced.

China

Sun Yatsen called himself a socialist and allied himself in 1905 with the Second Socialist International in Brussels. After the establishment of the republic, Sun repeated this self-identification. "Yes, ours is a socialist republic and we intend to follow socialistic principles," he told a journalist in May 1912. "All the leaders are genuine socialists." In October 1912, Sun spoke at length before the recently formed Chinese Socialist Party and was recognized as its "magnanimous mentor," though not a member.[74]

Despite this sympathy for socialism, Sun was no friend of labor. This apparent contradiction rested on two bases. The first was Sun's emphasis on

China's economic backwardness. As I argued in Chapter 2, Sun held the "social problem" of inequality to be equivalent to capitalist inequality. He did not believe that precapitalist labor was exploited, and therefore had little sympathy for the aspirations of peasants, artisans, and other precapitalist working classes that constituted the bulk of Chinese labor at the time. As for the small but growing class of proletarians, Sun treated their activism as a symptom of capitalism's social problems, not as a desirable solution to those problems. Labor activism would not be necessary in China, Sun implied, because intellectuals would devise preventative measures for capitalism's social problems.[75]

At the same time, Sun recognized the need for allies in the revolutionary struggle. Although the modern working class was too small to be of much use, Sun's Revolutionary Alliance sought the support of "secret societies," semicriminal, often lower-class organizations that served as informal representatives of popular aspirations, as idealized in the Chinese saying: "The officials draw their power from the law; the people, from the secret societies." These groups were not inherently sympathetic to the prodemocracy movement, but Sun and his fellow intellectuals were able to convert individual secret-society leaders to the prodemocracy cause, in part by emphasizing their shared anti-Manchu sentiments. In Zhejiang, secret societies were brought into revolutionary plans for 1907, but premature uprisings ruined the plot and the intellectuals' liaisons with the secret societies were killed. In Guangdong, intellectual revolutionaries arranged repeated plots involving secret societies from 1905 through early 1911, all of which came to naught. In Hunan and Guizhou, the revolutionaries had more success in maintaining alliances with rural secret societies, which adopted the platform of the Revolutionary Alliance and contributed significantly to the 1911 revolution.[76]

The appeal for popular support ultimately resulted in the formation of popular revolutionary armies, which fought alongside the rebel factions of the professional army (see Chapter 8). "[S]edan-chair bearers, transport coolies, vagrants and beggars all went one after the other to join the army," according to one account[77]—an individual rather than collective mobilization of the proletariat.

Yet Sun and many of the intellectuals who assumed state power after the 1911 revolution treated popular organizations, even their own revolutionary army, as a threat to the positivist social order. In Guangdong, the new democracy urged secret societies to give up their illegal activities. In Hunan and Hubei, where one secret-society leader organized a Peasant

Party to compete in the upcoming elections, the new government clashed repeatedly with ongoing secret-society activists. In Guizhou, secret societies playing prominent roles in the provincial government were subdued by invasion from the neighboring province of Yunnan.[78]

The same hostility reigned with regard to labor unrest. Labor activism intensified with the fall of the monarchy, most notably with the founding of a Labor Party that organized several large strikes among skilled workers in Shanghai. The party named Sun Yatsen its honorary chairman, but this did not guarantee sympathetic treatment by republican authorities. In July 1912, for example, municipal authorities in Shanghai barred women in the silk-reeling industry from joining a newly founded union. In May 1913, the authorities in Changsha allowed owners of a match factory to fire striking workers. In Guangdong, the stronghold of the prodemocracy movement, the police arrested "night-soil coolies" (workers carried feces in buckets to dumping sites outside town, in place of a sewer system) who had struck over new public health regulations. Sounding like a foreign diplomat (see Chapter 9), Sun criticized "the ignorant people who misunderstood equality and liberty" in agitating for workers' rights. Strikes, he said in an April 1912 speech dedicated to social revolution, are "not really a revolution"—a word that Sun reserved for positive connotations—"but merely a form of violence." Sun did not even object when Song Jiaoren, the strategist of the parliamentary Nationalist Party that inherited the mantle of Sun's Revolutionary Alliance, eliminated the socialist principle of "people's livelihood" from the party platform.[79]

In terms of power politics, the intellectuals' key shift with regard to workers was to disband the revolutionary armies. Thousands of poor Chinese who had joined military regiments in the fall of 1911 were now seen as a drain on the treasury and a threat to public order. Song Jiaoren had worried about this possibility just weeks before the outbreak of the revolution in fall 1911; he praised the recent democratic revolution in Portugal for sticking with professional troops. Vice President Li Yuanhong, a nonrevolutionary general who was drafted by the revolutionaries to lead the uprising in Hubei, complained in 1912: "When the civil war [that is, the prodemocracy uprising] began, troops were enlisted throughout last autumn and winter; they were without discipline and regarded crime as a title to merit, and anarchy as duty. To them mob law spelled equality and browbeating coercion was freedom."[80] Disbanding these troops proved tricky, because the soldiers naturally wanted to be paid their back wages, plus a severance bonus. Given the financial difficulties of the new democracy, these demands were not always met. Some of the troops rioted and looted to earn their pay, thereby fulfilling the fears and prejudices of the intellectuals.

As a result of this breach, few popular organizations assisted the new democracy when it came into armed conflict with Yuan Shikai in mid-1913. In Guangdong, the appeals of prodemocracy forces for aid went unanswered. In Shanghai, promises of high wages and opportunities for looting attracted some poor people into a reconstituted revolutionary army. But these promises were not enough to counter the greater paychecks and prospects for victory offered by Yuan's government and its foreign backers. By and large, workers simply sat out the brief civil war as the democratic experiment was destroyed.[81]

Contrary to recent social-scientific expectations, the size and density of the working class do not appear to predict democratization during this period, though independent countries were too few at that time to test the relationship statistically. Democratic revolutions of the early twentieth century occurred in countries with a relatively substantial working class in the industrial capitalist sense, such as Russia and Mexico, and in countries with very few such workers, such as Iran.

Where the working class existed in large numbers, portions of it were sometimes active in the democracy movement. In Russia, especially, strikes were crucial in forcing the tsar to grant democratic concessions. By contrast, the working class in the Ottoman Empire was not particularly politically active before democratization. Where the modern working class was small, the prodemocracy movement sometimes mobilized traditional working people and their organizations instead, such as the anjumans in Iran and secret societies in China.

When working-class activists joined democracy movements, they did so by allying with the intellectuals. The leader of the largest labor union in Russia consulted with "several intellectual Liberals" and invited "students and other educated people" to union meetings, where workers received their prodemocracy platform enthusiastically. Workers in Mexico flocked to Francisco Madero's prodemocracy campaign, despite his unwillingness to promise them material rewards. In Portugal, anarcho-syndicalists worried that workers had "abandoned the struggle"—that is, the path of revolution—and were joining the intellectuals' republican movement.

The intellectuals, for their part, were of two minds about the workers. On one hand, they glorified ordinary folk as oppressed and unfairly denied their democratic rights. On the other hand, they considered workers to be igno-rant and unworthy of full democratic rights. "The people will go where they are ordered," said one prodemocracy intellectual in Portugal. A Russian prodemocracy intellectual expressed concern about the "insurmountable barriers" that "the property-less and 'dark' strata of the population" had erected in their distrust of intellectuals. The leader of the Ottoman democ-racy movement refused to authorize mass mobilization for years out of fear that it would lead to uncontrolled bloodshed.

The intellectuals who took office in the new democracies continued these contradictory attitudes toward workers. In each country with a sig-nificant working class, the fall of dictatorship ignited working-class ac-tivism, with hundreds of strikes breaking out. The intellectuals did not suppress these strikes violently, at first, but the disorder displeased them. In Portugal, an official asked workers to call off their protests, on the grounds that "strikes are damaging the normalcy of the country and, should they spread, will be stirred up by enemies of the Republic." In China, prodemocracy leader Sun Yatsen chastised strikers as "ignorant people who misunderstood equality and liberty." The new democracies sought to intervene in labor relations, most explicitly in Mexico, where a Department of Labor was created to pressure workers and owners to ac-cept government-brokered compromises. In the textile industry, Mexico's largest modern sector and source of widespread strikes, workers who had been excluded from negotiations rejected the compromise and continued to strike.

After democratization, many working-class activists appear to have dis-engaged from the political arena and retreated to labor battles. No working-class party played a large role in the new parliaments. Leftists continued to debate the value of participation in "bourgeois democracy." Government officials demobilized their remaining working-class allies, such as the anjumans and popular militias in Iran, and the working-class groups in Mexico that offered to defend the new democracy from a threatened coup d'état in February 1913. Intellectuals turned most ag-gressively against the working class in Portugal, disenfranchising them in 1913 and sending in the military to break strikes in Setúbal, an act that impressed even the antidemocratic British ambassador. Ironically, when antidemocracy movements threatened the new regimes, only in Portugal did the working classes mobilize in defense. They took to the barricades and toppled the military government in 1915, just as they had toppled the monarchy in 1910.

7

Democracy and the Landowners

In the morality play of democratization, landowners are generally cast as the villains. The classic statement on this subject is Barrington Moore's *Social Origins of Dictatorship and Democracy*. While repudiating the language of heroes and villains, Moore identifies a particular sort of landownership as the primary foe of democracy: labor-repressive agrarian systems that "require political methods to extract the surplus [and] and keep the labor force in its place," as opposed to market mechanisms for hiring and firing rural workers. To the extent that landowners abandon labor repression and turn to commercial market relations, Moore argues, democracy has a better chance of emerging and succeeding.[1]

An alternative perspective suggests that landowners may under some conditions assist democratization. Otto Hintze, the best-known proponent of this thesis, argued in 1931 that the feudal privileges of the landed nobility restrained the autocratic power of the centralizing state. In this view, democracy in Europe grew out of the estate system of the Middle Ages, as landowners asserted their rights against the crown through regional and then national parliaments. For Hintze, this path is entwined with the legacies of Catholic Christianity and Roman imperial law, and is peculiar to Europe. However, later authors have extended the argument to other regions, usually in the obverse: non-Western countries may have had difficulty sustaining democracy because traditional elites (not necessarily labor-repressive landowners, to be sure) were unable to maintain strong institutions that could limit the power of the state.[2]

Both Moore and Hintze claim that agrarian elites are central to the emergence and survival of democracy. Was this so in the democratic revolutions of the early twentieth century? In his brief discussion of the Russian Revolution of 1905, Moore identifies the landed upper classes with the Black Hundreds, reactionary extremists who agitated violently against the new democracy; his discussion of China suggests that "landed upper classes did not develop any significant principled opposition to the Imperial system."[3] Both of these characterizations, however, overlook significant alliances between landowners and prodemocracy intellectuals.

Russia

Contrary to the stereotype, Russian landowners supported the democracy movement, albeit briefly. The roots of this counterintuitive phenomenon lie in the landed gentry's estrangement from the monarchy. The sources of this break dated back to the tsar's reforms of the 1860s, which included the emancipation of serfs and changes in land laws. These reforms represented a direct challenge to the gentry's dominance in the countryside, and in the following decades the gentry suffered a dramatic loss of power. By 1905, the gentry's landholdings had dropped more than 40 percent, and the percentage of gentry owning land fell by half, from 80 percent to just under 40. More than half of the landed gentry in 1905 owned relatively modest holdings (under 110 hectares/270 acres). The gentry were poorly trained for the emerging capitalist environment; only 29 percent operated their estates on capitalist principles, according to one sample. The image of decline should not be exaggerated, but it is clear that the Russian landed gentry was not nearly so dominant in the countryside in the early 1900s as it had been a half-century earlier. The landed gentry lost its grip on the state bureaucracy as well: in the top four ranks of the civil service, the proportion of landed gentry fell from 81 percent in 1853 to 28 percent in 1902.[4] A similar trend occurred in the military, as we will see in the next chapter. In 1897, the gentry appeared to be in such dire straits that the tsar convened a Special Conference on the Needs of the Nobility.

This perception of declining fortunes provided the backdrop for recurrent friction between the gentry and the state. This friction was manifested through the system of provincial assemblies, or *zemstvos*, that had been established in the mid-nineteenth century. Especially after the 1880s, voting regulations were designed to allow the gentry to dominate these assemblies, and the landed gentry tried to use the *zemstvos* as a counterweight against their decreasing power over the central government. The *zemstvos* challenged the state over tax collection, health and public works projects, administrative procedures, and public policy more generally. Dimitri N. Shipov, "the grand old man of the emerging *zemstvo* opposition movement," was so critical of the autocratic state that the minister of the interior voided his reelection as chair of the Moscow provincial *zemstvo* in 1904, a position he had held for more than a decade.[5] In a sense, these gentry-state tensions represented a return to a premodern model of conflict between a state-centralizing monarch and the regional authority of the nobility. However, the nobility in twentieth-century Russia had lost this contest, and eventually they realized it. In addition to demanding a devolution of state power to the provincial level, they increasingly supported the gentry-intellectuals' demands for democratization of the central state. The intellectuals' prodemocracy agenda coincided with the gentry's antistate agenda.

In 1904 and 1905, the gentry voted overwhelmingly in favor of the prodemocracy demands of the intellectuals. In November 1904 Shipov hosted a national meeting of *zemstvo* representatives, who were mainly gentry-intellectuals. Of 105 delegates, 98 voted to demand that the tsar grant a parliament. The provincial gentry did not repudiate this demand made on their behalf. In the next two months, 26 of 34 provincial *zemstvos* endorsed the call for a parliamentary body, though half of these were willing to settle for consultative, not legislative, powers. Eleven of 17 provincial noble assemblies did the same. In March 1905, 20 of 26 provincial "marshals of the nobility" voted to demand the rescinding of the gentry's—their own—electoral privileges in any forthcoming parliament. By the summer of 1905, one conservative gentry complained, "the deputies in a majority of *zemstvos* have suspended all normal activities and spend their time drafting all sorts of possible constitutional projects. . . . It is clear that a public activist, in order to preserve his own authority and popularity at this time, has to abandon his own convictions and vigorously support the demands of the radicals."[6]

A sign of this shift was the gentry's willingness to entertain land reform projects that involved the expropriation of gentry landholdings, albeit with compensation. In September 1905, a conference of *zemstvo* and city council representatives proposed the "alienation" of state-owned lands "and, in case of need, private lands with fair compensation to the landowner." "Our land, our property is not a high price to pay for our own—and the people's—political freedom," one gentry-intellectual argued in November 1905. Even the tsar's government began to develop modest land reform policies.[7]

After the October Manifesto, however, the landed gentry reversed course and distanced itself from the democracy movement. In part this may have been due to the posture of prodemocracy intellectuals, who apparently placed more importance on wooing popular support, in the coming era of electoral competition, than on retaining the support of landowners. For example, Pavel N. Miliukov stated at the founding of the Constitutional-Democratic (Kadet) Party in October 1905, "Our party will never stand in defense of [landlords' and industrialists'] interests!"[8] Underlying the split, however, was a growing realization among landowners that their antistate movement and the intellectuals' prodemocracy movement did not in fact share the same goals after all, beyond vague demands for a parliament. While the landed gentry wanted to limit the power of the central state, the prodemocracy intellectuals wanted an activist state, even more activist than the tsar's had been; one of their critiques of tsarism was its ineffectiveness in transforming society.

Also related to the gentry's shift was the resurgence of peasant uprisings in fall 1905, spring 1906, and spring 1907, coinciding with the announcement of the October Manifesto and the sitting of the first two parliaments. Peasants played a far more active role in the Russian democratic experiment than in any of the others in this study. "They are difficult to put down because there are not enough troops or Cossacks to go around," the tsar complained to his mother. Their land seizures and other protests lent an urgency to the democracy movement that other countries lacked, giving substance to the fear, as one newspaper put it in October 1905, that the "ubiquitous disquiet in the population is a volcano capable at any minute of spewing forth from its quaking depths disasters both terrible and unexpected."[9] Prodemocracy intellectuals worried about the reactionary potential of the peasants, as in this parable by a Jewish parliamentary representative:

> On the Sabbath, pious Jews must not strike a light, nor even ask a non-Jew to do it, though they may have it done for them. The better-off will let the light burn all night. But during a long winter night, such a Jew found that it had gone out. He wanted to read. So he woke up his peasant servant, and asked: "Ivan, would you like a drink?" "Sure, I would." "But it's so dark, I can't find the bottle." So Ivan lit a candle—exactly what the Jew wanted. But after Ivan had had his glass of vodka, in his innocence he put out the light. Be careful or Ivan will blow out your candle.[10]

But as the prodemocracy intellectuals in parliament considered assisting the peasants with land reform, the revival of peasant activism with each major step toward democratization drove the gentry to the right, convincing many of the unsuitability of democracy for Russia's rural population. The landed gentry turned against the new democracy as quickly and dramatically as they had demanded its founding. In January 1906, even before parliamentary elections were held, provincial *zemstvo*s began to back away from their democratic demands of the previous year. The electoral returns, in which peasants overwhelmingly rejected conservative and landowner candidates, surprised and disappointed the gentry; "nobody from personal experience suspected that the mass of the Russian populace was in any way imbued with radical political ideas," a conservative newspaper opined.[11]

In *zemstvo* elections of 1906 and 1907, the gentry turned more than half of the incumbents out of office; Kadets led 3 percent of the new *zemstvo*s (compared with 44 percent before this round of elections), while centrists and rightists led 88 percent (compared with 38 percent before). At the same time, representatives of the largest gentry landowners began to mobilize in early 1906 through a new organization called the United Nobility, which immediately established warm relations with the monarchy and expressed hostility toward the Kadets. Significantly, the United Nobility succeeded in mobilizing landed gentry while a Union of Landowners, organized in late 1905 to mobilize both gentry and commoner landowners, failed to attract much gentry support. The gentry may have been willing to countenance the removal of status barriers in 1905; they were no longer willing to do so in 1906.[12]

In short, the landed gentry returned to the role that social scientists expect it to play, that of reactionary intriguers against democracy. The primary issue that motivated this shift, not surprisingly, was land reform. In January 1906, gentry organizations got word that the state was preparing a preemptive land reform plan in advance of the meeting of the first parliament. They quickly mobilized opposition to the plan, sending delegations to lobby government officials and obtaining not just the abandonment of the plan but also the dismissal of the official who was designing it. The incident provided a precedent for the brief parliamentary period. The United Nobility "waged a fierce campaign against the Duma [parliament]," opposed the Kadet Party's land reform proposals, and argued to high state officials "that the Duma had to be dismissed immediately." In the summer of 1906, right-wing extremists called the Black Hundred, led by two landowners (as well as an antidemocracy physician), assassinated one of parliament's key agrarian experts, Mikhail Gertsenstein.[13]

In part, perhaps, because of the gentry's efforts, the land reform issue came to be the crucial sticking point between parliament and the monarchist state. The prodemocracy intellectuals in parliament maintained their basic position of 1905: land reform was both proper in its own right and necessary to forestall further peasant unrest. The government itself was preparing land reform schemes throughout this period, with the goals of forestalling peasant unrest and of turning communal peasants into individual smallholders, who were expected to make better citizens of an autocratic state. (The tsar's government identified peasant communal bodies as potential threats to the state, as did later social scientists.) Yet pressure from the landed gentry prevented the government from reaching an agreement with parliament over land reform. Indeed, the pretext for dismissal of the first parliament was a parliamentary resolution on land reform; one of the pretexts for dismissal of the second parliament was parliamentary committee work on land reform.[14]

When their efforts bore fruit with the dissolution of parliament, the landed gentry claimed credit and expressed relief and satisfaction. A *zemstvo* conference in June 1907, meeting a week after parliament had been dissolved a second time, voiced its approval of the act as well as its author, prime minister P. A. Stolypin, "a loyal servant of our Sovereign, who did not lose faith in this difficult time in the vital forces of the Russian land." The unofficial slogan of the conference—"Why should 500 *zemstvos* count for less than 500 Duma representatives?"—expressed the landed gentry's preference for oligarchy over democracy. Much of the landed gentry apparently agreed with the finance minister's statement, "Thank God, we have no parliament!" The gentry benefited hugely from the redesigned electoral laws issued in 1907. In one particularly egregious case, the laws in a county in Vlatka province raised the landowners' electoral representation from four to eight, while reducing the landowners' electorate from six to three (removing nongentry landowners).[15] However, the gentry did not abandon its antistate activism and continued to agitate against ongoing state encroachment on gentry prerogatives.

Iran

The major landowners of Iran enjoyed tremendous privileges in the period before 1906, considerably more privileges than landowners enjoyed in the other countries considered in this book. For the peasants on their land, the landowners were the state. They collected taxes, passing along a portion to provincial and central authorities. They settled disputes, in lieu of a legal system. They granted licenses for marriage, commercial transactions, and other activities. Moreover, large landholding had increased considerably during the nineteenth century, as the monarchy rewarded favorites with land and social-climbing merchants bought status through landowning.[16]

Nonetheless, landowners did not constitute a homogenous political unit, and they did not organize themselves into gentry or agricultural associations, as in some other countries at this time. Indeed, their families were so large that wealthy landowners of royal lineage could be found on all sides of controversies over democracy. Fath 'Ali Shah, who reigned in the first third of the nineteenth century, sired more than one hundred children, so Qajar princes were not uncommon. On the prodemocracy side, for example, stood the radical Qajar princes Yahya and Sulayman Mirza Iskandari, who—though probably not landowners themselves—represented the landowning nobility in the first two parliaments. While they were students at the largest modern school in Tehran, the Dar al-Funun, Sulayman organized the first student strike in Iran. Yahya later founded a modern-style school in Tehran, and they were both early members of the Society of Humanity (see Chapter 2), along with eighteen other Qajar princes. Both brothers were among the fifty-plus founders of the prodemocracy Revolutionary Committee in 1904. Yahya died of injuries sustained in the shah's prisons after the 1908 coup; Sulayman took his seat in parliament and came to lead the radical faction that pressed for significant land reforms, as described later. After the coup of December 1911, Sulayman was sent into internal exile. Decades later, he helped to found the Socialist Party of Iran.[17]

More typical of Iranian landowner politics were 'Abdulhusayn Farmanfarma and Muhammad Vali Khan Tunukabuni (Nasr al-Saltanah, later known as Sipahdar), two of the largest landowners in Iran. Farmanfarma had some European education through an Austrian military academy in Tehran and served as a military commander, provincial governor, and cabinet minister for decades. He had an interest in aspects of European culture, and when the democratic revolution broke out in Tehran, he conveyed his sympathies for the movement, spending large sums to ingratiate himself with the prodemocracy activists. Sipahdar also had modern military training in Tehran and a similar mix of government positions. He apparently had less interest than Farmanfarma in things European and was hostile to the religious protest movement in 1906 that later joined the prodemocracy movement, ordering troops to open fire on the crowd. He expressed enthusiasm for democracy only in late 1907, after the assassination of a conservative prime minister. In the fall of 1906, when the constitution was first announced, the shah had to browbeat his Qajar relatives into selecting representatives to fill the nobility's quota in parliament. A year later, out of fear for their lives, or a desire to save the monarchy and their own privilege, or perhaps genuine ideological conversion, large numbers of landowners and other antidemocracy notables joined prodemocracy groups in a matter of weeks. Sipahdar and thirty-one other prominent conservatives, for example, founded a group called the Leaders' Council and signed an open letter to the government urging recognition of the powers of parliament. Even the reactionary monarch Muhammad 'Ali Shah, by far the largest landowner in Iran, joined the Society of Humanity, pledging obedience to its ideals of democratic positivism. In parliament, landowner representatives, comprising about one-sixth of the total, went along with attempts to balance the budget primarily on the backs of landowners. They voted unanimously to nationalize tax collection, replacing landowner tax farmers with state agents and requiring certain landowner taxes to be paid in kind, rather than at discounted cash equivalents. Parliament also voted to reduce the salaries of court retainers, with thirteen princely landowners losing the bulk of the money.[18]

At the same time, parliament opposed more radical plans for land reform. Certain intellectuals proposed that the government forcibly purchase large landholdings and distribute them to peasants. None of these plans was even brought to a vote in parliament, despite letter-writing campaigns and sporadic revolts in the countryside. Parliament acted instead to order the repression of rebellion and the orderly collection of rural taxes. When peasants on Sipahdar's lands sent their grievances against him to parliament, no action was taken to address their concerns.[19]

Nonetheless, many landowners were appalled by the new taxes and by peasant activism in the new democracy. In Mazandaran, landowners complained that the new taxes were being enforced unfairly on those "who were poor and religious and harmless." As Farmanfarma told parliament: "Our peasants have no knowledge and do not know what the meaning of *mashrutiyat* is. They think it means hoarding other people's property and not paying the interest due the landlord according to the laws of the *shari'at*." A group of landowners in the northern province of Gilan, site of the largest rural rebellions in the country, telegraphed parliament to complain that "the peasants imagine that constitutional monarchy means immediate liberty."[20]

Among landowners, reactionaries soon regained the upper hand. Among the most prominent antidemocracy figures were Muhammad 'Ali Shah and his brother Malik Mansur (Shu'a al-Saltanah), who had called prodemocracy activism "a whirlpool of heresy" and sought to bribe religious scholars to oppose parliamentary rule. These men were rivals—Shu'a al-Saltanah had aspirations to inherit the throne in place of his brother—but they shared a hostility to the new democracy. Both men had their incomes cut severely by parliament's reduction of the court budget in 1907. In late 1907, Muhammad 'Ali Shah reneged on his pledges to uphold the constitution and imprisoned the prime minister, though widespread demonstrations and pressure from the British ambassador made him back down. He appointed Shu'a al-Saltanah and others to a Conciliation Committee that pretended to make peace with parliament.[21] Meanwhile, the shah plotted with his Russian Cossack officers (see Chapters 9 and 10) to prepare for a second attempt to disband parliament.

When this coup was achieved in June 1908, positions of power were given once again to reactionary landowners, including Sipahdar, who put aside his previous statement on behalf of parliament and led troops to Tabriz to subdue prodemocracy forces there. This attempt failed, and—for reasons that are unclear—Sipahdar switched sides once again, agreeing to serve as nominal commander of prodemocracy forces in northern Iran. He performed this role half-heartedly, according to observers, and told a Russian newspaper that his political convictions were still antidemocratic. Even though he planned to march on Tehran and defeat the shah, he said, "I am convinced that Iran needs absolutism."[22] In conjunction with Sardar As'ad's Bakhtiyari forces (see Chapter 5) and others, Sipahdar took Tehran in June 1909 and sent Muhammad 'Ali Shah, Shu'a al-Saltanah, and other reactionaries into exile, reestablishing parliamentary democracy. The former monarch's attempts to retake the throne the following year were repelled by government forces, including divisions under Sipahdar and other landowners.

The democracy that these elites envisioned was an orderly one in which the government enjoyed sufficient "power and authority" to deal with the country's challenges; this was how Sipahdar—then serving simultaneously as prime minister, minister of war, and minister of education—phrased it to parliament in his successful request for extraordinary executive powers. Sipahdar's diary entries for this period suggest that he considered himself a democrat, but would not brook opposition, much less popular mobilization.

Sipahdar wrote that he was "fed up" with Muhammad 'Ali's reactionary movement, and he was hurt that, despite his contributions to the reestablishment of democracy, "still they do not consider me a democrat!" Sipahdar considered his opponents in parliament, Sulayman Mirza's Democrat Party, to be acceptable in principle, but odious in practice. "I read the platform that they wrote, and it is not bad. Except for one or two points in this credo"—possibly the commitment to land reform and limits on landlords' power over peasants?[23]—"I'm very much in favor of the rest." Sipahdar continued:

> But these people who call themselves Democrats these days [are nothing but] two or three princes who gave up their asses a lot in their youth. These were, and are, the swindler charlatans of the city. And there is another group, all poor people and lascivious beggars who gather around them in the evening, and whom they send off to terrorize people for money. They sell and drink cognac and expend their energy on obscene acts, which you can imagine. What a shame that our democracy is becoming disreputable in the hands of these people.[24]

Landowner-democrats were also displeased when the state tried to exercise "power and authority" in ways that undermined their privileges. Most famously, they opposed efforts by the Iranian treasurer-general, an American named Morgan Shuster, to collect taxes. Landowners and other wealthy Iranians resented this attempt, according to a German diplomat, because it threatened "their most sacred possession: their freedom to steal and their freedom from taxes" (see Chapter 5). Farmanfarma, for example, advised the treasurer-general that it would be more prudent to proceed through consultation rather than confrontation. Sipahdar's diary called Shuster's methods "thievery" and accused parliament of "gobbling up and carrying off 15 million [tumans] of the nation's property over the past two years in the most indecent self-dealing activities." Sipahdar's solution was to turn over the government to "four intellectuals to reform things"—by which he meant himself and three select colleagues. He had no use for the intellectual pretensions of "Mr. Democrat Semocrat, [parliamentary] representative," and he disliked Sardar As'ad and the other coup-makers of December 1911. If the coup was not his, he had no use for it.[25] It is impossible to tell whether these comments reflected the views of Iranian landowners in general; in any case, major landowners played little role in the coup of 1911.

Ottoman Empire

Landowners played little organized role in the Ottoman politics of this period, either pro- or antidemocracy. This observation must be considered tentative, because source materials on the subject are sparse. Most studies of late Ottoman agriculture focus on long-term trends in land tenure, not short-term political activism. Unlike much of Europe, the state owned most arable land in the Ottoman Empire, renting it to small-scale cultivators and deputizing regional elites to collect taxes. Large-scale private landowning advanced somewhat in the late nineteenth century, but most land was still cultivated in small plots at the time of the 1908 revolution. A key question in the study of Ottoman agriculture is whether this system counts as "feudalism," since the income of agrarian elites came less from labor-exploitative landowning than from tax-collection and debt-peonage. For present purposes, in any case, the distinction is moot, because both systems relied on political repression to extract surplus, which was Barrington Moore's key criterion for antidemocratic agrarian elites.[26]

Despite their grip on the countryside, agrarian elites were in many ways weaker in the Ottoman Empire than in any other country that underwent democratization in the early twentieth century. They did not have regional councils that could resist the power of the central state, as in Russia and China. They did not control private armies, as in Iran. They did not have powerful agricultural associations to negotiate with the state and peasants, as in Portugal and Mexico.[27]

Perhaps as a result of this weakness, agrarian elites who were active in Ottoman politics of the early twentieth century tended to be prodemocracy. In Rumelia, large-scale landowners joined the Society for Union and Progress, and numerous Albanian notables cooperated with the Society as well. After the constitution was reinstated in 1908, many traditional elites voiced their agreement in what one Ottoman journalist called a "comedy of support for democracy." Among the most prominent prodemocracy activists was Prince Sabahaddin, the sultan's nephew, who had lived in exile in Europe since 1899. Sabahaddin was not himself a landowner, so far as I can tell, but as a member of the royal lineage, his family wealth was likely indebted in some way to the extraction of agrarian surplus. Nonetheless, Sabahaddin identified with intellectuals and championed the rights of peasants, as in his statement in 1906: "At the instigation of the intellectual class, the peasants are beginning to take note of their duties and their rights."[28]

Sabahaddin's political movement linked support for democracy with an emphasis on decentralization of power in the Ottoman Empire. This emphasis echoed the centrifugal demands of the *ayan* (regional elites) a century earlier, which had culminated in an accord with the sultan in 1808 that limited the authority of the central state in important regional matters. This accord was upended in subsequent decades by the centralization of the Ottoman state. In 1908, the upper house of parliament was named for the *ayan,* but the meaning of the term had changed. Now it simply meant "elite" and could refer to high-ranking government officials, military officers, prominent intellectuals, or other prestigious individuals. This Senate does not appear to have been dominated by landowners. In any case, the Senate did not oppose the lower chamber on many issues. Neither chamber, nor the administration, entertained serious land reform after democratization. The only agrarian reform to be effected after the reinstatement of the constitution was the partially reimbursed expropriation and distribution of the sultan's landholdings in September 1908. The program of the Society for Union and Progress, developed in the fall of 1908, proposed modest interventions into the agrarian scene, including proposals to reduce taxes, develop productivity through schooling in modern agricultural methods, and sell uncultivated state lands to smallholders by offering low-interest loans. The following year, when democracy had been undermined, the Society's new agrarian policy dropped land distribution, focusing only on agricultural schools and the right to sell land.[29]

Meanwhile, agrarian elites maintained their grip on the countryside. As one Anatolian peasant told an Ottoman journalist in 1909,

> Since there is no help from anywhere else we have to buy seed from the *ağa* [agrarian elite] at either 100–125 kuruş per bushel or return him three bushels for one. Those *ağa*s became a menace; they can have the peasant beaten by their toughs, have him jailed, or sometimes have him intimidated by the intervention of the state. In this way they collect their debt from those who cannot pay.

This report came a year after the proclamation of the Ottoman constitution, which had brought high hopes to the countryside, the same peasant reported. "We thought that everything could be rectified, taxes would be collected justly and peacefully, . . . [and] officials would not do things as they pleased. But so far nothing has happened." In one extreme case on the coast of the Black Sea, according to an Ottoman official, local elites "were all as it were in the position of being like a [nonofficial] government for each of their separate areas."[30]

There seem to have been few peasant revolts at this time. The only rural mobilization, it appears, was communal violence against Armenians in southern Anatolia and, to a lesser extent, Jews in Palestine during the mutiny and coup of April 1909. It is unclear from published sources whether peasants, landowners, and/or state officials were responsible for this violence. Similarly, it is unclear whether landowners might have sponsored Islamic antidemocratic movements. The intellectual Yusuf Akçura, among others, accused "feudal" elements of collaboration with religious reactionaries in the Istanbul mutiny of April 1909, which spurred the Society for Union and Progress's march on the capital and imposition of martial law. The only evidence I have seen of such collaboration refers to the role of the sultan, by far the largest landowner in the country, and no others.[31] The Society deposed the sultan one week after suppressing the mutiny.

The moderate political tone of the Ottoman agrarian elite can be tracked in the *Ottoman Agriculture and Commerce Newspaper*, which began publication in 1907 with a mission to improve the productivity of Ottoman agriculture. After the reinstatement of the constitution in 1908, the newspaper joined the general celebration, writing paeans to intellectuals, with whom the editor identified: "Oh! Many thanks to freedom for liberating the pens that were enslaved by the group of polecats and foxes known as censorship officials. Therefore, from now on, we shall try to serve our beloved nation's progress and uplift, and its happy future, by writing whatever we wish." Over the following months, the newspaper registered a variety of political grievances related to the new democracy's agricultural policies. However, the paper showed no sign of antidemocratic tendencies. And after the Society for Union and Progress's coup of April 1909, it did not rejoice in the suppression of parliament, but rather complained about the "silencing of thoughts" that it and other newspapers suffered at the hands of the martial law authorities.[32]

Portugal

King Manuel II abandoned Portugal on the second day of the 1910 uprising, sailing to exile in Gibraltar and then to England, but he did not abdicate. "I am not a leader of the democracy," he told a sympathetic British official. "I am a King and it is as a King I must manage my affairs." For two years he attempted to regain his throne by funding military incursions from Spain. These incursions were not intended to topple the democratic government militarily, but to trigger popular uprisings in rural areas, particularly in the north of Portugal, that were presumed to be sympathetic to the monarchy. No uprisings ensued, and the monarchist invaders were soon repulsed or captured. At the end of 1912, Manuel decided that these raids were no longer cost-effective. He cut off funding and called on his followers to refrain from further invasions. Even the British ambassador, sturdily pro-monarchist, agreed that "the republic seems to me more likely to perish by the internal quarrels of the factions which divide it than by an armed Royalist attack from without."[33]

It is an interesting question why, as in Iran, the monarchist cause in Portugal attracted so little support among the extremely traditional rural population. Barrington Moore has urged us to seek the fate of democracy in the strength of the labor-repressive landowning class, but such indications with regard to Portugal are unclear. On one hand, rising emigration in the late nineteenth century may have weakened the landowners' power over its workforce. Rising agrarian activism after the 1910 revolution may also have affected the balance of power in the countryside, with rural strikes exploding particularly in the Alentejo region and a national congress of rural workers meeting in April 1912.[34] On the other hand, the landowners had begun to organize collectively in Agricultural Societies, suggesting an increasing power. Although many of their feudal rights had been abolished a century earlier, in the liberal revolution of 1820, landowners still held peasants in an oppressive shareholding system called *enfiteuse*.

The new democracy posed a direct threat to the landowners' privileges. One of the democracy's early steps was to undermine the *enfiteuse* system by strengthening alternative land-rental arrangements. The landowners saw this as a direct attack on their prerogatives and mobilized to have the law repealed, arguing, "What good is land which has been freed?" Limited land reform measures were proposed in 1911, 1913, 1917, and 1925, focusing on the forced sale of certain uncultivated lands, but vocal opposition from landowners helped prevent their implementation. In addition, the positivists running the new democracy knew they had to raise revenues to fund the intellectual class project, and they identified "the large property-owner" as a class that "pays in general much less than it ought," as a parliamentary commission concluded.[35] A law to raise revenues through a property tax led the landowners' Agricultural Societies to hold a demonstration in late 1912 and conduct large-scale propaganda around the issue in early 1913, circulating "manifestos, pamphlets, leaflets, satires, and even newspapers, urging on citizens the refusal to pay the property tax." By 1913, another British diplomat reported, the "whole upper class [was] furious with the land laws and the new taxation."[36] Significantly, this landowner activism appears to have been unconnected with the monarchist activism of the same period.

The landowning class was therefore powerful enough to block many of the government's proposed attacks on its privileges, yet for more than a decade it did not become seriously involved in antidemocracy mobilization. The Portuguese case appears to hinge on the ideology of the landowning class, rather than on Moore-ish issues of class power. Many of those with the greatest stake in the old regime abandoned it without a fight. As one Portuguese monarchist complained of his peers:

> The monarchists, sadly, to be sure, recognized that the Republic has men of a moral and intellectual superiority that the Monarchy had never enjoyed, and that from this number came those who consti-tuted its first government. . . . In the majority, even a large majority, the monarchists concluded then that the Republic and its men, while not meriting support, merited . . . benevolent, even very benevolent, expectation.[37]

This attitude may have contributed to the poor showing that the nobility made both in monarchist fund-raising[38] and in the monarchist invasions, as the British ambassador reported:

> Some of the killed were boys still in their teens, belonging to the best families in this country, whom loyal and religious fervor, no doubt helped by the love and excitement of adventure, had led into this gal-lant forlorn hope, but if the mass of the Portuguese aristocracy had been animated by their spirit, a basis [for a monarchist restoration] might have been found, as in the days of Dom Pedro, in the north, from which the rest of the country could in time have been rewon.[39]

Even King Manuel, the largest landowner in the nation, had to defend himself against criticism from fellow monarchists "among whom it is being spread about that I am . . . disinterested in the Cause that I repre-sent, abandoning those who served and defended it with such dedication, sacrifice, and bravery." Many monarchists preferred Manuel's cousin Miguel, splitting the movement. A reconciliation was eventually reached, with Manuel—who had no children—agreeing that Miguel's children would succeed him. But the confusion did not end with this agreement. When World War I broke out, the Anglophile Manuel urged Portuguese monarchists to "put aside . . . every and any political consideration" and cooperate with the democratic regime in aiding Britain. Miguel and his supporters, Germanophiles, continued to conspire against the regime. "The monarchists do not want to listen to me and always do the contrary of what I tell them is the good of the Country," Manuel complained in 1915. "Everybody wants to give orders and nobody wants to obey," he opined in 1924.[40]

A further division in the monarchist cause separated the old nobility from the bourgeoisie. Although numerous capitalists had bought their way into the aristocracy in the late nineteenth century and others had become major landowners, a culture gap remained wide. Some monarchists found one another so distasteful that they were unwilling to work together; for example, Captain Henrique de Paiva Couceiro, who led the unsuccessful invasions, is reported by a sympathetic biographer to have been " 'disturbing' to the bourgeois and to the nobleman with the soul of the merchant," basing his conduct instead on "the unique Light of Portugal that illuminated the path of Duty." Paiva Couceiro was more comfortable appealing to the "traditions and unity" and "great pride" of right-wing military officers.[41]

Mexico

The landed elite in Mexico did not retain a system of aristocratic titles or control over the officer corps, as in other countries. Nor did they have peonage rights over their workers—in 1856–1857, these rights had been removed in a series of key policies known as La Reforma. Yet this legislation—like Portugal's agricultural reforms of the 1820s and Russia's emancipation of the serfs in the 1860s—did not succeed in transforming peons into smallholders. Rather, by freeing land from its traditional legal restraints and allowing it to be sold and bought, the Reforma unintentionally promoted the centralization of landholding and the creation of large-scale commercial estates, or haciendas. By the time of the revolution in 1910, there were more than eight thousand haciendas, several of them millions of hectares in size, averaging perhaps three thousand hectares each.[42] These estates took different forms in the various regions of Mexico, but they shared several characteristics that made them susceptible to rural revolts: First, owners of these estates gained land in ways that were viewed as illegitimate by traditional standards, exploiting peasants' lack of written title and taking advantage of their debts. Second, hacienda owners abandoned traditional communal leadership, as repressive as it had been, in favor of capitalist profit maximization. Third, in some regions hacienda owners faced organized opposition from peasant communities that had retained their customs and limited autonomy.

One such community in the central state of Morelos led a rural revolt in support of the democracy movement. Known by the name of its leader, Emiliano Zapata, the Zapatista revolt began as part of the national movement. Its leaders considered themselves the official democracy movement in Morelos and delayed their uprising waiting for accreditation from prodemocracy leader Francisco Madero. They were especially interested in the portion of the prodemocracy platform that promised to return unlawfully taken lands to their rightful owners—a limited but important land reform proposal. Yet when the democracy movement came to power, Zapata was not named to high office. Instead, Madero's assistants appointed the landowners' candidates in Morelos and hedged on the land reform proposal, urging peasants to reclaim their lands through legal procedures rather than armed occupation. As the new democracy sent troops to protect landowners, the Zapatistas resumed their revolt.[43]

The democratic regime was slow to implement even the limited, legalistic rural reforms that it had promised. Madero called for peasants to await the results of "a series of studies." José María Pino Suárez, a Maderista governor and soon to be elected vice president, urged peons to "remain in their present enslaved state to prevent brusque transitions that might injure their well-being." The radical wing of the democracy movement proffered land reform proposals in parliament, the most famous being Luis Cabrera's plan to restore peasants' communal ownership rights—a proposal influenced by his friend, the positivist Andre's Molina Enríquez.[44]

Yet in practice the democratic government ruled in cooperation with the large landowners, who shared the intellectuals' positivist vision of agricultural reform. In the west of Mexico, for example, the Jalisco National Agricultural Chamber offered to work with the new democratic government in early 1912 to study agricultural reforms along with "men of good will . . . independent and honorable, and friends of the study of arduous social problems," a nod to the intellectuals, perhaps. The chamber opposed "the rapid and indiscreet distribution of some lands and haciendas to lazy people," and suggested instead that "We must begin to work energetically to raise the intellectual and moral level of the disinherited classes and of our indigenous race. We must inject energy by means of elementary education and agricultural instruction, diffusing them as much as possible among the peasants."[45]

The landowners' cooperation with the democratic state reached beyond ideological overlap to coordinated defense of landed property against rural uprisings. The Zapatista revolt was echoed by widespread though largely small-scale protests throughout Mexico.[46] In view of the reduced power of the central government, it is somewhat surprising that this endemic discontent in the new democracy was not far greater. This observation suggests that Mexican landowners retained considerable power in the countryside, over and above their ability to appeal to the state for armed support. Yet—contrary to Barrington Moore's thesis—the predominance of labor-exploitative agriculture in the countryside did not undermine the new democracy.

Ironically, the greatest landowner threat to the new democracy came through a rebellion in Chihuahua led by Pascual Orozco, whose platform sought land reform. According to a Mexican government operative in Texas, Orozco was secretly funded by the largest landowners in Chihuahua, who tried to use the movement to regain control of the state and the nation.[47] Orozco's movement was defeated by General Victoriano Huerta, who would later topple the new democracy himself.

China

Barrington Moore's classic analysis of the rural determinants of democracy suggests that because China's landowners were unable to adapt to capitalist market conditions, they clung to premodern political forms: "During the period under discussion [late nineteenth and early twentieth centuries], the Chinese landed upper classes did not develop any significant principled opposition to the Imperial system. There were no doubt some who took up Western parliamentary notions as an intellectual plaything, but there was no political movement of opposition with substantial roots in Chinese conditions."[48] I propose that Moore's analysis is inaccurate, and that the Chinese landowning class was considerably more supportive of democracy than were its counterparts in the other new democracies covered in this study.

Unlike European aristocracies, Chinese landowners did not form a class of landed nobility. The Chinese aristocracy was abolished a millennium ago, and the Manchu nobility that ruled China since the seventeenth century did not colonize considerable acreage. Instead, large-scale landowning in China grew out of state officialdom, the entry into which was determined primarily by examinations (though also by purchase of office). The contrast with Russian landowners whose rights to land flowed from their noble blood could hardly be more pronounced. In China, the gentry—the term generally used to describe the class of Chinese landowner-officials—was under greater pressure to reproduce itself as a class in each generation than were landowning classes in other countries. This pressure resulted in a class solidarity based at least in part on achievement rather than inheritance, on knowledge rather than blood, and on continuous renewal rather than protection of the past.[49]

By the beginning of the twentieth century, however, the landowners' overlap with the traditional intelligentsia was beginning to break down. To begin with, the examination system now produced far more successful candidates than the state had official positions. In 1905, the state abolished the examination system altogether, and the gentry in response sent their children to modern-style schools, including five to ten thousand private students (in addition to government-scholarship students) to schools in Japan. As a sign of the gentry's willingness to repudiate its traditions, one report claims that in the province of Hubei, 40 percent or more of all degree holders—that is, men who had passed the traditional examinations—enrolled in programs to be "re-educated" in modern disciplines in the years 1906–1911.[50]

A further breakdown of the landowners' traditional solidarity resulted from their increasing participation in modern commerce. Barrington Moore may well be correct in suggesting that Chinese agriculture remained premodern, but landowners' economic position was no longer reliant solely on agriculture. Chapter 5 noted the ambiguity in distinguishing among state bureaucrats, landowners, and capitalists in the Chinese context. The clearest indication of the gentry's new economic role was its involvement with railroad construction in the last years of the old regime. In several provinces, gentry committed large sums of money through investments or taxes to bring railroad lines through their regions[51]—the sort of promotional activity more often associated with capitalist boosterism than with traditional landowning elites. The expropriation of several of these railroad investment companies by the central government in 1911 is commonly considered one of the precipitating events of the revolution.

Politically, too, important elements of the Chinese gentry played an unexpectedly progressive role, supporting limited democratization, not as an "intellectual plaything," in Moore's term, but—in their eyes—as a means to save the nation from the encroachments of foreign powers and the mismanagement of the Manchu rulers. According to Kang Youwei, a leading ideologue of gentry reformism, "The secret of the strength of Japan and Western countries lies solely in their adoption of constitutional government and convening of parliament. . . . This is the trend of history which has greatly changed the mood of the people. Surging waves and rolling waters [of revolution] are engulfing the great earth—a profoundly awesome trend!" According to Liang Qichao, Kang's influential student, "What is called monarchy is nothing but selfishness; what is called democracy is nothing but public-mindedness."[52] Despite this rhetoric, both men, as well as the bulk of the political activists among the gentry, sought a gradual transition to democracy, on the grounds that the Chinese people were not ready for the responsibility of popular sovereignty. This gradualism earned them the scorn of the young revolutionary intellectuals, but it was an ideology suited to the elitism of the gentry.

Gentry prodemocracy activism, in keeping with this gradualist ideology, contented itself with demanding suffrage for the gentry, within the context of a constitutional monarchy. Yet the nonrevolutionary nature of gentry activism made it no less strident. Gentry mobilized in "constitutional study groups" and other voluntary associations, issued a large number of prodemocracy pamphlets, actively petitioned the throne for reforms, and used the bully pulpit of the newly granted provincial assemblies *(ziyiju)* in the last years of the old regime as leverage for its demands. Indeed, the power struggle between these parliaments—elected and dominated by gentry—and the imperial government led the gentry even to support the revolution when it erupted in fall 1911. Throughout October and November, gentry-dominated provincial assemblies declared independence from monarchical rule in Beijing. In late November, representatives from these bodies met in Nanjing and claimed the authority to select Sun Yatsen as provisional president of the Republic of China, thereby ousting the monarchy. The improbable result was that much of China's landowning class not only supported democratic reforms as a means of saving the monarchy but also chose democracy over monarchy when the two came into conflict.[53]

The radicalization of the gentry was not the work of Sun Yatsen and other prodemocracy revolutionaries. These activists directed their efforts at the gentry's modern-educated children, not the parents. Indeed, one of Sun's earliest policy recommendations was a plan for radical land reform:

"For the rich . . . to enjoy the fertility of everything and to have a huge gap between them and the impoverished requires a method for equalization." Sun subsequently spoke of nationalizing landholdings, or at least nationalizing the rise in land values by taxing appreciation, a plan that Sun borrowed from the U.S. economist Henry George. Yet in the months after the gentry had selected him provisional president of the republic, Sun tamed down these plans: "In the past, one of the doctrines of this party, the T'ung-meng-hui [United Alliance], was the required level of equalized land rights, holding that if we could succeed in equalizing land rights, then we would have accomplished 70 or 80 percent of the social revolution. But there is one matter to which we must pay attention." Sun went on to reject land reform on the grounds that the state was not yet wealthy enough to compensate landholders for expropriation; instead, he proposed an ad valorem land tax. Yet, predictably, the gentry were opposed to higher taxes. In Hunan, a revolutionary finance minister demanded "contributions" from wealthy landowners; their representatives in the provisional Hunan parliament objected and the minister eventually lost his job. In Guangdong province, where the modern intellectuals controlled the new legislature, a law was proposed requiring landowners to reregister their holdings at current market values. The gentry exerted enough pressure on the provincial assembly to water down and postpone the implementation of this legislation, and it never went into effect. In Guangxi province, some landowners were said to prefer forfeiting their voting rights to registering their property values, for fear of taxation.[54]

Peasant revolts against taxes, regulations, and rents occurred in various parts of China under the new democracy. However, I have found little evidence that the gentry felt provoked to mobilize against democracy. In most provinces, land taxes were not proposed, and the more radical plans for land equalization were abandoned everywhere. In addition, the new democracy's weakened central government may have suited the gentry well, because it devolved considerable power upon local elites. A recent collection of case studies emphasizes the continuity of elite control in various parts of the country during the revolutionary period. In any case, the province where the gentry appears to have held the greatest power, Hunan, defended democracy against Yuan Shikai's coup in 1913 and was conquered by his armies. In the decades that followed, the Chinese gentry—like many intellectuals as well, as I will discuss in Chapter 10—abandoned the ideal of democracy and allied themselves with military rulers to maintain their privileged social position.[55] Yet we should not let this later stage cloud the startling fact that the landowning class in China was at one time remarkably open to the concept of democracy.

The democratic revolutions of the early twentieth century do not appear to have been won or lost in the countryside, as Barrington Moore and Otto Hintze lead us to expect. Although there was significant peasant activism in several of these countries—less so in the Ottoman Empire than elsewhere—the rise and demise of democracies were largely decided in cities. In addition, landowners were far more ambivalent about democracy in this period than Moore's analysis suggests. In Russia and China, landowning gentry controlled regional assemblies that lent crucial support for the democracy movement, albeit last minute and short-lived. At these moments, in keeping with Hintze's argument, the Russian *zemstvos* and the Chinese *ziyijus* sought limits on the power of the autocrat in order to preserve their own agrarian privileges. But these were not ancient assemblies acting as a feudal brake on the modernizing state, as in Hintze's analysis, but relatively recent creations (1864 and 1907, respectively) of the state itself. And in the other four democratic revolutions of the period, there were no comparable bodies. Aristocrats in Iran and the Ottoman Empire who supported the democracy movement did so as individual black sheep, therefore aristocratic landowners' institutional counterweight to autocracy does not seem to have been a prerequisite for democratization at this time.

After democratization, landowners played a variety of political roles, not just that of the antidemocratic villain. In Mexico, landowners cooperated with the new democracy to suppress peasant rebellions. In Iran, major landowners sided both with the new democracy and its opponents, sometimes in consecutive months. In the Ottoman Empire, landowners appear to have been largely silent on the issue of democracy. In Portugal and China, by contrast, they engaged actively in democratic politics, mobilizing demonstrations and parliamentary campaigns to oppose increased land taxes. Only in Russia did landowners revert en masse to the antidemocratic position. Landowning gentry formed a new organization, the United Nobility, that lobbied the monarchy consistently for the dismissal of parliament.

Russia stands out as well because it was the only new democracy of the period to consider extensive land reform. In the other new democracies, intellectuals weakened the land reform proposals that they had voiced before coming to office, except in Iran, where land reform had never been a significant part of the prodemocracy agenda. In Russia, by contrast, the forced distribution of landholdings—albeit with some compensation—seemed so inevitable after democratization that even the monarchy developed its own land reform plans. Intellectuals in parliament naturally considered these measures insufficient and developed their own, more sweeping proposals, which provided the excuse for the tsar to shut down the first and second parliaments and order election laws rewritten to privilege landowners.

Barrington Moore's classic analysis of the social origins of dictatorship and democracy skips over the democratic revolutions in Russia and China as though they were insignificant preludes to anticipated later outcomes. In the grand sweep of history, these experiments with democracy, and the others of the same period, were indeed brief. However, their rapid demise was not assumed by observers and participants. At the time, landowners and others debated democracy intensely. Some landowners engaged in democratic politics, some opposed democracy, and some stayed out of national politics altogether. Outside of Russia, however, landowners were not ultimately the factor that threatened the new democracies. For that dubious honor we must turn to modern military officers.

8

Democracy and the Military

Who will defend us from our defenders? As a government invests significant power in its armed forces, it also seeks mechanisms to keep those
arms from being used against itself. One set of mechanisms is organizational: the military may be kept sufficiently weak, divided, or engaged so
that it poses no serious threat to the government, should it want to. Another set of mechanisms is normative: key military personnel may be in-
culcated with such loyalty to the government that they have no desire to
overturn it, should they be capable of doing so.[1]

During the nineteenth century, the growing size and bureaucracy of the
militaries in many countries weakened both sets of mechanisms. On one
hand, militaries became far more unified and mightier than just a century
earlier. Instead of relatively small armies, the most powerful states managed massive troop forces. Huge infrastructures, including railways and
steamships in place of the old wagons and sailboats, transported these
troops. Giant centralized organizations trained the soldiers and housed
and fed them. Modern-style military academies educated a new sort of officer to serve in these vast bureaucratic apparatuses, an officer with technical expertise in engineering or strategy or logistics. States that did not
develop these institutions faced a real risk of being conquered and colonized by those that did. Yet states that did develop these institutions faced
a risk as well, as military organizations swelled disproportionately to other
state institutions. What would keep the military from conquering the rest
of the state?

At the same time, modern-trained officers were imbued with a worldview that privileged education and efficiency, as distinct from the aristocratic officers of an earlier age, who continued to dominate the officer
corps in many countries throughout the nineteenth century. The modern-
educated officers were becoming positivist intellectuals who worried that

196

the states they served did not match the ideals they served. One solution to this dilemma was to turn away from the sullying spheres outside of the military world, to "professionalize" through specialization in military affairs. This was the path described by Samuel Huntington's famous book *The Soldier and the State* (1957). Huntington's next big book, *Political Order in Changing Societies* (1968), described another path: an expansion of the military's mission through praetorian attempts to conquer their own state and transform the rest of society.[2]

In the early twentieth century, as the identity of the modern intellectual spread globally, some modern-educated officers associated themselves with this movement and its prodemocracy goals. Once the intellectuals helped them break the bonds of loyalty to the state, however, it was apparently much easier for them to take the next step and attempt to reorder the state and society along military lines.

Russia

In 1905, with virtually all social groups in revolt, even the landed gentry, the Russian monarchy's primary domestic support was the military. Yet the Russian military was tottering. It had just been routed by the Japanese, a large portion of its navy sunk, and its prestige and self-confidence destroyed. In addition, the war with Japan had pulled much of the nation's military forces to the eastern edge of the massive Russian Empire, thousands of miles from the center of the democracy movement in Russia's western regions. Beginning in late September, a railway strike prevented the return of troops from the Far East, and widespread lack of discipline among the soldiers cast doubt on their usefulness in suppressing dissent, even if they could be transported back to Europe.

The crippled state of the military was a major factor in the tsar's decision to grant democratic reforms in the October Manifesto of 1905. The tsar's military advisors informed him that the troops in European Russia were too few and too exhausted from months of clashes with civilians to reopen the striking railways, or even to guard the empty train stations in St. Petersburg. Grand Duke Nikolai Nikolaevich, the tsar's choice to lead a clampdown against the democracy movement, advised against such a policy. He pointed a revolver at his head and threatened to kill himself if the tsar did not sign the October Manifesto.[3]

The tsar's reliance on the military did not end with the pronouncement of the October Manifesto. In the following months, Russian peasants engaged in a flurry of rebellions. Strikes, threatening though ultimately limited in scope, broke out in the major cities. At the same time, the situation within the military deteriorated. Conscripts and reserves mounted hundreds of mutinies in the two months after the Manifesto, and peasant resistance hampered the mobilization of additional units. The government was so afraid of its soldiers' rebelliousness that it granted all of their demands, and then some: pay was more than doubled, food rations multiplied, clothing improved, bedding issued for the first time—along with handkerchiefs, "to show that soldiers were given not only what they demanded, but even a luxury that had not occurred to them," according to the minister of war.[4]

Because of the monarchy's concessions to soldiers, or just because of its good luck, the mutinies subsided rapidly in mid-December 1905, just in time to make soldiers available to suppress the Moscow uprising of that month. For the first time during the revolution, the military used heavy weapons on civilian protestors and destroyed large parts of the Presnia district, center of the textile industry and a stronghold of working-class activists. The massive application of force subdued the Moscow uprising and deterred future protests. After parliament was dismissed in the summer of 1906, representatives of Presnia refused to join a citywide protest: "We bore the brunt of the December [1905] strike; now it is your turn." Elite troops were combined with regular peasant-soldiers on punitive expeditions aimed against restive peasants and provincial strikers, and the government gained the upper hand for the first time in a year.[5]

The methods that succeeded during this period were codified in government policy, especially the bombardment of civilians (urban neighborhoods and peasant villages) and the use of "punitive trains" (military units based on rail cars that would commandeer the tracks during railway strikes). Both of these methods, but especially the use of artillery, represented a shift from reliance on large units of poorly trained conscripts to the use of smaller units of more highly trained troops. The military command still feared mutiny. One indication of this fear, as John Bushnell points out, was the mass of counterrevolutionary propaganda that it poured into the barracks—and their fears proved accurate, as a second wave of mutinies (again coinciding with peasant uprisings) broke out in the spring of 1906. In June 1906, the minister of war ordered district commanders to minimize the number of troops used in protest suppression for fear of "the total disintegration of the army and the loss of it as an organized military force."[6]

This shift from labor-intensive to capital-intensive military methods coincided with a shift within the military officer corps from landowner-cavalrymen to trained professionals. At the end of the nineteenth century, nobles still constituted more than half of the Russian military officer corps. However, the corps retained few of its traditional links with the landed gentry. Only a small proportion of gentry officers still owned land; crucial branches of the officer corps, particularly engineers and technical officers, were dominated by commoners; and the changing conduct of war required that virtually all officers receive specialized training at military schools or colleges. While they retained noble status, most military officers on the eve of the democratic experiment had more in common with other educated professionals than with landed gentry. In addition, the disastrous war with Japan brought the issue of military reform to the fore: a growing number of officers called for the increased education and professionalization of the officer corps, and even for universal literacy among soldiers. One of these reformists, General A. F. Rediger, was named minister of war in June 1905.[7]

After the October Manifesto, this professionalization led to the publication of the first independent daily military newspaper in Russia, *The Military Voice,* in early 1906. This newspaper linked themes of military reform with those of political reform and supported not only the existence of parliament but also parliament's right to control military affairs, a right that the monarchy jealously monopolized. The newspaper attained a certain popularity within the officer corps, to judge by the number of unsolicited letters from officers in the field. "Many [officers] saw in [parliament] one of the means to put the army on the path of broad reforms," according to one general. Even Rediger, the minister of war, shared the newspaper's support for parliamentary authority; he was one of the few tsarist ministers during this period to acknowledge and accept parliamentary oversight. Perhaps just as important, Rediger and other top officers resented the use of their troops as policemen and guards in the state's struggle against popular protests, fearing that such duties reduced soldiers' discipline and harmed the military's preparedness for national defense.[8]

Ultimately, however, *The Military Voice* and the prodemocracy officers were unable to shake the military's loyalty to the monarchy. Several factors were involved: First, Russian military men, even modern-educated professionals, had a long tradition of mutual hostility with civilian intellectuals, an animosity that dated back to the antimilitary literature of the 1880s. The democracy movement of 1905 produced an outpouring of antimilitary novels and articles, and many officers may have sympathized with the colonel in Turkestan who assassinated a local newspaper editor. Second, the solidary traditions of the officer corps emphasized the nonpolitical nature of their calling: "Almost without exception, military memoirists writing about the empire period between 1880 and 1914 have noted, in some cases ruefully, that the majority of Russian officers were strangers to politics, if not outright political illiterates." Third, many officers, including Rediger, feared the effects of officers' prodemocracy sentiments on rank-and-file soldiers, given the general atmosphere of indiscipline and mutiny. In the summer of 1906, Rediger banned *The Military Voice* from distribution among soldiers on these grounds. Fourth, the prodemocracy officers were not the ultimate authorities in the military; that position was still held by the tsar and his top advisers, who were hostile to democracy. In fact, at the time of Rediger's appointment in June 1905, the tsar had reorganized the general staff so as to increase the court's control of military affairs. *The Military Voice* pointed this out in its criticism of Rediger's action against the newspaper, noting that "his generals, his officers, his courts and his troops are controlled by the Ministry of the Interior [Stolypin]." In response, Rediger had the newspaper banned, depriving prodemocracy officers of their only, limited outlet.[9]

Ultimately, it would be absurd to expect the tsar's minister of war to side with the prodemocracy movement in a significant way. Any indications of such a move would have led to his immediate dismissal. A more meaningful hypothetical would have been the organization of a prodemocracy group of officers stemming from the officers' own military-reform movement. As we will see, this is precisely what occurred in Portugal and especially in the Ottoman Empire. In Russia, by contrast, the military-reform movement was not fully integrated into the democracy movement. Its goals of efficiency and discipline were just as easily accomplished under the authoritarian government of P. A. Stolypin as under a democratic regime.

Iran

Iran scarcely had a military in the early twentieth century. Its standing army was "completely useless from a military point of view" and served primarily "as a conduit for the transfer of financial resources [from the state] to favoured individuals and groups," who pocketed the military budget instead of hiring, training, and outfitting soldiers. According to a Russian officer who served in Iran, "The army of Iran exists only on paper." According to another, Iranian soldiers "make their living by begging, most of their weapons are rusted, and these wretches don't know how to shoot. The Iranian soldier cannot hit a target even from 20 paces." When it wished to apply force, Iran's central government relied instead on proxy troops controlled by major landowners, tribal leaders, and, in the case of the Iranian Cossack Brigade, the Russian government. With these sparse capabilities— the Cossacks comprised fewer than two thousand soldiers—the central government was unable to monopolize coercion anywhere outside the capital. In some regions, local forces levied their own "road taxes" with impunity. At least one regional force in the late nineteenth century, led by a princely governor, may have been superior to the central government's army. The military's condition had not been improved by a century of military reforms—indeed, Iran's military had "been 'reorganized' oftener than any similar body of troops in the world," according to an American observer.[10]

But military reform did succeed in generating a small body of modern-educated officers, trained by Austrians and other European officers. As in other countries at the time, some of these officers supported the democracy movement. A dozen were early members of the Society of Humanity, and when the democracy movement staged its historic sit-in at the British embassy in 1906, one officer suggested that the army would not block the movement, and might even join it. Intellectual activists hurried to the barracks to convince troops not to shoot prodemocracy protestors; soon the soldiers were removed from Tehran, except for a small guard protecting the sit-in. When the constitution was granted, the main military academy in Tehran became the symbolic center of democracy in Iran, site of the first elections in the country and temporary home of the first parliament. The director of the military school warned his teachers and students not to imitate this model in school affairs, as "there can be no democracy inside the Military Academy."[11]

Prodemocracy intellectuals had long bemoaned the state of the military and appealed to officers to join in creating a modern-style army. Malkum Khan, one of the chief inspirations of the prodemocracy movement, addressed this theme in two of his earliest manifestos. Hajji Sayyah, a founder of the prodemocracy Revolutionary Committee, complained that "there is no soldier or army in Iran except the name." Nevertheless, military reform was not a top priority in the new democracy. In mid-1907, a satirical newspaper published a cartoon showing "sorrowful, . . . weary looking soldiers [who] plead for their long overdue wages, saying they are hungry. The official replies that the Ministry of War does not have his own mint and treasury, but he will agree to make the payments from his own personal funds." Later in the year, the same newspaper published a more optimistic cartoon showing rows of neatly dressed soldiers swearing to sacrifice themselves for the protection of the country, but this was wishful thinking, as the new democracy had done nothing to strengthen the military or its budget. A reformist newspaper urged the government to do something quickly, as "everybody knows that all states and all nations need a military force now more than ever, even those states that abide by the wisdom of the Hague peace conference."[12]

In 1908, as the shah and his Russian supporters prepared to disband parliament, prodemocracy intellectuals continued their efforts to bring military officers over to their side, and believed that they had had some success. The previous fall, a number of high-ranking military officers had formed a group, the Commanders' Association, that pledged support for democracy.[13] The sincerity of this pledge was unclear, however, and none of these commanders moved to defend parliament when it was shelled and disbanded in June 1908 by the Cossack Brigade.

The sole military resistance to this coup d'état came from irregular troops in the provinces: popular militias in Azerbaijan and Gilan, assisted by small numbers of revolutionaries from the Russian Empire, and Bakhtiyari tribal forces in south-central Iran. Photos from the period show militiamen posing with rifles and crossed bandoleros of bullets over their chests, in a style identical to rebels of a few years later in Mexico. Despite the small size of these forces—the Bakhtiyaris numbered fewer than two thousand troops—the Iranian Army was unable to prevent the march on Tehran, which was captured in July 1909 after two days of fighting. The Cossack Brigade, contrary to its role in the coup of 1908, refused to fight, negotiated a surrender, and was kept intact.[14]

Tehran now housed four entirely separate armed forces, in addition to the army: a small number of Azerbaijani soldiers under the command of Sattar Khan and Baqir Khan; a larger number of Gilani forces under the command of the Armenian radical Yeprem Khan, who was named chief of police of Tehran; Bakhtiyari fighters, encamped near the city, under the command of a feuding array of tribal leaders, some of whom also served as cabinet ministers; and the Cossack Brigade, whose Russian officers continued to report both to the Iranian government and to the Russian military commander of the Caucasus.

Faced with tensions among these forces, the new democracy turned to military reform. To replace the unsystematic levy of conscripts, proposals were aired for a volunteer army or universal (male) military service. More successful proposals aimed to disband autonomous militias or incorporate them into the army and police. The Tehran police moved its stations out of the homes of local notables and into its own buildings, and got cabinet approval to subsidize an expanded and reorganized force through a tax on the sale of alcohol and opium. Still more proposals established two new armed forces: a government gendarmerie under the command of Swedish officers, which was intended to secure trade routes in southern Iran; and a treasury gendarmerie under the command of the American treasurer-general, which was intended to collect tax revenues.[15]

In some quarters, military support for democracy ran high. Twenty-three Iranian officers in the Cossack Brigade now expressed their enthusiasm for democracy, meeting with parliamentary leaders and issuing an open letter in which they pledged to defend parliament even if their Russian commanders ordered otherwise. The new treasury gendarmerie took steps to shore up the new democracy's finances, upsetting Russian sensibilities in the process. The Gilan militia organized expeditions to repel monarchist invasions on Iran's northern and western borders. Yet the Bakhtiyari commanders, for all their success in restoring democracy, were less eager to defend it. After holding out for financial incentives, they offered to cut a deal with the Russians.[16] In the fall of 1911, facing parliamentary intransigence and Russian ultimatums, the Bakhtiyari commanders sent Yeprem Khan to close down parliament, ending Iran's brief democratic period. Once again, as with the coup of 1908, none of the military officers who had pledged to defend the constitution took any action on its behalf.

The Bakhtiyari commanders who dismantled democracy in Iran were too fractious to plan or carry out authoritarian modernization, as military coup-makers attempted to do in Russia, the Ottoman Empire, and Portugal. Rather, as in China and Mexico, the coup led to a period of divided power. Only in the 1920s did Iran witness a concerted campaign of military-led modernization.[17]

Ottoman Empire

The Ottoman democracy movement had attracted modern-educated military officers since its beginnings in the late nineteenth century. These officers considered themselves intellectuals, as in the reference by one longtime prodemocracy officer, a professor at a military academy, to "intellectuals, especially educated military officers." Educated military officers were scornful of old-style commanders lacking modern training, whom they blamed for the weakness of the Ottoman national defense. "No commanders at that time had much contemporary knowledge and culture," another activist in the military recalled, though he also noted that one illiterate officer knew his job thoroughly and was respected by prodemocracy activists. "We need a committee [composed] of intellectuals," wrote another.[18]

When the democracy movement's leadership in exile in Europe decided to mobilize a revolutionary movement in 1907, it renewed efforts to recruit military officers. One pamphlet, published in Paris, called on "my comrades in arms in the army and navy" to fight to the death against dictatorship, in imitation of Russia, where "even young girls" stood courageously in defense of parliament. Apparently this campaign was quite successful, especially among junior officers in the Third Army, which was stationed in the Ottoman Empire's European provinces.[19]

Democratization in 1908 followed directly from the linkages forged between military officers and prodemocracy civilian intellectuals. In June 1908, military members of the Society for Union and Progress attempted to assassinate an Ottoman officer in Salonica who had been investigating the opposition movement. As a result, a number of prodemocracy officers in the Third Army came under suspicion and were transferred from Macedonia to Istanbul for investigation and possible court-martial. Instead of obeying, one officer, Ahmed Niyazi, fled into the countryside with a group of supporters. Another Society member assassinated the general who had been ordered to pursue Niyazi. Several days later, with several more military members of the Society roaming the hills of Macedonia, the Society began to issue demands for the reinstatement of the constitution. The sultan quickly backed down and announced the reinstatement of the constitution, including elections and limits on royal authority.[20] Significantly, he retained the right to appoint the ministers of war and the navy.

As in Russia, Ottoman military newspapers appeared soon after democratization, emphasizing national renewal and military modernization and hailing the Third Army for its "sacred struggle for freedom" against "the oppressive and absolutist government." Intellectuals credited the military as well for its role in democratization. A newspaper cartoon of the period, for example, showed a baby labeled "New Turkey" sitting on books labeled "The Constitution," which were balanced precariously on the bayonet of a soldier's rifle. A flurry of plays honoring prodemocracy officers were produced in the months after democratization.[21]

The new government instituted a series of reforms in the fall of 1908 to modernize the military, with particular attention to the promotion of educated officers. Within months, more than a thousand military academy graduates replaced noncommissioned officers who lacked modern educations. This scramble for positions reflected a cultural divide between schooled and experienced officers. "From now on, all officers will be trained in schools," wrote one modern-educated general. "Even our uneducated comrades cannot deny that the army today, and in the future, needs to train intelligent and capable officers." In the meantime, he proposed, "The hand must work as one. Educated and uneducated must not be differentiated from one another." The government proposed to retrain existing old-style officers, while admitting that the funding allotted for this task was "completely insufficient."[22]

Old-style officers were displeased with this treatment. They ridiculed the new officers as *merkepli* (donkey-riding), a play on the word *mektepli* (educated). On several occasions in the months after democratization, old-style officers mobilized small-scale protests: one unit refused to be transferred from Istanbul to Yemen, for example. "In those days, [military] discipline was in a state of complete bankruptcy," one officer recalled. The mutiny of April 1909 was the largest and most influential event in this series of protests. The event culminated in a mass rally led by the firebrand Islamic leader, Derviş Vahdeti, whose Islamic Unity Society and newspaper, *The Volcano*, demanded that the new democracy implement the Islamic legal precepts that Vahdeti and his colleagues considered most important. Vahdeti had little use for modern-educated intellectuals, calling them "cucumber people" (see Chapter 4). He seems to have preferred military rule: "We shall rely first on God, and then the soldier." During the mutiny of April 1909, Vahdeti congratulated soldiers for taking the place of their modern-educated officers: "There were no commanders leading them, no officers. Their officers were corporals, their commanders were glorious sergeants." The mutineers killed a number of educated officers, then confronted parliament with their grievances against the officers, as well as demands for the implementation of Islamic law.[23] Various parliamentary leaders and cabinet members, including the prime minister, resigned in response.

Modern-educated officers responded to the April uprising by suppressing both the mutiny and parliament. Already in February 1909, officers had expressed grievances with the new democracy. Dozens of them gathered in parliament to demand the removal of recently appointed ministers of the navy and army, and the dismissal of the prime minister. Parliament acquiesced. In April, modern-educated officers dispensed with parliamentary action altogether, preferring to remove the new prime minister by force. As they organized a special Action Army to "save" the constitution, military leaders indicated that they were as offended by the mutiny's rejection of educated officers' authority as by its rejection of the constitution: "The main aim of the conspiracy is against the military and the constitution," Mahmud Şevket Pasha, leader of the Action Army, telegraphed to the palace. "The actions of these men [in the mutiny] have subjected to a very great shame the sacred Ottoman military," wrote another Action Army general, on the eve of the conquest of Istanbul. Military action is needed "to cleanse this extraordinary blemish with all speed" and "restore the honour of the Ottoman military."[24]

The Action Army occupied Istanbul on April 24, 1909. The following week, the military court-martialed and executed the mutineers, including Derviş Vahdeti, replaced the prime minister, deposed the sultan, crowned his brother in his place, and declared martial law and a state of siege. With the Action Army still occupying the capital, parliament passed laws allowing the extended detention of "vagabonds" and other "suspected criminals," outlawing strikes, and limiting freedom of the press and public meetings. Two dozen high-ranking military officers had signed a report several weeks before the vote on the press bill making their position clear: "Everyone knows that the newspapers have abused the freedom of the press to no end, clouding minds and destroying unity among the elements [presumably ethnic groups]." The government needs "a plan other than remaining impotent and submitting to this rushing torrent of violent attacks and insults." As a result, one observer noted during the parliamentary debate on the press bill, "all the deputies seemed conscious of the fact that their business was to pass the Bill, and not to question its wisdom." A leader of the Society for Union and Progress allegedly boasted at a secret meeting, "At the present moment the reins of power are entirely in our hands and no one here present need fear that we are in any danger of losing control."[25] The regime maintained a charade of democratic rule. But for the next several decades, governments in the Ottoman Empire and almost all of its successor states would be decided by military intervention.

Portugal

Immediately after the toppling of the monarchy in 1910, *Military Review*, a magazine edited by prominent military officers, relaxed its ban on political themes in order to pledge its obedience to the new regime. Still, Paiva Couceira, the leader of the monarchist invasions of republican Portugal, saw his fellow military officers as natural allies. He was not entirely wrong. The ideology of military authoritarianism, linking institutional pride with monarchism and later fascism, was apparently dominant in the central military reproductive institution, the officer-training school. Under the new democracy the school continued to be "structurally monarchist, beginning with the greater part of the teaching corps and ending with the students themselves. Alas for those who had the courage to reveal themselves as republicans." "Numerous students have the audacity to declare themselves openly monarchist, loudly threatening those who are republicans," another student reported.[26]

Yet not all military officers were monarchist. Enough maintained loyalty to democracy for the monarchist incursions to be handily contained. The new regime tried to put officers in charge who were deemed sympathetic to democracy, in particular a group of officers known as the "Young Turks," who began a purge of monarchists in the military. The results were incomplete. Older officers resented the quick promotion of prodemocracy junior officers; radical enlisted men resented the continued employment of the older officers. "The soldiers want to come into the streets and the officer doesn't let them? He's a monarchist! A sergeant makes a request that isn't attended to . . . Monarchist! Monarchist!" Discipline deteriorated to the point where even staunchly prodemocracy officers labeled the situation "chaos" and implored soldiers to behave with "uniformity, decency, and composure."[27]

Moreover, the fighting ability of the military sank to near zero. A British naval attaché reported that the Portuguese navy, once the pride of this seafaring nation, was no longer seaworthy. "The result now is that the ships['] companies go in fear of their lives on the few occasions they are taken to sea, and are beginning to cry out for their old officers with a little experience, while the officers are frightened out of their lives of the men."[28] The army was so little respected by Portugal's allies Britain and France that when World War I broke out, they insulted Portugal by requesting weapons but no troops.

Their pride wounded, a number of officers resigned their commissions in early 1915 as a political protest against the democratic government, pledging their allegiance instead to an elderly general and military-school instructor, Joaquim Pimenta de Castro. In a legal coup d'état, the president selected Pimenta as the new prime minister. Pimenta had served as minister of war in the first year of the republic, but his support for democracy was suspect. As minister of war, Pimenta was considered lackadaisical in combating the first monarchist invasion, and he allegedly avoided the word *republic*. By 1915, in any case, Pimenta had "lost faith in the Republic," according to his wife's cousin, another army general. The president, an old friend, had to persuade him to take the premiership.[29] Once in office, Pimenta moved to consolidate power, refusing to allow parliament to meet, dissolving locally elected governments, postponing new elections, and giving every impression of creating a dictatorship.

King Manuel was thrilled. "It would be a great good for the Country if the present government lasts," he wrote to his former secretary, whom Pimenta had just released from prison in a wave of amnesties for monarchists. Manuel and his followers pinned their hopes on full-suffrage elections, in which the peasant majority would vote the monarchy back into power. The prospect of restoration appeared "inevitable," according to a monarchist newspaper. Yet the antidemocracy movement was so divided that one faction, the Miguelists, continued to agitate against the Pimenta regime, "contrary to the express orders of Dom Manuel, and despite the fact that their supporters held decisive influence in the . . . [Pimenta] government." In one bizarre scheme, the monarchist Paiva Couceiro appears to have courted the workers' movement,[30] attempting to forge the right-wing–left-wing alliance that the Portuguese republicans had invented several years earlier as an excuse for suppressing strikes (see Chapter 6).

All of these monarchist movements were flops. By mid-May, 1915, after less than five months in office, Pimenta was ousted by a military mutiny and popular uprising that restored the prodemocracy forces to power. The monarchist officers, as it turned out, had little control over their prodemocracy colleagues and subordinates. Other officers were upset by Germany's invasion of Portugal's African colonies, which drove them to renew their devotion to the alliance with Britain, while Pimenta's sympathies leaned toward Germany (see Chapter 9). Pimenta had been unwilling to believe that the military would betray him, his wife's cousin reported—but in the May 14 uprising, as it is known in Portuguese historiography, virtually all of the Lisbon regiments joined the democracy forces.[31]

The result was a stalemate: both the prodemocracy and antidemocracy factions in the Portuguese military had the power to disrupt, even to overturn governments they did not favor—a dictatorial government was installed for a time in 1918–1919 as well—but neither had the power to maintain governments they favored. Only in 1926 did the antidemocracy elements in the military decisively gain the upper hand, installing a fascist regime that lasted until 1974. The monarchists, having no other choice, lamely endorsed the fascists.[32]

Mexico

Soon after overthrowing the Díaz dictatorship, Francisco Madero attempted to win the loyalty of the top officers, all of whom had fought against him. He praised the army for its selflessness and discipline, cultivated leading generals with promotions and material considerations, and lavished weaponry purchases on the military. Significantly, even during the February 1913 coup, Madero believed that the military was staunchly on his side (as I will detail later). Perhaps because of this optimism, Madero placed little emphasis on maintaining the prodemocracy revolutionary forces that had brought him to power. Within two months of the dictator's departure, most of the revolutionaries had been mustered out. A small portion was retained under arms as a rural gendarmerie under the command of the regular military, and some revolutionaries were uncomfortably integrated into the military. Several revolutionary generals, upset by Madero's abandonment, threatened renewed military action, but Madero had them arrested. Some revolutionary armed forces that refused to lay down their arms turned against the democratic regime, accusing it of having been co-opted by the autocratic elements it had set out to displace. Emiliano Zapata, the most famous of these rebel leaders, refused to assist Madero during the February 1913 coup d'état.[33]

Madero miscalculated. The military officer corps developed no great affection for the new democracy. The reforms of the nineteenth century had broken the military's links with landed oligarchies, but the professionalism of the ranking officers and their dedication to national progress did not include devotion to democratic principles. The officers' esprit de corps expressed itself in the alumni association of the Colegio Militar, with 461 members in 1910. Félix Díaz, nephew of the longtime dictator, was a two-time president of this group. He adapted himself well to the fall of his uncle's regime, running for governor in Oaxaca, unsuccessfully, and then winning a seat in the national legislature. Though his public statements invariably supported the concept of democracy, his opposition to the Madero administration flirted with the limits of parliamentary criticism. In responses submitted for a U.S. newspaper interview, Díaz said he would prefer the hard-line law-and-order policies of his uncle, but that he lacked the personality to carry them out himself. If called to power, he said, "My primary force would be that of assuming complete responsibility, that is to say, I would not be bound by the compromises that shackle every plan of the [present] government, as well thought out as they may be." When he launched a revolt against the new democracy in October 1912, his plans called for the military officer corps to join his cause. He remained confident even as the federal army marched to Veracruz and surrounded his rebel forces. He wrote to the head of the federal forces, General Joaquin Beltrán, urging him to put their old military-school ties ahead of loyalty to the civilian government.[34]

Beltrán would have none of it. In his return letter, he placed his oath of loyalty above his old school ties. But his position was not popular within the military officer corps. A U.S. diplomat reported that the military "is unquestionably hostile to Madero." "At that time there were very few of us who had demonstrated our adhesion to the spirit of the cause [of democracy]," one officer recalled years later. "[A]ll the others were opposed. That's why almost the whole [military] was on the side of Huerta," the general who deposed the Madero administration in February 1913. By early 1913, a week before Díaz's second rebellion, Beltrán defensively reiterated his position in a letter to a newspaper editor: Public opinion seems to want the military to play the role of "a modern wild-card" and take responsibility for the country's fate, but any armed action could well split the military into warring factions, which would undermine the ultimate goal of maintaining the peace.[35]

Beltrán's fears were borne out on February 9, 1913, when antidemocracy officers and their supporters freed Félix Díaz and Bernardo Reyes from prison in an attempted coup d'état. Although the plot had been rumored for days and reported to the government by intelligence agents, Madero did little to prevent it and remained unconcerned even after it broke out.[36] The regiment at the presidential palace remained loyal— surprising Díaz, who again counted on military solidarity in place of strategic planning—and fired on the rebels, killing Reyes. Díaz and the remaining rebels fell back to a fortress in the center of the capital, the Ciudadela, where they holed up and waited for support to materialize.

From around the country, a variety of midlevel military officers telegrammed their support to Madero. General Felipe Angeles brought troops to Mexico City to help suppress the revolt. But the officer corps had largely gone over to the rebel side, most notably the newly appointed chief of staff, Victoriano Huerta. While Huerta had refused to participate in the coup plot, his loyalty to the democratic regime was limited. Madero was not the only senior figure ignorant of Huerta's dubious allegiance; Madero's secretary, normally very astute at identifying friends and opponents, said he was also taken in. Huerta may not have been loyal to Madero, but he apparently had no desire to serve under a Díaz presidency either. He coveted the presidency himself. Under pressure from U.S. and German ambassadors (see Chapter 9), Huerta and Díaz secretly agreed to dismiss the democratically elected Madero.[37] While negotiations continued, Huerta launched a fake attack on the rebel stronghold, sending loyal prodemocracy troops to their deaths. After ten days, Huerta took President Madero captive. Again, U.S. diplomatic pressure brought Huerta and Díaz to agree on a power-sharing plan, wherein Huerta would assume the provisional presidency, while Díaz would assume the regular presidency through election later in the year.

China

Modern elements in the Chinese military, as in the Ottoman Empire and Portugal, favored the democracy movement. Many of them received their military training in Japan, along with the civilian students who formed the vanguard of prodemocracy activism. Like their counterparts in the Ottoman Empire and Portugal, these modern-oriented officers objected to the inefficiency and personalistic authority of the old-style Chinese military, which they viewed as a danger to the unity of the empire. China had not won a foreign war in a century, during which time major portions of its landmass were ceded to other states, including Mongolia, Tibet, Manchuria, Formosa, and the so-called treaty ports placed under foreign sovereignty as a result of forcibly imposed treaties. Recognizing the need for a modern military organization after the humiliating defeat to Japan in 1894, the Chinese monarchy established New Army units and modern officer-training schools, as well as sponsoring officer training in Japan. These officers were the first in the military to sympathize with the prodemocracy movement.[38]

Like their civilian classmates, many had grand aspirations for rehabilitating China. Foreign-educated officers, according to an imperial official who in previous years had sponsored such students, "appear arrogant and overbearing because of their long stay overseas. Having extravagant expectations, they will not be happy with anything short of an exalted position and an attractive salary. They are loath to work under Chinese-educated divisional and regimental commanders." The U.S. ambassador commented in 1910: "While it is impossible to obtain reliable information with regard to the 'morale' of the army or the degree of its discipline, it would not be surprising if the example of Turkey were one day to be repeated here and the real revolution start[ed] with junior officers."[39]

As the U.S. ambassador anticipated, the Chinese Revolution of 1911 began with a secret military group, as in the Ottoman Empire, but it was nowhere nearly as well organized, and the group was strongest, not among the foreign-educated junior officers, but among Chinese-educated rank-and-file soldiers. In Hubei, where the revolution broke out first, as many as a third of these soldiers were reported to belong to revolutionary cells. Many modern-trained officers, "although not daring to participate in revolutionary activities, also did not dare to suppress them." Soldier grievances did not always mesh with the ideology of the democracy movement; often they were focused on more mundane issues such as pay and fair treatment by officers. A significant strain of military resentment—and an ugly side of the prodemocracy movement—involved nativist hostility toward the Manchus, leading to the slaughter of thousands of Manchu soldiers and their families during the revolution. Regardless of the soldiers' precise ideological motivations, several foreign observers noted a commitment to revolutionary battle that had been missing in recent Chinese military engagements, the "comic element" normal in Chinese warfare, as a British diplomat disparagingly put it. "[T]he one anxiety of the wounded in the hospitals was to get back into the fighting at the earliest possible moment. It is impossible to ignore the fact that these men were animated by zeal for a cause in which they thoroughly believed."[40]

After the revolution, modern-educated, especially foreign-educated, military officers received more than seven hundred general officer positions. Despite their youth, between 25 and 35 years of age, officers trained at Japanese military academies comprised about 30 percent of all generals in China in 1913. "The recent Revolution owes its success, and the Republic its creation, entirely to the efforts of military men," Sun Yatsen told a group of soldiers welcoming him to Guangdong in April 1912. At the same time, Sun lectured them to remain obedient to civilian authority. Sun combined the same themes in a September speech to army officers in Beijing: "It was the ardent support of right-minded military men and policemen in the various provinces that led to the overthrow of the dictatorship. . . . Our Republic is still in its infancy. You, our compatriots in the army and the police, should concern yourselves only with supporting and protecting it. Under no circumstances should you abuse or despoil it."[41]

Others shared Sun's concern, such as Li Yuanhong, who feared that provinces—almost half of them led by modern-educated military officers[42]—were acting too independently of the central government:

> A province is the territory of the man who rules it, the army is the possession of its general. This disposition finds imitation far and wide, as a sound is repeated by its echo. At the beginning it was a small matter, but in the end it has become like a spreading conflagration. For the measuring out and the partition of the country they care nothing.[43]

The specter of partition became a reality later in the decade, during the Warlord Period when central authority virtually disappeared in China. Yet during the new democracy, the problem was a different one. Modern-educated officers felt a greater affinity for Yuan Shikai's authoritarianism than for the ideal of democracy.

Yuan—like generals Mahmud Şevket Pasha in the Ottoman Empire, Victoriano Huerta in Mexico, and Joaquim Pimenta de Castro in Portugal—believed in modernity and progress, but aimed to achieve these goals through an authoritarian route. Though he had been trained in the traditional manner himself, Yuan "prided himself on the recognition he gave to returned students in the form of important appointments," according to his biographer, who counted dozens of Japanese-trained officers in Yuan's military command, some in top positions. Yuan consistently disparaged democratic government. In a public statement in late 1911, before taking office, he said, "I am not at all sure whether the Chinese people are well prepared to accept the citizenship of a republic." In his first months as president, he told the British ambassador that "a republic meant a deal of useless talking and very little work." Yuan "makes no mystery of his own conviction that the monarchic regime is the best for China," an Italian diplomat observed.[44]

In early 1913, Yuan began to work himself free from democratic control. He had the parliamentary opposition leader assassinated and stepped up negotiations with various European banking consortiums for a significant loan without parliamentary approval (see Chapter 9). When prodemocracy forces objected, Yuan applied military pressure, using the funds obtained from the European loan. Civil war, known as the Second Revolution in Chinese historiography, broke out in the summer of 1913.

The military, including a large majority of the modern-educated officers, sided with Yuan. Even officers who had been active in the democracy movement less than two years before, such as the army commanders in Guangdong, Shanxi, and Yunnan, abandoned the cause, though their decision may have had as much to do with an appraisal of the new democracy's poor odds of survival as with sympathy for Yuan's authoritarian ideology.[45]

Many modern-educated military officers supported democratization in the early twentieth century. They shared prodemocracy intellectuals' positivist worldview, and they felt a particular urgency for state reform because of their professional preoccupation with foreign military competition. For each country experiencing a democratic revolution in this period, foreign military intervention was a recent historical memory and an ongoing threat. The strongest link between military officers and the prodemocracy movement emerged in the Ottoman Empire, where modern-educated officers identified themselves as intellectuals and provided the leadership for the 1908 revolution. The weakest link was in Mexico, where no officers participated in the armed phase of the democratic revolution and the officers' esprit de corps worked largely toward antidemocratic ends. The other democratic revolutions witnessed conflict within the armed forces between pro- and antidemocratic elements, with the prodemocratic position aligning generally with modern military training.

Even prodemocracy officers were frequently disturbed by the turbulence of the new democracy. Unrest spread in many cases from the streets into the barracks, undermining the officers' authority. Those officers who entered politics during the democratic revolution may have found it easier to enter politics again to help undermine the new democracy. In each case, the new democracy wound up defending itself against its own military defenders. In Russia, the democracy movement put its hopes in A. F. Rediger, the reformist minister of war, who ultimately sided with the tsar against democracy. In Iran, democratic leaders supported the Bakhtiyari tribal leaders, whose military services restored democracy in 1909 and undermined it in 1911. Young Turk military officers brought democracy to the Ottoman Empire in 1908 and removed it in 1909. In Mexico, President Francisco I. Madero counted on General Victoriano Huerta to defend democracy against a coup by another general; instead, Huerta made a pact with the rebel and took power himself. The prodemocracy movement in China entrusted General Yuan Shikai with extensive executive power, just as the last Qing monarch had done, and Yuan abolished the democracy just as he had abolished the Qing dynasty. Only in Portugal was the military so evenly divided that neither prodemocracy nor antidemocracy officers were able to vanquish the other side decisively, with coups and counter-coups roiling the republic until the advent of fascism in 1926.

It is worth noting that these coups were unable to end the tumult that provided the key rationale for authoritarianism. Iran, Mexico, and China fell into extended periods of civil war; the Ottoman Empire faced rebellions and invasions and lost most of its territory; Russia's monarchy stumbled along for another decade before falling in 1917. Thus Portugal's unstable democracy was matched by the other cases' unstable autocracies. Military organizations proved disastrously incapable of reordering society at this time, and their attempts ultimately undermined the military organizations themselves.

9

Democracy and the Great Powers

The military weakness that characterized the democratic revolutions of the early twentieth century, described in the last chapter, points to the broader international context of these events. These revolutions occurred in countries that were desperately concerned about the prospect of foreign domination. In particular, they were concerned about the designs of the Great Powers of the era, especially Great Britain, whose far-flung empire and sea power made it a global presence at this time. Other regional powers worked to exert their influence on their neighbors: the United States in Latin America; Austria-Hungary, Germany, and Russia in the Balkans; Russia in Iran and Central Asia; Japan, Russia, the United States, and the European Powers in East Asia; plus all of the European Powers in Africa. I use the capitalized word *Powers* to refer to governments that frequently resorted to military operations abroad in their competition with one another for territorial control and other privileges and that routinely threatened military operations in diplomatic and commercial negotiations. In the early twentieth century, European Powers had colonized almost all of Africa and Asia, and the United States had occupied parts of Latin America and the Caribbean. The countries that had not been colonized were keenly aware that their turn might be next.

The military advantages of the Powers were considerable. In 1905 the military budget of Great Britain, for example, was more than two-thirds larger than that of China, more than seven times larger than that of the Ottoman Empire, and more than twenty times larger than those of the Iran, Mexico, and Portugal.[1] But military budgets were not the only factor: Russia was badly defeated in war with Japan in 1904, despite having a military budget more than three times larger. The records of the other new democracies were equally discouraging: none of them had won a war in many years, and all had been invaded or lost territory in the nineteenth century.

216

All had foreign military ships stationed at or visiting their ports, and the prospect of additional battles must not have seemed promising.

However, the influence of the Powers did not rest on military advantage alone. It was multiplied through the inferiority complex characterizing those regions that later came to be called the "developing world." Political and military leaders in these regions—as well as the emerging class of intellectuals who are the focus of this book—described their own societies and polities as dysfunctional and incompetent, in comparison with the regions that they called "civilized." Even those who were critical of significant features of European modernity, such as democracy or alleged sexual libertinism, sought to import many of the institutions of European modernity, especially military institutions.

This prism of perceived inferiority was evident in the minute attention paid to the Powers' policies by all of the major political movements in the weaker countries. Newspapers of the period ran constant coverage of European political events, and official debates frequently cited European experiences as evidence for their position. In Iran, for example, Ayatullah Muhammad Tabataba'i told the first sessions of the Iranian parliament that European institutions were the root of all good things: "I'd never seen the constitutional countries myself. But what I'd heard, and those who had seen the constitutional countries told me, the constitution is the cause of the security and flourishing of the country." Similarly, Ayatullah 'Abdullah Bihbihani praised European legislation and urged parliament only to be subtle about its mimicry: "I have a request to make. Never argue that in such and such a country they have done this or that, so let us do likewise! For the common people would not understand, and we would be offended. We now have laws, and we have the Qur'an. I do not mean that you should not mention this; you certainly should. But if you analyse the matter, you will find that what they [the foreigners] have done is based on wisdom and derived from the laws of the *shari'a*."[2]

The rest of this chapter seeks to demonstrate that democracy movements and their opponents scanned the horizon for hints of Great Power support at key moments in the trajectory of their democratic revolutions and often responded to the cues they perceived. This attentiveness gave the Powers considerable causal significance in the rise and fall of democratic revolutions in the early twentieth century. Until recent years, most theories of democratization downplayed such foreign factors. In the late twentieth century, however, a number of scholars have attempted to specify the import of international actors for the emergence and success of democratization. Some of these studies focus on the positive effects of these international factors, others focus on the negative effects. Still others, including the present study, suggest that international factors play both pro- and antidemocratic roles.[3] The focus in this analysis is the alignment of resources between domestic and international forces: the moments when internal pro- or antidemocracy movements managed to secure support from outside of the country, or managed at least to convince their allies and enemies that they had secured this support.

"*Vive la liberté des peuples!* is a strange and startling cry to ring out upon the serene air of ancient Iran," wrote the U.S. ambassador during the democratic revolution of 1906. "Who knows but that it may send an echo all around the world."[4] He and other officials of the Great Powers, by and large, welcomed the new democracies when they were first installed. In some cases, this welcome expressed the optimistic belief that backwards nations were gradually becoming civilized. This was the era of the white man's burden and the heyday of imperialism, one of the justifications for which was the improvement of the so-called backward races. Many Westerners viewed the spreading desire for Western-style constitutions, like the desire for Western-style clothes and other elements of "civilization," as a gratifying confirmation of the West's position as object of imitation. In public, Western leaders could only applaud the implementation of democracy—to do otherwise would have denied the superiority of Western political forms.

A few Western officials went beyond applause. In Iran, British diplomats actively encouraged the democracy movement—"I can't tell you how refreshing it is to hear the Persians [Iranians] talking about their new liberties and the things they are ready to do for their country," one of them wrote a colleague. British diplomats had offered sanctuary on the embassy grounds to thousands of prodemocracy activists even after the British government in London had directed its diplomats to limit such intervention. British *chargé d'affaires* Evelyn Grant Duff was so popular in Tehran as a result of his assistance that the British foreign secretary joked, "I expect every day to hear that Grant Duff has been proclaimed Shah."[5]

Other leaders of the Great Powers welcomed democratization for economic and geopolitical reasons. French government and business circles were jubilant over news of the October Manifesto, according to the Russian ambassador in Paris, because they felt that democratic concessions would help to restore order in Russia, preserving the country's value as an ally and investment opportunity. The British foreign office was pleased that the restoration of the Ottoman constitution might balance the pro-German affinities of the sultan's court with the pro-British affinities of the prodemocracy coalition: "If only this Young Turk party can consolidate itself and introduce a really good administration, they will have been playing our game entirely, but perhaps not the game of other more interested Powers."[6]

At the same time, most Great Power officials were skeptical, even scornful, of the new democracies' chances for survival. The racism of the period was brutal. At its mildest, this attitude manifested itself in concerns about the abruptness of the shift from authoritarian to democratic regimes. For example, the British ambassador to the Ottoman Empire wrote just days after the reinstatement of the constitution in 1908: "Altho' every one is a Young Turk now, (some say including the Sultan) it seems too much to believe that they will, for long, be able to live up to their motto of Liberty, Equality and Fraternity and that the Mahomedan can suddenly drop all his pre-conceived ideas and shake hands with his Christian countrymen as if they were one."[7] Others expressed their doubts in nastier language. To select from innumerable examples:

- U.S. official in Iran: "As a matter of fact, the [Iranian] people are not in a condition to appreciate the benefits of a constitutional form of government, and are much less fit to govern themselves than are the Filipinos."[8]
- U.S. diplomat in China: "The centralized system of government such as existed under the Manchu regimes, Chinese character considered, is the only form of government that will hold the Chinese. The republican form of government is as foreign to the Chinese people and as opposite to their peculiar makeup as earth is from heaven. They are wholly unfitted both by superstitious beliefs and dense ignorance on the one hand, and provincial and sectional hatreds on the other. They are not endowed with the intellect to enjoy the blessings of a free government, the principles of which are wholly unknown to the great majority of the people."[9]
- German ambassador in Mexico: "The cardinal error lies in his [President Madero's] . . . belief that he can rule the Mexican people as one would rule one of the more advanced Germanic nations. This raw people of half-savages without religion, with its small ruling stratum of superficially civilized mestizos can live with no regime other than enlightened despotism."

Kaiser Wilhelm of Germany noted in the margin of this last report: "Right!"[10]

These racist attitudes applied as well to Portugal. We may think of Portugal today, in the early twenty-first century, as a European nation, but its status was highly suspect at the beginning of the twentieth century, geographic position notwithstanding. A British embassy official in Portugal commented in his memoirs that "a nation of southern stock at the social stage of the Portuguese can be governed easily enough by a variety of combinations of political authority and of popular appeal, but a representative Chamber does not in itself contain the minimum of either." British ambassador Arthur Hardinge, who had served in Iran and the Ottoman Empire before coming to Lisbon, described the Portuguese as midway between Iranians and Europeans on the scale of intellectual development: unlike more civilized people, he wrote, the Portuguese tend to be "inaccurate persons—I have erased a harsher word" (the word *liars* is crossed out). At the same time, when compared with Iranians, the Portuguese have "developed a greater appreciation of the merits of strict accuracy," and their behavior is therefore more culpable than that of "my Persian friends, whose mendacities were more naive and childlike." Hardinge characterized the Portuguese as "not everyday Europeans": "I believe that if you found yourself face to face with this inert and corrupt mass you would be the first, now and then, to use the goad." Similarly, the British *chargé d'affaires* favored an "honest despotism" that would "pull this benighted and Godforsaken country out of the evil plight in which it wallows."[11]

Officials of the Great Powers were also derisive of modern-educated intellectuals in the "developing world," who were so closely associated with democracy movements and democratic revolutions. The German ambassador in Istanbul called prodemocracy intellectuals "those people who, filled—perhaps more infected—with Western European notions without deeper knowledge, dream of a 'Reformation' of their fatherland through the introduction of so-called parliamentary institutions after some European pattern." The British consul at Guangdong insulted the foreign-educated leaders of the democratic revolution for their "so-called foreign education" and "the crude notions of practical government and economics which they have brought from abroad."[12]

Great Power elitism often applied not just to the abilities of "backward" peoples but also to women and poor men in the Great Powers—in short, to democracy per se. Universal adult suffrage had not been adopted in any

European country by the early twentieth century, and many government officials considered it to be entirely undesirable. During the 1905 revolution in Russia, for example, Kaiser Wilhelm wrote to Tsar Nicholas complaining about British agitation for "infernal parliaments." Similarly, the Austria-Hungarian ambassador in Russia, Baron Alois von Aehrenthal, felt that democracy was imprudent in Austria-Hungary and ludicrous in less developed nations such as Russia. When the tsar granted the October Manifesto, Aehrenthal concluded, "Evidently [the tsar] has learned nothing and lives totally outside reality." In the Ottoman Empire, "The Ambassador of one great democracy . . . made no attempt to conceal his disgust with this unexpected parliamentarianism. Referring with contemptuous fury to these young revolutionaries, he called them by a term which, picturesque and popular as it may be in barracks, would hardly appeal to the ingenuous reader."[13]

Russian diplomats in Iran, the Ottoman Empire, and China systematically opposed democracy in these countries, as they were appointed by a tsar intent on opposing democracy in his own country. In Iran, a British diplomat noted, "The Russians are engaged in spoiling their own Duma at home and teaching the Shah how to spoil his Mejlis here." Ultimately, as I discuss later in this chapter, the Russians sent thousands of troops into Iran to press their interests and subdue the Iranian parliament. As to the Ottoman Empire, one Russian diplomat emphasized "the extreme ignorance of the great mass of the people, who were devoid of any political or social ideals," and others regretted that Russia was unable to intervene militarily when the opportunity arose. In China as well, the Russians considered military intervention. Russia's activities in these countries demonstrate its role as a semi-peripheral power. Relative to France and Britain, it was a debtor nation and militarily bankrupt. Relative to its Asian neighbors—with the exception of Japan, which had resoundingly defeated Russia in 1904, shocking the world—Russia could issue demands and military threats alongside its Great Power allies, France and Britain, so long as it had these core Powers' support.[14]

These contradictory sentiments—satisfaction at new nations joining the ranks of the "civilized" and suspicion about their ability to manage it— were frequently settled on economic and geopolitical grounds. In the early twentieth century, the Great Powers were engaged in high-stakes economic competition, viewed by all sides as vital for national survival. This competition involved securing world markets for manufactured goods, obtaining concessions for Great Power industries, and negotiating governmental loans. During this period, state officials increasingly identified their nation's foreign economic interests as crucial for national wellbeing. Herbert Feis has collected numerous examples of European states' energetic promotion of business dealings overseas. In Britain just before World War I, for instance, the foreign minister told parliament:

> I regard it as our duty, wherever *bona fide* British capital is forthcoming in any part of the world, and is applying for concessions to which there are no valid political objections, that we should give it the utmost support we can and endeavor to convince the foreign government concerned that it is to its interest as well as to our own to give the concessions for railways and so forth to British firms who carry them out at reasonable prices and in the best possible way.

The French minister told his parliament in 1911 that diplomatic intervention of behalf of French industry

> is a tradition to which we conform in the Ministry of Foreign Affairs. You can see from the statistics that we have obtained valuable results in this respect, especially for our great metallugical industries; it is generally thanks to the intervention of our Minister of Foreign Affairs in accord with the Ministers of Finance and Commerce that we have been able to secure important orders.

A leading German banker described an even more activist stance on the part of the German state:

> The Foreign Office has frequently stimulated the German banks to enter into competition for Italian, Austro-Hungarian, Turkish, Roumanian, Serbian, Chinese, Japanese, and South American loans. Even when the banks are approached from other quarters, the first move is to ask the consent of the Foreign Office for carrying on the negotiations. If the consent is given, then ministers, ambassadors, and consuls frequently support the representatives of the German banks by word and deed.[15]

The relations between the state and capitalists were not always smooth. The British minister's comment about "valid political objections" refers to occasions when the state wished to restrain investment for geopolitical reasons and reminded, cajoled, or threatened the private sector to subordinate its economic interests to national interests; on other occasions, the state sought to encourage investment for similar reasons. The British government ought to remember that "we scrupulously carried out their wishes to our own detriment and did all in our power to further their policy in Persia," a British banker in Tehran commented in 1909, after foregoing a loan to the shah at the request of British officials. Conversely, the government sometimes ceded to capitalists' interests, as in China in 1912, when the British ambassador called in a gunboat to support British opium importers, despite his personal opposition to the opium trade. In general, however, the state and capital shared similar interests.[16]

Where labor held significant political power, as in France and to a lesser extent in Britain after 1905, its representatives felt it necessary to place national interests ahead of class sympathies. This is most starkly evidenced by the about-face of French socialist Georges Clemenceau. Before entering the cabinet in early 1906, the journalist/politician editorialized frequently against the Russian monarchy. According to a tsarist Russian diplomat in Paris:

> [Clemenceau,] as soon as he entered into his duties as Minister of the Interior, paid a visit to the Russian ambassador to tell him that, as a member of the Government of the [French] Republic, he could not but consider Russia and its [monarchical] government with sympathy and confidence. And such is the political formula of all the heads of the radical-socialist "bloc" who come to power.[17]

Clemenceau and the French government acted on their sympathy for and confidence in the tsar with an extra-parliamentary loan, as I will detail later.

Similarly, in Great Britain, the growing enfranchisement of labor shifted the political landscape to the left, as the 1906 elections put the Labour Party in parliament and the Liberal Party in power, succeeding the conservative Unionists. The Liberals were less likely to go to war to protect Britain's interests, as had the Unionists in the Boer War, but they were nonetheless active in the protection of these interests, even when doing so meant the demise of new democracies. When Britain supported the Iranian coup d'état of July 1908, one British diplomat expressed his disillusionment. "I am seriously contemplating the possibility of throwing off my profession," wrote William Smart. "When a government turns aside from the straight path of equity and plunges into the crooked byway of pure politics, playing with the happiness of other nations, then it is time for honest men to disinterest themselves of the game and leave it to the professional politicians.[18]

Complicating the new democracies' foreign relations was their simultaneous effort to gain autonomy in economic and political matters. Officials of the Great Powers were sensitive to any such steps, viewing them
as threats to their own countries' privileges. A British diplomat in China,
for example, worried that "the idea of 'China for the Chinese' would
seem to be gaining ground. Students returning from Japan, America and
England all share the ardent desire to control the settlements and concessions in China and abolish extra-territoriality. They complain of the
treatment of Chinese by foreigners at Shanghai and other treaty ports,
and wish to keep in their own control the finances, railways, and other
enterprises of China." More sympathetically, a British official in Istanbul
noted several weeks after the Ottoman democratic revolution, "If all goes
well with the Constitution, and Turkey really regenerates herself on European lines, we [dragomans] are bound to disappear sooner or later, as
no civilised European Government would tolerate a class of foreign officials whose business it was to meddle directly in all their public offices."[19]

Overlaid on Great Power economic competition was conflict over military and political spheres of influence. For a decade before World War I,
the Powers considered combat among themselves all but inevitable, as a
series of international conflicts repeatedly brought Europe to the brink of
war. In 1905, it was the Moroccan Crisis, ultimately resolved at the Algeciras Conference in 1906. In 1908, it was the Bosnian Crisis, settled in
early 1909 by a German ultimatum to Russia. Then followed the Agadir
Crisis (1911), the Tripoli Crisis (1911), the First Balkan War (1912), and
the Second Balkan War (1913). Beyond the details loomed a keen sense
of general crisis. As the German ambassador in Paris noted in a quiet
conversation with a French official in 1905, "Our quarrel over Morocco
is only a detail and the Algeciras conference will soon have settled it. I'm
not worried on that score any longer. But there's a much greater issue
between our two countries, an issue which may result in many sorrows;
you know what it is."[20] The issue was competition over the Great
Powers' relative "place" in the world. Germany experienced tremendous
industrial growth at the end of the nineteenth century, but it came too
late to participate fully in the imperial conquests of the time; nonetheless,
Germany wished to gain a greater share of the spoils. Allied with Austria-
Hungary and more loosely with Italy, Germany pressed repeatedly for a
renegotiation of the global order. Britain and France led the defense of
the status quo and were allied to varying degrees with Russia, the United
States, and Japan—though these countries' governments had consid-

erable disagreements amongst themselves. In this international climate, the Great Powers were vitally concerned with domestic political developments in every country of the world. They felt they could not afford to remain neutral.

In the new democracies, the side the Great Powers would choose to ally themselves with—pro- or antidemocratic—was not a foregone conclusion. In almost every country, both sides sought Great Power support. And the Great Powers sided, on different occasions, with either side. But Great Power perceptions of global economic conflict generated a bias toward antidemocracy coalitions, with their emphasis on establishing order and the potential for military alliance. Of the six cases, the prodemocracy coalitions were able to overcome this bias only in Portugal, where the prodemocracy movement was better positioned to serve the economic and geopolitical interests of the country's primary Great Power patron.

Russia

France's financial pressure helped force Tsar Nicholas of Russia to proclaim limited democratic rights in the October Manifesto of 1905. For months, the tsar's government had been trying to secure a massive loan in France that would cover the expenses of the previous year's war with Japan. French banks were not eager to increase their exposure in Russia, and the French government was reluctant to pressure them to do so, for reasons unrelated to the Russian democracy movement. The effect of this reluctance was to limit the tsar's options in dealing with the democratic revolutionary movement. Even after the October Manifesto, the Russian monarchy continued to pursue the French loan. "I was convinced," Prime Minister Sergei Witte wrote in his memoirs, "that for Russia to survive the revolutionary crisis and for the Romanov dynasty to remain in power it was necessary quickly to bring back the troops that had been in Manchuria and to borrow enough money to tide us over several years."[21]

Unfortunately for the monarchists, parliament now had oversight of the budget, including loans. The tsarist government hurried to conclude a loan before parliament met for the first time, because, as Witte said, "it would be the greatest calamity to hand the question of a loan over to the *Duma* [parliament]."[22] Witte explained in terms that express his hostility to principles of democratic governance:

If the [tsarist] government asked the parliamentary chambers immediately for funds, as soon as they opened, it would put itself in an eminently uncomfortable position, given that it will find itself first of all in front of an undisciplined and politically uneducated mob. Under these conditions, it is highly important for us to conclude the liquidation loan with minimal delay, that is, in the course of the coming six weeks. This is vital.[23]

The Moroccan Crisis presented convenient leverage for the tsarist government. France had agreed to German demands for a multilateral conference on the fate of northwest Africa, to be held at the Spanish city of Algeciras. To maintain its sphere of influence in Morocco, however, France needed allies at the conference. The Russian finance minister, in Paris trying to negotiate a loan, wrote to Prime Minister Witte: "The success of my difficult mission would be noticeably favored if I were authorized to declare confidentially to Rouvier [the French prime minister] that, on the question of Morocco, France can count on the moral support of Russia."[24] The deal was struck.

Russian democrats were outraged. A member of the leading oppositional party in Russia wrote to the French prime minister:

No one doubts in Russia that it [the tsar's government] would like to procure the material means to govern as it pleases and suppress the national representation from the outset, after which the Duma will have already played its role, having served to attract money from Europe by making people believe falsely in the imminent coming to power of a regular regime.[25]

Russians in Paris as well as French socialists published open letters, lobbied the French government, and plastered the city with one hundred thousand handbills decrying the loan. Clemenceau, the French minister of the interior—and until recently a proponent of the Russian democracy movement—promised to paste posters over the handbills. French Minister of Finance Raymond Poincaré worried whether the tsar's government had the authority to obtain a loan without the approval of parliament. The Russian government commissioned a response by a respected Russian legal scholar, Feodor Martens, who indicated that the loan was legitimate and that parliament could not repudiate it. Russian constitutional law was not the primary concern, apparently, for the French government. When the Algeciras Conference had been settled to France's satisfaction,

Poincaré authorized the loan without waiting for Martens's legal opinion.[26]

The French government's geopolitical considerations concerning its competition with Germany even outweighed narrow economic calculations over the profitability of the Russian loan. French officials had been worrying for several years about the advisability of continued lending to the tsar. In early January 1905, the foreign bond office in the French Ministry of Finance recommended that the Russians be notified that "the limit of appeals to French credit has almost been reached, if it hasn't been already." According to one report, French bankers approved the 1906 Russian loan only "to oblige the prime minister." "To induce them to consent, Monsieur Rouvier did not appeal to their pockets, but dwelt on the political aspect, urging that it was France's duty to help the Russian Government [that is, the tsar] to restore order."[27]

Witte called this "the loan that saved Russia's financial strength," equating the nation with its monarchy. Prodemocracy activists in Russia agreed with Witte's assessment of the importance of the loan, if not with his political beliefs. Boycotts of French goods were organized in various parts of Russia. Maxim Gorky, the famous socialist author, expressed his anger at the French: "O great France, once the guide of civilization, do you realize the vileness of your act? Your money-grubbing hand has tried to stop a whole country from taking the road to freedom and culture."[28]

With its financial footing somewhat more secure, the tsar's government ignored parliament from the start and blocked virtually all legislation. On July 22, 1906, the tsar dissolved parliament and appointed P. A. Stolypin as prime minister with a mandate to crack down on dissidence. The following year, the Second Duma was also dissolved, and the election law was modified to ensure a more pliant legislature.[29] French financing had helped to bring about democratic reforms, and to undermine them.

Iran

In the summer of 1906, British diplomats in Tehran allowed Iranian protestors to stage a massive sit-in on the grounds of the embassy legation, where they were safe from government reprisals. As described in previous chapters, the protestors set up tents and hosted as many as fourteen thousand merchants, artisans, and intellectuals. From this base of operations, they negotiated the terms of the democratic revolution. Within a week of the shah's agreement to these terms, the sit-in dispersed. The British foreign minister was none too happy about his representatives' role in the affair. The *chargé d'affaires* in Tehran "should be told very plainly not to interfere between the Persian Government and the refugees and to confine his action to trying to persuade the latter to leave the Legation." British diplomats nonetheless persisted in harboring the democracy movement, "with almost insane enthusiasm," according to the unsympathetic manager of the British bank in Tehran.[30]

Two years later, in June 1908, Muhammad 'Ali Shah confronted parliament and its supporters in increasingly violent terms, accusing radicals of threatening the Iranian monarchy, "which the forefathers of my forefathers earned at the cost of their lives and with the strength of their swords." On June 23 the shah's soldiers surrounded and bombed the parliament building, dispersed the representatives, declared martial law, and banned all meetings. At the same time, the shah asked the tsar of Russia "to accept Persia under [his] patronage" and said he considered Iran to be in "the same relations to Russia as the emir of Bukhara"—that is to say, a semicolonial relationship. The tsar wrote back noncommittally. Nevertheless, foreign sponsorship of the crackdown was hardly subtle. The Russian monarchy viewed Iranian democracy as a challenge to the Russian position of dominance in northern Iran and an affront to the principle of absolute monarchical rule, which the tsar had only recently restored in Russia. The Iranian Cossack brigade, whose Russian officers reported both to the shah and to the Russian government, planned the coup with the full knowledge and approval of the Russian government.[31]

Britain acquiesced in the coup in order to maintain the recent Anglo-Russian agreement directed against Germany. The Anglo-Russian agreement had divided Iran into spheres of influence, so as to minimize friction in the region between the two allies. During the events leading to the coup, Iranian supporters of democracy telegraphed the British embassy in Tehran, appealing for assistance. British *chargé d'affaires* Charles M. Marling made no response, except to say that "it was not fitting or right that she [Britain] should interfere in the internal affairs of a free and independent people." Moreover, the British allowed themselves to believe that no plot was afoot. The day before the coup, Marling and the Russian ambassador met with Muhammad 'Ali Shah. The Russian ambassador disingenuously advised the shah to respect the parliament, and the shah disingenuously responded that he had "no hostile feelings" toward parliament. Marling appears to have accepted these statements at face value.[32]

After the coup, the sacrifice of Iranian democracy for the sake of the Russian alliance struck some of the British diplomats in Iran as odious (see the comments of William Smart, quoted earlier in this chapter). Even in London the Foreign Office resented the role it felt obliged to play. The foreign minister, one of his assistants wrote, "has constantly, during the past year, had to appear in the House of Commons as the advocate of the Russian Government [in Iranian affairs]. We have had to suppress the truth and resort to subterfuge at times to meet hostile public opinion."[33] In 1908, the British government was willing to undermine both Iranian democracy and British law in order to maintain the Russian alliance against Germany.

The prodemocracy forces survived the 1908 coup d'état and drove the shah from the country in 1909. Russia sided strongly with the shah and sought, in the words of the Russian foreign minister, to "make use of all the means in our power for the reconciliation of the shah and the [Iranian] nation." Russian troops crossed the border into Iran and advanced almost to Tehran, prepared to suppress the prodemocracy forces at the shah's request. Despite his offer of semicolonial status the previous year, the shah was apparently unwilling to request such humiliating assistance. Rather, his prime minister asked Russian forces to leave the country; if they did so, he wrote, the prodemocracy movement would subside: "The Qazvin revolutionaries would undoubtedly disperse and the Bakhtiyaris would certainly return to their homelands." In addition, the British refused to allow Russian troops to advance to Tehran in support of the shah—not so much because they opposed the shah as out of concern that Russia would permanently occupy and annex the capital, to the detriment of British interests in the region. The British foreign minister informed his Russian counterpart that he would call off the 1907 Anglo-Russian agreement if Russian troops entered Tehran in aid of the shah. In this way, Great Power competition temporarily aided the prodemocracy forces in Iran.[34]

Two years later, the ex-shah invaded Iran to try to regain his throne. To placate its British ally, the Russian government officially maintained strict neutrality in what it called an internal Iranian matter, but Russian officials throughout the north of Iran made no pretense of neutrality. As soon as Muhammad 'Ali had landed on Iran's Caspian coast, the Russian consul in nearby Astarabad told city officials—who were considering supporting the former monarch—"whatever cooperation and assistance you would like, the consulate will cooperate in this matter." In Tabriz, the

Russian consul forcibly freed a general accused of treason and refused to allow the elected government's army to maintain defenses inside the city. In Tehran, the consul generated an international crisis over the Iranian government's expropriation of one of Muhammad 'Ali's supporters, claiming that Russian interests were being damaged—a claim so flimsy that even the Russian ambassador in Tehran objected to the consul's actions. The Russian foreign ministry backed the consul and rebuked the ambassador. This final incident led Russia to send troops once again toward Tehran. Again, the British opposed the Russian occupation of the Iranian capital and prevented it by threatening to cancel the Anglo-Russian Agreement of 1907. Lacking the open assistance of Russian troops, Muhammad 'Ali's campaign failed to capture Tehran. He negotiated a sizable pension from the Iranian government and eventually retreated back into exile in Russia.[35]

Throughout this period, the Iranian parliament recognized the danger it was in and cast about for international assistance. The U.S. House of Representatives literally laughed at a telegram it received. The German government ignored numerous appeals from the Iranian government and cut a deal with Russia in August 1911 that recognized the Russian sphere of influence in northern Iran, in exchange for Russian recognition of Germany's railway plans in the Ottoman Empire. Morgan Shuster, the U.S. citizen who served as treasurer of Iran in 1911, warned Britain in an open letter that democracy was in the process of being undermined. Iranian prodemocracy activists in Europe wrote to their British friends, who revived the "Persian Committee" campaign to pressure the British foreign ministry into action. The British government was unmoved; the foreign minister refused even to explain his opposition.[36]

While the monarchists and parliament failed to mobilize much international support, a third group was far more successful. This was the Bakhtiyari tribal leadership, which appears to have joined the prodemocracy coalition in 1909 more for tribal power and glory than for democratic principles.[37] Bakhtiyari leaders assumed the prime ministry and other cabinet positions when the constitution was restored in 1909. By the end of 1911, however, their strengthened position—in control of both the state and an independent military force—served to undermine the new democracy. Russia piled up demands that the Iranian parliament refused to accept; the Bakhtiyari-led cabinet, caught between Russian demands and Iranian nationalism, chose to dismiss parliament itself, rather than risk having the Russians do so.

As was typical for the period, the cabinet sounded out the reaction of the Great Powers before acting. On November 21, 1911, the prime minister of Iran, Bakhtiyari tribal leader Samsam al-Saltanah, visited the Russian and British ambassadors to seek their opinion of his planned coup d'état. Both foreign ministries telegraphed their assent: "We certainly cannot encourage [a] coup d'état," wrote the British foreign minister, "but [we] have no more intention of interfering with a Bakhtiari coup d'état than with previous coups d'état in Persia." (The usual nod toward noninterference in the internal affairs of a sovereign state was particularly insincere in this case, because the British government was simultaneously engaged in preventing a coup d'état by the former shah, Muhammad 'Ali.) The Russian foreign ministry was more honest, hewing to the British line of nonencouragement but instructing the ambassador "not to repulse the Bakhtiaris and not to impel them to give up energetic actions against . . . the parliament desirable from our point of view."[38]

In a ceremony at the royal palace on December 20, 1911, the regent dissolved parliament, leaving Samsam al-Saltanah in effective control of the country, and called new elections. Elections were postponed, again with the approval of Britain and Russia, until 1914, by which time the Great Powers' military maneuvers in World War I had reduced the Iranian government to virtual colonial status. Thus the Iranian democratic revolution was undermined twice in three years: first by monarchists, then by its own tribal supporters, and both times with the active intervention of Russia and the clear assent of Britain.

Ottoman Empire

The Ottoman democratic revolution was launched in part by fears that the Great Powers were planning to carve up parts of the Ottoman Empire. News that King Edward of Britain and Tsar Nicholas of Russia were meeting in Reval (now Tallinn, the capital of Estonia) in June 1908 accelerated the Ottoman plans for revolution, prompted by concern that the Great Powers would iron out their differences more quickly than anticipated. The Reval meeting did not actually propose the dismemberment the Ottoman lands, but dismemberment ensued nonetheless. Within three months of democratization, the Ottoman Empire lost Bosnia-Herzegovina to Austria-Hungary, Crete to Greece, and Bulgaria to independence. Ottoman efforts to counter these losses embroiled the Ottoman government in Great Power politics.[39]

The possibility of further territorial losses provided the backdrop for the pro- and antidemocracy forces' scramble for foreign support in April 1909, when a mutiny erupted in Istanbul demanding Islamic government. The sultan responded by replacing the Society for Union and Progress's prime minister with a liberal from the opposition Freedom Party, perhaps as a prelude to re-exerting his own authority. The Freedom Party tried to secure a British or French loan that might imply foreign protection, with no success. In London, the Ottoman ambassador sought to convince the British Foreign Office that the new government was not a reactionary tool of the sultan.[40] In Istanbul, liberal parliamentary leader Ismail Kemal Bey approached the British ambassador and inquired about British intervention:

> He [the ambassador] did not entirely reject my suggestion that the British Government should intervene, but asked me who would propose such interference. When I replied that I would ask the Sultan to do so, he said such a demand from His Majesty would no longer carry any weight. In that case I said I would see to it that the request came from the Grand Vizier [the Prime Minister], and the Ambassador's reply was that in that case he would see what could be done. When I saw the Grand Vizier, Tewfik Pasha, on the matter the same evening, he was too upset by the situation to be able to take any resolution.[41]

The British ambassador was sympathetic to the liberal cause and took several small steps in support of the new liberal government, but sympathy only went so far. The Foreign Office in London recommended making no "great sacrifices" for the Ottomans and warned against acting "for the sake of Turkish friendship, which is ephemeral."[42]

British reticence to support the liberals was due to Great Power competition for influence in the Ottoman Empire. This was articulated some weeks after the Society's triumph, when London instructed its ambassador in Istanbul to "adopt a sympathetic attitude towards the Young Turks and be neither critical nor even impartial towards them. . . . [I]f they do not meet with sympathy and cannot lean on us they will soon learn to lean on some other Power, and the splendid position which we had at Constantinople a few months ago will be lost."[43]

The Society for Union and Progress was somewhat more successful in mobilizing foreign support. To put down the mutiny in Istanbul, the Society's military leaders virtually evacuated the troops from a large section of the Ottoman Empire's Balkan border, leaving the empire open to attack.

The empire's Balkan neighbors moved to take advantage of the opening. Bulgaria mobilized its army and threatened to invade in three days. Serbia hurried to make an alliance with Bulgaria to divvy up the spoils of the Ottoman Empire. To cover its unprotected borders, the Society urged the Great Powers to restrain their dependent states in the Balkans from invading while it marched on Istanbul.[44] The Powers were willing to oblige both because of their sympathy for the Society and their fear of a free-for-all in the Balkans should the Ottoman Empire disintegrate. Just a month earlier, the Powers had narrowly averted such a catastrophe over Austria's annexation of Bosnia. The Powers were hesitant to see the Balkan balance disturbed. Germany and Austria were hesitant because they had just arranged the balance to their advantage, and Russia and its allies, because they felt unprepared to stand up to Germany militarily.

Germany and Russia instructed their client states not to invade the unprotected Ottoman regions. The German ambassador in Sofia, Bulgaria, stated that "Germany would never tolerate an intervention of the Balkan states, which would reopen the whole of the Eastern question in the most dangerous manner." Russia encouraged Serbia to "maintain her self-control," and the Serbian foreign minister "expressed full readiness to follow . . . instructions."[45] As a result of this pressure from the Great Powers, the Balkan nations refrained from taking advantage as the Ottoman Third Army shuttled thousands of troops to Istanbul on commandeered trains. The military and its allies in the Society for Union and Progress invaded Istanbul on April 24 and quickly consolidated power, forcing parliament to approve martial law, limits on the freedom of the press, the replacement of the sultan by his brother, and other legislation.

Mexico

The Mexican democratic revolution of 1910–1911 was announced and planned in the United States. Few U.S. officials were pleased by the prospect of unrest and regime change in Mexico, but the U.S. government maintained a policy of "neutrality" that allowed the rebels to raise money, purchase weapons, recruit supporters, and publish newspapers on U.S. soil, despite requests by the autocratic government in Mexico to curtail oppositional activity in the United States. Eventually, the U.S. government ordered Madero's arrest for violation of neutrality laws, and Madero fled back to Mexico. The following month, U.S. President William Howard Taft also sent troops for maneuvers in Texas as a show of force in support of Porfirio Díaz, the dictatorial president of Mexico, in hopes that Díaz could cut a deal with leading oppositionists and maintain power. This deal did not materialize—indeed, the troop maneuvers were misinterpreted by many in Mexico as a sign of U.S. mistrust of Díaz's prospects—and the Mexican democracy movement marched south from the U.S. border toward Mexico City. Within months, Díaz had fled Mexico.[46]

Two years later, during the attempted coup d'état of February 1913, the U.S. government lent more decisive support to antidemocracy forces. Henry Lane Wilson, the U.S. ambassador in Mexico City, had long been skeptical of the feasibility of democracy in Mexico. By early 1912, his opposition to the democratic regime was so pronounced that even the U.S. State Department had begun to discount his negative reports. By early 1913, the State Department feared "an intention on the part of the Ambassador to force this government's hands in its dealings with the Mexican situation as a whole."[47]

Wilson does not appear to have had specific foreknowledge of Félix Díaz's February 1913 plot. Yet when the rebellion launched itself disastrously on February 9, Wilson moved quickly to assist it. His first line of action was to persuade General Victoriano Huerta, Madero's recently appointed chief of staff, to support the Díaz rebellion (see Chapter 8). Wilson, along with the German ambassador, encouraged the two leaders to agree to dismiss the democratically elected Madero. After ten days of negotiation and carnage, Huerta took President Madero captive. Wilson summoned Huerta and Díaz immediately to the U.S. embassy. "[A]fter enormous difficulties," Wilson reported to Washington, D.C., "I got them to agree to work in common." According to aides of Díaz, Wilson threatened to call in the U.S. Marines if either man balked. A pact was signed in the U.S. embassy whereby Huerta would assume the provisional presidency, while Díaz would assume the regular presidency through election later in the year. When the pact was signed, Wilson was thrilled. He imagined that he had restored the Díaz family to power, thereby ensuring U.S. interests in Mexico. According to a diplomatic witness, Wilson shouted at the embassy gate, "Long live Félix Díaz, idol of the foreigners!"[48]

Wilson's second line of action was to organize meetings of selected ambassadors in Mexico City to pressure President Francisco Madero to resign. "[The] American ambassador [is] working openly for Díaz," the German ambassador reported. "[He] told Madero in my presence he was doing so because Díaz is pro-American." Madero was outraged that foreign diplomats should intervene so blatantly in Mexican politics. He telegraphed an angry note to President Taft, complaining about Ambassador Wilson's behavior. Taft had already been warned of Wilson's hostility toward Mexican democracy. He was furious to learn that Wilson had threatened U.S. military intervention, because Wilson's requests for authority to do so had twice been rejected, on the grounds that U.S. interests in Mexico would suffer reprisals.[49]

On the other hand, the U.S. government judged its economic interests to be against Madero. For more than a year, U.S. authorities had been concerned that rising anti-American sentiment in Mexico was handicapping U.S. businesses in the country, particularly in regard to preferential treatment for Europeans. Authoritarian elements in Mexico apparently encouraged this sentiment to prove the new democracy's inability to govern, and to spur the United States to action. In September 1912, the U.S. government issued a stern warning about the mistreatment of U.S. citizens in Mexico, while Ambassador Wilson continued to stress the theme that there is "no possibility of our people receiving worse treatment than they are receiving at present." During the February 1913 coup, the Díaz forces presented themselves as better able to impose order on Mexico, for the protection and benefit of U.S. interests in the country.[50]

Taft sided with his ambassador against the Mexican president. "Your Excellency was somewhat misinformed," Taft wrote to Madero. To Ambassador Wilson, Taft wrote: "[I]t is left to you to deal with this whole matter of keeping Mexican opinion, both official and unofficial, in a salutary equilibrium between a dangerous and exaggerated apprehension [of U.S. intervention] and a proper degree of wholesome fear." Indeed, Taft viewed Madero's ouster with a certain sense of relief. With only two weeks remaining in his presidency, Taft wrote to his brother, "Mexico City did not promise a very pleasant problem, but fortunately with their treachery and throat-cutting, a light has broken in on the situation."[51]

On February 19, Huerta was named provisional president. Madero was killed several days later, allegedly while attempting to escape captivity. The promised elections never occurred, as Huerta consolidated his power over the following months and disbanded parliament in October 1913. Huerta was himself ousted the following year in an armed rebellion supported by the new U.S. administration. Some historians have taken the Díaz-Huerta coup as a momentary setback in an ongoing Mexican Revolution, and it is true that revolutionary and democratic movements continued through the 1910s. However, the fall of Madero signified the end of democratic rule in Mexico. The country got a new constitution in 1917, but successive governments saw little need to abide by it. With a few exceptions,[52] democratic elections would have to wait for decades.

China

In the fall of 1911, facing a widening rebellion, the Qing monarchy in China appealed to the Great Powers for an emergency loan. This appeal was refused. Many Great Power officials considered the Chinese people to be unfit for democratic self-government, as quoted above, but others "are entirely in sympathy with the rebels," according to an American in Beijing. The democracy movement, for its part, tried to calm Great Power concerns about democratization by promising to honor the monarchy's past foreign debt—but not any new debt incurred by the monarchy during the revolution.[53]

A year later, the European Powers were quicker to aid the antidemocracy movement in China. In early 1913, as parliament sought to establish control over the executive branch through oversight of Yuan Shikai's budget and cabinet, Yuan stepped up negotiations with various European banking consortiums for a significant loan without parliamentary approval, contrary to the provisional constitution. The European banks were hesitant to sign a loan outside of parliament, because this would mean clear involvement in an internal political struggle. But this was precisely why European diplomats wished to make such a loan: they considered Yuan a better guarantor of order, and therefore of European commercial interests in China. "[I]n making the loan we are virtually backing him against the rest of the field," wrote the British ambassador; the loan thereby ensures Britain's "freedom for economic enterprise." The German ambassador concurred: "The political importance of the loan's conclusion in giving Yuan Shikai moral support is as much appreciated in authoritative circles here as its financial importance in helping the government out of urgent financial misery."[54]

Parliament objected strenuously. Opposition leader Sun Yatsen warned European bankers that provinces controlled by the opposition would repudiate the loan. The evening that the loan was concluded, parliamentary leaders searched Beijing for the location of the signing ceremony. They found it, managed to gain entrance, and made a small speech on the unconstitutionality of the loan—all in vain. The next day, parliamentary leaders visited the French ambassador and asked him to block the loan, but he remained unmoved. Parliament officially declared the loan unconstitutional, and in the weeks after the signing, the opposition con tinued to lobby against the implementation of the loan. "I earnestly desire to preserve peace throughout the Republic," Sun Yatsen wrote in an open letter to the Great Powers, "but my efforts will be rendered ineffective if financiers will supply the Peking Government with money that would, and probably will, be used in waging war against the people."[55]

In late April 1913, Yuan met with the British ambassador to ask for the Great Powers' support in case of a civil war. The ambassador's answer must have been encouraging—"there could be no doubt," he said, "that the foreign representatives in Peking almost unanimously favored [Yuan's] retention in office." A week later, Yuan flatly rejected parliament's refusal to ratify the loan and said he "cannot tolerate the actions of these troublemakers," meaning members of parliament. At the same time, Yuan's prime minister announced that money from the Reorganization Loan would go toward a strengthened national police force, which would assist in destroying parliament later in the year. Troop movements began to threaten the provinces most hostile to Yuan's government, a step that British officials attributed directly to Yuan's improved financial position. In July 1913, the conflict came to a head, and civil war—called the Second Revolution in Chinese historiography—broke out. British diplomats encouraged Yuan to crush the rebellion without mercy and "make an example of the leaders. . . . He [Yuan] will never be able to consolidate his position unless he exercises the mail fist régime."[56] "I venture to submit," wrote the ranking British diplomat in Beijing,

> that it is desirable to consider what action may eventually become necessary in order to maintain over as wide an area as possible free trade and the open door, and what additional safeguards may be required in order to ensure the maintenance and welfare of the financial, commercial and political interests which Great Britain has at stake both in northern and southern China.[57]

Formal British action was not needed, as it turned out, though several British officials acted unofficially to support Yuan's military campaign.[58]

In this case, the Great Powers seem not to have been working in competition with one another, but rather in a coordinated front. This front had developed in the previous decade due to common interests in controlling China's foreign loans. As a result, China was informally divided into spheres of "special interest"—regions where each Power held a near-monopoly on major investment opportunities. Russia held this position in the north of

China, Germany in the northeast, Britain in the southeast, and France in the south. The French, who appear to have been dissatisfied with this arrangement, were rebuked by the British several times, including in one stern message in 1909 that a "return to the system of active international competition for every loan which the Chinese may desire to issue would be most unfortunate." The Chinese revolution threw this system of regional "special interests" into question, as the French and Japanese angled for improved positions.[59]

Sun Yatsen and other opposition leaders, rejected by Britain and the other Great Powers, played on the ambitions of the regional Powers. Various provincial leaders appealed to the United States, to no avail. Seeking Japanese support, Sun and his associates made several startling offers: China would cede the province of Manchuria to Japan; China would adopt Japanese currency; and even, when Sun's internal support had been destroyed by Yuan's forces, that China would be Japan's India! The British Foreign Office urged Japan not to get involved in the Chinese civil war, but the Japanese government had already decided that cooperation with Britain, its ally, was more important than making friends in China. With no international assistance, the opposition was crushed within a month. In late 1913, Yuan dismissed parliament altogether.[60]

Portugal

The Portuguese Republic is a deviant case among the democratic revolutions of 1905–1912 in that it survived, albeit haltingly, through World War I, only succumbing to coup d'état in 1926. The contrast between Portugal and the other cases shows how prodemocracy forces may, in some cases, manipulate Great Power rivalries to their advantage.

As in the other cases in this book, the Great Powers did not come to the rescue of the autocracy during the democratic revolution. British diplomats refused to summon warships to protect the king of Portugal, despite the "fixed idea at the [Portuguese] Court that if a revolutionary movement were attempted we [British] should intervene." Yet British and other foreign officials did not greet the new democracy warmly. Even the government of France, which supported republicanism ideologically, refused to recognize the new government before its ally Britain did. "Often, we [French] must forget that we are [also] a republic," a French diplomat told his Portuguese counterpart. British officials sympathized with the monarchists and delayed recognition of the republic for months.[61]

However, British sympathy for the monarchists never translated into concrete assistance. A half-year after his ouster, for instance, King Manuel spoke in London with Winston Churchill, the first lord of the admiralty:

> He began our talk by saying—Mr Ch[urchill]! I am not a leader of the democracy. I am a King and it is as a King I must manage my affairs. . . . He told me much about his views of Portugal & his hopes of returning soon by a *coup d'état*. I had to be extremely guarded so as not to raise false hopes, or encourage adventures in wh[ich] I sh[oul]d not share the risks.[62]

Hardinge, the British ambassador in Portugal, was similarly inclined:

> Personally I quite agree with the opinion expressed to me by Winston Churchill that we made a mistake in permitting the dethronement of the house of Braganza and the establishment in a country with which we have such peculiarly close relations of the present detestable régime, but having once taken the line that the misgovernment of Portugal is no concern of ours, it seems futile to be rude to its authors.[63]

Hardinge's dispatches to the British Foreign Office routinely contained phrases such as "if I had the honour of being one of King Manuel's advisers," but his advice was to play a waiting game, because "the republic seems to me more likely to perish by the internal quarrels of the factions which divide it than by an armed Royalist attack from without."[64]

The argument that carried the day was that of Sir Eyre Crowe, British assistant undersecretary of state, who held that the Portuguese Republic should not be driven into Germany's arms through British hostility.

> Our general relations with Portugal are likely to pass through a critical stage before long, and in view of possible complications with Germany which might easily arise in this connection, it is of some importance that we should preserve the good-will of the Portuguese government, who are in many ways showing a genuine desire both to cultivate the friendliest relations with us, and to meet our wishes and follow our advice in matters of good administration. The Portuguese alliance has a positive value for us. If we alienate Portuguese opinion, the Republic may throw herself into Germany's arms, which would create a situation calculated to hamper us in more ways than one.[65]

In early 1915, when General Joaquim Pimenta de Castro was appointed prime minister and moved to consolidate power, British officials sounded supportive. The undersecretary of state commented, "I trust Portugal has at last been endowed with a moderate and sensible government." Pimenta de Castro, however, was not sympathetic to Britain. Staunchly pro-German, he would not deign to seek British support. Yet Portugal was so firmly under British influence that Germany could do nothing to help. Even had Germany been able to help, it might not have wanted to. Germany coveted Portugal's overseas territories, and the two countries were engaged in a series of skirmishes in southern Africa. A strong government in Portugal, the German ambassador stated, "could make the cession of the colonies still more difficult."[66]

The prodemocracy forces, meanwhile, did not hesitate to seek British support. They promised to throw Portuguese military resources into the war against Germany, and prodemocracy leaders who had questioned the suffocating nature of the British alliance a few years earlier now hid their doubts.[67] Even capitalists who had been hostile to the new democracy for several years saw their interests as lying with Britain and therefore rallied temporarily to the democratic side.[68] Britain and Germany stood by as the democrats toppled Pimenta de Castro in a coup d'état of their own on May 14, 1915. The British ambassador noted days later:

> From the point of view of our interests the return to power of the Democratic party is on the whole advantageous[,] for ever since the beginning of the war [World War I] they have advocated the closest cooperation with Great Britain and the unconditional compliance with all requests from His Majesty's Government. . . . I have no reason to believe that General Pimenta de Castro's Government[,] if less enthusiastic, was in any way unfavourably disposed towards us, but their internal policy and their appointments of various officials with monarchist and sometimes Germano-phil sentiments were undoubtedly calculated to render such assistance as we might call on Portugal to give us, less certain and efficacious, especially in the colonies.[69]

The democratic revolutions of the early twentieth century were made and unmade by domestic forces. However, these forces worked actively to gain foreign support, which was crucial to the decision-making of national leaders in the new democracies. In most of the six democratic revolutions of the period, one or more Great Powers were perceived to side with the democracy movement. In Iran and Mexico, the Powers provided safe havens for the democratic opposition, which organized the final stages of their movement in the British legation grounds in Tehran and the U.S. border states. In Russia, China, and Portugal, the Powers refused the autocracy's last-minute requests for financial or military assistance.

Within a year or two after democratization, however, the Great Powers shifted their support to antidemocratic movements. In Russia and China, the Powers concluded significant loans that bypassed parliamentary oversight and allowed the suppression of the new democracy. In Iran, the Powers assented to two coup plots, one in 1908 and one 1911; in Mexico, the Powers forced two coup plotters to cooperate. In the Ottoman Empire, the Powers provided diplomatic cover for the march on Istanbul. Only in Portugal did the Powers stand by while coup plots failed.

The reasons for the Great Powers' switch lay in a combination of economic and ideological self-interest. On the ideological side, the Great Powers sought confirmation of their bias against the ability of "backward" peoples, to use a phrase that was common in that period, to govern themselves democratically. Strikes and demonstrations, unruly electoral campaigns, and violations of the rule of law—incidents that are characteristic of all new democracies, including the Great Powers'—were interpreted as proof of the countries' unpreparedness for democracy. On the economic side, the Great Powers considered their self-interest to be better served by autocratic regimes in the "developing" world. Signs of economic assertiveness in the new democracies—threats to cancel the Powers' monopolistic positions and privileges—were interpreted as indicators of a hostile economic environment.

Antidemocratic movements played on these Great Power biases. They promised security for foreign property, investment opportunities for foreign capital, and insulation from the demands of popular political participation. Among the first acts of the postdemocratic regimes was to promise the protection of foreigners and their property. This had been one of the first acts of the democracy movements as they came to power, as well.[70]

The importance of the Great Powers may be judged by the one new democracy that survived a major coup d'état in the early twentieth century. This was also the one case where the antidemocracy movement was unable or unwilling to attract Great Power support. In Portugal, General Joaquim Pimenta de Castro dismissed parliament and municipal councils in early 1915 and seemed set to establish an authoritarian regime. Unlike coup plotters in other new democracies of the period, however, he did not consult the Great Powers and seek their blessing and assistance. The

Power that could have helped him most effectively was Britain, given the occasional visits of British warships to Portuguese ports. Yet Pimenta de Castro's sympathies lay with Germany, which was both unable to provide much assistance and unlikely to do so, given Germany's conflict with Portugal over colonies in southern Africa. British officials decided their country's interest lay with the prodemocracy movement, and this alignment of international and domestic resources allowed the democracy movement to oust Pimenta de Castro and restore parliamentary democracy in May 1915.

10

Aftermath and Implications

In the aftermath of the democratic revolutions of the early twentieth century, intellectuals underwent a dramatic demobilization. The monarchs or generals who had undermined emerging democratic institutions also suppressed the intellectuals associated with those institutions. The intellectuals' newspapers were closed, their parties were driven from parliament, their state sinecures were purged, and many were driven into exile. The new authoritarians adopted parts of the intellectuals' hegemonic ideology—mass education and public health reform, for example—but without the former hegemons, who were incorporated selectively and only in subordinate roles. The intellectuals plunged into despair, and themes of hopeless bleakness emerged in the literatures of all of these countries in the wake of failed democracy. With their class mobilization in ruins, intellectuals began to criticize the collective identity of "intellectual."

The disillusionment of the intellectuals occurred in Europe and North America, as well as in the new democracies. Even before World War I, signs of fatigue were evident in the intellectuals' various political movements: Progressivism in the United States, Fabianism and New Liberalism in Britain, Solidarism and Interventionism in the Leftist Bloc in France. French intellectual Anatole France wrote in 1908 that "indifference and lassitude have overtaken the intellectuals who had thrown themselves so generously into the dangerous tumult of the [Dreyfus] Affair." Intellectuals in France "cherished magnificent illusions, and they are now experiencing cruel disappointments. That is why one must pardon their pusillanimity. Dreamers and thinkers founded upon the Dreyfus Affair the hope for a moral transformation, from which would emerge a marvelous renaissance of society. It was too much optimism. Their dream was beautiful; their awakening is painful." Young intellectuals in Europe began to turn in larger numbers from liberal positivism to idealist, spiritualist, and organicist

243

avant gardes, a trend that can be traced in France in the growing influence of the antipositivist philosopher Henri Bergson.[1]

After World War I, the intellectuals' disillusionment was even greater. Roberto Michels, writing on "Intellectuals" for the *Encyclopedia of the Social Sciences,* characterized his subjects as "largely demoralized" and undergoing "an intense spiritual self-criticism." Theodor Adorno recalled the early 1920s as a period of "anti-intellectual intellectuals" seeking authenticity through religion. Édouard Berth, who just before World War I critiqued intellectuals as "the harshest, the most nefarious, the most ruinous of aristocracies," prefaced his second edition in 1926 with a pitiful image of "intellectual and moral prostration" beneath the plutocratic captains of industry. V. I. Lenin, who expressed high hopes before the war that bourgeois intellectuals would turn revolutionary and enlighten the working class, now called them "not [the nation's] brains but its shit." In a best-selling book of the late 1920s, Julien Benda excoriated his fellow intellectuals for their "treason" against the ideals of the Dreyfusard movement. A handful of activists, arguing that "the class of intellectuals" had become "disinherited," tried to establish an international organization to promote their identity and represent their interests. "Intellectuals of all countries, unite!" wrote one of their spokespeople. Few intellectuals responded to the call.[2]

The decline of the intellectuals' collective identity during this period corresponded with their reluctance to pursue prodemocracy movements. In place of collective mobilization for democracy, intellectuals scattered, "looking for new gods," in the phrase of sociologist Teodor Shanin. If some intellectuals served in interwar governments, they no longer ruled in their own name, but rather in the name of the socialist working class, the nationalist bourgeoisie, or the fascist fatherland. This diversity of intellectual affiliations was one of the founding insights of the sociology of intellectuals in the 1920s, as expressed by Karl Mannheim: "Unattached intellectuals are to be found in the course of history in all camps." Mannheim's observation was truer in the 1920s than it would have been two decades earlier, when self-identifying intellectuals sided overwhelmingly with positivist democracy movements. But in the wake of the destruction of these movements, intellectuals abandoned their collective identity and scattered across the ideological spectrum.[3]

When the new democracies were dismantled, the authorities punished democracy's intellectual proponents. In Russia, hundreds were arrested and exiled; in several provinces, so many teachers were fired that schools had to be closed. The press was muzzled; bookstores in Warsaw and Moscow, for instance, were forced to remove all pictures relating to parliament. The professional unions that had formed the backbone of the prodemocracy movement were banned. The landed gentry, which had sponsored the growth of the intellectual class through *zemstvo* professional activities—statistical research, medical services, educational systems, and so on, whose practitioners were known as the "Third Element"—fired its activist intellectual employees. In some provinces, *zemstvo* spending was cut by as much as 50 percent.[4]

In other countries, where the new autocrats had fewer intellectuals to fire than in Russia, the main intellectual occupation to suffer was writing. In one failed democracy after another, autocrats shut down the press. After the 1908 coup that ended Iran's first democratic interlude, "the mushroom newspapers of the past two years have been practically suppressed," the U.S. ambassador reported with satisfaction. After the Iranian coup of 1911, independent newspapers were replaced by an official gazette that "display[ed] moderation and a true sense of Persia's real interests," in the opinion of the British ambassador. In the Ottoman Empire, too, military authorities quickly shut down large segments of the press. Within days of occupying Istanbul, they arrested the editors of two opposition newspapers. A restrictive new press law was pushed through parliament two months later, and by the following year, the number of periodicals had dropped from more than 300 to 130. In China, Yuan Shikai's government suppressed more than 70 newspapers—only 2 of 10 papers survived in Wuhan, for example—and issued new press regulations similar to the former monarchy's. In Mexico, Huerta's government threatened or bribed opposition newspapers.[5]

Beyond the loss of jobs, politically prominent intellectuals often had to flee for their lives. In Tabriz, a stronghold of the Iranian democratic revolution, antidemocratic forces and their Russian allies tortured and killed many of the intellectuals who remained in the city in the weeks after the coup of December 1911.[6] In Mexico, President Francisco I. Madero, Vice-President José María Pino Suárez, Chihuahua Governor Abraham González, and other officials were assassinated just after the 1913 coup, intimidating many prodemocracy intellectuals into acceptance of the new autocracy, or exile. In China, Sun Yatsen and many other activist intellectuals fled to Japan.

Intellectuals in the former democracies sank into despair. In the days after the dismissal of the second parliament, Russian intellectuals declared themselves "thunderstruck." One lamented the "fruitless struggle of ideas against reality"; one described "anger, often expressed indiscriminately, a lack of trust, disconnectedness"; another rejected earlier democratic ideals as "idolatry of the brutes." An activist in southern Russia complained that "the intellectuals sleep and wish to do nothing." A leading poet likened the situation to a nightmare in which he expected to be trampled by the hooves of a horse. According to a song from one student strike, "The epoch of barracks has again commenced, and the nightmare looms before us." Student leaders considered the activism of the following years to be a farce.[7]

Similar themes of doom were prominent in the literature of the postdemocratic period in each country. An opera in Iran brought its audience to tears with the lament, "These ruins of a cemetery are not our Iran. These ruins are not Iran, where is Iran?" Ashraf, an Iranian poet, wrote: "It is unclear whether you are dead or alive. Oh people, are you a eunuch or a slave? Is this a life that you are living? Death is better than this life. Why are you alive? Your ancestors weep at your condition, since you are the cause of laughter among nations." "Behold Iran, once exalted to heaven, become a ruin haunted by owls," wrote Pur-i Davud, another Iranian poet. An Ottoman author opined several months after the coup of April 1909: "My friend, sometimes the environment is like a bad omen, like a graveyard. What intelligence, what wisdom, what talent can survive there?" "The nation is suffering, the nation is dying!" wrote Tevfik Fikret, an Ottoman poet who had only four years earlier greeted the democratic revolution with another famous poem: "If only you knew what feelings, what desires, what joy rises up inside of me now, what ecstasy-inducing melodies rise up!" In Mexico, one of many exiled intellectuals wrote, "We no longer belong to Mexico. . . . It is the elders, by age and by blood, who rule and command there now." In Portugal, after the coup of 1926, the journal *School Federation* warned, "Black days await us. Days of hunger threaten us. Days of slavery await us."[8]

A Chinese writer suggested the metaphor of suffocation in a windowless iron house. "Now if you raise a shout to awake a few of the light sleepers, making these unfortunate few suffer the agony of irrevocable death, do you really think you are doing them a good turn?" Another Chinese author, who had worked in the Ministry of Education during the democratic period, offered the parable of a young intellectual who has a breakdown when he learns that his neighbors are cannibals: "A nation with four thousand years of man-eating history, and to think I've been living in it for so long and yet only now do I see what is really going on. . . . There may still be children who have never eaten man. Save them. . . . Save the children." Afterwards, he recovers and seeks a government position. Some young intellectuals in China committed suicide out of despair for their country. "[T]heir purposes misunderstood, their offers of service rejected, their ideals slipping away from them in a squalid and sordid environment, is it any wonder that they become filled with misgiving as to their future, and silently mutter resentment against the established order of things?"[9]

In this atmosphere of defeat, intellectuals asked themselves what had gone wrong: why had they failed in their attempt to lead their country to a new stage of historical development? Some answered with an angry denunciation of intellectuals and their supposed mission. There had always been some educated people opposed to the idea of the intellectual class and its association with democracy movements, but these numbers grew after the suppression of democracy. In Russia, this shift was exemplified by a controversial collection of essays entitled *Landmarks,* published in 1909. These essays formed part of a growing antipositivist movement, which existed in the late nineteenth century—one famous philosopher attacked "the class to which I have the misfortune of belonging" in a thesis entitled, "The Crisis in Western Philosophy: Against the Positivists"[10]—but only gained widespread support after the debacle of 1906–1907. The essays in *Landmarks* continued this tradition of antipositivism and intellectual self-hatred, as in the contribution by P. B. Struve:

> How lightly and boldly the intelligentsia [in 1905] pushed the exhausted, suffering masses onto the path of political and social revolution! This was not simply a political error or tactical lapse; it was a moral error. . . . Political foolishness and ineptitude compounded this fundamental moral error. If the intelligentsia possessed the form of religiosity without its content, its "positivism," on the contrary, was totally formless. Here were "positive" ideas that were in no way authentically positive, "scientific" ideas that lacked any knowledge of life and people, "empiricism" without experience, and "rationalism" without wisdom or even common sense.[11]

The significance of this critique lay in the author's own participation in the events that he denounced as morally and politically misguided. Struve, as editor of the journal *Liberation,* was one of the major players of the prodemocracy movement; though he was already critical of positivism in the years before 1905, he cooperated fully with prodemocracy positivists

such as Pavel N. Miliukov. In 1909, Struve's angry words rejected cooperation with the class-movement of the intellectuals. Indeed, Struve's
greatest hope for the future of Russia, he wrote, was that the intellectual
class might "cease to exist as a special cultural category." The essays in
Landmarks sparked tremendous debates among educated Russians.[12]

Miliukov and other liberal intellectuals responded with their own volume
on *Intellectuals in Russia,* defending their class movement and its
prodemocracy stance.[13] Perhaps more typical of the intellectuals' mood at
the time, however, was the resignation exemplified by Aleksandr A. Blok's
essay "The People and the Intelligentsia," first delivered as a lecture in late
1908, a year after the closing of the second duma. Blok, 28 years old at the
time and already a leading poet, had been caught up briefly in the excite-
ment of the democracy movement in 1905. Three years later, Blok's portrait of the intellectual class emphasizes its pathos. There are, he suggests,

> two realities: the people and the intelligentsia; a hundred and fifty
> million on the one hand, and a few hundred thousand on the other,
> unable to understand each other in the most fundamental things. . . .
> Once in a while, on the narrow line where the people and the intelli-
> gentsia communicate, great men and important events arise. These
> men and events always demonstrate, as it were, that the antagonism is
> deep and of long standing, that the problem of reconciliation is not
> an abstract but a practical problem, and that is must be solved in
> some special way, which we have not found as yet. The men who
> emerge from the masses and reveal the depths of the people's soul are
> immediately antipathetic to us, antipathetic because somehow in-
> comprehensible in their innermost being.[14]

Blok did not envision the disintegration of the intellectual class, as
Struve did, but self-criticism in its angry and resigned tropes encouraged
the process of disintegration. Similarly, in the Ottoman Empire, leading
prodemocracy intellectuals criticized their class from within. Yusuf
Akçura, writing about the recent democratic revolution in Portugal, ridiculed "the Turkish intellectual class" for believing "that societies are
moved by ideas, even by morality. In newspapers filled with troubling economic facts, it is common to find editorials written with a historical idealism worthy of 18-year-old girls." Unmanliness was a common trope of
intellectual insult at the time. From outside of the intellectual class came
even more vehement denunciations. During the democratic interlude itself,
Derviş Vahdeti, a seminary-trained scholar, criticized modern-educated in-

tellectuals as "cucumber people" (see Chapter 4). He was hanged after the mutiny of April 1909, but similar critiques became even more influential in the following years. Perhaps the most widely noted of these critiques was a poem by Mehmed Akif, "In the Pulpit of the Süleymaniye Mosque" (1912), that mocked modern "thinkers" and condemned the predominance of modern education over traditional training: "The teaching of knowledge imposed by force. That too is despotism!"[15]

In Iran, intellectuals did not so much abandon the identity of intellectuals as reshape it. They dropped the inclusive term *danishmandan* (knowledgeable ones), which they had used to combine modern-educated and seminary scholars, and replaced it with the more exclusively modern-oriented terms *munavvaran al-fikr* and later *raushanfikran*, both of which referred to enlightened thought (see Chapter 3). In China, a decade after the democratic revolution and a failed successor movement, one writer called himself "a superfluous man . . . castrated by advanced education." In the mid-1920s, educated members of the Chinese Communist Party developed the slogan, "Down with the intellectual class."[16]

In Mexico, novelist Mariano Azuela—once a prodemocracy activist—had a character denounce "literatoids" as "a herd of pen-wielding helots, swollen with venality; eunuchs forever moaning about peace, incapable of giving one drop of blood for their brothers, for their country, or for their own species; dolts who spend their whole lives burning incense to whoever fills their bellies, and who are quite pleased for their names to appear as so many more ciphers among the list of despicable, corrupt slaves, hardly worthy even to sing to their masters' concubines." That was in 1911, when the new democracy was still in power, and the character referred to in this way redeemed himself by dying for the cause of liberty. In a 1914 novella, after the coup, Azuela's verdict on intellectuals was if anything even more severe. As one of his characters asserted, without refutation:

The most ignominious shame that the revolution of 1910 has revealed is an abject intelligentsia [*intelectualidad*] that drags its belly through the mud, eternally licking the boots of anyone who occupies a higher position. We know that there are two classes of serfs in Mexico, the proletarians and the intellectuals [*intelectuales*]; but while the proletarians spill their blood in torrents to escape being serfs, the intellectuals soak the press with their filthy ruffian spittle. The ignorant poor make us shout in admiration, while the learned make us raise our handkerchiefs to our noses.[17]

Mexican antipositivists retained the category of intellectuals in a shrunken form that excluded prodemocracy activists, identifying themselves as *nosotros* (we). "The triumph of anti-intellectualism in Mexico is almost complete," wrote Adolfo Reyes, one of the leading figures in this movement, one year after the coup of 1913.[18]

Despite this sense of discouragement, prodemocracy movements revived briefly in each of the former democracies in the 1910s:

- Russian students engaged in a series of protests in 1910–1912, and intellectuals led the transitional democratic government in 1917 that abolished the monarchy. This second democratic interlude was ended by the Bolshevik Revolution several months later.
- An isolated instance of democratic competition emerged an Ottoman by-election in 1911, which was won by an opposition candidate, and the authoritarian Society for Union and Progress was temporarily ousted from the cabinet in 1912–1913, though this and other changes in government continued to be determined by force rather than democratic procedures.
- The Mexican prodemocracy movement defeated General Huerta in 1914 and held a constitutional convention in 1916–1917, producing a new democratic legal framework for the country. Elections started up again in the fall of 1916, and were held regularly for the following decades, though they were generally manipulated by the ruling party until the late twentieth century.
- Partial parliamentary elections were held in Iran in 1914, 1917–1921, and 1923–1924, but parliament's effectiveness was limited by British, Russian, and Iranian military intervention. General Riza Khan's coronation ultimately subjugated residual democratic procedures for the next decades.
- Beginning in 1918–1919, Chinese students organized themselves in intellectual and political circles hailing modernity, science, and democracy. This May Fourth Movement—named for several days of demonstrations beginning on May 4, 1919—lost its prodemocracy character by the time it became an official ideology in succeeding decades.

None of the autocrats who undermined the new democracies remained in power after World War I. Tsar Nicholas was deposed and murdered in 1917, and his prime minister, P. A. Stolypin, was assassinated in 1911. Muhammad 'Ali Shah was forced into exile twice, in 1909 and 1911, and the Bakhtiyari tribal leaders who led the Iranian coup of 1911 were out of power by 1913, though Samsam al-Saltanah returned to the premiership briefly in 1918. Mahmud Şevket Pasha was assassinated in 1913, and most of the leaders of the Society for Union and Progress were imprisoned or exiled under British occupation in 1918. Victoriano Huerta was swept from power in 1914. Yuan Shikai died in office in 1916.

The coup-makers passed from the scene, but the ideology of authoritarianism outlived the autocrats who had brought it to power. Like democratic thought in the decade and a half before World War I, antidemocratic ideologies spread globally in the decade and a half after World War I. Democratic movements continued in many places—for example, Claudia Wasserman notes significant parallels between Madero's movement in Mexico before World War I, Argentinian democracy movements before and after the war, and Brazilian movements of the 1920s. However, these were outnumbered by coups and revolutions that brought dictators of various sorts to power in many countries, including Mexico, Argentina, and Brazil. Dictators of this period included V. I. Lenin in Russia (1917), Riza Khan in Iran (1921), Benito Mussolini in Italy (1922), Alexander Tsankov in Bulgaria (1923), Miguel Primo de Rivera in Spain (1923), Mustafa Kemal in Turkey (1923), Ahmed Zogu in Albania (1925), Antanas Smetana in Lithuania (1926), Józef Piłsudski in Poland (1926), António Óscar Carmona in Portugal (1926), Chiang Kai-shek in China (1928), Plutarco Elías Calles in Mexico (1928), Petar Zivkovic in Yugoslavia (1929), José Félix Uriburu in Argentina (1932), Getúlio Vargas in Brazil (1932), Gyula Gömbös in Hungary (1932), and Adolf Hitler in Germany (1933). Other prominent antidemocratic movements emerged during the same period, such as the Rashtriya Swayemsevak Sangh, or National Volunteer Union, in India (1925) and the Muslim Brotherhood in Egypt (1928); and on the left, antidemocratic movements emerged in almost every country in the world.[19]

In the former democracies, significant numbers of prominent intellectuals joined these antidemocratic movements, forging ideologies of national or racial or religious authenticity to support right-wing dictators, and ideologies of revolutionary transformation to support left-wing dictators. In Iran, for example, young intellectuals turned from democratic ideologies to authoritarian ones. The author of the era's most extensive Islamic defense of democracy tried to have copies of his treatise destroyed. One group of intellectuals, former leaders of the democracy movement in exile in Berlin, published an influential newspaper that glorified Iran's (and Germany's) martial heritage. The writer 'Ishqi wrote in 1921, "When revolutionaries realize none of their institutions work according to previous plans and ideals, they certainly become disillusioned, thinking, 'It would have been better not to have made a revolution!' and this way of thinking makes them reactionaries." Others drifted toward communism and founded a socialist republic in northern Iran soon after the Bolshevik Revolution in Russia. In the Ottoman Empire, the Society for Union and Progress and its successors in the Turkish Republic dropped much of the earlier discourse about democracy, which had always been balanced with its other dominant theme, strong central government. Leaders of the Chinese democracy movement reverted to their earlier antidemocratic ideologies. Already in 1913, members of parliament were starting to reject competitive party politics and debate various schemes of enlightened despotism, and Sun Yatsen reverted from support for democratic institutions to his earlier insistence on the need for authoritarian government—not with Yuan Shikai in charge, of course, but rather himself.[20]

Prominent prodemocracy intellectuals later considered their democratic goals as unrealistic panaceas. A Portuguese prodemocracy military officer lamented that "the idea of the Republic slowly assumed the category of myth. Only by the fact of its proclamation, it would put an end to the stagnation of the national economy, the disorder of the public finances, the shameful contrasts between the misery of almost everybody and the senseless opulence of the few, the popular ignorance, in sum the impotence of politics ruled by men without faith and without hope." Similarly, Ottoman Turkish activist Hüsayin Cahid Yalçın later suggested that prodemocracy activists

> believed that in order to rescue the Ottoman Empire it would be sufficient merely to proclaim the constitution. . . . They were convinced that if freedom were given to all, to Turks and all the elements in brotherly fashion, and that if the parliament were convened and allowed to act, then all the complaints and evils would be abolished. The Turkish fatherland would live in comfort and prosperity; it would grow strong and be delivered from its foreign foes—all of this within their lifetimes.[21]

The new dictatorships made use of the intellectuals who were willing to shill for authoritarianism. Parts of the intellectuals' program were adopted, but not with them in charge. Primary education, for example, was expanded under Stolypin, Huerta, Yuan, and António Salazar, the fascist dictator in Portugal. Stolypin's vision of Russia's development, like the intellectuals', placed central emphasis on social reforms—but, crucially, his vision differed from theirs in placing such projects under the strict control of the autocratic state. "All the whining about the government's arbitrariness, about imaginary infringement upon academic autonomy and so on will not compel the government to deviate from establishing order [and] legality," Stolypin wrote angrily in response to criticism about his handling of the universities.[22]

By the 1920s, intellectuals in many countries had accommodated themselves to the need for a "revolutionary dictator," in the words of an Iranian journal, who would "break the influence of the traditional authorities" and forcibly modernize the "99 percent of the population [that] is under the electoral sway of the reactionary mullas." "In my view what China needs is an able and idealistic dictator," wrote a Chinese political scientist in 1934. "There are among us some people, including myself, who have undergone long periods of liberal education. These people naturally find undemocratic practices extremely distasteful. But if we want to make China into a strong modern nation, I fear there is no alternative except to throw aside our democratic conviction." This regime type was later labeled alliteratively as a "modernizing military" or "developmental dictatorship." The state-building projects of the democratic revolutions continued after the democratic elements had been suppressed. The democratic revolutions of the early twentieth century did not last long, but they represented a path not taken in a series of countries that suffered through authoritarian rule for the following half-century or more.[23]

The late twentieth century gave the intellectuals a second chance to lead democratic revolutions, but by then they had faded away. Just as the Russian Revolution of 1905 initiated a wave of democratizations, the Soviet reforms of the late 1980s started another wave at the end of the century. Democracy movements rose up in the Soviet client states of Eastern Europe, where communist regimes imploded in a "carnival of revolution," in Padraic Kenney's evocative phrase. The Soviet Union itself followed suit in 1991, dissolving into its constituent republics, some of which established democratic government. In China, a prodemocracy sit-in at Tiananmen Square was suppressed after seven weeks of global attention in 1989. In Africa, national conferences assembled in ten countries to chart democratic transitions, sometimes successfully. Dictator Omar Bongo of Gabon commented derisively on the "wind from the east"—that is, from the communist bloc—"that is shaking the coconut trees." In total, several dozen countries underwent democratization of varying degrees between 1989 and 1996.[24]

The run of democratic revolutions in the early twentieth century provided a dress rehearsal for these later democratizations in Russia, China, Mexico, and Iran, where late-twentieth-century prodemocracy activists summoned the imagery and legacy of their countries' earlier democratic revolutions. A few hundred diehard members of the Russian Constitutional Democrat Party waved their green flag with a white swan during the 1991 demonstrations that brought down the Soviet Union. Students at Tiananmen Square invoked the ideals of the May Fourth Movement of 1919, the last gasp of the democratic movement of 1911, and sold T-shirts with the May Fourth slogan, "Democracy and Science." The Iranian reform movement of the late 1990s frequently harkened back to the Constitutional Revolution. Opposition parties in Mexico claimed inspiration from Francisco Madero, the leader of the 1910–1911 revolution, by way of contrast with the single-party domination that became entrenched in subsequent decades.[25]

Beyond these echoes, democratization in the first and last decades of the twentieth centuries often took comparable forms. In both periods, mass movements—combined with Great Power encouragement—toppled long-standing dictatorships with startling speed. In both periods, the institutions of democracy were quickly installed and endowed with massive expectations, which they rarely met. In both periods, democracy was nearly a global norm, as a means to socioeconomic progress and as an end it itself. In the late twentieth century, this norm was visible both in leftist critiques of authoritarianism, as revolutionary socialism retreated to social democracy, and in free market ideologies such as the "Washington Consensus," which linked together political and economic liberalization.[26] As in the early twentieth century, when a second-tier Power, the monarchy in Russia, rejected the global democratic norm and sought to undermine it throughout Asia, the Communist Party in the People's Republic of China played a similar role in the late twentieth century, financing autocratic pariahs and hindering international efforts to promote democracy and human rights.

Not only were the waves of democratic revolution parallel in significant ways, but educated people also participated prominently in both. In the late twentieth century, university groups formed the organizational basis for the democracy movement in China, Côte d'Ivoire, Nigeria, and elsewhere.

Educated professionals organized the Democratic Russia movement, the New Forum and other prodemocracy groups in East Germany, as well as the antidictatorship referendum in Chile. In Communist Eastern Europe, especially, technocrats were a prime constituency for oppositional identities. The number of educated adults in each nondemocracy in 1988 was strongly correlated with the likelihood of that country undergoing democratization in the subsequent years.[27]

However, this was not the same class that had mobilized around the banner of the "intellectuals" in the early twentieth century. In the late twentieth century, educated people neither rallied to this identity nor attracted others to it. There was no worldwide spread of a term comparable in its resonance to the Dreyfusard *intellectuels*. Instead, prodemocracy activists seem to have adopted labels that hid their class origin, such as "civil society," "popular," "democratic," or "national." As in the independence movements of the middle decades of the twentieth century, educated people merged their own collective identity into that of the people they claimed to represent. Each country's national distinctiveness was combined with membership in a global system of citizens and consumers. In the Soviet Union, for example, prodemocracy activists wanted their country to be "normal" again—by which they meant that its government and society would look more like Western Europe, including not just free elections but also free markets for popular music and blue jeans. This identification of global fashion with global political ideology was not new. In 1912, for example, a Chinese newspaper commented,

> Now that the Republic has been newly established, everything is in imitation of Europe and the West. The reverence with which most young people regard Western products is very profound. The pigtail has been done away with, Western clothes have become fashionable, and there are none among the so-called enlightened girl-students who do not love Western products, to the extent that almost everything they wear from head to foot is a Western product.[28]

But just as intellectuals' class-formation project was largely abandoned in the West by the late twentieth century, self-identification as intellectuals ceased to be fashionable in democracy movements elsewhere as well. The intellectual class-in-itself was more numerous than ever, thanks to state-led educational expansion, but the class-for-itself had faded away.

The case of Iran provides a useful counterexample. Iran was one of the few countries in the late twentieth century where intellectuals continued to identify themselves as such. The seminarians who had ruled the Islamic republic since 1979 mistrusted nonclerical scholars and purged many of them from the country's universities in the early 1980s. Despite this treatment, or perhaps in part because of it, the intellectual (*raushanfikr*) remained a potent identity in Iran. In publications and professional organizations, self-proclaimed intellectuals emphasized their leadership role in society, their right to interpret religion autonomously from the seminarians, and, increasingly in the 1990s, their demand for democracy. The intellectual identity proved its popularity in 1997 when reformist politician Muhammad Khatami, himself a seminarian, associated himself with the intellectuals and won more than two-thirds of the vote for president. Numerous intellectuals also won in the parliamentary elections of 1998. The democracy movement soon unraveled, however, when Khatami and his intellectual supporters broke with the student activists who had helped to organize his campaign and opposed their calls for direct action to accelerate the pace of democratization. After several years of tepid reform, Khatami and most of his allies were removed from office, amid anxious debates among intellectuals over their failure to capitalize on the political opportunity. The salience of the intellectual class identity in Iran survived repeated failures at democratization.

Elsewhere, in the absence of a self-identified intellectual class, other classes took the lead in the democratic revolutions of the late twentieth century. Labor movements led the Solidarity prodemocracy movement in Poland—in conjunction with Polish intellectuals—and also in South Africa, Southern Europe, and various Latin American democracy movements. The bourgeoisie also played a prominent role in democratization in numerous countries.[29] Women's rights activists, environmentalists, ethnic autonomy movements, leftist military officers, and other movements were important in ways that they had not been in the democratic revolutions of the early twentieth century. No consistent global pattern appears to have emerged in this profusion of collective actors, by contrast with the singular global significance of intellectual class mobilization in the democratic revolutions of the early twentieth century, though perhaps a pattern will emerge from more detailed studies of the late twentieth century.

But if the intellectuals did not reprise their role in the late twentieth century, another crucial set of actors did: the Great Powers. At both ends of the twentieth century, Great Power rivalries were central to the making and unmaking of democratic revolutions. In the early twentieth century, as we saw in Chapter 9, pro- and antidemocratic movements placed a disproportionate emphasis on the support of the Powers, and the fate of the democratic revolutions hinged largely on the alignment of domestic and foreign resources. In the late twentieth century, as well, democracy movements frequently looked to the Powers for encouragement and diplomatic support. In Central Europe, activists appealed to Western colleagues through the framework of the Helsinki human rights process. In China, students in Tiananmen Square symbolized their appeal for U.S. support by erecting a large Goddess of Democracy statue, similar to the Statue of Liberty in New York. In many instances, though not in the case of the Tiananmen Square protests, significant Great Power support was forthcoming. In the former French colonies in Africa, for example, autocratic leaders were bluntly advised by the French president in June 1990 to democratize or lose their budget subsidies and military aid.

As in the early twentieth century, however, the Great Powers' ideological sympathy for democracy did not always translate into consistent support. If they deemed it necessary, the Powers would also abandon new democracies in deference to geopolitical rivalry. In the late twentieth century, rivalry centered on the United States, which ruled the seas just as Great Britain had earlier in the century. Jeffrey Garten, one of the architects of U.S. trade policy in the 1990s, called this rivalry "a cold peace" and predicted that competition among the United States, Europe, and Japan for market share in the rest of the world would dominate the post–Cold War era. With international economic *competitiveness* a buzzword in the political circles of North America and Western Europe,[30] Great Powers sometimes put aside their democratic ideals when they considered their economic interests to be in jeopardy, as the U.S. government did with the democratically elected President Jean-Bertrand Aristide in Haiti in 1991. The Great Powers rarely dismantled new democracies through armed intervention; as in the early twentieth century, the Powers got their way by supporting domestic antidemocratic movements, tipping the scale in subtle ways such as providing covert assistance and diplomatic cover. The Haitian coup of 1991, for example, was led by a salaried informant of the U.S. Central Intelligence Agency; the French and U.S. ambassadors saved Aristide's life, but they did not act to preserve his government. (Three years later, the U.S. military put Aristide back in power; in his second term as president, the U.S. ambassador again helped to save his life and remove him from power.)

The cunning of the Great Powers was on display in the democratic revolutions of the early and late twentieth century—cunning not just in the sense of cleverness, but also in the grander sense of alignment with the "cunning of history," G. W. F. Hegel's phrase for the inevitable path that mortals follow without necessarily meaning to. Throughout the twentieth century, the Great Powers were obsessed with getting on the right side of history. Each of them claimed to represent the future of humankind, which justified their machinations beyond the terms of self-interest. The Great Powers nurtured elaborate ideological systems, from elementary school civics lessons to scholarly treatises such as this one, that reflected and promoted the public values of the state. This apparatus became ever more professionalized over the course of the twentieth century, generating specialized industries dedicated to the alignment of Great Power causes with the course of global history. By the end of the twentieth century, squadrons of economists, resource specialists, and technical experts of all sorts were dispatched to the capitals of the world along with military advisers and "intelligence" operatives to make history happen the way it was supposed to. The cunning of history was no longer left to chance; like every other aspect of human life, it was subjected to scientific scrutiny and professional manipulation. Global democracy movements had their own specialized corps of Great Power expertise, a field called "democracy promotion" that thrived during the democratic revolutions of the late twentieth century.

These industries marked a rise in reflexivity. Like all modern professions, they were supposed to learn from their mistakes and cast aside old assumptions in light of the latest findings. They did not always live up to this noble self-image, but new careers were continually created by acknowledging old errors and offering innovative solutions. Debates over these issues were not confined to the specialists. At the end of the twentieth century, they were also the subject of increased public discussion on talk radio and weblogs, in addition to and sometimes in place of the older print and broadcast media. Whether the topic was Great Power involvement in tsunami warning systems or Great Power involvement in democratization, citizens were called upon to be familiar with past successes and failures and to have opinions about current policy and future lines of action.

Around the world, democracy movements also became much more reflexive about relations with the Great Powers over the course of the twentieth century. Democracy movements before World War I were basically amateurs when it came to foreign affairs. Pavel Miliukov, for example, was in the United States on a lecture tour when the prodemocracy movement began to take off in Russia in early 1905; rather than rush home or lobby foreign governments, he spent several months writing a book on the Russian crisis for American readers, then stopped off in Paris to arrange a French translation.[31] In the late twentieth century, by contrast, democracy movements had a century of experience to draw on. They had specialists who were savvy enough to fax press releases to the global media, politicians who were familiar enough about Great Power politics to appeal to various factions in Washington or London or Paris, and symbolism that played on global themes and concerns.

This trend of increased reflexivity countered the trend of intellectuals' self-effacement over the twentieth century. Intellectuals became more public about their tactics and more private about their class position: Even as they announced their Great Power strategies, they subsumed their class position in rhetoric about national unity. In the early twentieth century, prodemocracy intellectuals were clear about their identity as intellectuals but sometimes hid their alliances with the Great Powers. In the late twentieth century, prodemocracy activists were clear about their alliances with the Great Powers but hid—or lost—their identity as intellectuals.

This distinction makes it easier to study the democratic revolutions of the early twentieth century than the democratic revolutions of the late twentieth century. For the earlier period, we simply take the democracy movements at their word. Their own public statements at the time stand as evidence of their class identity and democratic positivist aspirations, while their relations with the Great Powers are recorded in diplomatic publications and archives. For the later period, the public statements paint a less coherent picture, and the archival material is not yet available for research. Prodemocracy groups that were more open about their class identity in the late twentieth century—business associations and trade unions, for example—thus receive somewhat more attention than intellectuals.

Our subjects' change in self-reporting affects not only researchers' ease of study, but also researchers' mode of analysis. When our analysis does not coincide with the self-understandings of the people we study, we need two explanations instead of one. The first explanation gives the substance: what we think is really going on. The second is an additional burden: why readers should accept our analysis instead of our subjects' analysis. We may accuse our subjects of trying to mislead us, or call them deluded, or claim access to information about our subjects that they did not have—in all of these strategies, we have to argue that our subjects were acting in ways that they themselves were not aware of. Certainly this is sometimes the case. But it may be less likely to be the case when our subjects make history and break with previous routines.[32]

One such break was the wave of democratic revolutions in the early twentieth century. The intellectuals who made these revolutions were highly aware of the historic shift they were engaged in and did not doubt their ability to break with the past, despite the obstacles. As a leading figure in the Chinese democracy movement said, "Opportunity invariably arises from being created and never from being awaited." An anonymous leaflet in Iran pointed out that no monarch can repress a "mass uprising" if it is widespread enough: "Would he kill everyone at once? He cannot!"[33] Intellectuals may have overestimated their historic destiny, given the rapidity with which their star ultimately fell. But while it lasted, their confidence mattered. It generated solidarity and motivation, and it succeeded in drawing intellectuals into prodemocracy activism. As a result, at that time, countries with more intellectuals were more likely than others to experience prodemocracy activism and political transitions. But this causal effect worked only as long as their confidence lasted, and then it stopped working.

The same is the case for the effect of the working class, the bourgeoisie, the middle class, "soft-liner" authoritarians, or any social group that may be considered the prime mover of democratization. These groups act collectively when they perceive themselves as a group, and when they believe that this group identity holds the key to the future of their country. When they lose this collective self-confidence, their causal importance ceases—collective identities may come and go with startling speed, regardless of whether underlying class characteristics remain stable. Identities are ultimately fads, even the most long-lasting of them, because they are based on individuals' attempts to identify peers and fit in with patterns that seem to be popular. When an identity seems to be losing popularity, all but the most stubborn stalwarts abandon it. This is not to trivialize the efforts of prodemocracy activists by suggesting all they need is more confidence. Rather, I propose that confidence is simultaneously the cause and effect of collective action.

Institutions of all sorts operate like this. They pattern social behavior as long as people consider them unavoidable, and when people sense that an institution is losing popularity, they abandon it. In this way, democracy movements, like everything else in society, enact explanation. That is, they act upon the identities, institutions, and expectations that scholars later come to call causal explanations. In an earlier study of the Iranian Revolution, I argued that some events are such dramatic breaches of routine that they cannot be "explained" in the usual way—the closer we study these events, the more evidence we discover of shifts in expectations and behaviors that were unthinkable before they happened. The alternative approach I proposed in that book was "anti-explanation," that is, analysis that emphasizes understanding people's experiences during such nonroutine events. Instead of explaining these events in terms of the institutions of social life, I suggested that it is truer to the experience of these events to examine people's responses to the perceived breakdown of the usual patterns of behavior.[34] This book offers another example of nonroutine events—democratic revolutions that rose and fell with startling rapidity—and another exploration of people's experiences during these episodes. However, the current study proposes an additional dimension to anti-explanation, which I will call "enacted explanation": the extent to which people believe that patterns of behavior exist and fulfill these beliefs by acting as if they did exist, with the result that they bring them into existence.

This book offers the extended example of intellectuals in the early twentieth century, who believed that their class, or anticlass, existed, and that it had a privileged mission in world history to establish the rule of democracy and expertise, notwithstanding the tension between these two halves of the democratic positivist ideology. To the extent that this belief was shared—among the intellectuals, the emerging bourgeoisie and working class, and other social groups—it was self-fulfilling. Nondemocratic countries with more intellectuals were more likely than those with fewer intellectuals to undergo democratic revolutions. But this correlation hides the enactment of the explanation. The pattern holds because people at the time thought it would hold: Afghans, Bukharans, and Khivans did not support democracy movements in large numbers because they did not consider their kingdoms to be the sort of place where such movements would succeed, while Iranians next door, by contrast, did conceive of their country as an appropriate site for democracy and of intellectuals as the appropriate carriers of democracy, and therefore supported the movement in large enough numbers to frighten the shah into granting a constitution. There's no escaping tautology in enacted explanations, and that is okay. For nonroutine events, explanations work only when our subjects believe in them and make them work.

Once a new democracy is established, its chief dilemma, according to this perspective, is to overcome expectations of failure. When democracy appears fragile, fewer people commit to its defense, and antidemocratic movements become bolder and broader, providing further evidence that democracy is fragile. This circular process is particularly endemic in poor countries, where democracy is often short-lived. As Adam Przeworski and his colleagues have noted, new democracies in the second half of the twentieth century lasted only eight years, on average, in the world's poorest countries.[35] I propose that democracies in poor countries were undermined, not because of poverty itself, or because of their too-small intelligentsias or proletariats or bourgeoisies, but rather because people expected democracy not to last in poor countries.

In the early twentieth century, antidemocracy movements frequently invoked stereotypes about the instability of the new democracies, and enough people believed in this image that they felt democracy would not survive, no matter what they did. So they stood aside as democracy collapsed. One common stereotype in the discourse of the period held that intellectuals were an inappropriate social basis for democracy. The democracy movement was weak "by its very nature," business leaders in Russia asserted, because "it is a party of the intelligentsia, shorn therefore of any economic strength" (see Chapter 5). Even some prodemocracy intellectuals and their allies came to share this concern. In Mexico, for example, an enthusiastic supporter of democracy became disgusted with the "debility and stultification" of student activists; in China, a Western-educated intellectual insulted the Western-educated intellectual as "puffed with book learning, self-conscious of his dignity and importance, and valuing himself 50 percent above par" (see Chapter 4). Many representatives of the Great Powers concurred, deriding local intellectuals as "superficially civilized" and "infected . . . with Western European notions without deeper knowledge" (see Chapter 9). These images were not based on detailed investigation or on comparison with the social bases of democracy elsewhere. But the accuracy of the image did not matter so much as its effect: the erosion of the brief hegemony of the intellectuals.

A second stereotype held that the revolutionary path to democracy was less stable than more gradual democratizations. The people were not "ready" for democracy, according to this view, and needed a longer period of tutelage before they could be expected to uphold the responsibilities of political participation. Hostile estimations of the people's abilities were common in the early twentieth century. "Our peasants have no knowledge and do not know what the meaning of *mashrutiyat* [constitutional democracy] is," a major Iranian landowner complained (see Chapter 7).

Even prodemocracy intellectuals shared this negative view of the people's abilities—though they felt that democracy, in the grip of the intellectuals, would provide better tutelage than autocracy (see Chapter 2). Again, the stereotype did not need to be based on solid evidence. If enough people believed that their country was not ready for democracy, then their belief would fulfill itself—crucially, if policymakers in the Great Powers set aside their democratic ideals and threw their support to the opponents of democracy. A telling example comes from a U.S. diplomat who arrived in Iran soon after the democratic revolution of 1906:

> On my arrival at Enzeli [an Iranian port on the Caspian Sea] I was told the following story by the Mehmandar, my official host: A few days before, a man in that city had been called to account by the authorities for insulting a woman in the street, and in defence he had appealed to the new Constitution. He asked to be informed as to what was meant by "freedom of speech" if he could not tell a person what he thought of him. Many similar stories are current, with or without foundation, and they serve to show how much is understood by the people of the real significance of a Constitution, for which no Persian word existed and one had to be invented.[36]

Apparently the diplomat was unimpressed with the constitutional protection afforded to freedom of speech in his own country. His willingness to accept disparaging stories at face value—even stories he suspected were dubious—suggests that they resonated deeply with his own stereotypes of Iran. The United States was not a major player in Iran at the time, so the ambassador's negative opinion of the Iranian potential for democracy did not greatly affect the course of events there. But the ambassador's stereotype mattered nonetheless. Months later, when the shah shelled parliament and began to arrest and kill his political opponents, several supporters of democracy sought refuge in the U.S. embassy. The ambassador reported proudly to Washington that he had turned them down.[37]

If democracy movements accepted these pessimistic stereotypes and expectations, they would never get off the ground. If everybody accepted their movements' optimism, new democracies would never fall. The unpredictable history of democratization is the outcome of these dueling expectations, and the activists who can be mobilized around them.

Notes

1. Introduction

1. Bing, *The Secret Letters of the Last Tsar*, page 185; Verner, *The Crisis of Russian Autocracy*, page 241; Mosolov, *At the Court of the Last Tsar*, page 90; Witte, *The Memoirs of Count Witte*, page 486.

2. Ascher, *The Revolution of 1905*, volume 1, page 231; Stockdale, *Paul Miliukov and the Quest for a Liberal Russia*, page 145.

3. Billington, *Fire in the Minds of Men*, page 507; *The Times*, October 31, 1905, page 5; *L'Aurore*, October 31, 1905, page 1.

4. *O Mundo*, November 1, 1905, page 2; *North-China Herald*, November 3, 1905, page 237; *Habl al-Matin* (Calcutta), November 6, 1905, page 23; Scalapino and Schiffrin, "Early Socialist Currents in the Chinese Revolutionary Movement," page 327 (see also Price, *Russia and the Roots of the Chinese Revolution*, pages 151–159, and Spector, *The First Russian Revolution*, pages 86–88); *Idjtihad*, December 1905, page 142.

5. *Habl al-Matin* (Calcutta), August 24, 1906, page 9; Browne, *The Persian Revolution of 1905–1909*, page 120; Sohrabi, "Global Waves, Local Actors," pages 56, 59; *Congress Presidential Addresses*, page 729; Khuri, *Modern Arab Thought*, page 207; Ferreira, *História Política da Primeira República Portuguesa*, volume 1, part 2, page 24.

6. Urióstegui Miranda, *Testimonios del Proceso Revolucionario de México*, page 60; Friedman, *Backward toward Revolution*, page 169; Karl, *Staging the World*, pages 182–186; Price, *Russia and the Roots of the Chinese Revolution*, pages 155, 185.

7. Kurzman, "Waves of Democratization"; Markoff, *Waves of Democracy*; O'Kane, *Paths to Democracy*; Palmer, *The Age of the Democratic Revolution*; Thompson, *Democratic Revolutions*.

8. Lenin, "The Right of Nations to Self-Determination," page 162; Bryce, *Modern Democracies*, pages 501–502; *The Positivist Review*, December 1, 1911, page 387.

9. Gheissari, "Despots of the World Unite," pages 367–369.

10. Exceptions, which study subsets of the wave considered here, include Foran, "Dependency and Resistance in the Middle East"; Hart, *Revolutionary*

Mexico; Price, *Russia and the Roots of the Chinese Revolution;* Sohrabi, "Constitutionalism, Revolution and State" and "Historicizing Revolutions"; and Spector, *The First Russian Revolution.*

11. Kurzman, "Waves of Democratization."

12. Ascher, *The Revolution of 1905,* volume 1, page 236; Edmondson, *Feminism in Russia,* page 50; Stites, *The Women's Liberation Movement in Russia,* page 204; Stockdale, *Paul Miliukov and the Quest for a Liberal Russia,* pages 144–145.

13. Edwards, "Women's Suffrage in China," pages 621, 634–637; Ono, *Chinese Women in a Century of Revolution,* pages 82–91; Strand, "Citizens in the Audience and at the Podium," pages 55–61.

14. Ballesteros García, *El Movimiento Feminista Portugués,* pages 60–64; Esteves, *As Origens do Sufragismo Português,* pages 51–78; Silva, "Feminismo em Portugal," page 892; Souza, "As Primeiras Deputadas Portuguesas," page 428.

15. Suffrage: Boli, "Human Rights or State Expansion," page 139; Flora, *State, Economy, and Society in Western Europe, 1815–1975,* volume 1; Mackie and Rose, *The International Almanac of Electoral History.* International observers: Bryce, *Modern Democracies;* Lecky, *Democracy and Liberty;* Ostrogorski, *Democracy and the Organization of Political Parties.* French revolution: Braga, *História das Ideias Republicanas em Portugal;* Shlapentokh, *The French Revolution in Russian Intellectual Life;* Sohrabi, "Global Waves, Local Actors," pages 51–52; Sohrabi, "Historicizing Revolutions," pages 1384–1385; Tavakoli-Targhi, "Asar-i Agahi az Inqilab-i Faransah"; Villegas Moreno, "De Junta Militar a Poder Constituyente," pages 255–258; Zhang, *China and the French Revolution,* pages 75–128. On the global spread of European liberal thought more generally, see Bayly, *The Birth of the Modern World,* pages 284–324. On Japan: Kreiser, "Der japanische Sieg über Russland"; Kurzman, "Weaving Iran into the Tree of Nations," pages 145–147; Laffan, "Mustafa and the Mikado"; Madero, *The Presidential Succession of 1910,* page 211; Sohrabi, "Global Waves, Local Actors," pages 53–56; Vaz, *Bernardino Machado,* pages 74–75; Worringer, " 'Sick Man of Europe' or 'Japan of the Near East'?" pages 207, 219–220. In Iran, *shurish* was later limited to the meaning of "uprising," and revolution came to be called *inqilab,* which had been used in the early twentieth century primarily as a negative term, along the lines of "unrest" (see *Qanun,* number 17 [circa 1891], page 2; *Nida-yi Vatan,* December 27, 1906, page 6; Mustashar al-Daulah, *Khatirat va Asnad,* volume 2, page 49; Sharif-Kashani, *Vaqa'at-i Ittifaqiyah dar Ruzgar,* volume 1, pages 303 and 351). Palmer, *The Age of the Democratic Revolution.*

16. *Osmanlı Ziraat ve Ticaret Gazetesi,* August 2, 1908, page 196; Knight, *The Mexican Revolution,* volume 1, page 247; *El Tiempo,* June 8, 1911, page 1; Harrison, *The Making of the Republican Citizen,* pages 29–30; Preuss, *Constitutional Revolution,* pages 25–40.

17. Reichman, *Railwaymen and Revolution,* page 231; Haravi-Khurasani, *Tarikh-i Paydayish-i Mashrutiyat-i Iran,* page 49; Gruening, *Mexico and Its Heritage,* pages 96–97.

18. *Álem*, February 18, 1909, pages 3, 5.

19. Huang, *Code, Custom, and Legal Practice in China*, pages 18–19.

20. Bohachevsky-Chomiak, *Feminists despite Themselves*, page 37; Kurzman, *The Unthinkable Revolution in Iran*.

21. Price, *Russia and the Roots of the Chinese Revolution*, page 155.

22. The middle class does not get its own chapter, for reasons elaborated in Chapter 5.

23. Rustow, "Transitions to Democracy"; O'Donnell and Schmitter, *Transitions from Authoritarian Rule;* Tilly, *Democracy*.

24. James, "The Social Value of the College Bred," page 319.

25. Kloppenberg, *Uncertain Victory*.

26. Kent, *Brains and Numbers*, page 34; Madero, *The Presidential Succession of 1910*, page 170.

27. Anderson, *Outcasts in Their Own Land*, page 261; Valente, *O Poder e o Povo*, pages 173, 88–89, 138–139; Brandão, *Memórias*, volume 2, page 87.

28. McDaniel, *Autocracy, Capitalism, and Revolution in Russia*, pages 128–129; Nazim al-Islam Kirmani, *Tarikh-i Bidari-yi Iranian*, volume 3, pages 272–274.

29. F. H. Villiers, British ambassador in Lisbon, to Arthur Hardinge, British ambassador in Brussels (soon to succeed Villiers in Lisbon), October 9, 1910, Great Britain, FO 371/1208.

30. Yeselson, *United States–Persian Diplomatic Relations*, pages 88–89; Richmond Pearson, U.S. ambassador in Tehran, to Elihu Root, U.S. secretary of state, August 22, 1906, United States, Department of State, numerical files M862, roll 138, case 1039 (for Islamic rebuttals to such comments, see the texts in Kurzman, *Modernist Islam*); Vincent-Smith, "Britain and Portugal," page 87.

31. Long, "French Attempts at Constitutional Reform in Russia," page 496; Heller, *British Policy towards the Ottoman Empire*, page 10.

32. Ascher, *The Revolution of 1905*, volume 2, pages 51–52, 178, 284; Emmons, *The Formation of Political Parties*, pages 167, 354–355; Valente, *O Poder e o Povo*, page 191; Almeida, *Saibam Quantos*, page 126; Valente, *O Poder e o Povo*, page 198; Knight, *The Mexican Revolution*, volume 1, pages 166–167; Friedman, "The Center Cannot Hold," pages 163–164 (see also Rhoads, *China's Republican Revolution*, pages 235–236).

33. Engelstein, *Moscow*, page 193; Pereira, "As Greves Rurais de 1911–12," page 498; Valente, *O Poder e o Povo*, pages 207–208; Hardinge, *A Diplomatist in Europe*, page 242; Ramírez Rancaño, *Burguesía Textil y Política*, pages 37–88; Li, *Hong Kong Surgeon*, page 48; Quataert, *Social Disintegration and Popular Resistance in the Ottoman Empire*, pages 129–137.

34. Lancelot D. Carnegie, British ambassador in Lisbon, to Edward Grey, British foreign minister, November 24, 1913, Great Britain, FO 800/71; McDaniel, *The Shuster Mission*, page 190; Pani, *Una Encuesta Sobre Educación Popular*, page 126; Bergère, "The Role of the Bourgeoisie," page 286.

35. Associação Comercial de Lisboa, *Relatório da Direcção . . . 1914*, page 83; Schwartzman, *The Social Origins of the Democratic Collapse*, pages 40–41; Göçek, *Rise of the Bourgeoisie;* Ahmad, "Unionist Relations."

36. Minute by Arthur Nicolson, British undersecretary of state, March 27, 1915, Great Britain, FO 371/2440; see also Vincent-Smith, "Britain and Portugal," page 295.

37. Blok, "The People and the Intelligentsia," page 363; Chehabi, "From Revolutionary Tasnif to Patriotic Surud," page 145; Tunaya, *Hürriyet İlanı*, page 64; Rutherford, *Mexican Society during the Revolution*, page 89; Mónica, *Educação e Sociedade no Portugal de Salazar*, page 179.

38. Schwarcz, *The Chinese Enlightenment*, page 13.

39. Read, *Religion, Revolution, and the Russian Intelligentsia;* Shatz and Zimmerman, *Vekhi (Landmarks);* Blok, "The People and the Intelligentsia," page 360; Atis, "Turkish Literature," pages 250–252; Ersoy, "Süleymâniye Kürsüsünde"; Katouzian, "Nationalist Trends in Iran," page 544; Schwarcz, *The Chinese Enlightenment*, page 186; Kurzman and Owens, "The Sociology of Intellectuals," pages 64–68.

40. For instance, Luebbert, *Liberalism, Fascism, or Social Democracy;* Moore, *The Social Origins of Dictatorship and Democracy;* Skocpol, *States and Social Revolutions.*

41. Kurzman, *The Unthinkable Revolution in Iran;* Kurzman, "Can Understanding Undermine Explanation?"

2. Intellectuals and the Discourse of Democracy

1. Etzioni-Halevy, *The Knowledge Elite and the Failure of Prophecy.*

2. Boggs, *Intellectuals and the Crisis of Modernity*, pages 15–27; Casanova, *The World Republic of Letters*, page 14.

3. Comte, "Plan of the Scientific Operations Necessary for Reorganizing Society," pages 252–255.

4. Ory and Sirinelli, *Les Intellectuels en France*, pages 5–6, 18; Sirinelli, *Intellectuels et Passions Françaises*, pages 30–31.

5. International attention: Veillard, "L'Affaire Dreyfus et l'Opinion Publique Internationale"; Feldman, *The Dreyfus Affair and the American Conscience;* La Puma, "L'Affaire Dreyfus dans la Presse Salentine"; Cadot, "Tchekhov et l'Affaire"; Bucur, "L'Affaire Dreyfus dans les Milieux Démocrates et Populaires Roumains." Iranian newspaper: *Habl al-Matin* (Tehran), June 22, 1907, page 2. Ottoman sultan: Refik, "Abdülhamid ve Dreyfüs Meselesi," page 2. Spain: Jareño López, *El Affaire Dreyfus en España*, page 154; Marichal, *El Intelectual y la Política en España*, pages 18, 25, 36. Arabic: Rida, "Al-Yahud fi Faransa wa fi Misr," page 55. Iran: Kurzman, *"Mashrutiyat, Meşrutiyet*, and Beyond"; Gheissari, *Iranian Intellectuals in the 20th Century*, pages 15–16; Daulatabadi, *Hayat-i Yahya*, volume 2, page 86. Central Asia: Behbudiy, "Padarkush," pages 74–76, 81; Cholpan, "Dokhtur Muhammadyor," page 136. Russia: Confino,

"On Intellectuals and Intellectual Traditions," page 138. China: *Min Bao*, April 3, 1906, page 1 (I thank Mei Zhou for translation and transliteration); Lippert, *Entstehung und Funktion einiger chinesischer marxistischer Termini*, page 316; Schwarcz, *The Chinese Enlightenment*, page 186.

6. Bauman, *Legislators and Interpreters*, page 8; Datta, *Birth of a National Icon*; Honoré, "Autour d'Intellectuel."
7. Thompson, *The Making of the English Working Class*, page 730; Catroga, *O Republicanismo em Portugal*, page 407; Malikzadah, *Tarikh-i Inqilab-i Mashrutiyat-i Iran*, volume 2, page 242; Yalçın, *Siyasal Anılar*, page 123; Pani, *Una Encuesta Sobre Educación Popular*, page 49.
8. Honoré, "Autour d'Intellectual," pages 156, 151.
9. Benda, *Dialogues à Byzance*, page 309.
10. International survey: Kotschnig, *Unemployment in the Learned Professions*. Similar arguments in 1800s: Bendix, *Force, Fate, and Freedom*, page 111; Brym, "Intellectuals," pages 15–17; Charle, *Naissance des "Intellectuels,"* page 59, and *Les Intellectuels en Europe*, pages 173–179; Levy, "Socialism and the Educated Middle Classes," page 161; O'Boyle, "The Problem of an Excess of Educated Men"; Pinto, "Les Intellectuels vers 1900," pages 144–146.
11. Charle, *Naissance des "Intellectuels,"* pages 60–61; Barrow, *Universities and the Capitalist State*, page 168; Weber, "Science as a Vocation," page 131.
12. Lima dos Santos, " 'Os Fabricantes dos Gozos da Inteligência,' " page 539. A hostile author used similar language to challenge the selfless self-image of the intellectuals: "what an aristocracy, the most baleful o[f] aristocracies, the intellectual aristocracy . . . you the eternal useless ones, the nonproducers, the state, the fashionable world, parasitism incarnate, and the most ferocious of parasites, for you exploit shamelessly, exploiting in the name of the modern lay Holy Spirit" (Nichols, *Treason, Tradition, and the Intellectual*, page 55).
13. Göçek, *Rise of the Bourgeoisie*, page 76.
14. Johnston, "The Origin of the Term 'Intellectuals,' " page 54.
15. Nichols, *Treason, Tradition, and the Intellectual*, pages 39–40.
16. Benda, *Dialogues à Byzance*, pages 323, 353, 360.
17. Comte, "Plan of the Scientific Operations Necessary for Reorganizing Society," page 251.
18. Spread of positivism: Simon, *European Positivism in the Nineteenth Century*; Woodward, *Positivism in Latin America*. Positivist liberalism: Kent, *Brains and Numbers*, pages 49, 34; Harp, *Positivist Republic*, page 176; Owram, *The Government Generation*, page 48; Catroga, "A Importância do Positivismo," page 287; Ramos, "A Formação da Intelligentsia Portuguesa," page 521.
19. Ory and Sirinelli, *Les Intellectuels en France*, pages 16–18.
20. Zola, *The Dreyfus Affair*, pages 158–189.
21. Blum, *Souvenirs sur l'Affaire*, page 103.
22. Dewey, *Democracy and Education*, page 86.
23. Fischer, *Russian Liberalism*, page 70; Riha, *A Russian European*, pages 40, 8, 75, 82; Billington, "The Intelligentsia and the Religion of Humanity," pages

813–815. By the end of the nineteenth century, Russian positivism had lost its Comtean fervor. A leading prodemocracy activist suggested that the younger generation of intellectuals was "carried away neither by 'materialism' nor 'atheism' nor 'positivism.' All this we outgrew. . . . But we did not have opposing faiths. We looked on everything with the eyes of skeptics" (Davies, "V. A. Maklakov," page 81).

24. Pipes, *Struve: Liberal on the Left*, pages 55, 296–297; Rosenthal and Bohachevsky-Chomiak, "Introduction," page 143; Read, *Power in Revolutionary Russia*, pages 26–27; Read, *Religion, Revolution, and the Russian Intelligentsia*, page 17; Loe, "Redefining the Intellectual's Role," page 300. Struve identified "the Russian classless intelligentsia" in 1903 as "the chief cadres of the liberal party" (Galai, *The Liberation Movement in Russia*, page 174). Pipes treats this positive evaluation of the intellectuals as a passing phase brought about by Struve's intense commitment to the democracy movement, and later undermined by his disillusionment with the movement after 1905.

25. Ascher, *The Revolution of 1905*, pages 115–116; Galai, *The Liberation Movement in Russia*, page 252.

26. Galai, *The Liberation Movement in Russia*, page 173.

27. Engineers: Rieber, *Merchants and Entrepreneurs in Imperial Russia*, page 355. Physicians: Hutchinson, *Politics and Public Health in Revolutionary Russia*, page 46. Teachers: Seregny, "Zemstvo Rabbits, Antichrists, and Revolutionaries," page 80.

28. Kassow, *Students, Professors, and the State in Tsarist Russia*, page 220.

29. Above-class and estate-less: Freeze, "The *Soslovie* (Estate) Paradigm and Russian Social History," pages 29–30; Pollard, "The Russian Intelligentsia," page 22; Rosenberg, "Kadets and the Politics of Ambivalence," page 140. Students: Fischer, *Russian Liberalism*, page 55; Pares, *Russia and Reform*, page 217. Sacrificing: Nahirny, *The Russian Intelligentsia*, pages 69–86. Shelgunov: Billington, "The Intelligentsia and the Religion of Humanity," page 812. Milyoukov, *Russia and Its Crisis*, page 560.

30. McClelland, *Autocrats and Academics*, page 70.

31. Newspaper: Pollard, "The Russian Intelligentsia," page 24. Vast majority: McClelland, *Autocrats and Academics*, page 70. Public enlightenment and public school teachers: Alston, *Education and the State in Tsarist Russia*, pages 173, 260–261. Recent analysis: Balzer, "The Problem of Professions in Imperial Russia," page 187.

32. Mendel, *Dilemmas of Progress in Tsarist Russia*, xii; Kovalewsky, *La Crise Russe*, page 135. Agrarian reforms: Léontovitsch, *Histoire du Libéralisme en Russie*; Maklakov, *The First State Duma*.

33. Mystique of *nauka*: McClelland, *Autocrats and Academics*, pages 61–74. Capitalists: Ruckman, *The Moscow Business Elite*, pages 197–198. Saratov landowner: Seregny, "Zemstvo Rabbits, Antichrists, and Revolutionaries," page 45. At the same time, prodemocracy Moscow capitalists were Slavophiles

and generally unsympathetic to Westernized intellectuals, whom one described as "clean shaven, in a Western jacket, having grabbed hold of some kind of higher education, in essence little cultivated, often a bribe-taker, though not by necessity, criticizing and condemning in secret everyone who stands above him, profoundly contemptuous of the peasant, one of the forerunners of the coming Russian intelligentsia" (Rieber, *Merchants and Entrepreneurs in Imperial Russia*, page 296).

34. Algar, *Mirza Malkum Khan*, pages 11–12, 27–33. This classic biography of Malkum Khan does not explore the Comtean tradition, though Comtean elements emerge in the biography's description of Malkum's activities and writings (Abrahamian, *Iran between Two Revolutions*, pages 65–67).

35. Algar, *Mirza Malkum Khan*, pages 29, 185–237, 247. Who is the greatest: *Qanun*, number 11, circa 1891, page 3, translation adapted from Menashri, *Education and the Making of Modern Iran*, page 34. A somewhat more generous reading of Malkum's work finds further references to popular sovereignty and attributes these opinions in part to Malkum's reading of John Stuart Mill (Hairi, *Shi'ism and Constitutionalism in Iran*, pages 39–41)—one of the thinkers who introduced democracy into positivism.

36. Algar, *Mirza Malkum Khan*, page 235; Kashani-Sabet, "Hallmarks of Humanism," page 1197; Menashri, *Education and the Making of Modern Iran*, page 34. Adamiyat: Abrahamian, *Iran between Two Revolutions*, page 77. Founding document: Adamiyat, *Fikr-i Azadi*, page 211.

37. Menashri, *Education and the Making of Modern Iran*, pages 39–40; Alavi, "Critical Writings on the Renewal of Iran."

38. Malkum: Bakhash, *Iran*, pages 332–333. Open letter: Nazim al-Islam Kirmani, *Tarikh-i Bidari-yi Iranian*, volume 1, page 59. Intellectuals of the country: Daulatabadi, *Hayat-i Yahya*, volume 2, page 42. Poet: Dihkhuda, *Namah'ha-yi Siyasi-yi Dikhuda*, page 71. Leading religious scholar: open letter of *Hujjat al-Islam* 'Abdullah Mazandarani, *Rahnima*, August 13, 1907, page 2.

39. Bayat, *Iran's First Revolution*, page 67 (the first portion of the quotation is translated somewhat differently in Menashri, *Education and the Making of Modern Iran*, page 37); *Habl al-Matin* (Calcutta), August 10, 1906, page 11.

40. Mardin, *Jön Türklerin Siyasî Fikirleri*, page 225; Swenson, "The Young Turk Revolution," page 112.

41. State officials: Khayr al-Din, *The Surest Path*, pages 74–75, 81, 165; Kemal, "And Seek Their Counsel in the Matter." Technical term: Sami, *Kamus-i Türki*, page 1352. Arabic and French roots: Hairi, *Shi'ism and Constitutionalism in Iran*, pages 182–189. Reservations about democracy: Mardin, *The Genesis of Young Ottoman Thought;* Davison, "The Advent of the Principle of Representation."

42. Few early constitutionalists: Korlaelçi, *Pozitivizmin Türkiye'ye Girişi*, pages 192–195. Ahmed Rıza: Hanioğlu, *The Young Turks in Opposition*, pages 294, 354; Fahri, *Auguste Comte ve Ahmet Rıza*, page 11.

43. Korlaelçi, *Pozitivizmin Türkiye'ye Girişi*, page 262 (see also Hanioğlu, *The Young Turks in Opposition*, page 208, and *Preparation for a Revolution*, pages 308–309); Çetin and Yıldız, *II Abdülhamid Han*, pages 290–291.

44. Hanioğlu, *The Young Turks in Opposition*, pages 205–208; Hanioğlu, *Preparation for a Revolution*, pages 308–311; Rıza, "L'Inaction des Jeunes-Turcs," page 98.

45. Korlaelçi, *Pozitivizmin Türkiye'ye Girişi*, page 257 (see also Hanioğlu, *The Young Turks in Opposition*, page 207); Swenson, "The Young Turk Revolution," page 239.

46. Hanioğlu, *The Young Turks in Opposition*, pages 200–203; Korlaelçi, *Pozitivizmin Türkiye'ye Girişi*, pages 252, 261; Kemal, "And Seek Their Counsel in the Matter"; Hanioğlu, *Preparation for a Revolution*, page 187 (see also pages 240–241); Refik, *İnkılab-ı Azim*, page 46.

47. Yalçın, *Siyasal Anılar*, page 123. Iranian newspaper: Nabavi, "Spreading the Word," page 311.

48. One of the few expressions of support from religious scholars occurred in a public meeting in Ottoman Albania during the rebellion (Gawrych, *The Crescent and the Eagle*, page 152). Cemaleddin Efendi, *Siyasi Hatıralar*, pages 43–47; Hanioğlu, *Preparation for a Revolution*, pages 306–307; Kara, *İslâmcıların Siyasi Görüşleri*, pages 66–69. Musa Kazım: Kurzman, *Modernist Islam*, page 176.

49. Order and work: Bell, *Portugal of the Portuguese*, page 200. Portuguese mentality: Almeida, *Quarenta Anos de Vida Literária e Política*, volume 2, page 77.

50. Braga, *Systema de Sociologia*.

51. Bell, *Portugal of the Portuguese*, page 198; Serrão, *Antologia do Pensamento Político Português*, volume 1, page 319; Valente, *O Poder e o Povo*, page 96; Braga, *História das Ideias Republicanas em Portugal*, page 114.

52. Braga, *Systema de Sociologia*, page 500; Ramos, "A Formação da Intelligentsia Portuguesa," page 525; Almeida, *Quarenta Anos de Vida Literária e Política*, volume 2, page 324; Vaz, *Bernardino Machado*, page 80.

53. Ramos, "A Formação da Intelligentsia Portuguesa," page 525.

54. Braga, *História das Ideias Republicanas em Portugal*, pages 148–149.

55. Braga, *História das Ideias Republicanas em Portugal*, pages 110–111; Vilela, *'Alma Nacional,'* page 2.

56. Vaz, *Bernardino Machado*, pages 75, 86; Almeida, *Quarenta Anos de Vida Literária e Política*, volume 2, pages 123–159; Tengarrinha, *História da Imprensa Periódica Portuguesa*, page 256.

57. Reyes, *Obras Completas de Alfonso Reyes*, volume 12, page 192; Vasconcelos, *Ulises Criollo*, volume 1, page 224; Cabrera, *Obras Completas*, volume 3, page 58.

58. Hunger at the gates: Palavicini, *Mi Vida Revolucionaria*, pages 16–17, translated in Cockcroft, *Intellectual Precursors of the Mexican Revolution*, page 44. Fine economically: Knight, *The Mexican Revolution*, volume 1, page 148.

Madero, *The Presidential Succession of 1910*, pages 18, 170. Our times demanded heroism: Vasconcelos, *Ulises Criollo*, volume 1, page 307.

59. Gómez Quiñones, *Porfirio Díaz, los Intelectuales y la Revolución*, page 209; Madero, *Epistolario (1900–1909)*, page 8.

60. Madero, *The Presidential Succession of 1910*, page 210; Córdova, *La Ideología de la Revolución Mexicana*, pages 111–112 *et passim*; González Navarro, "La Ideología de la Revolución Mexicana," page 631.

61. Hernández Luna, *Conferencias del Ateneo de la Juventud*, pages 37–38; Reyes, *Obras Completas*, volume 12, page 193.

62. Rojas Garcidueñas, *El Ateneo de la Juventud y la Revolución*, pages 76–77; García Morales, *El Ateneo de México*, page 150; Vasconcelos, *Ulises Criollo*, volume 2, pages 269, 356; Hernández Luna, *Conferencias del Ateneo de la Juventud*, pages 136–137; Haynes, "Orden y Progreso," page 259.

63. Translations: Liu, *Translingual Practice*; Masini, *The Formation of Modern Chinese Lexicon*. Mr. Democracy and Mr. Science: Kwok, *Scientism in Chinese Thought*, pages 67–68. Directly from English: Grieder, *Intellectuals and the State in Modern China*, pages 146–147 (on the entry of the term *democracy* into Chinese, see also Xiong, " 'Liberty,' 'Democracy,' 'President' ").

64. Sun, *Prescriptions for Saving China*, pages 48, 32–33, 38; Gasster, *Chinese Intellectuals and the Revolution of 1911*, page 138.

65. Sun, *Prescriptions for Saving China*, page 49. Sun also proposed a fifth branch, called "supervisory power," that would monitor the executive in the same way, he argued, that the judicial branch monitors ordinary citizens (Sun, *Prescriptions for Saving China*, page 50). It is not clear why the judicial branch could not be allowed to monitor both the executive branch and ordinary citizens.

66. Knowledge: Liu, *Translingual Practice*, page 322. No one jeers: Kwok, *Scientism in Chinese Thought*, pages 11, 37. Pseudonyms: Hu, "Hu Shih," page 248.

67. Kwok, *Scientism in Chinese Thought*, pages 12–13.

68. Sun, *Prescriptions for Saving China*, pages 39–50; Bernal, *Chinese Socialism to 1907*, page 66. Sun said he had developed these principles in the years before 1900 (Sun, "Autobiography of Dr. Sun Yat-sen," page 53), which is difficult to reconcile with this account of a major organizational meeting of the prodemocracy movement in August, 1905: "Someone asked Sun Wen [Sun Yatsen], 'When one day revolution succeeds, could you please tell us frankly whether you will choose monarchy or democracy?' There were at the meeting nearly three hundred people. The question came in the midst of a flowing speech. On hearing it, like splitting a piece of silk suddenly reaching its end, an abrupt silence overcame the gathering. Sun Wen and Huang Hsing did not know what to say. They were speechless and could not answer it. . . . Realizing the seriousness of the situation, [a colleague of Sun's] came over from where he was sitting and said, 'Revolution is a public affair of the whole nation. How can Sun . . . decide for democracy or monarchy?' " (Liew, *Struggle for Democracy*, page 47).

3. Intellectuals and Democratization

1. Kurzman and Leahey, "Intellectuals and Democratization," pages 944–950; Banks, *Cross-National Time Series Data Archive;* Kassow, *Students, Professors, and the State in Tsarist Russia,* pages 18–25.
2. Gregorian, *The Emergence of Modern Afghanistan,* pages 184, 187, 212, 213; Ahang, *Sayr-i Zhurnalizm dar Afghanistan,* page 31; Nawid, "State, Clergy, and British Imperial Policy in Afghanistan," page 598; Habibi, *Junbish-i Mashrutiyat dar Afghanistan,* page 42; Ghani, *A Review of the Political Situation in Central Asia,* page 65; Tarzi, *Chih Bayad Kard?*
3. Banks, *Cross-National Time Series Data Archive.* Uribe Uribe: Morales Benítez, *Liberalismo,* page 87 (see also Santa, *El Pensamiento Político de Rafael Uribe Uribe,* page 56); Uribe Uribe, *Obras Selectas,* pages 247, 285. Red and Blue: Deas, "Gramática y Poder"; Delpar, *Red against Blue,* page 48 *et passim.* Oath of faith: Farrell, "The Catholic Church and Colombian Education," page 309. War of a Thousand Days: Bergquist, *Coffee and Conflict in Colombia;* Delpar, *Red against Blue;* Villegas and Yunis, *La Guerra de los Mil Días.* Later, in the 1910s, Uribe Uribe urged Colombia not to disregard primary education in its rush to build a university-based "intellectual aristocracy" (Morales Benítez, *Liberalismo,* page 87; Uribe Uribe, *El Pensamiento Social de Uribe Uribe,* page 98).
4. Kurzman, *The Unthinkable Revolution in Iran,* pages 131–135.
5. Milyoukov, *Russia and Its Crisis,* pages vii–viii.
6. Milyoukov, *Russia and Its Crisis,* page 226. Intelligentsia: Pollard, "The Russian Intelligentsia," pages 17, 3; Fischer, *Russian Liberalism,* pages 51–52. Chekhov: Confino, "On Intellectuals and Intellectual Traditions in Eighteenth- and Nineteenth-Century Russia," page 138. Banquet campaign: Ascher, *The Revolution of 1905,* page 66. Orthodox clerics: Curtiss, *Church and State in Russia,* page 79.
7. Kennan, "The Last Appeal of the Russian Liberals," pages 59, 63.
8. Pollard, "The Russian Intelligentsia," page 21.
9. Galai, *The Liberation Movement in Russia,* page 80. Galai translates *intelligent* as "intellectual." For the original Russian, see Tatarov, "Materialy k Istorii Pervogo Syezda," page 157.
10. Galai, *The Liberation Movement in Russia,* pages 59–65.
11. I can't understand: Confino, "On Intellectuals and Intellectual Traditions in Eighteenth- and Nineteenth-Century Russia," page 125. No longer dominant: Fischer, *Russian Liberalism;* Manning, "*Zemstvo* and Revolution," pages 34–36. Higher education: Manning, *The Crisis of the Old Order in Russia,* pages 379–380. Trubetskoi: Pares, *Russia and Reform,* page 330.
12. Young Turks: Vucinich, "Politics, Universities, and Science," page 158. Vanguard: Kassow, *Students, Professors, and the State in Tsarist Russia,* page 84. St. Petersburg University: Morrissey, *Heralds of Revolution,* page 65. Cattle: McReynolds, *Russia at Play,* page 246. Students were so associated with oppositional politics that peasant activists were said to "have gone and turned

into students," according to an author writing in 1905 (Perrie, "The Russian Peasant Movement," page 135).

13. Castigated: Kassow, *Students, Professors, and the State in Tsarist Russia*, page 51; Pares, *Russia and Reform*, pages 216, 326–327. Organizing professionally and politically: Balzer, *Russia's Missing Middle Class;* Galai, *The Liberation Movement in Russia*, pages 110–111, 169, 188.

14. Galai, *The Liberation Movement in Russia*, pages 113–119; Fröhlich, *The Emergence of Russian Constitutionalism*, pages 238–239.

15. Kassow, *Students, Professors, and the State in Tsarist Russia*, pages 184, 195; Morrissey, *Heralds of Revolution*, pages 101–112.

16. Balzer, *Russia's Missing Middle Class;* Galai, *The Liberation Movement in Russia*, pages 223, 246–248; Sanders, "The Union of Unions," page 845. Balzer suggests that Russian professionals had two identities—loyal beneficiaries of the state and autonomous, self-organized guilds—but that the state's refusal to acknowledge the latter identity generated resentments that undermined the former (Balzer, "The Problem of Professions in Imperial Russia").

17. Galai, *The Liberation Movement in Russia*, page 235; McDaniel, *Autocracy, Capitalism, and Revolution in Russia*, pages 128–129.

18. Galai, *The Liberation Movement in Russia*, pages 253–260; Balzer, "The Problem of Professions in Imperial Russia," page 193; Stockdale, *Paul Miliukov and the Quest for a Liberal Russia*, page 139; Kassow, "Professionalism among University Professors," page 208.

19. Reichman, *Railwaymen and Revolution.*

20. Marxists: Elkin, "The Russian Intelligentsia on the Eve of the Revolution," pages 474–475. Minister of interior and Witte: Wcislo, *Reforming Rural Russia*, pages 141, 168. Statistics: Galai, *The Liberation Movement in Russia*, page 138; Johnson, "Liberal Professonals and Professional Liberals," page 355. Police and mobs: Ascher, *The Revolution of 1905*, pages 130, 253–257 (see also Seregny, "Zemstvo Rabbits, Antichrists, and Revolutionaries," pages 147–150).

21. Tents: Tafrishi-Husayni, *Ruznamah-yi Akhbar-i Mashrutiyat*, page 41. Not recognized: Martin, *Islam and Modernism*, page 93. Open-air school: Abrahamian, *Iran between Two Revolutions*, page 84. Socialist: Sheikholeslami and Dunning, "The Memoirs of Haydar Khan 'Amu Ughlu," page 37. Negotiations: Abrahamian, "The Crowd in the Persian Revolution," page 134, and *Iran between Two Revolutions*, page 85; Bayat, *Iran's First Revolution*, page 135; Browne, *The Persian Revolution*, page 122; Martin, *Islam and Modernism*, pages 94–96; Tafrishi-Husayni, *Ruznamah-yi Akhbar-i Mashrutiyat*, pages 41–42.

22. Numbers of intellectuals: Afary, *The Iranian Constitutional Revolution*, pages 37–38, 42; Arasteh, *Education and Social Awakening in Iran;* Atai, "The Sending of Iranian Students to Europe"; Menashri, *Education and the Making of Modern Iran.* Convicts for execution: Rejali, *Torture and Modernity*, pages 12, 26.

23. Masonic-type organization: Algar, *Mirza Malkum Khan,* page 39. Hatred: Hidayat, *Khatirat va Khatarat,* page 53. Ignoramuses: Ekhtiar, "The Dar al-Funun," page 206. Very wrong: Adamiyat, *Fikr-i Azadi,* page 203. Schools flourishing: Mostafi, *The Administrative and Social History of the Qajar Period,* volume 2, page 391.

24. Flaunted their identity: Gheissari, *Iranian Intellectuals in the 20th Century,* pages 15–16. I went to Europe: Algar, *Mirza Malkum Khan,* page 35. Two days in a modern school: Dihkhuda, *Namah'ha-yi Siyasi-yi Dikhuda,* page 71. Neither Western nor Eastern: Aghaoglu, "La Société Persane," pages 525–526. Chameleons: Alavi, "Critical Writings on the Renewal of Iran," page 245; Ekhtiar, "The Dar al-Funun," page 203. Outstanding group: Mostafi, *The Administrative and Social History of the Qajar Period,* volume 2, page 456.

25. Majd al-Islam Kirmani, *Tarikh-i Inqilab-i Mashrutiyat-i Iran,* page 87.

26. Algar, *Mirza Malkum Khan,* pages 36–53, 228–235; Menashri, *Education and the Making of Modern Iran,* page 39.

27. Abrahamian, *Iran between Two Revolutions,* pages 78–79; Malikzadah, *Tarikh-i Inqilab-i Mashrutiyat-i Iran,* volume 2, page 239.

28. Malikzadah, *Tarikh-i Inqilab-i Mashrutiyat-i Iran,* volume 2, page 241. The term used here for intellectual, *raushanfikr,* may be anachronistic in this context, because it only became widespread after the 1920s.

29. Nazim al-Islam Kirmani, *Tarikh-i Bidari-yi Iranian,* volume 1, page 6.

30. Bayat, *Iran's First Revolution,* page 110; Nazim al-Islam Kirmani, *Tarikh-i Bidari-yi Iranian,* volume 1, page 119.

31. A leading intellectual used the term *danishmandan* to refer to prodemocracy religious scholars in a parliamentary debate (Iran, *Muzakarat-i Majlis,* January 10, 1907, volume 1, page 53). The first usage of the term *munavvaran al-fikr* in Iran appears to have occurred in 1911 (Gheissari, *Iranian Intellectuals in the 20th Century,* pages 15–16). The first usage by an Iranian—writing in Istanbul—may have occurred in 1910 (Mamaqani, *Maslak al-Imam,* page 60).

32. Russian Orthdox education: Cunningham, *A Vanquished Hope: The Movement for Church Renewal in Russia,* pages 296–300; Freeze, *The Parish Clergy in Nineteenth-Century Russia,* pages 450–468. Islamic education: Kurzman, *Liberal Islam,* pages 8–10; Kurzman, *Modernist Islam, 1840–1940,* pages 9–14, 21–23. Less reform in Iran: Adamiyat, *Idi'uluzhi-yi Nahzat-i Mashrutiyat-i Iran,* page 148. Iranian scholars affected: Hairi, *Shi'ism and Constitutionalism in Iran;* Martin, *Islam and Modernism.* Revolutionary Committee: Abrahamian, *Iran between Two Revolutions,* page 78.

33. Afary, *The Iranian Constitutional Revolution, 1906–1911,* pages 52–53; Daulatabadi, *Hayat-i Yahya,* volume 2, pages 44–51; Malikzadah, *Tarikh-i Inqilab-i Mashrutiyat-i Iran,* volume 2, pages 320–326. Heretical offshoots: Bayat, *Iran's First Revolution,* pages 66–70, 112–115, 117–118.

34. Public face: Algar, *Religion and State in Iran,* pages 244–251. Bihbihani: Bayat, *Iran's First Revolution,* pages 127–129. Merchants: Martin, *Islam and*

Modernism, pages 90–91. Bihbihani on democracy: Arjomand, "The Ulama's Traditionalist Opposition to Parliamentarism, 1907–1909," page 177.

35. Bayat, *Iran's First Revolution*, page 128; Nazim al-Islam Kirmani, *Tarikh-i Bidari-yi Iranian*, volume 3, page 243.

36. Afary, *The Iranian Constitutional Revolution, 1906–1911*, pages 57–58; Bayat, *Iran's First Revolution*, pages 134–139; Martin, *Islam and Modernism*, pages 93–100. Evildoers: Daulatabadi, *Hayat-i Yahya*, volume 2, page 86.

37. Translation Bureau: Mardin, *The Genesis of Young Ottoman Thought*, pages 10–13. Protodemocratic interlude: Devereux, *The First Ottoman Constitutional Period;* Shaw and Shaw, *History of the Ottoman Empire and Modern Turkey*, volume 2, pages 174–187.

38. Military Medical School: Bleda, *İmparatorluğun Çöküşü*, page 57. Rıza Nur: Aktar, *İkinci Meşrutiyet Dönemi Öğrenci Olayları*, page 37; Göçek, *The Rise of the Bourgeoisie*, page 79.

39. Intellectual youth: Keramett Bey, "The Young Turk Movement," page 477. Field of education: Hanioğlu, *The Young Turks in Opposition*, page 207. Seventy-eight members and military officers: Karabekir, *İttihat ve Terakki Cemiyeti*, pages 306–307, 65. Rumelia cell: Niyazi, *Hatırat-ı Niyazi*, page 20.

40. Hanioğlu, *Preparation for a Revolution*, page 309.

41. *Şûra-yı Ümmet*, May 20, 1905, pages 1–2, parts translated in Hanioğlu, *The Young Turks in Opposition*, page 207. I thank Professor Hanioğlu for providing me with the original article.

42. Bleda, *İmparatorluğun Çöküşü*, page 17.

43. Erişirgil, *Bir Fikir Adamının Romanı*, pages 53–54.

44. Kurzman, *Modernist Islam*.

45. Not convinced: Karpat, "The Memoirs of N. Batzaria," page 292. Confident: Hanioğlu, *Preparation for a Revolution*, pages 261–265. Turkish Dreyfuses: Kara, *İslâmcıların Siyasî Görüşleri*, page 75.

46. Cruzeiro, "Os Professores da Universidade de Coimbra," page 530.

47. Manifesto of 1862: Braga, *História da Universidade de Coimbra*, volume 4, page 496. Protest of 1890: Sousa Lamy, *A Academia de Coimbra*, pages 149–150. Strike of 1907: Xavier, *História da Greve Académica de 1907*, page 94.

48. Sacred mission: Ramos, "A Formação da Intelligentsia Portuguesa"; Valente, *O Poder e o Povo*, page 145. Machado: Rodrigues, "Ideal Republicano e Reforma da Universidade de Coimbra," page 313.

49. Valente, *O Poder e o Povo*, pages 73–74, 88–89. Enlightened elements: Vilela, '*Alma Nacional*,' page 112.

50. Mid-nineteenth century: Hale, *Mexican Liberalism in the Age of Mora*. Late nineteenth century: Hale, *The Transformation of Liberalism in Late Nineteenth-Century Mexico*. Científicos and the revolution: Bulnes, *The Whole Truth about Mexico*, page 181; Tannenbaum, *Peace by Revolution*, page 116.

51. Cabrera, *Obras Completas*, volume 3, page 54.

52. Madero, *The Presidential Succession of 1910*, page 170.

278 | Notes to Pages 71–75

53. Guerra, *Le Mexique de l'Ancien Régime à la Révolution,* pages 203, 200.
54. Student Congress: Luis León, interviewed in 1965 in the James W. Wilkie and Edna Monzón Wilkie Oral History Interviews, Bancroft Library, University of California at Berkeley, page 10. Demonstration: Schmidt, "Power and Sensibility," page 182.
55. Nucleus: Córdova, *La Ideología de la Revolución Mexicana,* page 142. Schoolteachers: Cockcroft, "El Maestro de Primaria en la Revolución Mexicana." Youths: Bulnes, *The Whole Truth about Mexico,* page 138.
56. Cockcroft, *Intellectual Precursors of the Mexican Revolution,* pages 45–46.
57. Ayers, *Chang Chih-tung and Educational Reform in China,* page 226.
58. Borthwick, *Education and Social Change in China,* page 94; Chow, *The May Fourth Movement,* page 379; Ping, *The Chinese System of Public Education,* page 157.
59. Local schools: Borthwick, *Education and Social Change in China,* page 94. Japan: Hackett, "Chinese Students in Japan," page 142; see also Reynolds, *China,* page 48. Short-term courses: Wang, *Chinese Intellectuals and the West,* page 64. Serious students: Galt, "Oriental and Occidental Elements in China's Modern Education System," page 644. Quickie diplomas: Reynolds, *China,* page 98.
60. Shanghai: Rankin, *Early Chinese Revolutionaries,* page 81. Total collapse: Liew, *Struggle for Democracy,* page 22. Saviours: Mei, "The Returned Student in China," page 167. First taste of politics: Huang, *Chinese Students in Japan in the Late Ch'ing Period.*
61. Brown, *The Chinese Revolution,* page 81.
62. Simpson, *The Re-Shaping of the Far East,* page 222.
63. Teaching and Sichuan: Borthwick, *Education and Social Change in China,* pages 184, 119. More than half and stepping stone: Ping, *The Chinese System of Public Education,* pages 159–160, 154. Novels paid three yuan: Bao, *Chuan ying lou hui yi lu,* volume 2, page 388. I thank Rong Zhang for the translation.
64. Short supply: Bergère, *The Golden Age of the Chinese Bourgeoisie,* pages 41–42. Circular education: Borthwick, *Education and Social Change in China,* pages 77, 120–121.
65. Entrepreneurs: Grieder, *Intellectuals and the State in Modern China.* Maltreatment: Rankin, *Early Chinese Revolutionaries.* Jiangsu: Fincher, *Chinese Democracy,* page 235. Scholarly societies: Bergère, *The Golden Age of the Chinese Bourgeoisie,* pages 54, 57. British observer: Young, "Yuan Shih-k'ai's Rise to the Presidency," pages 429–430; but see Borthwick, *Education and Social Change in China,* page 148. Provinces most active: Wang, *Chinese Intellectuals and the West,* page 301.
66. Liew, *Struggle for Democracy,* page 123.
67. Billington, *Fire in the Minds of Men;* Weisberger, McLeod, and Morris, *Freemasonry on Both Sides of the Atlantic;* Zarcone, *Secret et Sociétés Secrètes.*

4. The New Democracy: Intellectuals in Power

1. Chernukha and Anan'ich, "Russia Falls Back, Russia Catches Up," page 92.
2. Seregny, "Zemstvo Rabbits, Antichrists, and Revolutionaries," page 173.
3. Ascher, P. A. *Stolypin*, pages 198–201.
4. Miliukov: McClelland, *Autocrats and Academics,* page 67. Party membership, elections, and education: Emmons, *The Formation of Political Parties,* pages 160–179, 354–356. Dregs and education: Ascher, *The Revolution of 1905,* pages 51–52, 178, 284.
5. Platform: Harcave, *First Blood,* pages 292–300. Track record: Zimmerman, "The Kadets and the Duma," page 129.
6. Censorship: McReynolds, *Russia at Play,* page 70. Tolstoi: Kassow, *Students, Professors, and the State in Tsarist Russia,* pages 288–289, 298–299; Tolstoi, *Vospominaniia;* Wartenweiler, *Civil Society and Academic Debate in Russia,* pages 50–56.
7. Civilized class: 'Ayn al-Saltanah, *Ruznamah-yi Khatirat,* volume 3, page 1802. Elect intellectuals: *Rahnima,* August 13, 1907, page 2. Education in parliament: Shaji'i, *Namayandagan-i Majlis-i Shura-yi Milli,* page 225. Few dozen schools: Menashri, *Education and the Making of Modern Iran,* page 60. Disproportionate influence: Afary, *The Iranian Constitutional Revolution,* pages 66–70. European terms and furniture: Bayat, *Iran's First Revolution,* page 156; *A'inah-yi Ghayb-nima,* July 11, 1907, page 2, in Najmabadi, *The Story of the Daughters of Quchan,* page 108.
8. Factions: Ettehadieh, "Origin and Development of Political Parties in Persia" and "Constitutional Revolution: Political Parties of the Constitutional Period." Never fully displaced monarchy: Sohrabi, "Constitutionalism, Revolution and State" and "Historicizing Revolutions." Hire graduates: Demorgny, *Essai sur l'Administration de la Perse,* pages 117–118. Legal reforms: Floor, "Change and Development in the Judicial System of Qajar Iran"; Greenfield, "Die geistlichen Schariagerichte in Persien"; Sohrabi, "Constitutionalism, Revolution and State," pages 302–303. Grim humour: Hairi, *Shi'ism and Constitutionalism in Iran,* page 85. Medical and public health reform: Menashri, *Education and the Making of Modern Iran,* pages 83–85; Iran, *Majmu'ah-yi Musavvabat,* pages 386–389; Floor, *Public Health in Qajar Iran,* pages 215–216, 222; Elgood, *A Medical History of Persia,* pages 531–532; Schayegh, "Science, Medicine, and Class in the Formation of Semi-Colonial Iran," page 332. Newspapers founded: Sa'idi Sirjani, "The Constitutional Revolution: The Press," pages 208–212. Strongest sign: Nabavi, "Spreading the Word," page 310. Budget: Demorgny, *Essai de Réformes et d'Enseignement Administratifs en Perse,* pages 50, 56; Issawi, *Economic History of Iran,* page 368.
9. Never any room for protest: *Habl al-Matin* (Calcutta), February 18, 1907. Supplementary Constitution: Browne, *The Persian Revolution,* page 375. Modest system: Iran, *Majmu'ah-yi Musavvabat,* page 402. Ministry of Sci-

ence and Arts: Arasteh, *Education and Social Awakening in Iran,* pages 223–226.

10. Arasteh, *Education and Social Awakening in Iran,* pages 226–230.

11. Arasteh, *Education and Social Awakening in Iran,* pages 229; Kani, *Sazman-i Farhangi-yi Iran,* pages 21–22.

12. Not enough intellectuals: Menashri, *Education and the Making of Modern Iran,* page 80. Budget: Turabi-Farsani, *Asnadi az Madaris-i Dukhtaran,* pages 6–7. Study abroad: Iran, *Majmu'ah-yi Musavvabat,* pages 509–513. These totals include 600 tumans for four college students from the Political School (January 4, 1911); 3,000 tumans for thirty additional college students (May 16, 1911); and 3,500 tumans for furniture in five primary schools (October 31, 1911). Not on a large scale: Sadiq, *Modern Persia and Her Education System,* page 21. Oblivion: Kashani-Sabet, *Frontier Fictions,* page 143.

13. Soroudi, "Poet and Revolution," page 34.

14. Chosen from our members: Hanioğlu, *Preparation for a Revolution,* page 286. Club of Educated Ottoman Youth: *The Levant Herald and Eastern Express,* August 1, 1908, page 308.

15. Social science: Şuayb, Cavid, and Tevfik, "Mukaddime ve Program," page 9. History and causal patterns: Zeki, "Auguste Comte," page 197; for a similar view, expressed a half-century earlier, see Hanioğlu, "Transformation of the Ottoman Intelligentsia and the Idea of Science," page 32. Education over experience: Sohrabi, "Constitutionalism, Revolution and State," page 517. Child crying: *Âlem,* April 7, 1909, page 1.

16. Tax collection: Sohrabi, "Constitutionalism, Revolution and State," page 518. Swinging a stick: *İstişare,* September 17, 1908, page 38; see also Hanioğlu, *Preparation for a Revolution,* page 287; Kansu, *The Revolution of 1908 in Turkey,* pages 149–151. One out of ten vacancies: Swenson, "The Young Turk Revolution," page 155. Not a single secretary remained: Türkgeldi, *Görüp İşittiklerim,* page 1. Interior Ministry: Biren, *II. Abdülhamid, Meşrutiyet ve Mütareke Devri Hatıralar,* volume 1, page 466. Rehiring old officials: Birinci, *Hürriyet ve İtilaf Fırkası,* page 30. It is also worth noting that religious scholars were often appointed to criminal law courts after 1908 (Miller, *Legislating Authority,* pages 93, 162–163).

17. Did not prepare us: Kayalı, *Arabs and Young Turks,* page 56. Parliamentary members coded from Güneş, *Türk Parlamento Tarihi,* volume 2, pages 221–679. This source indicates modern education for 142 out of 183 representatives for whom any educational background is listed (out of 228 representatives listed in total). British observer: Buxton, *Turkey in Revolution,* page 113. Talat Bey: Bleda, *İmparatorluğun Çöküşü,* page 88; Kutay, *Talat Paşa'nın Gurbet Hatıraları,* volume 1, pages 89–90.

18. Satirical newspaper: *Kalem,* April 1, 1909, page 10. State expenditures: Akarlı, "Economic Policy and Budgets in Ottoman Turkey," pages 471–473.

19. Literacy: Karpat, *Ottoman Population,* page 221; on the educational system more generally, see Fortna, *Imperial Classroom.* Above all: Swenson, "The

Young Turk Revolution," page 127. Newspapers: Aytekin, *İttihad ve Terakki Dönemi Eğitim Yönetimi*, page 142.

20. Grand Education Council: Ottoman Archives, MF.MKB, dosya 161, gömlek 2, August 23, 1908, and gömlek 123, August 29, 1908. The new council members simply ratified some of the decisions of the old council members, crossing out their signatures on a dozen documents and adding their own signatures below (dosya 162, gömleks 92–109, September 16, 1908). Principals: Ottoman Archives, İMF, vesika 12.B.1326, hususi 8, January 13, 1909. Raises: Ottoman Archives, İMF, vesika 27.Ş.1326, hususi 3, September 19, 1908; MF.MKB, dosya 163, gömlek 58, September 21, 1908.

21. Ottoman Empire, *Meclisi Mebusan Zabıt Ceridesi*, February 20, 1909, volume 1, page 740.

22. Ottoman Empire, *Devlet-i Aliyye-i Osmaniyye'nin 1325 Senesi Muvazene-i Umumiyye Kanuni*, section 5, page 85. The classic history of Ottoman and Turkish education, citing figures from the government accounting office, estimates a far greater increase of about 230 percent (Ergin, *Türkiye Maarif Tarihi*, volume 4, page 1331). Another well-informed source gives no credible figures for education expenditures during these years (Shaw, "Ottoman Expenditures," page 377).

23. Free and compulsory education: Tekeli and İlkin, *Osmanlı İmparatorluğu'nda Eğitim ve Bilgi Üretim Sisteminin Oluşumu ve Dönüşümü*, page 86. Budget: Ottoman Empire, *Devlet-i Osmaniyye'nin 1325 Senesine Mahsus Bütçesidir*, pages 119–129. Nail Bey: Ergin, *Türkiye Maarif Tarihi*, volume 4, page 1275.

24. Tuba tree: Ergin, *Türkiye Maarif Tarihi*, volume 4, pages 1276–1280; Tekeli and İlkin, *Osmanlı İmparatorluğu'nda Eğitim ve Bilgi Üretim Sisteminin Oluşumu ve Dönüşümü*, page 84. We cannot wait: Sakaoğlu, "Eğitim Tartışmaları," volume 2, page 482.

25. Unlike Iran, where debate emerged over "constitutionalism" *(mashrutiyat)* versus Islamic law *(mashru'iyat)*, Ottoman intellectuals used both terms interchangeably, as in a pronouncement from the Society for Union and Progress in August 1908 referring to the new order as a "just and Islamic government" *(hükumet-i meşruai adile)* (Tunaya, *Hürriyetin İlanı*, page 58). Certain Ottoman Islamists objected to this usage (Berkes, *The Development of Secularism in Turkey*, page 371).

26. Serfice: Ottoman Archives, MF.İST, dosya 6, gömlek 20, April 15, 1908, and gömlek 85, December 24, 1908. Parallel curricular shifts occurred at this time in the elite Administrative College in Istanbul, where courses on morals were replaced with political history, and traditional religious sciences were replaced with Islamic legal philosophy (Çankaya, *Yeni Mülkiye Tárihi*, volume 1, pages 330–331). Religious officials: Sohrabi, "Constitutionalism, Revolution and State," pages 584–585.

27. Examples of opposition: hostile parliamentary questioning of the minister of education (Ottoman Empire, *Meclisi Mebusan Zabıt Ceridesi*, February 20, 1909, volume 1, page 742), editorial in Konya (Aydın, "II. Meşrutiyet Döne-

minde Konya'da İslamci Muhalefetin Sesi," pages 36–37). Vahdeti: Koca-hanoğlu, "Derviş Vahdeti, II," page 49, and *Derviş Vahdeti ve Çavuşların İsyanı,* page 73; Cemaleddin Efendi, *Siyasi Hatıralarım,* pages 43–44.

28. Censorship abolished: Kabacalı, "Tanzimat ve Meşrutiyet Dönemlerinde Sansür," page 615. Two hundred new papers: Günyol and Mango, "Djarida," page 475; Hourani, *Arabic Thought in the Liberal Age,* page 280; Imbert, *La Rénovation de l'Empire Ottoman,* page 269; Kabacalı, "Tanzimat ve Meşrutiyet Dönemlerinde Sansür," page 615; Kayalı, *Arabs and Young Turks,* page 55; Khalidi, " 'Abd al-Ghani al-'Uraisi and *al-Mufid*," 39; Topuz, *100 Soruda Türk Basın Tarihi,* page 105; Watenpaugh, *Being Modern in the Middle East,* page 72. Past three decades: Duman, *İstanbul Kütüphaneleri Arap Harfli Süreli Yayınlar Toplu Kataloğu;* see also Göçek, *Rise of the Bourgeoisie,* page 130. Family newspapers: Kavcar, *II. Meşrutiyet Devrinde Edebiyat ve Eğitim,* page 32. Ears assailed: Abbott, *Turkey in Transition,* page 13; see also Ramsay, *The Revolution in Constantinople and Turkey,* page 63. Provincial newspaper: Arıkan, *İzmir Basınından Seçmeler,* volume 1, page 82. Plays: And, *Meşrutiyet Döneminde Türk Tiyatrosu,* pages 182–183; Yalçın, *II. Meşrutiyet'te Tiyatro Edebiyatı Tarihi,* pages 25–30, 135–140. Trade association: Brummett, *Image and Imperialism,* pages 31–32; Yalman, *Gördüklerim ve Gecirdiklerim,* page 62. Commission: Arat, *Histoire de la Liberté de la Presse en Turquie,* pages 81–82.

29. Vampire: Kabacalı, "Tanzimat ve Meşrutiyet Dönemlerinde Sansür," page 614. Hüseyin Hilmi: Ahmad, *The Young Turks,* page 40. Serbesti editor: Ahmad, *The Young Turks,* page 39; Aktar, *İkinci Meşrutiyet Dönemi Öğrenci Olayları,* pages 74–75; *Serbesti Gazetesi Muharriri Hasan Fehmi Efendinin Katlı.*

30. Police permission: Sohrabi, "Constitutionalism, Revolution and State," page 566. Administrative College: Çankaya, *Yeni Mülkiye Târihi,* volume 1, pages 333–335. Traitors and reactionaries: Birinci, *Hürriyet ve İtilaf Fırkası,* page 35. Students: Aktar, *İkinci Meşrutiyet Dönemi Öğrenci Olayları,* pages 78–79.

31. Marques, *Parlamentares e Ministros da 1a República.* See also Valente, *O Poder e o Povo,* page 223; Vidigal, *Cidadania, Caciquismo e Poder em Portugal,* page 77.

32. Xavier, *Memórias da Vida Pública,* pages 35–36, 38.

33. Teófilo Braga: Braga Paixão, "A Constituinte de 1911," page 27. Heroes of thought: Valente, *O Poder e o Povo,* page 191. Diploma is everything: Almeida, *Saibam Quantos,* page 126. Sardines and Botto Machado: Valente, *O Poder e o Povo,* page 198.

34. Almeida: Valente, *O Poder e o Povo,* pages 196–197.

35. Morgado, *Legislação Republicana,* pages 12–76, 134.

36. Education reforms and outcomes: Marques, *Nova História de Portugal,* volume 11, pages 539, 561, 532, 539, 531, 520; Marques, *Afonso Costa,* page 141. Form new men: Brandão, *Memórias,* volume 1, page 232. Budgets: Portugal, *Orçamento Geral* (1910–1911), capitulos 8–9; Portugal, *Orçamento Geral* (1911–1912), capitulos 7–8; Portugal, *Leis de Receita e de*

Despesa e Orçamentais (1914–1915), page 11. Later observers: Mónica, "Moulding the Minds of the People," page 3; Marques, *Afonso Costa*, pages 141–142.

37. Judicial review: Araújo, "A Construção da Justiça Constitucional Portuguesa," page 885. Newspapers: Marques, *Afonso Costa*, page 144. Beating the loins: Maia, "Liberdade de Imprensa," page 19.

38. Chinese oculists: Arthur Hardinge, British ambassador in Lisbon, to Edward Grey, British foreign minister, November 28, 1911, Great Britain, FO 371/1211. Opera moved: Marques, *Afonso Costa*, page 144; Sasportes, *História da Dança em Portugal*, page 228. Benefit for impoverished monarchists: Cabral, *As Minhas Memorias Políticas*, page 221; *O Mundo*, March 17, 1914, page 5, and ongoing coverage over the following week.

39. Plums of office: Knight, *The Mexican Revolution*, volume 1, pages 166–167. Lawyer over carpenter: Gavira, *General de Brigada Gabriel Gavira*, page 57. Cabinet: Camp, *Mexican Political Biographies*.

40. Manifest incapacity: Pani, *Mi Contribución al Nuevo Régimen*, page 29. Illiterate masses: Madero, *The Presidential Succession of 1910*, pages 208, 210.

41. Reform of 1911: Pani, *Una Encuesta Sobre Educación Popular*, pages 11–12. Budget increases: Mexico, *Ley de Ingresos*, 1910–1911, page 329, and 1912–1913, page 353. Provinces: Flores Torres, *Burguesía, Militares y Movimiento Obrero en Monterrey*, page 61; Beezley, "Madero," page 17; Deeds, "José María Maytorena and the Mexican Revolution in Sonora," page 32; LaFrance, *The Mexican Revolution in Puebla*, page 159; Pani, *Una Encuesta Sobre Educación Popular*, page 132.

42. Debate: Pani, *Una Encuesta Sobre Educación Popular*, pages 126, 17, 67–68, 77, 26. Federal spending: Mexico, *Ley de Ingresos*, 1910–1911, page 171, and 1912–1913, page 189. Landowner schools: Gabriel Vargas, parliamentary deputy from Jalisco, to Francisco I. Madero, president of Mexico, November 14, 1912, Mexico, Centro de Estudios de História de Mexico Condumex, fondo 915, carpeta 28, documento 2775.

43. Peasant movements: Womack, *Zapata and the Mexican Revolution*. Anti-U.S. speaker: Abascal, *Madero*, page 209. Pro-U.S. plotter: 290 students of the National Preparatory School, Mexico City, to Francisco Madero, president of Mexico, October 25, 1912, in Mexico, Archivo General de la Nación, Colección Revolución, tomo 1, Serie: Revolución y Régimen Maderista, caja 2, carpeta 26, expediente 588. Autophagism: *El Mañana*, January 14, 1913, in Rábago, *"El Mañana,"* volume 1, page 290.

44. Abascal, *Madero*, page 209.

45. Profound discontent: Guzmán, *Febrero de 1913*, page 43. Renovators: González Ramírez, *Manifiestos Políticos*, page 603. Student organization: Ezequiel Padilla, interviewed in 1964–1965 in the James W. Wilkie and Edna Monzón Wilkie Oral History Interviews, Bancroft Library, University of California at Berkeley, page 20.

46. Cabinet: Wang, *Chinese Intellectuals and the West,* page 89. Exhortation: Chang and Gordon, *All under Heaven,* pages 44–46. Telegraph rates: Link, *Mandarin Ducks and Butterflies,* pages 110–111.

47. In search of official position: Wu, *Recollections of the Revolution of 1911,* page 133. Thoughts of honours: Anonymous, "What the Chinese Are Thinking," pages 421–422; see also Harrison, *The Man Awakened from Dreams,* page 93. Heightened expectations: Fung, *The Military Dimension of the Chinese Revolution,* page 118; Wang, *Chinese Intellectuals and the West,* pages 94–95. Puffed with book learning: Mei, "The Returned Student in China," page 167. Power for reforms: Maybon, *La République Chinoise,* page 181.

48. Legal reform: Conner, "Lawyers and the Legal Profession during the Republican Period," pages 216, 219–220, 226; Xu, *Chinese Professionals and the Republican State,* pages 108–109. Actors: Dong, "Unofficial History and Gender Boundary Crossing," page 179. Cai Yuanpei: Rankin, *Early Chinese Revolutionaries,* pages 64–69; Duiker, *Ts'ai Yüan-p'ei,* pages 15–41.

49. Cai, *Cai Yuanpei quan ji,* pages 468–470. I thank Rong Zhang for the translation.

50. Dispatch of January 1912: Bailey, *Reform the People,* pages 139–142; Ping, *The Chinese System of Public Education,* page 111. Phonetic alphabet: Kwok, *Scientism in Chinese Thought,* page 35; Purcell, *Problems of Chinese Education,* page 105. Study abroad: Wu, *Recollections of the Revolution of 1911,* page 135. Budgets and new schools: Pott, "Modern Education," page 435. Enrollment: Huang, *Huang Yanpei Kao cha jiao yu ri ji,* volume 1, pages 157–158. Universities: Pott, "Education in China," page 240; Weston, *The Power of Position,* pages 79–96. Criticism of Cai: Bailey, *Reform the People,* pages 146–148; Duiker, *Ts'ai Yüan-p'ei,* pages 46–47. First step: Song, *Song Jiaoren xian sheng wen ji,* volume 2, page 189. Normal schools: Huang, *Huang Yanpei Kao cha jiao yu ri ji,* volume 1, pages 88–90. Lump of dough: Garrett, *Social Reformers in Urban China,* page 122. I thank Qin Hua for these translations.

51. Duiker, *Ts'ai Yüan-p'ei,* page 48; see also Bailey, *Reform the People,* pages 151–157.

52. Ten provincial governments: Ichiko, "The Role of the Gentry," pages 314–317. Sishu schools: Borthwick, *Education and Social Change in China,* page 83. Hunan: Esherick, *Reform and Revolution in China,* page 248. Chengdu: Stapleton, *Civilizing Chengdu,* page 187. Shandong: Huang, *Huang Yanpei Kao cha jiao yu ri ji,* volume 2, pages 11–12; I thank Qin Hua for the translation. Guangdong: Friedman, "The Center Cannot Hold," pages 162–164, 175, 178, 179; see Rhoads, *China's Republican Revolution,* pages 235–236. Queue-cutting: Li, *Hong Kong Surgeon,* page 48; see also Harrison, *The Making of the Republican Citizen,* pages 20–23, 30–40.

53. Friedman, "The Center Cannot Hold," pages 151, 227, 180, 199–221, 228–234, 241–246, 181; Rhoads, *China's Republican Revolution,* page 241, 257, 260.

54. Chang, "Political Participation and Political Elites," pages 303–312; Kupper, "Revolution in China," pages 374–390.
55. New assembly: Ch'en, *Yuan Shih-k'ai*, pages 178–179. Budget shifted: Huang, *Huang Yanpei Kao cha jiao yu ri ji*, volume 1, page 29 *et passim*. I thank Qin Hua for the translation.
56. *El País*, January 10, 1912.

5. Democracy and the Bourgeoisie

1. Marx and Engels, "Manifesto of the Communist Party," page 475.
2. Moore, *The Social Origins of Dictatorship and Democracy*, page 418. Late twentieth century: Bellin, "Contingent Democrats"; Cardoso, "Entrepreneurs and the Transition Process"; Conaghan and Malloy, *Unsettling Statecraft*, pages 86–97; Nam, "South Korea's Big Business Clientelism in Democratic Reform"; Parsa, "Entrepreneurs and Democratization"; Payne, *Brazilian Industrialists and Democratic Change*; Seidman, *Manufacturing Militance*, pages 91–142; Yılmaz, "Business Notions of Democracy."
3. Marx, "The Eighteenth Brumaire of Louis Bonaparte," pages 189–190.
4. Weber, "Bourgeois Democracy in Russia," page 109.
5. Capitalists rejecting democracy: Cardoso and Faletto, *Dependency and Development in Latin America*; O'Donnell, *Modernization and Bureaucratic-Authoritarianism*. Serve its interests: Alexander, *The Sources of Democratic Consolidation*; Bellin, "Contingent Democrats"; Rueschemeyer, Stephens, and Stephens, *Capitalist Development and Democracy*.
6. *O Trabalho Nacional*, January 15, 1915, page 2. See similar comments in *Journal de la Chambre de Commerce de Constantinople*, April 10, 1909, page 113; *Semana Mercantil*, February 3, 1913, page 2.
7. Lipset, *Political Man*, page vii.
8. Lipset, Seong, and Torres, "A Comparative Analysis of the Social Requisites of Democracy," page 166. Combination of definitions: Glassman, *The Middle Class and Democracy in Socio-Historical Perspective*; Luebbert, *Liberalism, Fascism, or Social Democracy*. Civil society: Ferguson, *Essay on the History of Civil Society*; Gellner, *Conditions of Liberty*. Portuguese business groups: União da Agricultura, Comércio e Indústria, *Livro para Actas Directoria*, number 1, pages 57–58, December 2, 1912 (capilha 3111); *O Trabalho Nacional*, May 15, 1915, page 130; Associação Comercial de Lisboa, *Relatório da Direcção Relativo ao Exercicio, Ano de 1915*, page 30. A later movement that did mobilize around an explicitly "middle class" identity, the French Social Party of the 1930s, did so with an antiliberal political platform (Boltanski, *The Making of a Class*, pages 56–57; Passmore, *From Liberalism to Fascism*, page 271).
9. Banks, *Cross-National Time Series Data Archive*; Gatrell, *The Tsarist Economy*; Von Laue, *Sergei Witte and the Industrialization of Russia*.
10. Pares, *Russia and Reform*, page 476.

11. Moscow businessmen: Owen, *Capitalism and Politics in Russia,* pages 100–101, 168, 269; Rieber, *Merchants and Entrepreneurs in Imperial Russia,* pages 298–299, 312. Morozov: Ascher, *The Revolution of 1905,* volume 1, page 76.

12. Moscow City Council: Owen, *Capitalism and Politics in Russia,* page 170. St. Petersburg: Menashe, "Industrialists in Politics," pages 353–354; Rieber, *Merchants and Entrepreneurs in Imperial Russia,* page 345; Surh, *1905 in St. Petersburg,* page 189. Odessa: Weinberg, *The Revolution of 1905 in Odessa,* page 101.

13. McDaniel, *Autocracy, Capitalism, and Revolution in Russia,* page 109; Menashe, "Industrialists in Politics," page 355; Owen, *Capitalism and Politics in Russia,* page 175; Rieber, *Merchants and Entrepreneurs in Imperial Russia,* page 345; Roosa, "Russian Industrialists, Politics, and Labor Reform in 1905," page 130.

14. Menashe, "Industrialists in Politics," page 356; see also Surh, *1905 in St. Petersburg,* pages 191–192.

15. Owen, *Capitalism and Politics in Russia,* pages 175–178; Rieber, *Merchants and Entrepreneurs in Imperial Russia,* pages 263–265; Roosa, "Russian Industrialists, Politics, and Labor Reform in 1905," page 131; Ruckman, *The Moscow Business Elite,* pages 195–201.

16. Roosa, "Russian Industrialists, Politics, and Labor Reform in 1905," page 142.

17. Menashe, "Industrialists in Politics," page 365.

18. Owen, *Capitalism and Politics in Russia,* pages 186–187; Rieber, *Merchants and Entrepreneurs in Imperial Russia,* page 312.

19. Cossacks: Engelstein, *Moscow,* pages 123–124; Menashe, "Industrialists in Politics," pages 365–366. Moderate Progressive Party: Harcave, *First Blood,* pages 298–299. Union of 17 October: Emmons, *The Formation of Political Parties,* pages 283, 355. Progressive Economic Party: Rieber, *Merchants and Entrepreneurs in Imperial Russia,* page 350.

20. McDaniel, *Autocracy, Capitalism, and Revolution in Russia,* page 131; Owen, *Capitalism and Politics in Russia,* page 199. Chetverikov: Menashe, "Industrialists in Politics," page 363; see also Owen, *Capitalism and Politics in Russia,* page 200.

21. Lockouts: Owen, *Capitalism and Politics in Russia,* page 199; Surh, *1905 in St. Petersburg,* page 368. Worthless and undesirable: Bonnell, *Roots of Rebellion,* page 196. Firings lead to strikes: Engelstein, *Moscow,* pages 170–171; Surh, *1905 in St. Petersburg,* pages 359–360. Blacklists: Bonnell, *Roots of Rebellion,* page 283. Survey: Ascher, *The Revolution of 1905,* volume 2, page 137. Epidemic flight: Engelstein, *Moscow,* pages 172, 218. Feeble reaction: Ascher, *The Revolution of 1905,* volume 2, pages 135–136, 235–236, 358–362.

22. Mine manager: McCaffray, *The Politics of Industrialization in Tsarist Russia,* page 182. Stock exchange: Owen, *Capitalism and Politics in Russia,* pages

185–186; Rieber, *Merchants and Entrepreneurs in Imperial Russia,* page 271. City council: Engelstein, *Moscow,* page 145; Owen, *Capitalism and Politics in Russia,* page 193. Executions: Owen, *Capitalism and Politics in Russia,* page 202. St. Petersburg society: McDaniel, *Autocracy, Capitalism, and Revolution in Russia,* page 131; Rieber, *Merchants and Entrepreneurs in Imperial Russia,* pages 348–350. Ekaterinoslav: Wynn, *Workers, Strikes, and Pogroms,* page 241.

23. Ascher, *The Revolution of 1905,* volume 2, page 349.

24. Central Asia: *Tujjar,* August 21, 1907. Printing and baking: Bonnell, *Roots of Rebellion,* pages 298–299, 307–308. Unions shut: Ascher, *The Revolution of 1905,* volume 2, page 362. Donbass: McCaffray, *The Politics of Industrialization in Tsarist Russia,* pages 211–212.

25. Hosking, *The Russian Constitutional Experiment,* page 191.

26. Banks, *Cross-National Time Series Data Archive;* Foran, *Fragile Resistance,* pages 107–151. Banking: Ashraf, "Historical Obstacles to the Development of a Bourgeoisie in Iran," page 69; Basseer, "Banking in Iran: History of Banking in Iran," page 699. Monopoly: Rabino, *Memories,* page 18.

27. Factory industry: Issawi, *The Economic History of Iran,* page 260. Chamber of commerce: Adamiyat and Natiq, *Afkar-i Ijtima'i,* pages 299–371; Mahdavi, *For God, Mammon, and Country,* pages 90–94. Strong bond: Issawi, *The Economic History of Iran,* page 68.

28. Sit-in: Bayat, *Iran's First Revolution,* pages 130–134; Martin, *Islam and Modernism,* pages 90–93; Tafrishi-Husayni, *Ruznamah-yi Akhbar-i Mashrutiyat,* pages 29–30. Delegation: Bayat, *Iran's First Revolution,* page 134–139; Martin, *Islam and Modernism,* pages 94–95. Strong bond: Abrahamian, "The Crowd in the Persian Revolution," page 149. Sani' al-Daulah: Demorgny, *Les Institutions Financières en Perse,* page 49.

29. Reuter concessions: Adamiyat, *Shurish bar Imtiyaz-Namah-yi Rizhi;* Keddie, *Religion and Rebellion in Iran;* Moaddel, "Shi'i Political Discourse and Class Mobilization in the Tobacco Movement of 1890–1892"; Natiq, *Bazarganan dar Dad-u-Sitad-i Bank-i Shahi va Rizhi-yi Tunbaku.* Customs fees: Gilbar, "The Big Merchants *(Tujjar)* and the Persian Constitutional Revolution of 1906," page 296. Overpricing: Bayat, *Iran's First Revolution,* pages 110–111; Browne, *The Persian Revolution,* pages 112–113; Martin, *Islam and Modernism,* pages 62–63.

30. Dear Merchant: Abrahamian, *Iran between Two Revolutions,* page 69. Isfahan: Dadkhah, "*Lebas-o Taqva.*" Swadeshi: Afary, *The Iranian Constitutional Revolution,* page 179; Bakhash, *Iran,* pages 350–351. Small capitalist class: Afary, *The Iranian Constitutional Revolution,* pages 128–129.

31. Schools: Bayat, *Iran's First Revolution,* page 49; Martin, *Islam and Modernism,* page 54. Amin al-Zarb: Daulatabadi, *Hayat-i Yahya,* volume 2, pages 41–42; Issawi, *The Economic History of Iran,* pages 43, 47; Bharier, *Economic Development in Iran,* page 16; Daulatabadi, *Hayat-i Yahya,* volume 1, page 192, volume 2, page 42; Enayat, "Amin al-Zarb," page 953. Sardar As'ad: Ferrier, *The History of the British Petroleum Company,* pages 76–83; Garthwaite, *Khans*

and Shahs, pages 109, 112; Khazeni, "The Bakhtiyari Tribes in the Iranian Constitutional Revolution," pages 381–382; Ross, *A Lady Doctor in Bakhtiari Land,* page 45; Sa'idi Sirjani, "Baktiari," page 543; Malikzadah, *Tarikh-i Inqilab-i Mashrutiyat-i Iran,* volume 1, page 9. Shining lamp of science: *Habl al-Matin* (Calcutta), November 13, 1905, page 7.

32. National bank: Issawi, *The Economic History of Iran,* page 46; *Tarikhchah-yi Si-Salah-yi Bank-i Milli-yi Iran,* pages 65–74. Parliament: Ashraf, *Mavani'-i Tarikhi,* pages 121–122. Concessionary terms: Bayat, *Iran's First Revolution,* pages 72–73; Ettehadieh, "Origin and Development of Political Parties in Persia," pages 193–194. Unappreciated: *Habl al-Matin* (Calcutta), January 14, 1907, pages 17–18.

33. Law would bring order: Kashani-Sabet, "Hallmarks of Humanism," page 1198. Southern Iran: *Habl al-Matin* (Calcutta), February 4, 1907, pages 14–15; March 11, 1907, pages 5–6; Floor, *A Fiscal History of Iran,* page 397. British observer: Wilson, *S. W. Persia,* page 197.

34. Raise taxes: Mustashar al-Daulah, *Khatirat va Asnad,* volume 2, pages 40–42. In no country: *Sur-i Israfil,* June 20, 1907, page 2. Customs duties: Floor, *A Fiscal History of Iran,* page 397; Floor, "The Merchants *(Tujjar)* in Qajar Iran," page 105; Amanat and Hekmat, "Merchants and Artisans," page 729; Seyf, "Obstacles to the Development of Capitalism," page 75. Heavily pledged: British ambassador in Tehran to Edward Grey, British foreign minister, September 9, 1909, in Great Britain, Cd. 5120, page 127 (for a more positive view of customs revenues, see Demorgny, *Les Institutions Financières en Perse,* pages 23–25). Money is needed: *Habl al-Matin* (Calcutta), February 6, 1907, page 21. Sani' al-Daulah, *Rah-i Nijat,* page 12. German diplomats: McDaniel, *The Shuster Mission,* page 190.

35. Customs revenues and mean value of dutiable imports, 1906–1911, as compared with the mean value of dutiable imports, 1901–1905, calculated from Bharier, *Economic Development in Iran,* page 71. Industrialization: Amanat and Hekmat, "Merchants and Artisans," pages 737–739. Disastrous situation: Sadiq, *Yadgar-i 'Umr,* page 20. Ruinous condition: Daulatabadi, *Hayat-i Yahya,* volume 2, page 274.

36. Soon wavered: Foran, "The Strengths and Weaknesses of Iran's Populist Alliance." Amin al-Zarb: Daulatabadi, *Hayat-i Yahya,* volume 2, page 303. Imperial Bank: Jones, *Banking and Empire in Iran,* volume 1, page 107. Hid weapons: Martin, *Islam and Modernism,* pages 161, 163–164. Loan to shah: Abrahamian, *Iran between Two Revolutions,* page 96. Sa'd al-Daulah: Adamiyat, *Fikr-i Azadi,* pages 231–235; Afary, *The Iranian Constitutional Revolution,* pages 66–67. Commented bitterly: Nazim al-Islam Kirmani, *Tarikh-i Bidari-yi Iranian,* volume 4, page 206. Merchants Association: Turabi-Farsani, *Tujjar, Mashrutiyat, va Daulat-i Mudirn,* page 167.

37. There is disagreement over the extent of business protest in Tehran after the closing of parliament in 1908. For the affirmative, see Amanat and Hekmat, "Merchants and Artisans," page 743; for the negative, see Bayat, *Iran's First*

Revolution, pages 233–234. Guild association: Turabi-Farsani, *Tujjar, Mashrutiyat, va Daulat-i Mudirn*, page 171. Sani' al-Mamalik: Sharif-Kashani, *Vaqa'at-i Ittifaqiyah*, volume 1, page 237. Tabriz and Isfahan: Ashraf, *Mavani'-i Tarikhi*, page 115. Forced contributions: A. C. Wratislaw, British consul-general in Tabriz, to G. Barclay, British minister in Tehran, November 18, 1908, in Great Britain, Cd. 4733, page 32. Even more rapacious: Abrahamian, "The Crowd in the Persian Revolution," page 143; Vijuyah, *Tarikh-i Inqilab-i Azarbayjan*, page 130; report of December 9, 1909, in Shaykh al-Islam, *Du Sanad*, page 80. Rousing calls: Vijuyah, *Tarikh-i Inqilab-i Azarbayjan*, page 131. Isfahan strike: Danishvar-'Alavi, *Tarikh-i Mashrutah-yi Iran*, pages 4–16. Bakhtiyaris: Danishvar-'Alavi, *Tarikh-i Mashrutah-yi Iran*, pages 20–21, 35; Garthwaite, *Khans and Shahs*, pages 116, 126; Khazeni, "The Bakhtiyari Tribes in the Iranian Constitutional Revolution," pages 383–389; Zaygham al-Daulah, *Tarikh-i Il-i Bakhtiyari*, page 595.

38. Sardar As'ad: Amirkhayzi, *Qiyam-i Azarbayjan*, page 488; Ettehadieh, "Origin and Development of Political Parties in Persia," page 395. British diplomats: Ettehadieh, "Origin and Development of Political Parties in Persia," page 415. British Chamber of Commerce: Kashani-Sabet, *Frontier Fictions*, page 141. Boycott: Afary, *The Iranian Constitutional Revolution*, pages 332–334; Malikzadah, *Tarikh-i Inqilab-i Mashrutiyat-i Iran*, volume 7, pages 1458–1459, 1465–1468. Back to business: Malikzadah, *Tarikh-i Inqilab-i Mashrutiyat-i Iran*, volume 7, pages 1474–1479.

39. Midhat Pasha, "Liberty Is the Key to Everything," page 200.

40. Midhat Pasha, "Liberty Is the Key to Everything," page 200; Kuran, *İnkılâp Tarihimiz ve Jön Türkler*, pages 238–242.

41. For an overview of late Ottoman economic development, see Quataert, *Ottoman Manufacturing*. International trade: Aybar, *Osmanlı İmperatorluğun Ticaret Muvazenesi*, page 17; Owen, *The Middle East in the World Economy*, pages 191, 201–203. Foreign investors: Göçek, *Rise of the Bourgeoisie*, page 112. Chambers of commerce: Hoell, "The *Ticaret Odası*." Later business groups criticized the business groups of this period as "existing only in name" (*Osmanlı Ziraat ve Ticaret Gazetesi*, September 13, 1908, page 305); the Istanbul Chamber of Commerce said it had achieved nothing worthwhile in its first twenty-six years (*İstanbul Ticaret ve Sanayi Odası Mecmuası*, January 1926, page 10).

42. Particular businessmen: Hanioğlu, *Preparation for a Revolution*, page 176. Diyarbakır: Parla, *The Social and Political Thought of Ziya Gökalp*, page 13. Trabzon: Kansu, *The Revolution of 1908 in Turkey*, page 57. Other intersections may have occurred in the Italian Masonic lodges that served as secure meeting places for prodemocracy activists in Salonica (Ramsaur, *The Young Turks*, page 107; Hanioğlu, *The Young Turks in Opposition*, pages 33–41). One intellectual later claimed that the entire bourgeoisie of Salonica joined the Society for Union and Progress, but this may have referred to the postrevolutionary period (Tekeli and İlkin, "İttihat ve Terakki Hareketinin Oluşumunda Selanik'in Toplumsal Yapısının Belirleyiciliği," pages 376–377).

43. Istanbul Chamber of Commerce: Nezihi, *50 Yıllık Oda Hayatı*, pages 150–151. I have guessed at the ethnic affiliation based on the names of the executive committee members. Similarly, the Edirne Chamber of Commerce, Agriculture, and Industry was directed in 1901 by two Muslims and six non-Muslims (*Edirne Ticaret ve Sanayi Odası Rehberi*, page 8). An Istanbul census in 1885 reported that the joint category of commerce, trade, and industry was 38 percent Muslim, 27 percent Armenian, and 25 percent Greek, in a city whose population was approximately half Muslim (Shaw, "The Population of Istanbul," pages 271, 266). Another source estimates the Turkish portion of capital throughout the empire at 15 percent in 1913 (Berberoglu, *Turkey in Crisis*, page 16). Alliances with ethnic groups: Hanioğlu, *Preparation for a Revolution*, pages 242–261. Which class: Ergli, "A Reassessment," page 51; see also Göçek, *Rise of the Bourgeoisie*, page 109.

44. British journalist: *The Times*, August 8, 1908, page 5; Kansu, *The Revolution of 1908 in Turkey*, pages 130–131. Business statements: Toprak, *Milli İktisat—Milli Burjuvazi*, pages 93–96, 84–85.

45. Not until World War I: Şener, "İttihat ve Terakki Cemiyetinin İktisadi ve Mali Politikaları," pages 208–212. British director: Blaisdell, *European Financial Control of the Ottoman Empire*, page 178. Railway projects: Tekeli and İlkin, "The Public Works Program," page 232; *Journal de la Chambre de Commerce de Constantinople*, January 23, 1909, pages 25–26. Tobacco concession: *Meclisi Mebusan Zabıt Ceridesi*, February 22, 1909, volume 1, page 727; Fulton, "France and the End of the Ottoman Empire," page 157. Longshoremen: Pears, *Forty Years in Constantinople*, pages 270–271.

46. Subsidies for chambers: *Osmanlı Ziraat ve Ticaret Gazetesi*, September 27, 1908, page 306, October 18, 1908, page 354; *Journal de la Chambre de Commerce de Constantinople*, March 13, 1909, page 81. Bad at commerce: *Journal de la Chambre de Commerce de Constantinople*, September 26, 1908, pages 301–302; February 27, 1909, pages 65–66; March 6, 1909, pages 73–75. Register and tax factories: Ottoman Archives, T.TNF.VRK, dosya 62, gömlek 9, January 16, 1909.

47. Toprak, *Milli İktisat—Milli Burjuvazi*, pages 31–32.

48. *Osmanlı Ziraat ve Ticaret Gazetesi*, March 26, 1909, pages 15–16; see also Toprak, *Milli İktisat—Milli Burjuvazi*, pages 25–26.

49. Lawlessness in customs offices: *Journal de la Chambre de Commerce de Constantinople*, August 22, 1908, pages 261–262; January 9, 1909, page 11. Budgetivores: *Journal de la Chambre de Commerce de Constantinople*, January 16, 1909, pages 17–18. Parliament on taxes: *Meclisi Mebusan Zabıt Ceridesi*, January 13, February 22, February 24, 1909, volume 1, pages 159–161, 565, 791. Cavid, "Kanun-u Esasimizin Maliye Kanunu Hakkındaki Mevaddı," page 25. Tax revenues up: Ahmad, "Vanguard of a Nascent Bourgeoisie," page 334. Cartoon of Finance Minister: *Âlem*, April 1, 1909, page 6.

50. Jerusalem: Campos, "A 'Shared Homeland' and Its Boundaries," pages 40, 42. Parliamentary elections: Boura, "The Greek Millet in Turkish Politics,"

page 195; Kayalı, *Arabs and Young Turks,* pages 86–87; Makedonski, "La Revolution Jeune-Turque," pages 138–145; Prätor, *Der arabische Faktor,* pages 39–42. By contrast with other groups, Jewish representation was boosted (Benbassa, *Haim Nahum,* page 152). Byzantine heritage: Clogg, "The Greek *Millet* in the Ottoman Empire," pages 196–197; Dakin, *The Greek Struggle in Macedonia,* pages 382–383. Conservative Armenian leadership: Ahmad, "Unionist Relations," page 419. Militants abandon violence: Arkun, "Les Relations Arméno-Turques et les Massacres de Cilicie de 1909," page 58; Dasnabedian, *History of the Armenian Revolutionary Federation,* page 90; Panayatopoulos, "The Hellenic Contribution," pages 45–46; Psilos, "From Cooperation to Alienation," pages 548–552. New chief rabbi: Benbassa, *Haim Nahum,* pages 14–17, 152–153, 160–163; Rodrigue, *French Jews, Turkish Jews,* pages 127, 129. See also Campos, "A 'Shared Homeland' and Its Boundaries," pages 290–297; Stein, *Making Jews Modern,* pages 76–77.

51. Two Greek newspapers: Ahmad, *The Young Turks,* page 43; Panayatopoulos, "The Hellenic Contribution," page 49. Massacre in Adana: Arkun, "Les Relations Arméno-Turques et les Massacres de Cilicie de 1909." Arab nationalism: Kayalı, *Arabs and Young Turks,* pages 79, 87–88; Nafi, *Arabism, Islamism and the Palestine Question,* pages 26–28. At least some Arab intellectuals cheered the Society for Union and Progress's actions of April 1909 (Campos, "A 'Shared Homeland' and Its Boundaries," page 58). Ottoman Jews: Benbassa, *Une Diaspora Sépharade en Transition,* pages 173–174; Farhi, "Documents on the Attitude of the Ottoman Government," pages 200–201; Molho, "The Zionist Movement in Thessaloniki," page 333.

52. Noble titles: Mónica, "Capitalistas e Industriais," page 845. Nauseous: Valente, *O Poder e o Povo,* page 245. Bourgeoisie displacing aristocrats: Marques, "Revolution and Counterrevolution in Portugal," page 408. Industrial production: Reis, "A Produção Industrial Portuguesa," page 925. Capitalist organizations: Schwartzman, *The Social Origins of Democratic Collapse,* page 145. Minutes of the founding of the joint business federation in Lisbon are available in União da Agricultura, Comércio e Indústria, *Livro para Actas Directoria,* number 1, 1912–1913 (capilha 3111).

53. Exposition catalog: Mónica, "Capitalistas e Industriais," page 836. Catechism: Oliveira, *O Operariado e a República Democrática,* page 49. Newspaper: Vilela, 'Alma Nacional,' page 105.

54. Support of the bourgeoisie: Trindade, *História da Associação Comercial de Lisboa,* page 68. Grandela: Gómez, *Contra-Revolução,* page 319. Safe of the nation: Bell, *Portugal of the Portuguese,* page 198. Ox that gores: Brandão, *Memórias,* volume 3, pages 35–36.

55. National industry: Schwartzman, *The Social Origins of Democratic Collapse,* pages 96, 163. Strikes: Reis, "A Produção Industrial Portuguesa," page 925. Balance our accounts: Braga Paixão, "A Constituinte de 1911," page 39.

56. União da Agricultura, Comércio e Indústria, Assembléa Geral, Conselho Consultivo, *Actas,* number 1, pages 49–50, February 24, 1913 (capilha 3109).

57. Properties tax: Arthur Hardinge, British ambassador in Lisbon, to Edward Grey, British foreign minister, November 23, 1911, Great Britain, FO 371/1210, and December 20, 1912, Great Britain, FO 371/1463. Finance minister: Portugal, *Diário da Câmara dos Deputados,* November 25, 1912, page 5. Business federation: União da Agricultura, Comércio e Indústria, draft letter of December 9, 1912 (capilha 2663, caixa 113); *Livro para Actas Directoria,* number 1, page 62, December 16, 1912 (capilha 3111).

58. Lancelot Carnegie, British ambassador in Lisbon, to Edward Grey, British foreign minister, November 24, 1913, Great Britain, FO 800/71.

59. União da Agricultura, Comércio e Indústria, *Livro para Actas Directoria,* number 1, page 83, March 17, 1913 (capilha 3111); Assemblêa Geral, Conselho Consultivo, *Actas,* number 1, pages 98–99, October 27, 1913; page 115, February 9, 1914; pages 129–131, April 6, 1914; pages 135–137, April 20, 1914 (capilha 3109).

60. *Commercio do Porto,* March 7, 1915, page 1; April 18, 1915, page 1; *Jornal do Commercio e das Colonias,* April 3, 1915, page 1 (see also *O Trabalho Nacional,* March 15, 1915, pages 65–67, and June 15, 1915, pages 161–163; Schwartzman, *The Social Origins of Democratic Collapse,* pages 40–41). Proprietors: Farelo Lopes, "Clientelismo, 'Crise de Participação' e Deslegitimação na I República," page 414.

61. Lack of continuity: Associação Comercial de Lisboa, *Actas da Direcção, 1913–1916,* pages 129–129a, March 11, 1915 (capilha 3053). No steps for Pimenta da Castro: Associação Comercial de Lisboa, *Actas da Direcção, 1913–1916,* pages 123–133, January–May 1915 (capilha 3053); and União da Agricultura, Comércio e Indústria, *Assemblêa Geral, Conselho Consultivo: Actas, 1913–1921,* pages 183–200, February–June 1915 (capilha 3110). Industrialist in Oporto: Chagas, *Diario de João Chagas,* volume 2, page 71. Crowning this very sad episode: Associação Comercial de Lisboa, *Actas da Direcção, 1913–1916,* page 146, August 11, 1915 (capilha 3053). Mid-1920s: Schwartzman, *The Social Origins of Democratic Collapse,* pages 145–149.

62. Bourgeoisie divided: Leal, *La Burguesía y el Estado Mexicano,* page 159. Madero family: Ross, *Francisco I. Madero,* page 101. Venustiano Carranza to Cristobal Ll. y Castillo, January 8, 1912, in Mexico, Archivo General de la Nación, Colección de Documentos del Instituto Nacional de Estudios Históricos de la Revolución Mexicana, caja 1, expediente 3. Chihuahua: Wasserman, "The Social Origins of the 1910 Revolution in Chihuahua"; Katz, *The Life and Times of Pancho Villa,* pages 60–62. Rodríguez Cabo: Vasconcelos, *Ulises Criollo,* volume 2, page 324.

63. *El Economista Mexicano,* November 26, 1910, page 177. On economic growth under the Porfiriato, see Cosío Villegas, *Historia Moderna de México: El Porfiriato,* volumes 7–8.

64. Zermeño, *Las Cámaras de Comercio en el Derecho Mexicano,* pages 27, 34.

65. Grave political events: Cámara Nacional de Comercio, *Actas de la Junta Directiva,* May 8, 1911, livro 1, page 85. Arming commerce: Cámara Nacional

de Comercio, *Actas de la Junta Directiva,* May 10, 1911, livro 1, page 85A. Malefactors: *Semana Mercantil,* May 15, 1911, page 305.
66. Córdova, *La Ideología de la Revolución Mexicana,* page 108.
67. Victoriano Carranza, manifesto to the people of Coahuila, Saltillo, August 1, 1911, Mexico, Centro de Estudios de Historia de Mexico Condumex, fondo 21, carpeta 1, legajo 38.
68. Cabinet: Camp, *Entrepreneurs and Politics in Twentieth-Century Mexico,* page 16. Monterrey: Flores Torres, *Burguesía, Militares y Movimiento Obrero en Monterrey,* page 59. Yucatán: Joseph, *Revolution from Without,* page 2. Jalisco: Craig, *The First Agraristas,* page 36. Mexico City: Cámara Nacional de Comercio, *Actas de la Junta Directiva,* November 15, 1911, livro 2, pages 17–17A.
69. Mining regulations: Bernstein, *The Mexican Mining Industry,* pages 95–96. Oil regulations: Knight, *U.S.-Mexican Relations,* page 78.
70. Ramírez Rancaño, *Burguesía Textil y Política en la Revolución Mexicana,* pages 50–55, 63, 70–87, 88–92.
71. General assembly: Minutes of the executive council, March 6, 1912, Cámara Nacional de Comercio de la Ciudad de México, *Actas de la Junta Directiva,* book 2, pages 36A–37; Collado, *La Burguesía Mexicana,* page 124. Chihuahua Chamber of Commerce, letter to Francisco I. Madero, president of Mexico, no date, in *El Comercio en la Historia de Chihuahua,* page 423. Félix Salinas, factory owner in Saltillo, Coahuila, to Federico González Garza, private secretary to President Francisco I. Madero, March 15, 1912, Mexico, Centro de Estudios de História de Mexico Condumex, fondo 915, carpeta 24, documento 2359.
72. *El Pueblo,* January 11, 1913, page 2.
73. Cámara Nacional de Comercio, *Actas de la Junta Directiva,* January 9, 1913, livro 2, page 79A.
74. Hire a lawyer: Cámara Nacional de Comercio, *Actas de la Junta Directiva,* January 9, 1913, livro 2, pages 79A–80. Madero and constitutions: *Multicolor,* June 22, 1911, page 1. U.S. consul reports: Niemeyer, *El General Bernardo Reyes,* pages 195–197. The better classes: *San Antonio Express,* October 11, 1911, pages 1, 4. Intelligence report: Anonymous memorandum, presumably February 1913, Mexico, Centro de Estudios de História de Mexico Condumex, fondo 915, carpeta 23, documento 2268. See also Harris and Sadler, "The 1911 Reyes Conspiracy," pages 29–38.
75. Self-proclaimed leader: Rodolfo Reyes, interviewed December 5, 1910, Havana, Cuba, in Mexico, *Documentos Históricos,* volume 5, page 117. Nervous system: Reyes, *De Mi Vida,* volume 1, page 201. Financiers: Licéaga, *Félix Díaz,* page 145. On Ocón, see Henderson, *Félix Díaz,* page 69; Meyer, *Huerta,* pages 72–73. On Braniff, see Collado, *La Burguesía Mexicana;* Hanrahan, *Documents on the Mexican Revolution,* volume 9, part 1, page 129. Taxi boss: Valades, "Los Secretos del Reyismo," December 4, 1932, section 2, page 2.

76. José López, Guadalajara, Jalisco, to Francisco I. Madero, February 15, 1913, Mexico, Archivo General de la Nación, Revolución y Régimen Maderista, carpeta 32, expediente 430.

77. Monterrey: Flores Torres, *Burguesía, Militares y Movimiento Obrero en Monterrey*, pages 77–78. Jalisco: Rodríguez García, *La Cámara Agrícola Nacional Jalisciense*, page 56. U.S. Chamber of Commerce: Collado, *La Burguesía Mexicana*, pages 131–132. Reyes-Díaz Club: Cámara Nacional de Comercio, *Actas de la Junta Directiva*, April 3, 1913, livro 2, pages 89A–90.

78. *El Economista Mexicano*, April 5, 1913, page 1; *Semana Mercantil*, March 17, 1913, page 161.

79. Feuerwerker, *China's Early Industrialization*; Hao, *The Commercial Revolution in Nineteenth-Century China*; Bergère, *The Golden Age of the Chinese Bourgeoisie*; Chan, *Merchants, Mandarins, and Modern Enterprise*.

80. Bergère, *The Golden Age of the Chinese Bourgeoisie*, pages 54, 57–58, 198.

81. Bergère, *The Golden Age of the Chinese Bourgeoisie*, page 255.

82. Reducing talk of socialism: Bergère, *The Golden Age of the Chinese Bourgeoisie*, page 257. A splinter group abandoned socialism around the same time in favor of anarchism, and later broke with the primary faction of the movement centered on Sun Yatsen (Bernal, "The Triumph of Anarchism over Marxism"). Merchant power and tax relief: Friedman, "The Center Cannot Hold," page 251. Assist development: Yen, *The Overseas Chinese and the 1911 Revolution*, page 340.

83. Bergère, *The Golden Age of the Chinese Bourgeoisie*, page 200.

84. Bergère, "The Role of the Bourgeoisie," page 256; Chang and Gordon, *All under Heaven*, pages 33–34.

85. Tianjin: Sheridan, *China in Disintegration*, page 45. British observers: Friedman, "The Center Cannot Hold," page 32. In Guangdong, more than in other coastal cities, the bourgeoisie was divided in its support of the democracy movement: a number of major merchants fled and had to be wooed back in early 1912 by promises to protect private property (Bergère, *The Golden Age of the Chinese Bourgeoisie*, pages 198–99; Friedman, "The Center Cannot Hold," pages 67–68). Hankou: Li, "A Re-Assessment," pages 78–79. Southeast Asia: Yen, *The Overseas Chinese and the 1911 Revolution*, pages 264–277.

86. Shanghai: Bergère, *The Golden Age of the Chinese Bourgeoisie*, page 198; see also Elvin, "The Revolution of 1911 in Shanghai," pages 140–155. Nature of the merchants: Friedman, "The Center Cannot Hold," page 19. Subsidized troops: Fewsmith, "The Emergence of Authoritarian-Corporatist Rule in Republican China," pages 102–103; Fincher, *Chinese Democracy*, page 237; Friedman, "The Center Cannot Hold," pages 37–38; Tsin, *Nation, Governance, and Modernity in China*, pages 90–91; Zhang, *Social Transformation in Modern China*, page 72. Loans: Bergère, *The Golden Age of the Chinese Bourgeoisie*, pages 198, 200; Friedman, "The Center Cannot Hold," page 114.

87. Government office: Bergère, *The Golden Age of the Chinese Bourgeoisie*, page 200; Dollar, *The Private Diary of Robert Dollar on His Recent Visits to China*, page 155. Internal customs taxes: Bergère, "The Role of the Bourgeoisie," page 275. Investment capital: Esherick, *Reform and Revolution in China*, page 247. Guangdong: Friedman, "The Center Cannot Hold," pages 249–251. Shanghai: Suzuki, "The Shanghai Silk-Reeling Industry during the Period of the 1911 Revolution," page 56. Major bank: Bergère, "The Role of the Bourgeoisie," pages 285–286. Small boom: Huang, "The Role of the 1911 Revolution in Promoting National Capitalist Industry," pages 126–131.
88. Morals campaigns: Friedman, "The Center Cannot Hold," pages 173, 182–183; Friedman, "Revolution or Just Another Bloody Cycle?" page 302; Ho, *Understanding Canton*, pages 236, 287. Public health measures: Friedman, "The Center Cannot Hold," pages 157–161. Sun, *Prescriptions for Saving China*, pages 64–65. Shanghai anecdote: Rudinger, *The Second Revolution in China*, pages 36–37.
89. French consul: Bergère, "The Role of the Bourgeoisie," page 286. Kidnapping: McElderry, *Shanghai Old-Style Banks*, pages 120–121. Taxes reimposed: Bergère, "The Role of the Bourgeoisie," page 278.
90. Guangdong: Friedman, "The Center Cannot Hold," pages 185, 244–245, 181; Rhoads, *China's Republican Revolution*, pages 262–263.
91. Great Britain, Cd. 7356, page 44; United States, *Papers*, 1913, page 122; Pu, "The Consortium Reorganization Loan to China," pages 494, 501; Rhoads, *China's Republican Revolution*, pages 261–262.
92. Friedman, "Revolution or Just Another Bloody Cycle?" page 470.
93. Friedman, "The Center Cannot Hold," pages 464–466; Rudinger, *The Second Revolution in China*, page 18.
94. Friedman, "The Center Cannot Hold," pages 463–464.
95. Boorman, *Biographical Dictionary of Republican China*, volume 1, page 38; Godley, *The Mandarin-Capitalists from Nanyang*, page 185; Bergère, *The Golden Age of the Chinese Bourgeoisie*, page 204.
96. Lenin, "The Right of Nations to Self-Determination," page 162.

6. Democracy and the Working Class

1. Rueschemeyer, Stephens, and Stephens, *Capitalist Development and Democracy*, page 59. Late twentieth century: Adler and Webster, "Challenging Transition Theory"; Collier, *Paths toward Democracy*; Collier and Mahoney, "Adding Collective Actors to Collective Outcomes"; Fishman, *Working-Class Organization and the Return to Democracy in Spain*; Keck, *The Workers' Party and Democratization in Brazil*; Osa, "Contention and Democracy"; Seidman, *Manufacturing Militance*; Wood, *Forging Democracy from Below*; Yashar, *Demanding Democracy*.
2. *Sixième Congrès Socialiste International*, pages 179, 200–205.
3. Friedman, "The Center Cannot Hold," page 125.

4. Blackwell, *The Industrialization of Russia*, page 44; Bonnell, *Roots of Rebellion*, page 22.
5. Galai, *The Liberation Movement in Russia*, page 161.
6. Schwarz, *The Russian Revolution of 1905*, pages 149, 315.
7. Marxified: Wildman, "The Russian Intelligentsia of the 1890s," page 179. Milyoukov, *Russia and Its Crisis*, page 340. Paris meeting: Galai, *The Liberation Movement in Russia*, pages 214–218.
8. Ascher, *The Revolution of 1905*, volume 1, pages 75–76; Surh, *1905 in St. Petersburg*, page 121, 140–167; Gapon, *The Story of My Life*, pages 133–140; McDaniel, *Autocracy, Capitalism, and Revolution in Russia*, page 268.
9. McDaniel, *Autocracy, Capitalism, and Revolution in Russia*, page 199; Lenin, "Two Tactics of Social Democracy," page 126.
10. Bonnell, *Roots of Rebellion*, page 165; see also Schwarz, *The Russian Revolution of 1905*, pages 316–319.
11. Ivanovo-Voznesensk: Ascher, *The Revolution of 1905*, volume 1, pages 145–146. On socialists and the democracy movement, see Bonnell, *Roots of Rebellion*; Keep, *The Rise of Social Democracy in Russia*; Schwarz, *The Russian Revolution of 1905*.
12. Reichman, *Railwaymen and Revolution*. Kadet Party: Engelstein, *Moscow*, pages 115, 125. Miliukov: Karpovich, "Two Types of Russian Liberalism," page 138. The extent of such sentiments: Bonnell, *Roots of Rebellion*, page 170.
13. Strike weakening: Engelstein, *Moscow*, pages 132–133. Ekaterinoslav: Wynn, *Workers, Strikes, and Pogroms*, pages 196–197. St. Petersburg: Surh, *1905 in St. Petersburg*, pages 334–335. Odessa: Weinberg, *The Revolution of 1905 in Odessa*, page 161.
14. No enemies on the left: Karpovich, "Two Types of Russian Liberalism," page 139. Big Group: Emmons, *The Formation of Political Parties*, pages 78–81.
15. Muromtsev: Engelstein, *Moscow*, pages 118–119. Ufa: Steinwedel, "The 1905 Revolution in Ufa," page 560. For what: Wynn, *Workers, Strikes, and Pogroms*, page 222. Ekaterinoslav: Reichman, *Railwaymen and Revolution*, page 233. Odessa: Weinberg, *The Revolution of 1905 in Odessa*, pages 200, 216. Moscow: Engelstein, *Moscow*, page 122. Embittered masses: Ascher, *The Revolution of 1905*, volume 1, pages 296–297.
16. Engelstein, *Moscow*, page 193. Neuberger, *Hooliganism*, page 102.
17. Limited participation: Ascher, *The Revolution of 1905*, volume 2, page 49; Emmons, *The Formation of Political Parties*, pages 288–292. Moscow bakery: Bonnell, *Roots of Rebellion*, page 310. After opening of parliament: Ascher, *The Revolution of 1905*, volume 2, pages 128–129. St. Petersburg: Bonnell, *Roots of Rebellion*, page 311. Worker organizations: Bonnell, *Roots of Rebellion*, pages 194–234. Strikes: Ascher, *The Revolution of 1905*, volume 2, pages 128, 136.
18. Labor legislation: Bonnell, *Roots of Rebellion*, pages 202–223. Gorky: France, *Trente Ans de Vie Sociale*, volume 2, pages 170–171.

19. Ascher, *The Revolution of 1905*, volume 2, pages 93, 77, 180, 193, 198, 95, 196, 198–199.

20. Ascher, *The Revolution of 1905*, volume 2, pages 205–206.

21. Active participation: Ascher, *The Revolution of 1905*, volume 2, pages 282–285. St. Petersburg: Bonnell, *Roots of Rebellion*, page 313. Election results: Ascher, *The Revolution of 1905*, volume 2, page 284; Levin, *The Second Duma*, page 67. Last-ditch negotiations: Ascher, *The Revolution of 1905*, volume 2, page 349; Ascher, *P. A. Stolypin*, page 199. Suppression: Swain, *Russian Social Democracy and the Legal Labour Movement*, page 31.

22. Tabriz group: Chaquèri, *La Social-Democratie en Iran*, pages 35–37, 39, 50; Chaqueri, *Origins of Social Democracy in Iran*, pages 148–151. Tehran group: Zamani, *Tarikhchah-yi Ahzab*, pages 159–160. Other social democrats in Iran also committed themselves to the support of democracy—see the Mashhad programme of September 10, 1907 (Chaqueri, *Origins of Social Democracy in Modern Iran*, page 125; Ettehadieh, "Origin and Development of Political Parties," page 564). Ettehadieh suggests (pages 108–111) that social democrats in Tehran may have merged organizationally with the democracy movement.

23. Recent estimate: Floor, *Industrialization in Iran*, pages 4–5; Floor, "Traditional Crafts and Modern Industry in Qajar Iran," page 345. A second author estimates twenty-four thousand modern-sector workers in 1914 (Foran, *Fragile Resistance*, pages 127, 241). Emerged after democratization: Amanat and Hekmat, "Merchants and Artisans," page 738. Electrical plants: Enayat, "Amin al-Zarb," page 953; Abrahamian, *Iran between Two Revolutions*, page 87. Railways: Bharier, *Economic Development in Iran*, page 15; Issawi, *The Economic History of Iran*, pages 155–159. Other industries: Floor, *Industrialization in Iran*, page 9, and "Traditional Crafts and Modern Industry," pages 334–336. Strikes: Floor, *Labour Unions*, pages 5–11. Tabriz: Sohrabi, "Constitutionalism, Revolution and State," pages 243–247, and "Historicizing Revolutions," page 1404.

24. Sit-in: Afshari, "The Pishivaran and Merchants," pages 133, 151–153; Foran, "The Strengths and Weaknesses of Iran's Populist Alliance," pages 805–806. Artisans and peasants: Afary, *The Iranian Constitutional Revolution*, pages 145–176. Coordinating committee: Ettehadieh, "Origin and Development of Political Parties," pages 230–232.

25. Right of association: Browne, *The Persian Revolution*, page 375. Natiq: Afary, *The Iranian Constitutional Revolution*, page 170. See other statements defending the popular associations in Ettehadieh, "Origin and Development of Political Parties," pages 250, 254. Ironworker: Browne, *The Persian Revolution*, page 127. People are not the same: *Sur-i Israfil*, May 30, 1907, page 3. Sewer of ignorance: Natiq, "Anjuman'ha-yi Shura'i," page 50.

26. Suffrage for illiterates: *Habl al-Matin* (Calcutta), August 24, 1906, page 3. Limited suffrage: Furughi, *Huquq-i Asasi*, page 37.

27. Electoral law: Afary, *The Iranian Constitutional Revolution*, pages 72–73; Floor, "Asnaf," page 777; Shaji'i, *Namayandagan-i Majlis-i Shura-yi Milli*,

page 187; Abrahamian, *Iran between Two Revolutions,* page 86; Browne, *The Persian Revolution,* pages 355–356. Adult male suffrage proposal: Bayat, *Iran's First Revolution,* pages 138–139; Nazim al-Islam Kirmani, *Tarikh-i Bidari-yi Iranian,* volume 3, pages 327–328. Rejecting wider electorate: Iran, *Muzakarat-i Majlis,* October 18, 1907, session 1, page 348.

28. Guild representatives in parliament: Ashraf, *Mavani'-i Tarikhi,* page 120. Grocer: *Asami-yi Namayandigan,* page 6; Ettehadieh, "Origin and Development of Political Parties," page 200.

29. Popular associations in Tehran: Chaqueri, *Origins of Social Democracy in Iran,* page 101; Lambton, "Persian Political Societies"; Sohrabi, "Constitutionalism, Revolution and State," page 238, and "Historicizing Revolutions," pages 1404–1405. Rely heavily: Sohrabi, "Constitutionalism, Revolution and State," pages 234–259, and "Historicizing Revolutions," pages 1402–1406. British account: Abrahamian, *Iran between Two Revolutions,* page 91. Threats of popular associations: Majd al-Islam Kirmani, *Tarikh-i Inhitat-i Majlis,* pages 49–51.

30. Armed groups: Martin, *Islam and Modernism,* pages 158–159. Fast drifting: Charles M. Marling, British chargé d'affaires in Tehran, to Edward Grey, British foreign minister, June 18, 1908, Great Britain, Cd. 4581, page 143. Talibuf: Ettehadieh, "Origin and Development of Political Parties," page 222; *Ruznamah-yi Milli,* November 21, 1906, page 1; Bayat, *Iran's First Revolution,* page 152; Katouzian, *State and Society in Iran,* page 48.

31. Fed up: Najmabadi, *The Story of the Daughters of Quchan,* pages 138–139. Flyer: Natiq, "Anjuman'ha-yi Shura'i," page 50.

32. Lost great hopes: Mustashar al-Daulah, *Khatirat va Asnad,* volume 1, pages 54–55. Taqizadeh: Malikzadah, *Tarikh-i Inqilab-i Mashrutiyat-i Iran,* volume 3, page 699.

33. Amirkhayzi, *Qiyam-i Azarbayjan,* page 410; Abrahamian, *Iran between Two Revolutions,* page 97.

34. Electoral Law of July 1, 1909, in Great Britain, Cd. 5120, page 94. Needs of the time: Mustashar al-Daulah, *Khatirat va Asnad,* volume 1, page 67. [Aleksandr] Isvolsky, Russian foreign minister, to Edward Grey, British foreign minister, January 16, 1909; and Grey to Isvolsky, February 3, 1909, in Great Britain, Cd. 4733, pages 39–41, 43. Most democratic: George H. Barclay, British ambassador in Tehran, to Edward Grey, British foreign minister, June 21, 1909, in Great Britain, Cd. 5120, page 30. Second parliament: Shaji'i, *Namayandagan-i Majlis-i Shura-yi Milli,* page 187.

35. Taxes: Afary, *The Iranian Constitutional Revolution,* pages 315–316. Reverse salt tax: Shuster, *The Strangling of Persia,* pages 33–34; Iran, *Majmu'ah-yi Musavvabat,* page 390. Assassination: Katouzian, *State and Society in Iran,* page 59–61; Keddie, "The Assassination of Amin as-Sultan."

36. Iran, *Majmu'ah-yi Musavvabat,* page 403; Iran, *Muzakarat-i Majlis,* August 4, 1911, session 2, page 1529.

37. Working class: Dumont, "À Propos de la 'Classe Ouvrière' Ottomane," page 240. World economy: Kasaba, *The Ottoman Empire and the World Economy;*

Keyder, *State and Class in Turkey,* pages 25–48; Quataert, *Ottoman Manufacturing in the Age of the Industrial Revolution.* Salonica: Dumont, "La Structure Sociale de la Communauté Juive de Salonique," page 376. Divisions: Dumont, "À Propos de la 'Classe Ouvrière' Ottomane," pages 241–246. Underground groups: Adanır, "The National Question"; Libaridian, *Modern Armenia,* pages 103–112; Ter Minassian, *Nationalism and Socialism in the Armenian Revolutionary Movement.* Alliance with these groups: Hanioğlu, *Preparation for a Revolution,* pages 191–209, 243–249.

38. Rıza, "L'Inaction des Jeunes-Turcs"; Hanioğlu, *Preparation for a Revolution,* page 224.

39. Scattered protests: Demirel, *İkinci Meşrutiyet Öncesi Erzurum'da Halk Hareketleri;* Hanioğlu, *Preparation for a Revolution,* pages 109–116, 238–239; Kansu, *The Revolution of 1908 in Turkey,* pages 29–77; Sohrabi, "Global Waves, Local Actors," pages 62–64. Istanbul and Uşak: Mentzel, "Nationalism and the Labor Movement in the Ottoman Empire," page 94; Quataert, "Machine Breaking and the Changing Carpet Industry of Western Anatolia," page 483.

40. Beirut: Burdett, *Arab Dissident Movements,* pages 21–22. Stop demonstrating: Aktar, *İkinci Meşrutiyet Dönemi Öğrenci Olayları,* page 66.

41. Stray dogs: Brummett, *Image and Imperialism in the Ottoman Revolutionary Press,* pages 264–265. Liberty limitless: Tevfik, "Hürriyet," page 21; see also Swenson, "The Young Turk Revolution," page 270; Tunaya, *Hürriyetin İlanı,* pages 54, 62. Ahmed Rıza: Hanioğlu, *Preparation for a Revolution,* page 311.

42. Izmir: Panayotopolous, "The Hellenic Contribution," page 39. Strike count: Güzel, "Tanzimat'tan Cumhuriyet'e İşçi Hareketi ve Grevler," pages 805–815. Extent of participation: Mentzel, "Nationalism and the Labor Movement in the Ottoman Empire," page 100; see also Karakışla, "The 1908 Strike Wave in the Ottoman Empire," page 155. Railway workers as model: Karakışla, "The Emergence of the Ottoman Industrial Working Class," pages 23–24; Toprak, "İlan-ı Hürriyet ve Anadolu Osmanlı Demiryolu Memurin," pages 45–50.

43. Quickly intervened: Onur, "1908 İşçi Hareketleri ve Jön Türkler"; Karakışla, "The 1908 Strike Wave in the Ottoman Empire," pages 172–173. Forbidding mass demonstrations: Panayatopoulos, "The Hellenic Contribution," page 40. Society members mediated: Dumont, "À Propos de la 'Class Ouvrière' Ottomane," page 249; Quataert, *Social Disintegration and Popular Resistance,* pages 113–118; Karakışla, "The 1908 Strike Wave in the Ottoman Empire," pages 157, 172–173. Platform and regulations: Mentzel, "Nationalism and the Labor Movement in the Ottoman Empire," pages 160–162, 168; Sohrabi, "Constitutionalism, Revolution and State," pages 549–550.

44. British diplomats: Panayatopoulos, "The Hellenic Contribution," page 42. Austrian strike: Quataert, *Social Disintegration and Popular Resistance,* pages 121–137; Campos, "A 'Shared Homeland' and Its Boundaries," pages 119–136.

45. New Zealand: Kadri, *Meşrutiyet'ten Cumhuriyet'e Hatıralarım,* pages 8–10. Socialist: Clogg, "The Greek *Millet* in the Ottoman Empire," page 207; Panayatopoulos, "The Hellenic Contribution," page 42. We will scare the capitalists: Toprak, *Milli İktisat—Milli Burjuvazi,* page 85. Social-democrat in parliament: Panayatopoulos, "The Hellenic Contribution," pages 48–49. Segments of Bulgarian and Greek leftists remained hostile to the new democracy (Adanïr, "The National Question," pages 42–48; Noutsos, "The Role of the Greek Community," page 83).

46. Written by railway executive: Dumont, "À Propos de la 'Classe Ouvrière' Ottomane à la Veille de la Révolution Jeune-Turque," page 250. New labor law: Mentzel, "Nationalism and the Labor Movement in the Ottoman Empire," pages 162–164. Ban unions: Karakışla, "The 1908 Strike Wave in the Ottoman Empire," page 171.

47. Salonica: Dumont, "Sources Inédites pour l'Histoire du Mouvement Ouvrier," page 385; Karakışla, "The Emergence of the Ottoman Industrial Working Class," page 25. Strikes drop: Güzel, "Tanzimat'tan Cumhuriyet'e İşçi Hareketi ve Grevler," page 818.

48. Industrial workers: Mónica, *Artesãos e Operários,* pages 13–14; Reis, "A Produção Industrial Portuguesa," page 920; Vincent-Smith, "Britain and Portugal," page 228. Two movements fall out: Ramos, "A Formação da Intelligentsia Portuguesa," pages 503, 508–509. O model-boss: Mónica, *Artesãos e Operários,* page 49.

49. Machado: Vaz, *Bernardino Machado,* page 76. Universal suffrage: Vilela, *'Alma Nacional,'* page 82. Borges: Valente, *O Poder e o Povo,* page 74. Holy propaganda: Ramos, "A Formação da Intelligentsia Portuguesa," page 498. Conservative majority: Vilela, *'Alma Nacional,'* page 110.

50. Valente, *O Poder e o Povo,* page 173.

51. Ferrão, *A Obra da República,* page 276; Oliveira, *O Operariado e a República Democrática,* page 210; Vilela, *'Alma Nacional,'* page 80.

52. Santos, "Na Transição do 'Constitucionalismo Monárquico' para o 'Constitucionalismo Republicano,'" page 684; Mónica, *Artesãos e Operários,* page 147; Valente, *O Poder e o Povo,* page 68.

53. The Strike: Valente, *O Poder e o Povo,* page 68. Working-class towns: Wheeler, *Republican Portugal,* page 55. Half the membership: Valente, *O Poder e o Povo,* pages 88–89, 138–139. Standing guard: Brandão, *Memórias,* volume 1, page 87.

54. Strikes: Marques, *Afonso Costa,* pages 135–136; see also alternative figures showing a similar pattern (Ventura, *O Sindicalismo no Alentejo,* page 20). The Syndicalist: Pereira, "As Greves Rurais de 1911–12," page 499; see also Barreto, "Jorge Coutinho e 'O Despertar dos Trabalhadores Rurais' (1911)."

55. Legalization of strikes: Oliveira, *O Operariado e a República Democrática,* pages 257–258. Joke-decree: Mónica, *Artesãos e Operários,* page 17. Explicit incitement: Almeida, *Saibam Quantos,* page 85. Metalworkers: Mónica, *Artesãos e Operários,* page 150.

56. Pretext to clamp down: Pereira, "As Greves Rurais de 1911–12," page 498; Valente, *O Poder e o Povo*, pages 207–208. Vigorous measures: Hardinge, *A Diplomatist in Europe*, page 242. Greater repression of worker activism than under monarchy: Valente, "Revoluções," page 22.

57. Machado: Valente, *O Poder e o Povo*, pages 181–182. Costa: Marques, *Afonso Costa*, pages 342–346. Cork workers: Schwartzman, *The Social Origins of Democratic Collapse*, page 96.

58. Charles Wingfield, British diplomat in Lisbon, to Edward Grey, British foreign minister, September 29, 1912, Great Britain, FO 371/1463.

59. Marques, *Afonso Costa*, page 137.

60. Strike numbers: Marques, *History of Portugal*, volume 2, page 161. Lancelot Carnegie, British ambassador in Lisbon, to Edward Grey, British foreign minister, February 17, 1914, Great Britain, FO 371/2085.

61. Mistake to shut workers out: Santos, *A Ordem Publica e o 14 de Maio*, page 79. Labor rhetoric: Pimenta de Castro, *O Dictador e a Affrontosa Dictadura*, page 38.

62. *El Tiempo*, July 21, 1911, page 3.

63. Anderson, *Outcasts in Their Own Land*, page 261. At other times Madero was somewhat more expansive in his appeals. On April 25, 1910, he promised worker-compensation legislation and said he would work to elevate workers' "material, intellectual, and moral level" (Córdova, *La Ideología de la Revolución Mexicana*, page 108). On May 29, 1910, he apparently promised higher wages directly (Ruiz, "Madero's Administration and Mexican Labor," page 29).

64. Anderson, *Outcasts in Their Own Land*, page 264.

65. Anderson, *Outcasts in Their Own Land*, pages 254–297; see also Lear, *Workers, Neighbors, and Citizens*, pages 128–135.

66. Knight, *The Mexican Revolution*, volume 1, pages 131, 139–150, 424; Cockcroft, *Mexico: Class Formation, Capital Accumulation, and the State*, pages 327–328.

67. Strikes break out: Ruiz, "Madero's Administration and Mexican Labor," page 26. U.S. consul: Knight, *The Mexican Revolution*, volume 1, page 425. January 1912: Carr, *El Movimiento Obrero y la Política en México*, volume 1, page 67.

68. Gilly, *The Mexican Revolution*, page 91; pronouncement of the Sociedad "Empleados Libres," December 6, 1911, in Mexico, Archivo General de la Nación, Fondo Francisco I. Madero, caja 64, documento 2691.

69. Carr, *El Movimiento Obrero y la Política en México*, volume 1, pages 67–68.

70. Mexico, *Documentos Históricos*, volume 5, page 423, translated in Rutherford, *Mexican Society during the Revolution*, page 28.

71. Strikers shot dead: Ruiz, "Madero's Administration and Mexican Labor," pages 37–38. German ambassador: LaFrance, *The Mexican Revolution in Puebla*, pages 195–199; Katz, *The Secret War in Mexico*, page 89.

72. Lear, *Workers, Neighbors, and Citizens*, pages 164–166, 204–212; Ramos-Escandón, "La Política Obrera del Estado Mexicano," pages 40–46; Ruiz,

"Madero's Administration and Mexican Labor," pages 32–36; Ramírez Rancaño, *Burguesía Textil y Política en la Revolución Mexicana,* pages 37–88.

73. Union at Río Bravo: Francisco I. Madero, president of Mexico, to Asociación "Solidaridad Obrera," Río Blanco, Veracruz, July 22, 1912, Mexico, Archivo General de la Nación, fondo Francisco I. Madero, caja 64, documento 2736. Mexico City union: Sociedad Mutualista "Empleados Libres," Mexico City, to Francisco I. Madero, president of Mexico, January 28, 1913, Mexico, Centro de Estudios de História de Mexico Condumex, fondo 915, carpeta 29, documento 2812. Miners demonstrate: Aguilar Camín, *La Frontera Nómada,* page 272. Lower-class volunteers: William W. Canada, U.S. consul in Vera Cruz, to U.S. Department of State, February 20, 1913, U.S. Library of Congress, Taft Papers, series 6, case 229, reel 376. Presidential palace: *El Artesano,* February 17, 1913 [extra edition], page 2.

74. Bernal, *Chinese Socialism to 1907;* Scalapino and Schiffrin, "Early Socialist Currents in the Chinese Revolutionary Movement"; Friedman, *Backward toward Revolution,* pages 17, 23–27.

75. Sun, *Prescriptions for Saving China,* pages 40, 44–48, 63–70.

76. Officials draw their power from the law: Davis, *Primitive Revolutionaries of China,* page 3. Shared anti-Manchu sentiments: Duara, *Rescuing History from the Nation,* pages 115–146; Lust, "Secret Societies, Popular Movements, and the 1911 Revolution," pages 177–184; Murray, *The Origins of the Tiandihui,* pages 118–119. Zhejiang: Rankin, *Early Chinese Revolutionaries,* pages 173–185. Guangdong: Rhoads, *China's Republican Revolution,* pages 110–121, 188–189. Hunan and Guizhou: Chesneaux, *Secret Societies in China,* pages 135–159; Esherick, *Reform and Revolution in China;* Shimizu, "The 1911 Revolution in Hunan and the Popular Movement."

77. Fung, *The Military Dimension of the Chinese Revolution,* page 233; McCord, *The Power of the Gun,* pages 120–127; Powell, *The Rise of Chinese Military Power,* pages 317–318; Shimizu, "The 1911 Revolution in Hunan and the Popular Movement," page 200; Esherick, *Reform and Revolution in China,* page 205.

78. Guangdong: Rhoads, *China's Republican Revolution,* page 229. Peasant Party: Esherick, *Reform and Revolution in China,* pages 250–252. Guizhou: Lust, "Secret Societies, Popular Movements, and the 1911 Revolution," pages 191–192; Sutton, *Provincial Militarism and the Chinese Republic,* pages 127–138.

79. Labor Party: Perry, *Shanghai on Strike,* pages 41–43. Shanghai: Suzuki, "The Shanghai Silk-Reeling Industry during the Period of the 1911 Revolution," page 57. Changsha: Esherick, *Reform and Revolution in China,* page 248. Guangdong: Li, *Hong Kong Surgeon,* page 48. Sun on ignorant people: Friedman, "The Center Cannot Hold," page 125. Not really a revolution: Sun, *Prescriptions for Saving China,* page 65. Platform: Friedman, *Backward toward Revolution,* page 15.

80. Tamada, "Sung Chiao-jen and the 1911 Revolution," page 200; Fung, *The Military Dimension of the Chinese Revolution,* page 237.

81. Guangdong: Rhoads, *China's Republican Revolution*, pages 261–263. Shanghai: Rudinger, *The Second Revolution in China*, pages 23–24, 118. Simply sat out: Rudinger, *The Second Revolution in China*.

7. Democracy and the Landowners

1. Moore, *The Social Origins of Dictatorship and Democracy*, pages 434, 419.
2. Hintze, "The Preconditions of Representative Government in the Context of World History." For contrasting versions of this argument, see Alavi, "The State in Post Colonial Societies," and Gellner, *Conditions of Liberty*.
3. Moore, *The Social Origins of Dictatorship and Democracy*, pages 491, 181.
4. Gentry landholding: Becker, *Nobility and Privilege in Late Imperial Russia*, pages 32,188, 38; Korelin, "The Social Problem in Russia," pages 142–143. Decline should not be exaggerated: Becker, *Nobility and Privilege in Late Imperial Russia*, pages 47–54; Munting, "Economic Change and the Russian Gentry." Bureaucracy: Manning, *The Crisis of the Old Order in Russia*, page 27.
5. Grand Old Man: Manning, *The Crisis of the Old Order in Russia*, page 57. Minister of interior: Fallows, "The Zemstvo and the Bureaucracy," page 226; Wcislo, *Reforming Rural Russia*, page 150.
6. Manning, *The Crisis of the Old Order in Russia*, pages 79, 115; Becker, *Nobility and Privilege in Late Imperial Russia*, pages 156–157.
7. Alienation of land: Ascher, *The Revolution of 1905*, volume 1, page 181. Our land: Manning, *The Crisis of the Old Order in Russia*, page 129. Modest land reform policies: Hennessy, *The Agrarian Question in Russia*.
8. Owen, *Capitalism and Politics in Russia*, page 196.
9. More active role: Perrie, "The Russian Peasant Movement." Difficult to put down: Harcave, *Count Sergei Witte and the Twilight of Imperial Russia*, page 205. A volcano: Wcislo, *Reforming Rural Russia*, page 172.
10. Namier, *1848: The Revolution of the Intellectuals*, page 21.
11. Back away from democratic demands: Becker, *Nobility and Privilege in Late Imperial Russia*, page 164; Wcislo, *Reforming Rural Russia*, page 201. Election returns: Emmons, *The Formation of Political Parties*, pages 244–247; Manning, *The Crisis of the Old Order in Russia*, page 210. Nobody suspected: Wcislo, *Reforming Rural Russia*, page 190.
12. *Zemstvo* elections: Manning, *The Crisis of the Old Order in Russia*, pages 390–391. United Nobility: Hosking and Manning, "What Was the United Nobility?" pages 142–183; Manning, *The Crisis of the Old Order in Russia*, pages 229–259. Union of Landowners: Rawson, *Russian Rightists and the Revolution of 1905*, pages 115–116.
13. United Nobility: Ascher, *The Revolution of 1905*, volume 2, page 196; see also Rawson, *Russian Rightists and the Revolution of 1905*, pages 116–123. Black Hundred: Laqueur, *Black Hundred*, pages 22–24.
14. Intellectuals on land reform: Ascher, *The Revolution of 1905*, volume 2, pages 171–177, 192–195, 319–322. Government land reform plans: Macey,

Government and Peasant in Russia. On later social scientists, see in particular Skocpol, *States and Social Revolutions.* Pretexts for dismissal: Ascher, *The Revolution of 1905,* volume 2, pages 192–195, 348.

15. *Zemstvo* conference: Manning, *The Crisis of the Old Order in Russia,* pages 258–259, 327–328. Redesigned election laws: Haimson, "Introduction," page 28.

16. Afary, *The Iranian Constitutional Revolution,* pages 161–162; Floor, *Agriculture in Qajar Iran,* pages 84–87; Lambton, *Landlord and Peasant in Iran,* pages 169, 179; Foran, *Fragile Resistance,* pages 119–120.

17. Yahya: Abrahamian, *Iran between Two Revolutions,* page 79; Bayat, *Iran's First Revolution,* page 43; Daulatabadi, *Hayat-i Yahya,* volume 1, page 275. Society of Humanity: Adamiyat, *Fikr-i Azadi,* pages 241–242. Revolutionary Committee: Bayat, *Iran's First Revolution,* page 72; Malikzadah, *Tarikh-i Inqilab-i Mashrutiyat-i Iran,* volume 1, page 239. Yahya's death: Browne, *The Persian Revolution,* page 208. Sulayman's exile: Malikzadah, *Tarikh-i Inqilab-i Mashrutiyat-i Iran,* volume 7, page 1479. I thank Ervand Abrahamian and Manoutchehr Eskandari-Qajar for sharing information on Yahya and Sulayman.

18. Farmanfarma'iyan, *Zindaginamah-yi 'Abdulhusayn Mirza Farmanfarma;* Mir et alia, "Farmanfarma, 'Abd-al-Hosayn Mirza"; Kurzman, "Weaving Iran into the Tree of Nations," pages 138–139; Bayat, *Iran's First Revolution,* page 164. Sipahdar: Khal'atbari, *Sharh-i Mukhtasar-i Zindagani-yi Sipahsalar-i A'zam;* Nazim al-Islam Kirmani, *Tarikh-i Bidari-yi Iranian,* volume 3, pages 245–246. Browbeat Qajar relatives: Sohrabi, "Constitutionalism, Revolution and State," pages 263–264. Joining prodemocracy groups: Bayat, *Iran's First Revolution,* pages 199–200; Natiq, "Anjuman'ha-yi Shura'i," page 51. Leaders' Council: Safa'i, *Rahbaran-i Mashrutah,* volume 1, page 293; Tunukabuni, *Yad-dasht'ha-yi Sipahsalar-i Tunukabuni,* pages 48–50. Shah joins Society of Humanity: Adamiyat, *Fikr-i Azadi,* pages 275–299. Parliament: Shaji'i, *Namayandagan-i Majlis-i Shura-yi Milli,* page 176; Afary, *The Iranian Constitutional Revolution,* pages 162–167; Ettehadieh, "Origin and Development of Political Parties in Persia," page 173; Nava'i, "Majlis-i Avval: Nakhustin Budjah"; Sohrabi, "Constitutionalism, Revolution and State," pages 284–288; Browne, *The Persian Revolution,* page 240; Haravi-Khurasani, *Tarikh-i Paydayish-i Mashrutiyat-i Iran,* page 107.

19. Land reform plans: Adamiyat, *Fikr-i Dimukrasi-yi Ijtima'i,* pages 65–91; Afary, *The Iranian Constitutional Revolution,* pages 86, 127–128, 151–162; Shafiei-Nasab, *Les Mouvements Révolutionnaires et la Constitution de 1906 en Iran,* pages 378–408. Few peasant revolts reached the attention of British diplomats (Kazemi and Abrahamian, "The Nonrevolutionary Peasantry of Modern Iran," pages 294–295). Repression of rebellion: Afary, *The Iranian Constitutional Revolution,* pages 160–161. Sipahdar's peasants: Iran, *Muzakarat-i Majlis,* September 9, 1907, session 1, page 287; Najmabadi, *The Story of the Daughers of Quchan,* pages 131, 136.

20. Landowners appalled: Sohrabi, "Constitutionalism, Revolution and State," pages 289–291. Mazandaran: Kazembeyki, *Society, Politics and Economics in Mazandaran*, page 171. Farmanfarma: Afary, *The Iranian Constitutional Revolution*, page 164. Gilan: Adamiyat, *Fikr-i Dimukrasi-yi Ijtima'i*, page 70.

21. Bayat, *Iran's First Revolution*, pages 132, 144; Browne, *The Persian Revolution*, page 197.

22. Sipahdar's diary gives no clear indication for his switch, though perhaps the reason was less ideological than disgust with the futility of the task assigned to him by the shah (Tunukabuni, *Yad-dasht'ha-yi Sipahsalar-i Tunukabuni*, pages 254–257). Half-heartedly: Browne, *The Persian Revolution*, page 438. I am convinced: Chaqueri, *Origins of Social Democracy in Modern Iran*, page 103.

23. Orderly democracy: Ettehadieh, "Origin and Development of Political Parties in Persia," pages 481–485. Sipahdar's diary: Tunukabuni, *Yad-dasht'ha-yi Sipahsalar-i Tunukabuni*, pages 300, 311. Land reform platform: Gharavi-Nuri, *Hizb-i Dimukrat-i Iran*, pages 227–228.

24. Tunukabuni, *Yad-dasht'ha-yi Sipahsalar-i Tunukabuni*, page 292. The vulgarity in this passage is elided in this later edition of Sipahdar's memoirs, but can be found in the earlier edition (Khal'atbari, *Zindigani-yi Sipahsalar-i A'zam*, page 45).

25. Shuster, *The Strangling of Persia*, pages 287–288, 298–301; Farmanfarma, *Guzidah'i az Majmu'ah-yi Asnad*, volume 1, page 97. Sipahdar's diary: Tunukabuni, *Yad-dasht'ha-yi Sipahsalar-i Tunukabuni*, pages 318, 293, 311, 310, 316–317.

26. Small plots: Gerber, *The Social Origins of the Modern Middle East;* Owen, *New Perspectives on Property and Land in the Middle East;* Quataert, "The Age of Reforms," pages 861–875. Feudalism: Berktay, "The Feudalism Debate"; Keyder and Tabak, *Landholding and Commercial Agriculture in the Middle East.* Antidemocratic agrarian elites: Moore, *The Social Origins of Dictatorship and Democracy*, pages 434–435.

27. A group of agricultural scientists, not landowners, formed an Ottoman Agricultural Society several weeks after democratization (*Osmanlı Ziraat ve Ticaret Gazetesi*, September 13, 1908, page 273).

28. Rumelia and Albania: Tekeli and İlkin, "İttihat ve Terakki Hareketinin Oluşumunda Selanik'in Toplumsal Yapısının Belirleyiciliği," page 377; Hanioğlu, *Preparation for a Revolution*, pages 254–258. Comedy of support: Aktar, *İkinci Meşrutiyet Dönemi Öğrenci Olayları*, page 66. Sabahaddin: Ege, *Prens Sabahaddin*, pages 3–10; Hanioğlu, *Preparation for a Revolution*, page 123.

29. Centralization: İnalcık, "Centralization and Decentralization in Ottoman Administration." Upper house: Tunaya, *Türkiye'de Siyasî Partiler*, page 248. Landowners' numbers in the Senate might have been limited by the Society for Union and Progress, which pressured the sultan not to appoint certain favorites of the old regime (Ahmad, *The Young Turks*, page 29). Agrarian

reforms: Fischbach, *State, Society and Land in Jordan,* page 54; Sohrabi, "Constitutionalism, Revolution and State," page 590. New agrarian policy: Ahmad, "The Agrarian Policy of the Young Turks," pages 278–279; Tunaya, *Türkiye'de Siyasî Partiler,* pages 209–211.

30. Anatolian peasant: Ahmad, "The Agrarian Policy of the Young Turks," pages 275–276. Black Sea coast: Meeker, *A Nation of Empire,* page 280.

31. Few revolts: Baer, "Landlord, Peasant and the Government"; Baer, "Fellah Rebellion in Egypt and the Fertile Crescent"; Kazemi and Waterbury, *Peasants and Politics in the Modern Middle East.* The agriculture-oriented newspaper *Osmanlı Ziraat ve Ticaret Gazetesi* paid little attention to peasant mobilization in 1908–1909. Communal violence: Arkun, "Les Relations Arméno-Turques et les Massacres de Cilicie de 1909"; Farhi, "Documents on the Attitude of the Ottoman Government," page 200. Akçura: Georgeon, *Aux Origines du Nationalisme Turc,* page 85. Sultan: Kocahanoğlu, *Derviş Vahdeti ve Çavuşların İsyanı,* pages 91, 178–181. On the extent of Abdülhamid's landholdings, see Quataert, "The Age of Reforms," page 868.

32. *Osmanlı Ziraat ve Ticaret Gazetesi,* August 2, 1908, page 196, and November 4, 1909, page 65.

33. I am a King: Churchill, *Winston S. Churchill,* volume 2, page 341. Incursons: Cabral, *Cartas d'El-Rei D. Manuel II,* page 190; Manuel Teixeira-Gomes, Portuguese ambassador in London, to Edward Grey, British foreign minister, July 12, 1912, Great Britain, FO 371/1461. Trigger uprisings: Malheiro-Dias, *O Estado Actual da Causa Monarchica,* volume 2, pages 18–19. Cut off funding: Benton, *The Downfall of a King,* page 152. Perish by internal quarrels: Arthur Hardinge, British ambassador in Lisbon, to Edward Grey, British foreign minister, July 15, 1912, Great Britain, FO 371/1462.

34. Ventura, *O Sindicalismo no Alentejo.*

35. Limited land reform: Schwartzman, *The Social Origins of Democratic Collapse,* pages 46, 104. Parliamentary commission: Queiroz, *Episódios da Vida do Político,* page 229.

36. Limited land reform: Schwartzman, *The Social Origins of Democratic Collapse,* pages 46, 104. Parliamentary commission: Queiroz, *Episódios da Vida do Político,* page 229. British diplomat: Young, *Portugal Old and Young,* page 290.

37. Gómez, *Contra-Revolução,* page 18.

38. Almeida, *Memórias do Sexto Marquês de Lavradio,* pages 196–197.

39. Arthur Hardinge, British ambassador in Lisbon, to Edward Grey, British foreign minister, July 15, 1912, Great Britain, FO 371/1462.

40. Manuel: Cabral, *Cartas d'El-Rei D. Manuel II,* page 375. Cooperate with England: Benton, *The Downfall of a King,* page 163. Always do the contrary: Cabral, *Cartas d'El-Rei D. Manuel II,* page 200. Nobody wants to obey: Almeida, *Memórias do Sexto Marquês de Lavradio,* page 253.

41. Become landowners: Mónica, "Capitalistas e Industriais," page 854; Schwartzman, *The Social Origins of Democratic Collapse,* page 30. Paiva Cou-

ceiro: Preto Cruz, *Paiva Couceiro*, page 119; Brandão, *Memórias*, volume 1, page 148.

42. Wolf, *Peasant Wars of the Twentieth Century*, pages 16–17.

43. Womack, *Zapata and the Mexican Revolution*.

44. Series of studies: Córdova, *La Ideología de la Revolución Mexicana*, page 190. Remain enslaved: Joseph and Wells, "Yucatán: Elite Politics and Rural Insurgency," page 119. Land reform proposals: Córdova, *La Ideología de la Revolución Mexicana*, page 138.

45. Rodríguez García, *La Cámara Agrícola Nacional Jalisciense*, page 78.

46. Knight, *The Mexican Revolution*, volume 1, pages 274–351.

47. Anonymous memoranda entitled "Revolutionary Information," from an agent moving between El Paso, Texas, and Douglas, Arizona, March–June 1912, Mexico, Centro de Estudios de História de Mexico Condumex, fondo 915, carpetas 24–27. See also Katz, *The Life and Times of Pancho Villa*, pages 131, 139–146.

48. Moore, *The Social Origins of Dictatorship and Democracy*, page 181.

49. On the system generally, see Chang, *The Chinese Gentry*, and Ho, *The Ladder of Success in Imperial China*.

50. Fincher, *Chinese Democracy*, page 126.

51. Huenemann, *The Dragon and the Iron Horse*, page 65; Lee, *China's Quest for Railway Autonomy*, page 148.

52. Kang Youwei: Hsiao, *A Modern China and a New World*, pages 202–203. Liang Qichao: Chang, *Liang Ch'i-ch'ao and Intellectual Transition in China*, pages 104–105.

53. Fincher, *Chinese Democracy;* Chang, "The Constitutionalists," pages 150–151 *et passim.* In provinces where the democrtic revolution was suppressed by the central government, the gentry prudently supported the monarchy (Ch'en, *The Military-Gentry Coalition*, pages 21–22; Enatsu, *Banner Legacy*, pages 97–108).

54. Sun: Bernal, *Chinese Socialism to 1907*, page 57. Henry George: Schiffrin, "Sun Yat-sen's Early Land Policy"; Bernal, *Chinese Socialism to 1907*. Provisional president: Sun, *Prescriptions for Saving China*, pages 65–67. Hunan: Esherick, *Reform and Revolution in China*, pages 239–241. Guangdong, Guangxi: Friedman, "The Center Cannot Hold," pages 199–221, 211.

55. Revolts: Bernhardt, *Rents, Taxes, and Peasant Resistance*, pages 163, 242; Madancy, *The Troublesome Legacy of Commissioner Lin*, pages 314–329; Young, *The Presidency of Yuan Shih-k'ai*, page 265. Continuity: Esherick and Rankin, *Chinese Local Elites and Patterns of Dominance*. Later decades: Ch'en, *The Military-Gentry Coalition*.

8. Democracy and the Military

1. For a recent review of the literature on this subject, see Feaver, "Civil-Military Relations."

2. Huntington, *The Soldier and the State* and *Political Order in Changing Societies.*

3. Ascher, *The Revolution of 1905,* volume 1, pages 226–228; Bushnell, *Mutiny amid Repression,* pages 71–72.

4. Bushnell, *Mutiny amid Repression,* page 112.

5. Heavy weapons: Engelstein, *Moscow,* pages 214–221. We bore the brunt: Ascher, *The Revolution of 1905,* volume 1, pages 313–321, volume 2, page 234. Punitive expeditions: Bushnell, *Mutiny amid Repression,* pages 109–140.

6. Bushnell, *Mutiny amid Repression,* pages 148–149, 163, 173, 196.

7. Officers: Becker, *Nobility and Privilege in Late Imperial Russia,* page 110; Manning, *The Crisis of the Old Order in Russia,* pages 27, 31–32. Reformists: Fuller, *Civil-Military Conflict in Imperial Russia,* pages 158–159.

8. Fuller, *Civil-Military Conflict in Imperial Russia,* pages 198–200, 226, *et passim.*

9. Fuller, *Civil-Military Conflict in Imperial Russia,* pages 26, 143–144, 159, 194, 208.

10. Completely useless: Cronin, *The Army and the Creation of the Pahlavi State in Iran,* page 4. Russian officer: Yakrangiyan, *Gulgun-i Kafanan,* pages 119, 138. Proxy troops: Kazemzadeh, "The Origin and Early Development of the Persian Cossack Brigade"; Tousi, "The Persian Army." Cossack numbers: Cronin, *The Army and the Creation of the Pahlavi State in Iran,* pages 56–57. Road taxes: Demorgny, *Les Institutions de la Police en Perse,* pages 89–92. Regional force: Walcher, "Creating a New Order." Reorganized oftener: Cresson, *Persia,* page 79; Rejali, *Torture and Modernity in Iran,* pages 37–38.

11. Modern-educated officers: Kadletz, "Reformwünsche und Reformwirklichkeit," pages 153–157; Kani, *Sazman-i Farhangi-yi Iran,* page 19; Karvar, "La Reforme de l'État," pages 67–72; Menashri, *Education and the Making of Modern Iran,* page 60. Dozen members: Adamiyat, *Fikr-i Azadi,* pages 241, 243–244. Army would not block: Haravi-Khurasani, *Tarikh-i Paydayish-i Mashrutiyat-i Iran,* page 68; Abrahamian, *Iran between Two Revolutions,* page 85. Barracks, military academy: Nazim al-Islam Kirmani, *Tarikh-i Bidari-yi Iranian,* volume 3, pages 243–244, 273, 368–408. Director of military academy: Hidayat, *Khatirat va Khatarat,* page 140.

12. Malkum: Algar, *Mirza Malkum Khan,* pages 31, 34–35. Hajji Sayyah: Malikzadah, *Tarikh-i Inqilab-i Mashrutiyat-i Iran,* volume 1, page 239. There is no soldier, not a top priority: Richard, "La Fondation d'une Armée Nationale en Iran," pages 45–46, 48. Cartoons: Balaghi, "Print Culture in Late Qajar Iran," page 173. Wisdom of Hague: *Nida-yi Vatan,* November 21, 1907, page 1.

13. Mustashar al-Daulah, *Khatirat va Asnad,* volume 1, page 55; Iran, *Muzakarat-i Majlis,* September 27 and 30, 1907, session 1, pages 329–331; Najmabadi, *The Story of the Daughters of Quchan,* pages 141–142.

14. Bakhtiyaris: Garthwaite, *Khans and Shahs,* page 115. Capturing Tehran: Zaygham al-Daulah Bakhtiyari, *Tarikh-i Il-i Bakhtiyari,* page 601. Cossack

Brigade: Frederic de Billier, U.S. chargé d'affaires in Tehran, to Philander C. Knox, U.S. secretary of state, July 18, 1909, United States, Department of State, numerical files M862, roll 484, case 5931, document 463; Rejali, *Torture and Modernity in Iran*, page 48.

15. Volunteer army: Kashani-Sabet, *Frontier Fictions*, pages 130–131. Universal service: Gharavi-Nuri, *Hizb-i Dimukrat-i Iran*, page 226. Militias: Ettehadieh, "Origin and Development of Political Parties in Persia," pages 276, 315–316, 434–435. Tehran police: Amini, *Tarikh-i Du-Hazar va Pansad Salah-yi Pulis-i Iran*, pages 34–35; Mukhtari, *Tarikh-i Haftad-Salah-yi Pulis-i Iran*, page 21. Gendarmeries: Cronin, *The Army and the Creation of the Pahlavi State in Iran*, pages 18–19; Shuster, *The Strangling of Persia*, page 40, *et passim*.

16. Twenty-three officers: Yakrangiyan, *Gulgun-i Kafanan*, pages 129–130. Treasury gendarmerie: McDaniel, *The Shuster Mission*, pages 173–174; Kazemzadeh, *Russia and Britain in Persia*, pages 613–622. Gilan militia: Berberian, *Armenians and the Iranian Constitutional Revolution*, pages 149–152. Bakhtiyaris: Afary, *The Iranian Constitutional Revolution*, page 323.

17. Cronin, *The Army and the Creation of the Pahlavi State in Iran*.

18. Since beginnings: Hanioğlu, *The Young Turks in Opposition*, pages 73–75. Some less-educated military officers also joined the movement, though this appears to have been the exception (Cemal, *Arnavutluk'tan Sakarya'ya Komitacılık Yüzbaşı Cemal'in Anıları*, page 14). Intellectual officers: Karabekir, *İttihat ve Terakki Cemiyeti*, page 65. No commanders: İnönü, *Hatıralar*, pages 48 and 56; see also Mardin, "Les Souvenirs d'Anciens Élèves," page 162. Committee of intellectuals: Alkan, *II. Meşrutiyet Devrinde Ordu ve Siyaset*, page 26.

19. Recruit officers: Hanioğlu, *Preparation for a Revolution*, pages 219–221. Pamphlet: Alkan, *II. Meşrutiyet Devrinde Ordu ve Siyaset*, page 15. Campaign successful: Akmeşe, *The Birth of Modern Turkey*, pages 51–53.

20. Hanioğlu, *Preparation for a Revolution*, pages 266–275.

21. Renewal and modernization: Akmeşe, *The Birth of Modern Turkey*, pages 64–86. Hailing Third Army: *Asker*, September 3, 1908, pages 5–6. Cartoon: Çeviker, *Meşrutiyet İmzasız Karikatürler Antolojisi*, page 57. Flurry of plays: And, *Meşrutiyet Döneminde Türk Tiyatrosu*, page 183.

22. Reforms: Moreau, "Les Réformes Militaires Jeunes-Turques de 1908," pages 60–68; Sohrabi, "Constitutionalism, Revolution and State," pages 526–527. Thousand graduates: Swenson, "The Young Turk Revolution," pages 332–333; Turfan, *The Rise of the Young Turks*, page 157. From now on: Refik, *İnkılab-ı Azim*, page 60. Completely insufficient: Ottoman Empire, *Devlet-i Aliyye-i Osmaniyye'nin 1325 Senesi Muvazene-i Umumiyye Kanuni*, "Masarif" (Expenditures) section, page 27.

23. Military rule: Alkan, *II. Meşrutiyet Devrinde Ordu ve Siyaset*, pages 50, 79–88, 76, 100; see also Turfan, *The Rise of the Young Turks*, pages 158, 235. Glorious

sergeants: Kocahanoğlu, *Derviş Vahdeti ve Çavuşların İsyanı*, page 153. Muti-neers: *Akşin, 31 Mart Olayı*, pages 53–86, 309–319; Farhi, "The Şeri'at as a Political Slogan"; Sohrabi, "Constitutionalism, Revolution and State," pages 470–487; Swenson, "The Military Rising in Istanbul"; Turfan, *The Rise of the Young Turks*, pages 238–239. This antidemocracy movement also drew sup-port from seminary students whose exemption from military conscription had been rescinded after democratization (Bein, "Politics, Military Conscription, and Religious Education in the Ottoman Empire," pages 296–297).

24. Alkan, *II. Meşrutiyet Devrinde Ordu ve Siyaset*, pages 88–97; Turfan, *The Rise of the Young Turks*, pages 153–155,139, 135–136.

25. Occupied Istanbul: Sarrou, *La Jeune Turquie et la Révolution*, pages 157, 159–160; Ahmad, *The Young Turks*, page 61; Shaw and Shaw, *History of the Ottoman Empire and Modern Turkey*, volume 2, pages 285–286; Sohrabi, "Constitutionalism, Revolution and State," pages 566–567, 569–570, 574–577. Report: Avcıoğlu, *31 Mart'ta Yabancı Parmağı*, page 134. Press bill: Abbott, *Turkey in Transition*, page 290. Not all bills supported by the military government passed; for example, a bill modifying the constitution to allow deputies to hold undersecretaryships failed, perhaps because of divisions within the ruling elite (Ahmad, *The Young Turks*, pages 50–52). Secret meeting: Great Britain, *British Documents*, volume 9, part 1, page 208. Slightly different versions of the speech appear in French in Pinon, *L'Europe et la Jeune Turquie*, page 100, and Basribeg de Dukagjin, *Le Monde Oriental*, page 53. The British version is quoted with varying degrees of credulity in Ahmad, *The Young Turks*, page 85; Lewis, *The Emergence of Modern Turkey*, page 214; and Zeine, *The Emergence of Arab Nationalism*, pages 86–87.

26. *Revista Militar*, November 1910, pages 871–875; Cardoso, *Memórias duma Época*, pages 13–14; Gómez, *Contra-Revolução*, page 411.

27. Young Turks: Cunha Leal, *As Minhas Memórias*, page 226. He's a monarchist: Brandão, *Memórias*, volume 1, page 141. Chaos: Valente, *O Poder e o Povo*, page 217.

28. A. H. Kelly, British naval attaché in Paris, to Arthur Hardinge, British ambas-sador in Lisbon, June 5, 1913, Great Britain, FO 371/1740.

29. Avoided word republic: Gómez, *Contra-Revolução*, page 120. Lost faith: Pi-menta de Castro, *As Minhas Memórias*, volume 1, page 406. Persuaded: Ar-riaga, *Na Primeira Presidência da República Portuguesa*, pages 138–139; Pi-menta de Castro, *O Dictador e a Affrontosa Dictadura*, pages 11–12.

30. A great good: Cabral, *Cartas d'El-Rei D. Manuel II*, page 197. Inevitable: Va-lente, "Revoluções," page 35. Miguelists and Paiva Couceiro: Ferrão, *O Inte-gralismo e a Republica*, pages 39, 40.

31. *Revista Militar*, January 1915, page 20; Pimenta de Castro, *As Minhas Memórias*, volume 1, pages 407–410.

32. Almeida, *Memórias do Sexto Marquês de Lavradio*, page 254.

33. Praised army: Knight, *The Mexican Revolution*, volume 1, pages 464–466. Prodemocracy forces: Lieuwen, *Mexican Militarism*, page 13; Katz, *The Life*

and Times of Pancho Villa, pages 162–164. Arrested: Cumberland, *Mexican Revolution,* pages 159–160. Zapata: King, *Tempest Over Mexico,* page 111; Womack, *Zapata and the Mexican Revolution,* page 161.

34. Alumni association: Félix Díaz, speech at annual meeting of La Asociación del Colegio Militar, September 13, 1910, Mexico, Centro de Estudios de História Condumex, fondo 621, carpeta 1, documento 65. My primary force: Interview with Félix Díaz, presumably 1912, in Mexico, Centro de Estudios de História Condumex, fondo 621, carpeta 1, documento 69; Licéaga, *Félix Díaz,* page 58. Letter to Beltrán: González Ramírez, *Manifiestos Políticos,* pages 566–567.

35. Beltrán letter: González Ramírez, *Manifiestos Políticos,* pages 567–568. Unquestionably hostile: Lieuwen, *Mexican Militarism,* page 13. One officer recalled: Jacinto Treviño, interviewed in 1964 in the James W. Wilkie and Edna Monzón Wilkie Oral History Interviews, Bancroft Library, University of California at Berkeley, page 11. Modern wild-card: *El Mañana,* February 4, 1913.

36. Intelligence agents: Anonymous memorandum, February 5, 1913, Mexico, Centro de Estudios de História de Mexico Condumex, fondo 915, carpeta 28, documento 2814. Remained unconcerned: Ross, *Francisco I. Madero,* pages 288–292; Sánchez Azcona, *La Etapa Maderista de la Revolución,* pages 71–72; Vasconcelos, *Ulises Criollo,* volume 2, page 439.

37. Telegrammed support: Mexico, Archivo General de la Nación, Revolución y Régimen Maderista, carpeta 32. Huerta: Meyer, *Huerta,* pages 46–50. Madero's secretary: Sánchez Azcona, *La Etapa Maderista de la Revolución,* page 70. Considerable pressure: Katz, *The Secret War in Mexico,* pages 98–99.

38. New Army: Fung, *The Military Dimension of the Chinese Revolution,* pages 12–61; Powell, *The Rise of Chinese Military Power.* Sympathetic to democracy: Esherick, *Reform and Revolution in China,* page 146; Fass, "The Role of the New-Style Army in the 1911 Revolution in China," page 187; Fung, *The Military Dimension of the Chinese Revolution,* pages 77–81, 120–121; McCord, *The Power of the Gun,* pages 46–59; Sutton, *Provincial Militarism and the Chinese Republic,* page 82 and forward.

39. Fung, *The Military Dimension of the Chinese Revolution,* pages 118, 194.

40. Hubei: Esherick, *Reform and Revolution in China,* page 171; Fung, *The Military Dimension of the Chinese Revolution,* pages 114–144; McCord, *The Power of the Gun,* page 63. Did not dare: McCord, *The Power of the Gun,* page 66. Anti-Manchu: Rhoads, *Manchus and Han,* pages 187–205. Comic element: Schiffrin, *Sun Yat-sen and the Origins of the Chinese Revolution,* page 276. The one anxiety: Fung, *The Military Dimension of the Chinese Revolution,* page 232.

41. General officer positions: Fung, *The Military Dimension of the Chinese Revolution,* page 249; Young, *The Presidency of Yuan Shih-k'ai,* page 61. Sun, *Prescriptions for Saving China,* pages 71–72, 87.

42. Ichiko, "The Role of the Gentry," pages 314–317.

43. Sheridan, *China in Disintegration*, pages 51–52.
44. Young, *The Presidency of Yuan Shih-k'ai*, pages 70, 60–63. Public statement: Ch'en, *Yuan Shih-k'ai*, page 92. Useless talking: Crane and Breslin, *An Ordinary Relationship*, page 57; Young, *The Presidency of Yuan Shih-k'ai*, page 81. Makes no mystery: Varè, *The Laughing Diplomat*, page 108.
45. Assassination: Ch'en, *Yuan Shih-k'ai*, page 130. Large majority: Fung, *The Military Dimension of the Chinese Revolution*, pages 248–249. Abandoned the cause: Gillin, *Warlord*, page 19; Rhoads, *China's Republican Revolution*, page 263; Sutton, *Provincial Militarism and the Chinese Republic*, pages 155–161; see also McCord, *The Power of the Gun*, pages 169–170.

9. Democracy and the Great Powers

1. Banks, *Cross-National Time Series Data Archive*.
2. Kurzman, "Weaving Iran into the Tree of Nations," page 148.
3. Downplaying foreign factors: Pridham, "International Influences in Democratic Transition," page 1; Schmitter, "The International Context of Contemporary Democratization," page 2; Skocpol, "A Critical Review," pages 28–33. Positive effects: Hyde-Price, "Democratization in Eastern Europe"; O'Loughlin *et alia*, "The Diffusion of Democracy"; Pridham, "International Influences in Democratic Transition"; Schmitter, "The International Context of Contemporary Democratization"; Smith, "Notes on the Study of the International Origins of Democracy"; Starr, "Democratic Dominoes." Negative effects: Chomsky, *Deterring Democracy*; Thomas, *The Rise of the Authoritarian State in Peripheral Societies*. Both effects: Rueschemeyer, Stephens, and Stephens, *Capitalist Development and Democracy*; Whitehead, "International Aspects of Democratization" and "Concerning International Support for Democracy in the South."
4. Yeselson, *United States–Persian Diplomatic Relations*, page 89.
5. Gwynn, *The Letters and Friendships of Sir Cecil Spring Rice*, pages 88, 78.
6. Long, "French Attempts at Constitutional Reform in Russia," page 496; Heller, *British Policy towards the Ottoman Empire*, page 10.
7. Great Britain, *British Documents*, volume 5, page 264.
8. Greaves, "Some Aspects of the Anglo-Russian Convention and Its Working in Persia," page 291.
9. Crane and Breslin, *An Ordinary Relationship*, pages 80–81.
10. Katz, *The Secret War in Mexico*, page 89.
11. Young, *Portugal Old and Young*, page 253; Arthur Hardinge, British ambassador in Lisbon, to Eyre Crowe, British assistant undersecretary of state, April 4, 1912, Great Britain, FO 371/1463. Not everyday Europeans, honest despotism: Vincent-Smith, "Britain and Portugal," pages 87, 100–101.
12. Germany, *Die Grosse Politik*, volume 25, part 2, page 557, translated in Ramsaur, *The Young Turks*, page 145; Friedman, "The Center Cannot Hold," page 216; Rhoads, *China's Republican Revolution*, page 243.

13. Semenoff, *Correspondance entre Guillaume II et Nicolas II,* pages 194–195; Heilbronner, "Aehrenthal in Defense of Russian Autocracy," page 384; Ostrorog, *The Turkish Problem,* page 68.

14. Iran: Gwynn, *The Letters and Friendships of Sir Cecil Spring Rice,* page 98. Ottoman Empire: Mandelstam, *Le Sort de l'Empire Ottoman,* page 22; Schreiner, *Entente Diplomacy and the World,* pages 271–272. China: Russia, *Un Livre Noir,* volume 1, page 153.

15. Feis, *Europe, The World's Banker,* pages 97, 127, 174.

16. Laves, *German Governmental Influence on Foreign Investments;* Platt, *Finance, Trade, and Politics in British Foreign Policy,* pages 7–8, 26, 298–299; Poidevin, *Les Relations Économiques et Financières entre la France et l'Allemagne,* page 250. To our own detriment: McLean, *Britain and Her Buffer State,* page 95. China: Baumler, *The Chinese and Opium under the Republic,* pages 81–83.

17. Russia, *Un Livre Noir,* volume 1, page 15; Long, "French Attempts at Constitutional Reform in Russia," page 497.

18. Bayat, *Iran's First Revolution,* page 244.

19. Schiffrin, *Sun Yat-sen, Reluctant Revolutionary,* page 178; Ryan, *The Last of the Dragomans,* page 68.

20. German ambassador: Paléologue, *Three Critical Years,* page 306; see also Newhall, *Clemenceau,* page 233. On the series of crises, see Dickinson, *The International Anarchy.*

21. Girault, *Emprunts Russes et Investissements Français en Russie,* pages 412–429; Crisp, "The Russian Liberals and the 1906 Anglo-French Loan to Russia," pages 500–501; Long, "The Economics of the Franco-Russian Alliance"; Witte, *The Memoirs of Counte Witte,* page 561.

22. Ascher, *The Revolution of 1905,* volume 2, page 58.

23. Germany, *Die Grosse Politik,* volume 21, part 1, page 195.

24. Renouvin, "Finance et Politique," page 510.

25. Crisp, "The Russian Liberals and the 1906 Anglo-French Loan to Russia," page 510; see also Ferenczi, *Aussenpolitik und Öffentlichkeit in Russland,* page 102–110.

26. Long, "Organized Protest against the 1906 Russian Loan," pages 31–32; Long, "French Attempts at Constitutional Reform in Russia," page 498; Girault, *Emprunts Russes et Investissements Français en Russie,* page 442; Long, "The Economics of the Franco-Russian Alliance," page 168.

27. Renouvin, "Finance et Politique," page 509; Girault, *Emprunts Russes et Investissements Français en Russie,* page 414; Michon, *The Franco-Russian Alliance,* page 153.

28. Witte, *The Memoirs of Count Witte,* page 561; Long, "French Attempts at Constitutional Reform in Russia," page 500; Ferenczi, *Aussenpolitik und Öffentlichkeit in Russland,* page 111. Troyat, *Gorky,* page 103.

29. Ascher, *The Revolution of 1905,* volume 2, page 58; Healy, *The Russian Autocracy in Crisis,* chapters 8–10; Hosking, *The Russian Constitutional Experiment,* page 44.

30. Bonakdarian, *Britain and the Iranian Constitutional Revolution of 1906–1911,* page 54; Rabino, *Memories,* page 13. Ja'fariyan, *Bast-Neshini,* tendentiously suggests that the British instigated and subsidized the entire democratization movement.

31. My forefathers earned: Qa'im Maqami, *Asnad-i Tarikhi-yi Vaqayi'-i Mashrutah-yi Iran,* page 38. Russian patronage: Smirnov, *Zapiski Vospitatelia Persidskogo Shakha,* pages 75–76. I thank Zumrad Ahmedjanova for translation assistance. Cossack Brigade: Browne, *The Persian Revolution,* pages 221–225, 432–436; Mamuntov, "Hukumat-i Tzar va Muhammad 'Ali Shah," pages 351–352.

32. Marling: Great Britain, *Parliamentary Papers,* Cd. 4581, pages 142, 127. The Iranian government was only notified of the Anglo-Russian agreement weeks after it was signed, with an understated cover letter: "I have the honor of sending you the enclosed text of the Agreement of August 18/31, 1907, entered into by Great Britain and Russia, inasmuch as this agreement treats matters that might interest the Persian Government" (Vilayati, *Tarikh-i Ravabit-i Khariji-yi Iran,* volume 1, page 17).

33. Greaves, "Some Aspects of the Anglo-Russian Convention and Its Working in Persia," page 85; McLean, *Britain and Her Buffer State,* page 101.

34. All the means in our power: Russia, *Kitab-i Naranji,* volume 2, pages 193, 221–222; Kazemzadeh, *Russia and Britain in Persia,* page 543. Undoubtedly disperse: Mustashar al-Daulah, *Khatirat va Asnad,* volume 2, page 246. British did not oppose the shah: Kazemzadeh, *Russia and Britain in Persia,* page 541; Lambton, "Persian Political Societies," pages 82–83; Russia, *Kitab-i Naranji,* volume 2, pages 199–200; but see also McLean, *Britain and Her Buffer State,* pages 91–92. British foreign minister: Schreiner, *Entente Diplomacy and the World,* pages 54–55. The two telegrams translated in this source disagree on the British minister's language but agree that the threat was serious. However, another source—a monograph by Ivan Zinoviev (at that time Russian ambassador in Istanbul, formerly Russian ambassador in Tehran)—quotes the British foreign minister as telling the Russians that troop advances would not harm Anglo-Russian relations (Zinoviev, *Inqilab-i Mashrutiyat-i Iran,* page 137).

35. Internal matter: Great Britain, *British Documents,* volume 10, part 1, pages 775–777. Astarabad: Afshar and Daryagasht, *Mukhabarat-i Astarabad,* volume 1, page 271. Tabriz: Kazemzadeh, *Russia and Britain in Persia,* pages 609–610. Russian ambassador rebuked: *Mezhdunarodnye Otnosheniia,* volume 18, part 2, pages 146 and forward; Kazemzadeh, *Russia and Britain in Persia,* pages 613–619; Siegel, *Endgame,* page 108. British oppose occupation: Great Britain, *British Documents,* volume 10, part 1, pages 823, 825; Great Britain, Cd. 6105, page 49; USSR, *Mezhdunarodnye Otnosheniia,* volume 19, part 1, pages 122–123.

36. Yeselson, *United States–Persian Diplomatic Relations,* page 119; Martin, *German-Persian Diplomatic Relations,* pages 179, 189, 194–195; Laves,

German Governmental Influence on Foreign Investments, pages 173–175; *The Times* [London], November 10 and 11, 1911, page 5 both days; Bonakdarian, *Britain and the Iranian Constitutional Revolution of 1906–1911;* McLean, "English Radicals, Russia, and the Fate of Persia," pages 344, 348.

37. Danishvar-'Alavi, *Tarikh-i Mashrutah-yi Iran,* pages 35–36; Foran, "Dependency and Resistance in the Middle East," page 183; Garthwaite, *Khans and Shahs,* page 126; Zaygham al-Daulah Bakhtiyari, *Tarikh-i Il-i Bakhtiyari,* page 595.

38. Samsam al-Saltanah: Garthwaite, *Khans and Shahs,* page 122; Great Britain, *British Documents,* volume 10, part 1, page 837; McDaniel, *The Shuster Mission and the Persian Constitutional Revolution,* page 191; USSR, *Mezhdunarodnye Otnosheniia,* volume 19, part 1, pages 50–51. No more intention: Great Britain, *British Documents,* volume 10, part 1, page 841. Actively preventing: Kazemzadeh, *Russia and Britain in Persia,* pages 601, 607, 641; Greaves, "Some Aspects of the Anglo-Russian Convention and Its Working in Persia," page 293. Russian foreign ministry: Kazemzadeh, *Russia and Britain in Persia,* page 639.

39. Hanioğlu, *Preparation for a Revolution,* pages 262–263, 266–267; Schmitt, *The Annexation of Bosnia;* Ünal, "Ottoman Policy during the Bulgarian Independence Crisis."

40. Sullivan, "Stamboul Crossings," pages 139–140; Djevad Bey, Ottoman ambassador in London, to Rifaat Pasha, Ottoman foreign minister, April 15, 1909, Ottoman Archives, HR.SYS, dosya 337, gömlek 1.

41. Ismail Kemal Bey, *The Memoirs of Ismail Kemal Bey,* page 344.

42. Sympathetic: Ahmad, *The Young Turks,* page 44; Great Britain, *British Documents,* volume 5, page 316; Mikić, *Austro-Ugarska i Mladoturci,* page 190. No great sacrifices: Bridge, *Great Britain and Austria-Hungary,* page 136.

43. Heller, *British Policy towards the Ottoman Empire,* pages 30–31; Ünal, "Britain and Ottoman Domestic Politics," page 22.

44. Bulgaria: Akşin, *31 Mart Olayı,* page 84; France, *Documents Diplomatiques,* volume 12, pages 210–211; Nadi, *İhtilal ve İnkılab-ı Osmani,* page 114. Serbia: Aleksić-Pejković, *Odnosi Srbije sa Franzuskom i Engleskom,* page 501; Ćorović, *Relations between Serbia and Austria-Hungary,* pages 514–515; Rossos, *Russia and the Balkans,* page 23. Restrain dependent states: Rappoport, *Au Pays des Martyrs,* page 113. A representative of the Society for Union and Progress also bluffed to Bulgaria and Serbia that Austria-Hungary would not permit interference (France, *Documents Diplomatiques,* volume 12, page 221; Great Britain, *British Documents,* volume 5, pages 788, 798). I have found no evidence in the published literature that Austria-Hungary had agreed to guarantee the peace; in fact, there is much evidence to suggest that the Dual Monarchy did not wish to get involved (for instance, Austria, *Österreich-Ungarns Aussenpolitik,* volume 20, pages 3, 24–27, 75).

45. German ambassador: France, *Documents Diplomatiques,* volume 12, page 221. Russia: Schreiner, *Entente Diplomacy and the World,* page 275. Serbia: USSR, "Turetskaia Revoliutsiia," part 3, page 37.

46. Neutrality: Carman, *United States Customs and the Madero Revolution;* Hanrahan, *Documents on the Mexican Revolution,* volume 1. Maneuvers: William Howard Taft to E. P. Mitchell, editor of the *New York Sun,* March 29, 1911, U.S. Library of Congress, Taft Papers, series 7, case 118, reel 456. Misinterpreted: Cumberland, *Mexican Revolution,* pages 132–134.

47. Skeptical: Calvert, *The Mexican Revolution,* page 110; Ross, *Francisco I. Madero,* page 237. So pronounced: Calvert, *The Mexican Revolution,* page 111. Force this government's hands: Haley, *Revolution and Intervention,* page 57; Katz, *The Secret War in Mexico,* page 94; Ross, *Francisco I. Madero,* page 279; Scholes and Scholes, *The Foreign Policies of the Taft Administration,* page 96.

48. Wilson and German ambassador: Katz, *The Secret War in Mexico,* pages 98–99. Got them to agree: Hanrahan, *Documents on the Mexican Revolution,* volume 4, page 58; United States, *Papers,* 1913, page 721. Call in Marines: Katz, *The Secret War in Mexico,* pages 107–108; memorandum by M. F. González, aide to Félix Díaz, presumably mid-1913, Mexico, Centro de Estudios de História Condumex, fondo 621, carpeta 1, documento 69 en reverso. Provisional presidency: United States, *Papers,* 1913, pages 722–723. Idol of the foreigners: Márquez Sterling, *Los Últimos Días del Presidente Madero,* page 479. Two days before the rebellion, Wilson suggested that the U.S. government's attitude toward Madero be "strengthened"—suggesting a get-tough stance—in order to "prevent drastic and heroic action." Henry Lane Wilson, U.S. ambassador in Mexico City, to Stephen Bonsal, writer, February 7, 1913, United States, Library of Congress, Bonsal Papers, container 4.

49. Selected ambassadors: Blasier, "The United States and Madero," pages 211–213; Calvert, *The Mexican Revolution,* pages 142–143; Katz, *The Secret War in Mexico,* pages 99–101; Mexico, *Documentos Históricos,* volume 9, pages 230–231; Meyer, *Huerta,* page 54. German ambassador: Katz, *The Secret War in Mexico,* page 103. Telegraph to Taft: United States, *Papers,* 1913, pages 710–711. Taft furious: Blasier, "The United States and Madero," page 230. Specifically rejected: United States, *Papers,* 1913, pages 704, 706, 708, 710.

50. Handicapping U.S. businesses: Hanrahan, *Documents on the Mexican Revolution,* volume 6; Hart, "Social Unrest," pages 79–84. Preferential treatment: United States, *Papers,* 1912, page 826. Authoritarian elements: Bell, *The Political Shame of Mexico,* pages 220–222. Stern warning: United States, *Papers,* 1912, pages 842–846. No possibility: Henry Lane Wilson, U.S. ambassador to Mexico (on leave in New York), to Philander Knox, U.S. secretary of state, December 24, 1912, U.S. Library of Congress, Knox Papers, container 20. Protection of U.S. interests: Hanrahan, *Documents on the Mexican Revolution,* volume 4, pages 15–16.

51. Misinformed: Mexico, *Documentos Históricos,* volume 9, page 99; United States, *Papers,* 1913, page 715. Salutary equilibrium: United States, *Papers,* 1913, page 717. Treachery and throat-cutting: William Howard Taft, U.S.

president, to Charles P. Taft, the president's brother, a newspaper owner in Cincinnati, February 20, 1913, U.S. Library of Congress, Taft Papers, series 3, reel 126.

52. Richmond, *Venustiano Carranza's Nationalist Struggle*, page 150.

53. Qing appeal refused: Bastid, "La Diplomatie Française et la Révolution Chinoise de 1911"; Chan Lau, "British Policy of Neutrality during the 1911 Revolution in China"; Edwards, *British Diplomacy and Finance in China*, page 159; Rea, "The Financial History of the Revolution," pages 343–345; Reid, *The Manchu Abdication and the Powers*, pages 242–279; Woodhouse, *The Chinese Hsinhai Revolution*, pages 90–142. Sympathy with the rebels: Croly, *Willard Straight*, page 420. Honor past debt: Bergère, "The Role of the Bourgeoisie," page 258; Friedman, "The Center Cannot Hold," page 42.

54. Parliamentary oversight: Yu, *Party Politics in Republican China*, pages 84–116. Loan negotiations: Young, *The Presidency of Yuan Shih-k'ai*, pages 286–287. Banks hesitant: Edwards, *British Diplomacy and Finance in China*, page 174; Young, *The Presidency of Yuan Shih-k'ai*, page 128. British ambassador: Chan, "British Policy in the Reorganization Loan to China," pages 372, 370. German ambassador: Pu, "The Consortium Reorganization Loan to China," page 501.

55. Provinces would repudiate loan: Edwards, *British Diplomacy and Finance in China*, page 174. Signing ceremony: Farjenel, *Through the Chinese Revolution*, pages 302–305. French ambassador: France, *Documents Diplomatiques*, volume 6, page 458. Declared unconstitutional: Pu, "The Consortium Reorganization Loan to China," page 512. Open letter: *The Times* [London], May 3, 1913, page 7.

56. Ambassador's answer: Friedman, "The Center Cannot Hold," page 389; Chan Lau, *Anglo-Chinese Diplomacy*, page 69. Chan Lau notes (pages 70–71) that the British ambassador was similarly supportive in a subsequent meeting with Yuan in early June 1913. Flatly rejected: Pu, "The Consortium Reorganization Loan to China," page 518. Troublemakers: Li, *The Political History of China*, page 292. Police force: Fincher, *Chinese Democracy*, pages 233–234. Troop movements: Great Britain, Cd. 7356, page 32. Make an example: Lowe, *Great Britain and Japan*, page 104.

57. Lowe, *Great Britain and Japan*, page 107.

58. Friedman, "The Center Cannot Hold," pages 438–450; Tyler, *Pulling Strings in China*, pages 234–237.

59. Common interests: Edwards, *British Diplomacy and Finance in China*, pages 114–137. French rebuked: Platt, *Finance, Trade, and Politics in British Foreign Policy*, page 298.

60. United States: Crane and Breslin, *An Ordinary Relationship*, pages 132–133. Offers to Japan: Jansen, *The Japanese and Sun Yat-Sen*, pages 165–166, 188–189; Young, *The Presidency of Yuan Shih-k'ai*, pages 119, 128. British Foreign Office: Lowe, *Great Britain and Japan*, page 105; Nish, *Alliance in Decline*, page 100. Had already decided: Lowe, *Great Britain and Japan*, page

101; Young, *The Presidency of Yuan Shih-k'ai*, page 133. One month after the Chinese parliamentary forces had been crushed, British representatives to the Great Power cartel controlling Chinese finances ceded to Japanese desire for freedom of investment in Chinese industrial and railway loans (Platt, *Finance, Trade, and Politics in British Foreign Policy*, page 301). I have not been able to determine if this concession constituted *quid pro quo* for Japanese refusal to support the Chinese parliamentary forces.

61. Fixed idea: F. H. Villiers, British ambassador in Lisbon, to Arthur Hardinge, British ambassador in Brussels, October 9, 1910, Great Britain, FO 371/1208. See also Prestage, "Reminiscences of Portugal," page 8. We must forget: Derou, *Les Relations Franco-Portugaises*, page 20.

62. Churchill, *Winston S. Churchill*, volume 2, page 341.

63. Arthur Hardinge, British ambassador in Madrid, to Eyre Crowe, British assistant undersecretary of state, November 22, 1913, Great Britain, FO 371/1741; also see Vincent-Smith, "Britain and Portugal, 1910–16," page 103.

64. Arthur Hardinge, British ambassador in Lisbon, to Edward Grey, British foreign minister, July 15, 1912, Great Britain, FO 371/1462.

65. Minute by Eyre Crowe, British assistant undersecretary of state, on Arthur Hardinge, British ambassador in Lisbon, to Edward Grey, British foreign minister, March 16, 1912, Great Britain, FO 371/1463; also in Great Britain, *British Documents*, volume 10, part 2, page 451; and Vincent-Smith, "Britain and Portugal," page 91.

66. I trust: Minute by Arthur Nicolson, British undersecretary of state, March 27, 1915, Great Britain, FO 371/2440; see also Vincent-Smith, "Britain and Portugal," page 295. Pro-German: Pimenta de Castro, *O Dictador e a Affrontosa Dictadura*, page 50; Vincent-Smith, "Britain and Portugal," pages 290–291. Germany could do nothing: Germany, *Die Grosse Politik*, volume 37, part 1, page 105. Series of skirmishes: "Guerra Mundial (1a), Protestos da Alemanha, 1914–1916," Portugal, Arquivo Histórico-Diplomático, 3o piso, armário 7, maço 36; *Revista Militar*, January 1915, pages 19–41. German ambassador: Germany, *Die Grosse Politik*, volume 37, part 1, page 27.

67. Bragança-Cunha, *Revolutionary Portugal*, pages 181–182.

68. Schwartzman, *The Social Origins of Democratic Collapse*, pages 130–131.

69. Lancelot Carnegie, British ambassador in Lisbon, to Edward Grey, British foreign minister, May 20, 1915, Great Britain, FO 371/2442.

70. Postdemocratic regimes: *De Cómo Vino Huerta*, pages 218–223; Lowe, *Great Britain and Japan*, page 98; Tinayre, "Notes d'Une Voyageuse en Turquie," part 4, page 586. Democracy movements: *British Documents on the Origins of the War*, volume 5, page 251, volume 8, page 73; Crane and Breslin, *An Ordinary Relationship*, pages 42–43; Lambton, "Persian Political Societies," pages 44–45; O'Shaughnessy, *Diplomatic Days*, page 55.

10. Aftermath and Implications

1. France, *Trente Ans de Vie Sociale,* volume 2, page 259; Binet, "Une Enquête," pages 169–170; Agathon, *Les Jeunes Gens d'Aujourd'hui,* pages 116–117, 270.

2. Michels, "Intellectuals," pages 123–124; Adorno, *The Jargon of Authenticity,* pages 3–4; Berth, *Les Méfaits des Intellectuels,* pages 74, 29; Lenin, "What Is to Be Done?" pages 24–25; Koenker and Bachman, *Revelations from the Russian Archives,* page 229; Benda, *The Treason of the Intellectuals;* Lévy, *Intellectuels, Unissez-Vous!,* page 6.

3. Shanin, *The Roots of Otherness,* volume 2, page 208; Mannheim, *Ideology and Utopia,* page 158; Kurzman and Owens, "The Sociology of Intellectuals," page 67.

4. Ascher, *The Revolution of 1905,* volume 2, pages 250, 361–362; Levin, "June 3, 1907," page 247; Manning, *The Crisis of the Old Order in Russia,* page 277; Seregny, *Russian Teachers and Peasant Revolution,* page 200. On the Third Element more generally, see Emmons and Vucinich, *The Zemstvo in Russia.*

5. John B. Jackson, U.S. ambassador in Tehran, to Elihu Root, U.S. secretary of state, July 2, 1908, United States, National Archives, Department of State, numerical files, M862, roll 483, case 5931, document 99; Afary, *The Iranian Constitutional Revolution,* page 336; Great Britain, Cd. 6264, pages 78, 113; Ottoman Archives, Zabtiye Nezareti Evrakı (ZB), dosya 602, gömlek 49, May 4, 1909; Kabacalı, "Tanzimat ve Meşrutiyet Dönemlerinde Sansür," page 615; Topuz, *100 Soruda Türk Basın Tarihi,* page 105; Xu, *Chinese Professionals and the Republican State,* page 174; Young, *The Presidency of Yuan Shih-k'ai,* page 143; Garciadiego Dantán, "The Press and the Mexican Revolution," pages 7–8.

6. See the gruesome photographs in Browne, *The Reign of Terror at Tabriz.*

7. Levin, "June 3, 1907," page 257; Ascher, *The Revolution of 1905,* volume 2, page 361; McDaniel, *Autocracy, Capitalism, and Revolution in Russia,* page 291; Shanin, *The Roots of Otherness,* volume 2, page 208; Wynn, *Workers, Strikes, and Pogroms,* page 254; Blok, "The People and the Intelligentsia," page 363; Morrissey, *Heralds of Revolution,* pages 136, 139.

8. Chehabi, "From Revolutionary *Tasnif* to Patriotic *Surud,*" page 145 (for an alternative translation, see Soroudi, "Poet and Revolution," page 258); Ajudani, *Ya Marg ya Tajaddud,* page 241; Browne, *The Press and Poetry of Modern Persia,* pages 290–291; Tunaya, *Hürriyet İlanı,* page 64; Fikret, *Bütün Şiirler,* pages 661, 480; Guzmán and Reyes, *Medias Palabras,* page 111; Mónica, *Educação e Sociedade no Portugal de Salazar,* page 179.

9. Schwarcz, *The Chinese Enlightenment,* page 13; Lu, "Diary of a Madman"; Wu, *Recollections of the Revolution of 1911,* pages 141–142; Mei, "The Returned Student in China," page 168.

10. Rosenthal and Bohachevsky-Chomiak, "Introduction," page 8.

11. Struve, "The Intelligentsia and Revolution," page 125.

12. Pipes, *Struve: Liberal on the Left;* Flikke, *Democracy or Theocracy;* Struve, "The Intelligentsia and Revolution," page 128; Read, *Religion, Revolution, and the Russian Intelligentsia,* pages 141–142.

13. Heuman, *Kistiakovsky,* page 98; Read, *Religion, Revolution, and the Russian Intelligentsia,* pages 142–143; Riha, *A Russian European,* pages 175–177.

14. Blok, "The People and the Intelligentsia," page 360. On Blok's participation in the democratic revolution, see Pyman, *The Life of Aleksandr Blok,* volume 1, pages 210–217.

15. Georgeon, *Aux Origines du Nationalisme Turc,* page 116; Ersoy, "Süleymâniye Kürsüsünde," pages 150, 155–159. On the trope of unmanliness, see Forth, *The Dreyfus Affair and the Crisis of French Manhood;* Kurzman, *Modernist Islam,* page 25; Mosse, *The Image of Man.*

16. Lee, "The Romantic Temper of May Fourth Writers," page 73; Schwarcz, *The Chinese Enlightenment,* page 186.

17. Azuela, *Obras Completas,* volume 2, pages 786–787, 844; Rutherford, *Mexican Society during the Revolution,* page 93.

18. *Nosotros,* March 1914, page 220.

19. Wasserman, *Palavra de Presidente.* On the spread of antidemocratic ideologies, see Larsen, *Fascism Outside Europe;* Rees and Thorpe, *International Communism and the Communist International, 1919–43;* Worley, *In Search of Revolution.*

20. Iran: Samadzadeh, "The Emergence of Iranian Bonapartism." Destroy treatise: Hairi, *Shi'ism and Constitutionalism in Iran,* pages 124, 158–159. German journal: Kashani-Sabet, *Frontier Fictions,* pages 148–150; Ghahari, *Nationalismus und Modernismus in Iran.* 'Ishqi: Matin-asgari, "Sacred City Profaned," page 199. Socialist republic: Chaqueri, *The Soviet Socialist Republic of Iran.* China: Friedman, *Backward toward Revolution,* pages 46–47.

21. Cunha Leal, *As Minhas Memórias,* page 185; Swenson, "The Young Turk Revolution," page 112 (see also Mango, *Atatürk,* page 75).

22. Ascher, *P. A. Stolypin,* page 246.

23. Abrahamian, *Iran between Two Revolutions,* page 124; Liew, *Struggle for Democracy,* page 201; Huntington, *Political Order in Changing Societies;* Gregor, *Italian Fascism and Developmental Dictatorship.* On state-building, see Sohrabi, "Constitutionalism, Revolution and State" and "Historicizing Revolutions."

24. Kurzman, "Waves of Democratization"; Kenney, *A Carnival of Revolution;* Robinson, "The National Conference Phenomenon in Francophone Africa"; Decalo, "The Process, Prospects, and Constraints of Democratization in Africa," page 7. Several dozen countries: Diamond, *Developing Democracy,* pages 24–25, 60; Kurzman and Leahey, "Intellectuals and Democratization," page 969.

25. Elliot, "Three Days in August," page 297; Calhoun, *Neither Gods nor Emperors,* pages 1, 54, 243; Ansari, "Continuous Regime Change from Within," page 54; Kadivar, *Baha-yi Azadi,* page 105; Khatami, *Islam, Liberty and*

Development, page 41; Fox Quesada, *A Los Pinos,* page 13; Cárdenas Solórzano, *Nuestra Lucha Apenas Comienza,* page 33.

26. Rose and Ross, "Socialism's Past, New Social Democracy, and Socialism's Futures"; Williamson, "Democracy and the 'Washington Consensus.'"

27. Calhoun, *Neither Gods nor Emperors;* Cherrington, *China's Students;* Bailly, *La Restauration du Multipartisme en Côte d'Ivoire,* pages 109–120; Williams, "Intellectuals and the Crisis of Democratization in Nigeria"; Garcelon, "The Estate of Change"; Torpey, *Intellectuals, Socialism, and Dissent;* Puryear, *Thinking Politics.* Technocrats: Kurzman and Owens, "The Sociology of Intellectuals," page 78. Correlation: Kurzman and Leahey, "Intellectuals and Democratization," pages 968–972.

28. Eglitis, *Imagining the Nation;* Kenney, *A Carnival of Revolution,* pages 91–120; Li, *China's Silk Trade,* pages 121–122.

29. Karabel, "Polish Intellectuals and the Origins of Solidarity"; Kurzman and Leahey, "Intellectuals and Democratization," page 940.

30. Garten, *A Cold Peace* and *The Big Ten;* Jacquemin and Pench, *Europe Competing in the Global Economy;* Thurow, *Head to Head* (for a critique of this trend, see Krugman, *Pop Internationalism*).

31. Stockdale, *Paul Miliukov and the Quest for a Liberal Russia,* page 127.

32. Kurzman, "Can Understanding Undermine Explanation?"

33. Friedman, *Backward toward Revolution,* page 52; Sohrabi, "Constitutionalism, Revolution and State," page 344.

34. Kurzman, *The Unthinkable Revolution in Iran.*

35. Przeworski *et alia, Democracy and Development,* page 98.

36. John B. Jackson, U.S. ambassador in Tehran, to Elihu Root, U.S. secretary of state, January 15, 1908, United States, National Archives, Department of State, numerical files, M862, roll 483, case 5931, document 18.

37. Jackson to Root, June 29, 1908, United States, National Archives, Department of State, numerical files, M862, roll 483, case 5931, document 96.

Acknowledgments

I am very pleased to thank the National Science Foundation (grant SES-9911267), Georgia State University, the University of North Carolina at Chapel Hill, and the Institute for Advanced Study in Princeton, New Jersey, for their support of this project. For assistance with research and translation on four continents, I am honored to thank Zumrad Ahmed-janova, Farahnaz Amirkhani, Jennifer Bair, Luis Francisco de Carvalho, Betigül Ercan, Rhonda Evans, Catarina de Frois, Veronica Gushin, Patrick Heller, Hu Ying, Qin Hua, Rebecca Karl, Yonca Köksal, Lynn Owens, Margaret Phillips, Jennifer Rothchild, Mahmud Sadri, Zahide Sandıkçı, Tiago Canunes dos Santos, Josepha Schiffman, Yektan Türkyılmaz, Zeynep Türkyılmaz, Veljko Vujacic, Rong Zhang, Mei Zhou, Cangüzel Zülfikar, and numerous helpful librarians and archivists in Istanbul, Lisbon, London, Mexico City, Tehran, and throughout the United States. For reading and commenting on portions of the manuscript, I am extremely grateful to Deborah Barrett, Anne Emanuelle Birn, Ken Bollen, Victoria Bonnell, Houchang Chehabi, Laura Engelstein, John Foran, Patrick Heller, Evelyne Huber, Ralph LaRossa, John Markoff, Donald Reitzes, Kathleen Schwartzman, Neil Smelser, Nader Sohrabi, Mohamed Tavakoli-Targhi, and John Voll. I suspect that some of these colleagues may have forgotten the assistance they rendered over this project's dozen years, but I am humbled by the memory of the embarrassing mistakes and oversights they tried to help me avoid.

Bibliography

Archival Documents

Great Britain: Public Record Office, London: Foreign Office Files, FO 371 (Political Files, Portugal, 1910–1915); FO 800 (Papers of Sir Edward Grey, Sir Walter Langley); FO 899 (Cabinet Papers, 1914–1915).

Mexico: Archivo General de la Nación (General Archive of the Nation), Mexico City: Fondo del Presidente Francisco I. Madero (Files of President Francisco I. Madero); Colección Revolución, tomo 1, Revolución y Régimen Maderista (Revolution Collection, volume 1, Revolution and the Madero Regime).

Mexico: Bancroft Library, University of California at Berkeley: James W. Wilkie and Edna Wilkie Oral History Interviews, 1964–1965.

Mexico: Cámara Nacional de Comercio de la Ciudad de Mexico (National Chamber of Commerce of Mexico City): Actas de la Junta Directiva (Minutes of the Executive Council).

Mexico: Centro de Estudios de História de Mexico Condumex (Condumex Center for the Study of the History of Mexico), Mexico City: Fondo 621 (Félix Díaz), Fondo 915 (Federico González Garza).

Ottoman Empire: Türkiye Cumhuriyeti Başbakanlık, Devlet Arşivleri Genel Müdürlüğü, Osmanlı Arşivi Daire Başkanlığı (Prime Ministership of the Republic of Turkey, General Directorate of State Archives, Ottoman Archives Administration), Istanbul: Bab-ı Âli Evrak Odası (Prime Minister's Records Office), Dahiliye Nezareti (Interior Ministry), Hariciye Nezareti, Siyasi Kısım (HR.SYS, Foreign Ministry, Political Section); İrade Maarif (İMF, Education Decrees); Maarif Nezareti, İstatistik Kalemi (MF.İST, Education Ministry, Statistics Office); Maarif Nezareti, Meclis-i Kebir-i Maarif (MF.MKB, Education Ministry, Grand Education Council); Ticaret ve Nafia Nezareti, Evrak Odası (T.TNF.VRK, Ministry of Commerce and Public Works, Documents Bureau); Şura-yı Devlet Tasnifi (Council of State Files), Ticaret Nezareti (Ministry of Commerce), Yıldız Esas Evrakı (Yıldız Palace Basic Records), Zabtiye Nezareti (Police Ministry).

Portugal: Arquivo Histórico-Diplomático, Ministro de Negócios Estrangeiros (Historical-Diplomatic Archive, Ministry of Foreign Affairs), Lisbon: Movimento

Militar em Lisboa, Jan.–Maio 1915 (Military Movement in Lisbon, Jan.–May 1915); Guerra Mundial (1a), Protestos da Alemanha, 1914–1916 (First World War, German Protests, 1914–1916).

Portugal: Arquivos Nacionais da Torre do Tombo (Tombo Tower National Archives), Lisbon: Ministro do Interior (Interior Ministry).

Portugal: Associação Comercial de Lisboa/Câmara de Comercio (Commercial Association of Lisbon/Chamber of Commerce), Lisbon: Actas da Direcção (Minutes of the Executive Committee); Assemblêa Geral, Conselho Consultivo, and Actas da Directoria da União da Agricultura, Comercio, e Industria (General Assembly, Consultative Council, and Minutes of the Executive Committee of the Union of Agriculture, Commerce, and Industry).

United States: Library of Congress Manuscript Division, Washington, DC: Papers of Stephen Bonsal, Philander C. Knox, and William Howard Taft.

United States: National Archives and Records Administration, College Park, Maryland: Department of State, record group 59, numerical files M705 (Portugal), M862 (Persia).

Published Government Documents

Austria. 1930. *Österreich-Ungarns Aussenpolitik von der Bosnischen Krise 1908 bis zum Kriegsausbruch 1914* (Austria-Hungarian Foreign Policy from the 1908 Bosnian Crisis to the 1914 Outbreak of War), volumes 19–20, edited by Ludwig Bittner and Hans Uebersberger. Vienna and Leipzig, Austria: Österreichischer Bundesverlag für Unterricht, Wissenschaft und Kunst.

France. 1933–1954. *Documents Diplomatiques Français (1871–1914)* (French Diplomatic Documents, 1871–1914), second series, volume 12; third series, volume 6. Paris, France: Ministère des Affaires Étrangères, Commission de Publications des Documents Relatifs aux Origines de la Guerre de 1914; Imprimerie Nationale; Alfred Costes.

Germany. 1925–1926. *Die Grosse Politik der Europäischen Kabinette, 1871–1914* (The Foreign Policy of the European Cabinets, 1871–1914), volume 21, part 1, and volume 37, part 1, edited by Johannes Lepsius, Albrecht Mendelssohn Bartholdy, and Friedrich Thimme. Berlin, Germany: Deutsche Verlagsgesellschaft für Politik und Geschichte m.b.H.

Great Britain. 1909–1914. Cd. 4581 (Persia, 1909); Cd. 4733 (Persia, 1909); Cd. 5120 (Persia, 1910); Cd. 6105 (Persia, 1912); Cd. 7356 (China, 1914). In House of Commons, *Sessional Papers*. London, England: His Majesty's Stationery Office.

Great Britain. 1928–1936. *British Documents on the Origins of the War, 1898–1914*, volumes 5, 9 (part 1), and 10 (parts 1 and 2), edited by G. P. Gooch and Harold Temperley. London, England: His Majesty's Stationery Office.

Iran. No date. *Majmu'ah-yi Musavvabat-i Majlis-i Shura-yi Milli dar Chahar Daurah-yi Taqniniyah* (Collection of Laws of the National Consultative Assembly in Four Legislative Sessions). Tehran, Iran: Matba'ah-yi Majlis.

Iran. [1907–1911] 1946. *Muzakarat-i Majlis* (Parliamentary Proceedings), volumes 1–2. Tehran, Iran: Chapkhanah-yi Majlis.

Mexico. 1910–1912. *Ley de Ingresos y Presupuesto de Egresos del Erario Federal* (Law of Income and Plan of Expenditures of the Federal Budget). Mexico City, Mexico: Tipografía de la Oficina Impresora de Estampillas, Palacio Nacional.

Mexico. 1965. *Documentos Históricos de la Revolución Mexicana* (Historical Documents of the Mexican Revolution), volumes 8–9, edited by the Comisión de Investigaciones Históricas de la Revolución Mexicana, under the direction of Josefina E. de Fabela. Mexico City, Mexico: Editorial Jus.

Ottoman Empire. 1909. *Devlet-i Aliyye-yi Osmaniyye'nin 1325 Senesi Muvazene-yi Umumiyye Kanuni ve Esbab-i Mücbe Layihası* (The Public Budget Law of the Exalted Ottoman State for 1909–1910 and Memorandum on the Necessity Thereof). Istanbul, Ottoman Empire: Matbaa-yı Osmaniye.

Ottoman Empire. 1909. *Devlet-i Osmaniyye'nin 1325 Senesine Mahsus Bütçesidir* (The Ottoman State Budget for 1909–1910). Istanbul, Ottoman Empire: Matbaa-yı Amire.

Ottoman Empire. [1908–1909] 1982. *Meclisi Mebusan Zabıt Ceridesi* (Minutes of the Parliamentary Representatives), volume 1. Ankara, Turkey: TBMM Basımevi.

Portugal. 1910–1911. *Orçamento Geral e Proposta de Lei das Receitas e das Despesas Ordinarias e Extraordinarias do Estado na Metropole para o Anno Economico de 1910–1911/1911–1912* (General Budget and Legislative Proposal for Revenues and Ordinary and Extraordinary Expenses of the State in the Metropole for the Fiscal Year 1910–1911/1911–1912). Lisbon, Portugal: Imprensa Nacional.

Portugal. 1910–1915. *Diário da Câmara dos Deputados* (Minutes of the Chamber of Deputies). Lisbon, Portugal: Imprensa Nacional.

Portugal. 1914. *Leis de Receita e de Despesa e Orçamentais de 30 de Junho de 1914 para o Ano Económico de 1914–1915 e Respectivos Orçamentos* (Laws of Revenue and Expense and Budgets of June 30, 1914, for the Fiscal Year 1914–1915, and the Respective Budgets). Lisbon, Portugal: Imprensa Nacional.

Russia. [1911–1913] 1987–1988. *Kitab-i Naranji: Guzarish'ha-yi Siyasi-yi Vizarat-i Kharajah-yi Rusiyah-yi Tzari Dar-barah-yi Inqilab-i Mashrutah-yi Iran* (The Orange Book: Political Reports of the Russian Tsarist Foreign Ministry regarding the Constitutional Revolution of Iran), 3 volumes, edited by Ahmad Bashiri. Tehran, Iran: Nashr-i Nur.

Russia. [1922]. *Un Livre Noir: Diplomatie d'Avant-Guerre d'Après les Documents des Archives Russes* (A Black Book: Prewar Diplomacy according to Russian Archival Documents), volume 1, 1910–1912. Paris, France: Librairie du Travail.

USSR. 1930–1931. "Turetskaia Revoliutsiia 1908–1909 gg." (The Turkish Revolution of 1908–1909), 3 parts. *Krasnyi Arkhiv* (Red Archives), volume 43, pages 3–54; volume 44, pages 3–39; volume 45, pages 27–52.

USSR. 1938–1939. *Mezhdunarodnye Otnosheniia v Epokhu Imperializma: Doku-menti iz Arkhivov Tsarskogo i Vremennogo Pravitel'stva 1878–1917* (International Relations in the Epoch of Imperialism: Documents from the Archives of the Tsar and the Provisional Government 1878–1917), second series, volumes 18 (part 2) and 19 (part 1). [Moscow, USSR]: Gosudarstvennoe Izdatel'stvo Politicheskoi Literatury.

United States of America. 1914–1920. *Papers Relating to the Foreign Relations of the United States,* volumes 1909–1913. Washington, DC: Government Printing Office.

Periodicals

A'inah-yi Ghayb-nima (The Mystery-Displaying Mirror), Tehran, Iran.

Âlem (The World), Istanbul, Ottoman Empire.

Anjuman (City Council), Tabriz, Iran.

El Artesano (The Artisan), Mexico City, Mexico.

Asker (The Soldier), Istanbul, Ottoman Empire.

L'Aurore (The Dawn), Paris, France.

Commercio do Porto (Commerce of Porto), Oporto, Portugal.

El Economista Mexicano. (The Mexican Economist), Mexico City, Mexico.

Habl al-Matin (The Strong Bond), Calcutta, India.

Habl al-Matin (The Strong Bond), Tehran, Iran.

Idjtihad (Rational Interpretation), Cairo, Egypt.

İstanbul Ticaret ve Sanayi Odası Mecmuası (Journal of the Istanbul Chamber of Commerce and Industry), Istanbul, Turkey.

İstişare (Consultation), Istanbul, Ottoman Empire.

Jornal do Commercio e das Colonias (Journal of Commerce and Colonies), Lisbon, Portugal.

Journal de la Chambre de Commerce de Constantinople (Journal of the Constantinople Chamber of Commerce), Istanbul, Ottoman Empire.

Kalem (The Pen), Istanbul, Ottoman Empire.

The Levant Herald and Eastern Express, Istanbul, Ottoman Empire.

El Mañana (Tomorrow), Mexico City, Mexico.

Min Bao (The People), Tokyo, Japan.

Multicolor (Multicolor), Mexico City, Mexico.

O Mundo (The World), Lisbon, Portugal.

Nida-yi Vatan (The Call of the Homeland), Tehran, Iran.

North-China Herald, Shanghai, China.

Nosotros (We), Mexico City, Mexico.

Osmanlı Ziraat ve Ticaret Gazetesi (Ottoman Commerce and Agriculture Newspaper), Istanbul, Ottoman Empire.

El País (The Country), Mexico City, Mexico.

The Positivist Review, London, England.

El Pueblo (The People), Teziutlán, Puebla, Mexico.

Qanun (The Law), London, England.
Rahnima (The Guide), Tehran, Iran.
Revista Militar (Military Review), Lisbon, Portugal.
Ruznamah-yi Milli (The National Newspaper), Tabriz, Iran.
San Antonio Express, San Antonio, Texas.
Semana Mercantil (Mercantile Week), Mexico City, Mexico.
Sur-i Israfil (The Trumpet of Israfil), Tehran, Iran.
Şûra-yı Ümmet (The National Council), Paris, France.
El Tiempo (The Times), Mexico City, Mexico.
The Times, London, England.
O Trabalho Nacional (The National Labor), Oporto, Portugal.
Tujjar (Merchants), Tashkent, Russian Turkistan.

Books and Papers

Abascal, Salvador. 1983. *Madero: Dictador Infortunado, Anti-Agrarista, Autor de la Reforma Política* (Madero: Unfortune Dictator, Opponent of Agrarian Reform, Author of the Political Reform). Mexico City, Mexico: Editorial Tradición.

Abbott, G. F. 1909. *Turkey in Transition.* London, England: Edward Arnold.

Abrahamian, Ervand. 1969. "The Crowd in the Persian Revolution." *Iranian Studies,* volume 2, pages 128–150.

———. 1982. *Iran Between Two Revolutions.* Princeton, New Jersey: Princeton University Press.

Adamiyat, Firaydun. 1961. *Fikr-i Azadi va Muqadamah-yi Nahzat-i Mashrutiyat* (Thoughts of Liberty and the Preliminaries to the Constitutionalist Movement). Tehran, Iran: Intisharat-i Sukhan.

———. 1975. *Fikr-i Dimukrasi-i Ijtima'i dar Nahzat-i Mashrutiyat-i Iran* (Social Democratic Thought in the Iranian Constitutionalist Movement). Tehran, Iran: Intisharat-i Payam.

———. 1976. *Idi'uluzhi-yi Nahzat-i Mashrutiyat-i Iran* (Ideology of the Constitutionalist Movement of Iran), volume 1. Tehran, Iran: Intisharat-i Payam.

———. 1981. *Shurish bar Imtiyaz-Namah-yi Rizhi: Tahlil-i Siyasi* (Uprising against the Regie Concession). Tehran, Iran: Payam.

Adamiyat, Firaydun, and Huma Natiq. 1977. *Afkar-i Ijtima'i va Siyasi va Iqtisadi dar Asar-i Muntashir Na-Shudah-yi Dauran-i Qajar* (Social, Political, and Economic Thought in Unpublished Works of the Qajar Era). Tehran, Iran: Intisharat-i Agah.

Adanır, Fikret. 1994. "The National Question and the Genesis and Development of Socialism in the Ottoman Empire: The Case of Macedonia." Pages 27–48 in Mete Tunçay and Erik Jan Zürcher, editors, *Socialism and Nationalism in the Ottoman Empire, 1876–1923.* London, England: British Academic Press.

Adler, Glenn, and Eddie Webster. 1995. "Challenging Transition Theory: The Labor Movement, Radical Reform, and Transition to Democracy in South Africa." *Politics and Society,* volume 23, pages 75–106.

Adorno, Theodor. [1964] 1973. *The Jargon of Authenticity,* translated by Knut Tarnowski and Frederic Will. Evanston, Illinois: Northwestern University Press.

Afary, Janet. 1996. *The Iranian Constitutional Revolution, 1906–1911.* New York, New York: Columbia University Press.

Afshar, Iraj, and Muhammad Rasul Daryagasht, editors. 1984. *Mukhabarat-i Astarabad: Guzarish'ha-yi Husaynquli Maqsudlu, Vakil al-Daulah* (Correspondence from Astarabad: The Reports of Husaynquli Maqsadlu, Vakil al-Daulah), volume 1. Tehran, Iran: Nashr-i Tarikh-i Iran.

Afshari, Mohammad Reza. 1983. "The Pishivaran and Merchants in Precapitalist Iranian Society: An Essay on the Background and Causes of the Constitutional Revolution." *International Journal of Middle East Studies,* volume 15, pages 133–155.

Agathon [Henri Massis and Alfred de Tarde]. [1913] 1995. *Les Jeunes Gens d'Aujourd'hui* (Young People of Today). Paris, France: Imprimerie Nationale.

[Aghaoglu,] Ahmed-Bey. 1893. "La Société Persane: Le Gouvernment de la Perse et l'État d'Ésprit des Persans" (Persian Society: The Government of Persia and the State of the Spirit of the Persians). *La Nouvelle Revue* (The New Review), October 1, 1893, pages 509–527.

Aguilar Camín, Héctor. 1985. *La Frontera Nómada: Sonora y la Revolución Mexicana* (The Nomadic Frontier: Sonora and the Mexican Revolution). Mexico City, Mexico: CONAFE and Siglo XXI Editores.

Ahang, Muhammad Kazim. 1970. *Sayr-i Zhurnalizm dar Afghanistan* (The Development of Journalism in Afghanistan). Kabul, Afghanistan: Anjuman-i Tarikh va Adab.

Ahmad, Feroz. 1969. *The Young Turks: The Committee of Union and Progress in Turkish Politics, 1908–1914.* Oxford, England: Clarendon Press.

———. 1980. "Vanguard of a Nascent Bourgeoisie: The Social and Economic Policy of the Young Turks 1908–1918." Pages 329–350 in Osman Okyar and Halil İnalcık, editors, *Social and Economic History of Turkey (1071–1920).* Ankara, Turkey: Meteksan Limited Şirketi.

———. 1982. "Unionist Relations with the Greek, Armenian, and Jewish Communities of the Ottoman Empire, 1908–1914." Pages 401–434 in Benjamin Braude and Bernard Lewis, editors, *Christians and Jews in the Ottoman Empire,* volume 1. New York, New York: Holmes and Meier.

———. 1983. "The Agrarian Policy of the Young Turks, 1908–1918." Pages 275–288 in Jean-Louis Bacqué-Grammont and Paul Dumont, editors, *Économie et Sociétés dans l'Empire Ottoman (Fin du XVIIIe–Début du XXe Siècle)* (Economy and Societies in the Ottoman Empire, End of the Eighteenth to the Beginning of the Twentieth Century). Paris, France: Éditions du Centre National de la Recherche Scientifique.

Ajudani, Masha'llah. 2002. *Ya Marg ya Tajaddud: Daftari dar Shi'r va Adab-i Mashrutah* (Death or Renewal: Notes on Constitutionalist Poetry and Literature). London, England: Fasl-e Ketab.

Akarlı, Engin. 1992. "Economic Policy and Budgets in Ottoman Turkey, 1876–1909." *Middle Eastern Studies*, volume 28, pages 443–476.

Akmeşe, Handan Nezir. 2005. *The Birth of Modern Turkey: The Ottoman Military and the March to World War I*. London, England: I. B. Tauris

Akş, Sina. 1972. *31 Mart Olayı* (The March 31 Incident). Istanbul, Turkey: Sinan Yayınları.

Aktar, Yücel. 1990. *İkinci Meşrutiyet Dönemi Öğrenci Olayları, 1908–1918* (Student Incidents during the Second Constitutional Period). Istanbul, Turkey: İletişim.

Alavi, Bozorg. 1983. "Critical Writings on the Renewal of Iran." Pages 243–254 in Edmund Bosworth and Carole Hillebrand, editors, *Qajar Iran: Political, Social and Cultural Change, 1800–1925*. Edinburgh, Scotland: Edinburgh University Press.

Alavi, Hamza. 1972. "The State in Post Colonial Societies: Pakistan and Bangladesh." *New Left Review*, number 74, pages 59–81.

Aleksić-Pejković, Ljiljana. 1965. *Odnosi Srbije sa Franzuskom i Engleskom, 1903–1914* (Relations of Serbia with France and England, 1903–1914). Belgrade, Yugoslavia: Édition de l'Institut d'Histoire.

Alexander, Gerard. 2002. *The Sources of Democratic Consolidation*. Ithaca, New York: Cornell University Press.

Algar, Hamid. 1969. *Religion and State in Iran, 1785–1906: The Role of the Ulama in the Qajar Period*. Berkeley, California: University of California Press.

———. 1973. *Mirza Malkum Khan: A Study in the History of Persian Modernism*. Berkeley, California: University of California Press.

Alkan, Ahmet Turan. 1992. *II. Meşrutiyet Devrinde Ordu ve Siyaset* (The Army and Politics during the Second Constitutional Period). Ankara, Turkey: Cedid Neşriyat.

Almeida, António José de. 1933. *Quarenta Anos de Vida Literária e Política* (Forty Years of Literary and Political Life), volume 2. Lisbon, Portugal: J. Rodrigues.

Almeida, Fialho d'. 1920. *Saibam Quantos . . . Cartas e Artigos Políticos* (They Know So Much . . . Political Letters and Articles), 3rd edition. Lisbon, Portugal: Livraria Classica Editora de A. M. Teixeira.

Almeida, José Luiz de. 1947. *Memórias do Sexto Marquês de Lavradio* (Memoirs of the Sixth Marquess of Lavradio). Lisbon, Portugal: Edições Atica.

Alston, Patrick L. 1969. *Education and the State in Tsarist Russia*. Stanford, California: Stanford University Press.

Amanat, A., and H. Hekmat. 1981. "Merchants and Artisans in the Developmental Processes of Nineteenth-Century Iran." Pages 725–750 in A. L. Udovitch, editor, *The Islamic Middle East, 700–1900*. Princeton, New Jersey: Darwin Press.

Amini, D. [1966?] *Tarikh-i Du-Hazar va Pansad Salah-yi Pulis-i Iran* (The 2,500-Year History of the Police of Iran). [Tehran, Iran?]: No publisher listed.

Amirkhayzi, Isma'il. 1960. *Qiyam-i Azarbayjan va Sattar Khan* (The Azarbaijan Uprising and Sattar Khan). Tabriz, Iran: Kitabfurushi-yi Tihran.

And, Metin. 1971. *Meşrutiyet Döneminde Türk Tiyatrosu (1908–1923)* (Turkish Theater during the Constitutionalist Period, 1908–1923). Ankara, Turkey: Türkiye İş Bankası Kültür Yayınları.

Anderson, Rodney D. 1976. *Outcasts in Their Own Land: Mexican Industrial Workers, 1906–1911.* Dekalb, Illinois: Northern Illinois University Press.

Anonymous. 1912. "What the Chinese Are Thinking," translated by Evan Morgan. *The Chinese Recorder,* volume 43, pages 421–423.

Ansari, Ali M. 2003. "Continuous Regime Change from Within." *Washington Quarterly,* volume 26, pages 53–67.

Arasteh, A. Reza. 1969. *Education and Social Awakening in Iran, 1850–1968.* Leiden, Netherlands: E. J. Brill.

Arat, Ali Alpaslan. 1969. *Histoire de la Liberté de la Presse en Turquie* (History of the Freedom of the Press in Turkey). Istanbul, Turkey: Yönet Matbaası.

Araújo, António. 1995. "A Construção da Justiça Constitucional Portuguesa: O Nascimento do Tribunal Constitucional" (The Construction of Portuguese Constitutional Justice: The Birth of the Constitutional Court). *Análise Social* (Social Analysis), number 134, pages 881–946.

Arıkan, Zeki. 2001. *İzmir Basınından Seçmeler, 1872–1922* (Selections from the Izmir Press, 1872–1922), volume 1. Izmir, Turkey: İzmir Büyükşehir Belediyesi Kültür Yayını.

Arjomand, Said Amir. 1981. "The Ulama's Traditionalist Opposition to Parliamentarism, 1907–1909." *Middle Eastern Studies,* volume 17, pages 174–190.

Arkun, Aram. 1999. "Les Relations Arméno-Turques et les Massacres de Cilicie de 1909" (Armenian-Turkish Relations and the Massacres of Cilicia in 1909). Pages 57–74 in *L'Actualité du Génocide des Arméniens* (The Actuality of the Genocide of Armenians). Créteil, France: Edipol.

Arriaga, Manuel d'. 1916. *Na Primeira Presidência da República Portuguesa* (In the First Presidency of the Portuguese Republic). Lisbon, Portugal: Teixeira.

Asami-yi Namayandagan-i Majlis-i Shura-yi Milli (Names of the Representatives of the National Consultative Assembly). 1977. Tehran, Iran: No publisher listed.

Ascher, Abraham. 1988, 1992. *The Revolution of 1905,* 2 volumes. Stanford, California: Stanford University Press.

———. 2001. *P. A. Stolypin: The Search for Stability in Late Imperial Russia.* Stanford, California: Stanford University Press.

Ashraf, Ahmad. 1969. "Historical Obstacles to the Development of a Bourgeoisie in Iran." *Iranian Studies,* volume 2, pages 54–79.

———. 1980. *Mavani'-i Tarikhi-yi Rushd-i Sarmayah-dari dar Iran: Daurah-yi Qajariyah* (Historical Obstacles to the Development of Capitalism in Iran: The Qajar Era). Tehran, Iran: Intisharat-i Zaminah.

Associação Comercial de Lisboa. 1915. *Relatório da Direcção Relativo ao Exercício do Ano de 1914* (Report of the Executive Committee regarding Activities of the Year 1914). Lisbon, Portugal: Tip. do Anuario Comercial.

———. 1916. *Relatório da Direcção Relativo ao Exercicio, Ano de 1915* (Report of the Executive Committee regarding Activities of the Year 1915). Lisbon, Porgual: Tip. do Anuario Comercial.

Atai, Mohammad Farhad. 1992. "The Sending of Iranian Students to Europe, 1811–1906." Ph.D. dissertation, Department of Near Eastern Studies, University of California, Berkeley.

Atis, Sarah G. Moment. 1995. "Turkish Literature." Pages 245–254 in John L. Esposito, editor, *Oxford Encyclopedia of the Modern Islamic World*, volume 4. New York, New York: Oxford University Press.

Avcıoğlu, Doğan, 1969. *31 Mart'ta Yabancı Parmağı* (Foreign Fingerprints in the 31 March [Incident of 1909]). Ankara, Turkey: Bilgi Yayınevi.

Aybar, Celal. 1939. *Osmanlı İmperatorluğun Ticaret Muvazenesi, 1878–1913* (Trade Balance of the Ottoman Empire, 1878–1913). Ankara, Turkey: Zerbamat Basımevi.

Aydın, Hakan. 2007. "II. Meşrutiyet Döneminde Konya'da İslamci Muhalefetin Sesi" (A Voice of Islamist Opposition in Konya in the Second Constitutional Period). *Sosyal Bilimler Enstitüsü Dergisi* (Review of the Institute of Social Sciences), number 17, pages 33–52.

Ayers, William. 1971. *Chang Chih-tung and Educational Reform in China*. Cambridge, Massachusetts: Harvard University Press.

'Ayn al-Saltanah, Qahraman Mirza Salur. 1998. *Ruznamah-yi Khatirat-i 'Ayn al-Saltanah* (Daily Memoirs of 'Ayn al-Saltanah), edited by Mas'ud Salur and Iraj Afshar, volume 3. Tehran, Iran: Intisharat-i Asatir.

Aytekin, Halil. 1991. *İttihad ve Terakki Dönemi Eğitim Yönetimi* (Educational Administration in the Union and Progress Era). Ankara, Turkey: Gazi Üniversitesi Basın-Yayın Yüksekokulu Matbaası.

Azuela, Mariano. 1958. *Obras Completas* (Complete Works), 3 volumes. Mexico City, Mexico: Fondo de Cultura Económica.

Baer, Gabriel. 1982. "Fellah Rebellion in Egypt and the Fertile Crescent." Pages 253–323 in Gabriel Baer, *Fellah and Townsman in the Middle East*. London, England: Frank Cass.

———. 1983. "Landlord, Peasant and the Government in the Arab Provinces of the Ottoman Empire in the 19th and Early 20th Century." Pages 261–274 in Jean-Louis Bacqué-Grammont and Paul Dumont, editors, *Économie et Sociétés dans l'Empire Ottoman (Fin du XVIIIe–Début du XXe Siècle)* (Economy and Societies in the Ottoman Empire, End of the Eighteenth to the Beginning of the Twentieth Century). Paris, France: Éditions du Centre National de la Recherche Scientifique.

Bailey, Paul J. 1990. *Reform the People: Changing Attitudes towards Popular Education in Early Twentieth-Century China*. Vancouver, Canada: University of British Columbia Press.

Bailly, Diégou. 1995. *La Restauration du Multipartisme en Côte d'Ivoire* (The Restoration of Multi-Partyism in Côte d'Ivoire). Paris, France: Éditions L'Harmattan.

Bakhash, Shaul. 1978. *Iran: Monarchy, Bureaucracy and Reform under the Qajars, 1858–1896*. London, England: Ithaca Press.

Balaghi, Shiva. 2001. "Print Culture in Late Qajar Iran: The Cartoons of *Kashkul.*" *Iranian Studies,* volume 34, pages 165–181.

Ballesteros García, Rosa María. 2001. *El Movimiento Feminista Portugués: Del Despertar Republicano a la Exclusión Salazarista, 1909–1947* (The Portuguese Feminist Movement: From the Republican Awakening to the Salazarist Exclusion, 1909–1947). Málaga, Spain: Universidad de Málaga.

Balzer, Harley D. 1991. "The Problem of Professions in Imperial Russia." Pages 183–198 in Edith W. Clowes, Samuel D. Kassow, and James L. West, editors, *Between Tsar and People: Educated Society and the Quest for Public Identity in Late Imperial Russia.* Princeton, New Jersey: Princeton University Press.

———, editor. 1996. *Russia's Missing Middle Class: The Professions in Russian History.* Armonk, New York: M. E. Sharpe.

Banks, Arthur S. 1996. *Cross-National Time Series Data Archive.* Binghamton, New York: Center for Social Analysis, State University of New York at Binghamton.

Bao Tianxiao. 1990. *Chuan ying lou hui yi lu* (Memoirs of Bao Tianxiao's Studio), 3 volumes. Taipei, Taiwan: Long wen chu ban she.

Barreto, José. 1984. "Jorge Coutinho e 'O Despertar dos Trabalhadores Rurais' (1911)" (Jorge Coutinho and 'The Despair of the Rural Laborers,' 1911). *Análise Social* (Social Analysis), number 83, pages 523–540.

Barrow, Clyde W. 1990. *Universities and the Capitalist State: Corporate Liberalism and the Reconstruction of American Higher Education, 1894–1928.* Madison, Wisconsin: University of Wisconsin Press.

Basribeg de Dukagjin. 1919. *Le Monde Oriental et le Problème de la Paix* (The Oriental World and the Problem of Peace). Paris, France: Perrin et Cie.

Basseer, Potkin. 1989. "Banking in Iran: History of Banking in Iran." Pages 698–708 in Ehsan Yarshater, editor, *Encyclopaedia Iranica,* volume 3. London, England: Routledge and Kegan Paul.

Bastid, Marianne. 1969. "La Diplomatie Française et la Révolution Chinoise de 1911" (French Diplomacy and the Chinese Revolution of 1911). *Revue d'Histoire Moderne et Contemporaine* (Review of Modern and Contemporary History), volume 16, pages 221–245.

Bauman, Zygmunt. 1987. *Legislators and Interpreters: On Modernity, Post-Modernity, and Intellectuals.* Cambridge, England: Polity.

Baumler, Alan. 2007. *The Chinese and Opium under the Republic.* Albany, New York: State University of New York Press.

Bayat, Mangol. 1991. *Iran's First Revolution: Shi'ism and the Constitutional Revolution of 1905–1909.* New York, New York: Oxford University Press.

Bayly, C. A. 2004. *The Birth of the Modern World, 1780–1914: Global Connections and Comparisons.* Malden, Massachusetts: Blackwell.

Becker, Seymour. 1985. *Nobility and Privilege in Late Imperial Russia.* DeKalb, Illinois: Northern Illinois University Press.

Beezley, William H. 1979. "Madero: The 'Unknown' President and His Political Failure to Organize Rural Mexico." Pages 1–24 in George Wolfskill and Douglas W. Richmond, editors, *Essays on the Mexican Revolution: Revisionist Views of the Leaders*. Austin, Texas: University of Texas Press.

Behbudiy, Mahmud Khoja. [1911] 1986. "Padarkush" (The Patricide), in Edward A. Allworth, "Murder as Metaphor in the First Central Asian Drama." *Ural-Altaischer Jahrbücher/Ural-Altaic Yearbook*, volume 58, pages 72–83.

Bein, Amit. 2006. "Politics, Military Conscription, and Religious Education in the Ottoman Empire." *International Journal of Middle East Studies*, volume 38, pages 283–301.

Bell, Aubrey. 1915. *Portugal of the Portuguese*. London, England: Sir I. Pitman.

Bell, Edward I. 1914. *The Political Shame of Mexico*. New York, New York: McBride, Nast.

Bellin, Eva. 2000. "Contingent Democrats: Industrialists, Labor, and Democratization in Late-Developing Countries." *World Politics*, volume 52, pages 175–205.

Benbassa, Esther. 1993. *Une Diaspora Sépharade en Transition: Istanbul, XIXe–XXe siècle* (A Sephardic Disapora in Transition: Istanbul, Nineteenth–Twentieth Centuries). Paris, France: Cerf.

———. 1995. *Haim Nahum: A Sephardic Chief Rabbi in Politics, 1892–1923*, translated by Miriam Kochan. Tuscaloosa, Alabama: University of Alabama Press.

Benda, Julien. 1900. *Dialogues à Byzance* (Dialogues in Byzantium). Paris, France: Éditions de la Revue Blanche.

———. [1927] 1928. *The Treason of the Intellectuals*, translated by Richard Aldington. New York, New York: William Morrow.

Bendix, Reinhard. 1984. *Force, Fate, and Freedom: On Historical Sociology*. Berkeley, California: University of California Press.

Benton, Russell E. 1977. *The Downfall of a King: Dom Manuel II of Portugal*. Washington, DC: University Press of America.

Bérard, Victor. 1913. *La Mort de Stamboul: Considérations sur le Gouvernement des Jeunes-Turcs* (The Death of Istanbul: Considerations on the Government of the Young Turks). Paris, France: Librairie Armand Colin.

Berberian, Houri. 2001. *Armenians and the Iranian Constitutional Revolution of 1905–1911*. Boulder, Colorado: Westview.

Berberoglu, Berch. 1982. *Turkey in Crisis*. London, England: Zed.

Bergère, Marie-Claire. 1968. "The Role of the Bourgeoisie." Pages 229–295 in Mary Clabaugh Wright, editor, *China in Revolution: The First Phase, 1900–1913*. New Haven, Connecticut: Yale University Press.

———. 1989. *The Golden Age of the Chinese Bourgeoisie, 1911–1937*. Cambridge, England: Cambridge University Press.

Bergquist, Charles W. 1978. *Coffee and Conflict in Colombia, 1886–1910*. Durham, North Carolina: Duke University Press.

Berkes, Niyazi. 1964. *The Development of Secularism in Turkey*. Montreal, Canada: McGill University Press.

Berktay, Halil. 1987. "The Feudalism Debate: The Turkish End: Is 'Tax vs. Rent'

Necessarily the Product and Sign of a Modal Difference?" *Journal of Peasant Studies,* volume 14, pages 291–333.

Bernal, Martin. 1968. "The Triumph of Anarchism over Marxism, 1906–1907." Pages 97–142 in Mary Clabaugh Wright, editor, *China in Revolution: The First Phase, 1900–1913.* New Haven, Connecticut: Yale University Press.

———. 1976. *Chinese Socialism to 1907.* Ithaca, New York: Cornell University Press.

Bernhardt, Kathryn. 1992. *Rents, Taxes, and Peasant Resistance: The Lower Yangzi Region, 1840–1950.* Stanford, California: Stanford University Press.

Bernstein, Marvin D. 1964. *The Mexican Mining Industry, 1890–1950.* Albany, New York: State University of New York.

Berth, Édouard. 1926. *Les Méfaits des Intellectuels* (The Misdeeds of the Intellectuals), 2nd edition. Paris, France: Marcel Rivière.

Bharier, Julian. 1971. *Economic Development in Iran, 1900–1970.* London, England: Oxford University Press.

Billington, James H. 1960. "The Intelligentsia and the Religion of Humanity." *American Historical Review,* volume 65, pages 807–821.

———. 1980. *Fire in the Minds of Men: Origins of the Revolutionary Faith.* New York, New York: Basic Books.

Binet, Alfred. 1908. "Une Enquête sur l'Évolution de l'Enseignement de la Philosophie" (An Investigation of the Evolution of Philosophy Teaching). *L'Année Psychologique* (Psychological Yearbook), volume 14, pages 152–231.

Bing, E. J., editor. 1938. *The Secret Letters of the Last Tsar.* New York, New York: Longmans.

Biren, Mehmet Tevfik. 1993. *II. Abdülhamid, Meşrutiyet ve Mütareke Devri Hatıraları* (Memoirs of the Periods of Abdülhamid II, the Constitution, and the Armistice), 2 volumes. Istanbul, Turkey: Arma Yayınları.

Birinci, Ali. 1990. *Hürriyet ve İtilaf Fırkası: II. Meşrutiyet Devrinde İttihat ve Terakki'ye Karşı Çıkanlar* (The Freedom and Entente Party: Opponents of [the Society for] Unity and Progress during the Second Constitutional Period). Istanbul, Turkey: Dergah Yayınları.

Blackwell, William L. 1994. *The Industrialization of Russia: A Historical Perspective,* 3rd edition. Arlington Heights, Illinois: Harlan Davidson.

Blaisdell, Donald C. 1929. *European Financial Control of the Ottoman Empire.* New York, New York: Columbia University Press.

Blasier, Cole. 1972. "The United States and Madero." *Journal of Latin American Studies,* volume 4, pages 207–231.

Bleda, Mithat Şükrü. 1979. *İmparatorluğun Çöküşü* (The Collapse of the Empire). Istanbul, Turkey: Remzi Kitabevi.

Blok, Alexander. [1908] 1978. "The People and the Intelligentsia." Pages 359–363 in Marc Raeff, editor, *Russian Intellectual History: An Anthology.* Atlantic Highlands, New Jersey: Humanities Press.

Blum, Léon. 1935. *Souvenirs sur l'Affaire* (Memories of the [Dreyfus] Affair). Paris, France: Gallimard.

Boggs, Carl. 1993. *Intellectuals and the Crisis of Modernity*. Albany, New York: State University of New York Press.

Bohachevsky-Chomiak, Martha. 1988. *Feminists despite Themselves: Women in Ukrainian Community Life, 1884–1939*. Edmonton, Canada: Canadian Institute of Ukrainian Studies, University of Alberta.

Boli, John. 1987. "Human Rights or State Expansion: Cross-National Definitions of Constitutional Rights, 1870–1970." Pages 133–49 in George M. Thomas, John W. Meyer, Francisco O. Ramirez, and John Boli, *Institutional Structure: Constituting State, Society, and the Individual*. Newbury Park, California: Sage.

Boltanski, Luc. 1987. *The Making of a Class: Cadres in French Society*, translated by Arthur Goldhammer. Cambridge, England: Cambridge University Press; Paris, France: Éditions de la Maison des Sciences de l'Homme.

Bonakdarian, Mansour. 2006. *Britain and the Iranian Constitutional Revolution of 1906–1911: Foreign Policy, Imperialism, and Dissent*. Syracuse, New York: Syracuse University Press.

Bonnell, Victoria E. 1983. *Roots of Rebellion: Workers' Politics and Organizations in St. Petersburg and Moscow, 1900–1914*. Berkeley, California: University of California Press.

Boorman, Howard L., editor. *Biographical Dictionary of Republican China*, volume 1. New York, New York: Columbia University Press.

Borthwick, Sally. 1983. *Education and Social Change in China: The Beginnings of the Modern Era*. Stanford, California: Hoover Institution Press.

Boura, Catherine. 1999. "The Greek Millet in Turkish Politics: Greeks in the Ottoman Parliament (1908–1918)." Pages 193–206 in Dimitri Gondicas and Charles Issawi, editors, *Ottoman Greeks in the Age of Nationalism: Politics, Economy, and Society in the Nineteenth Century*. Princeton, New Jersey: Darwin Press.

Braga, Teófilo [Theophilo]. [1880] 1983. *História das Ideias Republicanas em Portugal* (The History of Republican Ideas in Portugal). Lisbon, Portugal: Vega.

———. 1884. *Systema de Sociologia* (System of Sociology). Lisbon, Portugal: Typographia Castro Irmão.

———. 1902. *História da Universidade de Coimbra* (History of the University of Coimbra), volume 4. Lisbon, Portugal: Academia Real das Sciencias.

Braga Paixão, Vítor. 1976. "A Constituinte de 1911 (Teófilo, Afonso, Sidónio)" (The Constituent Assembly of 1911: Teófilo [Braga], Afonso [Costa], Sidónio [Pais]). *Anais da Academia Portuguesa da História* (Annals of the Portuguese Academy of History), volume 23, number 2, pages 9–50.

Bragança-Cunha, V. de. 1937. *Revolutionary Portugal (1910–1936)*. London, England: James Clarke.

Brandão, Raul. 1919. *Memórias* (Memoirs), volume 1. Porto, Portugal: Edição da "Renascença Portuguesa."

———. 1925. *Memórias* (Memoirs), volume 2. Paris, France: Livrarias Aillaud e Bertrand.

———. 1933. *Memórias* (Memoirs), volume 3, *Vale de Josafat* (The Valley of Josafat). Lisbon, Portugal: Seara Nova.

Bridge, F. R. 1972. *Great Britain and Austria-Hungary, 1906–1914: A Diplomatic History*. London, England: London School of Economics and Political Science, Weidenfeld and Nicolson.

Brown, Arthur Judson. 1912. *The Chinese Revolution*. New York, New York: Student Volunteer Movement for Foreign Missions.

Browne, Edward G. [1910] 1995. *The Persian Revolution, 1905–1909*. Washington, DC: Mage.

———. 1912. *The Reign of Terror at Tabriz*. Manchester, England: Taylor, Garnett, Evans.

———. 1914. *The Press and Poetry of Modern Persia*. Cambridge, England: Cambridge University Press.

Brummett, Palmira. 2000. *Image and Imperialism in the Ottoman Revolutionary Press, 1908–1911*. Albany, New York: State University of New York Press.

Bryce, James. 1922. *Modern Democracies*, 2 volumes. New York, New York: Macmillan.

Brym, Robert J. 2001. "Intellectuals, Sociology of." Pages 7631–7635 in Neil J. Smelser and Paul B. Balates, editors, *International Encyclopedia of the Social and Behavioral Sciences,* volume 11. Oxford, England: Elsevier Science.

Bucur, Marin. 1983. "L'Affaire Dreyfus dans les Milieux Démocrates et Populaires Roumains" (The Dreyfus Affair in Democratic and Popular Romanian Circles). Pages 93–100 in Géraldi Leroy, editor, *Les Écrivains et l'Affaire Dreyfus* (Writers and the Dreyfus Affair). Paris, France: Presses Universitaires de France.

Bulnes, Francisco. 1916. *The Whole Truth about Mexico,* translated by Dora Scott. New York, New York: M. Bulnes Book.

Burdett, A. L. P., editor, 1996. *Arab Dissident Movements, 1905–1955,* volume 1. Farnham Common, England: Archive Editions.

Bushnell, John. 1985. *Mutiny amid Repression: Russian Soldiers in the Revolution of 1905–1906*. Bloomington, Indiana: Indiana University Press.

Buxton, Charles Roden. 1909. *Turkey in Revolution*. London, England: T. Fisher Unwin.

Cabral, Antonio. 1932. *As Minhas Memorias Políticas* (My Political Memoirs), volume 4. Lisbon, Portugal: Livraria Popular de Francisco Franco.

———. 1933. *Cartas d'El-Rei D. Manuel II* (Letters of King Dom Manuel II). Lisbon, Portugal: Livraria Popular de F. Franco.

Cabrera, Luis. 1975. *Obras Completas* (Complete Works), volume 3, *Obras Políticas* (Political Works). Mexico City, Mexico: Ediciones Oasis.

Cadot, Michel. 1983. "Tchekhov et l'Affaire" (Chekhov and the [Dreyfus] Affair). Pages 85–92 in Géraldi Leroy, editor, *Les Écrivains et l'Affaire Dreyfus* (Writers and the Dreyfus Affair). Paris, France: Presses Universitaires de France.

Cai Yuanpei. 1968. *Cai Yuanpei quan ji* (Collected Works of Cai Yuanpei). Tainan, Taiwan: Wang jia ju ban she.

Calhoun, Craig. 1994. *Neither Gods nor Emperors: Students and the Struggle for Democracy in China*. Berkeley, California: University of California Press.

Calvert, Peter. 1968. *The Mexican Revolution, 1910–1914: The Diplomacy of Anglo-American Conflict*. Cambridge, England: Cambridge University Press.

Camp, Roderic A. 1989. *Entrepreneurs and Politics in Twentieth-Century Mexico*. New York, New York: Oxford University Press.

———. 1991. *Mexican Political Biographies, 1884–1935*. Austin, Texas: University of Texas Press.

Campos, Michelle U. 2003. "A 'Shared Homeland' and Its Boundaries: Empire, Citizenship and the Origins of Sectarianism in Late Ottoman Palestine, 1908–1913." Ph.D. dissertation, Department of History, Stanford University.

Çankaya, Ali. 1968–1970. *Yeni Mülkiye Târihi ve Mülkiyeliler* (History of the New Administrative College and Its Graduates), 8 volumes. Ankara, Turkey: Mars Matbaası.

Cárdenas Solórzano, Cuauhtémoc. 1988. *Nuestra Lucha Apenas Comienza* (Our Struggle Is Just Beginning). Mexico City, Mexico: Editorial Nuestro Tiempo.

Cardoso, Fernando H. 1986. "Entrepreneurs and the Transition Process: The Brazilian Case." Pages 137–153 in Guillermo O'Donnell, Philippe C. Schmitter, and Laurence Whitehead, editors, *Transitions from Authoritarian Rule: Comparative Perspectives*. Baltimore, Maryland: Johns Hopkins University Press.

Cardoso, Fernando Henrique, and Enzo Faletto. 1979. *Dependency and Development in Latin America*, translated by Marjory Mattingly Urquidi. Berkeley, California: University of California Press.

Cardoso, Sá. 1973. *Memórias duma Época* (Memories of an Epoch). Lisbon, Portugal: Edição do Autor.

Carman, Michael Dennis. 1976. *United States Customs and the Madero Revolution*. El Paso, Texas: Texas Western Press, University of Texas at El Paso.

Carr, Barry. 1976. *El Movimiento Obrero y la Política en México, 1910–1929* (The Workers' Movement and Politics in Mexico, 1910–1929), volume 1. Mexico City, Mexico: SepSetentas.

Casanova, Pascale. 2004. *The World Republic of Letters*, translated by M. B. DeBevoise. Cambridge, Massachusetts: Harvard University Press.

Catroga, Fernando. 1977. "A Importância do Positivismo na Consolidação da Ideologia Republicana em Portugal" (The Importance of Positivism in the Consolidation of the Republican Ideology in Portugal). *Biblos*, volume 53, pages 285–327.

———. 1991. *O Republicanismo em Portugal: Da Formação ao 5 de Outubro 1910* (Republicanism in Portugal: From the Beginning to October 5, 1910), 2 volumes. Coimbra, Portugal: Faculdade de Letras.

Cavid, Mehmed. 1908. "Kanun-u Esasimizin Maliye Kanunu Hakkındaki Mevaddı" (Our Constitution's Articles on Finance Law). *Ulûm-u İktisadiye ve İctimaiye Mecmuası* (Journal of Economic and Social Sciences), volume 1, pages 25–33.

Cemal. 1996. *Arnavutluk'tan Sakarya'ya Komitacılık Yüzbaşı Cemal'in Anıları* (The Memoirs of Revolutionary Captain Cemal, from Albania to Sakarya). Ankara, Turkey: Kebikeç Yayınları.

Cemaleddin Efendi. 1990. *Siyasi Hatıralarım* (My Political Memoirs), edited by Selim Kutsan. Istanbul, Turkey: Nehir Yayınları.

Çeviker, Turgut. 1989. *Meşrutiyet İmzasız Karikatürler Antolojisi* (Anthology of Unsigned Cartoons from the Constitutional Period). Istanbul, Turkey: Adam Yayınları.

Çetin, A. Alâaddin, and Ramazan Yıldız, editors. 1976. *II Abdülhamid Han: Devlet ve Memleket Görüşlerim* (Abdülhamid II: My Views on State and Country). Istanbul, Turkey: Çığır Yayınları.

Chagas, João. 1930. *Diario de João Chagas* (The Diary of João Chagas), volume 2. Lisbon, Portugal: Parceria António Maria Pereira.

Chan, K. C. 1971. "British Policy in the Reorganization Loan to China, 1912–13." *Modern Asian Studies,* volume 5, pages 355–372.

Chan, Wellington K. K. 1977. *Merchants, Mandarins, and Modern Enterprise in Late Ch'ing China.* Cambridge, Massachusetts: East Asian Research Center, Harvard University.

Chan Lau, Kit-ching. 1970. "British Policy of Neutrality during the 1911 Revolution in China." *Journal of Oriental Studies,* volume 8, pages 357–379.

———. 1978. *Anglo-Chinese Diplomacy in the Careers of Sir John Jordan and Yüan Shih-k'ai.* Hong Kong: Hong Kong University Press.

Chang, Chung-li. 1955. *The Chinese Gentry: Studies on Their Role in Nineteenth-Century Chinese Society.* Seattle, Washington: University of Washington Press.

Chang, Hao. 1971. *Liang Ch'i-ch'ao and Intellectual Transition in China, 1890–1907.* Cambridge, Massachusetts: Harvard University Press.

Chang, P'eng-yüan. 1968. "The Constitutionalists." Pages 143–183 in Mary Clabaugh Wright, editor, *China in Revolution: The First Phase, 1900–1913.* New Haven, Connecticut: Yale University Press.

———. 1978. "Political Participation and Political Elites in Early Republican China: The Parliament of 1913–1914," translated by Andrew J. Nathan. *Journal of Asian Studies,* volume 37, pages 293–313.

Chang, Sidney H., and Leonard H. D. Gordon. 1991. *All under Heaven: Sun Yat-sen and His Revolutionary Thought.* Stanford, California: Hoover Institution Press.

Chaquèri, Cosroe. 1979. *La Social-Démocratie en Iran* (Social Democracy in Iran). Florence, Italy: Edition Mazdak.

———. 1995. *The Soviet Socialist Republic of Iran, 1920–1921.* Pittsburgh, Pennsylvania: University of Pittsburgh Press.

———. 2001. *Origins of Social Democracy in Modern Iran.* Seattle, Washington: University of Washington Press.

Charle, Christophe. 1990. *Naissance des "Intellectuels" (1880–1900)* (Birth of the "Intellectuals," 1880–1900). Paris, France: Éditions de Minuit.

———. 1996. *Les Intellectuels en Europe au XIXe Siècle* (Intellectuals in Europe in the Nineteenth Century). Paris, France: Éditions du Seuil.

Chehabi, Houchang. 1999. "From Revolutionary *Tasnif* to Patriotic *Surud:* Music and Nation-Building in Pre–World War II Iran." *Iran,* volume 37, pages 143–154.

Ch'en, Jerome. 1972. *Yuan Shih-k'ai,* 2nd edition. Stanford, California: Stanford University Press.

————. 1979. *The Military-Gentry Coalition: China under the Warlords.* Toronto, Canada: University of Toronto-York University Joint Centre on Modern East Asia.

Chernukha, Valentina G., and Boris V. Anan'ich. 1995. "Russia Falls Back, Russia Catches Up: Three Generations of Reformers." Pages 55–96 in Theodore Taranovski, editor, *Reform in Modern Russian History: Progress or Cycle?* Washington, DC: Woodrow Wilson Center Press; New York, New York: Cambridge University Press.

Cherrington, Ruth. 1991. *China's Students: The Struggle for Democracy.* London, England: Routledge.

Chesneaux, Jean. 1971. *Secret Societies in China in the Nineteenth and Twentieth Centuries,* translated by Gillian Nettle. Ann Arbor, Michigan: University of Michigan Press.

Cholpan, Abdulhamid Sulayman. [1914] 1992. "Dokhtur Muhammadyor" (Doctor Muhammadyar), edited by Sirojiddin Ahmad and Ulughbek Dolimov. *Sharq Yulduzi* (Eastern Star), number 1, pages 132–138.

Chomsky, Noam. 1991. *Deterring Democracy.* London, England: Verso.

Chow, Tse-tsung. 1964. *The May Fourth Movement: Intellectual Revolution in Modern China.* Cambridge, Massachusetts: Harvard University Press.

Churchill, Randolph S. 1967. *Winston S. Churchill,* volume 2, *Young Statesman, 1900–1914.* Boston, Massachusetts: Houghton Mifflin.

Clogg, Richard. 1982. "The Greek *Millet* in the Ottoman Empire." Pages 185–207 in Benjamin Braude and Bernard Lewis, editors, *Christians and Jews in the Ottoman Empire,* volume 1. New York, New York: Holmes and Meier.

Cockcroft, James D. 1967. "El Maestro de Primaria en la Revolución Mexicana" (The Primary Teacher in the Mexican Revolution). *História Mexicana* (Mexican History), volume 16, pages 565–587.

————. 1968. *Intellectual Precursors of the Mexican Revolution, 1900–1913.* Austin, Texas: University of Texas Press.

————. 1983. *Mexico: Class Formation, Capital Accumulation, and the State.* New York, New York: Monthly Review Press.

Collado, María del Carmen. 1987. *La Burguesía Mexicana: El Emporio Braniff y su Participación Política, 1865–1920* (The Mexican Bourgeoisie: The House of Braniff and Its Political Participation, 1865–1920). Mexico City, Mexico: Siglo Veintiuno Editores.

Collier, Ruth Berins. 1999. *Paths toward Democracy: The Working Class and Elites in Western Europe and South America.* Cambridge, England: Cambridge University Press.

Collier, Ruth Berins, and James Mahoney. 1997. "Adding Collective Actors to Collective Outcomes: Labor and Recent Democratization in South America and Southern Europe." *Comparative Politics,* volume 29, pages 285–303.

Comte, Auguste. [1822] 1969. "Plan of the Scientific Operations Necessary for Reorganizing Society." Pages 248–282 in Philip Rieff, editor, *On Intellectuals: Theoretical Studies, Case Studies.* Garden City, New York: Doubleday.

Conaghan, Catherine M., and James M. Malloy. 1994. *Unsettling Statecraft: Democracy and Neoliberalism in the Central Andes*. Pittsburgh, Pennsylvania: University of Pittsburgh Press.

Confino, Michael. 1972. "On Intellectuals and Intellectual Traditions in Eighteenth- and Nineteenth-Century Russia." *Daedalus*, volume 101, pages 117–149.

Congress Presidential Addresses, From the Foundation to the Silver Jubilee, First Series. 1935. Madras, India: G. A. Natesan.

Conner, Alison W. 1994. "Lawyers and the Legal Profession during the Republican Period." Pages 215–248 in Kathryn Bernhardt and Philip C. C. Huang, editors, *Civil Law in Qing and Republican China*. Stanford, California: Stanford University Press.

Córdova, Arnaldo, 1973. *La Ideología de la Revolución Mexicana* (The Ideology of the Mexican Revolution). Mexico City, Mexico: Ediciones Era.

Ćorović, Vladimir. [1936]. "Relations between Serbia and Austria-Hungary in the XX Century," translated by Stoyan Gavrilović. Unpublished and undated manuscript at the Hoover Institution Archives, Stanford University.

Cosío Villegas, Daniel. 1974. *Historia Moderna de México: El Porfiriato* (Modern History of Mexico: The Era of Porfirio Díaz), volumes 7–8, *La Vida Económica* (Economic Life), 2nd edition. Mexico City, Mexico: Editorial Hermes.

Craig, Ann L. 1983. *The First Agraristas: An Oral History of a Mexican Agrarian Reform Movement*. Berkeley, California: University of California Press.

Crane, Daniel M., and Thomas A. Breslin. 1986. *An Ordinary Relationship: American Opposition to Republican Revolution in China*. Miami, Florida: University Presses of Florida, Florida International University Press.

Cresson, W[illiam] P. 1908. *Persia: The Awakening East*. Philadelphia, Pennsylvania: J. B. Lippincott.

Crisp, Olga. 1961. "The Russian Liberals and the 1906 Anglo-French Loan to Russia." *The Slavonic and East European Review*, volume 29, pages 497–511.

Croly, Herbert. 1924. *Willard Straight*. New York, New York: Macmillan.

Cronin, Stephanie. 1997. *The Army and the Creation of the Pahlavi State in Iran, 1910–1926*. London, England: Tauris Academic Studies.

Cruzeiro, Maria Eduardo. 1992. "Os Professores da Universidade de Coimbra na Segunda Metade do Século XIX" (The Professors of the University of Coimbra in the Second Half of the Nineteenth Century). *Análise Social* (Social Analysis), numbers 116–117, pages 529–537.

Cumberland, Charles C. 1952. *Mexican Revolution: Genesis under Madero*. Austin, Texas: University of Texas Press.

Cunha Leal, [Francisco]. 1966. *As Minhas Memórias: Romance duma Época, duma Família e duma Vida de 1888 a 1917* (My Memories: The Story of an Epoch, a Family, and a Life, from 1888 to 1917). Lisbon, Portugal: Self-published.

Cunningham, James W. 1981. *A Vanquished Hope: The Movement for Church Renewal in Russia, 1905–1906*. Crestwood, New York: St. Vladimir's Seminary Press.

Curtiss, John S. 1940. *Church and State in Russia: The Last Years of the Empire, 1900–1914.* New York, New York: Columbia University Press.

Dadkhah, Kamran M. 1992. *"Lebas-o Taqva* [Dress and Piety]: An Early Twentieth-Century Treatise on the Economy." *Middle Eastern Studies,* volume 28, pages 547–559.

Dakin, Douglas. 1966. *The Greek Struggle in Macedonia, 1897–1913.* Thessalonica, Greece: Institute for Balkan Studies.

Danishvar-'Alavi, Nurullah. 1951. *Tarikh-i Mashrutah-yi Iran va Junbish-i Vatan-Parastan-i Isfahan va Bakhtiyari* (Constitutional History of Iran and the Movement of the Isfahan and Bakhtiyari Patriots). Tehran, Iran: Kitabkhanah-yi Danish.

Dasnabedian, Hratch. 1990. *History of the Armenian Revolutionary Federation, Dashnaktsutiun, 1890–1924,* translated by Bryan Fleming and Vahe Habeshian. Milan, Italy: Oemme Edizioni.

Datta, Venita. 1999. *Birth of a National Icon: The Literary Avant-Garde and the Origins of the Intellectual in France.* Albany, New York: State University of New York Press.

Daulatabadi, Yahya. [1950] 1992. *Hayat-i Yahya* (The Life of Yahya), 4 volumes. Tehran, Iran: Intisharat-i 'Attar; Intisharat-i Firdausi.

Davies, David A. 1972. "V. A. Maklakov and the Westernizer Tradition in Russia." Pages 78–89 in Charles W. Timberlake, editor, *Essays on Russian Liberalism.* Columbia, Missouri: University of Missouri Press.

Davis, Fei-ling. 1971. *Primitive Revolutionaries of China: A Study of Secret Societies in the Late Nineteenth Century.* Honolulu, Hawaii: University Press of Hawaii.

Davison, Roderic H. 1990. "The Advent of the Principle of Representation in the Government of the Ottoman Empire." Pages 96–111 in *Essays in Ottoman and Turkish History, 1774–1923.* Austin, Texas: University of Texas Press.

De Cómo Vino Huerta y Cómo se Fué (On How Huerta Came [to Power] and How He Left). [1914] 1975. Mexico City, Mexico: Ediciones El Caballito.

Deas, Malcolm. 1994. "Gramática y Poder: La Hegemonía de los Letrados" (Grammar and Power: The Hegemony of the Educated). *Mundo Nuevo* (New World), volume 17, numbers 63–64, pages 41–58.

Decalo, Samuel. 1992. "The Process, Prospects, and Constraints of Democratization in Africa." *African Affairs,* volume 91, page 7–35.

Deeds, Susan M. 1976. "José María Maytorena and the Mexican Revolution in Sonora." *Arizona and the West,* volume 18, pages 21–40 and 125–148.

Delpar, Helen. 1981. *Red against Blue: The Liberal Party in Colombian Politics, 1862–1899.* University, Alabama: University of Alabama Press.

Demirel, Muammer, 1990. *İkinci Meşrutiyet Öncesi Erzurum'da Halk Hareketleri (1906–1907)* (Popular Movements in Erzerum Before the Second Constitutional Period, 1906–1907). Ankara, Turkey: Kültür Bakanlığı.

Demorgny, Gustave. 1913. *Essai sur l'Administration de la Perse* (Essay on the Administration of Persia). Paris, France: Ernest Leroux.

———. 1914. *Les Institutions de la Police en Perse* (Police Institutions in Persia). Paris, France: Ernest Leroux.

———. 1915. *Essai de Réformes et d'Enseignement Administratifs en Perse* (Essay on Administrative Reforms and Instruction in Persia). Paris, France: Ernest Leroux.

———. 1915. *Les Institutions Financières en Perse* (Financial Institutions in Persia). Paris, France: Ernest Leroux.

Derou, Jean. 1986. *Les Relations Franco-Portugaises à l'Époque de la Première République Parlementaire Libérale (5 Octobre 1910–28 Mai 1926)* (Franco-Portuguese Relations during the First Liberal Parliamentary Republic, October 5, 1910–May 28, 1926). Paris, France: Publications de la Sorbonne.

Devereux, Robert. 1963. *The First Ottoman Constitutional Period: A Study of the Midhat Constitution and Parliament.* Baltimore, Maryland: Johns Hopkins Press.

Dewey, John. [1916] 1944. *Democracy and Education.* New York, New York: Free Press.

Diamond, Larry. 1999. *Developing Democracy: Toward Consolidation.* Baltimore, Maryland: Johns Hopkins University Press.

Dickinson, G. Lowes. 1926. *The International Anarchy, 1904–1914.* London, England: Allen and Unwin.

Dihkhuda, 'Ali Akbar. 1979. *Namah'ha-yi Siyasi-yi Dihkhuda* (Political Letters of Dihkhuda), edited by Iraj Afshar. Tehran, Iran: Ruzbihan.

Dollar, Robert. 1912. *The Private Diary of Robert Dollar on His Recent Visits to China.* San Francisco, California: Robert Dollar Co.

Dong, Madeleine Yue. 2005. "Unofficial History and Gender Boundary Crossing in the Early Republic." Pages 169–187 in Bryna Goodman and Wendy Larson, editors, *Gender in Motion: Divisions of Labor and Cultural Change in Late Imperial and Modern China.* Lanham, Maryland: Rowman and Littlefield.

Duara, Prasenjit. 1995. *Rescuing History from the Nation: Questioning Narratives of Modern China.* Chicago, Illinois: University of Chicago Press.

Duiker, William J. 1977. *Ts'ai Yüan-p'ei: Educator of Modern China.* University Park, Pennsylvania: Pennsylvania State University Press.

Duman, Hasan. 1986. *İstanbul Kütüphaneleri Arap Harfli Süreli Yayınlar Toplu Kataloğu, 1828–1928* (Union Catalog of the Periodicals in Arabic Script in the Libraries of Istanbul, 1828–1928). Istanbul, Turkey: İslâm Tarih, Sanat, ve Kültür Araştırma Merkezi.

Dumont, Paul. 1977. "À Propos de la 'Classe Ouvrière' Ottomane à la Veille de la Révolution Jeune-Turque" (About the Ottoman "Working Class" on the Eve of the Young Turk Revolution). *Turcica,* volume 9, pages 229–251.

———. 1980. "Sources Inédites pour l'Histoire du Mouvement Ouvrier et des Courants Socialistes dans l'Empire Ottoman au Début du XXe Siècle" (Unpublished Sources for the History of the Worker Movement and Socialist Currents in the Ottoman Empire at the Start of the Twentieth Century). Pages 383–396 in Osman Okyar and Halil İnalcık, editors, *Türkiye'nin Sosyal ve Ekonomik Tarihi (1071–1920)* (Social and Economic History of Turkey, 1071–1920). Ankara, Turkey: Meteksan.

————. 1980. "La Structure Sociale de la Communauté Juive de Salonique à la Fin du Dix-Neuvième Siècle" (The Social Structure of the Jewish Community of Salonica at the End of the Nineteenth Century). *Revue Historique* (Historical Review), number 263, pages 351–393.

Edirne Ticaret ve Sanayi Odası Rehberi: Yüzüncü Yıl Anısına, 1885–1985 (Guide to the Edirne Chamber of Commerce and Industry, in Commemoration of its Centennial, 1885–1985). 1985. Istanbul, Turkey: ARBA.

Edmondson, Linda Harriet. 1984. *Feminism in Russia, 1900–17.* Stanford, California: Stanford University Press.

Edwards, E. W. 1987. *British Diplomacy and Finance in China, 1895–1914.* Oxford, England: Clarendon.

Edwards, Louise. 2000. "Women's Suffrage in China: Challenging Scholarly Conventions." *Pacific Historical Review,* volume 69, pages 617–638.

Ege, Nezahet Nurettin. 1977. *Prens Sabahaddin: Hayatı ve İlmî Müdafaaları* (Prince Sabahaddin: His Life and Scholarly Arguments). Istanbul, Turkey: Fakülteler Matbaası.

Eglitis, Daina Stukuls. 2002. *Imagining the Nation: History, Modernity, and Revolution in Latvia.* University Park, Pennsylvania: Pennsylvania State University Press.

Ekhtiar, Maryam D. 1994. "The Dar al-Funun: Educational Reform and Cultural Development in Qajar Iran." Ph.D. dissertation, Department of Near Eastern Languages and Literatures, New York University.

El Comercio en la Historia de Chihuahua (Commerce in Chihuahua History). 1991. Chihuahua, Mexico: Cámara Nacional de Comercio, Servicios y Turismo de Chihuahua.

Elgood, Cyril. 1951. *A Medical History of Persia.* Cambridge, England: Cambridge University Press.

Elkin, Boris. 1960. "The Russian Intelligentsia on the Eve of the Revolution." *Daedalus,* volume 89, pages 472–486.

Elliot, Iain. 1994. "Three Days in August: On-the-Spot Impressions." Pages 289–300 in Victoria E. Bonnell, Ann Cooper, and Gregory Freidin, editors, *Russia at the Barricades: Eyewitness Accounts of the August 1991 Coup.* Armonk, New York: M. E. Sharpe.

Elvin, Mark. 1984. "The Revolution of 1911 in Shanghai." *Papers on Far Eastern History,* number 29, pages 119–161.

Emmons, Terence. 1983. *The Formation of Political Parties and the First National Elections in Russia.* Cambridge, Massachusetts: Harvard University Press.

Emmons, Terence, and Wayne S. Vucinich, editors. 1982. *The Zemstvo in Russia: An Experiment in Local Self-Government.* Cambridge, England: Cambridge University Press.

Enatsu, Yoshiki. 2004. *Banner Legacy: The Rise of the Fengtian Local Elite at the End of the Qing.* Ann Arbor, Michigan: Center for Chinese Studies, University of Michigan.

Enayat, Anne. 1985. "Amin al-Zarb." Pages 953–954 in Ehsan Yarshater, editor, *Encyclopaedia Iranica,* volume 1. London, England: Routledge and Kegan Paul.

Engelstein, Laura. 1982. *Moscow, 1905: Working-Class Organization and Political Conflict.* Stanford, California: Stanford University Press.

Ergin, Osman. [1943] 1977. *Türkiye Maarif Tarihi* (The History of Education in Turkey). Istanbul, Turkey: Eser Matbaası.

Ergli, Doğu. 1975. "A Reassessment: The Young Turks, Their Politics, and Anti-Colonial Struggle." *Balkan Studies,* volume 16, pages 26–72.

Erişirgil, M. Emin. 1951. *Bir Fikir Adamının Romanı: Ziya Gökalp* (A Thinker's Novel: Ziya Gökalp). Istanbul, Turkey: İnkılap Kitabevi.

Ersoy, Mehmet Akif. [1912] 1990. "Süleymâniye Kürsüsünde" (In the Süley-maniye [Mosque] Pulpit). Pages 129–162 in M. Ertuğrul Düzdağ, editor, *Safahat* (Collected Works). Ankara, Turkey: Kültür Bakanlığı.

Esherick, Joseph W. 1976. *Reform and Revolution in China: The 1911 Revolution in Hunan and Hubei.* Berkeley, California: University of California Press.

Esherick, Joseph W., and Mary Backus Rankin. 1990. *Chinese Local Elites and Patterns of Dominance.* Berkeley, California: University of California Press.

Esteves, João. 1998. *As Origens do Sufragismo Português: A Primeira Organização Sufragista Portuguesa, a Associação de Propaganda Feminista (1911–1918)* (The Origins of Portuguese Suffragism: The First Portuguese Suffragist Organization, The Association for Feminist Propaganda, 1911–1918). Lisbon, Portugal: Editorial Bizâncio.

Ettehadieh [Ettehadiyeh] (Nezam Mafi), Mansoureh. 1979. "Origin and Development of Political Parties in Persia, 1906–1911." Ph.D. dissertation, Department of History, University of Edinburgh.

———. 1993. "Constitutional Revolution: Political Parties of the Constitutional Period." Pages 199–202 in Ehsan Yar-Shater, editor, *Encyclopaedia Iranica,* volume 6. Costa Mesa, California: Mazda.

Etzioni-Halevy, Eva. 1985. *The Knowledge Elite and the Failure of Prophecy.* London, England: George Allen and Unwin.

Fahri, Fındıkoğlu Z. 1962. *Auguste Comte ve Ahmet Rıza* (Auguste Comte and Ahmed Rıza). Istanbul, Turkey: Fakülteler Matbaası.

Fallows, Thomas. 1982. "The Zemstvo and the Bureaucracy, 1890–1904." Pages 177–241 in Terence Emmons and Wayne S. Vucinich, editors, *The Zemstvo in Russia: An Experiment in Local Self-Government.* Cambridge, England: Cambridge University Press.

Farelo Lopes, Fernando. 1991. "Clientelismo, 'Crise de Participação' e Deslegitimação na I República" (Clientelism, "Crisis of Participation," and Deligitimation in the First [Portuguese] Republic). *Análise Social* (Social Analysis), number 111, pages 401–415.

Farhi, David. 1971. "The Şeri'at as a Political Slogan—or the 'Incident of the 31st Mart.'" *Middle Eastern Studies,* volume 7, pages 275–300.

———. 1975. "Documents on the Attitude of the Ottoman Government towards the Jewish Settlement in Palestine after the Revolution of the Young Turks, 1908–1909." Pages 190–210 in Moshe Ma'oz, editor, *Studies on Palestine during the Ottoman Period.* Jerusalem, Israel: Magnes Press.

Farjenel, Fernand. 1915. *Through the Chinese Revolution,* translated by Margaret Vivian. London, England: Duckworth.

Farmanfarma, 'Abdulhusayn Mirza. 1987. *Guzidah'i az Majmu'ah-yi Asnad-i 'Abdulhusayn Mirza Farmanfarma: 1325–1340 Hijri-yi Qamari* (Selected Documents of 'Abdulhusayn Mirza Farmanfarma, 1907–1922), edited by Mansurah Ittihadiyah (Nizam Mafi) and Sirus Sa'dvandiyan, 3 volumes. Tehran, Iran: Nashr-i Tarikh-i Iran.

Farmanfarma'iyan, Mihrmah. 1998. *Zindaginamah-yi 'Abdulhusayn Mirza Farmanfarma* (Biography of 'Abdulhusayn Mirza Farmanfarma). Tehran, Iran: Intisharat-i Tus.

Farrell, Robert V. 1974. "The Catholic Church and Colombian Education, 1886–1930." Ph.D. dissertation, Department of Education, Columbia University.

Fass, Josef. 1962. "The Role of the New-Style Army in the 1911 Revolution in China." *Archiv Orientální: Journal of the Czechoslovak Oriental Institute,* volume 30, pages 183–191.

Feaver, Peter D. 1999. "Civil-Military Relations." *Annual Review of Political Science,* volume 2, pages 211–241.

Feis, Herbert. 1930. *Europe, The World's Banker, 1870–1914.* New Haven, Connecticut: Yale University Press; London, England: H. Milford, Oxford University Press.

Feldman, Egal. 1981. *The Dreyfus Affair and the American Conscience, 1895–1906.* Detroit, Michigan: Wayne State University Press.

Ferenczi, Caspar. 1982. *Aussenpolitik und Öffentlichkeit in Russland 1906–1912* (Foreign Policy and the Public Sphere in Russia, 1906–1912). Husum, West Germany: Matthiesen Verlag.

Ferguson, Adam. [1767] 1995. *Essay on the History of Civil Society.* Cambridge, England: Cambridge University Press.

Ferrão, Carlos. 1964. *O Integralismo e a Republica: Autópsia dum Mito* (Integralism and the Republic: Autopsy of a Myth), 2 volumes. Lisbon, Portugal: Inquérito.

———. 1966. *A Obra da República* (The Work of the Republic). Lisbon, Portugal: Editorial "O Seculo."

Ferreira, David. 1973. *História Política da Primeira República Portuguesa* (Political History of the First Portuguese Republic), volume 1, part 2. Lisbon, Portugal: Livros Horizonte.

Ferrier, R. W. 1982. *The History of the British Petroleum Company,* volume 1. Cambridge, England: Cambridge University Press.

Feuerwerker, Albert. 1958. *China's Early Industrialization: Shen Hsuan-Huai (1844–1916) and Mandarin Enterprise.* Cambridge, Massachusetts: Harvard University Press.

Fewsmith, Joseph. 1980. "The Emergence of Authoritarian-Corporatist Rule in Republican China: The Changing Pattern of Business Association in Shanghai." Ph.D. dissertation, Department of Political Science, University of Chicago.

Fikret, Tevfik. 2001. *Bütün Şiirler* (Complete Poems), edited by İsmail Parlatır and Nurullah Çetin. Ankara, Turkey: Türk Dil Kurumu Yayınları.

Fincher, John H. 1981. *Chinese Democracy: The Self-Government Movement in Local, Provincial and National Politics, 1905–1914*. London, England: Croom Helm; Canberra, Australia: Australia National University Press.

Fischbach, Michael R. 2000. *State, Society, and Land in Jordan*. Leiden, Netherlands: Brill.

Fischer, George. 1958. *Russian Liberalism: From Gentry to Intelligentsia*. Cambridge, Massachusetts: Harvard University Press.

Fishman, Robert M. 1990. *Working-Class Organization and the Return to Democracy in Spain*. Ithaca, New York: Cornell University Press.

Flikke, Geir. 1994. *Democracy or Theocracy: Frank, Struve, Berdjaev, Bulgakov, and the 1905 Russian Revolution*. Oslo, Norway: Universitetet i Oslo, Slavisk-Baltisk Avdeling.

Floor, Willem M. 1976. "The Merchants *(Tujjar)* in Qajar Iran." *Zeitschrift der Deutschen Morgenlandischen Gesellschaft* (Journal of the German Orientalist Society), volume 126, pages 101–135.

———. 1983. "Change and Development in the Judicial System of Qajar Iran (1800–1925)." Pages 113–147 in Edmund Bosworth and Carole Hillebrand, editors, *Qajar Iran: Political, Social and Cultural Change, 1800–1925*. Edinburgh, Scotland: Edinburgh University Press.

———. 1984. *Industrialization in Iran, 1900–1941*. Durham, England: University of Durham Centre for Middle Eastern and Islamic Studies.

———. 1985. *Labour Unions, Law and Conditions in Iran (1900–1941)*. Durham, England: University of Durham Centre for Middle Eastern and Islamic Studies.

———. 1987. "Asnaf." Pages 772–779 in Ehsan Yarshater, editor, *Encyclopaedia Iranica*, volume 2. London, England: Routledge and Kegan Paul.

———. 1991. "Traditional Crafts and Modern Industry in Qajar Iran." *Zeitschrift der Deutschen Morgenlandischen Gesellschaft* (Journal of the German Orientalist Society), volume 141, pages 317–352.

———. 1998. *A Fiscal History of Iran in the Safavid and Qajar Periods, 1500–1925*. New York, New York: Bibliotheca Persica Press.

———. 2003. *Agriculture in Qajar Iran*. Washington, DC: Mage.

———. 2004. *Public Health in Qajar Iran*. Washington, DC: Mage.

Flora, Peter. 1973. "Historical Processes of Social Mobilization: Urbanization and Literacy, 1850–1965." Pages 213–258 in S. N. Eisenstadt and Stein Rokkan, editors, *Building States and Nations*, volume 1. Beverly Hills, California: Sage.

———. 1983. *State, Economy, and Society in Western Europe, 1815–1975*, volume 1. Frankfurt am Main, West Germany: Campus Verlag; Chicago, Illinois: St. James Press.

Flores Torres, Oscar. 1991. *Burguesía, Militares y Movimiento Obrero en Monterrey, 1909–1923* (Bourgeoisie, the Military, and the Workers' Movement in Monterrey, 1909–1923). Monterrey, Mexico: Facultad de Filosofía y Letras de la Universidad Autónoma de Nuevo León.

Foran, John. 1991. "The Strengths and Weaknesses of Iran's Populist Alliance: A Class Analysis of the Constitutional Revolution of 1905–1911." *Theory and Society,* volume 20, pages 785–823.

———. 1993. "Dependency and Resistance in the Middle East, 1800–1925." *Political Power and Social Theory,* volume 8, pages 107–140.

———. 1993. *Fragile Resistance: Social Transformation in Iran from 1500 to the Revolution.* Boulder, Colorado: Westview.

Forth, Christopher E. 2004. *The Dreyfus Affair and the Crisis of French Manhood.* Baltimore, Maryland: Johns Hopkins University Press.

Fortna, Benjamin C. 2002. *Imperial Classroom: Islam, the State, and Education in the Late Ottoman Empire.* New York, New York: Oxford University Press.

Fox Quesada, Vicente. 1999. *A Los Pinos: Recuento Autobiográfico y Político* (To Los Pinos: Autobiographical and Political Account). Mexico City, Mexico: Océano.

France, Anatole. 1953. *Trente Ans de Vie Sociale* (Thirty Years of Social Life), volume 2. Paris, France: Éditions Émile-Paul Frères.

Freeze, Gregory L. 1983. *The Parish Clergy in Nineteenth-Century Russia: Crisis, Reform, Counter-Reform.* Princeton, New Jersey: Princeton University Press.

———. 1986. "The *Soslovie* (Estate) Paradigm and Russian Social History." *American Historical Review,* volume 91, pages 11–36.

Friedman, Edward. 1968. "The Center Cannot Hold: The Failure of Parliamentary Democracy in China from the Chinese Revolution of 1911 to the World War in 1914." Ph.D. dissertation, Department of Government, Harvard University.

———. 1970. "Revolution or Just Another Bloody Cycle? Swatow and the 1911 Revolution." *Journal of Asian Studies,* volume 29, pages 289–307.

———. 1974. *Backward toward Revolution: The Chinese Revolutionary Party.* Berkeley, California: University of California Press.

Fröhlich, Klaus. 1981. *The Emergence of Russian Constitutionalism, 1900–1904.* The Hague, Netherlands: Martinus Nijhoff.

Fuller, William C., Jr. 1985. *Civil-Military Conflict in Imperial Russia, 1881–1914.* Princeton, New Jersey: Princeton University Press.

Fulton, L. Bruce. 1984. "France and the End of the Ottoman Empire." Pages 141–171 in Marian Kent, editor, *The Great Powers and the End of the Ottoman Empire.* London, England: George Allen and Unwin.

Fung, Edmund S. K. 1980. *The Military Dimension of the Chinese Revolution: The New Army and Its Role in the Revolution of 1911.* Vancouver, Canada: University of British Columbia Press.

[Furughi,] Muhammad 'Ali Khan bin Zuka' al-Mulk. 1908. *Huquq-i Asasi, ya'ni Adab-i Mashrutiyat-i Duvval* (The Constitution, or Customs of Constitutionalism in the States [of the World]). Tehran, Iran: Self-published.

Galai, Shmuel. 1973. *The Liberation Movement in Russia, 1900–1905.* Cambridge, England: Cambridge University Press.

Galt, Howard S. 1928. "Oriental and Occidental Elements in China's Modern Education System," part 3. *Chinese Social and Political Review,* volume 12, pages 627–647.

Gapon, George. 1905. *The Story of My Life*. London, England: Chapman and Hall.

Garcelon, Marc. 1997. "The Estate of Change: The Specialist Rebellion and the Democratic Movement in Moscow, 1989–1991." *Theory and Society*, volume 26, pages 39–85.

García Morales, Alfonso. 1992. *El Ateneo de México, 1906–1914* (The Atheneum of Mexico, 1906–1914). Sevilla, Spain: Escuela de Estudios Hispano-Americanos de Sevilla.

Garciadiego Dantán, Javier. 2000. "The Press and the Mexican Revolution." University of Chicago, Mexican Studies Program, Center for Latin American Studies, Working Paper Series, Number 5.

Garrett, Shirley S. 1970. *Social Reformers in Urban China: The Chinese YMCA, 1895–1926*. Cambridge, Massachusetts: Harvard University Press.

Garten, Jeffrey E. 1992. *A Cold Peace: America, Japan, Germany, and the Struggle for Supremacy*. New York, New York: Times Books.

———. 1997. *The Big Ten: The Big Emerging Markets and How They Will Change Our Lives*. New York, New York: Basic Books.

Garthwaite, Gene R. 1983. *Khans and Shahs: A Documentary Analysis of the Bakhtiyari in Iran*. Cambridge, England: Cambridge University Press.

Gasster, Michael. 1969. *Chinese Intellectuals and the Revolution of 1911*. Seattle, Washington: University of Washington Press.

Gatrell, Peter. 1986. *The Tsarist Economy, 1850–1917*. London, England: B. T. Batsford.

Gavira, Gabriel. 1933. *General de Brigada Gabriel Gavira: Su Actuación Politico-Militar Revolucionaria* (Brigade General Gabriel Gavira: His Revolutionary Politico-Military Performance). Mexico City, Mexico: Talleres, Tipograficos de A. del Bosque.

Gawrych, George. 2006. *The Crescent and the Eagle: Ottoman Rule, Islam and the Albanians, 1874–1913*. London, England: I. B. Tauris.

Gellner, Ernest. 1994. *Conditions of Liberty: Civil Society and Its Rivals*. New York, New York: Allen Lane, The Penguin Press.

Georgeon, François. 1980. *Aux Origines du Nationalisme Turc: Yusuf Akçura (1876–1935)* (At the Origins of Turkish Nationalism: Yusuf Akçura, 1876–1935). Paris, France: Éditions ADPF.

Gerber, Haim. 1987. *The Social Origins of the Modern Middle East*. Boulder, Colorado: Lynne Rienner; London, England: Mansell.

Ghahari, Keivandokht. 2001. *Nationalismus und Modernismus in Iran in der Periode zwischen dem Zerfall der Qagaren-Dynastie und der Machtfestigung Reza Schahs: Eine Untersuchung Über die intellektuellen Kreise um die Zeitschriften Kaweh, Iranşahr und Ayandeh* (Nationalism and Modernism in Iran in the Period between the Fall of the Qajar Dynasty and the Rise of Reza Shah: An Investigation into the Intellectual Circles around the Journals *Kavah*, *Iranshahr*, and *Ayandah*). Berlin, Germany: Schwarz.

Ghani, Abdul. [1921] 1980. *A Review of the Political Situation in Central Asia*. Lahore, Pakistan: Aziz.

Gharavi-Nuri, 'Ali. 1973. *Hizb-i Dimukrat-i Iran: Daurah-yi Duvvum-i Majlis-i Shura-yi Milli* (The Democrat Party of Iran: The Second Session of the National Consultative Assembly). Tehran, Iran: Chapkhanah-yi Firdausi.

Gheissari, Ali. 1998. *Iranian Intellectuals in the 20th Century.* Austin, Texas: University of Texas Press.

———. 2005. "Despots of the World Unite! Satire in the Iranian Constitutional Press: The *Majalleh-ye Estebdad,* 1907–1908." *Comparative Studies of South Asia, Africa and the Middle East,* volume 25, pages 360–376.

Gilbar, Gad G. 1977. "The Big Merchants (*Tujjar*) and the Persian Constitutional Revolution of 1906." *Asian and African Studies,* volume 11, pages 275–303.

Gillin, Donald G. 1967. *Warlord: Yen Hsi-shan in Shansi Province, 1911–1949.* Princeton, New Jersey: Princeton University Press.

Gilly, Adolfo. 1983. *The Mexican Revolution,* translated by Patrick Camiller. London, England: Verso Editions and NLB.

Girault, René. 1973. *Emprunts Russes et Investissements Français en Russie, 1887–1914* (Russian Loans and French Investments in Russia, 1887–1914). Paris, France: Librairie Armand Colin.

Glassman, Ronald M. 1995. *The Middle Class and Democracy in Socio-Historical Perspective.* Leiden, Netherlands: E. J. Brill.

Göçek, Fatma Müge. 1996. *Rise of the Bourgeoisie, Demise of Empire: Ottoman Westernization and Social Change.* New York, New York: Oxford University Press.

Godley, Michael R. 1981. *The Mandarin-Capitalists from Nanyang.* Cambridge, England: Cambridge University Press.

Gómez, Hipólito de la Torre. 1980. *Contra-Revolução: Documentos para a História da Primeira República Portuguesa* (Counter-Revolution: Documents for the History of the First Portugese Republic). Lisbon, Portugal: Perspectivas e Realidades.

Gómez Quiñones, Juan. [1983]. *Porfirio Díaz, los Intelectuales y la Revolución* (Porfirio Díaz, the Intellectuals, and the Revolution). Mexico City, Mexico: Ediciones el Caballito.

González Navarro, Moisés. 1961. "La Ideología de la Revolución Mexicana" (The Ideology of the Mexican Revolution). *História Mexicana* (Mexican History), volume 10, pages 628–636.

González Ramírez, Manuel. 1957. *Manifiestos Políticos, 1892–1912* (Political Manifestos, 1892–1912). Mexico City, Mexico: Fondo de Cultura Económica.

Greaves, Rose Louise. 1968. "Some Aspects of the Anglo-Russian Convention and Its Working in Persia, 1907–1914." *Bulletin of the School of Oriental and African Studies,* volume 31, pages 69–91 and 290–308.

Greenfield, James. 1934. "Die geistlichen Schariagerichte in Persien" (The Religious *Shari'a* Courts in Persia). *Zeitschrift für vergleichende Rechtswissenschaft* (Journal of Comparative Legal Studies), volume 48, pages 157–167.

Gregor, A. James. 1979. *Italian Fascism and Developmental Dictatorship.* Princeton, New Jersey: Princeton University Press.

Gregorian, Vartan. 1969. *The Emergence of Modern Afghanistan; Politics of Reform and Modernization, 1880–1946.* Stanford, California: Stanford University Press.

Grieder, Jerome B. 1981. *Intellectuals and the State in Modern China: A Narrative History.* New York, New York: Free Press.

Gruening, Ernest. 1928. *Mexico and Its Heritage.* New York, New York: Century.

Guerra, François-Xavier. 1985. *Le Mexique de l'Ancien Régime à la Révolution* (Mexico from the Old Regime to the Revolution), 2 volumes. Paris, France: Éditions L'Harmattan and Publications de la Sorbonne.

Güneş, İhsan. 1997, 1998. *Türk Parlamento Tarihi, I. ve II. Meşrutiyet* (The History of the Turkish Parliament, First and Second Parliamentary Periods), 2 volumes. Ankara, Turkey: Türkiye Büyük Millet Meclisi Basımevi Müdürlüğü.

Günyol, Vedad, and Andrew Mango. 1965. "Djarida. iii. Turkey." Pages 473–476 in B. Lewis, Ch. Pellat, and J. Schacht, editors, *Encyclopedia of Islam,* 2nd edition, volume 2. Leiden, Netherlands: E. J. Brill; and London, England: Luzac.

Güzel, Şehmus. 1985. "Tanzimat'tan Cumhuriyet'e İşçi Hareketi ve Grevler" (The Worker Movement and Strikes from the Tanzimat to the Republic). Pages 803–828 in *Tanzimat'tan Cumhuriyet'e Türkiye Ansiklopedisi* (Encyclopedia of Turkey from the Tanzimat to the Republic), volume 3. Istanbul, Turkey: İletişim Yayınları.

Guzmán, Martín Luis. 1963. *Febrero de 1913* (February 1913). Mexico City, Mexico: Empresas Editoriales.

Guzmán, Martín Luis, and Alfonso Reyes. 1991. *Medias Palabras: Correspondencia, 1913–1959* (Half Words: Correspondence, 1913–1959), edited by Fernando Curiel. Mexico City, Mexico: Universidad Nacional Autónoma de México.

Gwynn, Stephen, editor. 1929. *The Letters and Friendships of Sir Cecil Spring Rice: A Record.* Boston, Massachusetts: Houghton Mifflin.

Habibi, 'Abd al-Hayy. 1993. *Junbish-i Mashrutiyat dar Afghanistan* (The Constitutionalist Movement in Afghanistan). Qum, Iran: Ihsani.

Hackett, Roger F. 1949. "Chinese Students in Japan, 1900–1910." *Papers on China,* volume 3, pages 134–169.

Haimson, Leopold H. 1979. "Introduction: The Russian Landed Nobility and the System of the Third of June." Pages 1–29 in Haimson, editor, *The Politics of Rural Russia, 1905–1914.* Bloomington, Indiana: Indiana University Press.

Hairi, Abdul-Hadi. 1977. *Shi'ism and Constitutionalism in Iran.* Leiden, Netherlands: E. J. Brill.

Hale, Charles A. 1968. *Mexican Liberalism in the Age of Mora, 1821–1853.* New Haven, Connecticut: Yale University Press.

———. 1989. *The Transformation of Liberalism in Late Nineteenth-Century Mexico.* Princeton, New Jersey: Princeton University Press.

Haley, P. Edward. 1970. *Revolution and Intervention: The Diplomacy of Taft and Wilson with Mexico, 1910–1917.* Cambridge, Massachusetts: MIT Press.

Hanioğlu, M. Şükrü. 1987. "Transformation of the Ottoman Intelligentsia and the Idea of Science." *Anuarul Institutului de Istorie şi Arheologie "A. D.*

Xenopol" (Yearbook of the "A. D. Xenopol" Institute of History and Archeology), volume 24, pages 29–34.

————. 1995. *The Young Turks in Opposition*. New York, New York: Oxford University Press.

————. 2001. *Preparation for a Revolution: The Young Turks, 1902–1908*. New York, New York: Oxford University Press.

Hanrahan, Gene Z., editor. 1976–1985. *Documents on the Mexican Revolution*, 9 volumes. Salisbury, North Carolina: Documentary Publications.

Hao, Yen-p'ing. 1986. *The Commercial Revolution in Nineteenth-Century China: The Rise of Sino-Western Mercantile Capitalism*. Berkeley, California: University of California Press.

Haravi-Khurasani, Muhammad Hasan Adib. 1953. *Tarikh-i Paydayish-i Mashrutiyat-i Iran* (History of the Establishment of the Constitution in Iran). Mashhad, Iran: Self-published.

Harcave, Sydney. 1964. *First Blood: The Russian Revolution of 1905*. New York, New York: Macmillan.

————. 2004. *Count Sergei Witte and the Twilight of Imperial Russia*. Armonk, New York: M. E. Sharpe.

Hardinge, Arthur. 1927. *A Diplomatist in Europe*. London, England: Jonathan Cape.

Harp, Gillis J. 1995. *Positivist Republic: Auguste Comte and the Reconstruction of American Liberalism, 1865–1920*. University Park, Pennsylvania: Pennsylvania State University Press.

Harris, Charles H., III, and Louis R. Sadler. 1988. "The 1911 Reyes Conspiracy: The Texas Side." Pages 27–50 in Harris and Sadler, *The Border and the Revolution: Clandestine Activities of the Mexican Revolution, 1910–1920*. Silver City, New Mexico: High-Lonesome Books.

Harrison, Henrietta. 2000. *The Making of the Republican Citizen: Political Ceremonies and Symbols in China, 1911–1929*. Oxford, England: Oxford University Press.

————. 2005. *The Man Awakened from Dreams: One Man's Life in a North China Village, 1857–1942*. Stanford, California: Stanford University Press.

Hart, John Mason. 1987. *Revolutionary Mexico: The Coming and Process of the Mexican Revolution*. Berkeley, California: University of California Press.

————. 1998. "Social Unrest, Nationalism, and American Capital in the Mexican Countryside, 1876–1920." Pages 72–88 in Daniel Nugent, editor, *Rural Revolt in Mexico: U.S. Intervention and the Domain of Subaltern Politics*, expanded edition. Durham, North Carolina: Duke University Press.

Haynes, Keith Allen. 1991 "*Orden y Progreso:* The Revolutionary Ideology of Alberto J. Pani." Pages 259–279 in Roderic A. Camp, Charles A. Hale, and Josefina Zoraida Vázquez, editors, *Los Intelectuales y el Poder en México* (Intellectuals and Power in Mexico). Mexico City, Mexico: El Colegio de México; Los Angeles, California: University of California, Los Angeles, Latin American Center Publications.

Healy, Ann Erickson. 1976. *The Russian Autocracy in Crisis, 1905–1907.* Hamden, Connecticut: Archon.

Heilbronner, Hans. 1969. "Aehrenthal in Defense of Russian Autocracy." *Jahrbücher für Geschichte Osteuropas* (Yearbook of East European History), volume 17, pages 380–396.

Heller, Joseph. 1983. *British Policy towards the Ottoman Empire, 1908–1914.* London, England: Frank Cass.

Henderson, Peter V. N. 1981. *Félix Díaz, the Porfirians, and the Mexican Revolution.* Lincoln, Nebraska: University of Nebraska Press.

Hennessy, Richard. 1977. *The Agrarian Question in Russia, 1905–1907.* Giessen, West Germany: Wilhelm Schmitz Verlag.

Hernández Luna, Juan. 1962. *Conferencias del Ateneo de la Juventud* (Speeches of the Atheneum of Youth). Mexico City, Mexico: Centro de Estudios Filosóficos, Universidad Nacional Autónoma de México.

Heuman, Susan Eva. 1998. *Kistiakovsky: The Struggle for National and Constitutional Rights in the Last Years of Tsarism.* Cambridge, Massachusetts: Harvard Ukrainian Research Institute.

Hidayat, Mahdi Quli Khan (Mukhbir al-Saltanah). [1950] 1996. *Khatirat va Khatarat* (Memories and Concerns). Tehran, Iran: Zavvar.

Hintze, Otto. 1975. "The Preconditions of Representative Government in the Context of World History." Pages 302–353 in Felix Gilbert, editor, *The Historical Essays of Otto Hintze.* New York, New York: Oxford University Press.

Ho, Ping-ti. 1962. *The Ladder of Success in Imperial China: Aspects of Social Mobility, 1368–1911.* New York, New York: Columbia University Press.

Ho, Virgil K. Y. 2005. *Understanding Canton: Rethinking Popular Culture in the Republican Period.* Oxford, England: Oxford University Press.

Hoell, Margaret Stevens. 1973. "The *Ticaret Odası*: Origins, Functions, and Activities of the Chamber of Commerce of Istanbul, 1885–1899." Ph.D. dissertation, Department of History, Ohio State University.

Honoré, Jean-Paul. 1983. "Autour d'Intellectuel" (On the Intellectual). Pages 149–157 in Géraldi Leroy, editor, *Les Écrivains et l'Affaire Dreyfus* (Writers and the Dreyfus Affair). Paris, France: Presses Universitaires de France.

Hosking, Geoffrey A. 1973. *The Russian Constitutional Experiment.* Cambridge, England: Cambridge University Press.

Hosking, Geoffrey A., and Roberta Thompson Manning. 1979. "What Was the United Nobility?" Pages 142–183 in Leopold H. Haimson, editor, *The Politics of Rural Russia, 1905–1914.* Bloomington, Indiana: Indiana University Press.

Hourani, Albert. 1962. *Arabic Thought in the Liberal Age, 1798–1939.* London, England: Oxford University Press.

Hsiao, Kung-Chuan. 1975. *A Modern China and a New World: K'ang Yu-wei, Reformer and Utopian, 1858–1927.* Seattle, Washington: University of Washington Press.

Hu Shih. 1931. "Hu Shih." Pages 235–263 in Albert Einstein *et alia*, *Living Philosophies.* New York, New York: Simon and Schuster.

Huang, Fu-ch'ing. 1982. *Chinese Students in Japan in the Late Ch'ing Period*, translated by Katherine P. K. Whitaker. Tokyo, Japan: Centre for East Asian Cultural Studies.

Huang, Philip C. C. 2001. *Code, Custom, and Legal Practice in China: The Qing and the Republic Compared*. Stanford, California: Stanford University Press.

Huang Yanpei. 1915. *Huang Yanpei kao cha jiao yu ri ji* (Huang Yanpei's Diary on His Educational Investigation Trip), 2 volumes. Shanghai, China: Shang wu yin shu guan.

Huang, Yiping. 1986. "The Role of the 1911 Revolution in Promoting National Capitalist Industry." Pages 119–137 in Chün-tu Hsüeh, editor, *The Chinese Revolution of 1911: New Perspectives*. Hong Kong: Joint Publishing.

Huenemann, Ralph William. 1984. *The Dragon and the Iron Horse: The Economics of Railroads in China, 1876–1937*. Cambridge, Massachusetts: Council on East Asian Studies, Harvard University.

Huntington, Samuel P. 1957. *The Soldier and the State: The Theory and Politics of Civil-Military Relations*. Cambridge, Massachusetts: Harvard University Press.

———. 1968. *Political Order in Changing Societies*. New Haven, Connecticut: Yale University Press.

Hutchinson, John F. 1990. *Politics and Public Health in Revolutionary Russia, 1890–1918*. Baltimore, Maryland: Johns Hopkins University Press.

Hyde-Price, Adrian G. V. 1994. "Democratization in Eastern Europe: The External Dimension." Pages 220–252 in Geoffrey Pridham and Tatu Vanhanen, editors, *Democratization in Eastern Europe: Domestic and International Perspectives*. London, England: Routledge.

Ichiko, Chūzō. 1968. "The Role of the Gentry: An Hypothesis." Pages 297–313 in Mary Clabaugh Wright, editor, *China in Revolution: The First Phase, 1900–1913*. New Haven, Connecticut: Yale University Press.

Imbert, Paul. 1909. *La Rénovation de l'Empire Ottoman* (The Renovation of the Ottoman Empire). Paris, France: Librairie Academique, Perrin.

İnalcık, Halil. 1977. "Centralization and Decentralization in Ottoman Administration." Pages 27–52 in Thomas Naff and Roger Owen, editors, *Studies in 18th Century Islamic History*. Carbondale, Illinois: Southern Illinois University Press.

İnönü, İsmet. 1985. *Hatıralar* (Memoirs), edited by Sabahattin Selek. Ankara, Turkey: Bilgi Yayınları.

Ismail Kemal Bey. 1920. *The Memoirs of Ismail Kemal Bey*, edited by Sommerville Story. London, England: Constable.

Issawi, Charles, editor. 1971. *The Economic History of Iran, 1800–1914*. Chicago, Illinois: University of Chicago Press.

Jacquemin, Alexis, and Lucio R. Pench, editors. 1997. *Europe Competing in the Global Economy: Reports of the Competitiveness Advisory Group*. Cheltenham, England: Edward Elgar.

Ja'fariyan, Rasul. 1999. *Bast-Nashini: Mashrutah-Khwahan dar Safarat-i Inglis* (Sit-In: The Constitutionalists at the English Legation). Tehran, Iran: Mu'asasah-yi Mutala'at-i Tarikh-i Mu'asir-i Iran.

James, William. [1907] 1912. "The Social Value of the College Bred." Pages 309–325 in *Memories and Studies*. London, England: Longmans, Green.

Jansen, Marius B. 1967. *The Japanese and Sun Yat-Sen*. Cambridge, Massachusetts: Harvard University Press.

Jareño López, Jesús. 1981. *El Affaire Dreyfus en España, 1894–1906* (The Dreyfus Affair in Spain, 1894–1906). Murcia, Spain: Editorial Godoy.

Johnson, Robert E. 1982. "Liberal Professonals and Professional Liberals: The Zemstvo Statisticians and Their Work." Pages 343–363 in Terence Emmons and Wayne S. Vucinich, editors, *The Zemstvo in Russia: An Experiment in Local Self-Government*. Cambridge, England: Cambridge University Press.

Johnston, Reginald F. 1934. *Twilight in the Forbidden City*. London, England: Victor Gollancz.

Johnston, William M. 1974. "The Origin of the Term 'Intellectuals' in French Novels and Essays of the 1890s." *Journal of European Studies*, volume 4, pages 43–56.

Jones, Geoffrey. 1986. *Banking and Empire in Iran: The History of the British Bank of the Middle East*, volume 1. Cambridge, England: Cambridge University Press.

Joseph, Gilbert M. 1982. *Revolution from Without: Yucatán, Mexico and the United States, 1880–1924*. Cambridge, England: Cambridge University Press.

Joseph, Gilbert M., and Allen Wells. 1990. "Yucatán: Elite Politics and Rural Insurgency." Pages 93–131 in Thomas Benjamin and Mark Wasserman, editors, *Provinces of the Revolution: Essays on Regional Mexican History, 1910–1929*. Albuquerque, New Mexico: University of New Mexico Press.

Kabacalı, Alpay. 1985. "Tanzimat ve Meşrutiyet Dönemlerinde Sansür" (Censorship in the Tanzimat and Constitutional Periods). Pages 607–616 in *Tanzimat'tan Cumhuriyet'e Türkiye Ansiklopedisi* (The Encyclopedia of Turkey from the Tanzimat to the Republic), volume 3. Istanbul, Turkey: İletişim Yayınları.

Kadivar, Muhsin. 1999. *Baha-yi Azadi: Difaʿiyat-i Muhsin Kadivar dar Dadgah-i Vizhah-yi Ruhaniyat* (The Price of Freedom: The Defense Statements of Muhsin Kadivar before the Special Clergy Court). Tehran, Iran: Nashr-i Nay.

Kadletz, Karl. 1980. "Reformwünsche und Reformwirklichkeit: Modernisierungsversuche Persiens mit Österreichischer Hilfe durch Naser od-Din Sah" (Reform Hopes and Reform Reality: Nasir al-Din Shah's Attempt to Modernize Persia with Austrian Assistance). *Wiener Beiträge zur Geschichte der Neuzeit* (Viennese Contributions in Modern History), volume 7, pages 147–173.

Kadri, Hüseyin Kazım. 1991. *Meşrutiyet'ten Cumhuriyete Hatıralarım* (My Memoirs, from the Constitutional Period to the Republic). Istanbul, Turkey: İletişim Yayınları

Kani, ʿAli. 1954. *Sazman-i Farhangi-yi Iran* (Cultural Organization in Iran). Tehran, Iran: Intisharat-i Danishgah-i Tehran.

Kansu, Aykut. 1997. *The Revolution of 1908 in Turkey*. Leiden, Netherlands: E. J. Brill.

Kara, İsmail. 1994. *İslâmcıların Siyasî Görüşleri* (The Islamists' Political Views). Istanbul, Turkey: İz Yayıncılık.

Karabekir, Kazim. 1995. *İttihat ve Terakki Cemiyeti, 1896–1909* (Society for Union and Progress, 1896–1909), 2nd edition. Istanbul, Turkey: Emre Yayınları.

Karabel, Jerome. 1993. "Polish Intellectuals and the Origins of Solidarity: The Making of an Oppositional Alliance." *Communist and Post-Communist Studies,* volume 26, pages 25–46.

Karakışla, Yavuz Selim. 1992. "The 1908 Strike Wave in the Ottoman Empire." *Turkish Studies Association Bulletin,* volume 16, pages 153–177.

———. 1995. "The Emergence of the Ottoman Industrial Working Class, 1839–1923." Pages 19–34 in Donald Quataert and Erik Jan Zürcher, editors, *Workers and the Working Class in the Ottoman Empire and the Turkish Republic, 1839–1950.* London, England: Tauris Academic Studies in Association with the International Institute of Social History, Amsterdam.

Karl, Rebecca E. 2002. *Staging the World: Chinese Nationalism at the Turn of the Twentieth Century.* Durham, North Carolina: Duke University Press.

Karpat, Kemal H. 1975. "The Memoirs of N. Batzaria: The Young Turks and Nationalism." *International Journal of Middle Eastern Studies,* volume 6, pages 276–299.

———. 1985. *Ottoman Population, 1830–1914: Demographic and Social Characteristics.* Madison, Wisconsin: University of Wisconsin Press.

Karpovich, Michael. 1955. "Two Types of Russian Liberalism: Maklakov and Miliukov." Pages 129–143 in Ernest J. Simmons, editor, *Continuity and Change in Russian and Soviet Thought.* Cambridge, Massachusetts: Harvard University Press.

Karvar, Anousheh. 2004. "La Reforme de l'État et la Modernisation de l'Armée Persane au 19e Siècle: Un Processus Inachevé" (The Reform of the State and the Modernization of the Persian Army in the Nineteenth Century: An Unfinished Process). *Oriento Moderno* (Modern Orient), volume 23, pages 67–83.

Kasaba, Reşat. 1988. *The Ottoman Empire and the World Economy: The Nineteenth Century.* Albany, New York: State University of New York Press.

Kashani-Sabet, Firoozeh. 1999. *Frontier Fictions: Shaping the Iranian Nation, 1804–1946.* Princeton, New Jersey: Princeton University Press.

———. 2000. "Hallmarks of Humanism: Hygiene and Love of Homeland in Qajar Iran." *American Historical Review,* volume 105, pages 1171–1203.

Kassow, Samuel D. 1989. *Students, Professors, and the State in Tsarist Russia.* Berkeley, California: University of California Press.

———. 1996. "Professionalism Among University Professors." Pages 197–221 in Harley D. Balzer, editor. *Russia's Missing Middle Class: The Professions in Russian History.* Armonk, New York: M. E. Sharpe.

Katouzian, Homayoun [Homa]. 1979. "Nationalist Trends in Iran, 1921–1926." *International Journal of Middle East Studies,* volume 10, pages 533–551.

———. 2000. *State and Society in Iran: The Eclipse of the Qajars and the Emergence of the Pahlavis.* London, England: I. B. Tauris.

Katz, Friedrich. 1981. *The Secret War in Mexico: Europe, the United States, and the Mexican Revolution.* Chicago, Illinois: University of Chicago Press.

———. 1998. *The Life and Times of Pancho Villa.* Stanford, California: Stanford University Press.

Kavcar, Cahit. 1974. *II Meşrutiyet Devrinde Edebiyat ve Eğitim, 1908–1923* (Literature and Education in the Second Constitutional Period, 1908–1923). Ankara, Turkey: Üniversitesi Basımevi.

Kayalı, Hasan. 1997. *Arabs and Young Turks: Ottomanism, Arabism, and Islamism in the Ottoman Empire, 1908–1918.* Berkeley, California: University of California Press.

Kazembeyki, Mohammad Ali. 2003. *Society, Politics and Economics in Mazandaran, Iran, 1848–1914.* London, England: RoutledgeCurzon.

Kazemi, Farhad, and Ervand Abrahamian. 1978. "The Nonrevolutionary Peasantry of Modern Iran." *Iranian Studies,* volume 11, pages 259–304.

Kazemi, Farhad, and John Waterbury, editors. 1991. *Peasants and Politics in the Modern Middle East.* Miami, Florida: Florida International University Press.

Kazemzadeh, F[iruz]. 1956. "The Origin and Early Development of the Persian Cossack Brigade." *American Slavic and East European Review,* volume 15, pages 351–363.

———. 1968. *Russia and Britain in Persia, 1864–1914.* New Haven, Connecticut: Yale University Press.

Keck, Margaret E. 1992. *The Workers' Party and Democratization in Brazil.* New Haven, Connecticut: Yale University Press.

Keddie, Nikki R. 1966. *Religion and Rebellion in Iran: The Tobacco Protest of 1891–1892.* London, England: Cass.

———. 1971. "The Assassination of the Amin as-Sultan (Atabak-i A'zam), 31 August 1907." Pages 315–329 in C. E. Bosworth, editor, *Iran and Islam.* Edinburgh, Scotland: Edinburgh University Press.

Keep, John L. H. 1963. *The Rise of Social Democracy in Russia.* Oxford, England: Clarendon Press.

Kemal, Namık. [1868] 2002. "And Seek Their Counsel in the Matter," translated by M. Şükrü Hanioğlu. Pages 144–148 in Charles Kurzman, editor, *Modernist Islam: A Source-Book, 1840–1940.* New York, New York: Oxford University Press.

Kennan, George. 1887. "The Last Appeal of the Russian Liberals." *Century Illustrated Monthly Magazine,* volume 35, number 1, pages 50–63.

Kenney, Padraic. 2002. *A Carnival of Revolution: Central Europe, 1989.* Princeton, New Jersey: Princeton University Press.

Kent, Christopher. 1978. *Brains and Numbers: Elitism, Comtism, and Democracy in Mid-Victorian England.* Toronto, Canada: University of Toronto Press.

Keramett Bey, Salih. 1924. "The Young Turk Movement." Pages 476–490 in Eliot Grinnell Mears, editor, *Modern Turkey.* New York, New York: Macmillan.

Keyder, Çağlar. 1987. *State and Class in Turkey: A Study in Capitalist Development.* London, England: Verso.

Keyder, Çağlar, and Faruk Tabak, editors. 1991. *Landholding and Commercial Agriculture in the Middle East*. Albany, New York: State University of New York Press.

Khal'atbari, 'Abdulsamad. 1949. *Sharh-i Mukhtasar-i Zindagani-yi Sipahsalar-i A'zam Muhammad Vali Khan Khal'atbari Tunukabuni* (A Brief Biography of the Sipahsalar-i A'zam, Muhammad Vali Khan Khal'atbari Tunukabuni). Tehran, Iran: no publisher listed.

Khalidi, Rashid. 1981. "'Abd al-Ghani al-'Uraisi and *al-Mufid:* The Press and Arab Nationalism before 1914." Pages 38–61 in Marwan R. Buheiry, editor, *Intellectual Life in the Arab East, 1890–1939*. Beirut, Lebanon: American University of Beirut.

Khatami, Mohammad. 1998. *Islam, Liberty and Development*. Binghamton, New York: Institute of Global Cultural Studies, Binghamton University.

Khayr al-Din. [1867] 1967. *The Surest Path*, translated by Leon Carl Brown. Cambridge, Massachusetts: Center for Middle Eastern Studies, Harvard University.

Khazeni, Arash. 2005. "The Bakhtiyari Tribes in the Iranian Constitutional Revolution." *Comparative Studies of South Asia, Africa and the Middle East*, volume 25, pages 377–398.

Khuri, Ra'if. [1943] 1983. *Modern Arab Thought: Channels of the French Revolution to the Arab East*, translated by Ihsan 'Abbas. Princeton, New Jersey: Kingston Press.

King, Rosa E. 1935. *Tempest over Mexico: A Personal Chronicle*. Boston, Massachusetts: Little, Brown.

Kloppenberg, James T. 1986. *Uncertain Victory: Social Democracy and Progressivism in European and American Thought, 1870–1920*. New York, New York: Oxford University Press.

Knight, Alan. 1986. *The Mexican Revolution*, volume 1, *Porfirians, Liberals and Peasants*. Cambridge, England: Cambridge University Press.

———. 1987. *U.S.-Mexican Relations, 1910–1940: An Interpretation*. San Diego, California: Center for U.S.-Mexican Studies, University of California, San Diego.

———. 1989. "Los Intelectuales en la Revolución Mexicana" (Intellectuals in the Mexican Revolution). *Revista Mexicana de Sociología* (Mexican Review of Sociology), volume 51, pages 25–65.

Kocahanoğlu, Osman Selim. 2000. "Derviş Vahdeti, II" (Derviş Vahdeti, Part 2). *Tarih ve Toplum* (History and Society), number 202, pages 45–57.

———. 2001. *Derviş Vahdeti ve Çavuşların İsyanı* (Derviş Vahdeti and the Sergeants' Rebellion). Istanbul, Turkey: Temel Yayınları.

Koenker, Diane P., and Ronald D. Bachman, editors. 1997. *Revelations from the Russian Archives: Documents in English Translation*. Washington, DC: Library of Congress.

Korelin, Avenir P. 1995. "The Social Problem in Russia, 1906–1914: Stolypin's Agrarian Reform." Pages 139–162 in Theodore Taranovski, editor, *Reform in*

Modern Russian History: Progress or Cycle? Washington, DC: Woodrow Wilson Center Press; New York, New York: Cambridge University Press.

Korlaelçi, Murtaza. 1986. *Pozitivizmin Türkiye'ye Girişi* (Positivism's Entry into Turkey). Istanbul, Turkey: İnsan Yayınları.

Kotschnig, Walter. 1937. *Unemployment in the Learned Professions: An International Study of Occupational and Educational Planning.* London, England: Humphrey Milford, Oxford University Press.

Kovalewsky, Maxime. 1906. *La Crise Russe: Notes et Impressions d'un Témoin* (The Russian Crisis: Notes and Impressions of an Eyewitness). Paris, France: Librairie Générale de Droit et de Jurisprudence.

Kreiser, Klaus. 1981. "Der japanische Sieg über Russland (1905) und sein Echo unter den Muslimen" (The Japanese Victory over Russia [1905] and Its Echo among the Muslims). *Die Welt des Islams* (The World of Islam), volume 21, pages 209–239.

Krugman, Paul. 1996. *Pop Internationalism.* Cambridge, Massachusetts: MIT Press.

Kupper, Samuel Yale. 1973. "Revolution in China: Kiangsi Province, 1905–1913." Ph.D. dissertation, Department of History, University of Michigan.

Kuran, Ahmed Bedevi. 1945. *İnkılâp Tarihimiz ve Jön Türkler* (The History of Our Revolution and the Young Turks). Istanbul, Turkey: Tan Matbaası.

———. 1959. *Osmanlı İmparatorluğunda İnkılâp Hareketleri ve Milli Mücadele* (Revolutionary Movements in the Ottoman Empire and the National Struggle). Istanbul, Turkey: Çeltüt Matbaası.

Kurzman, Charles, editor. 1998. *Liberal Islam: A Sourcebook.* New York, New York: Oxford University Press.

———. 1998. "Waves of Democratization." *Studies in Comparative International Development,* volume 33, pages 37–59.

———, editor. 2002. *Modernist Islam, 1840–1940: A Sourcebook.* New York, New York: Oxford University Press.

———. 2004. "Can Understanding Undermine Explanation? The Confused Experience of Revolution." *Philosophy of the Social Sciences,* volume 34, pages 328–351.

———. 2004. *The Unthinkable Revolution in Iran.* Cambridge, Massachusetts: Harvard University Press.

———. 2005. "Weaving Iran into the Tree of Nations." *International Journal of Middle East Studies,* volume 37, pages 137–166.

———. 2006. "*Mashrutiyat, Meşrutiyet,* and Beyond: Parallels and Intersections in the Constitutional Revolutions of 1905–1912." Paper presented at the Centenary Conference of the Iranian Constitutional Revolution, University of Oxford, August 1.

Kurzman, Charles, and Erin Leahey. 2004. "Intellectuals and Democratization, 1905–1912 and 1989–1996." *American Journal of Sociology,* volume 109, pages 937–986.

Kurzman, Charles, and Lynn Owens. 2002. "The Sociology of Intellectuals." *Annual Review of Sociology,* volume 28, pages 63–90.

Kutay, Cemal. 1983. *Talat Paşa'n Gurbet Hatıraları* (Overseas Memoirs of Talat Pasha), 2nd edition, 3 volumes. Istanbul, Turkey: Kültür Matbaası.

Kwok, D. W. Y. 1965. *Scientism in Chinese Thought, 1900–1950*. New Haven, Connecticut: Yale University Press.

La Puma, Léonardo. 1983. "L'Affaire Dreyfus dans la Presse Salentine (Italie Méridionale, Région des Pouilles)" (The Dreyfus Affair in the Salentine Press [Southern Italy, Apulia Region]). Pages 47–55 in Géraldi Leroy, editor, *Les Écrivains et l'Affaire Dreyfus* (Writers and the Dreyfus Affair). Paris, France: Presses Universitaires de France.

Laffan, Michael. 1999. "Mustafa and the Mikado: A Francophile Egyptian's Turn to Meiji Japan." *Japanese Studies*, volume 19, pages 269–286.

LaFrance, David G. 1989. *The Mexican Revolution in Puebla, 1908–1913*. Wilmington, Delaware: Scholarly Resources Books.

Lambton, Ann K. S. 1963. "Persian Political Societies, 1906–1911." *Middle Eastern Affairs*, number 3, pages 41–89.

———. 1969. *Landlord and Peasant in Iran*. London, England: Oxford University Press.

Laqueur, Walter. 1993. *Black Hundred: The Rise of the Extreme Right in Russia*. New York, New York: Harper Collins.

Larsen, Stein Ugelvik, editor. 2001. *Fascism Outside Europe: The European Impulse against Domestic Conditions in the Diffusion of Global Fascism*. New York, New York: Columbia University Press.

Laves, Walter Herman Carl. [1927] 1977. *German Governmental Influence on Foreign Investments, 1871–1914*. New York, New York: Arno.

Leal, Juan Felipe. 1972. *La Burguesía y el Estado Mexicano* (The Bourgeoisie and the Mexican State). Mexico City, Mexico: Ediciones 'El Caballito.'

Lear, John. 2001. *Workers, Neighbors, and Citizens: The Revolution in Mexico City*. Lincoln, Nebraska: University of Nebraska Press.

Lecky, William Edward Hartpole. 1896. *Democracy and Liberty*, 2 volumes. New York, New York: Longmans, Green.

Lee, En-Han. 1977. *China's Quest for Railway Autonomy, 1904–1911*. Singapore: Singapore University Press.

Lee, Ou-fan. 1972. "The Romantic Temper of May Fourth Writers." Pages 69–84 in Benjamin I. Schwartz, editor, *Reflections on the May Fourth Movement*. Cambridge, Massachusetts: East Asian Research Center, Harvard University.

Lenin V. I. [1902] 1975. "What Is to Be Done?" Pages 12–114 in Robert C. Tucker, editor, *The Lenin Anthology*. New York, New York: W. W. Norton.

———. [1905] 1975. "Two Tactics of Social Democracy in the Democratic Revolution." Pages 120–147 in Robert C. Tucker, editor, *The Lenin Anthology*. New York, New York: W. W. Norton.

———. [1914] 1975. "The Right of Nations to Self-Determination." Pages 153–180 in Robert C. Tucker, editor, *The Lenin Anthology*. New York, New York: W. W. Norton.

Léontovitsch, Victor. [1957] 1987. *Histoire du Libéralisme en Russie* (The History of Liberalism in Russia), translated by Ole Hansen-Løve. Paris, France: Fayard.

Levin, Alfred. 1940. *The Second Duma: A Study of the Social-Democratic Party and the Russian Constitutional Experiment.* New Haven, Connecticut: Yale University Press; London, England: H. Milford, Oxford University Press.

————. 1964. "June 3, 1907: Action and Reaction." Pages 231–273 in Alan D. Ferguson and Alfred Levin, editors, *Essays in Russian History.* Hamden, Connecticut: Archon Books.

Levy, Carl. 1987. "Socialism and the Educated Middles Classes in Western Europe, 1870–1914." Pages 154–191 in Ron Eyerman, Lennart G. Svensson, and Thomas Söderqvist, editors, *Intellectuals, Universities, and the State in Western Modern Societies.* Berkeley, California: University of California Press.

Lévy, Roger. 1931. *Intellectuels, Unissez-Vous!* (Intellectuals, Unite!). Paris, France: Marcel Rivière.

Lewis, Bernard. 1965. *The Emergence of Modern Turkey.* London, England: Oxford University Press.

Li, Chien-nung. 1956. *The Political History of China, 1840–1928,* translated by Ssu-yu Teng and Jeremy Ingalls. Princeton, New Jersey: D. Van Nostrand.

Li, Lillian M. 1981. *China's Silk Trade: Traditional Industry in the Modern World, 1842–1937.* Cambridge, Massachusetts: Council on East Asian Studies, Harvard University.

Li Shu. 1983. "A Re-Assessment of Some Questions Concerning the 1911 Revolution." Pages 67–127 in Hu Sheng, Liu Danian, and others, *The 1911 Revolution: A Retrospective after 70 Years.* Beijing, China: New World Press.

Li Shu-fan. 1964. *Hong Kong Surgeon.* New York, New York: E. P. Dutton.

Libaridian, Gerard. 2004. *Modern Armenia: People, Nation, State.* New Brunswick, New Jersey: Transaction.

Licéaga, Luis. 1958. *Félix Díaz* (Félix Díaz). Mexico City, Mexico: Editorial Jus.

Lieuwen, Edwin. 1968. *Mexican Militarism: The Political Rise and Fall of the Revolutionary Army.* Albuquerque, New Mexico: University of New Mexico Press.

Liew, K. S. 1971. *Struggle for Democracy: Sung Chiao-jen and the 1911 Chinese Revolution.* Berkeley, California: University of California Press.

Lima dos Santos, M. de Lourdes. 1983. " 'Os Fabricantes dos Gozos da Inteligência': Alguns Aspectos da Organização do Mercado de Trabalho Intelectual no Portugal de Oitocentos" (Manufacturers of the Delights of Intelligence: Certain Aspects of the Organization of Intellectual Labor Market in Nineteenth Century Portugal). *Análise Social* (Social Analysis), number 75, pages 7–28.

Link, E. Perry, Jr. 1981. *Mandarin Ducks and Butterflies: Popular Fiction in Early Twentieth-Century Chinese Cities.* Berkeley, California: University of California Press.

Lippert, Wolfgang. 1979. *Entstehung und Funktion einiger chinesischer marxistischer Termini* (Emergence and Function of Certain Chinese Marxist Terms). Wiesbaden, West Germany: Franz Steiner Verlag.

Lipset, Seymour Martin. 1981. *Political Man: The Social Bases of Politics*, expanded edition. Baltimore, Maryland: Johns Hopkins University Press.

Lipset, Seymour Martin, Kyoung-Ryung Seong, and John Charles Torres. 1993. "A Comparative Analysis of the Social Requisites of Democracy." *International Social Science Journal*, volume 136, pages 155–175.

Liu, Lydia H. 1995. *Translingual Practice: Literature, National Culture, and Translated Modernity—China, 1900–1937*. Stanford, California: Stanford University Press.

Loe, Mary Louise. 1991. "Redefining the Intellectual's Role: Maksim Gorky and the Sreda Circle." Pages 288–307 in Edith W. Clowes, Samuel D. Kassow, and James L. West, editors, *Between Tsar and People: Educated Society and the Quest for Public Identity in Late Imperial Russia*. Princeton, New Jersey: Princeton University Press.

Long, James W. 1968. "The Economics of the Franco-Russian Alliance, 1904–1906." Ph.D. dissertation, Department of History, University of Wisconsin.

———. 1972. "Organized Protest against the 1906 Russian Loan." *Cahiers du Monde Russe et Soviétique* (Annals of the Russian and Soviet World), volume 13, pages 24–39.

———. 1975. "French Attempts at Constitutional Reform in Russia." *Jahrbücher für Geschichte Osteuropas* (Yearbook of East European History), volume 23, pages 496–503.

Lowe, Peter. 1969. *Great Britain and Japan, 1911–15*. London, England: Macmillan.

Lu Hsün. [1918] 1974. "Diary of a Madman." Pages 1–12 in Harold R. Isaacs, editor, *Straw Sandals: Chinese Short Stories, 1918–1933*. Cambridge, Massachusetts: MIT Press.

Luebbert, Gregory. 1991. *Liberalism, Fascism, or Social Democracy*. New York, New York: Oxford University Press.

Lust, John. 1972. "Secret Societies, Popular Movements, and the 1911 Revolution." Pages 165–200 in Jean Chesneaux, editor, *Popular Movements and Secret Societies in China, 1840–1950*. Stanford, California: Stanford University Press.

Macey, David A. J. 1987. *Government and Peasant in Russia, 1861–1906: The Prehistory of the Stolypin Reforms*. Dekalb, Illinois: Northern Illinois University Press.

Mackie, Thomas T., and Richard Rose. 1991. *The International Almanac of Electoral History*, 3rd edition. Houndsmills, England: Macmillan.

Madancy, Joyce A. 2003. *The Troublesome Legacy of Commissioner Lin: The Opium Trade and Opium Suppression in Fujian Province, 1820s to 1920s*. Cambridge, Massachusetts: Harvard University Asia Center.

Madero, Francisco I. 1963. *Epistolario (1900–1909)* (Collected Letters, 1900–1909). Mexico City, Mexico: Ediciones de la Secretaria de la Hacienda.

———. [1908] 1990. *The Presidential Succession of 1910*, translated by Thomas B. Davis. New York, New York: Peter Lang

Mahdavi, Shireen. 1999. *For God, Mammon, and Country: A Nineteenth-Century Persian Merchant*. Boulder, Colorado: Westview.

Maia, Álvaro. 1928. "Liberdade de Imprensa . . ." (Freedom of the Press . . .). Pages 13–22 in *Uma Hora de Jornalismo: Aspectos Anecdotas e Inconfidências da Vida Profissional* (One Hour of Journalism: Anecdotal and Secret Aspects of Professional Life). Lisbon, Portugal: Edição da Caixa de Previdência do Sindicato dos Profissionais da Imprensa da Lisboa.

Majd al-Islam (Kirmani), Ahmad. 1972. *Tarikh-i Inhitat-i Majlis* (History of the Degeneration of Parliament). Isfahan, Iran: Danishgah-i Isfahan.

———. 1972. *Tarikh-i Inqilab-i Mashrutiyat-i Iran* (History of the Constitutional Revolution of Iran), volume 1, *Safarnamah-yi Kalat* (Travelogue of Kalat). Isfahan, Iran: Danishgah-i Isfahan.

Makedonski, Stojan. 1974. "La Révolution Jeune-Turque et les Premières Élections Parlementaires de 1908 en Macédoine et en Thrace Orientale" (The Young Turk Revolution and the First Parliamentary Elections of 1908 in Macedonia and Eastern Thrace). *Études Balkaniques* (Balkan Studies), volume 10, number 4, 133–145.

Maklakov, Vasilij A. 1964. *The First State Duma: Contemporary Reminiscences*, translated by Mary Belkin. Bloomington, Indiana: Indiana University Press.

Malheiro-Dias, C. 1912. *O Estado Actual da Causa Monarchica* (The Current State of the Monarchical Cause), serialized in 20 parts. [Lisbon, Portugal]: José Bastos.

Malikzadah, Mahdi. 1984. *Tarikh-i Inqilab-i Mashrutiyat-i Iran* (History of the Constitutional Revolution of Iran), 7 volumes in 3. Tehran, Iran: 'Ilmi.

Mamaqani, Asadullah. 1910. *Maslak al-Imam fi Salamat al-Islam* (The Imami School and the Welfare of Islam). Istanbul, Ottoman Empire: Matba'ah-yi Shams.

Mamuntov, N. P. [1930] 1985. "Hukumat-i Tzari va Muhammad 'Ali Shah: Khatirat-i N. P. Mamuntuf" (The Tsarist Government and Muhammad 'Ali Shah: The Memoirs of N. P. Mamuntuf), translated by Marhum Sharfuddin Qahramani. Pages 265–410 in Humayun Shahidi, editor, *Bumbaran-i Majlis-i Shura-yi Milli* (The Shelling of the National Consultative Assembly). Tehran, Iran: Sazman-i Intisharat-i Ashkan.

Mandelstam, André. 1917. *Le Sort de l'Empire Ottoman* (The Departure of the Ottoman Empire). Lausanne, Switzerland: Librairie Payot.

Mango, Andrew. 1999. *Atatürk*. London, England: John Murray.

Mannheim, Karl. [1929] 1985. *Ideology and Utopia*, translated by Louis Wirth and Edward Shils. San Diego, California: Harcourt Brace Jovanovich.

Manning, Roberta T. 1979. "Zemstvo and Revolution: The Onset of the Gentry Reaction, 1905–1907." Pages 30–66 in Leopold H. Haimson, editor, *The Politics of Rural Russia, 1905–1914*. Bloomington, Indiana: Indiana University Press.

———. 1982. *The Crisis of the Old Order in Russia: Gentry and Government*. Princeton, New Jersey: Princeton University Press.

Mardin, Şerif. 1962. *The Genesis of Young Ottoman Thought.* Princeton, New Jersey: Princeton University Press.

———. 1964. *Jön Türklerin Siyasî Fikirleri, 1895–1908* (The Political Thought of the Young Turks, 1895–1908). Ankara, Turkey: Türkiye İş Bankası Kültür Yayınları.

———. 1983. "Les Souvenirs d'Anciens Élèves" (The Memoirs of Graduates). Pages 162–166 in Jean-Louis Bacqué-Grammont and Paul Dumont, editors, *Économie et Sociétés dans l'Empire Ottoman (Fin du XVIIIe–Début du XXe Siècle)* (Economy and Societies in the Ottoman Empire, End of the Eighteenth to the Beginning of the Twentieth Century). Paris, France: Éditions du Centre National de la Recherche Scientifique.

Marichal, Juan. 1990. *El Intelectual y la Política en España (1898–1936)* (The Intellectual and Politics in Spain, 1898–1936). Madrid, Spain: Publicaciones de la Residencia de Estudiantes.

Markoff, John. 1996. *Waves of Democracy.* Thousand Oaks, California: Pine Forge Press.

Marques, A. H. de Oliveira. 1969. "Revolution and Counterrevolution in Portugal: Problems of Portuguese History, 1900–1930." Pages 403–418 in *Studien Über die Revolution* (Studies of the Revolution), edited by Manfred Kossok. Berlin, East Germany: Akademie-Verlag.

———. 1972. *Afonso Costa* (Afonso Costa). Lisbon, Portugal: Editora Arcádia.

———. 1972. *History of Portugal,* volume 2, *From Empire to Corporate State.* New York, New York: Columbia University Press.

———, editor. 1991. *Nova História de Portugal* (New History of Portugal), volume 11, *Portugal da Monarquia para a República* (Portugal from Monarchy to Republic). Lisbon, Portugal: Editorial Presença.

———, editor. 2000. *Parlamentares e Ministros da 1a República (1910–1926)* (Parliamentarians and Ministers of the First Republic, 1910–1926). Lisbon and Porto, Portugal: Assembleia da República, Edições Afrontamento.

Márquez Sterling, M[anuel]. 1917. *Los Últimos Días del Presidente Madero: Mi Gestión Diplomática en México* (The Final Days of President Madero: My Diplomatic Service in Mexico). Havana, Cuba: Imprenta "El Siglo XX."

Martin, Bradford G. 1959. *German-Persian Diplomatic Relations, 1873–1912.* Gravenhage, Netherlands: Mouton.

Martin, Vanessa A. 1989. *Islam and Modernism: The Iranian Revolution of 1906.* London, England: I. B. Tauris.

Marx, Karl. [1852] 1974. "The Eighteenth Brumaire of Louis Bonaparte." Pages 143–249 in David Fernbach, editor, *Surveys from Exile.* New York, New York: Vintage Books.

Marx, Karl, and Friedrich Engels. [1848] 1978. "Manifesto of the Communist Party." Pages 469–500 in Robert C. Tucker, editor, *The Marx-Engels Reader,* 2nd edition. New York, New York: W. W. Norton.

Masini, Federico. 1993. *The Formation of Modern Chinese Lexicon and Its Evolution toward a National Language: The Period from 1840 to 1898.* Berkeley, California: Journal of Chinese Linguistics Monograph Series.

Matin-asgari, Afshin. 2000. "Sacred City Profaned: Utopianism and Despair in Early Modernist Persian Literature." Pages 186–211 in Rudi Matthee and Beth Baron, editors, *Iran and Beyond*. Costa Mesa, California: Mazda.

Maybon, Albert. 1914. *La République Chinoise* (The Chinese Republic). Paris, France: Colin.

McCaffray, Susan P. 1996. *The Politics of Industrialization in Tsarist Russia: The Association of Southern Coal and Steel Producers, 1874–1914.* DeKalb, Illinois: Northern Illinois University Press.

McClelland, James C. 1979. *Autocrats and Academics: Education, Culture, and Society in Tsarist Russia*. Chicago, Illinois: University of Chicago Press.

McCord, Edward A. 1993. *The Power of the Gun: The Emergence of Modern Chinese Warlordism*. Berkeley, California: University of California Press.

McCullagh, Francis. 1910. *The Fall of Abd-ul-Hamid*. London, England: Methuen.

McDaniel, Robert A. 1974. *The Shuster Mission and the Persian Constitutional Revolution*. Minneapolis, Minnesota: Bibliotheca Islamica.

McDaniel, Tim. 1988. *Autocracy, Capitalism, and Revolution in Russia*. Berkeley, California: University of California Press.

McElderry, Andrea Lee. 1976. *Shanghai Old-Style Banks (Ch'ien-Chuang), 1800–1935: A Traditional Institution in a Changing Society*. Ann Arbor, Michigan: University of Michigan Center for Chinese Studies.

McLean, David. 1978. "English Radicals, Russia, and the Fate of Persia." *English Historical Review*, volume 93, pages 338–352.

———. 1979. *Britain and Her Buffer State: The Collapse of the Persian Empire, 1890–1914.* London, England: Royal Historical Society.

McReynolds, Louise. 2003. *Russia at Play: Leisure Activities at the End of the Tsarist Era*. Ithaca, New York: Cornell University Press.

Meeker, Michael E. 2002. *A Nation of Empire: The Ottoman Legacy of Turkish Modernity*. Berkeley, California: University of California Press.

Mei, Hua-Chuan. 1917. "The Returned Student in China." *The Chinese Recorder,* volume 48, number 3, pages 158–175.

Menashe, Louis. 1968. "Industrialists in Politics: Russia in 1905." *Government and Opposition,* volume 3, pages 352–368.

Menashri, David. 1992. *Education and the Making of Modern Iran*. Ithaca, New York: Cornell University Press.

Mendel, Arthur P. 1961. *Dilemmas of Progress in Tsarist Russia*. Cambridge, Massachusetts: Harvard University Press.

Mentzel, Peter Carl. 1994. "Nationalism and the Labor Movement in the Ottoman Empire, 1872–1914." Ph.D. dissertation, Department of History, University of Washington.

Meyer, Michael C. 1972. *Huerta: A Political Portrait*. Lincoln, Nebraska: University of Nebraska Press.

Michels, Roberto. 1932. "Intellectuals." Pages 118–126 in Edwin R. A. Seligman, editor, *Encyclopedia of the Social Sciences,* volume 8. New York, New York: Macmillan.

Michon, Georges. 1929. *The Franco-Russian Alliance, 1891–1917*, translated by Norman Thomas. New York, New York: Macmillan.

Midhat, Pasha. [1879] 1983. "Liberty Is the Key to Everything." Pages 199–200 in Ra'if Khuri, editor, *Modern Arab Thought: Channels of the French Revolution to the Arab East*, translated by Ihsan 'Abbas. Princeton, New Jersey: Kingston Press.

Mikić, Djordje. 1983. *Austro-Ugarska i Mladoturci, 1908–1912* (Austria-Hungary and the Young Turks, 1908–1912). Banja Luka, Yugoslavia: Institut za Istoriju u Banja Luci.

Miller, Ruth A. 2005. *Legislating Authority: Sin and Crime in the Ottoman Empire and Turkey*. New York, New York: Routledge.

Milyoukov, Paul. [1905] 1906. *Russia and Its Crisis*. Chicago, Illinois: University of Chicago Press.

Mir, Cyrus, and Encyclopaedia Iranica. 1999. "Farmanfarma, 'Abd-al-Hosayn Mirza." Pages 196–199 in Ehsan Yarshater, editor, *Encyclopaedia Iranica*, volume 9. New York, New York: Bibliotheca Persica Press.

Moaddel, Mansour. 1992. "Shi'i Political Discourse and Class Mobilization in the Tobacco Movement of 1890–1892." *Sociological Forum*, volume 7, pages 447–468.

Molho, Rena. 1997. "The Zionist Movement in Thessaloniki, 1899–1919." Pages 327–350 in I. K. Hassiotis, editor, *The Jewish Communities of Southeastern Europe*. Thessaloniki, Greece: Institute for Balkan Studies.

Mónica, Maria Filomena. 1978. *Educação e Sociedade no Portugal de Salazar* (Education and Society in Salazar's Portugal). Lisbon, Portugal: Editorial Presença.

———. 1981. "Moulding the Minds of the People: Views on Popular Education in 20th Century Portugal." *Iberian Studies*, volume 10, pages 3–14.

———. 1986. *Artesãos e Operários: Indústria, Capitalismo e Classe Operária em Portugal (1870–1934)* (Artisans and Workers: Industry, Capitalism, and the Working Class in Portugal, 1870–1934). Lisbon, Portugal: Edições do Instituto de Ciências Sociais da Universidade de Lisboa.

———. 1987. "Capitalistas e Industriais (1870–1914)" (Capitalists and Industrialists, 1870–1914). *Análise Social* (Social Analysis), number 99, pages 819–863.

Moore, Barrington. 1966. *The Social Origins of Dictatorship and Democracy*. Boston, Massachusetts: Beacon.

Morales Benítez, Otto. 1985. *Liberalismo: Destino de la Patria* (Liberalism: Destiny of the Fatherland), 2nd edition. Bogota, Columbia: Plaza y Janés.

Moreau, Odile. 1997. "Les Réformes Militaires Jeunes-Turques de 1908: Évolution ou Révolution?" (The Young Turk Military Reforms of 1908: Evolution or Revolution?). *Cahiers du Centre d'Études d'Histoire de la Défense* (Annals of the Center for Studies of the History of Defense), number 5, pages 53–73.

Morgado, E., editor. 1910. *Legislação Republicana ou As Primeiras Leis e Disposições da República Portugueza* (Republic Legislation, or the First Laws and

Decrees of the Portuguese Republic). Lisbon, Portugal: Empreza do Almanach Palhares.

Morrissey, Susan K. 1998. *Heralds of Revolution: Russian Students and the Mythologies of Radicalism.* New York, New York: Oxford University Press.

Mosolov, A. A. [1934] 1935. *At the Court of the Last Tsar,* edited by A. A. Pilenco, translated by E. W. Dickes. London, England: Methuen.

Mosse, George L. 1996. *The Image of Man: The Creation of Modern Masculinity.* New York, New York: Oxford University Press.

Mostafi, Abdollah. 1997. *The Administrative and Social History of the Qajar Period: The Story of My Life,* translated by Nayer Mostofi Glenn, 3 volumes. Costa Mesa, California: Mazda.

Mukhtari, Pasha Liva'. 1950. *Tarikh-i Haftad-Salah-yi Pulis-i Iran* (Seventy-Year History of the Police of Iran). Tehran, Iran: Chapkhanah-yi Artish.

Munting, Roger. 1992. "Economic Change and the Russian Gentry, 1861–1914." Pages 234–243 in Linda Edmondson and Peter Waldron, editors, *Economy and Society in Russia and the Soviet Union, 1860–1930.* New York, New York: St. Martin's Press.

Murray, Dian H., in collaboration with Qin Baoqi. 1994. *The Origins of the Tiandihui: The Chinese Triads in Legend and History.* Stanford, California: Stanford University Press.

Mustashar al-Daulah. 1983. *Khatirat va Asnad-i Mustashar al-Daulah* (The Memoirs and Documents of Mustashar al-Daulah), edited by Iraj Afshar, 2 volumes. Tehran, Iran: Intisharat-i Firdausi; Intisharat-i Farhangi; Intisharat-i Iran va Islam.

Nabavi, Negin. 2005. "Spreading the Word: Iran's First Constitutional Press and the Shaping of a 'New Era.'" *Critique: Critical Middle Eastern Studies,* volume 14, pages 307–321.

Nadi, Yunus. 1909. *İhtilal ve İnkılab-ı Osmani, 31 Mart–14 Nisan 1325* (The Ottoman Revolt and Revolution, April 14–28, 1909). Istanbul, Ottoman Empire: Matbaa-yı Cihan.

Nafi, Basheer M. 1998. *Arabism, Islamism and the Palestine Question, 1908–1941.* Reading, England: Ithaca Press.

Nahirny, Vladimir C. 1962. "The Russian Intelligentsia: From Men of Ideas to Men of Convictions." *Comparative Studies in Society and History,* volume 4, pages 405–435.

Najmabadi, Afsaneh. 1998. *The Story of the Daughters of Quchan: Gender and National Memory in Iranian History.* Syracuse, New York: Syracuse University Press.

Nam, Chang-Hee. 1995. "South Korea's Big Business Clientelism in Democratic Reform." *Asian Survey,* volume 35, pages 357–366.

Namier, Lewis. 1944. *1848: The Revolution of the Intellectuals.* London, England: Oxford University Press.

Natiq, Huma. 1983. "Anjuman'ha-yi Shura'i dar Inqilab-i Mashrutah" (Consultative Committees in the Constitutional Revolution). *Alifba* (Alphabet), number 4, pages 48–65.

———. 1994. *Bazarganan dar Dad-u-Sitad ba Bank-i Shahi va Rizhi-yi Tan-*

baku: Bar Payah-yi Arshiv-i Amin al-Zarb (Merchants' Dealings with the Imperial Bank and the Tobacco Concession: On the Basis of the Amin al-Zarb Archive). Tehran, Iran: Tus.

Nava'i, 'Abdulhusayn. 1948. "Majlis-i Avval: Nakhustin Budjah-yi Saliyanah-yi Kishvar'ra Chigunah Tasvib Kard" (The First Parliament: How the Country's First Annual Budget Was Approved). *Ittila'at-i Mahanah* (The Monthly News), volume 1, number 8, pages 19–22.

Nawid, Senzil. 1997. "State, Clergy, and British Imperial Policy in Afghanistan during the 19th and Early 20th Centuries." *International Journal of Middle East Studies,* volume 29, pages 581–605.

Nazim al-Islam Kirmani, Muhammad. 1968. *Tarikh-i Bidari-yi Iranian* (History of the Awakening of the Iranians), edited by ['Ali Akbar] Sa'idi Sirjani, 5 volumes in 2. Tehran, Iran: Intisharat-i Bunyad-i Farhang-i Iran.

Neuberger, Joan. 1993. *Hooliganism: Crime, Culture, and Power in St. Petersburg, 1900–1914.* Berkeley, California: University of California Press.

Newhall, David S. 1991. *Clemenceau: A Life at War.* Lewiston, New York: E. Mellen Press.

Nezihi, Hakkı. 1932. *50 Yıllık Oda Hayatı, 1882–1932* (The Chamber's Fifty-Year Life, 1882–1932). Istanbul, Turkey: Sanayii Nefise Matbaası.

Nichols, Ray. 1978. *Treason, Tradition, and the Intellectual: Julien Benda and Political Discourse.* Lawrence, Kansas: Regents Press of Kansas.

Niemeyer, E. V., Jr. 1966. *El General Bernardo Reyes* (General Bernardo Reyes). Monterrey, Mexico: Biblioteca de Nuevo Leon.

Nish, Ian H. 1972. *Alliance in Decline: A Study in Anglo-Japanese Relations, 1908–23.* London, England: Athlone Press.

Niyazi, Ahmed. 1913. *Hatırat-ı Niyazi.* Istanbul, Ottoman Empire: Sabah Matbaası.

Noutsos, Panagiotis. 1994. "The Role of the Greek Community in the Genesis and Development of the Socialist Movement in the Ottoman Empire: 1876–1925." Pages 77–88 in Mete Tunçay and Erik Jan Zürcher, editors, *Socialism and Nationalism in the Ottoman Empire, 1876–1923.* London: British Academic Press.

O'Boyle, Leonor. 1970. "The Problem of an Excess of Educated Men in Western Europe (1800–1850)." *Journal of Modern History,* volume 42, pages 471–495.

O'Donnell, Guillermo A. 1973. *Modernization and Bureaucratic-Authoritarianism.* Berkeley, California: Institute of International Studies, University of California, Berkeley.

O'Donnell, Guillermo, and Philippe C. Schmitter. 1986. *Transitions from Authoritarian Rule: Tentative Conclusions about Uncertain Democracies.* Baltimore, Maryland: Johns Hopkins University Press.

O'Kane, Rosemary H. T. 2004. *Paths to Democracy: Revolution and Totalitarianism.* London, England: Routledge.

O'Loughlin, John, Michael D. Ward, Corey L. Lofdahl, Jordin S. Cohen, David S. Brown, David Reilly, Kristian S. Gleditsch, and Michael Shin. 1998. "The Diffusion of Democracy, 1946–1994." *The Annals of the Association of American Geographers,* volume 88, pages 545–575.

O'Shaughnessy, Edith. 1917. *Diplomatic Days*. New York, New York: Harper.

Ocampo López, Javier. 1990. *Qué es el Liberalismo Colombiano* (What Colombian Liberalism Is). Bogota, Colombia: Plaza y Janés.

Oliveira, César. 1974. *O Operariado e a República Democrática (1910–1914)* (The Working Class and the Democratic Republic, 1910–1914), 2nd edition. Lisbon, Portugal: Seara Nova.

Ono Kazuko. 1989. *Chinese Women in a Century of Revolution, 1850–1950*. Stanford, California: Stanford University Press.

Onur, Hakkı. 1977. "1908 İşçi Hareketleri ve Jön Türkler" (1908 Worker Movements and the Young Turks) *Yurt ve Dünya* (Home and World), volume 2, pages 277–295.

Ory, Pascal, and Jean-François Sirinelli. 1986. *Les Intellectuels en France de l'Affaire Dreyfus à Nos Jours* (Intellectuals in France from the Dreyfus Affair to Our Day). Paris, France: Armand Colin.

Osa, Maryjane. 1998. "Contention and Democracy: Labor Protest in Poland, 1989–1993." *Communist and Post-Communist Studies*, volume 31, pages 29–42.

Ostrogorski, M. 1902. *Democracy and the Organization of Political Parties*, translated by Frederick Clarke, 2 volumes. New York, New York. Macmillan.

Ostrorog, Léon. 1919. *The Turkish Problem: Things Seen and a Few Deductions*. London, England: Chatto and Windus.

Owen, Roger. 1993. *The Middle East in the World Economy, 1800–1914*, revised edition. London, England: I. B. Tauris.

———, editor. 2000. *New Perspectives on Property and Land in the Middle East*. Cambridge, Massachusetts: Center for Middle Eastern Studies, Harvard University.

Owen, Thomas C. 1981. *Capitalism and Politics in Russia: A Social History of the Moscow Merchants, 1855–1905*. Cambridge, England: Cambridge University Press.

Owram, Doug. 1986. *The Government Generation: Canadian Intellectuals and the State, 1900–1945*. Toronto, Canada: University of Toronto Press.

Palavicini, Félix F. 1937. *Mi Vida Revolucionaria* (My Revolutionary Life). Mexico City, Mexico: Ediciones Botas.

Paléologue, Maurice. 1957. *Three Critical Years (1904–05–06)*. New York, New York: Robert Speller.

Palmer, R. R. 1959–1964. *The Age of the Democratic Revolution: A Political History of Europe and America, 1760–1800*. Princeton, New Jersey: Princeton University Press.

Panayatopoulos, Alkiriades. 1980. "The Hellenic Contribution to the Ottoman Labor and Socialist Movement after 1908." *Études Balkaniques* (Balkan Studies), volume 16, pages 38–57.

Pani, Alberto J. 1918. *Una Encuesta Sobre Educación Popular* (An Inquest into Popular Education). Mexico City, Mexico: Poder Ejecutivo Federal, Departamiento de Aprovisionamientos Generales, Dirección de Talleres Gráficos.

———. 1936. *Mi Contribución al Nuevo Régimen (1910–1933)* (My Contribution to the New Regime, 1910–1933). Mexico City, Mexico: Editorial "Cultura."

Pares, Bernard. 1907. *Russia and Reform.* London, England: Archibald Constable.

Parla, Taha. 1985. *The Social and Political Thought of Ziya Gökalp, 1876–1924.* Leiden, Netherlands: E. J. Brill.

Parsa, Misagh. 1995. "Entrepreneurs and Democratization: Iran and the Philippines." *Comparative Studies in Society and History,* volume 37, pages 803–830.

Passmore, Kevin. 1997. *From Liberalism to Fascism: The Right in a French Province, 1928–1939.* Cambridge, England: Cambridge University Press.

Payne, Leigh. 1994. *Brazilian Industrialists and Democratic Change.* Baltimore, Maryland: Johns Hopkins University Press.

Pears, Edwin. 1916. *Forty Years in Constantinople.* New York, New York: Appleton.

Pereira, Ana Paula de Brito. 1983. "As Greves Rurais de 1911–12: Uma Leitura Através da Imprensa" (The Rural Strikes of 1911–1912: A Reading of the Press). *Análise Social* (Social Analysis), numbers 77–79, pages 477–511.

Perrie, Maureen. 1972. "The Russian Peasant Movement of 1905–1907: Its Social Composition and Revolutionary Significance." *Past and Present,* volume 57, pages 123–155.

Perry, Elizabeth J. 1993. *Shanghai on Strike: The Politics of Chinese Labor.* Stanford, California: Stanford University Press.

Pimenta de Castro, Gonçalo Pereira. [1945]. *As Minhas Memórias* (My Memoirs), volume 1. Porto, Portugal: Livraria Progredior.

Pimenta de Castro, Joaquim Pereira. 1915. *O Dictador e a Affrontosa Dictadura* (The Dictator and the Dictatorial Affront). Weimar, Germany: Impr. W. G. Humbold.

Ping, Kuo Wen. 1915. *The Chinese System of Public Education.* New York, New York: Teachers College, Columbia University.

Pinon, René. 1911. *L'Europe et la Jeune Turquie* (Europe and Young Turkey). Paris, France: Perrin et Cie.

Pinto, Louis. 1983. "Les Intellectuels vers 1900: Une Nouvelle Classe Moyenne" (The Intellectuals around 1900: A New Middle Class). Pages 140–155 in Georges Lavau, Gérard Grunberg, and Nonna Mayer, editors, *L'Univers Politique des Classes Moyennes* (The Political Universe of the Middle Classes). Paris, France: Presses de la Fondation Nationale des Sciences Politiques.

Pipes, Richard. 1970. *Struve: Liberal on the Left, 1870–1905.* Cambridge, Massachusetts: Harvard University Press.

Platt, D. C. M. 1968. *Finance, Trade, and Politics in British Foreign Policy, 1815–1914.* Oxford, England: Clarendon Press.

Poidevin, Raymond. 1969. *Les Relations Économiques et Financières entre la France et l'Allemagne* (Economic and Financial Relations between France and Germany). Paris, France: A. Colin.

Pollard, Alan P. 1964. "The Russian Intelligentsia: The Mind of Russia." *California Slavic Studies*, volume 3, pages 1–32.

Pott, Francis Lister Hawks. 1913. "Education in China." *China Mission Year Book*, volume 4, pages 235–246.

———. 1946. "Modern Education." Pages 427–440 in Harley Farnsworth MacNair, editor, *China*. Berkeley, California: University of California Press.

Powell, Ralph L. 1955. *The Rise of Chinese Military Power, 1895–1912*. Princeton, New Jersey: Princeton University Press.

Prätor, Sabine. 1993. *Der arabische Faktor in der jungtürkischen Politik: Eine Studie zum osmanischen Parlament der II. Konstitution (1908–1918)* (The Arab Factor in Young Turk Politics: A Study of the Ottoman Parliament of the Second Constitution, 1908–1918). Berlin, Germany: Klaus Schwarz.

Prestage, Edgar. 1953. "Reminiscences of Portugal." Pages 1–11 in H. V. Livermore, editor, *Portugal and Brazil: An Introduction*. Oxford, England: Clarendon Press.

Preto Cruz, Francisco Manso. 1944. *Paiva Couceiro: Político-Militar-Colonial* (Paiva Couceiro: Politician, Soldier, Colonialist), volume 1, *Política Internacional* (International Politics), 2nd edition. Lisbon, Portugal: Edição do Autor.

Preuss, Ulrich K. 1995. *Constitutional Revolution: The Link between Constitutionalism and Progress*. Atlantic Highlands, New Jersey: Humanities Press International.

Price, Don C. 1971. *Russia and the Roots of the Chinese Revolution, 1896–1911*. Cambridge, Massachusetts: Harvard University Press.

Pridham, Geoffrey. 1991. "International Influences in Democratic Transition: Problems of Theory and Practice in Linkage Politics." Pages 1–44 in Geoffrey Pridham, editor, *Encouraging Democracy: The International Context of Regime Transition in Southern Europe*. New York, New York: St. Martin's.

Przeworski, Adam, *et alia*. 2000. *Democracy and Development: Political Institutions and Well-Being in the World, 1950–1990*. Cambridge, England: Cambridge University Press.

Psilos, Christopher. 2005. "From Cooperation to Alienation: An Insight into Relations between the Serres Group and the Young Turks during the Years 1906–9." *European History Quarterly*, volume 35, pages 541–558.

Pu, Shu. 1950. "The Consortium Reorganization Loan to China, 1911–1914: An Episode in Pre-War Diplomacy and International Finance." Ph.D. dissertation, Department of History, University of Michigan.

Purcell, Victor. 1936. *Problems of Chinese Education*. London, England: K. Paul, Trench, Trubner.

Puryear, Jeffrey. 1994. *Thinking Politics: Intellectuals and Democracy in Chile, 1973–1988*. Baltimore, Maryland: Johns Hopkins University Press.

Pyman, Avril. 1979. *The Life of Aleksandr Blok*, volume 1. Oxford, England: Oxford University Press.

Qa'im Maqami, Jahangir, editor. 1969. *Asnad-i Tarikhi-yi Vaqayi'-i Mashrutah-yi Iran: Namah'ha-yi Zahir al-Daulah* (Historical Documents of the Constitutional Events of Iran: The Letters of Zahir al-Daulah). Tehran, Iran: Kitabkhanah-yi Tahuri.

Quataert, Donald. 1983. *Social Disintegration and Popular Resistance in the Ottoman Empire, 1881–1908*. New York, New York: New York University Press.

———. 1986. "Machine Breaking and the Changing Carpet Industry of Western Anatolia, 1860–1908." *Journal of Social History,* volume 19, pages 473–489.

———. 1993. *Ottoman Manufacturing in the Age of the Industrial Revolution.* Cambridge, England: Cambridge University Press.

———. 1994. "The Age of Reforms, 1812–1914." Pages 759–943 in Halil İnalcık with Donald Quataert, editors, *An Economic and Social History of the Ottoman Empire, 1300–1914.* Cambridge, England: Cambridge University Press.

Queiroz, Vasco de Barros. 1985. *Episódios da Vida do Político: Thomé José de Barros Queiroz* (Episodes from the Life of a Politician: Thomé José de Barros Queiroz). Lisbon, Portugal: Editorial Eva.

Rábago, Jesús M. [1913]. *"El Mañana": Periódico Político, Junio 15 de 1911 a Febrero 28 de 1913* ("The Morning": Political Newspaper, June 15, 1911, to February 28, 1913). Mexico City, Mexico: El Mañana.

Rabino, Joseph. 1937. *Memories, 1843–1915.* Cairo, Egypt: D. Spada.

Ramírez Rancaño, Mario. 1987. *Burguesía Textil y Política en la Revolución Mexicana* (Textile Bourgeoisie and Politics in the Mexican Revolution). Mexico City, Mexico: Instituto de Investigaciones Sociales, Universidad Nacional Autónoma de México.

Ramos, Rui. 1992. "A Formação da Intelligentsia Portuguesa (1860–1880)" (The Formation of the Portuguese Intelligentsia, 1860–1880). *Análise Social* (Social Analysis), numbers 116–117, pages 483–528.

Ramos-Escandón, Carmen. 1987. "La Política Obrera del Estado Mexicano de Díaz a Madero" (The Labor Policy of the Mexican State from Díaz to Madero). *Mexican Studies,* volume 3, pages 19–47.

Ramsaur, Ernest Edmondson, Jr. 1957. *The Young Turks: Prelude to the Revolution of 1908.* Princeton, New Jersey: Princeton University Press.

Ramsay, W. M. 1909. *The Revolution in Constantinople and Turkey: A Diary.* London, England: Hodder and Stoughton.

Rankin, Mary Backus. 1971. *Early Chinese Revolutionaries: Radical Intellectuals in Shanghai and Chekiang, 1902–1911.* Cambridge, Massachusetts: Harvard University Press.

Rappoport, Alfred. 1927. *Au Pays des Martyrs: Notes et Souvenirs d'un Ancien Consul Général d'Autriche-Hongrie en Macédoine (1904–1909)* (In the Land of Martyrs: Notes and Memories of a Former Austria-Hungarian Consul-General in Macedonia, 1904–1909). Paris, France: Librairie Universitaire J. Gamber.

Rawson, Don C. 1995. *Russian Rightists and the Revolution of 1905.* Cambridge, England: Cambridge University Press.

Rea, Geo. Bronson. 1912. "The Financial History of the [Chinese] Revolution: The Power of Money." *Far Eastern Review*, volume 8, pages 337–381.

Read, Christopher. 1979. *Religion, Revolution, and the Russian Intelligentsia, 1900–1912: The Vekhi Debate and Its Intellectual Background.* New York, New York: Barnes and Noble.

———. 1990. *Power in Revolutionary Russia: The Intelligentsia and the Transition from Tsarism to Communism.* New York, New York: St. Martin's Press.

Rees, Tim, and Andrew Thorpe, editors. 1998. *International Communism and the Communist International, 1919–43.* Manchester, England: Manchester University Press.

Refik, Ahmed. 1918. *İnkılab-ı Azim (11 Temmuz 1324)* (The Great Revolution of July 24, 1908). Istanbul, Ottoman Empire: Asr Matbaası.

Refik, Mustafa. 1899. "Abdülhamid ve Dreyfüs Meselesi" (Abdülhamid and the Dreyfus Affair). *Osmanlı Mecmuası* (The Ottoman Journal), volume 2, number 43, September 1, 1899, page 2.

Reichman, Henry. 1987. *Railwaymen and Revolution: Russia, 1905.* Berkeley, California: University of California Press.

Reid, John Gilbert. 1935. *The Manchu Abdication and the Powers, 1908–1912.* Berkeley, California: University of California Press.

Reis, Jaime. 1986. "A Produção Industrial Portuguesa, 1870–1914: Primeira Estimativa de um Índice" (Portuguese Industrial Production, 1870–1914: First Estimate of an Index). *Análise Social* (Social Analysis), number 94, pages 903–928.

Rejali, Darius M. 1994. *Torture and Modernity: Self, Society, and State in Modern Iran.* Boulder, Colorado: Westview.

Renouvin, Pierre. 1960–1961. "Finance et Politique: L'Emprunt Russe d'Avril 1906 en France" (Finance and Politics: The Russian Loan of April 1906 in France). *Études Suisses d'Histoire Générale* (Swiss Studies in General History), volume 18, pages 507–515.

Reyes, Alfonso. 1960. *Obras Completas de Alfonso Reyes* (Complete Works of Alfonso Reyes), volume 12. Mexico City, Mexico: Letras Mexicanas, Fondo de Cultura Económica.

Reyes, Rodolfo. 1929. *De Mi Vida: Memorias Políticas* (From My Life: Political Memoirs), volume 1. Madrid, Spain: Biblioteca Nueva.

Reynolds, Douglas R. 1993. *China, 1898–1912: The Xinzheng Revolution and Japan.* Cambridge, Massachusetts: Harvard University Council on East Asian Studies.

Rhoads, Edward J. M. 1975. *China's Republican Revolution: The Case of Kwangtung, 1895–1913.* Cambridge, Massachusetts: Harvard University Press.

———. 2000. *Manchus and Han: Ethnic Relations and Political Power in Late Qing and Early Republican China, 1861–1928.* Seattle, Washington: University of Washington Press.

Richard, Yann. 1989. "La Fondation d'une Armée Nationale en Iran" (The Founding of a National Army in Iran). Pages 43–67 in Yann Richard, editor,

Entre l'Iran et l'Occident: Adaptation et Assimilation des Idées et Techniques Occidentales en Iran (Between Iran and the West: Adaptation and Assimilation of Western Ideas and Technologies in Iran). Paris, France: Éditions de la Maison des Sciences de l'Homme.

Richmond, Douglas W. 1983. *Venustiano Carranza's Nationalist Struggle, 1893–1920.* Lincoln, Nebraska: University of Nebraska Press.

Rida, Rashid. 1898. "Al-Yahud fi Faransa wa fi Misr" (The Jew in Egypt and France), *al-Manar* (The Beacon), volume 1, number 2, March 18, pages 53–55.

Rieber, Alfred J. 1982. *Merchants and Entrepreneurs in Imperial Russia.* Chapel Hill, North Carolina: University of North Carolina Press.

Riha, Thomas. 1969. *A Russian European: Paul Miliukov in Russian Politics.* Notre Dame, Indiana: University of Notre Dame Press.

Rıza, Ahmet. 1903. "L'Inaction des Jeunes-Turcs" (The Inaction of the Young Turks). *Revue Occidentale* (Occidental Review), series 2, volume 27, pages 91–98.

Robinson, Pearl T. 1994. "The National Conference Phenomenon in Francophone Africa." *Comparative Studies in Society and History,* volume 36, number 3, pages 575–610.

Rodrigue, Aron. 1990. *French Jews, Turkish Jews: The Alliance Israélite Universelle and the Politics of Jewish Schooling in Turkey, 1860–1925.* Bloomington, Indiana: Indiana University Press.

Rodrigues, Alice Correia Godinho. 1985. "Ideal Republicano e Reforma da Universidade de Coimbra" (The Republican Ideal and Reform of the University of Coimbra). *Revista de História das Ideias* (Journal of the History of Ideas), volume 7, pages 313–333.

Rodríguez García, Rubén. 1990. *La Cámara Agrícola Nacional Jalisciense: Una Sociedad de Terratenientes en la Revolución Mexicana* (The National Agricultural Chamber of Jalisco: An Organization of Landowners in the Mexican Revolution). Mexico City, Mexico: Instituto Nacional de Estudios Históricos de la Revolución Mexicana.

Rojas Garcidueñas, José. 1979. *El Ateneo de la Juventud y la Revolución* (The Atheneum of Youth and the Revolution). Mexico City, Mexico: Biblioteca del Instituto Nacional de Estudios Históricos de la Revolución Mexicana.

Roosa, Ruth Amende. 1975. "Russian Industrialists, Politics, and Labor Reform in 1905." *Russian History,* volume 2, pages 124–148.

Rose, Brad, and George Ross. 1994. "Socialism's Past, New Social Democracy, and Socialism's Futures." *Social Science History,* volume 18, pages 439–469.

Rosenberg, William G. 1972. "Kadets and the Politics of Ambivalence, 1905–1917." Pages 139–163 in Charles W. Timberlake, editor, *Essays on Russian Liberalism.* Columbia, Missouri: University of Missouri Press.

Rosenthal, Bernice Glatzer, and Martha Bohachevsky-Chomiak. 1982. "Introduction." Pages 1–40 in Bohachevsky-Chomiak and Rosenthal, editors, *A Revolution of the Spirit: Crisis of Value in Russia, 1890–1918,* translated by Marian Schwartz. Newtonville, Massachusetts: Oriental Research Partners.

Ross, Elizabeth N. Macbean. 1921. *A Lady Doctor in Bakhtiari Land*. London, England: Leonard Parsons.

Ross, Stanley, R. 1955. *Francisco I. Madero: Apostle of Mexican Democracy*. New York, New York: Columbia University Press.

Rossos, Andrew. 1981. *Russia and the Balkans: Inter-Balkan Rivalries and Russian Foreign Policy, 1908–1914*. Toronto, Canada: University of Toronto Press.

Ruckman, Jo Ann. 1984. *The Moscow Business Elite: A Social and Cultural Portrait of Two Generations, 1840–1905*. Dekalb, Illinois: Northern Illinois University Press.

Rudinger, St. Piero. 1914. *The Second Revolution in China, 1913: My Adventures of the Fighting around Shanghai, the Arsenal, Woosung Forts*. Shanghai, China: Shanghai Mercury.

Rueschemeyer, Dietrich, John D. Stephens, and Evelyn Huber Stephens. 1992. *Capitalist Development and Democracy*. Cambridge, England: Polity Press; Chicago, Illinois: University of Chicago Press.

Ruiz, Ramón Eduardo. 1976. "Madero's Administration and Mexican Labor." Pages 187–203 in James W. Wilkie, Michael C. Meyer, and Edna Monzón de Wilkie, editors, *Contemporary Mexico: Papers of the IV International Congress of Mexican History*. Berkeley, California: University of California Press.

Rustow, Dankwart A. 1970. "Transitions to Democracy: Toward a Dynamic Model." *Comparative Politics*, volume 2, pages 337–363.

Rutherford, John. 1971. *Mexican Society during the Revolution: A Literary Approach*. Oxford, England: Clarendon.

Ruznamah-yi Anjuman-i Tabriz (The Newspaper of the Council of Tabriz), 2 volumes. 1995, 1997. Tehran, Iran: Kitabkhanah-yi Milli-yi Jumhuri-yi Islami-yi Iran; Ustandari-yi Azarbayjan-i Sharqi.

Ryan, Andrew. 1951. *The Last of the Dragomans*. London, England: G. Bles.

Sa'idi-Sirjani, 'Ali Akbar. 1989. "Baktiari." Pages 543–548 in Ehsan Yarshater, editor, *Encyclopaedia Iranica*, volume 3. London, England: Routledge and Kegan Paul.

———. 1993. "The Constitutional Revolution: The Press." Pages 202–212 in Ehsan Yarshater, editor, *Encyclopaedia Iranica*, volume 6. Costa Mesa, California: Mazda.

Sadiq, 'Isa. 1959. *Yadgar-i 'Umr* (Memories of Life). Tehran, Iran: Shirkat-i Sahami-yi Tab'-i Kitab.

Sadiq, Issa Khan. 1931. *Modern Persia and Her Education System*. New York, New York: Teachers College, Columbia University.

Safa'i, Ibrahim. 1984. *Rahbaran-i Mashrutah* (Leaders of the Constitutional Period), 2 volumes. Tehran, Iran: Javidan.

Sakaoğlu, Necdet. 1985. "Eğitim Tartışmaları" (Educational Debates). Pages 478–484 in *Tanzimat'tan Cumhuriyet'e Türkiye Ansiklopedisi* (The Encyclopedia of Turkey from the Tanzimat to the Republic), volume 2. Istanbul, Turkey: İletişim Yayınları.

Samadzadeh, Mehrdad Faiz. 1989. "The Emergence of Iranian Bonapartism, 1905–1921." *Studies in History*, volume 5 (new series), pages 211–269.

Sami, Şemseddin. 1899. *Kamus-i Türki* (Turkish Dictionary). Istanbul, Turkey: İkdam Matbaası.

Sánchez Azcona, Juan. 1960. *La Etapa Maderista de la Revolución* (The Madero Stage of the Revolution). Mexico City, Mexico: Biblioteca del Instituto Nacional de Estudios Históricos de la Revolución Mexicana.

Sanders, Jonathan. 1985. "The Union of Unions: Political, Economic, Civil and Human Rights Organizations in the 1905 Russian Revolution." Ph.D. dissertation, Department of History, Columbia University.

Sani' al-Daulah, Murtaza Quli Khan. [1907] 1984. *Rah-i Nijat*, edited by Huma Rizvani. Tehran, Iran: Nashr-i Tarikh-i Iran.

Santa, Eduardo. 1980. *El Pensamiento Político de Rafael Uribe Uribe* (The Political Thought of Rafael Uribe Uribe). Bogota, Colombia: Ediciones Tercer Mundo.

Santos, Fernando Piteira. 1982–1983. "Na Transição do 'Constitucionalismo Monárquico' para o 'Constitucionalismo Republicano': A Crise do Partido Socialista e a Crise do Partido Republicano" (In Transition from "Monarchical Constitutionalism" to "Republican Constitutionalism": The Crisis of the Socialist Party and the Crisis of the Republican Party). *Análise Social* (Social Analysis), numbers 72–74, pages 673–685.

Santos, Machado. 1916. *A Ordem Publica e o 14 de Maio* (Public Order and the 14th of May). Lisbon, Portugal: Papelaria e Tipografia Liberty.

Sarrou, Auguste. 1912. *La Jeune Turquie et la Révolution* (Young Turkey and the Revolution). Paris, France: Berger-Levrault.

Sasportes, José. 1970. *História da Dança em Portugal* (History of Dance in Portugal). Lisbon, Portugal: Fundação Calouste Gulbenkian.

Scalapino, Robert A., and Harold Schiffrin. 1959. "Early Socialist Currents in the Chinese Revolutionary Movement." *The Journal of Asian Studies*, volume 18, pages 312–342.

Schayegh, Cyrus. 2004. "Science, Medicine, and Class in the Formation of Semi-Colonial Iran, 1900s–1940s." Ph.D. dissertation, Department of Middle East and Asian Languages and Cultures, Columbia University.

Schiffrin, Harold. 1957. "Sun Yat-sen's Early Land Policy." *Journal of Asian Studies*, volume 16, pages 549–564.

———. 1968. *Sun Yat-sen and the Origins of the Chinese Revolution*. Berkeley, California: University of California Press.

——— 1980. *Sun Yat-sen, Reluctant Revolutionary*. Boston, Massachusetts: Little, Brown.

Schmidt, Henry C. 1989. "Los Intelectuales de la Revolución desde Otra Perspectiva" (The Intellectuals of the Revolution from Another Perspective). *Revista de Sociología Mexicana* (Mexican Review of Sociology), volume 51, pages 67–86.

———. 1991. "Power and Sensibility: Toward a Typology of Mexican Intellectuals and Intellectual Life, 1910–1920." Pages 173–188 In Roderic A. Camp, Charles A. Hale, and Josefina Zoraida Vázquez, editors, *Los Intelectuales y el Poder en México* (Intellectuals and Power in Mexico). Mexico City, Mexico: El Colegio de México.

Schmitt, Bernadotte E. [1937] 1970. *The Annexation of Bosnia, 1908–1909*. New York, New York: Howard Fertig.

Schmitter, Philippe. 1993. "The International Context of Contemporary Democratization." *Stanford Journal of International Affairs*, volume 2, pages 1–34.

Scholes, Walter V., and Marie V. Scholes. 1970. *The Foreign Policies of the Taft Administration*. Columbia, Missouri: University of Missouri Press.

Schreiner, George Abel, editor. 1921. *Entente Diplomacy and the World*, translated by B. de Siebert. New York, New York: Knickerbocker Press.

Schwarcz, Vera. 1986. *The Chinese Enlightenment: Intellectuals and the Legacy of the May Fourth Movement of 1919*. Berkeley, California: University of California Press.

Schwartzman, Kathleen C. 1989. *The Social Origins of Democratic Collapse: The First Portugese Republic in the Global Economy*. Lawrence, Kansas: University Press of Kansas.

Schwarz, Solomon M. 1967. *The Russian Revolution of 1905: The Workers' Movement and the Formation of Bolshevism and Menshevism*, translated by Gertrude Vakar. Chicago, Illinois: University of Chicago Press.

Seidman, Gay W. 1994. *Manufacturing Militance: Workers' Movements in Brazil and South Africa, 1970–1985*. Berkeley, California: University of California Press.

Semenoff, Marc, editor. 1924. *Correspondance entre Guillaume II et Nicolas II, 1894–1914* (Correspondence between Wilhelm II and Nicholas II, 1894–1914). Paris, France: Librairie Plon.

Şener, Abdüllatif. 1990. "İttihat ve Terakki Cemiyetinin İktisadi ve Mali Politikaları (1908–1918)" (The Society for Union and Progress's Economic and Financial Policies, 1908–1918). *Hacettepe Üniversitesi İktisadi ve İdari Bilimler Fakültesi Dergisi* (Hacettepe University Economic and Administrative Sciences Faculty Review), volume 8, pages 203–232.

Serbesti Gazetesi Muharriri Hasan Fehmi Efendinin Katlı (The Murder of *Freedom* Newspaper Journalist Hasan Fehmi). 1909. Istanbul, Ottoman Empire: No publisher listed.

Seregny, Scott J. 1989. *Russian Teachers and Peasant Revolution: The Politics of Education in 1905*. Bloomington, Indiana: Indiana University Press.

———. 1989. "Zemstvo Rabbits, Antichrists, and Revolutionaries: Rural Teachers in Saratov Province, 1890–1907." Pages 113–138 in Rex A. Wade and Scott J. Seregny, editors, *Politics and Society in Provincial Russia: Saratov, 1590–1917*. Columbus, Ohio: Ohio State University Press.

Serrão, Joel. 1970. *Antologia do Pensamento Político Português* (Anthology of Portuguese Political Thought), volume 1, *Liberalismo, Socialismo, Republicanismo* (Liberalism, Socialism, Republicanism). Oporto, Portugal: Editorial Inova.

Seyf, Ahmad. 1998. "Obstacles to the Development of Capitalism: Iran in the Nineteenth Century." *Middle Eastern Studies*, volume 34, pages 54–82.

Shafiei-Nasab, Djafar. 1991. *Les Mouvements Révolutionnaires et la Constitution de 1906 en Iran* (Revolutionary Movements and the Constitution of 1906 in Iran). Berlin, Germany: Klaus Schwarz Verlag.

Shaji'i, Zahra. 1965. *Namayandagan-i Majlis-i Shura-yi Milli Dar Bist-o-Yak Dowrah-yi Qanun-Guzari* (National Consultative Assembly Representatives from Twenty-One Legislative Sessions). Tehran, Iran: Intisharat-i Mu'asasah-yi Mutala'at va Tahqiqat-i Ijtima'i.

Shanin, Teodor. 1985–1986. *The Roots of Otherness: Russia's Turn of Century*, 2 volumes. New Haven, Connecticut: Yale University Press.

Sharif-Kashani, Muhammad Mahdi. 1983. *Vaqa'at-i Ittifaqiyah dar Ruzgar* (Daily Events), edited by Mansurah Ittihadiyah (Nizam Mafi) and Sirus Sa'dvandiyan, 3 volumes. Tehran, Iran: Nashr-i Tarikh-i Iran.

Shatz, Marshall S., and Judith E. Zimmerman, editors. [1909] 1994. *Vekhi (Landmarks): A Collection of Articles about the Russian Intelligentsia*. Armonk, New York: M. E. Sharpe.

Shaw, Stanford J. 1978. "Ottoman Expenditures and Budgets in the Late Nineteenth and Early Twentieth Centuries." *International Journal of Middle East Studies*, volume 9, pages 373–378.

———. 1979. "The Population of Istanbul in the Nineteenth Century." *International Journal of Middle East Studies*, volume 10, pages 265–277.

Shaw, Stanford J., and Ezel Kural Shaw. 1977. *History of the Ottoman Empire and Modern Turkey*, volume 2, *Reform, Revolution, and Republic: The Rise of Modern Turkey, 1808–1975*. Cambridge, England: Cambridge University Press.

Shaykh al-Islam, Mirza 'Abdulamir. 1977. *Du Sanad az Inqilab-i Mashrutiyat-i Iran* (Two Documents from the Constitutional Revolution of Iran). [Tehran, Iran]: Tuka.

Sheikholeslami, Reza, and Wilson Dunning. 1973. "The Memoirs of Haydar Khan 'Amu Ughlu." *Iranian Studies*, volume 6, pages 21–51.

Sheridan, James E. 1975. *China in Disintegration: The Republican Era in Chinese History, 1912–1949*. New York, New York: Free Press.

Shimizu Minoru. 1984. "The 1911 Revolution in Hunan and the Popular Movement." Pages 193–208 in Etō Shinkichi and Harold Z. Schiffrin, editors, *The 1911 Revolution in China: Interpretive Essays*. Tokyo, Japan: University of Tokyo Press.

Shlapentokh, Dmitry. 1996. *The French Revolution in Russian Intellectual Life, 1865–1905*. Westport, Connecticut: Praeger.

Shuster, W. Morgan. 1912. *The Strangling of Persia*. New York, New York: Century.

Siegel, Jennifer. 2002. *Endgame: Britain, Russia, and the Final Struggle for Central Asia*. London, England: I. B. Tauris.

Silva, Maria Regina Tavares da. 1983. "Feminismo em Portugal na Voz de Mulheres Escritoras do Início do Século XX" (Feminism in Portugal in the Voice of Women Writers of the Early Twentieth Century). *Análise Social* (Social Analysis), numbers 77–79, pages 875–907.

Simon, W. M. 1963. *European Positivism in the Nineteenth Century*. Ithaca, New York: Cornell University Press.

Simpson, Bertram Lenox. 1905. *The Re-Shaping of the Far East*, volume 2. New York, New York: Macmillan.

Sirinelli, Jean-François. 1990. *Intellectuels et Passions Françaises: Manifestes et Pétitions au XXe Siècle* (French Intellectuals and Passions: Manifestos and Petitions in the Twentieth Century). Paris, France: Fayard.

Sixième Congrès Socialiste International Tenu à Amsterdam du 14 au 20 Août 1904: Comte-Rendu Analytique (Sixth International Socialist Congress, held in Amsterdam on August 14–20, 1904: Analytical Proceedings), 1904. Brussels, Belgium: Secrétariat Socialiste International.

Skocpol, Theda. 1973. "A Critical Review of Barrington Moore's *Social Origins of Dictatorship and Democracy.*" *Politics and Society,* volume 4, pages 1–34.

———. 1979. *States and Social Revolutions: A Comparative Analysis of France, Russia, and China.* Cambridge, England: Cambridge University Press.

Smirnov, K. N. 2002. *Zapiski Vospitatelia Persidskogo Shakha, 1907–1914 Gody* (Notes of the Persian Shah's Tutor, 1907–1914), edited by Nugzar Konstantinovich Ter-Oganov. Tel Aviv, Israel: Ivrus.

Smith, Tony. 1994. "Notes on the Study of the International Origins of Democracy." Pages 346–368 in *America's Mission: The United States and the Worldwide Struggle for Democracy in the Twentieth Century.* Princeton, New Jersey: Princeton University Press.

Sohrabi, Nader. 1995. "Historicizing Revolutions: Constitutional Revolutions in the Ottoman Empire, Iran, and Russia, 1905–1908." *American Journal of Sociology,* volume 100, pages 1383–1447.

———. 1996. "Constitutionalism, Revolution and State: The Young Turk Revolution of 1908 and the Iranian Constitutional Revolution of 1906 with Comparisons to the Russian Revolution of 1905." Ph.D. dissertation, Department of Sociology, University of Chicago.

———. 2002. "Global Waves, Local Actors: What the Young Turks Knew about Other Revolutions and Why It Mattered." *Comparative Studies in Society and History,* volume 44, pages 45–79.

Song Jiaoren, 1982. *Song Jiaoren xian sheng wen ji* (Essays by Song Jiaoren), 2 volumes. Taipei, Taiwan: Zhongguo guo min dang zhong yang wei yuan hui dang shi wei yuan hui.

Soroudi, Sorour. 1979. "Poet and Revolution: The Impact of Iran's Constitutional Revolution on the Social and Literary Outlook of the Time." *Iranian Studies,* volume 12, pages 3–41 and 239–273.

Sousa Lamy, Alberto. 1990. *A Academia de Coimbra, 1537–1990* (The Academy of Coimbra, 1537–1990). Lisbon, Portugal: Rei dos Livros.

Souza, Maria Reynolds de. 1986. "As Primeiras Deputadas Portuguesas" (The First Portuguese Female Deputies). Pages 427–444 in *A Mulher na Sociedade Portuguesa* (Women in Portuguese Society), volume 2. Coimbra, Portugal: Instituto de História Económica e Social, Faculdade de Letras da Universidade de Coimbra.

Spector, Ivan. 1962. *The First Russian Revolution: Its Impact on Asia.* Englewood Cliffs, New Jersey: Prentice-Hall.

Stapleton, Kristin. 2000. *Civilizing Chengdu: Chinese Urban Reform, 1895–1937.* Cambridge, Massachusetts: Harvard University Asia Center.

Starr, Harvey. 1991. "Democratic Dominoes: Diffusion Approaches to the Spread of Democracy in the International System." *Journal of Conflict Resolution,* volume 35, pages 356–381.

Stein, Sarah Abrevaya. 2004. *Making Jews Modern: The Yiddish and Ladino Press in the Russian and Ottoman Empires.* Bloomington, Indiana: Indiana University Press.

Steinwedel, Charles. 2000. "The 1905 Revolution in Ufa: Mass Politics, Elections, and Nationality." *Russian Review,* volume 59, pages 555–576.

Stites, Richard. 1978. *The Women's Liberation Movement in Russia: Feminism, Nihilism, and Bolshevism, 1860–1930.* Princeton, New Jersey: Princeton University Press.

Stockdale, Melissa Kirschke. 1996. *Paul Miliukov and the Quest for a Liberal Russia, 1880–1918.* Ithaca, New York: Cornell University Press.

Strand, David. 2002. "Citizens in the Audience and at the Podium." Pages 44–69 in Merle Goldman and Elizabeth J. Perry, editors, *Changing Meanings of Citizenship in Modern China.* Cambridge, Massachusetts: Harvard University Press.

Struve, Petr B. [1909] 1994. "The Intelligentsia and Revolution." Pages 115–129 in Marshall S. Shatz and Judith E. Zimmerman, editors, *Vekhi (Landmarks): A Collection of Articles about the Russian Intelligentsia.* Armonk, New York: M. E. Sharpe.

Şuayb, Ahmed, Mehmed Cavid, and Rıza Tevfik. 1908. "Mukaddime ve Program" (Introduction and Program). *Ulûm-u İktisadiye ve İctimaiye Mecmuası* (Journal of Economic and Social Sciences), volume 1, pages 1–10.

Sullivan, Charles Donald. 1977. "Stamboul Crossings: German Diplomacy in Turkey, 1908 to 1914." Ph.D. dissertation, Department of History, Vanderbilt University.

Sun Yatsen. [1919] 1933. "Autobiography of Dr. Sun Yat-sen." Pages 44–82 in *Sun Yat-sen: His Political and Social Ideals,* edited by Leonard Shihlien Hsü. Los Angeles, California: University of Southern California Press.

———. 1994. *Prescriptions for Saving China: Selected Writings of Sun Yat-sen,* edited by Julie Lee Wei, Ramon H. Myers, and Donald G. Gillin. Stanford, California: Hoover Institution Press.

Surh, Gerald D. 1989. *1905 in St. Petersburg: Labor, Society, and Revolution.* Stanford, California: Stanford University Press.

Sutton, Donald S. 1980. *Provincial Militarism and the Chinese Republic: The Yunnan Army, 1905–25.* Ann Arbor, Michigan: University of Michigan Press.

Suzuki, Tomoo. 1984. "The Shanghai Silk-Reeling Industry during the Period of the 1911 Revolution," translated by Okui Yaeko. Pages 49–59 in Etō Shinkichi and Harold Z. Schiffrin, editors, *The 1911 Revolution in China: Interpretive Essays.* Tokyo, Japan: University of Tokyo Press.

Swain, Geoffrey. 1983. *Russian Social Democracy and the Legal Labour Movement, 1906–14.* London, England: Macmillan.

Swenson, Victor R. 1968. "The Young Turk Revolution: A Study of the First Phase of the Second Turkish Constitutional Regime from June 1908 to May

1909." Ph.D. dissertation, School of Advanced International Studies, Johns Hopkins University.

———. 1970. "The Military Rising in Istanbul, 1909." *Journal of Contemporary History,* volume 5, number 4, pages 171–184.

Tafrishi-Husayni, Ahmad. 1973. *Ruznamah-yi Akhbar-i Mashrutiyat va Inqilab-i Iran* (Diary of News of the Constitution and the Revolution of Iran), edited by Iraj Afshar. Tehran, Iran: Amir Kabir.

Tamada, Noriko. 1968. "Sung Chiao-jen and the 1911 Revolution." *Papers on China,* volume 21, pages 184–229.

Tannenbaum, Frank. [1933] 1971. *Peace by Revolution: An Interpretation of Mexico.* Freeport, New York: Books for Libraries Press.

Tarikhchah-yi Si-Salah-yi Bank-i Milli-yi Iran, 1307–1337 (The Thirty-Year History of the National Bank of Iran, 1928–1958). 1959. Tehran, Iran: Bank-i Milli-yi Iran.

Tarzi, Mahmud. 1912. *Chih Bayad Kard?* (What Is to Be Done?). Kabul, Afghanistan: Siraj al-Akhbar.

Tatarov, I. 1928. "Materialy k Istorii Pervogo Syezda" (Materials for the History of the First Union). *Proletarskaya Revolyutsiya* (Proletarian Revolution), number 3, pages 154–163.

Tavakoli-Targhi, Mohamad. 1990. "Asar-i Agahi az Inqilab-i Faransah dar Shikl-Giri-yi Angarah-yi Mashrutiyat dar Iran" (The Constitutionalist Imaginary in Iran and the Ideals of the French Revolution.) *Iran-Namah* (Persian Journal of Iranian Studies), volume 8, pages 411–439.

Tekeli, İlhan, and Selim İlkin. 1980. "İttihad ve Terakki Hareketinin Oluşumunda Selanik'in Toplumsal Yapısının Belirleyiciliği" (Social Structural Determination of the Union and Progress Movement's Origins in Salonica). Pages 351–382 in Osman Okyar and Halil İnalcık, editors, *Türkiye'nin Sosyal ve Ekonomik Tarihi (1071–1920): Social and Economic History of Turkey (1071–1920).* Ankara, Turkey: Meteksan Limited Şirketi.

———. 1986. "The Public Works Program and the Development of Technology in the Ottoman Empire in the Second Half of the Nineteenth Century." *Turcica,* volume 28, pages 195–234.

Temo, İbrahim. 1987. *İbrahim Temo'nun İttihad ve Terakki Anıları* (İbrahim Temo's Union and Progress Memoirs). Istanbul, Turkey: Arba.

Tengarrinha, José. 1989. *História da Imprensa Periódica Portuguesa* (History of the Portuguese Periodical Press), 2nd edition. Lisbon, Portugal: Editoral Caminho.

Ter Minassian, Anaide. 1984. *Nationalism and Socialism in the Armenian Revolutionary Movement (1887–1912),* translated by A. M. Berrett. Cambridge, Massachusetts: Zoryan Institute.

Tevfik, Rıza. 1909. "Hürriyet: İngiliz Hakîm-i Meşhuru Con Stu'art Mill Hürriyeti Nasıl Anlıyor?" (Liberty: How the Famous English Philosopher John Stuart Mill Understands Liberty), *Ulûm-u İktisadiye ve İctimaiye Mecmuası* (Journal of Economic and Social Sciences), volume 2, pages 19–39 and 190–237.

Thomas, Clive Y. 1984. *The Rise of the Authoritarian State in Peripheral Societies.* New York, New York: Monthly Review Press.

Thompson, E. P. 1963. *The Making of the English Working Class*. New York, New York: Vintage Books.

Thompson, Mark R. 2004. *Democratic Revolutions: Asia and Eastern Europe*. London, England: Routledge.

Thurow, Lester. 1992. *Head to Head: The Coming Economic Battle among Japan, Europe, and America*. New York, New York: Morrow.

Tilly, Charles. 2007. *Democracy*. Cambridge, England: Cambridge University Press.

Tinayre, Marcelle. 1909. "Notes d'Une Voyageuse en Turquie" (Notes of a Traveler in Turkey). *Revue des Deux Mondes* (Review of the Two Worlds), July 15, pages 309–337; August 1, pages 549–577; September 1, pages 41–74; October 1, pages 556–599; November 1, pages 147–180.

Tolstoi, Ivan. 1997. *Vospominaniia Ministra Narodnogo Prosveshcheniia Grafa I. I. Tolstogo, 31 Oktiabria 1905g.–24 Aprelia 1906g.* (Memoirs of Count I. I. Tolstoi, Minister of Public Education, 31 October 1905–24 April 1906). Moscow, Russia: "Greko-Latinskii Kabinet" IU. A. Shichalina.

Toprak, Zafer. 1988. "İlan-ı Hürriyet ve Anadolu Osmanlı Demiryolu Memurin ve Müstahdemini Cemiyet-i Uhuvvetkaranesi" (The Declaration of Freedom and the Anatolian Railroad Employees' Association). *Tarih ve Toplum* (History and Society), number 57, pages 45–50.

———. 1995. *Milli İktisat—Milli Burjuvazi* (National Economy, National Bourgeoisie). Istanbul, Turkey: Tarih Vakfı Yurt Yayınları.

Topuz, Hıfzı. 1973. *100 Soruda Türk Basın Tarihi* (The History of Turkish Publishing in 100 Questions). Istanbul, Turkey: Gerçek Yayınevi.

Torpey, John C. 1995. *Intellectuals, Socialism, and Dissent: The East German Opposition and Its Legacy*. Minneapolis, Minnesota: University of Minnesota Press.

Tousi, Reza Ra'iss. 1988. "The Persian Army, 1880–1907." *Middle Eastern Studies*, volume 24, pages 206–229.

Trindade, Luis. 2000. *História da Associação Comercial de Lisboa: Da Fundação Nacionalista à Integração Europeia* (History of the Commercial Association of Lisbon: From Nationalist Foundation to European Integration). Lisbon, Portugal: Câmara do Comércio e Indústria/Associação Comercial de Lisboa.

Troyat, Henri. 1989. *Gorky*, translated by Lowell Bair. New York, New York: Crown.

Tsin, Michael. 1999. *Nation, Governance, and Modernity in China: Canton, 1900–1927*. Stanford, California: Stanford University Press.

Tunaya, Tarik Z. 1952. *Türkiye'de Siyasî Partiler, 1859–1952* (Political Parties in Turkey, 1859–1952). Istanbul, Turkey: Doğan Kardeş Yayınları.

———. 1959. *Hürriyet İlanı: İkinci Meşrutiyetin Siyasî Hayatına Bakışlar* (The Proclamation of Liberty: Views of Political Life in the Second Constitutional Period). Istanbul, Turkey: Baha Matbaası.

Tunukabuni, Sipahdar Muhammad Vali ibn Habib Allah. 1999. *Yaddasht'ha-yi Muhammad Vali Khan Tunukabuni (Sipahsalar-i A'zam)* (Memoirs of Muhammad Vali Khan Tunukabuni, the Sipahsalar-i A'zam), edited by Allahyar Khal'atbari and Fazlullah Iraji Kajuri. Tehran, Iran: Danishgah-i Shahid Bihishti.

Turabi-Farsani, Suhayla. 1999. *Asnadi az Madaris-i Dukhtaran az Mashrutiyat ta Pahlavi* (Documents on Girls' Schools from the Constitutional Revolution to the Pahlavi Era). Tehran, Iran: Sazman-i Asnad-i Milli-yi Iran.

———. 2005. *Tujjar, Mashrutiyat, va Daulat-i Mudirn* (Merchants, Constitutionalism, and the Modern State). Tehran, Iran: Nashr-i Tarikh-i Iran.

Turfan, M. Naim. 2000. *The Rise of the Young Turks: Politics, the Military and Ottoman Collapse.* London, England: I. B. Tauris.

Türkgeldi, Ali Fuad. 1951. *Görüp İşittiklerim* (Things I've Seen and Heard), 2nd edition. Ankara, Turkey: Türk Tarih Kurumu Basımevı.

Tyler, William Ferdinand. 1929. *Pulling Strings in China.* London, England: Constable.

Ünal, Hasan. 1998. "Ottoman Policy during the Bulgarian Independence Crisis, 1908–9: Ottoman Empire and Bulgaria at the Outset of the Young Turk Revolution." *Middle Eastern Studies,* volume 34, number 4, pages 135–176.

———. 2001. "Britain and Ottoman Domestic Politics: From the Young Turk Revolution to the Counter-Revolution, 1908–9." *Middle Eastern Studies,* volume 37, number 2, pages 1–22.

Uribe Uribe, Rafael. 1960. *El Pensamiento Social de Uribe Uribe* (The Social Thought of Uribe Uribe). Bogota, Colombia: República de Colombia, Ministerio de Trabajo.

———. 1979. *Obras Selectas* (Selected Works). Bogota, Colombia: Camara de Representantes de Colombia.

Urióstegui, Miranda, Píndaro. 1970. *Testimonios del Proceso Revolucionario de México* (Testimony of the Revolutionary Process in Mexico). Xochimilco, Mexico: Telleres de Argrin.

Valades, José C. 1932. "Los Secretos del Reyismo" (The Secrets of the Reyes Movement). *La Prensa* (The Press; San Antonio, Texas), October 23–December 4.

Valente, Vasco Pulido. 1976. *O Poder e o Povo: A Revolução de 1910* (The People and the Power: The Revolution of 1910). Lisbon, Portugal: Publicações Dom Quixote.

———. 1992. "Revoluções: A 'República Velha' (Ensaio de Interpretação Política)" (Revolutions: The "Old Republic," an Essay of Political Interpretation). *Análise Social* (Social Analysis), number 115, pages 7–63.

Varè, Daniele. 1938. *The Laughing Diplomat.* New York, New York: Doubleday, Doran.

Vasconcelos, José. [1935] 1982. *Ulises Criollo* (Creole Ulysses), 2 volumes. Mexico City, Mexico: Fondo de Cultura Económica.

Vaz, Angelo. 1950. *Bernardino Machado: Sentimentos, Ideias e Factos do seu Tempo* (Bernardino Machado: Sentiments, Ideas, and Facts of his Time). Oporto, Portugal: Comércio do Porto.

Veillard, Jean-Yves. 1994. "L'Affaire Dreyfus et l'Opinion Publique Internationale" (The Dreyfus Affair and International Public Opinion). Pages 258–266 in Laurent Gervereau and Christophe Prochasson, editors, *L'Affaire*

Dreyfus et le Tournant du Siècle (1894–1910) (The Dreyfus Affair and the Turn of the Century, 1894–1910). Nanterre, France: Bibliothèque de Documentation Internationale Contemporaine.

Ventura, António. 1977. *O Sindicalismo no Alentejo: A "Tournée" de Propaganga de 1912* (Syndicalism in Alentejo: The Propaganda Campaign of 1912). Lisbon, Portugal: Seara Nova.

Verner, Andrew M. 1990. *The Crisis of Russian Autocracy: Nicholas II and the 1905 Revolution.* Princeton, New Jersey: Princeton University Press.

Vidigal, Luis. 1988. *Cidadania, Caciquismo e Poder em Portugal, 1890–1916* (Citizenship, Clientelism, and Power and in Portugal, 1890–1916). Lisbon, Portugal: Livros Horizonte.

Vijuyah, Muhammad Baqir. 1976. *Tarikh-i Inqilab-i Azarbayjan va Balva-yi Tabriz* (History of the Revolution in Azarbaijan and the Disturbance in Tabriz). Tehran, Iran: Amir Kabir.

Vilayati, 'Ali Akbar. 1991. *Tarikh-i Ravabit-i Khariji-yi Iran* (History of the Foreign Relations of Iran), volume 1. Tehran, Iran: Daftar-i Mutala'at-i Siyasi va Bayn-al-milli.

Vilela, Mário. 1977. *'Alma Nacional,' Revista Republicana (1910): Linguagem e Ideologia* ("Soul of the Nation," Republic Journal, 1910: Language and Ideology). Oporto, Portugal: Livraria Civilização.

Villegas, Jorge, and José Yunis. 1978. *La Guerra de los Mil Días* (The War of a Thousand Days). Bogota, Colombia: C. Valencia.

Villegas Moreno, Gloria. 1992. "De Junta Militar a Poder Constituyente: La Revolución Francesa, Paradigma de la Convención Revolucionaria Mexicana" (From Military Junta to Constituent Power: The French Revolution, Paradigm of the Mexican Revolutionary Convention). Pages 255–272 in Solange Alberro *et alia,* editors, *La Revolución Francesa en México* (The French Revolution in Mexico). Mexico City, Mexico: El Colegio de México, Centro de Estudios Mexicanos y Centroamericanos.

Vincent-Smith, J. D. 1971. "Britain and Portugal, 1910–16." Ph.D. dissertation, Department of History, London School of Economics and Political Science, University of London.

Von Laue, Theodore H. 1963. *Sergei Witte and the Industrialization of Russia.* New York, New York: Columbia University Press.

Vucinich, Alexander. 1976. *Social Thought in Tsarist Russia: The Quest for a General Science of Society, 1861–1917.* Chicago, Illinois: University of Chicago Press.

Walcher, Heidi A. 2001. "Creating a New Order: Repercussions of Military Modernization and Militarism in 19th Century Iran." Paper presented at the XXVIII. Deutscher Orientalistentag (28th Congress of the German Oriental Society), March 26–30, 2001, Bamberg, Germany.

Wang, Y. C. 1966. *Chinese Intellectuals and the West, 1872–1949.* Chapel Hill, North Carolina: University of North Carolina Press.

Wartenweiler, David. 1999. *Civil Society and Academic Debate in Russia, 1905–1914.* New York, New York: Oxford University Press.

Wasserman, Claudia. 2002. *Palavra de Presidente* (The President's Word). Porto Alegre, Brazil: Editora da Universidade, Universidade Federal do Rio Grande do Sul.

Wasserman, Mark. 1980. "The Social Origins of the 1910 Revolution in Chihuahua." *Latin American Research Review,* volume 15, pages 15–38.

Watenpaugh, Keith David. 2006. *Being Modern in the Middle East: Revolution, Nationalism, Colonialism, and the Arab Middle Class.* Princeton, New Jersey: Princeton University Press.

Wcislo, Francis William. 1990. *Reforming Rural Russia: State, Local Society, and National Politics, 1855–1914.* Princeton, New Jersey: Princeton University Press.

Weber, Max. [1906] 1995. "Bourgeois Democracy in Russia." Pages 41–147 in Gordon C. Wells and Peter Baehr, editors, *The Russian Revolutions.* Ithaca, New York: Cornell University Press.

———. [1919] 1946. "Science as a Vocation." Pages 129–156 in Hans H. Gerth and C. Wright Mills, editors, *From Max Weber.* New York, New York: Oxford University Press.

Weinberg, Robert. 1993. *The Revolution of 1905 in Odessa.* Bloomington, Indiana: Indiana University Press.

Weisberger, R. William, Wallace McLeod, and S. Brent Morris, editors. 2002. *Freemasonry on Both Sides of the Atlantic: Essays Concerning the Craft in the British Isles, Europe, the United States, and Mexico.* Boulder, Colorado: East European Monographs.

Weston, Timothy B. 2004. *The Power of Position: Beijing University, Intellectuals, and Chinese Political Culture, 1898–1929.* Berkeley, California: University of California Press.

Wheeler, Douglas L. 1978. *Republican Portugal: A Political History, 1910–1926.* Madison, Wisconsin: University of Wisconsin Press.

Whitehead, Laurence. 1986. "International Aspects of Democratization." Pages 3–46 in Guillermo O'Donnell, Philippe C. Schmitter, and Laurence Whitehead, editors, *Transitions from Authoritarian Rule: Comparative Perspectives.* Baltimore, Maryland: Johns Hopkins University Press.

———. 1996. "Concerning International Support for Democracy in the South." Pages 243–273 in Robin Luckham and Gordon White, editors, *Democratization in the South: The Jagged Wave.* Manchester, England: Manchester University Press.

Wildman, Allan K. 1960. "The Russian Intelligentsia of the 1890s." *The American Slavic and East European Review,* volume 19, pages 157–179.

Williams, Adebayo. 1998. "Intellectuals and the Crisis of Democratization in Nigeria: Towards a Theory of Postcolonial Anomie." *Theory and Society,* volume 27, pages 287–307.

Williamson, John. 1993. "Democracy and the 'Washington Consensus.'" *World Development,* volume 21, pages 1329–1336.

Wilson, Arnold. 1941. *S. W. Persia: A Political Officer's Diary, 1907–1914.* London, England: Oxford University Press.

Witte, Sergei Iulevich. [1921] 1990. *The Memoirs of Count Witte*, translated by Sidney Harcave. Armonk, New York: M. E. Sharpe.

Wolf, Eric R. 1969. *Peasant Wars of the Twentieth Century*. New York, New York: Harper.

Womack, John. 1968. *Zapata and the Mexican Revolution*. New York, New York: Knopf.

Wood, Elisabeth Jean. 2000. *Forging Democracy from Below: Insurgent Transitions in South Africa and El Salvador*. Cambridge, England: Cambridge University Press.

Woodhouse, Eiko. 2004. *The Chinese Hsinhai Revolution: G. E. Morrison and Anglo-Japanese Relations, 1897–1920*. London, England: RoutledgeCurzon.

Woodward, Ralph Lee, Jr., editor. 1971. *Positivism in Latin America, 1850–1900*. Lexington, Massachusetts: Heath.

Worley, Matthew, editor. 2004. *In Search of Revolution: International Communist Parties in the Third Period*. London, England: I. B. Tauris.

Worringer, Renée. 2004. " 'Sick Man of Europe' or 'Japan of the Near East'? Constructing Ottoman Modernity in the Hamidian and Young Turk Eras." *International Journal of Middle East Studies*, volume 36, pages 207–230.

Wu Yuzhang. [1962] 1981. *Recollections of the Revolution of 1911*, 4th edition. Beijing, China: Foreign Languages Press.

Wynn, Charters. 1992. *Workers, Strikes, and Pogroms: The Donbass-Dnepr Bend in Late Imperial Russia, 1870–1905*. Princeton, New Jersey: Princeton University Press.

Xavier, Alberto. 1950. *Memórias da Vida Pública* (Memories of Public Life). Lisbon, Portugal: Livraria Ferin.

———. 1962. *História da Greve Académica de 1907* (History of the Academic Strike of 1907). Coimbra, Portugal: Coimbra Editora.

Xiong Yuezhi. 2001. " 'Liberty,' 'Democracy,' 'President': The Translation and Usage of Some Political Terms in Late Qing China." Pages 69–89 in Michael Lackner, Iwo Amelung, and Joachim Kurtz, editors, *New Terms for New Ideas: Western Knowledge and Lexical Change in Late Imperial China*. Leiden, Netherlands: Brill.

Xu Xiaoqun. 2001. *Chinese Professionals and the Republican State: The Rise of Professional Associations in Shanghai, 1912–1937*. Cambridge, England: Cambridge University Press.

Yakrangiyan, Husayn. 1957. *Gulgun-i Kafanan: Gushah'i az Tarikh-i Nizami-yi Iran* (The Rosy Shrouded Ones: One Corner of the Military History of Iran). Tehran, Iran: 'Ilmi.

Yalçın, Alemdar. 1985. *II. Meşrutiyet'te Tiyatro Edebiyati Tarihi* (History of Theatrical Literature in the Second Constitutional Period). Ankara, Turkey: Gazi Üniversitesi Basın-Yayın Yüksek Okulu Matbaası.

Yalçın, Hüseyin Cahit. 1976. *Siyasal Anılar* (Political Memoirs), edited by Rauf Mutluay. Istanbul, Turkey: Türkiye İş Bankası Yayınları.

Yalman, Ahmed Emin. 1970. *Gördüklerim ve Gecirdiklerim, 1888–1918* (My Observations and Experiences, 1888–1918), volume 1. Istanbul, Turkey: Yenilik Basımevi.

Yashar, Deborah J. 1997. *Demanding Democracy: Reform and Reaction in Costa Rica and Guatemala, 1870s–1950s.* Stanford, California: Stanford University Press.

Yen, Ch'ing-huang. 1976. *The Overseas Chinese and the 1911 Revolution, With Special Reference to Singapore and Malaya.* Kuala Lumpur, Malaysia: Oxford University Press.

Yeselson, Abraham. 1956. *United States–Persian Diplomatic Relations, 1883–1921.* New Brunswick, New Jersey: Rutgers University Press.

Yılmaz, Hakan. 1999. "Business Notions of Democracy: The Turkish Experience in the 1990s." *Cahiers d'Études sur la Mediterranée Orientale et le Monde Turco-Iranien* (Annals of the Study of the Eastern Mediterranean and the Turco-Iranian World), volume 27, pages 183–194.

Young, Ernest P. 1968. "Yuan Shih-k'ai's Rise to the Presidency." Pages 419–442 in Mary Clabaugh Wright, editor, *China in Revolution: The First Phase, 1900–1913.* New Haven, Connecticut: Yale University Press.

———. 1977. *The Presidency of Yuan Shih-k'ai.* Ann Arbor, Michigan: University of Michigan Press.

Young, George. 1917. *Portugal Old and Young: An Historical Study.* Oxford, England: Clarendon Press.

Yu, George T. 1966. *Party Politics in Republican China: The Kuomintang, 1912–1924.* Berkeley, California: University of California Press.

Zamani, Safar. 2000. *Tarikhchah-yi Ahzab va Hizb-i Dimukrat-i Iran* (A Brief History of the Parties and the Democrat Party of Iran). Tehran, Iran: Vazhah-Ara.

Zarcone, Thierry. 2002. *Secret et Sociétés Secrètes en Islam: Turquie, Iran et Asie Centrale, XIXe–XXe Siècles* (Secret and Secret Societies in Islam: Turkey, Iran, and Central Asia, Nineteenth–Twentieth Centuries). Milan, Italy: Archè.

Zaygham al-Daulah Bakhtiyari, Iskandar Khan 'Ukkashah. 1986. *Tarikh-i Il-i Bakhtiyari* (History of the Bakhtiyari Tribe), edited by Farid Muradi. [Tehran, Iran]: Intisharat-i Farhangsara.

Zeine, Zeine N. 1966. *The Emergence of Arab Nationalism.* Beirut, Lebanon: Khayats.

Zeki, Salih. 1908. "Auguste Comte." *Ulûm-u İktisadiye ve İctimaiye Mecmuasi* (Journal of Economic and Social Sciences), volume 1, pages 163–197.

Zermeño, Francisco T. 1964. *Las Cámaras de Comercio en el Derecho Mexicano* (Chambers of Commerce in Mexican Law). Mexico City, Mexico: Cámara Nacional de Comercio de la Ciudad de México.

Zhang, Xin. 2000. *Social Transformation in Modern China: The State and Local Elites in Henan, 1900–1937.* Cambridge, England: Cambridge University Press.

Zhang Zhilian, editor. 1990. *China and the French Revolution.* Oxford, England: Pergamon Press.

Zimmerman, Judith E. 1972. "The Kadets and the Duma, 1905–1907." Pages 119–138 in Charles W. Timberlake, editor, *Essays on Russian Liberalism.* Columbia, Missouri: University of Missouri Press.

Zinoviev, Ivan Alekseevich. 1983. *Inqilab-i Mashrutiyat-i Iran: Nazarat-i Yak Diplumat-i Rus-i Havadis-i Iran dar Sal'ha-yi 1905 ta 1911* (The Constitutional Revolution of Iran: The Perspective of a Russian Diplomat on the Events of Iran in the Years 1905–1911), translated by Abulqasim I'tisami. [Tehran, Iran]: Iqbal.

Zola, Émile. 1996. *The Dreyfus Affair: 'J'Accuse' and Other Writings,* edited by Alain Pagès, translated by Eleanor Levieux. New Haven, Connecticut: Yale University Press.

Index

Abdülhamid II, 4, 26, 41, 67, 77, 85, 88, 184–85, 204, 206, 219, 232–33
Abu Bakr, 42
'Adalat, Husayn, 38
Adamiyat, 'Abbas Quli Khan Qazvini, 38
Adorno, Theodor, 244
Aerenthal, Alois von, 221
Afary, Janet, 22
Afghanistan, 5, 53–54, 261
Africa, 5, 105, 208, 216, 223, 226, 240, 242, 253–54, 256–57
Ahmed Rıza, 41, 51, 85, 157, 158
Akçura, Yusuf, 185, 248
Akif, Mehmed, 249
Albania, 86, 183, 251, 272n48
'Ali ibn Abi Talib, 42
Almeida, António José, 45, 90, 162
Amin al-Sultan, 'Ali Asghar Khan, Atabak-i A'zam, 156
Amin al-Zarb, Muhammad Husayn, 116, 118, 139
Anarchism and anarchists, 48, 142, 161–62, 164, 167, 294n82
Anderson, Rodney, 166
Angeles, Felipe, 210
Arabs, 4, 26, 65, 123–24, 158, 160, 251, 291n51
Argentina, 5, 251
Aristide, Jean-Bertrand, 257
Aristotle, 107
Armenians, 18, 120, 123–24, 151, 157, 185, 202, 290n43
Ascher, Abraham, 22
Ashraf, 246
Ateneo de la Juventud, 47
Austria, 5

Austria-Hungary, 5, 15, 17, 19, 108, 159–60, 179, 201, 216, 221, 224, 231, 233, 315n44
'Ayn al-Daulah, 66
Azuela, Mariano, 249

Bakhtiyaris, 100, 116, 119, 181, 202–3, 214, 229–31, 251
Baqir Khan, 81, 155, 202
Belgium, 62
Belov, V., 14, 59
Beltrán, Joaquin, 210
Benda, Julien, 28, 30, 244
Bérenger, Henry, 30
Bergère, Marie-Claire, 134
Bergson, Henri, 244
Berlin, 3
Berth, Édouard, 244
Bihbihani, 'Abdullah, 65–66, 217
Blok, Aleksandr A., 248
Bogucharskii, V. Y., 58
Bombarda, Miguel, 162
Bongo, Omar, 253–54
Borges, França, 161
Bosnia-Herzegovina, 17, 159, 224, 231, 233
Bourgeoisie, 9–10, 11, 13–14, 16–19, 21, 28, 32, 35, 37, 46, 56, 57, 59, 63–64, 70, 81, 95, 105–43, 146, 148, 151, 155, 159–62, 167, 172, 188, 191, 218, 222–23, 240, 244, 256, 259, 260–62, 270–71n33, 288n37, 289n41–42, 294n85
Braga, Teófilo, 43–45, 51, 90
Braniff, Tomás, 133
Brazil, 251